Second Canadian edition

Becoming a Teacher

Forrest W. Parkay
Washington State University

Beverly Hardcastle Stanford
Azusa Pacific University

John P. Vaillancourt
Acadia University

Heather C. Stephens
Acadia University

PEARSON

Toronto

This book is dedicated to our students—
their spirit continually renews us
and inspires confidence in the future
of teaching in Canada and America

National Library of Canada Cataloguing in Publication

Becoming a teacher / Forrest Parkay ... [et al.].—2nd Canadian ed.

Previous ed. written by: Forrest Parkay, Beverly Hardcastle Stanford and Thomas D. Gougeon
Includes bibliographical references and index.
ISBN 0-205-35714-8

1. Teaching—Vocational guidance—Canada. 2. Education—Study and teaching—
Canada. 3. Teachers—Canada—Attitudes. I. Parkay, Forrest W. II. Parkay, Forrest W.
Becoming a teacher.

LB1775.B42 2005   371.1'0023'71   C2003-906564-2

ISBN 0-205-35714-8

Vice President, Editorial Director: Michael J. Young
Executive Acquisitions Editor: Christine Cozens
Marketing Manager: Ryan St. Peters
Developmental Editor: Jennifer Murray
Production Editor: Martin Tooke
Copy Editor: Emma Gorst
Proofreader: Bonnie Di Malta
Production Coordinator: Anita Heyna
Page Layout: Arlene Edgar
Photo Research: Sandy Cooke
Art Director: Mary Opper
Cover and Interior Design: Anthony Leung
Cover Image: Jim Craigmyle/Masterfile

4 5 6 7 8 9   09 08 07 06 05

Printed and bound in the USA.

Contents

Part Two

Foundations of Teaching 74

Dear Mentor 74

3 Ideas and Events That Have Shaped Education in Canada 76

12 Education Issues for the Twenty-First Century 434

Preface

We hope that you share our belief that teaching is the world's most important profession. We also hope that you recognize the service Pearson Education Canada has provided to preservice Canadian teachers through the publication of this first comprehensive guide to the Canadian educational landscape. The demand for a Canadian book of this type has been evident for many years. However, until we accepted Pearson Canada's challenge to produce this text, instructors at Canadian universities and colleges were faced with a bleak choice: use an American text without any Canadian flavour, use a host of smaller Canadian texts and booklets that touch on selected topics while ignoring many others, or inundate their students with a flood of photocopied handouts. The broad range of topics covered in this Canadian edition of *Becoming a Teacher* overcomes these problems. Additionally, the twelve chapters mesh easily with the standard academic term. Canadian examples, historical data, and statistics are included throughout and, because of its breadth of topic, instructors can customize *Becoming a Teacher* for use within a variety of courses.

To facilitate your students' journey toward becoming professional teachers, this Canadian edition of *Becoming a Teacher* emphasizes the concept of mentoring. For example, the "Dear Mentor" feature that opens each part provides practical advice from highly accomplished teachers for meeting the complex challenges of teaching. This popular feature presents the responses of experienced mentor teachers to questions and concerns raised by preservice teachers much like the students who will be using this book. In their responses, the mentors, including award-winning teachers, provide practical and wise advice.

Throughout this Canadian edition of *Becoming a Teacher*, we highlight teacher leadership, since today's teachers are assuming diverse leadership roles beyond the classroom. For instance, in Chapter 10, "Teachers as Educational Leaders," readers learn about the exciting new leadership roles that await teachers.

"Teaching with Technology" (Chapter 9) provides an up-to-date overview of how educational technologies are influencing schools and the profession of teaching. This chapter describes how teachers are using computer-assisted instruction (CAI); microcomputer-based laboratories (MBL); newsgroups, chat rooms, and research assignments on the internet; home-school communication systems; and high-quality hypermedia simulations. Also, each chapter has a new feature, "Technology Highlights," that illustrates how educational technology is related to chapter content.

"Where Do You Stand?" and "Case to Consider" give opportunities to reflect on the realities of teaching and on controversial trends and issues that have aroused public opinion and attracted media attention. Among the issues addressed in these features are violence in schools, vouchers and school choice, character education, psychological assessments of teaching candidates, school uniforms, and increased standardized testing.

Organization of the Book

This Canadian edition of *Becoming a Teacher* has been extensively revised. To allow for expanded coverage of critical trends and issues in education, we have organized the book into four parts: "Part One: The Teaching Profession," "Part Two: Foundations of Teaching," "Part Three: The Art of Teaching," and "Part Four: Your Teaching Future."

Chapters 1 and 2, which make up Part One, are on the theme of teachers and teaching. After reading these chapters, students will be better able to determine whether teaching is a good career choice for them. Among the topics we address are why people choose to teach, the challenges and realities of teaching, the knowledge and skills needed to become a teacher, and how to establish mentoring relationships.

Chapters 3 to 5 in Part Two take up the foundations of education, which every professional teacher needs to know. These foundational areas include the philosophical, historical, social, cultural, political, financial, and legal dimensions of Canadian education. Philosophical and historical foundations are treated in "Ideas and Events That Have Shaped Education in Canada" (Chapter 3).

Chapters 6 to 9, which make up Part Three, examine student characteristics and the worlds of the classroom and the school. Here, readers learn about characteristics of students at different stages of development, students as learners, the dynamics of classroom life, the curricula that are taught in schools, and teaching with technology.

Finally, in Part Four, Chapters 10 to 12, we discuss issues and trends that will impact each student's quest to become an effective teacher, especially the expanding leadership role of teachers, planning for a successful first year of teaching, international education in a changing world, and the teacher's role in shaping the future of education.

Other Features and Learning Aids

Included in *Becoming a Teacher* are many features we believe will help prepare students for rewarding futures as professional teachers. To guide their study, "Focus Questions" at the beginning of each chapter reflect the questions addressed in that chapter. Opening scenarios present decision-making or problem-solving situations to reflect upon and resolve. These situations are referred to again in the chapter and give readers an opportunity to apply new learning in specific problem-solving contexts.

To inspire preservice teachers with the experiences of outstanding teachers, each odd-numbered chapter features "Teaching for Excellence," a section that profiles Canadian teachers who have won a Prime Minister's Award for Teaching Excellence. These individuals' philosophies and professional contributions reflect a commitment to touching others' lives through teaching. A "Professional Reflection" feature in each chapter gives readers an opportunity to reflect on their beliefs and values and on the issues teachers face. This feature is designed to give practice in the applied reflective inquiry that should characterize every teacher's professional life.

In addition, the book includes in its chapter-ending material a "Teacher's Database" feature with online activities for using the vast resources of the internet to facilitate professional growth. The internet has transformed teaching and learning in many schools and classrooms; advanced telecommunications will continue to change the way teachers teach and assess students' learning.

This edition of *Becoming a Teacher* continues the popular "Professional Portfolio" feature that will enable preservice teachers to document their growth and accomplishments over time. Each chapter includes guidelines for creating a portfolio entry that readers can actually use when they begin teaching; in addition, students may wish to use selected portfolio entries during the process of applying for a first teaching position.

As a further study aid, key terms and concepts are boldfaced in the text and listed with page cross-references at the ends of chapters. A glossary at the end of the book helps readers quickly locate the definitions of key terms and concepts and the text pages on which they appear.

Other end-of-chapter learning aids in this edition include a concise summary and suggested applications and activities. Applications and activities include journal-writing opportunities in "Teacher's Journal" and field experiences in "Observations and Interviews." In "Teacher's Journal," we continue a feature that has proved useful and popular with instructors who ask students to keep a teacher's journal to encourage active reflection as they learn about teaching. The short, optional journal-writing activities are based on the "writing-to-learn" and "writing-across-the-curriculum" concepts.

Supplements

To help both instructors and students get the most out of *Becoming a Teacher*, we have provided a number of useful supplements:

■ **Instructor's Resource Manual** in which, for each chapter of the text, a Chapter-at-a-Glance organizer correlates chapter outlines, learning objectives, and teaching supplements; an Annotated Lecture Outline provides examples, discussion questions, and student activities; suggestions for additional readings and media extend chapter learning; and handout masters provide additional lecture support materials.

■ A **Test Bank** of more than 1000 questions, including multiple choice items, true/false items, essay questions, case studies, and authentic assessments, plus text page references and answer feedback.

■ The **Companion website**, a restricted-access website available only to students who purchase the text new, offers a case study, audio clips, activities, weblinks, key terms and concept checks, and a practise test with answer feedback for each chapter of the text.

Acknowledgments

Many members of the Pearson Canada team provided expert guidance and support during the preparation of this Canadian edition of *Becoming a Teacher*. Clearly, Adrienne Shiffman, our developmental editor, heads the list. From suggestions for revision, feedback on draft manuscripts, and skilful coordination of the revision process, from beginning to end, Adrienne's cheerful manner, and ability to spot a misplaced comma at fifty paces, is deeply appreciated. The authors also extend a very special thanks to all the other members of the Pearson Canada team for their steadfast support throughout the prepublication period.

The authors extend a special thanks to educators working in schools, teacher professional organizations, and departments of education throughout Canada whom we consulted during the preparation of *Becoming a Teacher*. Invariably, they were courteous and helpful. A very common reaction among them was their delight that someone was going to make use of their material. We also wish to thank the *Education Law Reporter,* which generously gave us permission to use material from their excellent journal and website.

We are also very grateful to the authors of the US edition of *Becoming a Teacher 5th Ed.* for the superb foundation they provided for us and upon which we built this Canadian edition. Working with other writers' material placed a huge responsibility upon us. Throughout, we have tried to be consistent in writing style and true to their overall intent—judiciously cutting here, modifying something there, and inserting appropriate Canadian material whenever it was available.

We especially wish to thank our reviewers, who provided concise, helpful suggestions during the developmental stages of this book: Dick Baker, Concordia University College of Alberta; Patricia Bowslaugh, Brandon University; Kim Calder, University College of the Cariboo; Bill Gadsby, University of Winnipeg; Noel Hurley, University of Windsor; Ken Pudlas, Trinity Western University; and Campbell Ross, Grande Prairie Regional College.

The authors also appreciate the support of colleagues at Acadia University in this revision process. Acadia is a progressive institution that has the distinction of being the first fully wired laptop university in the country. This emphasis on technology provided material for the scenario in the opening chapter of the text. Special thanks to Dr. Heather Hemming, Director of the Acadia University School of Education at Acadia University, who provided ongoing support for the project.

The Canadian Teachers' Federation and Industry Canada's Prime Minister's Awards for Teaching Excellence were generous in their permission to reprint a wide array of information on teaching in Canada. In particular, we would like to salute the Award for Teaching Excellence recipients who are featured in selected chapters.

Both Heather Stephens and John Vaillancourt thank the many individuals who provided them with inspiration and assistance in the preparation of the Canadian edition of this textbook. Heather particularly appreciates the contributions made by her graduate students who continually teach her about the art and craft of teaching. The following graduate students provided material for the book: James Turner, Anna Gosse, Sonya Bracken-Vanderhoeden, Marie Church, Ann Robichaud, Rona Howald, and Cheryl Scotland-Moxon. Finally, the support of her partner, David Lacey, is acknowledged; the many hours of time spent on the project were made easier by his encouragement and sense of humour.

Heather Stephens
John Vaillancourt

part one

The Teaching Profession

dear mentor

On Determining Whether Teaching Is the Right Profession for You

Dear Mentor,

As a new college graduate, I am searching for the right profession. Others have encouraged me to teach because I work well with children, but how might I truly know whether teaching is the right profession for me? I definitely desire to be a teacher, yet will my first year be the determining factor?

Sincerely,
J. Casey Medlock

D ear Casey:

As a 23-year veteran teacher, I am always excited to share my experiences with those who are considering my profession for themselves. You are wise to ask whether teaching is right for you, but more important, you should ask whether you are right for teaching! An ability to work with students is certainly the most important characteristic of the teaching persona but many others are also important. Some other questions you might ask are

- Do I enjoy the company of children enough to spend most of my day with them?
- Do I have a limitless supply of energy, patience, and perseverance?
- Do I enjoy learning and am I able to be a model of lifelong learning for my students?
- Am I willing to learn from my students and use what they teach me to improve my ability as a teacher?
- Am I a person of strong convictions who can demonstrate those convictions in every aspect of my life?
- Can I focus on what is important and positive in my work while some around me seem to focus on negativism and dissension?
- Am I willing to be a strong advocate for the teaching profession, who is unwilling to accept the status quo and is prepared to fight to strengthen the profession, despite difficult odds?
- Can I always make the needs of my students the central reason for all that I do in teaching?

In response to your second question, whether your first year will be the determining factor in your success, the answer is both yes and no. I believe that the first year of any new experience has the potential to be a "make or break" year. This is one reason why I have chosen to teach Kindergarten. Some children, like my son, find their Kindergarten year such an abysmal experience that teachers and parents are never able to readjust their thinking and excite them about school. I have, therefore, made it my goal to ensure an enjoyable, productive Kindergarten year for all of my students. What was true for my son in Kindergarten seems also to be true for many new teachers—the first year sets the pattern for the rest. Furthermore, in education, the least experienced teachers have traditionally been placed in the most difficult situations. For some, this baptism by fire ignites a tenacity and strength that catapults them into "legendary teacher" status. But for too many, it either turns them away from teaching altogether or disillusions them, making them apathetic, ineffective teachers. I would say that if a teacher survives the first year and can look back with any feelings of accomplishment and a desire to return and try again, then he or she has potential to do well in the field. I doubt that you will find any teacher who believes his or her first year of teaching was the best. Becoming a good teacher is definitely a combination of innate ability, excellent preparation, an abundance of "on the job training," and stubborn persistence.

In a society that too often equates success with wealth and recognition, it is sometimes difficult for teachers to see themselves as successful, since they usually do not earn six figures and receive little acclaim for a job whose importance and responsibilities exceed those of almost all other professions. Those teachers who consider themselves successful have learned early in their careers to identify and celebrate their accomplishments! Helping one child is a reward in itself; helping many children is a measurement of great prosperity!

My 23 years of teaching have contained many peaks, plateaus, and valleys. But when I look into the faces of my students, I have never doubted the importance of my work. To teach is to impact directly the entire course of human destiny. It is an awesome responsibility, an incredible challenge, and a limitless opportunity for satisfaction and reward.

Sincerely,

Andy Baumgartner

1

Teaching: Your Chosen Profession

The best part of teaching is being a "learning catalyst." I love it when I can introduce my students to a project or concept and then "take the ball and run with it." My goal is accomplished when they go beyond what I know and I start learning from them.

—Sonya Vanderhoeden-Bracken
Teacher of Senior Mathematics
Laurentian Regional High School
Lachute, Quebec

**focus
questions**

1. Why do you want to teach?

2. What are the challenges of teaching?

3. What is teaching really like?

4. What does society expect of teachers?

5. How do good teachers view their work?

Your first interview for a job as a teacher is today, and you can hardly believe that it was only two years ago that you began to take courses to become a teacher. Several questions about your readiness for teaching occupy your mind while you walk from the staff parking lot toward the school, which is one of the newer educational facilities in the province and is recognized as a technologically innovative school. "Am I ready? Do I have what it takes to become a good teacher? Can I handle the stress? Do I have sufficient skills to use educational technology in my classroom?"

Approaching the main entrance, you look at the dozens of students playing on the open field next to the building. Their joyful, exuberant sounds this warm early September morning remind you of your own school days. Some children are moving constantly, running in tight circles and zigzags as they yell and motion to friends who are also on the move. Others stand near the entrance in groups of two or three, talking and milling about as they wait for the bell signalling the start of the first day of school.

At the bottom of the long stairs leading up to a row of green metal doors, you overhear the conversation of three students.

"It's such a great movie. What time do you want to meet?" the taller of two girls asks. Before her friends can respond, she adds, "My aunt's going to pick me up at four o'clock, so I should be home by four-thirty."

"Let's meet at five o'clock," the other girl says. "I can be ready by then."

You notice a young man in a wheelchair appear from around a corner; he jokes and laughs with two other students about skipping classes on this first day of school. As more students arrive, it is obvious that adolescents with special needs are integrated into the student body in a seamless way. Reaching the top of the stairs, you open a door and walk through the entrance out into a brightly lit hallway.

A large permanent sign asks all visitors to report to the main office and you realize that the main office is directly in front of you. To the right of the office door is a bulletin board proclaiming in large red block letters, "Welcome back, students!" Beneath that greeting, in smaller black letters, is another message: "It's going to be a great year!"

Inside the office, you approach the counter on which sits a plastic sign that says "Welcome" in four languages: English, French, Arabic, and Chinese. You introduce yourself to the school's head secretary. He remains seated behind a grey steel desk covered with loose papers.

"I have an appointment with Ms Carmichael," you inform him. "It's about a replacement for Mr. Medina."

"Good. She's expecting you. Why don't you have a seat over there?" He motions for you to sit on the couch across from the teachers' mailboxes. "She's working with some teachers on setting up a meeting of our School Advisory Council. She should be finished in just a few minutes."

While waiting for Ms Carmichael, you think about questions you might be asked. Why did you choose to become a teacher? What is your philosophy of education? How would you integrate technology into your curriculum? What is your approach to classroom management? How would you meet the needs of students from different cultural and linguistic backgrounds? How would you set up a program in your major content area? How familiar are you with provincial curriculum documents? What experience do you have in working with students with special needs? In what extracurricular areas could you make contributions? How would you involve parents in the classroom? What are your strengths? Why should the district hire you?

Reflecting on these questions, you admit they are actually quite difficult. Your answers, you realize, could determine whether or not you get the job.

Though predictable, the interview questions just posed are surprisingly challenging. Why did you decide to become a teacher? How will you meet the needs of all students? What do you have to offer students? The answers to these and similar questions depend on the personality and experiences of the person responding. However, they are questions that professional teachers recognize as important and worthy of careful consideration.

The primary purpose of this book is to orient you within the world of education and to help you begin to formulate answers to such questions. In addition, this book will help you answer your own questions about the career you have chosen. What is teaching really like? What are the trends and issues in the profession? What problems can you expect to encounter in the classroom? What kind of rewards do teachers experience?

We begin this book by asking you to examine why you want to become a teacher because we believe that "good teachers select themselves" (Carmichael, 1981, 113). They know why they want to teach and what subjects and ages they want to teach. They are active in the choosing process, aware of the options, informed about the attractions and obstacles in the field, and anxious to make their contributions to the profession.

Why Do You Want to Teach?

People are drawn to teaching for many reasons. For some, the desire to teach emerges early and is nurtured by positive experiences with teachers during the formative years of childhood. For others, teaching is seen as a way of making a significant contribution to the world and experiencing the joy of helping others grow and develop. And for others, life as a teacher is attractive because it is exciting, varied, and stimulating.

Desire to Work with Children and Young People

Though the conditions under which teachers work may be challenging, their salaries modest, and members of their communities unsupportive, most teach simply because they care about students. Figure 1.1, based on the Canadian Teachers' Federation (CTF) Workplace Survey (2001), indicates that the most important factor influencing teachers' choice of profession is related to the love of children and teaching.

Figure 1.1

Why do teachers enter the profession?

Source: Based on a survey by Environics for the Canadian Teachers' Federation. Canadian Teachers' Federation June 2001 Workplace Survey.

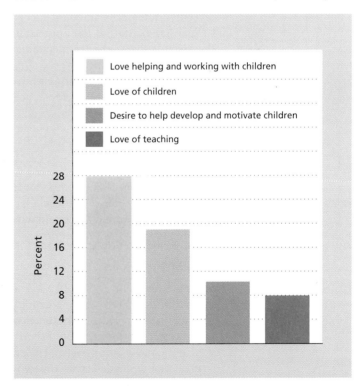

The day-to-day interactions between teachers and students build strong bonds. Daily contact also enables teachers to become familiar with the personal as well as the academic needs of their students, and this concern for students' welfare and growth outweighs the difficulties and frustrations of teaching. Like the following teachers, they know they can make a difference in students' lives:

> When I was struggling as a kid, one of my teachers was really there for me. She listened to me and supported me when nobody else believed in me. I want to pay her back by helping others like me (Zehm and Kottler 1993, 35).

> [Students] need someone to recognize their uniqueness and specialness and respect it and nurture it (Hansen 1995, 132).

Others, no doubt, love students because they appreciate the unique qualities of youth. They enjoy the liveliness, curiosity, freshness, openness, and trust of young children; or the abilities, wit, spirit, independence, and idealism of adolescents. Like the following teacher, they want to be connected to their students: "... I now know that I teach so I can be involved in my students' lives, in their real life stories" (Henry et al. 1995, 69).

Teachers also derive significant rewards from meeting the needs of diverse learners. Canadian classrooms include 10 to 15 percent of students who have special educational needs, and another 25 percent who arrive with problems and needs arising from their socio-economic background or from a lack of proficiency in English or French (CTF 2003). While Canadian students come from increasingly diverse racial and ethnic backgrounds and those with special needs are increasing in number, effective teachers recognize that their classrooms are enriched by the varied backgrounds of students. To enable you to experience the satisfaction of helping all students learn, significant portions of this book are devoted to **student variability** (differences among students in regard to their developmental needs, interests, abilities, and disabilities) and **student diversity** (differences among students in regard to gender, race, ethnicity, culture, and socioeconomic status). An appreciation for such diversity will help you to experience the rewards that come from enabling each student to make his or her unique contribution to classroom life.

The opportunity to work with young people, whatever their stage of development and whatever their life circumstances, is a key reason people are drawn to teaching and remain in the profession.

Love of Teaching

The CTF Workplace Survey asked teachers why they remained in teaching. The results indicate that for four in ten teachers, the most important factor influencing their decision is that they love helping and working with children (2001). Why do teachers find teaching so satisfying? What does it mean to *love* teaching?

Love of Subject

Some teachers who expressed a love of teaching may have meant that they love teaching in their discipline. The opportunity to continually learn more in one's profession and to share that knowledge with students is a definite attraction. Most of us can recall teachers who were so excited about their subjects that they were surprised when students were not equally enthusiastic. The affinity of such teachers toward their subjects was so great that we tended to see the two as inseparable—saying, for instance, "Ms Gilbert the French teacher" or "Mr Montgomery the math teacher." Though other factors may draw teachers to their work, a love of subject is clearly one of them.

Love of the Teaching Life

For those teachers who always enjoyed school, it is often the life of a teacher that has appeal—to be in an environment that encourages a high regard for education and the life of the mind, and to have daily opportunities to see students become excited about learning. Albert Einstein, for example, regretted that he did not devote his career to the teaching life:

> Believe it or not, one of my deepest regrets [is that I didn't teach]. I regret this because I would have liked to have had more contact with children. There has always been something about the innocence and freshness of young children that appeals to me and brings me great enjoyment to be with them. And they are so open to knowledge. I have never really found it difficult to explain basic laws of nature to children. When you reach them at their level, you can read in their eyes their genuine interest and appreciation (quoted in Bucky 1992, 99).

Love of the Teaching–Learning Process

To love teaching can also mean to love the act of teaching and the learning that can follow. Many teachers, like the following high school special education teacher, focus on the process rather than on the subject or even the students: "I enjoy what I do.... I've been teaching long enough that when the fun stops ... I'll get out. But it hasn't stopped yet, after 34 years. Every day is different. Every day is interesting" (Godar 1990, 244). Persons with this orientation are attracted by the live, spontaneous aspects of teaching and are invigorated by the need to think on their feet and to capitalize on teachable moments when they occur. "[T]hey possess a variety of schemata for seeing what is important, [and they] have a broad repertoire of moves with which to quickly and gracefully act on the situation that they see" (Eisner 1998, 200).

Influence of Teachers

It seems reasonable to assume that the process of becoming a teacher begins early in life. In fact, a Metropolitan Life Survey of 1002 graduates who began teaching in a public school in 1990–91 reported that 52 percent decided to become teachers before college (Louis Harris and Associates 1990). Although it is not true that some people are born teachers, their early life experiences often encourage them to move in that direction. A teacher's influence during the formative years may have been the catalyst. In most cases, the adults who have the greatest influence on children—beyond their parents or guardians—are their teachers.

Evidence also suggests that those who become teachers are often more influenced by their teachers as people than as subject-matter experts. "It is the human dimension that gives all teachers ... their power as professional influencers" (Zehm and Kottler 1993, 2). Behind the decision to become a teacher is often the inspirational memory of earlier teachers to whom one continues to feel connected in a way that goes beyond the subjects they taught.

Table 1.1 lists the minimum requirements for individuals to enter the teaching profession in Canada. General requirements for entrance into the teaching profession in most Canadian provinces is a Grade 12 high school diploma and four years of post-secondary education. Exceptions to this rule are Ontario, Quebec, and Nova Scotia. In addition to the academic requirements, teacher education programs frequently interview candidates to determine their suitability for the teaching profession. Positive qualities for prospective teacher education candidates include a good command of French or English, good health, emotional stability, enthusiasm, and an interest in and enjoyment of children and youth (CTF 1999). In most programs, this interview is the

Table 1.1

Minimum requirements to enter the teaching profession and lowest entry salaries (last updated August 1999)

Province or Territory	Last Year of Secondary Education	Minimum Years of Post-Secondary	Lowest Entry Designation	Lowest Entry-Level Salary	Requirements
NF	Grade 12	4	Certificate Level IV	$26 487 (Provincial)	A four-year (120 credit hours) degree in education. Restrictions are in place regarding content of the degree.
PE	Grade 12	4	Certificate Level IV	$26 958 (Provincial)	A Bachelor of Education with a minimum of four years university training.
NS	Grade 12	4	Class 5	$31 135 (Provincial)	An undergraduate degree (minimum three years) and a Bachelor of Education.
NB	Grade 12	4	Certificate 4	$29 562 (Provincial)	An approved four-year New Brunswick university degree, including teacher education or equivalent.
QC	Grade12	4	17 years of age	$30 222 (Provincial)	Graduation from the two year CEGEP program after Grade 11, plus a four-year Teacher Education degree.
ON	Grade 12	4	Category A1	$33 421 (Ottawa/ Carleton) $29 835 (Thames Valley) $31 445 (Toronto)	Generally, requirements include an acceptable three- or four-year university degree and at least the equivalent of one full year of teacher college acceptable to the Ontario College of Teachers.
NB	Grade 12	4	Class 4	$33 366 (Winnipeg)	Senior matriculation or equivalent, plus five years of study in a degree program, including at least one year of professional study. An undergraduate Bachelor's degree or equivalent is required.
SK	Grade 12	4	Class IV	$30 588 (Provincial)	A minimum of four years of recognized post-secondary education, and: a Professional "A" Certificate or a Professional "B" Certificate; or Vocational Teacher's Certificate, or Technical Teacher's Certificate, and additional training so that only one year of university education is required to complete a four-year degree.
AB	Grade12	4	Category 4	$33 188 (Edmonton Public) $32 676 (Calgary Public)	A four-year Bachelor of Education degree or four years of university education and one year of professional teacher education from an institution acceptable to the Alberta Minister of Education.

Table 1.1 continued

Province or Territory	Last Year of Secondary Education	Minimum Years of Post-Secondary	Lowest Entry Designation	Lowest Entry-Level Salary	Requirements
BC	Grade12	4	Category 4	$35 409 (Vancouver)	Completion of a minimum four-year program, or equivalent, of post-secondary professional and academic or specialist studies beyond 12, or equivalent, including appropriate basic teacher education acceptable to the College of Teachers.
YK	Grade 12	4	Category IV	$43 727 (Territorial)	Four years post-secondary education.
NT	Grade 12	4	Level 5	$46 226 (Territorial)	Junior matriculation (Grade 11) plus five years of teacher education or Senior matriculation plus four years of teacher education.

Source: Canadian Teachers' Federation. "Becoming a Teacher." Retrieved January 18, 2003 from www.ctf-fce.ca/E/TIC/becoming.htm

sole means of screening out mentally unhealthy people. Should formal psychological assessments be used to further assist in the screening process? Would using such tests lead to lawsuits against the colleges and universities that conduct them? Can a psychological instrument measure who is likely to be a good or poor teacher?

Desire to Serve

Many choose to teach because they want to serve others; they want the results of their labor to extend beyond themselves and their families. Some decide to select another program or leave teaching in order to earn more money elsewhere, only to return to teaching, confiding that they found the other program or work lacking in meaning or significance. Being involved in a service profession is their draw to the field. Twenty-nine percent of Canadian teachers surveyed reported the major factors for remaining in education to be the love of the profession and job satisfaction, followed by the desire to make a difference (15 percent) (CTF 2001).

For many teachers, the decision to serve through teaching was influenced by their experiences as volunteers. During admission interviews, teacher education program applicants often cite their volunteer work in Boy Scouts, Girl Guides, summer camps, church activities, and other child and youth organizations as influential in their decision to enter the teaching profession.

Explore more deeply your reasons for becoming a teacher. The Professional Reflection feature on page 13 focuses on several characteristics that may indicate your probable satisfaction with teaching as a career.

Should psychological assessments be used to identify students who should not become teachers?

Psychological assessments should be used to identify students who should not become teachers.

With our increasing knowledge about how the brain develops and its responsiveness to stimuli in the environment, especially for the young, we realize the power that teachers have to impact students' cognitive and emotional development for good or ill. Teachers who appear threatening to students can impact their learning as well as their sense of emotional well-being. A teacher who has problems with authority, a quick temper, insensitivity to the feelings of others, or poorly-defined personal boundaries, can be a menace to children and youth. Psychological assessments should be used to screen out teacher education candidates with these characteristics.

Just as extra psychological screening is needed for pilots and air traffic controllers, so too is it needed for people who work with the minds of our children and youth. In all three groups, if the individuals in positions of power fail to live up to their responsibilities or make mistakes, the consequences can be serious. The substitute teacher who exposed himself to a class of Grade Twos, the physical education teacher who had sexual relations with students, and the Grade 5 teacher who regularly ridiculed and humiliated students in class should not have been permitted to teach in the first place. Psychological assessments of them would have revealed their mental health problems and prevented them from entering the profession.

Psychological assessments should not be used to disqualify students who want to become teachers.

Psychological assessments should not be used to disqualify prospective teachers because they could screen out potentially superb teachers and could admit others likely to fail in a classroom. How can an assessment measure something that years of education research have failed to determine, the ingredients of a good teacher? If psychological assessments are used, will teachers begin to look alike, measured against a narrowly defined profile? How can instruments measure the rich array of personalities that motivate students to learn and love learning?

Psychological assessments are costly in terms of both money and personnel time. Evaluators who interview teacher education program candidates require extensive and expensive training. Not many colleges and universities can afford such a time- and cost-intensive approach.

The legalities of screening out candidates on the basis of a psychological assessment is another obvious concern. Could teacher education institutions be sued by people who believe that they were denied admission to their programs on false grounds?

An assessment instrument or process is not able to measure the psychological dimension that encompasses what today's teachers need: "interpersonal skills, willingness to confront and deal with social and cultural complexity, self-awareness and disposition toward reflection, cosmopolitanism, and a well-developed social conscience" (Griffin 1999, 10). An interview process similar to that proposed by Martin Haberman is more likely to get us closer to the mark. In attempting to predict the best candidates for teaching successfully in urban schools, Haberman (1996) proposes asking questions that address classroom situations and test character traits such as perseverance, resourcefulness, and ability to tolerate ambiguities. For instance, candidates are asked what they would do if a student didn't turn in his or her homework. Then they are asked, "What if that didn't work?" After a reply, again, "What if that didn't work either?" Such an approach is more likely to identify who should not be in a classroom than a psychological assessment.

Where do you stand on this issue?

1. What support can you give for your position?

2. How would you measure up in the homework question exercise?

3. What other situational and character-trait testing questions can you suggest to someone wanting to use Haberman's evaluation approach?

4. What legal challenges might be raised about psychological assessments for teacher candidates? What ethical challenges might be raised?

Recommended Sources

Beauchamp, L. & Parsons, J. (2000). *Teaching from the inside out*. Edmonton, AB: Duval House Publishing.

Dolmage, W.R. (1996). *So you want to be a teacher: The guide to teaching as a career choice in Canada*. Toronto, ON: Harcourt Brace and Company, Canada.

Griffin, G. A. (1999). Changes in teacher education: looking to the future. In G. A. Griffin (Ed). *The education of teachers: ninety-eighth yearbook of the National Society for the Study of Education.* Chicago: The University of Chicago Press.

Professional Reflection — Assessing your reasons for choosing to teach

For each of the following characteristics, indicate on a scale from 1 to 5 the extent to which it applies to you.

	Very applicable				Not at all applicable
1. Love of learning	1	2	3	4	5
2. Success as a student	1	2	3	4	5
3. Good sense of humour	1	2	3	4	5
4. Positive attitudes toward students	1	2	3	4	5
5. Tolerance toward others	1	2	3	4	5
6. Patience	1	2	3	4	5
7. Good verbal and writing skills	1	2	3	4	5
8. Appreciation for the arts	1	2	3	4	5
9. Experiences working with children (camp, church, tutoring, etc.)	1	2	3	4	5
10. Other teachers in family	1	2	3	4	5
11. Encouragement from family to enter teaching	1	2	3	4	5
12. Desire to serve	1	2	3	4	5

Total score

Now that you have completed the self-assessment, calculate your total score; the highest score = 60, the lowest = 12. Interpret the results of your self-assessment with caution. A high score does not necessarily mean that you will be dissatisfied as a teacher, nor does a low score mean that you will be highly satisfied.

Practical Benefits of Teaching

Not to be overlooked as attractions to teaching are its practical benefits. Teachers' hours and vacations are widely recognized as benefits. Though the number of hours most teachers devote to their work goes far beyond the number of hours they actually spend at school, their schedules do afford them a measure of flexibility not found in other professions. For example, teachers with school age children can often be at home when their children are not in school, and nearly all teachers, regardless of their years of experience, receive the same generous vacation time: holiday breaks and a long summer vacation. For Canadian teachers, the official classroom day usually runs from 8:30 or 9:00 AM to 3:30 or 4:00 PM. Weekends and statutory holidays are free, and vacations usually include a Christmas and spring break of a week or more, and eight weeks in the summer.

Salaries and Benefits

Although intangible rewards represent a significant attraction to teaching, teachers are demanding that the public acknowledge the value and professional standing of teaching by supporting higher salaries. Though there is still a general consensus that teachers are underpaid, teacher salaries are becoming more competitive with other occupations; in fact, salaries are becoming one of the attractions for the profession.

In seven Canadian provinces and the territories, basic salary scales and fringe benefits are established through negotiations between teacher associations or unions and the governments. In many areas, further bargaining concerning **fringe benefits** and work conditions takes place at the individual board level. The CTF "Salaries and Fringe Benefits" document states that all negotiations take place at the board level in Alberta, Manitoba, and Ontario (2002).

Canadian salary schedules are frequently based on a combination of years of service and level of post-secondary education, with additional allowances paid for those in administrative positions. "For 2001–2002, the minimum salary for a teacher with one university degree, including teacher training (Grade 12 plus four years post-secondary education) ranges from approximately $28 000 to $50 000 annually, depending upon the jurisdiction and experience. The maximum salary for the same level of training ranges from $38 000 to $70 000 (CTF 2002)."

Fringe benefits negotiated in collective agreements may include the following:

- Compassionate leave
- Supplementary medical insurance
- Cumulative sick leave
- Long term disability insurance
- Maternity leave
- Sabbatical and study leave
- Life insurance
- Dental insurance (CTF 2002).

Canadian Teacher Supply and Demand

The Survey of Canadian School Boards, conducted by Vector Research for the CTF in July 2000, showed that 51 percent of Canadian school boards surveyed indicated that they found it increasingly difficult to attract qualified candidates for full-time teaching jobs, with rural areas most affected. Two-thirds of the boards anticipated difficulty in hiring teachers in the next year. The top three factors contributing to this situation were teacher retirement, increased number of students with special needs, and fewer teacher education program graduates. Additional key findings included the following:

- Teacher shortages in science, French, technology, and mathematics.
- Difficulty recruiting and retaining beginning teachers in Northwest Territories and Ontario school boards.

- Problems attracting and keeping a pool of qualified substitute teachers.
- Hiring difficulties anticipated by 100 percent of school boards in Newfoundland and Labrador and the Territories for 2001.

Across Canada, research is taking place to improve understanding of demographic patterns that will affect teacher supply and demand. Examples include "Nova Scotia Public Education Teacher Demand and Supply," a research paper released by the Nova Scotia Department of Education in January 2000; and "Teacher Supply/Demand in Newfoundland and Labrador: 1998–2010," completed in 1998 by Dr. Robert Crocker of the Faculty of Education at Memorial University of Newfoundland.

Job Opportunities for Teachers from Diverse Groups

During the first part of the twenty-first century, there will be exceptional job opportunities for teachers from diverse racial and ethnic backgrounds and for teachers with disabilities. The changing Canadian demographics will be increasingly reflected in the student population. There are current projected increases in Aboriginal students in the western provinces and the territories and growing diversity in Canada's urban areas. For example, there is a growing Aboriginal student population in Saskatchewan that will provide challenges for staffing First Nations and public schools. For a society to understand cultural and ethnic diversity, teachers need to reflect that diversity. The CTF admits that there is a dearth of information available on how the diversity of the Canadian teaching force reflects the diversity of the student population (2002). However, it is known that visible minorities and people of Aboriginal heritage are under-represented as teachers and administrators in Canadian schools (Canadian Coalition for the Rights of Children 1999). Clearly, students from diverse racial, ethnic, and cultural backgrounds and students with disabilities benefit from having role models with whom they can easily identify. In addition, teachers from diverse groups and teachers with disabilities may have, in some instances, an enhanced understanding of student diversity and student variability that they can share with other teachers (CTF 2000).

What Are the Challenges of Teaching?

Like all professions, teaching has undesirable or difficult aspects. As one high school social studies teacher put it: "Teaching is not terrible. It's great. I love it. It just feels terrible sometimes" (Henry et al. 1995, 119).

Prospective teachers need to consider the problems as well as the pleasures they are likely to encounter. You need to be informed about what to expect if you are to make the most of your professional preparation program. With greater awareness of the realities of teaching, you can more purposefully and meaningfully (1) reflect on and refine your personal philosophy of education, (2) acquire teaching strategies and leadership techniques, and (3) develop a knowledge base of research and theory to guide your actions. In this manner, you can become a true professional—free to savour the joys and satisfactions of teaching and confident of your ability to deal with its frustrations and challenges. Table 1.2 shows that teachers must deal with a variety of problems in the schools.

Classroom Management and Increasing Violence

For three of the five years from 1994 to 1998, the public ranked lack of discipline as the most important problem facing the schools in the annual Gallup Polls of the Public's

Attitudes toward the Public Schools. For the other two years, the public ranked fighting, violence, and gangs as the most important. Not surprisingly, discipline and increased crime and violence among youth are strong concerns for teacher education students. Before teachers can teach they must manage their classrooms effectively. Even when parents and the school community are supportive and problems are relatively minor, dealing with discipline can be a disturbing, emotionally draining aspect of teaching. Moreover, the last few years of the 1990s were marked by frequent reports of random, horrific violence in and around schools. Thirty-six percent of parents in 1998 feared for their oldest child's safety while at school; in 1977, only 25 percent of parents had such fears (Rose and Gallup 1998). Several communities previously immune to such tragedies were recently thrust into the national spotlight as a result of violent incidents: Littleton, Colorado; Paducah, Kentucky; and Taber, Alberta to name a few. Though such acts of violence in schools are rare, the possibility of experiencing such events can cause additional job-related stress for teachers.

In addition, many schools have high **teacher–student ratios**, which can make classroom management more difficult. Feeling the press of overcrowding and valiantly resisting the realization that they cannot meet the needs of all their students, teachers may try to work faster and longer to give their students the best possible education. All too often, however, they learn to put off, overlook, or otherwise attend inadequately to many students each day. The Workplace Survey (CTF 2001) reports that 14 percent of teachers surveyed felt that class size and being overworked were among the most stressful parts of their job. The problem of high teacher–student ratios becomes even more acute when complicated by the high **student-mobility rates** in many schools. In such situations, teachers have trouble not only in meeting students' needs but also in recognizing students and remembering their names! As you will see, developing a leadership plan, a learning environment, and communication skills will help you face the challenges of classroom management.

Social Problems That Impact Students

Many social problems affect the lives and learning of many children and youth, such as substance abuse, teen pregnancy, homelessness, poverty, family distress, child abuse and neglect, violence and crime, suicide, and health problems such as HIV/AIDS and fetal alcohol syndrome. The social problems that place students at risk of school failure are not always easy to detect. Students' low productivity, learning difficulties, and attitude problems demand teacher attention; yet teachers may be unaware of the source of those difficulties. Even when teachers do recognize the source of a problem, they may lack the resources or expertise to offer help. Teachers feel frustrated by the wasted potential they observe in their students. In addition, when the public calls for schools to curb or correct social problems, that expectation can increase the stress teachers experience. The Workplace Survey reports that six in ten teachers surveyed felt that their job was more stressful than two years before, and student behaviour and discipline issues were the most stressful parts of their work. Further, 56 percent of teachers reported an increase in the amount of time they spend dealing with the "personal, non-academic problems of their students" (CTF 2001).

Canada's Rural and Urban Challenges

Teacher education programs are working to better prepare education students for the challenges they will face in rural and urban schools.

Table 1.2

Teacher's perceptions of the frequency of discipline problems

About how often do each of the problems listed occur at the school where you teach?

Most of the Time/Fairly Often

	All Teachers			Elementary Teachers			High School Teachers		
	1997	1989	1984	1997	1989	1984	1997	1989	1984
	%	%	%	%	%	%	%	%	%
Schoolwork/homework assignments not completed	71	79	76	68	76	73	78	85	80
Behaviour that disrupts class	58	87	47	65	60	48	45	50	47
Talking back to, disobeying teachers	50	45	43	54	45	42	43	44	43
Truancy/being absent from school	41	45	47	35	32	29	57	67	62
Sloppy or inappropriate dress	40	45	37	36	43	33	51	49	41
Cheating on tests	27	45	40	19	33	29	47	64	51
Stealing money or personal property belonging to other students, teachers, or staff	21	21	32	21	26	25	25	40	39
Vandalizing school property	20	25	29	18	20	22	25	34	35
Skipping classes	18	29	35	9	18	16	41	59	57
Using drugs at school	15	14	17	5	5	6	39	30	29
Theft of school property	14	15	23	13	13	18	15	19	29
Selling drugs at school	9	14	13	3	1	4	26	32	24
Racial fights	6	6	4	5	5	3	6	9	5
Carrying of knives, firearms, or other weapons at school	5	4	8	3	3	5	7	8	10
Drinking alcoholic beverages at school	4	6	10	1	1	2	10	14	17
Sexual activity at school	4	6	8	1	1	3	8	13	12
Taking money or property by force, using weapons or threats	2	2	2	2	2	2	2	2	2
Physical attacks on teachers or staff	2	2	1	2	2	1	2	2	1

Note: Figures add to more than 100 percent because of multiple answers.

Source: From Carol A. Langdon, "The Fourth Phi Delta Kappa Poll of Teachers' Attitudes toward the Public Schools," *Phi Delta Kappan,* November 1997, p. 213. Used by permission of the author and publisher. Copyright 1997, Phi Delta Kappa.

Data from the Canadian Youth in Transition Survey (Statistics Canada 2002) found that students from urban schools in Canada performed significantly better in reading than students from rural schools. Rural students were more likely to come from families with lower socio-economic backgrounds, and the parents tended to be less educated and less likely to be employed in professional occupations. The study shows that the difference between rural and urban reading performance is most strongly related to community differences. Compared to the urban communities, rural communities are characterized by lower levels of education, fewer jobs, and jobs that were, on average, lower earning and less likely to require a university degree (Statistics Canada 2002). Inner city schools also place special demands on teachers, especially in the area of teaching literacy.

Urban schools need resources to support the large number of children that come from impoverished circumstances. Toronto, for example, has nearly twice as many families with incomes under $10 000 compared to other Ontario cities. Not only that, its high rents force tenants to spend almost twice as much of their income on housing. As such, there is a large troubled student sector that requires extensive professional and paraprofessional services from the school board. These include assistance of youth counsellors, halls monitors, and attendance counsellors.

The publication *Every Kid Counts* (2001), an initiative of the Vancouver Elementary School Teachers' Association, details efforts of inner city activists and provides advocacy materials and guidance strategies to schools and community groups in Vancouver and beyond.

Schools in inner city areas must have teachers who care about children living in poverty and who are willing to make the extra efforts to meet their diverse needs. Many teachers and administrators leave these schools after a year or two because of the immense pressure of the social and educational environment. Beginning teachers need to become familiar with the literature on family literacy of children in poverty. In addition, teacher education programs need to emphasize the importance of developing school-family-community partnerships for student success.

Aboriginal Education in Inner Cities

Aboriginal Education in Winnipeg Inner City High Schools (2002) describes the life experiences and cultural values of many Aboriginal students and their families as very different from those they experience in schools, which are run largely by non-Aboriginal, middle class people. The report discusses the marginalization of Aboriginal students through curriculum that does not reflect their cultural values or daily realities. Incidences of racism—both overt (name-calling and stereotyping) and institutional—are prevalent. There are few Aboriginal teachers, and little Aboriginal content in the curriculum. Many Aboriginal students resist and reject this middle-class, non-Aboriginal curriculum. The paper states, "What Aboriginal people have said to us about the educational system is not that Aboriginal people should be forced to change in order to fit into and succeed in school, but rather that the educational system needs to change" (p. 3).

Canada's Sprawling Geography

Canada's large land mass provides challenges in terms of furnishing equitable educational services to small and isolated communities, especially those in the north. Northern and geographically isolated school boards have difficulty attracting and maintaining staff, and providing appropriate educational experiences is costly. The educational systems of these regions must be developed to meet the needs of the students in the context of their communities. The culture of the local communities must be valued and should shape the curriculum. Teachers need to be prepared to meet the special challenges of these regions. Initiatives that encourage young people to become teachers and to remain in their home communities are important. One example of a small school in Fort Providence, Northwest Territories, is the Déh Gah Elementary and Secondary School. Déh Gah is "committed to provide a balanced educational experience; one that is academically strong while incorporating traditional values." It is important to maintain community schools, as in the case of the Charles Yohin School in Nahanni Butte, also in the Northwest Territories. Built of logs with two large classrooms and a mezzanine, the school currently has an enrollment of 18 students, from Kindergarten to Grade 10.

In recent years, technology has had a positive effect on the ability of such schools to communicate and reach out to other areas of the country. Joseph Burr Tyrell School, located in remote Fort Smith, NT, is one such school that has used technology to increase contact with its Canadian peers. The school is working to bridge the distance gap and communicate with such schools as Harry Camsell School in Hay River, NT. Grade 6 students at the school are working on a "Frontier Earth" project, in which they research the effects of global warming and share their findings with students at Harry Camsell. Grade 4 students are now interested in accessing the "Space" project databases Harry Camsell students have already created. Technology will continue to assist schools in isolated areas to make important connections.

Diverse Populations

Canada is becoming increasingly diverse in its population, and such diversity enriches the school systems as well as providing challenges. Large urban areas, such as Vancouver and Toronto, have large populations of immigrants from Asia, Africa, and Latin America that have joined the more established populations with European roots, as well as Aboriginal people. The report on the future of education in Ontario, *The Schools We Need: A New Blueprint for Ontario* (Leithwood, Fullan, & Watson 2003), contends that 59 percent of immigrants to Canada moved to Ontario in 2001, and the vast majority of these settled in the Toronto area. The report argues that the Toronto student population is one of the most diverse found anywhere in the world.

The *Response to the Education Tax Credit* (2001) report, by the Toronto District School Board (TDSB) states the following:

- Approximately 53 percent of TDSB secondary students do not speak English as their first language. In elementary schools, 41 percent of students have a language other than English as their first language.
- More than 80 languages are represented in TDSB schools. Languages from all over the world, such as Urdu, Serbian, Spanish, Swahili, and Cantonese, are spoken by TDSB students.
- More than 47 000 (24 percent) of elementary students were born outside of Canada, in more than 175 different countries.
- More than 11 500 (12 percent) of secondary students have been in Canada for three years or less.

Immigrant students need intake workers and translation services, and their families need school community advisors. It is the public school's responsibility to support the diversity of cultures and tradition; the curriculum and the teaching staff need to address the cognitive and social needs of all learners. (Toronto Parent Network 2001).

Need for Family and Community Support

Support from parents and the community can make a significant difference in the teacher's effectiveness in the classroom. Increasingly, there has been a realization that school, parents, and community must work together so that children and youth develop to their maximum potential academically, socially, emotionally, and physically. Parents who talk with their children, help with homework, read to them, monitor their television viewing, and attend meetings of the Parent Teacher Organization (PTO) and school open houses can enhance their children's ability to succeed in school (Henry 1996; Moore 1992; Fuligni and Stevenson 1995). Similarly, communities can support schools by providing essential social, vocational, recreational, and health support services to students and their families. The CTF Workplace Survey reveals that stress and workload related issues are the most frequently stated reasons that influence Canadian teachers' decisions to leave the profession (CTF 2001).

A low rate of parental participation in their children's schooling is reflected in the 1994 Gallup Poll of the Public's Attitudes toward the Public Schools, which reported that less than 50 percent of the parents of public school students attended a PTA (Parent-Teacher Association) meeting during the academic year, and in the 1995 poll, which reported that only 38 percent of parents attended a school board meeting during the past school year. Nevertheless, the 1997 poll revealed that 69 percent of the public would be willing to work as an unpaid volunteer in local schools—a significant increase compared to 1992, when 59 percent indicated their willingness to volunteer. In Canada, demographic information states that teachers have the confidence of 80 percent of the population (CTF 2000).

Long Working Hours and Job Stress

The official working hours for teachers are attractive, but the real working hours are another matter. Not built into contracts are the after-hours or extra assignments found at all levels of teaching—from recess duty and parent conferences, to high school club advisorships and coaching. Also not obvious are the hours of preparation that occur before and after school—frequently late into the night and over the weekend. Over 90 percent of teachers work more than 40 h per week, with the largest percentage working more than 55 h per week (Louis Harris and Associates 1995).

The need to complete copious amounts of paperwork, including record keeping, may be the most burdensome of the teacher's non-teaching tasks. On average, teachers spend ten hours per week on school-related responsibilities not directly related to teaching (Louis Harris and Associates 1995, 68). Other non-teaching tasks include supervising student behaviour on the playground, at extracurricular events, and in the halls, study halls, and lunchrooms; attending faculty meetings, parent conferences, and open houses; and taking tickets or selling at concessions for athletic events. Individually, such assignments and responsibilities may be enjoyable; too many of them at once, however, become a burden and consume the teacher's valuable time.

In addition to long working hours, factors such as students' lack of interest, conflicts with administrators, public criticism, overcrowded classrooms, lack of resources, and isolation from other adults cause some teachers to experience high levels of stress. Unchecked, acute levels of stress can lead to job dissatisfaction, emotional and physical exhaustion, and an inability to cope effectively—all classic symptoms of teacher **burnout**. To cope with stress and avoid burnout, teachers report that activities in seven areas are beneficial: social support, physical fitness, intellectual stimulation, entertainment, personal hobbies, self-management, and supportive attitudes (Gmelch and Parkay 1995, 46–65).

Gaining Professional Empowerment

In an interview with journalist Bill Moyers, noted Harvard educator Sara Lawrence Lightfoot eloquently describes why teachers desire **professional empowerment**:

[Teachers are] saying, "I haven't had the opportunity to participate fully in this enterprise." Some teachers are speaking about the politics of teachers' voice. They're saying, "We want more control over our lives in this school." Some of them are making an even more subtle point—they're talking about voice as knowledge. "We know things about this enterprise that researchers and policy makers can never know. We have engaged in this intimate experience, and we have things to tell you if you'd only learn how to ask, and if you'd only learn how to listen" (Moyers 1989, 161).

Although some teachers may experience frustration in their efforts to gain professional empowerment, efforts to empower teachers and to "professionalize" teaching are leading to unprecedented opportunities for today's teachers to extend their leadership roles beyond the classroom.

What Is Teaching Really Like?

In this section we examine six basic **realities of teaching** that illustrate why teaching is so demanding and why it can be so exciting, rewarding, and uplifting. And when we say that teaching is demanding, we mean more than the fact that Ms Masih's third-period math students just can't seem to learn how to compute the area of a triangle; or that Mr. LeBlanc's Grade 6 English class can't remember whether to use *there* or *their*; or even that 35 percent of teachers in 1995 reported they were "under great stress" almost every day or several days a week (Louis Harris and Associates 1995, 55). Although there are many frustrating, stressful events with which teachers must cope, the difficulty of teaching goes much further, or deeper, than these examples suggest.

Reality 1: The Unpredictability of Outcomes

The outcomes of teaching, even in the best of circumstances, are neither predictable nor consistent. Any teacher, beginner or veteran, can give countless examples of how the outcomes of teaching are often unpredictable and inconsistent. Life in most classrooms usually proceeds on a fairly even keel—with teachers able to predict, fairly accurately, how their students will respond to lessons. Adherence to the best laid lesson plans, however, may be accompanied by students' blank stares, yawns of boredom, hostile acting out, or expressions of befuddlement. On the other hand, lack of preparation on the teacher's part does not necessarily rule out the possibility of a thoroughly exciting class discussion, a real breakthrough in understanding for an individual student or the entire class, or simply a good, fast-paced review of previously learned material. In short, teachers are often surprised at students' reactions to classroom activities.

Students' Responses

Contrary to the popular notion that teaching consists entirely of specific competencies or observable behaviours that have predetermined effects on students, the reactions of students to any given activity cannot be guaranteed. Furthermore, teachers, unlike other professionals, cannot control all the results of their efforts.

One example of the unpredictability of teaching is given in a teacher intern's description of setting up an independent reading program in his middle-school classroom. Here we see how careful room arrangement and organization of materials do not ensure desired outcomes, and how a teacher learned to adjust to one reality of teaching.

One of the challenges of teaching in the 21st century will be to keep abreast of new technologies that can enhance students' learning. Therefore, it will be important throughout your teacher education program to evaluate your ability to use newly emerging technology. Most colleges and universities offer a wide range of courses and training in the use of technology. To make a self-assessment of your current level of technological literacy, compare your skills with those highlighted in the following case illustration of a teacher education student at Acadia University in Wolfville, Nova Scotia, Canada.

A Day in the Life of …

Jude wakes up in the morning, turns on his laptop computer, sends an email to his parents, checks the sports scores from last night to find that the university basketball team won their game, accesses his group discussion topic for the first class of the day from the virtual bulletin board, adds his thoughts to the ongoing electronic exchanges, and grabs his CD-ROM of readings for the course.

He arrives at his first class, Reading in the Content Areas, finds a seat at one of the tables, takes out his laptop, and connects to the internet. The professor for the course circulates among the students, her computer docked into the teaching station. On a large projection screen is a Microsoft PowerPoint slide that features the topic for the day, the use of web quests as a teaching tool in secondary classrooms. The URL for a website for this topic has been sent to students prior to the class so Jude quickly brings up the site. After the professor explains the history and philosophy behind web quests, small groups form according to content areas. Groups then choose a web quest in their content area and critique it as a possible teaching resource according to a set of criteria. The group discussions are animated and the professor circulates around the room to facilitate the group work. During the class, the professor switches the computer docking station to show a video about reading strategies and the use of technology in the process. After class, groups will be required to continue their critique and to send their completed assignment via an email attachment. The professor reminds the group that the multimedia project is due for next class.

After lunch, Jude goes to his Education Issues class where the professor discusses the electronic case study discussion on censorship. The discussion focuses on several key points. One of Jude's classmates wonders which books are most frequently censored in schools, and the professor asks someone in the class to find that information. An internet search takes Jude to the National Council of Teachers of English (NCTE) site that lists the most frequently banned books and offers guidelines on this issue to educators.

At four o'clock, Jude returns to his room, connects to the internet, checks email, and orders two online articles from the library. He then attaches his contribution to a group project and sends it to the other group

I wanted everything looking perfect. For two more hours, I placed this here and stuffed that in there…. There were stacks of brand-new books sitting on three odd shelves and a metal display rack…. I coded the books and arranged them neatly on the shelves. I displayed their glossy covers as if the room was a [chain bookstore].

A few weeks after setting up the reading program, however, this teacher observes that

The orderly environment I thought I had conceived was fraught with complications. For example, the back rows of the classroom were inaccessible regions from which paper and pencil pieces were hurled at vulnerable victims, and there were zones where, apparently, no teacher's voice could be heard…. The books … remained in chaos. Novels turned up behind shelves, on the sidewalks outside,

members for feedback. He goes off to the dining hall where his student card is electronically swiped before he picks up his meal.

After dinner, Jude logs on to the internet again, and sends his unit lesson plans to his cooperating teacher at the school where he starts his field experience next week. He is proud of the learning object he has designed for one of the lessons. For his final task of the evening, he goes to a URL where he views some scenes from a Virtual Learning Environment that simulate the experience of a Grade 7 teacher. Jude emails home, checks the online edition of the local paper, and logs off for the night.

The task for the next day is to complete the electronic portfolio CD-ROM for use when applying for teaching positions.

Acadia University is an example of an innovative and technologically advanced Canadian school. All students enrolled at Acadia University lease an IBM ThinkPad, which they are allowed to take anywhere with them—from the classroom, to residence, or home for vacations. In addition, each student is provided with an email account. The university campus has over 5200 on-campus data connections; students can connect from classrooms, residences, and other locations throughout the campus and off-campus students use a dial-up service. The students and faculty use the technology in a number of ways from classroom applications, to out-of-class communication and instant messaging. Professors may put class notes on Microsoft PowerPoint and post course materials on the Automated Courseware Management Environment (ACME). Email is used to communicate outside class, set up appointments, post announcements, and exchange files. The university promises, "You will learn to access the world's knowledge, use today's technology, and develop the advanced technological skills you will need to adapt to ever-changing study and work environments." (Irwin 2003)

In universities across Canada, teachers of tomorrow are being prepared in a similar way for the technology-laden future by learning to keep abreast of change. Canadian teacher-training programs recognize the challenges future teachers face and they are focusing on preparing future educators to use and integrate technology into their curriculum in a meaningful way.

and in the trash can. And still, at least once a week, I dutifully arranged them until I was satisfied. But something was happening. It was taking less and less for me to be satisfied.... [I] loosened up (Henry et al. 1995, 73–76).

Contrary to the preceding example, unpredictability in the classroom is not always bad. Another teacher intern describes her unexpected success at setting up a writing workshop at an urban middle school with a large population of at-risk students. One day she began by telling her students that

"We're going to be starting something new these six weeks.... We will be transforming this classroom into a writing workshop." What was I trying to do here? They're not writers.... Raymond stared down at *Where's Waldo*. Michael was engrossed in an elaborate pencil drum solo. Edwina powdered her nose and under her eyes.

"Listen to me, you guys," I said, trying not to lose it before we even started. "We're starting something completely different, something you never get a chance to do in your other classes."

A few heads turned to face me. Veronica slugged Edwina, and Edwina slid her compact into her back pocket.

"What, Miss ... chew gum?"

In spite of her initial reservations, this teacher made the following observations the next day—the first day of the writing workshop.

Today, it's all clicking.

"Aw, man, I told you I don't understand that part. Why does that guy in your story ... Chris ... say that it's too early to rob the store?" David pleads. "It doesn't make sense."

Raymond tips his desk forward and smiles. "It's too early because they want to wait until the store's almost closed."

"Well, then, you've got to say that. Right, Miss?"

I lean against the door frame and try not to laugh. I listen to the conversations around me. Yes, they're loud and they're talking and they're laughing. But they're learning. My students are involved in their writing, I say to myself and shake my head (Henry et al. 1995, 54–55).

Philip Jackson describes the unpredictability of teaching in his well-known book *Life in Classrooms*: "[As] typically conducted, teaching is an opportunistic process.... Neither teacher nor students can predict with any certainty exactly what will happen next. Plans are forever going awry and unexpected opportunities for the attainment of educational goals are constantly emerging" (Jackson 1990, 166).

In what ways must this classroom teacher face the reality of unpredictable outcomes? What are five other basic realities that all teachers face in their work?

Results in the Future

Teachers strive to effect changes in their students for the future as well as for the here and now. In *Life in Classrooms*, Jackson labels this the preparatory aspect of teaching. In addition to having students perform better on next Monday's unit exam or on a criterion-referenced test mandated by the province, teachers expect students to apply their newly acquired skills and knowledge at some indeterminate, usually distant, point in the future.

Just as months or years may pass before the results of teaching become clear, teachers may wait a long time before receiving positive feedback from students. The following comment by a Kindergarten teacher illustrates the delayed satisfaction that can characterize teaching:

> About a month ago I had a 22-year-old boy knock on the door. He said, "Miss R?" I said, "Yes." He is now in England, an architect; he's married and has a little girl. I thought, "This is not happening to me. I had you in Kindergarten." If you teach high school and a kid comes back and he's married in two or three years, that's expected, but 16 years or 18 years—first year in Kindergarten. It's rewarding ... be it one year, or ten years down the road.... There are daily satisfactions—"She got it!"—that's a reward in itself, but I think it's a little bit down the road that you get your satisfaction (Cohn and Kottkamp 1993, 42–43).

Reality 2: The Difficulty of Assessing Students' Learning

It is difficult to assess what students learn as a result of being taught. The ultimate purpose of teaching is to lead the student to a greater understanding of the things and ideas of this world. But, as even the most casual appraisal of human nature will confirm, it is very difficult, perhaps impossible, to determine precisely what another human being does or does not understand. Although the aims or intentions of teaching may be specified with exacting detail, one of the realities of teaching, as the following junior high school teacher points out, is that some of what students learn may be indeterminate and beyond direct measurement:

> There is no clear end result.... That frustrates me. I want so badly for my joy [of teaching] to be neatly tied up so that I can look at it admiringly.... I want so badly to *see* my successes—I don't know, give me certificates or badges or jelly beans. Then I can stack them up, count them, and rate myself as a teacher (Henry et al. 1995, 68–69).

Advocates of national testing stress the need for objective measurement of school and student performance. Proponents of national testing stress that it is an accurate measure of Canada's public school system and a valuable method to compare results across schools, school boards, provinces or territories, and nations. Teachers' concerns about national testing include the interpretation of results, and the areas of learning that cannot be measured by such tests. (CTF n.d.)

We have miles of computer printouts with test data but very little knowledge of what lies behind a child's written response, little understanding of how the child experiences the curriculum. As one educational researcher concludes: "The inaccessibility of data is similar both in science and in learning. We cannot directly 'see' subatomic particles, nor can we 'see' the inner-workings of the mind and emotions of the child. Both are inferential: both are subject to human interpretation" (Costa 1984, 202).

On the one hand, then, teachers must recognize their limited ability to determine what students actually learn; on the other, they must continuously work to become aware of the latest approaches to assessing students' learning. Figure 1.2 presents a set of guiding principles for teachers to follow in developing a student-centred approach to classroom assessment.

Figure 1.2

The principles of sound assessment: a critical blend

Source: Adapted from Richard J. Stiggins, *Student-Centered Classroom Assessment,* 2nd ed. Upper Saddle River, NJ: Merrill, 1997, p. 10.

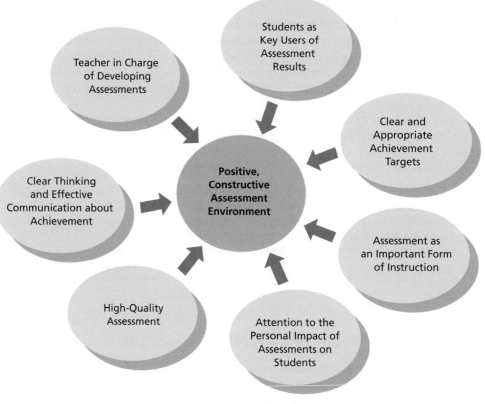

Reality 3: The Need for Student-Teacher Partnership

The teacher's ability to influence student behaviour is actually quite limited. The very fact that we refer to the teaching–learning process indicates the extent to which classroom events are "jointly produced" (Doyle 1986, 395) and depend upon a teacher–student partnership. According to Arthur Combs (1979, 234–35) in a book aptly titled *Myths in Education: Beliefs That Hinder Progress and Their Alternatives*:

> A teacher's influence on all but the simplest, most primitive forms of student behaviour, even in that teacher's own classroom, cannot be clearly established. The older children get, the less teachers can influence even those few, primitive forms of behaviour. The attempt to hold teachers responsible for what students do is, for all practical purposes, well nigh impossible.

At best, a teacher tries to influence students so that they make internal decisions to behave in the desired manner—whether it be reading the first chapter of *The Shipping News* by Friday or solving ten addition problems during a mathematics lesson. Teaching is a uniquely demanding profession, therefore, because the work of teachers is evaluated not in terms of what teachers do but in terms of their ability "to help the students become more effective as learners," to "become active seekers after new development" (Joyce and Weil 2000, 408, 399).

This reality underscores the need for a partnership between teacher and learners, including learners who are culturally diverse.

Reality 4: The Impact of Teachers' Attitudes

With the role of teacher also comes the power to influence others by example. Educational psychologist Anita E. Woolfolk (1998, 223) states that "teachers serve as models for a vast range of behaviours, from pronouncing vocabulary words, to reacting to the seizure of an epileptic student, to being enthusiastic about learning." Clearly, students learn much by imitation, and teachers are models for students. In the primary grades, teachers are idolized by their young students. At the high school level, teachers have the potential to inspire students' emulation and establish the classroom tone by modelling expected attitudes and behaviours.

In *The Tact of Teaching: The Meaning of Pedagogical Thoughtfulness*, Max van Manen (1991, 167) states the importance of teachers' attitudes toward students:

> An educator needs to believe in children. Specifically, he or she needs to believe in the possibilities and goodness of the particular children for whom he or she has responsibility. My belief in a child strengthens that child—provided of course that the child experiences my trust as something real and as something positive.

A high school social studies teacher expresses the same idea in this manner: "[The] relationship between teachers and students is becoming one of the most important aspects of teaching. [In] a world of broken homes and violence, the encouragement of their teachers may be the only thing students can hold onto that makes them feel good about themselves" (Henry et al. 1995, 127).

Teachers also model attitudes toward the subjects they teach and show students, through their example that learning is an ongoing, life-enriching process that does not end with diplomas and graduations. Their example confirms the timeless message of Sir Rabindranath Tagore that is inscribed above the doorway of a public building in India: "A teacher can never truly teach unless he is still learning himself. A lamp can never light another lamp unless it continues to burn its own flame."

Reality 5: The Drama and Immediacy of Teaching

Interactive teaching is characterized by events that are rapid-changing, multidimensional, and irregular. We have already discussed how the outcomes of teaching are unpredictable and inconsistent. Yet the challenges of teaching go beyond this. The face-to-face interactions teachers have with students—what Jackson (1990, 152) has termed **interactive teaching**—are themselves rapid-changing, multidimensional, and irregular. "Day in and day out, teachers spend much of their lives 'on stage' before audiences that are not always receptive ... teachers must orchestrate a daunting array of interpersonal interactions and build a cohesive, positive climate for learning" (Gmelch and Parkay 1995, 47).

When teachers are in the **preactive teaching** stages of their work—preparing to teach or reflecting on previous teaching—they can afford to be consistently deliberate and rational. Planning for lessons, grading papers,

How do teacher's attitudes affect students' learning? In what ways are teachers significant role models for students?

reflecting on the misbehaviour of a student—such activities are usually done alone and lack the immediacy and sense of urgency that characterize interactive teaching. While actually working with students, however, you must be able to think on your feet and respond appropriately to complex, ever-changing situations. You must be flexible and ready to deal with the unexpected. During a discussion, for example, you must operate on at least two levels. On one level, you respond appropriately to students' comments, monitor other students for signs of confusion or comprehension, formulate the next comment or question, and be alert for signs of misbehaviour. On another level, you ensure that participation is evenly distributed among students, evaluate the content and quality of students' contributions, keep the discussion focused and moving ahead, and emphasize major content areas.

During interactive teaching, the awareness that you are responsible for the forward movement of the group never lets up. Teachers are the only professionals who practice their craft almost exclusively under the direct, continuous gaze of up to 30 or 40 clients. Jackson (1990, 119) sums up the experience: "The *immediacy* of classroom events is something that anyone who has ever been in charge of a roomful of students can never forget."

Reality 6: The Uniqueness of the Teaching Experience

Teaching involves a unique mode of being between teacher and student—a mode of being that can be experienced but not fully defined or described. On your journey to become a teacher, you will gradually develop your capacity to listen to students and to convey an authentic sense of concern for their learning. Unfortunately, there is no precise, easy-to-follow formula for demonstrating this to students. You will have to take into account your personality and special gifts to discover your own best way for showing this concern.

One reason it is difficult to describe teaching is that an important domain of teaching, **teachers' thought processes**, including professional reflection, cannot be observed directly. Figure 1.3 shows how the unobservable domain of the teacher's "interior reflective thinking" interacts with and is influenced by the observable domain of the teacher's "exterior reflective action." Teachers' thought processes include their theories and beliefs about students and how they learn, their plans for teaching, and the decisions they make while teaching. Thought processes and actions can be constrained by the physical setting of the classroom or external factors such as the curriculum, the principal, or the community. On the other hand, teachers' thought processes and actions may be influenced by unique opportunities, such as the chance to engage in curriculum reform or school governance. The model also illustrates a further complexity of teaching—namely, that the relationships between teacher behaviour, student behaviour, and student achievement are reciprocal. What teachers do is influenced not only by their thought processes before, during, and after teaching but also by student behaviour and student achievement. This complexity contributes to the uniqueness of the teaching experience.

What Does Society Expect of Teachers?

The prevailing view within our society is that teachers are public servants accountable to the people. As a result, society has high expectations of teachers—some would say too high. Entrusted with our nation's most precious resource, its children and youth, today's teachers are expected to have advanced knowledge and skills and

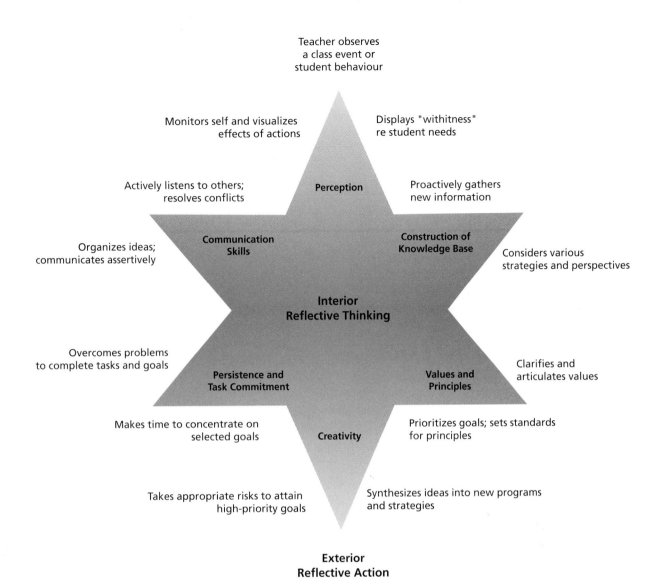

Teacher observes
a class event or
student behaviour

Monitors self and visualizes
effects of actions

Displays "withitness"
re student needs

Actively listens to others;
resolves conflicts

Perception

Proactively gathers
new information

Organizes ideas;
communicates assertively

**Communication
Skills**

**Construction of
Knowledge Base**

Considers various
strategies and perspectives

**Interior
Reflective Thinking**

Overcomes problems
to complete tasks and goals

**Persistence and
Task Commitment**

**Values and
Principles**

Clarifies and
articulates values

Makes time to concentrate on
selected goals

Creativity

Prioritizes goals; sets standards
for principles

Takes appropriate risks to attain
high-priority goals

Synthesizes ideas into new programs
and strategies

**Exterior
Reflective Action**

high academic and ethical standards. Although promoting students' academic progress has always been their primary responsibility, teachers are also expected to further students' social, emotional, and moral development and to safeguard students' health and well-being. Increasingly, the public calls on teachers and schools to address social problems and risk factors that affect student success.

The Public Trust

Teaching is subject to a high degree of public scrutiny and control. The level of trust that the public extends to teachers as professionals varies greatly. The public appears to have great confidence in the work that teachers do. Because of its faith in the teaching profession, the public invests teachers with considerable power over its children. For the most part, parents willingly allow their children to be influenced by teachers and expect their children to obey and respect teachers. However, the public trust increases and decreases in response to social and political changes that lead to waves of educational reform.

Figure 1.3

A model of reflective action in teaching

Source: Judy W. Eby, *Reflective Planning, Teaching, and Evaluation: K–12,* 2nd ed. Upper Saddle River, NJ: Merrill, 1996, p. 14. © 1996. Reprinted by permission of Prentice-Hall, Inc., Upper Saddle River, NJ.

Teacher Competency and Effectiveness

Society believes that competent, effective teachers are important keys to a strong system of education. Accordingly, teachers are expected to be proficient in the use of instructional strategies, curriculum materials, advanced educational technologies, and classroom management techniques. They are also expected to have a thorough understanding of the developmental levels of their students and a solid grasp of the content they teach. To maintain and extend this high level of skill, teachers are expected to be informed of exemplary practices and to demonstrate a desire for professional development.

Teacher competency and effectiveness includes the responsibility to help all learners succeed. Though today's students come from a diverse array of backgrounds, society expects teachers to hold strong beliefs about the potential for all children. Regardless of their students' ethnicity, language, gender, socioeconomic status, family backgrounds and living conditions, abilities, or disabilities, teachers have a responsibility to ensure that all students develop to their fullest potential. To accomplish this, teachers are expected to have a repertoire of instructional strategies and resources to create meaningful learning experiences that promote students' growth and development.

Teacher Accountability

Teachers must "be mindful of the social ethic—their public duties and obligations—embodied in the practice of teaching ..." (Hansen 1995, 143). Society agrees that teachers are primarily responsible for promoting students' learning, though it is not always in agreement about what students should learn. In any case, society expects teachers to understand how factors such as student backgrounds, attitudes, and learning styles can affect achievement; and it expects that teachers will create safe and effective learning environments. Society also believes that teachers and schools should be accountable for equalizing educational opportunity and maintaining high professional standards.

Teacher accountability also means meeting high standards of conduct. Teachers are no longer required to sign statements such as the following, taken from a 1927 contract: "I promise to sleep at least eight hours a night, to eat carefully, and to take every precaution to keep in the best of health and spirits, in order that I may be better able to render efficient service to my pupils" (Waller 1932, 43). Nevertheless, society does expect teachers to hold high standards of professional ethics and personal morality and to model behaviours that match those standards.

How Do Good Teachers View Their Work?

Most Canadian teachers across the country feel good about their jobs. Of 11 000 teachers surveyed (Kuehn n.d.) overall sources of satisfaction from their work included student respect for them as a teacher (92 percent), financial rewards (51 percent), and being well-respected in their community (49 percent). Eighty-seven percent of teachers agreed that "teaching is a worthwhile job," 89 percent said they are "proud to be a teacher," and 77 percent said that they "look forward to coming to work each day" (Larry Kuehn n.d.).

Good teachers derive greatest satisfaction when they are effective in promoting students' learning—when they "make a difference" in students' lives. When you recall your most effective teachers, you probably think of particular individuals, not idealizations of the teacher's many roles. What good teachers do can be described in terms of five **modes of teaching**, which are more general and significant than a discussion of roles.

You may recognize these modes in your observations of teachers and in the writings of gifted teachers when they reflect on their work. You may even acknowledge these modes of teaching as deeper reasons for becoming a teacher.

A Way of Being

In becoming a teacher, you take on the role and let it become a part of you. Increasingly, the learning of facts can be achieved easily with good books, good TV, CD-ROMs, and access to the Internet. What cannot be done in these ways is teaching styles of life, teaching what it means to be, to grow, to become actualized, to become complete. The only way a teacher can teach these qualities is to possess them. "They become living examples for their students, showing that what they say is important enough for them to apply to their own lives. They are attractive models who advertise, by their very being, that learning does produce wondrous results" (Zehm and Kottler 1993, 16).

A Creative Endeavour

Teaching is a creative endeavour in which teachers are continually shaping and reshaping lessons, events, and the experiences of their students. In *The Call to Teach*, David Hansen (1995, 13) describes the creative dimensions of teaching this way: "In metaphorical terms, teaching is ... more than carrying brick, mortar, and shovel. Rather, it implies being the architect of one's classroom world."

With careful attention to the details of classroom life, effective teachers artistically develop educative relationships with their students; they "read" the myriad events that emerge while teaching and respond appropriately. One high school teacher, identified as highly successful by her principal, reported: "I have to grab the kids that don't want to do math at all and somehow make them want to do this work. I'm not sure how I do it, but kids just want to do well in my class. For some mysterious reason, and I don't care why, they really want to do well."

A Live Performance

Teaching is a live performance with each class period, each day, containing the unpredictable. Further, teachers are engaged in live dialogues with their classes and individual students. The experience of teaching is thus an intense, attention-demanding endeavour—an interactive one that provides minute-to-minute challenges.

Some teachers embrace the live performance aspect of teaching more than others, believing that within it lies true learning. They recognize that teaching "... is full of surprises; classroom lessons that lead to unexpected questions and insights; lessons that fail despite elaborate planning; spur-of-the-moment activities that work beautifully and that may change the direction of a course; students who grow and learn; students who seem to regress or grow distant" (Hansen 1995, 12).

A Form of Empowerment

Power is the dimension of teaching most immediately evident to the new teacher. It is recognized in the first-grader's awed "Teacher, is this good?" on through the high school senior's "How much will this paper count?" Customarily, teachers get respect, at least initially; the deference derives from their power to enhance or diminish their students' academic status and welfare.

What are the modes of teaching that define the essence of good teaching and distinguish gifted teachers? Which mode of teaching might this photo represent?

Even in the most democratic classrooms, teachers have more influence than students because they are responsible for what happens when students are with them, establishing the goals, selecting the methods, setting the pace, evaluating the progress, and deciding whether students should pass or fail. How you use this power is critical. As you know, students at any level can be humiliated by teachers who misuse their power or convey negative expectations to students. A student teacher in a Grade 5 class comments on the impact negative expectations can have on students:

They [students] can sense how a teacher feels, especially how she feels about them personally. Students often find themselves locked into a role that they have played for so long they don't know how to get out of it. Students deserve the right to have an education. They should not have to worry about what negative comments their teachers are saying about them (Rand and Shelton-Colangelo 1999, 107).

An Opportunity to Serve

To become a teacher is to serve others professionally—students, the school, the community, and the country, depending on how broad the perspective is. Most who come to teaching do so for altruistic reasons. The altruistic dimension of teaching is at the heart of the motivation to teach. The paycheque, the public regard, and the vacations have little holding power compared to the opportunity to serve. As the authors of *On Being a Teacher* observe:

Very few people go into education in the first place to become rich or famous. On some level, every teacher gets a special thrill out of helping others.... [The] teachers who flourish, those who are loved by their students and revered by their colleagues, are those who feel tremendous dedication and concern for others—not just because they are paid to do so, but because it is their nature and their ethical responsibility (Zehm and Kottler 1993, 8–9).

Prime Minister's Award for Teaching Excellence Recipients: George Findlay, Renee Boyce, and Lindsay Johnston.

Taking students outside the traditional classroom walls expands their horizons and allows them to experience learning in non-traditional ways. The three teachers profiled in this Teaching for Excellence feature show their students a world of opportunities to prepare them for lifelong learning beyond the classroom.

George Findlay

Princess Elizabeth Public School, Windsor, Ontario

Subjects Taught: Grades 6, 7, and 8

At the very time of their lives when they need to be learning about the range of possibilities that life offers them and about the incredible potential they have within them, children are trapped in a routine round of fact processing, explains George Findlay, who teaches students in the transition years (Grades 6, 7, and 8) at Princess Elizabeth Public School. Findlay tries to counter the feeling he sees in too many kids, that they will stay in a routine school-bound existence until they are 17 or 18 and then leave to take a routine-bound job for the rest of their lives.

For Findlay, hope and opportunities lie around every corner—even at the local campground. "It may seem a simple—even a corny—thing to take a class on a three-day camping trip," he says, "but the benefits are huge." Children learn valuable lessons far beyond the curriculum, about working and about reaching outside their immediate experiences, he explains. "For children in my school, going to a campground or a large building downtown, paying for their own meal, and figuring out how to tip in a restaurant can be very educational experiences."

Lindsay Johnston

Calgary Science Centre School, Calgary, Alberta

Subjects Taught: Science

In elementary school, Lindsay Johnston says, the most important thing a child can learn about science is that it is accessible. In the controlled environment that is all too common inside the classroom, students often learn that science is something closed. "Can you imagine a 10-year-old child believing that they can't do science?" asks Johnston incredulously. Unfortunately, she has, and it is her desire to counter that impression that drives her work at the Science Centre School—a very un-classroom-like setting.

Johnston and her students adopted a natural area a kilometre from the school for a year. They studied the wildlife and plants, and they hiked, bicycled and picnicked, getting to know every corner of the green space. When there was a local dispute about making the area more commercial, the students immersed themselves in the related social issues, such as land use in urban areas. Even at a young age, the students began to see how their learning is connected to the real world.

Renee Boyce

Bishops College, St. John's, Newfoundland

Subjects Taught: Physics

At the high school level, Renee Boyce worried about opening doors for her high school students who feared physics courses. This teacher countered widespread fear by printing a pamphlet telling students exactly what they needed to "do physics." An enthusiastic advocate for the subject, Boyce says that the "mystique that surrounds physics—Newton, Einstein, and Hawking struggling with the basic stuff of the universe—is exactly what captivates kids and fills them with wonder, giving them the drive to master the concepts and the math." This includes getting them out of the classroom, and into the real world that led scientists to start asking questions in the first place. For example, her students learn about navigation on the deck of an oceanographic vessel while they are learning about the ocean floor and currents.

Source: Reproduced with the permission of the Minister of Public Works and Government Services, 2003. Prime Minister's awards for teaching excellence: Exemplary practices. *Beyond the Classroom Walls*. Retrieved 22 January 2003, from pma-ppm.ic.gc.ca/exemplary/1999/Beyond.html

Whatever forms the altruistic rewards of teaching take, they ennoble the profession and remind teachers of the human significance of their work.

Teaching for Excellence

Many of our country's most talented youth and dedicated veterans in the teaching field retain the desire to teach. In part, the desire endures because teachers have been positively influenced by one or more teachers of their own, who enriched, redirected, or significantly changed their lives. The desire also endures because teachers recognize the many joys and rewards the profession offers.

Reflecting on dedicated teachers and their contributions to our lives, we are guided to teaching for the benefit it brings to others. Every year, the Prime Minister's Awards for Teaching Excellence recognizes the efforts of outstanding teachers in all disciplines who provide students with "the tools to become good citizens, to grow and prosper as individuals, and to contribute to Canada's growth, prosperity and well-being" (Industry Canada 1998, iv). Specifically, nominees are recognized for excelling in "some or all of the following areas: exemplary teaching practices; student interest and participation; student achievement/performance; student skills development; and teacher commitment and leadership" (Industry Canada). This textbook acknowledges recipients of the Prime Minister's Awards for Teaching Excellence in selected chapters in a special feature called *Teaching for Excellence*.

SUMMARY

Why Do You Want to Teach?

- An important reason for becoming a teacher is a desire to work with children and young people.

- Other reasons include a passion for teaching based on a love of subject, the teaching life, or the teaching–learning process; the influence of teachers in one's past; and a desire to serve others and society.

- Practical benefits of teaching include on-the-job hours at school, vacations, increasing salaries and benefits, job security, and a feeling of respect in society.

- In contrast to the diversity of student enrollments, the backgrounds of today's teachers are less diverse; thus teachers from diverse racial and ethnic backgrounds and teachers with disabilities will experience exceptional job opportunities for the foreseeable future.

What Are the Challenges of Teaching?

- Working conditions for teachers can be difficult and stressful; however, for most teachers satisfactions outweigh dissatisfactions.

- Though problems in schools vary according to size of community, location, and other factors, teachers in most schools face five challenges: classroom management, social problems that impact students, need for family and community support, long working hours and job stress, and need for professional empowerment.

- Maintaining discipline and avoiding school-based violence are major concerns among preservice teachers.

- Social problems that impact the lives of many children and youth include substance abuse, teen pregnancies, homelessness, poverty, family distress, child abuse, violence and crime, suicide, and health problems such as HIV/AIDS and fetal alcohol syndrome.

- Though job-related factors cause some teachers to experience high levels of stress, stress-reduction activities can help teachers cope and avoid burnout.

What Is Teaching Really Like?

- The outcomes of teaching, even in the best of circumstances, are neither predictable nor consistent.

- It is difficult to assess what students learn as a result of being taught.

- The teacher's ability to influence student behaviour is actually quite limited.

- With the role of teacher also comes the power to influence others by example.

- Interactive teaching is characterized by events that are rapid-changing, multidimensional, and irregular.

- Teaching involves a unique mode of being between teacher and student—a mode of being that can be experienced but not fully defined or described.

What Does Society Expect of Teachers?

- Society has high expectations of the teachers to whom it entrusts its children and youth.

- Society expects teachers to be competent and effective, and it holds teachers accountable for student achievement, for helping all learners succeed, and for maintaining high standards of conduct.

How Do Good Teachers View Their Work?

- Helping students learn and making a difference in students' lives provide teachers with their greatest satisfaction.

- The essence of good teaching can be described in terms of modes of teaching illustrating what good teachers do.

- Five modes of teaching are teaching as a way of being, a creative endeavour, a live performance, a form of empowerment, and an opportunity to serve.

KEY TERMS AND CONCEPTS

burnout, 20
fringe benefits, 14
interactive
    teaching, 27
modes of teaching, 30
preactive teaching, 27

professional
    empowerment, 20
professional portfolio, 37
realities of teaching, 21
student diversity, 8
student-mobility rates, 16

student variability, 8
teacher accountability, 30
teacher–student ratios, 16
teachers' thought
    processes, 28

Teacher's Journal

1. Consider your reasons for deciding to become a teacher. How do they compare with those described in this chapter?

2. Describe a former teacher who has had a positive influence on your decision to teach. In what ways would you like to become like that teacher?

3. What is your impression of the public's image of teachers in your province, territory, or community today? What factors might be contributing to the kind of attention or lack of attention teachers are receiving?

4. Think about a time when a teacher truly motivated you to learn. What did that teacher do to motivate you? Do you believe other students in the class had the same reaction to this teacher? Why or why not?

5. Recall and describe specific experiences you had with teachers in elementary school, middle school or junior high school, or high school. Were you ever made uncomfortable because of a teacher's power over you? Were you ever ridiculed or diminished by a teacher? Or have you experienced the opposite—being elevated by a teacher's regard for you?

Teacher's Database

1. Make a list of recent portrayals of teachers in the movies, television, and other media. Analyze the portrayals in terms of the type of teacher image they present—positive, neutral, or negative.

2. Clip articles in a major newspaper that relate to one of the focus questions in this chapter. Analyze the clippings as sources of information and examples you can use to develop an answer to that question.

3. While you are on the web, use your favourite search engine and search for information by key words or topics such as: teacher burnout, cost of living, moonlighting, accountability, teacher–student ratios, and tenure.

Observations and Interviews

1. As a collaborative project with classmates, visit a local school and interview teachers to learn about their perceptions of the rewards and challenges of teaching. Share your findings with other groups in your class.

2. Arrange to observe a teacher's class. During your observation, note evidence of the five modes of teaching discussed in this chapter.

3. Ask your instructor to arrange group interviews between students in your class and students at the local elementary, middle, junior, and senior high schools. At each interview session, ask the students what characterizes good and not so good teachers. Also, ask the students what advice they would give to beginning teachers.

4. During an observation of a teacher's class, note evidence of the six realities of teaching discussed in this chapter. How many realities are evident during your observation? Which reality is most prevalent? Least prevalent?

5. Visit a first-year teacher (possibly a graduate from your institution) and ask about his or her first impressions of becoming a teacher. What aspects of teaching were difficult? Which easy? What surprises did this first-year teacher encounter? How would this person have prepared differently?

Professional Portfolio

To help you in your journey toward becoming a teacher, each chapter in this text-book includes suggestions for developing your **professional portfolio,** a collection of evidence documenting your growth and development while learning to become a teacher. At the end of this course you will be well on your way toward a portfolio that documents your knowledge, skills, and attitudes for teaching and contains valuable resources for your first teaching position.

For your first portfolio entry, expand on Teacher's Journal entry #1, which asks you to consider your reasons for becoming a teacher. In your entry (or videotaped version), identify the rewards of teaching for you. Identify the satisfactions. Also, describe the aspects of teaching that you will find challenging.

2

Learning to Teach

The mediocre teacher tells.
The good teacher explains.
The superior teacher demonstrates.
The great teacher inspires.
—William A. Ward

focus questions

1. What essential knowledge do you need to teach?

2. What are five ways of viewing the teacher knowledge base?

3. How are Canadian teachers educated and certified?

4. What can you learn from observing in classrooms?

5. How can you gain practical experience for becoming a teacher?

6. How can you develop your teaching portfolio?

7. How can you benefit from mentoring relationships?

8. What opportunities for continuing professional development will you have?

The room was filled with the chatter of writing workshop. Nat puzzled over two crayons in his hand, one of them blue: "Mrs. Hankins, ain't you had you a blue bicycle when you was a little-girl-teacher?" Nat had a way of naming me for what I was: always a teacher—or was it always a little girl? I answered Nat's present question, remembering my past blue bicycle and a childhood story about it that I had shared with the children recently.

Perhaps it was one of those "tell-me-about-when-you-were-little" moments that brought writing memoirs to the forefront of my teaching journal. Perhaps it was the need to make some sense of the cacophonous days with my three special students, Nat, Loretta, and Rodney, who had all been damaged in utero by drugs or alcohol. The original impetus for these writings is lost to me now, but, as Lucy Calkins (1991, 169) says, writing memoirs "has everything to do with rendering the ordinariness of our lives so that it becomes significant." The past seemed to wrap itself around my present-day questions, and as the number of memoirs grew, my journal became a place for uncovering the significant....

I wrote up a study of Nat, Loretta, and Rodney's journey through Kindergarten and presented parts of the study at a conference. After the presentation, I wrote the following reflection in my journal:

So, I keep this journal. It was easier when no one else knew or cared that I wrote. It's a teaching journal. It's a personal journal. It's a research journal. It's both a personal and teaching journal because John Dewey first and Lucy Calkins later taught me to reflect on my day and my life in the same breath. It's both a teaching and research journal because I no longer believe that teaching can be separated from research. (Perhaps it CAN be but it shouldn't be.) The question is ... I guess ... Can it be both personal and research journal? That's what people really want me to defend. But how can I tell people what my heart and head do together in my classroom? (journal entry, April)

I wrote at nap time, while waiting for faculty meetings to begin, during the last ten minutes before turning out the light each night, and on the backs of church bulletins or napkins in restaurants. I had never heard of field notes at the time. I read recently a definition of ethnographic field notes as "the systematic ways of writing what one observes and learns while participating in the daily rounds of the lives of others" (Emerson, Fretz, and Shaw 1995, 18). As the year progressed, I fell into a system of sorts as I recorded the "lives of others." My journal served, then, as the field notes of a teacher. Mine were records of what Emerson et al. (1995) call "head-notes"—mental notes—"hard notes"—direct observations—and "heartnotes"—my feelings and reflections....

When I began seriously listening to my life, my teaching life, I also began to listen to my students' lives at a different level.... I became more tolerant of those who were different from me. When I began to stop and examine the flashes of memory that jolted me, I became a more patient teacher. I more often saw the students and their parents as people; people walking in and out of pain, in and out of joy, in and out of socially constructed prisons (Hankins 1998, 81, 83, 93).*

*Source: Excerpts from Karen Hale Hankins, "Cacophony to Symphony: Memoirs in Teacher Research," *Harvard Educational Review, 68*:1 (Spring 1998), pp. 80–95. Copyright & copy; 1998 by the President and Fellows of Harvard College. All rights reserved.

In the preceding excerpt from Karen Hale Hankin's article "Cacophony to Symphony: Memoirs in Teacher Research," Hale describes how reflective journal writing enabled her to see significant connections between her personal history and her present experiences in the classroom. By purposely examining her "mental notes," "direct observations," and "feelings and reflections," Hankins learned how to "reach and teach" the students with whom she once felt she had little in common. Her ability to reflect upon her experiences in the classroom and her appreciation for the interconnectedness of teaching and research are the hallmarks of a professional teacher. Furthermore, her reflections are reminders that teaching is a complex act—one that requires thoughtfulness, insight into the motivations of others, and good judgment.

What Essential Knowledge Do You Need to Teach?

Students preparing to become teachers must have three kinds of knowledge before they can manage effectively the complexities of teaching: knowledge of self and students, knowledge of subject, and knowledge of educational theory and research. It is to this essential knowledge that we now turn.

Self-Knowledge

Effective teachers are aware of themselves and sensitive to the needs of their students. Although it is evident that teachers should understand their students as fully and deeply as possible, it is less evident that this understanding depends on their level of self-knowledge. If teachers are knowledgeable about their needs (and, most important, able to take care of those needs), they are better able to help their students. As Arthur Jersild (1955, 3), one of the first educators to focus attention on the connection between the teacher's personal insight and professional effectiveness, pointed out, a teacher's self-understanding and self-acceptance are prerequisites for helping students to know and accept themselves.

Teachers' self-evaluations often are influenced by emotions that teachers may experience when they teach, such as anxiety or loneliness. Promoting anxiety are the realities of teaching outlined in Chapter 1. For example, three conditions that cloud teachers' efforts are (1) the interminable nature of teaching (i.e., their work is never completed), (2) the intangible and often unpredictable characteristics of teaching results, and (3) the inability to attribute learning results to specific teachers' instruction. Unlike architects, lawyers, and doctors, teachers can never stand back and admire their work. If a student does well, that success rightfully belongs to the student.

Teachers thus need to develop the ability to tolerate ambiguities and to reduce their anxieties about being observably effective. Without this ability, a teacher "can feel that one is 'wrong,' 'missing something,' a 'bad fit' with students and with teaching itself. One can feel that one's circumstances are unfair, that one is giving but not receiving. One can feel helpless, not knowing what to do, not even knowing how to get the frustration out of mind let alone how to resolve it in practice" (Hansen 1995, 60).

Teachers can also experience loneliness or psychological isolation, since most of their time is spent interacting with children and youth, not adults. Though increased opportunities for professional collaboration and networking are reducing teacher isolation, teachers are behind classroom doors most of the day, immersed in the complexities of teaching and trying to meet the diverse needs of their students. Most teachers would welcome more interaction with their colleagues, especially time to observe one another. Without opportunities to receive feedback from one's peers, teachers are deprived of an important catalyst for professional growth. As Elliot Eisner puts it: "The result of professional isolation is the difficulty that teachers encounter in learning what they themselves do in their own classrooms when they teach. [How] can a teacher learn that he or she is talking too much, not providing sufficient time for student reflection, raising low-order questions, or is simply boring students? Teachers unaware of such features of their own performance are in no position to change them" (1998, 160–61). Additionally, by observing how a colleague responds to the challenges of teaching, the observer has an opportunity to reflect on his or her approaches to meeting those same challenges. For example, a Grade 4 teacher came to the following insight as a result of observing his teaching partner: "Being a teacher is so much more than an extensive repertoire of strategies and techniques. [To] be a teacher is to find a way to live within an environment filled with dilemmas" (Hole 1998, 419).

Knowledge of Students

Knowledge of students is also important. Student characteristics such as their aptitudes, talents, learning styles, stage of development, and their readiness to learn new material are a part of the essential knowledge teachers must have. The importance of this knowledge is evident in comments made by an intern at a middle school: "To teach a kid well you have to know a kid well.... teaching middle school takes a special breed of teachers who understand the unique abilities and inabilities ... [of] those undergoing their own metamorphosis into teenagers" (Henry et al. 1995, 124–25). Teachers gain this kind of knowledge through study, observation, and constant interaction. Without considerable understanding of children and youth, teachers' efforts to help students learn and grow can be inappropriate and, in some cases, counterproductive. Teachers' expectations of students directly affect student achievement. The following Professional Reflection activity is designed to guide you in reflecting on opportunities you have already had to acquire knowledge about learners.

Professional Reflection   Inventorying your knowledge of children and youth

To be accepted into a teacher preparation program, you may be required by your college or university to have prior experiences working with children and youth. For instance, to be admitted to any of Nova Scotia's four teacher education programs, all applicants must have a significant amount of supervised work (paid or volunteer) in a "teaching" capacity with children or adolescents. The knowledge of children and youth acquired through such experiences provides an excellent foundation upon which to begin your preparation for becoming a teacher.

Use the following outline to inventory your experiences working with children and youth. Your experiences might include working with service clubs such as Scouts, 4-H, and youth groups; volunteering at a child care center; coaching a sport as part of a parks and recreation program; or tutoring young children in reading or mathematics.

After completing your inventory, reflect on your experiences. During which experiences were you functioning, at least partially, in the role of "teacher"? For example, did you have to demonstrate the skills involved in a particular sport? As a member of a club in high school, did you explain club activities to new members or to parents? While holding a leadership position in a group, were you expected to function as a "role model" to other members of the group?

Setting	Activity	Participants' Age and Sex	Your Role	Date
Example:				
Summer sports program	Taught swimming	Coed, ages 6–8	Camp counsellor	Summer 2000
1.				
2.				
3.				

Knowledge of Subject

With the title of *teacher* comes an assumption of knowledge. Those outside the field of education expect a teacher to be a ready reference for all sorts of information. Clearly, teachers who have extensive knowledge of their subjects are better equipped to help their students learn. However, knowledge of subject matter does not translate into an understanding of *how* to share that knowledge with students—a point illustrated in a case study that focused on "Mary," an undergraduate literature major enrolled in a teacher education program at a major university. By any standards, Mary was a subject-matter expert—she was valedictorian of a large, urban high school; had straight A's in the literature courses she had taken; and had a sophisticated understanding of literature, especially poetry. The case study revealed that Mary had little understanding of classroom activities that would show her students *how* to read with sophistication and concluded that "some prospective teachers may come to teacher education unaware of how they have learned the processes they use and that render them expert. Unaided by their disciplines in locating the underpinnings of their expertise, these skilled, talented, and desirable recruits may easily become, ironically, those who can *do* but who cannot *teach*" (Holt-Reynolds 1999, 43).

Extensive knowledge of subject matter is, by itself, insufficient. Effective, successful teachers possess what is sometimes called **pedagogical content knowledge**. They have an understanding of how students can efficiently learn facts, concepts, generalization and skills. They also have learned how to use various teaching techniques—such as simulations, demonstrations, and illustrations—to maximize student learning.

Knowledge of Methods for Applying Educational Theory and Research

Theories about learners and learning guide the decision making of professional teachers. Not only do such teachers know that a certain strategy works, but they also know *why* it works. Because they recognize the importance of theories, they have at their disposal a greater range of options for problem solving than teachers who have not developed their repertoire of theories. Your ultimate goal as a professional is to apply theoretical knowledge to the practical problems of teaching.

To illustrate the usefulness of research on students' learning, we present six teaching strategies that Barak Rosenshine (1995, 267) recommends, based on his and others' research on cognitive processing, studies of teachers whose students have higher achievement gains than students of other teachers, and research on cognitive strategies.

1. Present new material in small steps so that the working memory does not become overloaded.
2. Help students develop an organization for the new material.
3. Guide student practice by (a) supporting students during initial practice and (b) providing for extensive student processing.
4. When teaching higher level tasks, support students by providing them with cognitive strategies.
5. Help students to use cognitive strategies by providing them with procedural prompts (e.g., questions students ask themselves while learning new material—"who," "what," "why," "when," etc.) and modelling the use of procedural prompts.
6. Provide for extensive student practice.

Which type of knowledge do teachers need more—subject-matter knowledge or professional knowledge?

If you know your subject well, can you teach it well? If you know how to teach well, can you teach anything? Which of the two forms of knowledge is more important for teachers—subject-matter knowledge or professional knowledge?

Individuals preparing to become teachers usually specialize in either elementary or secondary education—although some provinces have a middle school stream for those who wish to teach at the Grade 6 to 8 level. In general, students enrolled in elementary programs are given a broad range of methodological courses in how to teach language arts, social studies, mathematics, and science. On the other hand, students enrolled in secondary programs, where depth of subject knowledge is more critical, are usually given subject-specific methodological courses in only one or two areas. Some educators believe that schools of education should place emphasis on pedagogy, stressing the importance of teaching skills and knowledge about learning, brain research, and communication. Others are still emphatic that it is more important that teachers be well-educated individuals who have an in-depth knowledge of the subjects that they teach. Where do you stand on this issue?

Subject-matter knowledge is most needed.

In addition to the argument that teachers need to be prepared with subject-matter knowledge in order to meet students' curricular needs is the recognition that teachers model to their students what an educated person is. For all teachers, but especially those at the elementary school level, what they teach most is themselves: who they are. Day in and day out, they show students their values, beliefs, and knowledge, even as they teach the subject matter they are required to teach. The illustrations they offer, the language they use, and the perspectives they take draw on their personal knowledge base.

Marva Collins, a teacher who stretched the minds of children with the writings of Aristotle and Shakespeare, was successful in her teaching in large measure because of who she was and what she knew. Her knowledge of history, economics, and literature, especially poetry, enriched the learning of her elementary school children. Similarly, Jaime Escalante attracted attention and became the subject of a popular film, *Stand and Deliver*, because of his success teaching his economically stressed students to perform impressively well on the Scholastic Achievement Test in calculus. Most who followed his story would agree that his effectiveness was more attributable to his personal spirit, his in-depth knowledge of mathematics, and his understanding of history and culture, than to his knowledge of pedagogy per se.

Subject-matter expertise is thus more important for teachers because they must offer students much more than limited, superficial information about increasingly complex topics, and because they should model to students what an educated person is.

Professional knowledge is most needed.

Today, some educational scholars support returning to a greater emphasis on professional knowledge. They base their position on research results such as the following:

- Many studies have found positive relationships between education coursework and teacher performance in the classrooms. These relationships are stronger and more consistent than those between subject matter knowledge and teacher performance (Darling-Hammond, Wise, and Klein 1995, 24).
- The premise is that subject-matter knowledge alone is not enough. To paraphrase author Walker Percy's observation, "Some people get all A's and flunk life," in education, some people get all A's and flunk teaching. Academic knowledge does not translate automatically to teaching effectiveness.

Proponents of greater professional knowledge for teachers observe that teaching has become an increasingly complex and challenging endeavour. Students in today's classrooms are more diverse than ever in their cultural backgrounds, educational needs, and communication and learning styles. As Linda Darling-Hammond (1999, 222–223) observes:

In a typical classroom of 25 students, today's teacher will have at least four or five students with specific educational needs that require professional expertise previously reserved to a few specialists... [and] will need considerable knowledge to develop curriculum and teaching strategies that address the wide range of learning approaches, experiences, and prior levels of knowledge the other students bring with them, and an understanding of how to work within a wide range of family and community contexts.

Professional knowledge is thus more important for teachers because simply knowing a subject well does not guarantee being able to transmit it well, especially in light of the diverse and complex needs of students in today's classrooms.

Where do you stand on this issue?

1. What arguments can you give to defend your position?

2. What compromise position would be feasible and effective?

---

3. How can students best learn each type of knowledge?

4. What other questions are raised within each position—for instance, how specific should subject matter knowledge be? Should one know all of "science" or only "biology"?

5. Which type of professional knowledge is most needed for new teachers and which would be more useful later in a teacher's career?

Recommended Sources

Darling-Hammond, L., Wise, A. E., and Klein, S. P. (1995). *A license to teach: Building a profession for 21st-century schools.* Boulder:Westview Press.

Darling-Hammond, L. (1999). Educating teachers for the next century: Rethinking practice and policy. In *The education of teachers: Ninety-eighth yearbook of the National Society for the Study of Education,* Part 1. Chicago: University of Chicago Press.

Research on students' learning is not intended to set forth, in cookbook fashion, exactly what teachers should do to increase students' learning. Instead, it may be helpful to think of educational research as providing teachers with rules of thumb to guide their practice. For example, Rosenshine, Meister, and Chapman (1996, 198) point out that, in spite of extensive research on the effectiveness of procedural prompts, "at the present time, developing procedural prompts appears to be an art. [It] is difficult to derive any prescriptions on how to develop effective procedural prompts for cognitive strategies in reading, writing, and subject matter domains." Finally, noted educational psychologist Lee Cronbach (quoted in Eisner, 1998, 112) may have put it best when he said "[educational research] is to help practitioners use their heads."

What kinds of basic knowledge and skills do teachers need to do their jobs well? How will you acquire and develop knowledge and skills in these areas?

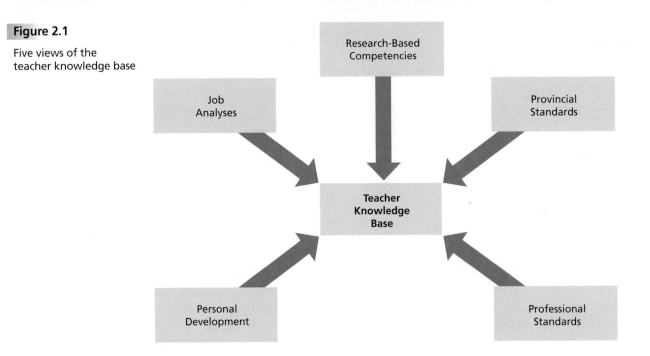

Figure 2.1

Five views of the teacher knowledge base

Job
Analyses

Research-Based
Competencies

Provincial
Standards

Teacher
Knowledge
Base

Personal
Development

Professional
Standards

What Are Five Ways of Viewing the Teacher Knowledge Base?

Just as people hold different expectations for schools and teachers, there are different views on the knowledge and abilities teachers need to teach well. The complexities of teaching make it difficult to describe in exact detail the **knowledge base** on which teaching as a profession rests. This difficulty results, in part, because there is no universally accepted definition of what good teaching is. Educational researchers are still learning *what* good teachers know and *how* they use that knowledge. Five widespread views of teachers' knowledge and abilities are portrayed in Figure 2.1.

A Personal Development View

One view of what teachers need to know and be able to do places primary emphasis on who the teacher is as a person. According to this view, teachers should be concerned with developing themselves as persons so that they may learn to use themselves more effectively. The importance of personal development is described as follows by the authors of *On Being a Teacher:* "... teachers who appear in charge of their own lives, who radiate power, tranquility, and grace in their actions, are going to command attention and respect. People will follow them anywhere.... What we are saying is that you have not only the option, but also the imperative, to develop the personal dimensions of your functioning, as well as your professional skills" (Zehm and Kottler 1993, 15).

What this approach requires, then, is that teachers continually develop their powers of observation and reflection so that they can most effectively respond to the needs of students. Teaching becomes an authentic, growth-oriented encounter between teacher and students. An important dimension of this **personal development view** is the teacher's need for self-knowledge, particularly in regard to oneself as a learner.

Research-Based Competencies

Since the late 1980s, most provinces, or the school districts within them, have developed their own lists of **research-based competencies** that beginning teachers must demonstrate. These competencies are derived from educational research that has identified what effective teachers do. Typically, many provinces have developed *behavioural indicators* for each competency, which trained observers use to determine to what extent teachers actually exhibit the target behaviours in the classroom. Teachers are required to demonstrate effective pedagogical behaviours in a number of domains: planning and preparation, effective classroom management, control of student conduct, instructional organization and development, presentation of subject matter, verbal and non-verbal communication, and testing (student preparation, administration, and feedback).

Provincial Standards

In addition to sets of research-based competencies for evaluating practicing teachers, some provinces have developed performance-based standards for what new teachers should know and be able to do. Known as **outcome-based** or **performance-based teacher education**, the new approach is based on several assumptions:

- Outcomes are demonstrations of learning rather than a list of teaching specializations, college courses completed, or concepts studied.
- Outcomes are performances that reflect the richness and complexity of the teacher's role in today's classrooms—not discrete, single behaviours.
- Demonstrations of learning must occur in authentic settings—that is, settings similar to those within which the teacher will teach.
- Outcomes are culminating demonstrations of what beginning teachers do in real classrooms.

Typically, outcome-based standards are developed with input from teachers, teacher educators, provincial department of education personnel, and various professional associations. However, outcome-based standards are not without their critics. Sharp criticism of the Atlantic Provinces Education Foundation (APEF) outcomes-based curriculum (see Appendix 2.1) is articulated by Dr David MacKinnon, author of *A Wolf in Sheep's Clothing: The Erosion of Democracy* in Education (Portelli and Solomon 2001, 136).

> [A]n outcomes-based approach to education provides an inadequate foundation for public education. Behavioral outcomes, by definition, are confined to that which is observable and measurable … [P]rojects like the APEF initiative are necessarily incomplete and, perhaps, unwittingly misguided … [T]he APEF initiative is a reductionist and anti-democratic exercise at increasing system accountability.

A Job-Analysis Approach

Another view of what teachers need to know and be able to do is based on the job analyses that some school districts conduct. Typically, a **job analysis** begins with a review of existing job descriptions and then proceeds to interviews with those currently assigned to the job and their supervisors regarding the activities and responsibilities associated with the job. These data are then analyzed to identify the dimensions of the job. Finally, interview questions based on the dimensions are developed and used by district personnel responsible for hiring.

The following excerpt from a study by the Urban Network to Improve Teacher Education (UNITE), an organization comprised of both Canadian and American universities, illustrates the knowledge, skills, and attitudes needed by successful urban teachers.

Twenty-two teachers and five administrators were involved in focus group interviews conducted during the study. Over half of the 27 participants have been working in the field of education for less than five years, although four have been teaching in their present school for over 15 years. On average, the participants graduated from a faculty of education 11 years ago. The teachers interviewed represented all grade levels, from Kindergarten to senior secondary, and represented a variety of subject areas and roles within a school community (eg., physical education, visual arts, resource teacher, special education teacher). All but one of the participants received their preservice education in the province of Ontario.

Characteristics of a Successful Urban Teacher

Eight characteristics were identified in all focus group interviews as being important for teachers to possess in order to be successful in an urban school. These eight characteristics are discussed in order of the degree of emphasis placed on them by the focus group participants.

Empathy—Because most teachers never experience many of the traumas and issues that their students deal with on a daily basis, they strongly believed that teachers in urban schools need to be empathetic. They mentioned the importance of "not placing your morals, judgments and values on the students and parents," and "making greater attempts at trying to understand the different cultures and religions."

Respect for the students—Teachers need to respect students and to operate on the belief that all students have the right to learn, and to achieve success. Participants stated that teachers in urban schools should not compromise expectations and that they should "believe that all students have a future."

Flexibility—Teachers in urban schools need to be flexible. Teachers reported that this flexibility was necessary when dealing with such things as curriculum guidelines, programming, evaluation, classroom disruptions, and student behaviour. One teacher stated, "You set up a wonderful day, and then it isn't working, and you have to step back and reassess. It's constant."

Self-care—In order to be a successful teacher in an urban school, participants stressed the need for caring for their personal needs. Since urban schools "really challenge you, you have to make sure you take care of the whole you, emotionally, physically, personally, and manage your stress. You have to find the balance."

Patience—Teachers in urban schools need to be patient. Dealing with the diverse population of students, and all of the other challenges previously mentioned, the need for 'infinite patience' was believed to be necessary in order to be successful as a teacher in an urban school.

Sense of humour—Participants in the focus group interviews strongly believed that in order to be a successful teacher in an urban school one must possess a sense of humour. One teacher described this need in connection with self-care, stating, "If you don't have the ability to laugh, you run the risk of becoming emotionally drained."

Collegiality—Another important characteristic for teachers in urban schools is collegiality and peer support. Participants described the need, in urban schools, for staff to work together, to "share their ups and downs," to share their resources, and to be there to support one another.

highlights

What technology-related knowledge and skills do teachers need?

Today, thousands of teachers and students routinely use desktop and laptop computers with built-in modems, faxes, and CD-ROM players; camcorders; optical scanners; speech and music synthesizers; laser printers; digital cameras; and data projectors. In addition, they use sophisticated software for email, word processing, desktop publishing, presentation graphics, spreadsheets, databases, and multimedia applications.

To prepare teachers to use these new technologies, many teacher education programs and provincial departments of education have developed information technology competency guidelines for classroom teachers. For example, many teachers are now expected to have technology skills in three areas: basic computer/technology operations and concepts, personal and professional use of technology, and integration of technology into a standards-based curriculum. The following competencies are among the most common. How many of these competencies do you possess, and what steps can you take to acquire those you do not have?

1. Media Communications and Integration

   - Set up and operate video media [eg., videocassette recorders (VCRs) and digital video disks (DVDs)]
   - Connect video output devices and other presentation systems to computers and video sources for large-screen display
   - Use painting, drawing, and authoring tools
   - Plan, create, and use linear and non-linear multimedia presentations
   - Use imaging devices such as scanners, digital cameras, and/or video cameras with computer systems and software

2. Telecommunications

   - Connect to the internet or an online service
   - Use internet search engines
   - Use a web browser to access and use resources on the internet
   - Download and print resources from the internet
   - Use URL management tools (eg., bookmarks or favourites)
   - Telnet to a remote computer on the internet
   - Connect to and use resources from university libraries
   - Use email (compose, send, retrieve, read, reply to sender, reply to all, and forward)
   - Attach files to email messages
   - Retrieve and use attachments (eg., view, read, save and print)
   - Configure and use email distribution lists relevant to professional information needs
   - Create and use group addresses for email
   - Collaborate with peers through available tools (eg., email, websites, threaded and other online discussions)

Source: Adapted from Colorado Technology Competency Guidelines for Classroom Teachers and School Media Specialists, Education Telecommunications Unit, Colorado, Department of Education, January, 1999.

High energy level—In order to deal with the plethora of daily challenges facing urban school teachers, interview participants stated that these teachers need to have high energy levels. A number of participants extended this characteristic to include a willingness "to make the commitment of time, energy and effort it takes to work in a school like this."

Source: UNITE article reprinted with permission from Patricia J. Rawson Wheeler. Retrieved November 1, 2003 from www.umanitoba.ca/publications/cjeap/issue1/issue6.htm

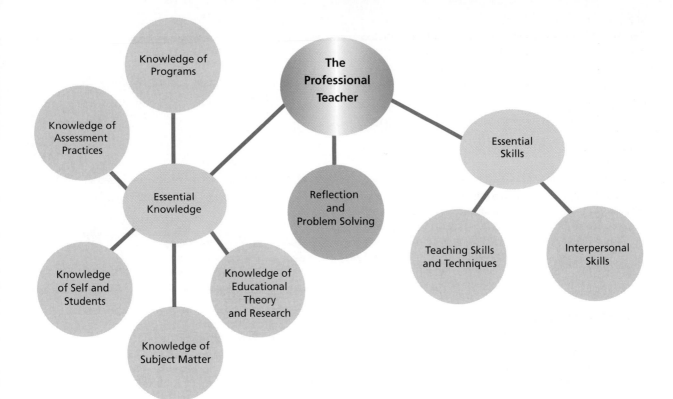

Figure 2.2

Essential knowledge and skills for the professional teacher.

Professional Views

While there are differing opinions regarding what teachers should be able to do, it seems evident that becoming a teacher is complex and demanding. For example, as part of its supervision policy, Manitoba's St. Boniface School Division No. 4 (now Louis Riel School Division) lists the following skills as essential to good practice (St. Boniface 1995).

- Classroom Learning Environment: The teacher provides appropriate learning resources, ... makes effective use of space ... [and] provides stimulating and creative experiences.
- Classroom Management: The teacher establishes a positive classroom environment ... promotes self-esteem ... [and] plans and organizes for success.
- Contribution to the Total School Environment: The teacher contributes to students ... parents/guardians and community partnerships ... the school ... colleagues ... [and] the St. Boniface System.
- Instructional Process: The teacher implements Manitoba Education, school and Board expectations and policies for curriculum and program planning ... understands the learner ... [and] employs a repertoire of instructional strategies.
- Interpersonal Relations: The teacher interacts positively with students ... with colleagues ... [and] with parents and community.
- Student Evaluation: The teacher understands the purpose of assessment and evaluation ... [and] implements a variety of assessment and evaluation strategies.

How Are Canadian Teachers Educated and Certified?

Because education is a provincial rather than a federal responsibility, each province has been free to elect its preferred method for educating those intent on pursuing careers as professional teachers. The result has been a patchwork quilt of Bachelor of Education programs, each with its own specific admission requirements, and each with its own particular curriculum.

Additionally, while the academic body bestows the Bachelor of Education degree on its graduates, each province and territory has a teacher certification body that establishes the requirements, which must be met before a teaching license will be awarded. In some provinces, such as Newfoundland and Nova Scotia, the certifying agency is each province's department of education. However, in other jurisdictions, such as BC and Ontario, independent agencies such as the British Columbia College of Teachers and the Ontario College of Teachers are responsible for teacher certification.

Most provinces and territories issue teaching certificates based upon the qualifications of the applicant. In general, the higher the level of certification, the higher the remuneration. (See Appendix 2.2, "Saskatchewan: Teacher Salary Classification"). Most provinces also give teachers annual raises for each of their first ten years of teaching experience. Saskatchewan has five levels of teacher certification and, as Table 2.2 indicates, has ten steps for years of experience.

In 2003 the Ontario Ministry of Education introduced the Ontario Teacher Qualifying Test (OTQT) as part of its teacher certification process (See Appendix 2.3).

Table 2.1

Salaries effective September 1, 2003, in dollars

Step	Class C	Class I-III	Class IV	Class V	Class VI
1	32 273	32 273	38 700	40 895	43 570
2		33 697	40 911	43 191	45 973
3		35 122	43 121	45 487	48 376
4		36 546	45 331	47 783	50 779
5		37 971	47 542	50 079	53 182
6		39 395	49 752	52 374	55 585
7		40 820	51 962	54 670	57 988
8		42 244	54 173	56 966	60 391
9		43 669	56 383	59 262	62 794
10		45 093	59 500	62 464	66 103

Source: Saskatchewan Teachers' Federation.

This is the first time any Canadian educational jurisdiction has administered what is effectively a teacher competency test to those whom it grants teaching certificates. The *Quality in the Classroom Act*, 2001, which provides the legislative requirements for the OTQT, also sets performance appraisal standards and processes for Ontario school districts to use in evaluating their teachers. The stated purposes of the new performance appraisal system (Ontario Ministry of Education 2002, 3) are as follows:

- To ensure that students receive the benefit of an education system staffed by teachers who are performing their duties satisfactorily
- To provide fair, effective and consistent teacher evaluation in every school
- To promote professional growth

For more information, see the sample "Rubric to Describe the Levels of Performance" for the "Domain Teaching Practice," Appendix 2.4, at the end of this chapter.

In Manitoba, Alberta, and Ontario, teacher associations negotiate their contracts at the regional or local level. In all other provinces and territories the negotiations are conducted between the teachers' associations and department of education personnel. Salary scales are quite variable. In some provinces a teacher with an approved undergraduate degree, with an additional eight-month Bachelor of Education degree, can earn an annual salary of $30 000 to $50 000; in other jurisdictions the same level of certification would result in annual pay of $40 000 to $70 000. The highest rates of teacher pay are offered by the Yukon, Nunavut, and the Northwest Territories, where starting salaries are $55 000 to $60 000.

Canadian Schools of Education: A Variety of Models

Concurrent Program

Students enrol in a Bachelor degree and take both regular academic courses and education courses at the same time. Most such programs are of four years' duration and provide their graduates with the least expensive route to a teaching degree. However, the majority of students in concurrent programs must decide at a very early stage in their lives that teaching is their chosen profession.

Eight-Month Post-Degree Program

This is by far the most common model. Applicants for admission to a school of education first obtain a three- or four-year undergraduate degree which contains the appropriate academic prerequisites as established by the university or department of education. Successful applicants then take a specified number of courses specifically designed to assist them with their teaching practice. As part of their program they also spend a specified amount of time—usually five to eight weeks—working with associate teachers in the field. Critics of eight-month programs argue that they do not provide sufficient time for student teachers to learn all of the things necessary for them to be truly effective educators. In addition, provinces with more comprehensive Bachelor of Education programs will sometimes decline to grant teaching licenses to those who have graduated from such programs.

Twelve-Month Post-Degree Programs

There are relatively few twelve-month Bachelor of Education programs available within Canada. Twelve-month programs have more coursework for students to complete and provide more time for fieldwork in classrooms. They are also more expensive for students but, as they are completed within an extended academic year, graduates of such programs can be employed as teachers in September of the year in which they graduate.

Two-Year Post-Degree Programs

At present, only Nova Scotia and Prince Edward Island have two-year post-degree Bachelor of Education programs. Applicants to these programs first obtain a three-year or four-year undergraduate degree, and then complete two academic years of educational studies in combination with 20 or more weeks of field experience. Some colleges and universities also offer two or more of the models described above. Hyperlinks to all of Canada's teacher education programs can be found at the following URL: www.oise.utoronto.ca/~mpress/eduweb/faculties.html

What Can You Learn from Observing in Classrooms?

Classroom observations are a vital element of many **field experiences**. Students report that these experiences aid them greatly in making a final decision about entering the teaching field. Most become more enthusiastic about teaching and more motivated to learn the needed skills, although a few decide that teaching is not for them. Recognizing the value of observations, many teacher education programs are increasing the amount of field experiences and placing such fieldwork earlier in students' programs.

Focused Observations

Observations are more meaningful when they are focused and conducted with clear purposes. Observers may focus on the students, the teacher, the interactions between the two, the structure of the lesson, or the setting. More specifically, for example, observers may note differences between the ways boys and girls or members of different ethnic groups communicate and behave in the classroom. They may note student interests and ability levels, study student responses to a particular teaching strategy, or analyze the question and response patterns in a class discussion.

Observations may also be guided by sets of questions related to specific areas. For instance, since beginning teachers are frequently frustrated by their lack of success in interesting their students in learning, asking questions specifically related to motivation can make an observation more meaningful and instructive. Figure 2.3 on page 56 presents a helpful set of focused questions on motivation. Similar questions can be generated for other focus areas such as classroom management, student involvement, questioning skills, evaluation, and teacher–student rapport.

Observation Instruments

A wide range of methods can be used to conduct classroom observations, ranging from informal, qualitative descriptions to formal, quantitative checklists. With reform efforts to improve education in Canada has come the development of instruments to facilitate the evaluation of teacher performance, a task now widely required of school administrators. Students preparing to teach can benefit by using these evaluative instruments in their observations.

Ruth's Dilemma

This case recounts a dilemma typical for many who decide to enter the teaching field. Ruth, who worked in the same department as one of the authors, faced this decision at the time this textbook was being written.

Ruth knew it was time to begin the process to become a teacher. She wondered what had influenced her decision most—her love of English literature, her youngest son's graduation from high school, or the fact that she was surrounded daily by people teaching or taking education classes. As secretary to the School of Education's associate dean, she oversaw the details of class schedules, textbook orders, room assignments, program evaluations, faculty teaching loads, and students' petitions, all to help smooth the way for others to become teachers. Now she had decided to enter the field herself.

She had applied to the program, outlined a plan, and sought her dean's permission to proceed. The former school superintendent was sincere in his encouragement. Certainly she could leave the office early on Tuesdays to attend classes. And what level did she plan to teach? High school or elementary? Ruth wasn't sure.

The question remained even after she had made several elementary and high school classroom observations in her Introduction to Teaching class. The answer wasn't as clear for Ruth as it seemed to be for many of her classmates. Like many of them, she had wanted to be a teacher for as long as she could remember, but unlike them, she had given up the idea because she was unable to gain the needed financial support until she learned that staff could participate in the university's degree completion program. Also, like a number of her classmates, a teacher had inspired her—her high school English teacher had made the subject come alive for her.

By the end of this course, she would have to choose between preparing to teach at the secondary or elementary school level, and her dilemma remained. She loved English literature. Whenever she talked about the books she had read, she felt that words were inadequate for capturing the experience. With other students in class, she thought

How Can You Gain Practical Experience for Becoming a Teacher?

A primary aim of teacher education programs is to give students opportunities to experience, to the extent possible, the real world of the teacher. Through field experiences and carefully structured experiential activities, preservice teachers are given limited exposure to various aspects of teaching. Observing, tutoring, instructing small groups, analyzing video cases, operating instructional media, performing student teaching, and completing various non-instructional tasks are among the most common experiential activities.

out loud about the problem: "In high school you have so many students. How could you possibly get to know 120, 150, or more students? It's just not possible. Just think about it. Over a hundred! You couldn't get to know all of them and not many very well. How much of an impact could I have on their lives?"

"In elementary school, it's different," she continued. "You really can get to know the children well. You would be with them every day, all day, all school year. And there wouldn't be that many, maybe 25 or 30. Even less in some places—only 18 or 21 in a class. You'd even know their families. And you certainly could have an impact on their lives. But then the curriculum isn't that interesting. I would miss teaching literature."

Ruth knew that at the end of her first education course she would have to decide between the two. The classes in the remainder of her program were focused on either elementary or secondary teaching, and she could not do both.

Questions

1. Should Ruth become a high school English teacher or teach children at the elementary level? On what basis should she make her decision?

2. Is teaching a generic skill or art that can be applied to any level, or does it require distinctive skills geared to the students' ages and educational needs?

3. What factors other than teaching skills need to be considered when making this decision? Do the two levels draw upon different personality strengths? Is there a greater demand for teachers at one level than at the other? How do salaries and benefits compare for the two levels?

4. How do motivations to teach vary with the stage of life in which the decision to become a teacher is made?

5. What research activities might help someone decide whether to teach at the elementary or the secondary level?

Classrom Experiences

Because of the need to provide opportunities to put theory into practice before student teaching, many teacher education programs enable students to participate in microteaching, teaching simulations, analyses of video cases, field-based practica and clinical experiences, and classroom aide programs.

Microteaching

Introduced in the 1960s, **microteaching** was received enthusiastically and remains a popular practice. The process calls for students to teach brief, single-concept lessons to

Intrinsic Motivation	Extrinsic Motivation
What things seem to interest students at this age?	How do teachers show their approval to students?
Which activities and assignments seem to give them a sense of pride?	What phrases do teachers use in their praise?
When do they seem to be confused? bored? frustrated?	What types of rewards do teachers give (eg., grades, points, tangible rewards)?
What topics do they talk about with enthusiasm?	What reward programs do you notice (eg., points accumulated toward free time)?
In class discussions, when are they most alert and participating most actively?	What warnings do teachers give?
What seems to please, amuse, entertain, or excite them?	What punishments are given to students?
What do they joke about? What do they find humorous?	How do teachers arouse concern in their students?
What do they report as being their favourite subjects? favorite assignments?	How do students motivate other students?
What do they report as being their least favourite subjects and assignments?	What forms of peer pressure do you observe?
How do they respond to personalized lessons (e.g., using their names in exercises)?	How do teachers promote enthusiasm for an assignment?
How do they respond to activity-oriented lessons (eg.,fieldwork, project periods)?	How do teachers promote class spirit?
How do they respond to assignments calling for presentations to groups outside the classroom (eg., parents, another class, the chamber of commerce)?	How do teachers catch their students' interest in the first few minutes of a lesson?
How do they respond to being given a choice in assignments?	Which type of question draws more answers—recall or open-ended?
	How do teachers involve quiet students in class discussions?
	How do teachers involve inactive students in their work?
	In what ways do teachers give recognition to srudents' accomplishments?

Figure 2.3

Guiding questions for observing motivation

a small group (five to ten students) while concurrently practicing a specific teaching skill, such as positive reinforcement. Often the microteaching is videotaped for later study.

As originally developed, microteaching includes the following six steps:

1. Identify a specific teaching skill to learn about and practice.
2. Read about the skill in one of several pamphlets.
3. Observe a master teacher demonstrate the skill in a short movie or on videotape.
4. Prepare a three- to five-minute lesson to demonstrate the skill.
5. Teach the lesson, which is videotaped, to a small group of peers.
6. Critique, along with the instructor and student peers, the videotaped lesson.

Simulations

As an element of teacher training, **teaching simulations** provide opportunities for vicarious practice of a wide range of teaching skills. In simulations, students analyze teaching situations that are presented in writing, on audiotape, in short films, or on videotape. Typically, students are given background information about a hypothetical school or classroom and the pupils they must prepare to teach. After this orientation, students role-play the student teacher or the teacher who is confronted with the problem situation. Following the simulation, participants discuss the appropriateness of solutions and work to increase their problem-solving skills and their understanding of the teacher's multifaceted role as a decision maker.

With recent advances in computer technology, some teacher education programs now use computer-based simulations that enable students to hone their classroom planning and decision-making skills. Students at Acadia University in Nova Scotia, for example, learn to deal with classroom management problems within an interactive virtual learning environment. In addition, continuing progress in the development of virtual reality technology suggests that preservice teachers will soon be able to practice their skills with computer-simulated "students" who learn by interacting with humans (VanLehn et al. 1994; Sigalit and VanLehn 1995).

Video Cases

Teacher education students who view, analyze, and then write about video cases have an additional opportunity to appreciate the ambiguities and complexities of real-life classrooms, to learn that "there are no clear-cut, simple answers to the complex issues teachers face" (Wasserman 1994, 606). Viewing authentic video cases enables students to see how "teaching tradeoffs and dilemmas emerge in the video 'text' as do the strategies teachers use, the frustrations they experience, the brilliant and less-brilliant decisions they make" (Grant, Richard, and Parkay 1996, 5).

Practica

A **practicum** is a short-term field-based experience (usually about two weeks long) that allows teacher education students to spend time observing and assisting in classrooms. Though practica vary in length and purpose, students are often able to begin instructional work with individuals or small groups. For example, a cooperating teacher may allow a practicum student to tutor a small group of students, read a story to the whole class, conduct a spelling lesson, monitor recess, help students with their homework, or teach students a song or game.

Classroom Assistants

Serving as a teacher assistant is another popular means of providing field experience before student teaching. A teacher assistant's role depends primarily on the unique needs of the school and its students. Generally, assistants work under the supervision of a certified teacher and perform duties that support the teacher's instruction. Assisting teachers in classrooms familiarizes teacher education students with class schedules, record-keeping procedures, and students' performance levels, and provides ample opportunity for observations. In exchange, the classroom teacher receives much needed assistance.

Student Teaching

The most extensive and memorable field experience in teacher preparation programs is the period of student teaching. As *The Student Teacher's Handbook* points out, student teaching "is the only time in a teaching career that one is an apprentice under the close guidance of an experienced mentor" (Schwebel et al. 1996, 4). Depending on the province, Bachelor of Education students may be required to have as few as five weeks of student teaching or, as in Nova Scotia, as many as fifteen weeks before being

certified as teachers. The nature of student teaching varies considerably among teacher education programs. Typically, a student is assigned to a cooperating (or master) teacher in the school, and a university supervisor makes periodic visits to observe the student teacher. Some programs even pay student teachers during the student teaching experience.

Student teaching is a time of responsibility. As one student teacher put it, "I don't want to mess up [my students'] education!" It is also an opportunity for growth, a chance to master critical skills. Time is devoted to observing, participating in classroom activities, and actively teaching. The amount of time one actually spends teaching, however, is not as important as one's willingness to reflect carefully on the student teaching experience. Two excellent ways to promote reflection during student teaching are journal writing and maintaining a reflective teaching log.

Student Teacher Journal Writing

Many supervisors require student teachers to keep a journal of their classroom experiences so that they can engage in reflective teaching and begin the process of criticizing and guiding themselves. The following two entries—the first written by a student teacher in a Grade 4 classroom, the second by a student teacher in a high school English class—illustrate how journal writing can help student teachers develop strategies for dealing with the realities of teaching.

What strategies can you use to make your student teaching experience truly valuable? In what sense will you remain a student teacher throughout your career?

> Today I taught a geography lesson and the kids seemed so bored. I called on individuals to read the social studies text, and then I explained it. Some of them really struggled with the text. Mr. H. said I was spoon-feeding them too much. So tomorrow I am going to put them into groups and let them answer questions together rather than give them the answers. This ought to involve the students in the learning a bit more and enable some of the better readers to help out those who have difficulty, without the whole class watching. I feel bad when I see those glazed looks on their faces. I need to learn how to be more interesting (Pitton 1998, 120).

> I had good feedback on small groups in their responses to questions on *Of Mice and Men*. They were to find a paragraph that might indicate theme and find two examples of foreshadowing. We found five!

> The short story unit was awful during fourth hour. The kids just didn't respond. I quickly revamped my approach for the next hour. Fifth hour did seem to go better. (Mostly though, I think it was just that I was more prepared, having had one class to try things out.) I can see how experience really helps. Now that I've tried the story "The Tiger or the Lady," I would use the same material, but I would know HOW to use it more effectively! (Pitton 1998, 143).

Relatively unstructured, open-ended journals, such as the ones from which these entries were selected, provide student teachers with a medium for subjectively exploring the student teaching experience.

Reflective Teaching Logs

To promote the practice of reflecting more analytically, some supervisors ask their student teachers to use a more directed and structured form of journal keeping, the reflective teaching log. In this form a student lists and briefly describes the daily sequence of activities, selects a single episode to expand on, analyzes the reason for selecting it and what was learned from it, and considers the possible future application of that knowledge.

To illustrate the reflective teaching approach to keeping a log, we share here a partial entry for one episode that was recounted and critiqued by a college student tutoring a student in French. The entry is of particular interest because it provides us with a glimpse of a college student's first experience with a pupil's difficulty in understanding subject matter.

Log #1: February 14, 1991 (10:00–10:30am)

Sequence of Events: Worked with Richy on his French.

Episode: Because I wasn't sure of Richy's level, I asked him a few questions to see what he knew. His homework exercises involved work like reflexives, irregular verbs, and vocabulary. But when he and I started reviewing, he didn't remember the very basics of conjugation. He said, "I know this stuff, I just need review." We reviewed the conjugation of regular verbs. I set up a chart of *er* and *ir* endings and had him fill in the correct forms. He kept saying, "I just don't remember," or "Oh yeah, I knew that." His facial expressions reflected concentration and perhaps frustration. At times, he would just stare at the page until I gave him a hint. His forehead was scrunched up and he fidgeted a bit with his hands and legs. After working on the regular endings, he wanted to get a drink. I told him to go ahead....

Analysis: I guess that I was just shocked at how little Richy knew. What we went over was the most simple form of French grammar and in a way he was acting as if he had no idea what we were doing. I was surprised, like I said, but only on the inside. I just helped him along, showing him why the concepts made sense. I had no idea how we were going to do his homework assignments since they were considerably more difficult ... (Posner 1993, 116–117).

Though student teaching will be the capstone experience of your teacher education program, the experience should be regarded as an *initial* rather than a terminal learning opportunity—your first chance to engage in reflection and self-evaluation for a prolonged period.

Gaining Experience in Multicultural Settings

Canadian schools will enrol increasing numbers of students from diverse cultural backgrounds during the twenty-first century. As this trend continues, it is vitally important that those entering the teaching profession achieve an understanding of children's differing backgrounds. As a result, many teacher education programs now have courses that deal with equity issues. Such courses help prepare student teachers for the diversity that exists in almost every classroom.

As a teacher you can be assured that you will teach students from backgrounds that differ from your own—including students from the more than 100 racial and ethnic groups in Canada, and students who are poor, gifted, or have disabilities. You will have the challenge of reaching out to all students and teaching them that they are persons of worth and that they can learn. You will also be confronted with the difficult challenge of being sensitive to differences among students, while at the same time treating all equally and fairly. To prepare for these realities of teaching, you should make every effort to gain experiences in multicultural settings.

Supply Teaching

On completion of a teacher education program and prior to securing a full-time teaching assignment, many students choose to gain additional practical experience in classrooms by **supply teaching** or **substitute teaching**. Others, unable to locate full-time positions, decide to supply, knowing that many districts prefer to hire from their pool of supply teachers when full-time positions become available. Supply teachers replace regular teachers who are absent due to illness, family responsibilities, personal reasons, or professional workshops and conferences.

Each day, thousands of supply teachers are employed in schools across Canada. For example, during one school year at the fifteen high schools in a large urban district, the total number of absences for 1200 regular teachers equalled 14 229 days. Multiplying this figure by five (the number of classes per day for most high school teachers) yields 71 145 class periods taught by supply teachers that year (St. Michel 1995).

Qualifications for supply teachers vary from province to province. An area with a critical need for supply teachers will often relax its requirements to provide classroom coverage. In many districts, it is possible to supply without regular certification *if no fully certified teacher can be located*. Some districts have less stringent qualifications for short-term, day-to-day supply teachers and more stringent ones for long-term, full-time assignments. In many districts, the application process for supply teachers is the same as that for full-time applicants; in others, the process may be somewhat briefer. Often, supply teachers are not limited to working in their area of certification; however, schools try to avoid making out-of-field assignments. If you decide to supply, contact the schools in your area to learn about the qualifications and procedures for hiring supply teachers.

In spite of the significant role supply teachers play in the day-to-day operation of schools, "... research tells us that they receive very little support, no specialized training, and are rarely evaluated.... In short, the substitute will be expected to show up to each class on time, maintain order, take roll, carry out the lesson, and leave a note for the regular teacher about the classes and events of the day without support, encouragement, or acknowledgement" (St. Michel 1995, 6–7). While working conditions such as these are certainly challenging, supplying can be a rewarding, professionally fulfilling experience. Figure 2.4 presents several advantages and disadvantages of supplying.

Figure 2.4

Advantages and disadvantages of supplying

Source: John F. Snyder, "The Alternative of Substitute Teaching." In *1999 Job Search Handbook for Educators.* Evanston, IL: American Association for Employment in Education, p. 38.

Advantages and Disadvantages of Substitute Teaching

Advantages
- Gain experience without all the nightly work and preparation
- Compare and contrast different schools and their environments
- Be better prepared for interviews by meeting administrators and teachers
- Teach and learn a variety of material
- Get to know people—network
- See job postings and hear about possible vacancies
- Gain confidence in your abilities to teach
- Practice classroom management techniques
- Learn about school and district politics—get the "inside scoop"
- Choose which days to work—flexible schedule

Disadvantages
- Pay is not as good as full-time teaching
- No benefits such as medical coverage, retirement plans or sick days
- Lack of organized representation to improve wages or working conditions
- May receive a cool reception in some schools
- Must adapt quickly to different school philosophies
- Lack of continuity—may be teaching whole language one day; phonetics the next

How Can You Develop Your Teaching Portfolio?

Now that you have begun your journey toward becoming a teacher, you should acquire the habit of assessing your growth in knowledge, skills, and attitudes. Toward this end, you may wish to collect the results of your reflections and self-assessment in a **professional portfolio**. A professional portfolio is a collection of work that documents an individual's accomplishments in an area of professional practice. An artist's portfolio, for example, might consist of a résumé, sketches, paintings, slides and photographs of exhibits, critiques of the artist's work, awards, and other documentation of achievement. Recently, new approaches to teacher evaluation have included the professional portfolio. Teacher education programs at several universities now use portfolios as one means of assessing the competencies of candidates for teacher certification.

Portfolio Contents

What will your portfolio contain? Written materials might include the following: lesson plans and curriculum materials, reflections on your development as a teacher, journal entries, writing assignments made by your instructor, sample tests you have prepared, critiques of textbooks, evaluations of students' work at the level for which you are preparing to teach, sample letters to parents, and a résumé. Non-print materials might include video- and audiotapes featuring you in simulated teaching and role-playing activities, audiovisual materials (transparencies, charts, or other teaching aids), photographs of bulletin boards, charts depicting room arrangements for cooperative learning or other instructional strategies, sample grade book, certificates of membership in professional organizations, and awards.

Your portfolio should represent your *best work* and give you an opportunity to become an advocate of *who you are* as a teacher. Because a primary purpose of the professional portfolio is to stimulate reflection and dialogue, you may wish to discuss what entries to make in your portfolio with your instructor or other teacher education students. In addition, the following questions from *How to Develop a Professional Portfolio: A Manual for Teachers* (Campbell et al. 1996) can help you select appropriate portfolio contents:

What questions might you ask a mentor teacher about developing your professional portfolio?

Would I be proud to have my future employer and peer group see this? Is this an example of what my future professional work might look like? Does this represent what I stand for as a professional educator? If not, what can I revise or rearrange so that it represents my best efforts? (p. 5).

Using a Portfolio

In addition to providing teacher education programs with a way to assess their effectiveness, portfolios can be used by students for a variety of purposes. Campbell et al. (1996, 7–8) suggest that a portfolio may be used as

1. A way to establish a record of quantitative and qualitative performance and growth over time.
2. A tool for reflection and goal setting as well as a way to present evidence of your ability to solve problems and achieve goals.
3. A way to synthesize many separate experiences; in other words, a way to get the "big picture."
4. A vehicle for you to collaborate with professors and advisors in individualizing instruction.
5. A vehicle for demonstrating knowledge and skills gained through out-of-class experiences, such as volunteer experiences.
6. A way to share control and responsibility for your own learning.
7. An alternative assessment measure within the professional education program.
8. A potential preparation for national, regional, and state accreditation.
9. An interview tool in the professional hiring process.
10. An expanded résumé to be used as an introduction during the student teaching experience.

How Can You Benefit from Mentoring Relationships?

When asked "What would have been most helpful in preparing you to be a teacher?" one first-year suburban high school teacher responded with: "I wish I had one [a mentor] here.... There are days that go by and I don't think I learn anything about my teaching, and that's too bad. I wish I had someone" (Dollase 1992, 138). In reflecting on how a mentor contributed to his professional growth, Forrest Parkay defined **mentoring** as

> ... an intensive, one-to-one form of teaching in which the wise and experienced mentor inducts the aspiring protégé [one who is mentored] into a particular, usually professional, way of life.... [T]he protégé learns from the mentor not only the objective, manifest content of professional knowledge and skills but also a subjective, non-discursive appreciation for *how* and *when* to employ these learnings in the arena of professional practice. In short, the mentor helps the protégé to "learn the ropes," to become socialized into the profession (Parkay 1988, 196).

An urban middle school intern's description of how his mentor helped him develop effective classroom management techniques exemplifies "learning the ropes": "'You've got to develop your own sense of personal power,' [my mentor] kept saying. 'It's not something I can teach you. I can show you what to do. I can model it. But I don't know, it's just something that's got to come from within you'" (Henry et al. 1995, 114).

Table 2.2

Problem-solving approaches used by a mentor

Prescription giving	Remedy given by the mentor with a rationale, examples, alternatives, parameters of use, or rules
Personal storytelling	The mentor gives an example of his or her own classroom experiences to set a context for the prescription
Rehearsal	Verbal practice or rehearsal by the mentor and novice teacher of a strategy to be implemented in the classroom the next day, together with problem anticipation and troubleshooting
Role-playing	Playing and reversal of roles by the mentor and novice teacher reflecting problem situations or concerns of the novice teacher; both teacher and student roles are played
Modelling	Verbalization by the mentor of a teaching strategy or interaction technique with demonstration
Oral blueprinting	Oral planning by the novice teacher with critique and refinement by the mentor
Replay	Reconstruction of the day's events by the novice teacher with probing and clarifying questions and feedback from the mentor

Source: J. A. Ponticel and S. J. Zepeda. "Making Sense of Teaching and Learning: A Case Study of Mentor and Beginning Teacher Problem Solving," in D. J. McIntyre and D. M. Byrd, eds., *Preparing Tomorrow's Teachers: The Field Experience: Teacher Education Yearbook IV.* Thousand Oaks, CA: Corwin Press, p.127. Copyright © 1996 by Corwin Press. Reprinted by permission of Corwin Press, Inc.

Those who have become highly accomplished teachers frequently point out the importance of mentors in their preparation for teaching. A **mentor** can provide moral support, guidance, and feedback to students at various stages of professional preparation. In addition, a mentor can model for the protegé an analytical approach to solving problems in the classroom. Table 2.2 shows several problem-solving approaches a mentor can demonstrate to a novice teacher.

What Opportunities for Continuing Professional Development Will You Have?

Professional development is a lifelong process; any teacher, at any stage of development, has room for improvement. Many school systems and universities have programs in place for the continuing professional development of teachers. Indeed, teachers are members of a profession that provides them with a "… continuous opportunity to grow, learn, and become more expert in their work" (Lieberman 1990, viii).

Self-Assessment for Professional Growth

Self-assessment, or **reflection,** is a necessary first step in pursuing opportunities for professional growth. The simplest level of reflection occurs when, after a particular lesson has been taught, a teacher asks such questions as: How did that lesson go?

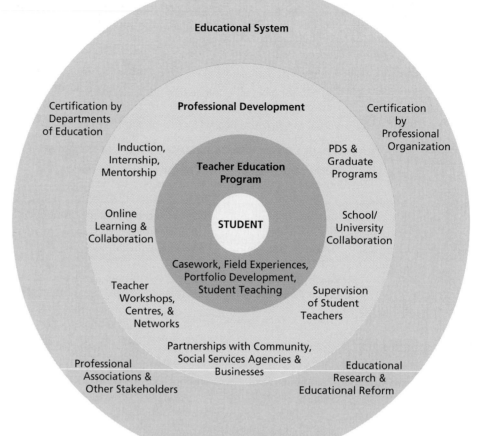

What might have been done to improve it? What were the good lesson elements which should be retained when I next teach it again? A deeper level of reflection might include such questions as: How has that lesson contributed to my students' overall educational growth? Is society as a whole in any way better off as a consequence of what my students just learned?

Several questions can help you make appropriate choices as a teacher: In which areas am I already competent? In which areas do I need further development? How will I acquire the knowledge and skills I need? How will I apply new knowledge and practice new skills? Answers to such questions will lead you to a variety of sources for professional growth: teacher workshops, teacher centres, professional development schools, the opportunity to supervise and mentor student teachers, and graduate programs. Figure 2.5 illustrates the relationship of these professional development experiences to your teacher education program.

Teacher Workshops

The quality of **in-service workshops** is uneven, varying with the size of school district budgets and the imagination and knowledge of the administrators and teachers who arrange them. It is significant that the most effective in-service programs tend to be the ones that teachers request—and often design and conduct.

Some workshops focus on topics that all teachers (regardless of subject or level) can benefit from: classroom management, writing across the curriculum, multicultural education, and strategies for teaching students with learning disabilities in the general education classroom, for example. Other workshops have a sharper focus and are intended for teachers of a subject at a certain level—for example, whole language techniques for middle school students, discovery learning for high school science students, and student-centred approaches to teaching literature in the high school classroom.

Teacher Centres

Teacher centres provide opportunities for teachers "to take the lead in the decision making and implementation of staff development programs based on the needs of teachers. Within limits they provide opportunities for teachers to have a level of control over their own professional development. In contrast to in-service programs, the initiatives undertaken are more clearly directed by teachers. Some centres cooperate with a local or neighbouring college of education and include members of the faculty on their planning committees.

Many teachers find teacher centres stimulating because they offer opportunities for collegial interaction in a quiet, professionally oriented setting. Teachers often find that The busy, hectic pace of life in many schools provides little time for professional dialogue with peers. Furthermore, in the teacher centre, teachers are often more willing to discuss openly areas of weakness in their performance. As one teacher put it:

> At the teacher centre I can ask for help. I won't be judged. The teachers who have helped me the most have had the same problems. I respect them, and I'm willing to learn from them. They have credibility with me.

Supervision and Mentoring of Student Teachers

After several years in the classroom, teachers may be ready to stretch themselves further by supervising student teachers. Some of the less obvious benefits of doing so are that teachers must rethink what they are doing so that they can explain and sometimes justify their behaviours to someone else, learning about themselves in the process. Furthermore, because they become a model for their student teachers, they continually strive to offer the best example. In exchange, they gain an assistant in the classroom—another pair of eyes, an aid with record keeping—and more than occasionally, fresh ideas and a spirit of enthusiasm.

Graduate Study

A more traditional form of professional development is to do graduate study. With the recent reforms, many provinces now require teachers to take some graduate courses to keep their certifications and knowledge up to date. Some teachers take only courses that are of immediate use to them; others use their graduate study to prepare for new teaching or administrative positions; and still others pursue doctoral work in order to teach prospective teachers or others in their discipline at the college level.

Study on the Internet

If you have access to the **internet,** you can locate many possibilities for continuing professional development. Teachers use the internet to exchange ideas and experiences and to acquire additional expertise in teaching or to share their expertise with others.

See the Appendix "Professional Development Opportunities on the Internet," on this book's website. Also at the website is a periodically updated list of professional development opportunities available online for teachers. If you decide to visit any of these sites, remember that web addresses change frequently or are taken off the internet. The web addresses given throughout this book were active at the time of printing. It is estimated that 10 000 websites are added to the internet every day, so you should regularly do internet searches using keywords related to education to gather the latest information and resources.

SUMMARY

What Essential Knowledge Do You Need to Teach?

- Professional teachers reflect upon their classroom experiences.
- Teachers need three kinds of knowledge: knowledge of self and students, knowledge of subject, and knowledge of educational theory and research.
- Teachers' self-knowledge influences their ability to understand students.
- The ambiguities of teaching can cause teachers to experience anxiety.
- Teachers can experience loneliness because they are isolated from adults.
- Teachers must know their students' aptitudes, talents, learning styles, stage of development, and readiness to learn new material.
- Teachers must understand their subjects deeply so that they can modify instructional strategies based on students' perception of content.
- Knowledge of educational theory enables professional teachers to know why certain strategies work.
- Educational research provides teachers with rules of thumb for practice.

What Are Five Ways of Viewing the Teacher Knowledge Base?

- There is no universally accepted definition of "good" teaching.
- The teacher knowledge base (essential knowledge and abilities) can place primary emphasis on personal development, research-based competencies, provincial or territorial standards, job analyses, or the views of professional organizations.
- Many provinces have developed standards for outcome-based or performance-based teacher education. Outcomes are based on what beginning teachers do in real classrooms.
- The job-analysis view of teaching is based on identifying job dimensions— the knowledge, skills, and attitudes teachers need.
- Effective teachers are guided by reflection and a problem-solving orientation.

How Are Canadian Teachers Educated and Certified?

- Provincial departments of education and independent professional organizations both set criteria for the certification of teachers.

What Can You Learn from Observing in Classrooms?

- The opportunity to observe in classrooms helps some students make a final decision about becoming a teacher.

- Many teacher education programs are providing students with more and earlier opportunities to observe in classrooms.

- Distance-learning classrooms, using compressed video, link teacher education programs to schools off campus.

- Observations can focus on a particular aspect of classroom life or be guided by a set of questions related to a specific area, such as how the teacher motivates students.

- Observation instruments range from informal, qualitative descriptions to formal, quantitative checklists.

How Can You Gain Practical Experience for Becoming a Teacher?

- Teacher education students can gain practical experience through focused classroom observations, microteaching, teaching simulations, analyses of video cases, field-based practica and clinical experiences, and classroom assistant programs.

- Distance-learning classrooms, using compressed video, link teacher education programs to schools off-campus.

- In microteaching, students practice specific skills by teaching brief lessons that are later analyzed.

- Computer simulations and virtual reality—as well as written, videotaped, and audiotaped cases—are being used for teaching simulations.

- Journal writing and reflective teaching logs increase the benefits of the student teaching experience.

- To prepare to teach students from diverse backgrounds, teacher education students should actively seek field experiences in multicultural settings.

- Supply teaching provides additional practical experience after completing a teacher education program.

How Can You Develop Your Teaching Portfolio?

- A portfolio documents professional growth and development over time.
- A portfolio can be organized around specific outcomes or standards.
- Portfolio contents should represent one's best work.
- Professional portfolios can be used in teacher evaluation, self-evaluation, and hiring.

How Can You Benefit from Mentoring Relationships?

- Ask for advice from teachers you admire.
- Mentoring can be a source of professional growth for experienced teachers.
- Mentoring enables the protegé to "learn the ropes."

What Opportunities for Continuing Professional Development Will You Have?

■ Self-assessment is necessary to select appropriate professional development experiences.

■ Opportunities for professional development include teacher workshops, teacher centres, professional development schools, supervision and mentoring of student teachers, graduate study, and the internet.

KEY TERMS AND CONCEPTS

field experiences, 53
in-service
   workshops, 64
internet, 65
job analysis, 47
knowledge base, 46
mentor, 63
mentoring, 62
microteaching, 55
observations, 53

outcome-based teacher
   education, 47
pedagogical content
   knowledge, 43
performance-based teacher
   education, 47
personal development
   view, 46
practicum, 57
professional portfolio, 60

reflection, 63
reflective teaching
   log, 59
research-based
   competencies, 47
self-assessment, 63
substitute teaching, 60
supply teaching, 60
teacher centres, 65
teaching simulations, 56

APPLICATIONS AND ACTIVITIES

Teacher's Journal

1. What does self-knowledge mean to you? Why is self-knowledge important in teaching? What steps can you take to achieve greater self-knowledge?

2. As a teacher, you will encounter challenges related to student variability (differences in developmental needs, interests, abilities, and disabilities) and student diversity (differences in gender, race, ethnicity, culture, and socioeconomic status). To begin thinking about how you will acquire and use knowledge about your students, write a brief profile of yourself as a student in elementary school, in middle school or junior high school, and in high school.

3. Reflect on your education as a teacher. What are your primary concerns about the preparation you are receiving? What experiences do you think will be most helpful to you as you move toward becoming a teacher? What qualities would you look for in a mentor?

4. On the basis of your field experiences to date and the information in Chapters 1 and 2, ask yourself these questions and respond in your journal: Do I have the aptitude to become a good teacher? Am I willing to acquire the essential knowledge and skills teachers need? Do I really want to become a teacher?

Teacher's Database

1. Find out more about the use of technology to enhance teaching and learning. Join one of the internet teacher discussion groups that deal with the educational use of information technology.

2. Instead of using "outside experts" to deliver professional development workshops to teachers, some school districts and teacher associations have implemented teacher networks in which teachers address problems of mutual concern. For example, the Nova Scotia Teachers Union organizes an annual conference specifically designed to assist new teachers with the problems they encounter. You can visit the Nova Scotia Teachers Union website at www.nstu.ca/ for more information.

Observations and Interviews

1. Think about areas for focused observations of teaching, such as classroom management, student involvement, questioning techniques, evaluation, or teacher–student rapport. For one or more areas, brainstorm and order in logical sequence a set of questions you could use to guide your next observations. Include a list of questions to ask the teacher whom you will observe.

2. As a collaborative project with classmates, interview students who have completed student teaching at your university. What tips do they have for developing a positive relationship with a cooperating teacher? For establishing rapport with students? For developing confidence in presenting lessons?

3. Arrange to interview a school administrator about the knowledge, skills, and aptitude he or she thinks teachers must have. Which of the knowledge and skills discussed in this chapter does the administrator mention? Does he or she mention knowledge and skills not discussed in this chapter?

4. Observe a teacher in the classroom for the purpose of identifying examples that help to answer the following questions. How does the teacher demonstrate or use knowledge of self and students? Knowledge of subject matter? Knowledge of educational theory and research?

5. Observe a classroom in which there is likely to be some teacher–student interaction (for example, questions and answers, discussion, or oral review and feedback). On the basis of the data you collect, what conclusions can you draw about life in this classroom?

Professional Portfolio

1. Create a plan for developing your portfolio. What specific outcomes or standards will you use to organize your portfolio entries? What artifacts will you use to demonstrate your professional growth and development?

2. Evaluate the products of your studies in education so far in your preparation for becoming a teacher. Identify a few examples of your best work to include in your portfolio. Also, evaluate your Teacher's Journal, Teacher's Database, and Observations and Interviews for possible inclusions in your portfolio.

Appendix 2.1

Broad focus	General curriculum outcomes
Speaking and listening	1. Students will speak and listen to, explore, extend, and reflect on their thoughts, ideas, feelings and experiences. 2. Students will be able to communicate information and ideas effectively and clearly, and to respond personally and critically. 3. Students will be able to interact with sensitivity and respect, considering the situation, audience, and purpose.
Reading and viewing	1. Students will be able to select, read, and view with understanding a range of literature, information, media, and visual texts. 2. Students will be able to interpret, select, and combine information using a variety of stategies, resources, and technologies. 3. Students will be able to respond personally to a range of texts. 4. Students will be able to respond critically to a range of texts, applying their understanding of language, form, and genre.
Writing and other ways of representing	1. Students will be able to use writing and other ways of representing to explore, clarify, and reflect on their thoughts, feelings, experiences, and learning; and to use their imagination. 2. Students will be able to create texts collaboratively and independently, using a variety of forms for a range of audiences and purposes. 3. Students will be able to use a range of strategies to develop effective writing and other ways of representing, and to enhance their clarity, precision, and effectiveness.

Source: Based on *Nova Scotia Education and Culture*, n.d., pp. 16–35.

Appendix 2.2

Teachers in Saskatchewan schools, which are regulated by *The Education Act, 1995*, are classified for salary purposes based on their post-secondary education and the type of teaching certificate they hold. Section 200, *The Education Act* 1995, gives authority to the Board of Education for initial classification. The salary paid in each class is determined by the provincial collective agreement.

Classifications

Class C: Teachers will be placed in this class if they hold a probationary certificate but lack the two years of approved post-secondary education required for Class I.

Class I Requirements: A teacher in Class I is required to hold a valid Probationary Certificate and to have completed two years of recognized post-secondary education.

Class II Requirements: A teacher in Class II is required to hold: (i) a valid: (a) Standard "A" Certificate; or (b) Standard "B" Certificate (Endorsed); and to have completed a minimum of two years of recognized post-secondary education; or (ii) a valid Probationary Certificate, and to have completed a minimum of three years of recognized post-secondary education.

Class III Requirements: A teacher in Class III is required to hold: (i) a valid: (a) Standard "A" Certificate; or (b) Standard "B" Certificate (Endorsed) or (c) Vocational Teacher's Certificate (Endorsed); or (d) Technical Teacher's Certificate (Endorsed); and to have completed a minimum of three years of recognized post-secondary education; or (ii) a valid Probationary Certificate, and to have completed a minimum of four years of recognized post-secondary education including a bachelor's degree.

Class IV Requirements: A teacher in Class IV is required to have completed a minimum of four years of recognized post-secondary education and hold: (i) a valid: (a) Professional "A" Certificate; or (ii) Professional "B" Certificate (Endorsed) or (iii) a valid (a) Vocational Teacher's Certificate (Endorsed); or (b) Technical Teacher's Certificate (Endorsed); and to have completed sufficient additional training that only one year of university education is required to complete a four-year degree.

Class V Requirements: A teacher in Class V is required to have completed a minimum of five years of recognized post-secondary education and hold: (i) a valid: (a) Professional "A" Certificate, a Bachelor of Education (B.Ed.) degree, or a degree recognized as equivalent to a B.Ed. degree, and a second bachelor's degree; or (ii) a valid Professional "A" Certificate, an approved bachelor's degree, and one year of graduate study; or (iii) a valid Professional "A" Certificate and an approved four-year bachelor's degree other than a B.Ed. degree; or (iv) a valid Professional "B" Certificate and an approved four-year bachelor's degree other than a B.Ed. degree; or (v) a valid: (a) Vocational Teacher's Certificate (Endorsed); or (b) Technical Teacher's Certificate (Endorsed); and a B.Ed. or equivalent degree.

Class VI Requirements: A teacher in Class VI is required to have completed a minimum of six years of recognized post-secondary education and hold: (i) a valid Professional "A" Certificate, a B.Ed. degree, a second bachelor's degree and one year of graduate study; or (ii) a valid Professional "A" Certificate, a B.Ed. degree, and two years of graduate study; or (iii) a valid Professional "A" Certificate, an Honours degree and a B.Ed. degree; or (iv) a valid Professional "A" Certificate, an approved bachelor's degree and a Masters of Education degree (v) a valid (a) Vocational Teacher's Certificate (Endorsed); or (b) Technical Teacher's Certificate (Endorsed); and a B.Ed. degree and one year of graduate study.

Source: "Teacher Salary Classification in Saskatchewan," Reprinted by permission of the Saskatchewan Teachers' Federation, p. 2. Retrieved October 3, 2003 from www.stf.sk.ca/prof_growth/pdf/teacher_classification.pdf

Appendix 2.3

Q. What does the OTQT assess?

A.
- The knowledge and skills judged to be important to carry out essential occupational responsibilities competently
- Whether individuals possess occupation-relevant knowledge and skills at the time of entry into their occupation or profession

Q. What is included in the OTQT?

A.
- The test has 36 multiple-choice questions that focus specifically on a particular theory, strategy, technique, term, concept, act, or regulation related to classroom instruction in Ontario.
- The test also has four case studies, each with short-answer question (a total of 14).
- Two case studies are seen by all test candidates, who are asked to write answers to the six questions associated with these case studies.
- The other two case studies and the eight questions associated with them are matched to the candidate's certification level—Primary/Junior, Junior/Intermediate, or Intermediate/Senior. In other words, each candidate will respond to a total of four case studies—two general ones and two for the candidate's specific certification level.
- The test covers content areas such as the Ontario Curriculum, Planning Instruction, Human Development, Classroom Management, The Use of Technology, Acts and Regulations, Instructional Skills, Motivation and Communication, Diversity and Students with Special Needs, Assessment, Reflections on Teaching, and Parents, Colleagues, and Resources.

Q. What is a case study?

A. A case study consists of a teaching scenario of 800 to 1000 words. Typically a case study focuses on a teacher's experience with a class or on the learning experiences of a student or group of students. Each case study is followed by three or four open-ended questions that encourage synthesizing of knowledge, much as new teachers have to do in the day-to-day work of teaching. A sample of a case study is included later in this booklet. Answers to the case study questions included here are actual responses of student-participants from a pilot test.

Q. How are the case studies used on the test?

A. Each case study describes a classroom situation and is followed by a set of questions. You will be asked to provide a brief written answer for each question. For example, you may be asked to:
- Analyze a student's behaviour
- Suggest next steps in a classroom management situation
- Discuss the merits and disadvantages of certain types of assessments
- Describe ways of communicating with parents
- Suggest teaching strategies to meet expectations based on the Ontario curriculum
- Your answer should be brief and relevant to the question being asked. The quality and relevance of your response are the keys to a high score.

Source: © Queen's Printer of Ontario. (2002). *Ontario Teacher Qualifying Test Information Booklet*, Ontario Ministry of Education, 2002–2003, p.4. Reprinted with permission.

Appendix 2.4

Domain: Teaching Practice

Competencies	Levels of Performance			
	Exemplary	Good	Satisfactory	Unsatisfactory
Teachers use their professional knowledge and understanding of the curriculum, legislation, teaching practices and classroom management strategies to promote the learning and achievement of their pupils.	The teacher always demonstrates use of professional knowledge and understanding of students, curriculum, legislation, teaching practices and classroom management strategies to promote the learning and achievement of his or her students.	The teacher consistently demonstrates use of professional knowledge and understanding of students, curriculum, legislation, teaching practices and classroom management strategies to promote the learning and achievement of his or her students.	The teacher generally demonstrates use of professional knowledge and understanding of students, curriculum, legislation, teaching practices and classroom management strategies to promote the learning and achievement of his or her students.	The teacher infrequently demonstrates use of professional knowledge and understanding of students, curriculum, legislation, teaching practices and classroom management strategies to promote the learning and achievement of his or her students.
Teachers communicate effectively with pupils, parents and colleagues.	The teacher is always effective in communicating with pupils, parents, and colleagues.	The teacher is consistently effective in communicating with pupils, parents, and colleagues.	The teacher is generally effective in communicating with pupils, parents, and colleagues.	The teacher is infrequently effective in communicating with pupils, parents, and colleagues.
Teachers adapt and refine their teaching practices through continuous learning and reflection, using a variety of sources and resources.	The teacher always adapts and refines teaching practice through continuous learning and reflection, using a variety of sources and resources.	The teacher consistently adapts and refines teaching practice through continuous learning and reflection, using a variety of sources and resources.	The teacher generally adapts and refines teaching practice through continuous learning and reflection, using a variety of sources and resources.	The teacher infrequently adapts and refines teaching practice through continuous learning and reflection, using a variety of sources and resources.
Teachers consistently use appropriate technology in their teaching practices and related professional responsibilities.	The teacher always uses appropriate technology in teaching practice and related professional responsibilities.	The teacher consistently uses appropriate technology in teaching practice and related professional responsibilities.	The teacher generally uses appropriate technology in teaching practice and related professional responsibilities.	The teacher infrequently uses appropriate technology in teaching practice and related professional responsibilities.

Source: Queen's Printer of Ontario. (2002). *Teacher performance appraisal manual and approved forms and guidelines*. Toronto: Ontario Ministry of Education, p. 75. Reprinted with permission.

part two

Foundations of Teaching

dear mentor

On Keeping Up with a Rapidly Changing Profession

Dear Mentor,

With all we see in the news media about modernizing and changing education to fit today's political agenda, how can educators be sure they are teaching students the "right" curriculum? How can I, as a teacher, be sure that I can keep up with the rapidly changing times? Is it possible that I can find the answers to these questions by studying the history, philosophy, and governance of education?

Sincerely,

Elizabeth Acevedo

Dear Elizabeth:

The questions you pose concerning curriculum and the rapidly changing times and forces in education today are probably among the most difficult for educators to deal with, but at the same time they are part of what makes education so exciting in this era of technology and the information age. I suggest you start with the curriculum that every provincial and territorial school system in Canada has established. These curricula are based on values and knowledge that are grounded in the history of education and in the education philosophies that have been developed through study and research. These values are also the foundation on which you should build your personal teaching style and philosophy.

I think it is also important to recognize that curricula are not static. They are not rigidly bound to just tradition and accepted values. A good curriculum has to be a vibrant, almost living device that allows us to teach the basic ideas, theories, and learning strategies, as well as to incorporate today's growing body of knowledge which is expanding exponentially because of computers and technology. I think that this makes education particularly exciting. To cite just one example, the amount of research done in the past decade concerning the brain and learning is revolutionizing the way we teach today. As educators we have to keep up with this research and use it in the best way possible to educate our students.

This leads me to your second question: How can a teacher be sure to keep up with the rapidly changing times? I think we should take the medical profession as a good example of how and why we must keep up with our ever-changing field. Just as a good doctor follows the advancements made in medicine by reading professional journals, attending professional conferences, and sharing practices and ideas with colleagues, we as educators have to do the same. We must realize that as professional educators, we have a responsibility to our students to provide them with the best education possible, and we cannot do this unless we are constantly learning, and studying, and improving our profession. We have to make a commitment to learning and  incorporate it into our professional development, as well as to instill it into our students' thinking. After all, I think a good teacher would want to be a learner for life and would want to encourage his or her students to be lifelong learners, too.

I hope these thoughts will help you in your quest to become a good teacher. Your questions already indicate that you possess the reflective abilities that all good educators must have. Best of luck to you in the future.

Sincerely,

Joe Bacewicz

3

Ideas and Events That Have Shaped Education in Canada

Educational philosophy is a way not only of looking at ideas, but also of learning how to use ideas in better ways.

—Howard A. Ozmon and Samuel M. Craver
Philosophical Foundations of Education,
6th ed., 1999

focus questions

1. What determines your educational philosophy?

2. What are the branches of philosophy?

3. What are five modern philosophical orientations to teaching?

4. What psychological orientations have influenced teaching philosophies?

5. How can you develop your educational philosophy?

6. What cultural traditions have led to the development of the Canadian educational landscape?

7. What were teaching and schools like in Canada prior to 1875?

8. What patterns did Canadian education develop from 1875 to 1918?

9. What is the history of schooling for First Nations peoples?

10. What educational advancements took place between the Great Wars (1918–1939)?

11. What are the major characteristics of today's Canadian system of education?

12. How are Canadian schools funded?

13. What are some current trends in Canadian education?

14. What are some other types of Canadian schools?

Y ou are having an animated conversation in the teacher's lounge with four colleagues, Manjit, Yuliya, Kim, and Claude about educational reform and the changes sweeping across our nation's schools. The discussion was sparked by a television special everyone watched last night about new approaches to teaching and assessing students' learning.

"I was really glad to see teachers portrayed in a professional light," you say. "The message seemed to be 'Let's get behind teachers and give them the support and resources they need to implement new ideas and technologies. Effective schools are important to our nation's well-being.'"

"I think it's just a case of schools trying to jump on the bandwagon," Claude says. "All this talk about restructuring schools, developing partnerships with the community, and using technology—they're supposed to be the silver bullets that transform education. These ideas just take time away from what we should be doing, and that's teaching kids how to read, write, and compute. If we don't get back to what really matters, our country is going to fall apart ... that's my educational philosophy."

"But times have changed; the world is a different place," Manjit says. "Look at how the internet has changed things in just a few years. We can't return to the 'good old days.' Students need to learn how to learn; they need to learn how to solve problems that we can't even imagine today."

"Just a minute," Yuliya interjects. "I don't think the 'good old days' ever were. That's a nostalgia trap. What kids need is to see how education is the key to understanding themselves and others. If we can't get along as human beings on this planet, we're in trouble. Look at the ethnic cleansing in Kosovo, the killing in Rwanda, Angola, Northern Ireland.... Sure, we've got the internet and all this technology, but as a species we haven't evolved at all."

"Of course we can't return to the past," Kim says, "but we can learn a lot from it. That's one of the main purposes of education ... to see how the great ideas can help us improve things. Like I tell my students, there isn't one problem today that Shakespeare didn't have tremendous insights into 400 years ago—racism, poverty, war."

"Well, all I know is that when I started teaching 30 years ago, we taught the basics," Claude says. "It was as simple as that. We were there to teach, and the kids, believe it or not, were there to learn. Nowadays, we have to solve all of society's problems—eliminate poverty, racism, crime, or whatever."

Claude pauses a moment and then turns his attention to you. "What do you think ... what's your educational philosophy?"

What do you say?

Manjit is correct when she says we cannot return to the past, to the "good old days." On the other hand, Kim is also correct when she says we should learn from the past. We cannot understand schools today without a look at what they were yesterday. The current system of public and private education in Canada is an ongoing reflection of its philosophical and historical foundations and of the aspirations and values brought to this country by its founders and generations of settlers. Developing an appreciation for the ideas and events that have shaped education in Canada is an important part of your education as a professional.

Still, you may wonder, what is the value of knowing about the philosophy and history of Canadian education? Will that knowledge help you to be a better teacher? First, knowledge of the ideas and events that have influenced our schools will help you evaluate current proposals for change more effectively. You will be in a better position to evaluate changes if you understand how schools have developed and how current proposals might relate to previous change efforts. Second, awareness of ideas and events that have influenced teaching is a hallmark of professionalism in education.

The first half of this chapter presents several basic philosophical concepts that will help you answer five important questions that teachers must consider as they develop an educational philosophy:

1. What should the purposes of education be?
2. What is the nature of knowledge?
3. What values should students adopt?
4. What knowledge is of most worth?
5. How should learning be evaluated?

The second half presents brief overviews of how education developed in Canada's major geographical regions. This chapter will discuss the philosophical concepts, social forces, and events that, in our judgment, have had the greatest impact on education in our country.

What Determines Your Educational Philosophy?

In simplest terms, **educational philosophy** consists of what you believe about education—the set of principles that guides your professional action. Every teacher, whether he or she recognizes it, has a philosophy of education—a set of beliefs about how human beings learn and grow and what one should learn in order to live the good life. Teachers differ, of course, in regard to the amount of effort they devote to the development of their personal philosophy or educational platform. Some feel that philosophical reflections have nothing to contribute to the actual act of teaching. (This stance, of course, is itself a philosophy of education.) Other teachers recognize that teaching, because it is concerned with *what ought to be*, is basically a philosophical enterprise.

Your behaviour as a teacher is strongly connected to your personal beliefs and your beliefs about teaching and learning, students, knowledge, and what is worth knowing (see Figure 3.1). Regardless of where you stand in regard to these five dimensions of teaching, you should be aware of the need to reflect continually on *what* you believe and *why* you believe it.

Beliefs about Teaching and Learning

One of the most important components of your educational philosophy is how you view teaching and learning. In other words, what is the teacher's primary role? Is the teacher a subject matter expert who can efficiently and effectively impart knowledge to students? Is the teacher a helpful adult who establishes caring relationships with students and nurtures their growth in needed areas? Or is the teacher a skilled technician who can manage the learning of many students at once?

Some teachers emphasize the individual student's experiences and cognitions. Others stress the student's behaviour. Learning,

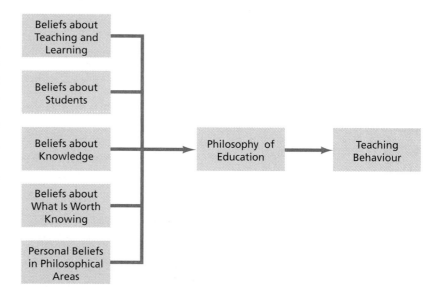

Figure 3.1

The influence of the teacher's educational beliefs on teaching behaviour

How can the web enhance your study of and interest in the philosophy and history of education?

The web has dramatically increased the amount of information that is easily available to anyone with a computer. The web, in a manner perhaps more dramatic than the invention of the printing press in the middle of the fifteenth century, has brought limitless information and expertise to people around the globe.

However, you might wonder, is there any connection between the web and the philosophy and history of education? Can the web enhance your study of and interest in these two areas? Prior to the availability of the web, it may have been more difficult for a student to develop an interest in the philosophy and history of education and to see their relevance to becoming a teacher. Only the most diligent students had the time, energy, and interest to do library research in these areas. Moreover, the outcomes of their research were limited to the size of the library collections they were using.

Today, however, the web makes available to you in a digitized form a huge amount of human culture. This means that you can easily access *more* information that is *more relevant* to your interests, experiences, and professional goals. The web makes available to you not only vast information on the philosophy and history of education, but also an extensive collection of original primary sources. Some internet sites you might visit are:

http://education.guardian.co.uk/netclass/schools/history/0,5607,80402,00.html

http://fcis.oise.utoronto.ca/~daniel_schugurensky/assignment1/1907montessori.html

http://gsnlists.org/pipermail/k12opps/2000-November/000280.html

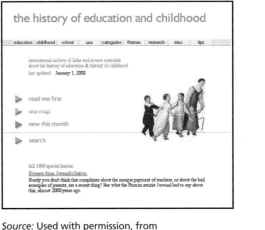

Source: Used with permission, from www.socsci.kun.nl/ped/whp/histeduc

according to the first viewpoint, is seen as the changes in thoughts or actions that result from personal experience; that is, learning is largely the result of internal forces within the individual. In contrast, the other view defines learning as the associations between various stimuli and responses. Here, learning results from forces that are external to the individual.

Beliefs about Students

Your beliefs about students will have a great influence on how you teach. Every teacher formulates an image in her or his mind of what students are like—their dispositions, skills, motivation levels, and expectations. What you believe students are like is based on your unique life experiences, particularly your observations of young people and your knowledge of human growth and development.

Negative views of students may promote teacher–student relationships based on fear and coercion rather than on trust and helpfulness. Extremely positive views may risk not providing students with sufficient structure and direction and not communicating sufficiently high expectations. In the final analysis, the truly professional teacher—the one who has a carefully thought-out educational philosophy—recognizes that, although children differ in their predispositions to learn and grow, they all *can* learn.

Beliefs about Knowledge

How a teacher views knowledge is directly related to how she or he goes about teaching. If teachers view knowledge as the sum total of small bits of subject matter or discrete facts, their students will most likely spend a great deal of time learning that information in a straightforward, rote manner.

Other teachers view knowledge more conceptually, that is, as consisting of the big ideas that enable us to understand and influence our environment. Such teachers would want students to be able to explain how legislative decisions are made in the provincial capital, how an understanding of the eight parts of speech can empower the writer and vitalize one's writing, and how chemical elements are grouped according to their atomic numbers.

Finally, teachers differ in their beliefs as to whether students' increased understanding of their own experiences is a legitimate form of knowledge. Knowledge of self and one's experiences in the world is not the same as knowledge about a particular subject, yet personal knowledge is essential for a full, satisfying life.

Beliefs about What Is Worth Knowing

As we saw in this chapter's opening scenario, teachers have different ideas about what should be taught. Claude believes it is most important that students learn the basic skills of reading, writing, and computation. These are the skills they will need to be successful in their chosen occupations, and it is the school's responsibility to prepare students for the world of work. Kim believes that the most worthwhile content is to be found in the classics or the Great Books. Through mastering the great ideas from sciences, mathematics, literature, and history, students will be well prepared to deal with the world of the future. Duncan is most concerned with students learning how to reason, communicate effectively, and solve problems. Students who master these cognitive processes will have learned how to learn—and this is the most realistic preparation for an unknown future. Last, Manjit is concerned with developing the whole child and teaching students to become self-actualizing. Thus, the curriculum should be meaningful and contribute to the student's efforts to become a mature, well-integrated person.

What Are the Branches of Philosophy?

To provide you with further tools to formulate and clarify your educational philosophy, this section presents brief overviews of six areas of philosophy that are of central concern to teachers: metaphysics, epistemology, axiology, ethics, aesthetics, and logic. Each area focuses on one of the questions that have concerned the world's greatest philosophers for centuries: What is the nature of reality? What is the nature of knowledge and is truth ever attainable? According to what values should one live? What is good and what is evil? What is the nature of beauty and excellence? What processes of reasoning will yield consistently valid results?

Metaphysics

Metaphysics is concerned with explaining, as rationally and as comprehensively as possible, the nature of reality (in contrast to how reality *appears*). What is reality? What is the world made of? These are metaphysical questions. Metaphysics also is concerned with the nature of being and explores questions such as, What does it mean to exist? What is humankind's place in the scheme of things? Metaphysical questions such as these are at the very heart of educational philosophy. As two educational philosophers put it: "Our ultimate preoccupation in educational theory is with the most primary of all philosophic problems: metaphysics, the study of ultimate reality" (Morris and Pai 1994, 28).

Metaphysics has important implications for education because the school curriculum is based on what we know about reality. And what we know about reality is driven by the kinds of questions we ask about the world. In fact, any position regarding what schools should teach has behind it a particular view of reality, a particular set of responses to metaphysical questions.

Epistemology

The next major set of philosophical questions that concerns teachers is called **epistemology**. These questions focus on knowledge: What knowledge is true? How does knowing take place? How do we know that we know? How do we decide between opposing views of knowledge? Is truth constant, or does it change from situation to situation? What knowledge is of most worth? How you answer the epistemological questions that confront all teachers will have significant implications for your teaching. First, you will need to determine what is true about the content you will teach; then you must decide on the most appropriate means of conveying this content to students. Even a casual consideration of epistemological questions reveals that there are many ways of knowing about the world, at least five of which are of interest to teachers:

1. *Knowing Based on Authority*—for example, knowledge from the sage, the poet, the expert, the ruler, the textbook, or the teacher.
2. *Knowing Based on Divine Revelation*—for example, knowledge in the form of supernatural revelations from the sun god of early peoples, the many gods of the ancient Greeks, or the Judeo-Christian god.
3. *Knowing Based on Empiricism (Experience)*—for example, knowledge acquired through the senses, the informally-gathered empirical data that direct most of our daily behaviour.
4. *Knowing Based on Reason and Logical Analysis*—for example, knowledge inferred from the process of thinking logically.
5. *Knowing Based on Intuition*—for example, knowledge arrived at without the use of rational thought.

Axiology

The next set of philosophical problems concerns values. Teachers are concerned with values because "school is not a neutral activity. The very idea of schooling expresses a set of values. [We] educate and we are educated for some purpose we consider good. We teach what we think is a valuable set of ideas. How else could we construct education?" (Nelson, Carlson and Palonsky 2000, 304).

Among the axiological questions teachers must answer for themselves are: What values should teachers encourage students to adopt? What values raise humanity to our highest expressions of humaneness? What values does a truly educated person hold?

Axiology highlights the fact that the teacher has an interest not only in the *quantity* of knowledge that students acquire but also in the *quality* of life that becomes possible because of that knowledge. Extensive knowledge may not benefit the individual if he or she is unable to put that knowledge to good use. This point raises additional questions: How do we define quality of life? What curricular experiences contribute most to that quality of life? All teachers must deal with the issues raised by these questions.

Ethics

While axiology addresses the question "What is valuable?" **ethics** focuses on "What is good and evil, right and wrong, just and unjust?"

A knowledge of ethics can help the teacher solve many of the dilemmas that arise in the classroom. Frequently, teachers must take action in situations where they are unable to gather all of the relevant facts and where no single course of action is totally right or wrong. For example, a student whose previous work was above average plagiarizes a term paper: Should the teacher fail the student for the course if the example of swift, decisive punishment will likely prevent other students from plagiarizing? Or should the teacher, following her hunches about what would be in the student's long-term interest, have the student redo the term paper, and risk the possibility that other students might get the mistaken notion that plagiarism has no negative consequences? Another ethical dilemma: Is an elementary mathematics teacher justified in trying to increase achievement for the whole class by separating two disruptive girls and placing one in a mathematics group beneath her level of ability?

What might this teacher want her students to learn about aesthetics? How were aesthetic values reflected in the K–12 curricula you experienced?

Aesthetics

The branch of axiology known as **aesthetics** is concerned with values related to beauty and art. Although we expect that teachers of music, art, drama, literature, and writing regularly have students make judgments about the quality of works of art, we can easily overlook the role that aesthetics ought to play in *all* areas of the curriculum.

- Treat all thoughts as in need of development.
- Respond to all answers with a further question (that calls on the respondent to develop his or her thinking in a fuller and deeper way).
- Treat all assertions as a connecting point to further thoughts.
- Recognize that any thought can only exist fully in a network of connected thoughts. Stimulate students—by your questions—to pursue those connections.
- Seek to understand—where possible—the ultimate foundations for what is said or believed.
- Recognize that all questions presuppose prior questions and all thinking presupposes prior thinking. When raising questions, be open to the questions they presuppose.

Figure 3.2

The spirit and principles of Socratic questioning

Source: Richard Paul and Linda Eider, "The Art of Socratic questioning," *Critical Thinking,* Fall 1995, 16.

Aesthetics can also help the teacher increase his or her effectiveness. Teaching, because it may be viewed as a form of artistic expression, can be judged according to artistic standards of beauty and quality. In this regard, the teacher is an artist whose medium of expression is the spontaneous, unrehearsed, and creative encounter between teacher and student.

Logic

Logic is the area of philosophy that deals with the process of reasoning and identifies rules that will enable the thinker to reach valid conclusions. The two kinds of logical thinking processes that teachers most frequently have students master are *deductive* and *inductive* thinking. The deductive approach requires the thinker to move from a general principle or proposition to a specific conclusion that is valid. By contrast, inductive reasoning moves from the specific to the general. Here, the student begins by examining particular examples that eventually lead to the acceptance of a general proposition. Inductive teaching is often referred to as discovery teaching—by which students discover, or create, their own knowledge of a topic.

Perhaps the best-known teacher to use the inductive approach to teaching was the Greek philosopher Socrates (ca. 470–399 BC). His method of teaching, known today as the Socratic method, consisted of holding philosophical conversations (dialectics) with his pupils. The legacy of Socrates lives in all teachers who use his questioning strategies to encourage students to think for themselves. Figure 3.2 presents guidelines for using **Socratic questioning** techniques in the classroom.

What Are Five Modern Philosophical Orientations to Teaching?

Five major philosophical orientations to teaching have been developed in response to the branches of philosophy we have just examined. These orientations, or schools of thought, are perennialism, essentialism, progressivism, existentialism, and social reconstructionism. The following sections present a brief description of each of these orientations, moving from those that are teacher-centred to those that are student-centred (see Figure 3.3).

Perennialism

Perennialism, as the term implies, views truth as constant, or perennial. The aim of education, according to perennialist thinking, is to ensure that students acquire knowledge of unchanging principles or great ideas. Like Karen, whom you met briefly in this chapter's opening scenario, perennialists believe that the great ideas continue to have the most potential for solving the problems of any era.

Socrates
(ca. 470–399 BC)

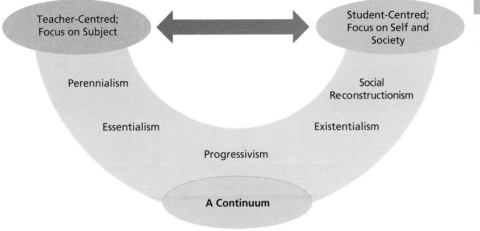

Figure 3.3

Five philosophical orientations to teaching

The curriculum, according to perennialists, should stress students' intellectual growth in the arts and sciences. To become "culturally literate," students should encounter in these areas the best, most significant works that humans have created. Thus, a high school English teacher would require students to read Melville's *Moby Dick* or any of Shakespeare's plays rather than a novel on the current best-seller list.

Similarly, science students would learn about the three laws of motion or the three laws of thermodynamics rather than build a model of the space shuttle.

Perennialist Educational Philosophers

Two of the best known advocates of the perennialist philosophy have been Robert Maynard Hutchins (1899–1977) and, more recently, Mortimer Adler, who together developed an undergraduate curriculum based on the study of the Great Books and discussions of these classics in small seminars. Noted educational philosopher Mortimer Adler, along with Hutchins, was instrumental in organizing the Great Books of the Western World curriculum. Through focusing study on over 100 enduring classics, from Plato to Einstein, the Great Books approach aims at the major perennialist goal of teaching students to become independent and critical thinkers. It is a demanding curriculum, and it focuses on the enduring disciplines of knowledge rather than on current events or student interests.

Robert Maynard Hutchins (1899–1977)

Essentialism

Essentialism, which has some similarities to perennialism, is a conservative philosophy of education. It was originally formulated by William C. Bagley (1874–1946), an American professor of education, as a criticism of progressive trends in schools. Essentialists, like Claude, whom you met in this chapter's opening scenario, believe that human culture has a core of common knowledge that schools are obligated to transmit to students in a systematic, disciplined way. Unlike perennialists, who emphasize a set of external truths, essentialists stress what they believe to be the essential knowledge and skills (often termed "the basics") that productive members of our society need to know.

William C. Bagley (1874–1946)

According to essentialist philosophy, schooling should be practical and provide children with sound instruction that prepares them to live life; schools should not try to influence or set social policies. Critics of essentialism, however, charge that such a tradition-bound orientation to schooling will indoctrinate students and rule out the possibility of change. Essentialists respond that, without an essentialist approach, students will be indoctrinated in humanistic and/or behavioural curricula that run counter to society's accepted standards and need for order.

Progressivism

Progressivism is based on the belief that education should be child-centred rather than focused on the teacher or the content area. The writing of John Dewey (1859–1952) in the 1920s and 1930s contributed a great deal to the spread of progressive ideas. Briefly, Deweyan progressivism is based on three central assumptions:

1. The content of the curriculum ought to be derived from students' interests rather than from the academic disciplines.
2. Effective teaching takes into account the whole child and his or her interests and needs in relation to cognitive, affective, and psychomotor areas.
3. Learning is essentially active rather than passive.

Progressive Strategies

John Dewey
(1859–1952)

The progressive philosophy also contends that knowledge that is true in the present may not be true in the future. Hence, the best way to prepare students for an unknown future is to equip them with problem-solving strategies that will enable them to discover meaningful knowledge at various stages of their lives.

Educators with a progressive orientation give students a considerable amount of freedom in determining their school experiences. Contrary to the perceptions of many, though, progressive education does not mean that teachers do not provide structure or that students are free to do whatever they wish. Progressive teachers begin where students are and, through the daily give-and-take of the classroom, lead students to see that the subject to be learned can enhance their lives.

In a progressively oriented classroom, the teacher serves as a guide or resource person whose primary responsibility is to facilitate student learning. The teacher helps students learn what is important to them rather than passing on a set of so-called

How might you explain what is happening in this classroom from the perspective of progressivism? From the perspective of perennialism? From the perspective of essentialism?

enduring truths. Students have many opportunities to work cooperatively in groups, often solving problems that the group, not the teacher, has identified as important.

Existentialism

Existential philosophy is unique in that it focuses on the experiences of the individual. Other philosophies are concerned with developing systems of thought for identifying and understanding what is common to *all* reality, human existence, and values. **Existentialism**, on the other hand, offers the individual a way of thinking about *my* life, what has meaning for *me*, what is true for *me*. In general, existentialism emphasizes creative choice, the subjectivity of human experiences, and concrete acts of human existence over any rational scheme for human nature or reality.

The writings of Jean-Paul Sartre (1905–1980), well-known French philosopher, novelist, and playwright, have been most responsible for the widespread dissemination of existential ideas. According to Sartre (1972), every individual first exists and then he or she must decide what that existence is to mean. The task of assigning meaning to that existence is the individual's alone; no preformed philosophical belief system can tell one who one is. It is up to each of us to decide who we are.

Jean-Paul Sartre
(1905–1980)

Life, according to existential thought, has no meaning, and the universe is indifferent to the situation humankind finds itself in. Moreover, "existententialists [believe] that too many people wrongly emphasize the optimistic, the good, and the beautiful—all of which create a false impression of existence" (Ozmon and Craver 1999, 253). With the freedom that we have, however, each of us must commit him- or herself to assign meaning to his or her *own* life. As Maxine Greene, an eminent philosopher of education whose work is based on existentialism, states: "We have to know about our lives, clarify our situations if we are to understand the world from our shared standpoints ..." (1995, 21). The human enterprise that can be most helpful in promoting this personal quest for meaning is the educative process. Teachers, therefore, must allow students freedom of choice and provide them with experiences that will help them find the meaning of their lives. This approach, contrary to the belief of many, does not mean that students may do whatever they please; logic indicates that freedom has rules, and respect for the freedom of others is essential.

Existentialists judge the curriculum according to whether or not it contributes to the individual's quest for meaning and results in a level of personal awareness that Greene (1995) terms "wide-awakeness." The ideal curriculum is one that provides students with extensive individual freedom and requires them to ask their own questions, conduct their own inquiries, and draw their own conclusions.

Maxine Greene
(b. 1917)

Social Reconstructionism

As the name implies, **social reconstructionism** holds that schools should take the lead in changing or reconstructing society. Theodore Brameld (1904–1987), acknowledged as the founder of social reconstructionism, based his philosophy on two fundamental premises about the post–World War II era: (1) We live in a period of great crisis, most evident in the fact that humans now have the capability of destroying civilization overnight, and (2) humankind also has the intellectual, technological, and moral potential to create a world civilization of "abundance, health, and humane capacity" (Brameld 1959, 19). In this time of great need, then, social reconstructionists like Yuliya, whom we met in this chapter's opening scenario, believe that schools should become the primary agent for planning and directing social change. Schools should not only *transmit* knowledge about the existing social order; they should seek to *reconstruct* it as well.

George Counts
(1889–1974)

Social Reconstructionism and Progressivism

Social reconstructionism has clear ties to progressive educational philosophy. Both provide opportunities for extensive interactions between teacher and students and among students themselves. Furthermore, both place a premium on bringing the community, if not the entire world, into the classroom. Student experiences often include field trips, community-based projects of various sorts, and opportunities to interact with people beyond the four walls of the classroom.

According to Brameld and social reconstructionists such as George Counts, who wrote *Dare the School Build a New Social Order?* (1932), the educative process should provide students with methods for dealing with the significant crises that confront the world: war, economic depression, international terrorism, hunger, inflation, and ever-accelerating technological advances. The logical outcome of such education would be the eventual realization of a worldwide democracy (Brameld 1956). Unless we actively seek to create this kind of world through the intelligent application of present knowledge, we run the risk that the destructive forces of the world will determine the conditions under which humans will live in the future.

What Psychological Orientations Have Influenced Teaching Philosophies?

In addition to the five philosophical orientations to teaching described in previous sections of this chapter, several schools of psychological thought have formed the basis for teaching philosophies. These psychological theories are comprehensive world views that serve as the basis for the way many teachers approach teaching practice. Psychological orientations to teaching are concerned primarily with understanding the conditions that are associated with effective learning. In other words, what motivates students to learn? What environments are most conducive to learning? Chief among the psychological orientations that have influenced teaching philosophies are humanistic psychology, behaviourism, and constructivism.

Humanistic Psychology

Humanistic psychology emphasizes personal freedom, choice, awareness, and personal responsibility. As the term implies, it also focuses on the achievements, motivation, feelings, actions, and needs of human beings. The goal of education, according to this orientation, is individual self-actualization.

Humanistic psychology is derived from the philosophy of **humanism**, which developed during the European Renaissance and Protestant Reformation and is based on the belief that individuals control their own destinies through the application of their intelligence and learning. People "make themselves." The term "secular humanism" refers to the closely related belief that the conditions of human existence relate to human nature and human actions rather than to predestination or divine intervention.

In the 1950s and 1960s, humanistic psychology became the basis of educational reforms that sought to enhance students' achievement of their full potential through self-actualization (Maslow 1954, 1962; Rogers 1961). According to this psychological orientation, teachers should not force students to learn; instead, they should create a climate of trust and respect that allows students to decide what and how they learn, to question authority, and to take initiative in "making themselves." Teachers should be what noted psychologist Carl Rogers calls "facilitators," and the classroom should be a place "in which curiosity and the natural desire to learn can be nourished and enhanced" (1982, 31). Through their non-judgmental understanding of students, humanistic teachers encourage students to learn and grow.

Behaviourism

Behaviourism is based on the principle that desirable human behaviour can be the product of design rather than accident. According to behaviourists, it is an illusion to say that humans have a free will. Although we may act as if we are free, our behaviour is really *determined* by forces in the environment that shape our behaviour. "We are what we are and we do what we do, not because of any mysterious power of human volition, but because outside forces over which we lack any semblance of control have us caught in an inflexible web. Whatever else we may be, we are not the captains of our fate or the masters of our soul" (Power 1982, 168).

Founders of Behaviouristic Psychology

John B. Watson (1878–1958) was the principal originator of behaviouristic psychology and B. F. Skinner (1904–1990) its best-known promoter. Watson first claimed that human behaviour consisted of specific stimuli that resulted in certain responses. In part, he based this new conception of learning on the classic experiment conducted by Russian psychologist Ivan Pavlov (1849–1936). Pavlov had noticed that a dog he was working with would salivate when it was about to be given food. By introducing the sound of a bell when food was offered and repeating this several times, Pavlov discovered that the sound of the bell alone (a conditioned stimulus) would make the dog salivate (a conditioned response). Watson came to believe that all learning conformed to this basic stimulus-response model (now termed classical or type S conditioning).

B. F. Skinner
(1904–1990)

Skinner went beyond Watson's basic stimulus-response model and developed a more comprehensive view of conditioning known as operant (or type R) conditioning. Operant conditioning is based on the idea that satisfying responses are conditioned, unsatisfying ones are not. In other words, "The things we call pleasant have an energizing or strengthening effect on our behaviour" (Skinner 1972, 74). Thus the teacher can create learners who exhibit desired behaviours by following four steps:

1. Identify desired behaviours in concrete (observable and measurable) terms.
2. Establish a procedure for recording specific behaviours and counting their frequencies.
3. For each behaviour, identify an appropriate reinforcer.
4. Ensure that students receive the reinforcer as soon as possible after displaying a desired behaviour.

Constructivism

In contrast to behaviourism, **constructivism** focuses on processes of learning rather than on learning behaviour. According to constructivism, students use cognitive processes to *construct* understanding of the material to be learned—in contrast to the view that they *receive* information transmitted by the teacher. Constructivist approaches support student-centred rather than teacher-centred curriculum and instruction. The student is the key to learning.

Unlike behaviourists who concentrate on directly observable behaviour, constructivists focus on the mental processes and strategies that students use to learn. Our understanding of learning has been extended as a result of advances in **cognitive science**—the study of the mental processes students use in thinking and remembering. By drawing from research in linguistics, psychology, anthropology, neurophysiology, and computer science, cognitive scientists are developing new models for how people think and learn.

Teachers who base classroom activities on constructivism know that learning is an active, meaning-making process, that learners are not passive recipients of information. In fact, students are continually involved in making sense out of activities around them. Thus the teacher must *understand students' understanding* and realize that students' learning is influenced by prior knowledge, experience, attitudes, and social interactions.

How Can You Develop Your Educational Philosophy?

As you read the preceding brief descriptions of five educational philosophies and three psychological orientations to teaching, perhaps you felt that no single philosophy fit perfectly with your image of the kind of teacher you want to become. Or, there may have been some element of each approach that seemed compatible with your own emerging philosophy of education. In either case, don't feel that you need to identify a single educational philosophy around which you will build your teaching career. In reality, few teachers follow only one educational philosophy, and, as Figure 3.4 shows, educational philosophy is only one determinant of the professional goals a teacher sets.

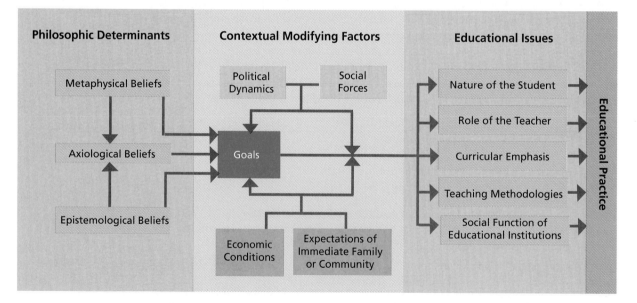

Figure 3.4

The relationship of philosophy to educational practice

Source: George R. Knight, *Issues & Alternatives in Educational Philosophy, 3rd ed.* Berrien Springs, MI: Andrews University Press, p. 34.

These children are active learners in a real or relevant context, and they are constructing their own meanings through direct experience. How might this lesson be seen as an eclectic blend of progressive, existential, and constructivist ideals?

Most teachers develop an *eclectic* philosophy of education, which means they develop their own unique blending of two or more philosophies. The self-knowledge you glean from the philosophical constructs presented in the first half of this chapter will provide a useful framework for studying the six periods in the historical development of schools that follow. For example, you will be able to see how philosophical orientations to education waxed and waned during each period—whether it was the perennialism and essentialism that characterized colonial schools, the progressivism of the 1920s and 1930s, the essentialism of the 1950s and 1980s, the humanism and social reconstructionism of the 1960s, or the constructivism of the 1990s.

What Cultural Traditions Have Led to the Development of the Canadian Educational Landscape?

The Canadian educational landscape has roots which can be traced to four cultural traditions. The earliest schools of New France were, for example, quite naturally modelled after the educational practices common in France. Later, after the fall of Quebec and the rise to governmental supremacy of the British, practices common to English schools were introduced. Later still, after the American Revolution of 1776 and the resultant emigration of the Loyalists to Canada, educational practices based upon the American model were given support. And finally, during the 1760–1840 period, thousands of Scots immigrated to Canada, bringing with them their strong regard for schools based upon democracy and merit. In areas of the country where only one cultural tradition was common, as in New Brunswick, where the Loyalists initially had the field to themselves, development of a coherent educational system was accomplished with a comparative degree of ease. However, in Nova Scotia, where the Scottish, English, and American traditions were all represented, several systems vied for supremacy with the consequence that factionalism, tumult and discord enriched the level of educational discourse.

The French Tradition

During the period 1650–1700, most adult citizens of New France—an area which extended from Cape Breton to the Great Lakes—had received their education in France. In the **French tradition**, the dominant educational philosophy was based upon the traditions of the Roman Catholic Church. Elementary **parochial schools**, known as **petites écoles**, were relatively common in most areas of France. While there was a general belief among the upper classes that the children of the lower classes should be educated, their education was to deal with only the most rudimentary of facts. Girls and boys attended separate schools, with the boys' education tending to be of a better quality. Instruction in the curriculum (catechism, singing, arithmetic, reading, writing, and grammar) was delivered by the parish priests or their assistants.

Funding for the support of the *petites écoles* was provided by the church and those parents who could afford to make contributions. Teacher colleges, also known as **normal schools**, were starting to appear, and several religious orders, most notably the Jesuits priests and the Ursuline nuns, were becoming involved in the educational process. Secondary schools, while not common, did exist and were almost exclusively the responsibility of specific religious orders.

The English Tradition

During the period 1760–1840, the English school system emerged. The **English tradition** reflected the beliefs and attitudes of the upper classes and had two salient characteristics. First, education was primarily a responsibility of the church rather than the state; second, education a was a function of class rather than merit. Education for the lower classes was primarily provided by the Church of England, although other organizations did have some modest involvement. While charitable groups sometimes provided schooling for the poor, some children attended **dame-schools** run by widows and housewives, who taught within their own homes and collected small fees from their students' parents. At the other end of the educational spectrum were the "public" schools reserved for the privileged and the wealthy.

There were various religious groups who wanted to improve the quality of education given to the lower classes, most notably, the Puritans, who eventually decamped to the American colonies. The group with the most outstanding success, however, was the Society for the Propagation of the Gospel in Foreign Parts (SPG). While its main goal was the teaching of the Bible for the benefit of overseas British settlers, the SPG soon involved itself with the development of schools in Canada and other parts of the British Empire.

The American Tradition

The United States' educational system, the **American tradition**, had its primary roots in English culture. The settlers initially tried to develop a system of schooling that paralleled the British two-track system. If students from the lower classes attended school at all it was at the elementary level for the purpose of studying an essentialist curriculum of reading, writing, and computation and receiving religious instruction. Students from the upper classes had the opportunity to attend Latin grammar schools, where they were given a college-preparatory education that focused on subjects such as Latin and Greek classics. Above all, the American colonial curriculum stressed religious objectives.

Generally, no distinction was made between secular and religious life in the colonies. The religious motives that impelled the Puritans to endure the hardships of settling in a new land were reflected in the schools' curricula. The primary objective of elementary schooling was to learn to read so that one might read the Bible and religious catechisms and thereby achieve salvation.

In the period immediately following the American Revolution of 1776, thousands of Loyalists fled to Canada. However, because they had a strong distrust of all things republican, and because they were staunchly loyal to Britain, the Loyalists tended to reinforce the provincial elites who were predominantly Anglicans in control of government counsels. In reality, the American influence upon early Canadian education was essentially a modified, somewhat more practical, version of the English influence. During the many nineteenth-century battles fought for control of Canadian schools, the Loyalists usually supported the entrenched "family compacts" who favoured the English educational tradition. It was a struggle they were destined to lose.

The Scottish Tradition

At the time of the great Scottish migration (1760–1840), the **Scottish tradition** of education, based upon a combination of parish and burgh (town) schools, had several characteristics which led to its easy transference to the New World. The first of these characteristics is of primary importance, for it resulted in the Scots having an educational impact which far outweighed their actual numbers as a percentage of the Canadian population. In Scotland almost every child attended a school, which frequently had students from *all ranks of society*. The class-based system of education found in England was absent. In addition, both male and female students often attended the same school, and had done so for hundreds of years. The practice of having separate schools for boys and girls, a dominant characteristic of the French educational tradition, was absent. Additionally, many Scottish schools provided education at both the elementary and secondary levels. There was no great divide between the two. Rather than placing a strong emphasis upon the classics as the foundation of the curriculum, subjects such as science and art were also taught. In combination with its strong democratic tradition, the characteristics of the Scottish educational system would flourish in Canada's frontier environment.

What Were Teaching and Schools Like in Canada Prior to 1875?

Canada can be roughly divided into five geographical regions: Atlantic Canada, Quebec, Ontario, the west, and the north. As each region was settled at a different time by immigrants from a variety of cultural, linguistic, and religious backgrounds, it is not surprising that the school systems which evolved had their own individual characteristics. In the early years almost all schooling was controlled by religious authorities. However, as Canada's population increased in size, and as economic development became more important to the life of the citizenry, the state began to take a greater interest in educational matters. This increased interest led to the two great educational questions of the eighteenth and nineteenth centuries: Who would control the schools? Who would pay for their maintenance and operation? These questions were largely answered by 1875—but how they were answered differed from one geographical region to another.

Quebec

1608–1760

The earliest Quebec schools were modelled exactly after the *petites écoles* of the mother country. There were separate schools for girls and boys with instruction usually provided by members of religious orders. However, lay teachers who met the moral and competency requirements of the clergy were present in small numbers. Student attendance (by those who had access to a school) varied and most students left soon after learning the rudiments of reading, writing, and arithmetic. Financial support for the *petites écoles* was provided by the church, the students' parents, and in some cases by the King of France. If an educational issue required resolution, an appeal was made to the bishop of Quebec. Indeed, it was not until after 1760 that any civil laws concerning the schools came into existence.

The *petites écoles* provided a very basic education. As early as 1635, however, when the population of New France numbered less than a thousand, the Jesuits established the Collège de Québec. For the next 150 years it remained the only secondary school in French North America. Its curriculum followed the French model, with courses in philosophy, grammar, rhetoric, mathematics, and the humanities.

An interesting development during the latter part of the 1600s was the establishment of craft and trade schools for those young men who were not suited by inclination, education, or personal circumstances, to a career in religion or one of the other professions. These schools, which offered courses in such varied subjects as carpentry, masonry, and shoemaking, provided a valuable service to a developing colony with a need for a skilled workforce. While the craft and trade schools had the support of both the secular and religious authorities, it was the latter who were responsible for their administration and support.

From 1700 until 1760, the pattern of education in New France underwent little change. The various religious societies continued to provide a modest degree of schooling to those children who lived in or near urban communities; children in rural areas had very limited access to schools and many received no education of any kind. However, the ecclesiastical school system established by the religious orders formed the basis for the system which would evolve after the start of British rule.

1760–1875

Jean-Baptiste Meilleur, first superintendent of education in Lower Canada (1842–1855).

During the first 30 years of British rule, Protestant settlers from England, Scotland, Ireland, and other British colonies settled in the urban areas of Quebec. During this period, a few Anglo-Protestant schools were established through the initiative of interested clergy and lay persons. Nothing resembling a coherent school system for either the English-speaking or French-speaking citizens was evident. Education was still an essentially private or church-sponsored enterprise.

The first tentative steps towards the establishment of a centralized school system took place in the last ten years of the eighteenth century, when citizens of all religious groups recognized that economic and social development required a sound educational system. But there were some immediate problems. Should the schools be English or French; Protestant or Roman Catholic? Should the state or the church control the schools? And, most importantly, who should pay for the maintenance and operation of the educational system which would be established? It would take an additional 75 years of acrimonious political and social debate before these questions could be answered.

By 1875, all the elements of a systematic school system were in place. In actuality there were two distinct and totally separate school systems: one for Protestants, and one for Roman Catholics. While religious groups would continue to operate their schools, it would be the state, via a centralized bureaucracy, which would establish teaching standards, set curriculum and, through taxation based upon local assessment, pay for school maintenance and teacher salaries. The state would also provide grants for the establishment of normal schools for the training of teachers. And, by the late 1850s, three such schools had been successfully established. While this separate system of schools was a political solution acceptable to both religious groups, it created a divide between them which lasted well into the twentieth century.

Atlantic Canada

Despite their geographical proximity, the school systems which developed in the four Atlantic Provinces were the result of significantly different influences. During the formative years of its educational system, Nova Scotia had a population which was predominantly Scottish in origin, whereas New Brunswick was composed primarily of Loyalists. Both Prince Edward Island and Newfoundland had populations which were much more varied. The degree of difficulty each province would experience in its drive to establish a comprehensive school system became a function of the cultural traditions within each, and of how these cultural traditions interacted.

Nova Scotia

In 1710 the British conquered the French Garrison at Port Royal, and in 1713 the Treaty of Utrecht gave all of Nova Scotia to England. Later, after the British founded Halifax in 1749, they initiated the infamous expulsion of the Acadians in 1755. Shortly after the expulsion, 8000 New England citizens (traditionally referred to as the Planters) accepted the Governor of Nova Scotia's invitation that they move to Nova Scotia and take over the now vacant farm lands of the departed Acadians. These new settlers brought with them their tradition of self-government in church and state matters.

Prior to the arrival of the Planters, most of the schools which did exist were administered by the Church of England's Society for the Propagation of the Bible (SPG). While the quality of education provided by these schools was very limited, the SPG had strong connections with government officials. Therefore, in an effort to keep the Planters from establishing their own schools, during 1766 the SPG had the House of Assembly pass *An Act Concerning Schools and Schoolmasters*. This act, designed to protect the Church of England's monopoly over education, ironically marks the first official recognition that education was actually the responsibility of the state.

In the ten years following the 1776 American War of Independence, the Loyalists formed a second, larger wave of American immigrants to Nova Scotia. At approximately the same time, an even larger group of Scottish settlers started their migration to the province. The Scots arrived in such numbers that they quickly became the largest, and eventually most influential, faction within the colony.

By 1800, there was recognition that an effective school system was needed for an ever-expanding population. However, the questions which needed to be answered were somewhat simpler in nature. Should the state or the Church of England control the schools? Who should pay for the maintenance and operation of the educational system that would be established? The numerical strength of the Scots provided the answers to these questions. By 1875, after the usual series of acrimonious debates in the legislature, there was agreement that the state would be responsible for the governance and maintenance of schools, and that financial support for schools would be through

Sir John William Dawson, first superintendent of education in Nova Scotia (1850–1853) and later president of McGill University (1855–1893).

taxation based upon local assessment. It was also agreed that a coeducational normal school should be established at Truro. The Planters and the Loyalists had a strong affinity for democratically operated schools, while the Scots had a high regard for the benefits of a school education for everyone. Working in tandem, these two traditions completely overwhelmed the influence of the British, who wanted control of schools to be a function of the Church of England.

New Brunswick

Prior to 1783, New Brunswick was sparsely settled. There were pockets of Acadians who had fled there as a result of their expulsion from Nova Scotia, and a few New England Planters were also present in small numbers. Therefore, when large numbers of Loyalists arrived in the 1775–1785 period, they quickly became the dominant group within the colony. The school system envisaged by the Loyalists, most of whom were Anglicans, was one in which church and state would work together in support of the aristocratic English tradition. Initially, this is what took place. The Society for the Propagation of the Bible (SPG) had the full support of the Executive Council of the legislature, and such grammar schools and other institutions of higher learning had their enrolments limited to members of the Anglican Church.

Unfortunately for the Loyalists, settlers from other areas of the world started arriving in large numbers during the period 1815–1825. In particular, there was a great influx of immigrants from Ireland. Scots, business people from other parts of the British Empire, and settlers from non-Anglican denominations were also becoming increasingly common, with up to one-third of the citizenry composed of Roman Catholics. Additionally, the children of the first Loyalists tended to have educational and social ideas which differed from those of their parents. All groups saw the need for tax assessment in support of free schools, an educational bureaucracy to govern the schools, and a normal school to provide qualified and effective teachers. After years of confused and rancorous debate, the situation began to improve. A normal school was established in 1847, as was a Board of Education. However, it was not until 1871 that the *Common School Act* made provision for free, non-sectarian schools supported by taxation based upon local assessment. Roman Catholics, who had diligently lobbied for separate schools supported by public funds, were deeply offended by the *Act*'s failure to grant their request.

Prince Edward Island

The early history of education in Prince Edward Island (PEI) is one of unrelenting sectarian strife. Acadians missed by the expulsion formed a small part of the population, but there were also Loyalists, Irish, Roman Catholic and Protestant Scots, and English immigrants. In the early part of the 1800s a small number of private schools were in existence. In general, they were operated by itinerant schoolmasters who made their services available to the residents of PEI's ethnic communities.

In 1800 there were fewer than 5000 people in the colony, a number which grew to 70 000 by 1855. Roman Catholics comprised approximately 40 percent of the population, while various Protestant denominations formed the remainder. It was this approximate balance between the two religious groups that lay at the heart of the sectarian warfare and dominated discussion in the provincial legislature. The fundamental issue upon which the two groups could not agree concerned authorization of the Bible for use in PEI public schools. Both groups recognized the needs for establishing a comprehensive system of schools, but the "Bible Question" hindered progress. Coincident with the Bible debate was the question of whether Prince Edward Island should join Confederation. The Roman Catholics tied the two issues together by saying that

Teaching for Excellence

Prime Minister's Award for Teaching Excellence Recipients: Blake Seward and Carmie MacLean.

Blake Seward
Smith Falls District Collegiate, Smith Falls, Ontario
Subjects Taught: Grade 9 to OAC History

Teaching Philosophy

Take students to the site; make history come to life

Outstanding Achievements

Blake Seward brought the relevance of history to life with an inspiring, unusual project—*Lest We Forget*. Grade 10 students were each given the name of a fallen soldier listed on the World War I section of the local cenotaph [monument] and given three weeks to find as much information as possible about the person. Students initially accessed regimental information from government websites, and quickly discovered that many names were misspelled and missing. Students searched relatives' attics, old newspapers and finally the National Archives of Canada for primary research material. The final result is a permanent written record of an almost—but not quite (thanks to Seward and his students)—forgotten band of men and period of history. Students received an award from the Minister of Veteran Affairs for their research and an Ontario Heritage award.

Seward is now working with the National Archives of Canada to expand the project. So far, several schools have signed up, with the formal launch taking place in September of 2003.

The history department has grown under Seward's leadership to be the largest in the school. He has redesigned and reintroduced the American History course, overseen the development of the World Issues and World Religions courses, written curriculum for several history courses, and is planning to launch a senior-level philosophy course.

Rave Reviews

"Students are like bloodhounds: they can sniff out a fake from the very first lesson of the year. But there is no fear that such a thing could occur in Blake's class."

—*Colleague*

"I believe that this project [*Lest We Forget*] is very important because not only does it inspire learning on several different levels, but it also invokes a deep respect for those who fought for our freedom, something that is not often felt by my generation."

—*Student*

Carmie MacLean
Tusarvik School, Repulse Bay, Nunavut
Subjects Taught: Grade 6, All Subjects

Teaching Philosophy

- Share the joy and excitement of lifelong learning with a community—children and their extended families—that, not that many years ago, was nomadic, focused mainly on day-to-day survival.
- Make every effort to ensure students think about learning—even after school hours and outside school walls.
- Balance understanding of many cultural differences with clear high expectations for students.

Outstanding Achievements

Created numerous incentives to improve English skills of Inuktitut-speaking students:
- An email account for all students with required literacy skills.
- Personal letters each week to students in response to their journal entries
- A daily letter to the class outlining new topics, discussing moral or behaviour issues, commenting on performance on tests, or introducing new vocabulary, which ensures students start each school day with reading that is personal, applicable, and pertinent.

Students who use English mainly at school and often have little opportunity to practice their skills at home improve their reading by at least one grade by the end of the year.

MacLean adjusts teaching strategies as necessary to address the learning styles and culture of the North while improving the academic skills of students. For example,

(continued on next page)

MacLean launched a campaign making homework completion a normal expectation of daily school life. The campaign includes lunchtime reminder notes to parents for missing homework, special draws for prizes, a daily visual record maintained by the students, and school-wide homework challenges with PA announcements and coloured bar graphs displayed in the office area.

MacLean also spearheaded an initiative to improve chronic low attendance. One month's perfect attendance earns Saturday morning blueberry muffin baking at MacLean's home, and photos of students displayed in the school foyer, a true incentive in a place where personal photos are rare. These efforts resulted in the outstanding accomplishment of three students having perfect attendance for one whole year.

Rave Reviews

"She is as solid as the rock we walk on in our barren-ground community."

—*Fellow teacher*

"My students, who are presently in Grade 9, still cannot read or write as well as Carmie's but neither did they have the benefit of Carmie's teaching for the last three years."

—*Colleague*

Source: Reproduced with the permission of the Minister of Public Works and Services. Prime Minister's Awards for Teaching Excellence. Retrieved October 4, 2003 from pma-ppm.ic.gc.ca/bio02-e.asp?prov=on and pma-ppm.ic.gc.ca/bio00-e.asp?prov=nu

the union should be opposed unless they were given a constitutional right to **separate schools**. Such a guarantee was not given, and in 1873 Prince Edward Island joined the Confederation of Canada. Shortly thereafter, the Public School Act was passed. This act established the office of Superintendent of Education, decreed that taxation based upon local assessment would support free, non-denomination schools, and created an improved Board of Education for administration of the new system of schooling.

Newfoundland and Labrador

While Prince Edward Island experienced a great deal of sectarian strife during its journey towards a system of publicly funded, non-sectarian schools, the situation in Newfoundland was more protracted and bitter, by several orders of magnitude. The roots of Newfoundland's educational system are similar to the roots of other systems in Canada. The first schools were established and operated by the Society for the Propagation of the Bible, and other groups soon began to provide schooling for the island's children. Roman Catholics, Methodists, and other Protestant groups established schools in various communities, and private schools also sprang up. However, for reasons deeply locked in Newfoundland's cultural history, the state's battle for free, non-denominational schools was lost. In 1874 the legislature gave its formal approval to funding all of the parochial schools which had been founded. Separate schools for everyone became part of the established educational order. Of all the British North American colonies, Newfoundland was the only one to develop such a unique educational model. It would be late in the twentieth century before this parochial system of schools was discontinued.

Labrador, with its harsh climate and very scattered and nomadic Inuit population, also had a church-based system of schooling. In the second half of the 1700s, the Church of the United Brethren (also known as the Moravian Church) took an interest in converting and educating the indigenous Inuit population. The Moravians carried

The Little Red School House

During the early days of Canadian education, any available room in a church, tavern, or public meeting house was pressed into service as a school. If a community did go to the trouble and expense of building a school, the structure was usually made of five-metre long, rough-cut logs. In very few instances was it ever painted red. The ceiling was relatively low and a simple fireplace was the only source of heat. Students were required to supply the firewood. During the winter months those who sat furthest from the fireplace were often uncomfortably cold.

The older students sat on simple benches arranged around three of the walls. In some cases these benches were accompanied by crude desks. Arranged around the centre of the room were more deskless, backless benches for the younger children. Other than a desk for the teacher, the room was almost completely empty. There were no blackboards, no maps, no reference books, and no teaching aids. However, quill pens were common and the students would practice their writing skills for as long as two hours each day. In cases where paper was scarce, birch bark was used. Writing slates, which the students would often "erase" by spitting and wiping them, became relatively common after 1825.

Textbooks were in very short supply and the modern concept of a "class set" was unknown. Students would bring to school any textbook which they might have been able to buy or borrow. Those who could not supply a textbook shared with students who did. The few textbooks which were available were often of American origin, a feature of much annoyance to the Loyalist faction.

The teaching strategies were simple. In many cases students were required to memorize and then recite material assigned to them by the teacher. Instruction of groups within the school was rare. In most cases the teacher dealt with individual students.

The strap was freely used to maintain discipline, and, depending on the seriousness of the offence, a specific number of lashes was administered to the offender. Arriving at school with dirty hands might result in two lashes, fighting might result in five, but swearing or playing cards at school would engender even more.

The teacher was usually an unmarried young woman who, if she did marry and became pregnant, would be expected to resign her position. The administration of the school was usually in the hands of three male trustees—some of whom might be illiterate.

---

out their work with skill and energy and helped to make their Inuit students literate in their own language. Unlike Newfoundland, where numerous religious groups vied for the souls and minds of the citizens, the Moravians carried out their work without competition from any other church.

Ontario

Prior to the arrival of approximately 6000 Loyalists in 1884–1886, Upper Canada (Ontario) had very few settlers. While most of the new Loyalist settlers were farmers, among them were small numbers of well-educated individuals with a high regard for good schooling. These Loyalists wanted their children to have access to American grammar (secondary) schools in addition to the locally supported non-denominational schools. Their educational concerns received support from a second wave of American settlers who, enticed by offers of free land grants, arrived in large numbers during

The District School in Cornwall, Ontario, ca. 1810.

the 20 years preceding the War of 1812. However, while these two groups of American settlers constituted a majority of the population, the government was primarily in the hands of British officials, who believed that the state should control education while leaving its administration to Church of England officials. As most of the population had religious affiliations which were non-Anglican, it is not surprising that a struggle between the English and American traditions developed.

In 1816 the passage of the *Common School Act* suggested that the free schools might come into existence with a minimum of difficulty. This act, which permitted any community with sufficient resources to establish a public school towards which the government would make an annual grant for a teacher's salary, was undermined by the 1820 *Common School Act*, which reduced the government grant. It effectively neutralized the Act of 1816 and established a pattern which would last for another 25 years. where acts regarding schools would be passed, and later rescinded or rendered irrelevant by later acts. While Upper Canada would not be spared the legislative struggles which had dogged the other Canadian provinces, it did continue to make incremental steps towards a comprehensive educational system. By the early 1840s, progress towards a centralized bureaucracy had been made, and provisions for a normal school had been put in place. Local assessment in support of schools was effectively introduced in 1846 and, the *School Act* having been passed in 1843, members of religious groups were permitted to operate their own schools. Interestingly, the impetus for separate schools came not from Roman Catholics, but from adherents of the Church of England and other protestant groups. By the early 1870s the major features common to Ontario's present system of schooling had been established.

The West of Canada

The Prairies

Until 1869, western Canada was under the control of the Hudson Bay Company, which had the fur trade as its exclusive interest. Prior to 1810, most of those living in what would eventually become Manitoba, Saskatchewan, and Alberta were either First Nations peoples or French-speaking Catholic Metis. However, in 1811, Thomas Douglas, the fifth Earl of Selkirk, made the first concerted effort to colonize this area. He wanted to provide relief to distressed Scottish farmers while also providing the Hudson Bay Company with a source of food and labour. To this end he established the agriculturally-based Red River Settlement near present-day Winnipeg. Early attempts to provide the settlers with a school were unsuccessful and it would be almost 40 years before a Presbyterian school was established for them. In the interim, such schools as did exist for the French-speaking population were run by Roman Catholic priests or their French-Canadian lay recruits. By 1820 Roman Catholics had access to three schools, while Protestants had access to none.

Between 1820 and 1870, the population of the prairies experienced a slow but steady growth and a concurrent increase in the number of schools. In general, the schools which were established

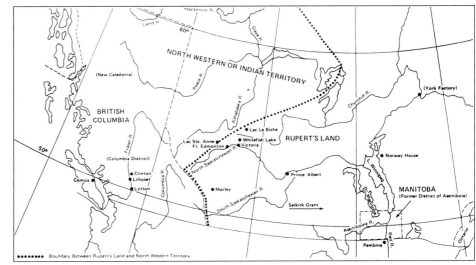

Figure 3.5

Centres where Western schools were established prior to 1873.

Source: Reprinted with permission from the University of Toronto Press.

during this period were of a sectarian nature. By 1840 the Roman Catholics and Methodists were active in what is presently northern Alberta. By the late 1860s Saskatchewan also had a small number of Protestant schools. Despite the parochial nature of these prairie schools, 20 years after Manitoba joined Confederation in 1870, the province decreed that all schools should be non-denominational. Alberta and Saskatchewan, on the other hand, would eventually recognize separate schools based upon religious affiliation.

British Columbia

Like the prairies, British Columbia was initially under the control of the Hudson Bay Company. Prior to 1858 the non-indigenous population was less than a thousand. As a result, the first British Columbia school was not established until 1849. Nine years later, the gold rush of 1858 brought about dramatic changes. Thousands of gold seekers from all parts of the world descended on the territory and brought an end to the influence of the Hudson Bay Company. The new arrivals, who were of numerous cultural and ethnic backgrounds, immediately began to agitate for schools which were both non-denominational and free. Unlike other areas of Canada, where protracted battles for control of the schools had been waged by primarily sectarian interests, the conflict in BC was remarkably brief. The *Common School Act* of 1865, supplemented by the common *School Ordinance* of 1869, decreed that BC schools would be both free and non-sectarian. The state was now firmly in control of the educational system.

Confederation and the British North America Act of 1867

As Canada's colonial period came to an end, political figures from all parts of England's remaining North American provinces discussed a confederation that would bind them together as one nation. The **British North America Act (BNA Act)** of 1867 was the legal instrument used to set out the federal and provincial responsibilities of those provinces that wished to become part of this new country. Under Article 93 of this agreement, education was to be a provincial responsibility (see Figure 3.6). Careful reading of

Figure 3.6

The British North
America Act 1867

Education

93. In and for each Province the Legislature may exclusively make Laws in relation to Education, subject and according to the following Provisions:

(1) Nothing in any such Law shall prejudicially affect any Right or Privilege with respect to Denominational Schools which any Class of Persons have by Law in the Province at the Union;

(2) All the Powers, Privileges, and Duties at the Union, by Law conferred and imposed in Upper Canada on the Separate Schools and School Trustees of the Queen's Roman Catholic Subjects shall be and the same are hereby extended to the Dissentient Schools of the Queens's Protestant and Roman Catholic Subjects in Quebec:

Where in any Province a System of Separate or Dissentient Schools Exists by Law at the Union or is hereafter established by the Legislature of the Province, an appeal shall lie to the Governor General in Council from any Act or Decision of any Provincial Authority affecting a Right or Privilege of the Protestant or Roman Catholic Minority of the Queen's Subjects in relation to Education:

In case any such Provincial Law as from Time to Time seems to the Governor General in Council requisite for the due Execution of the Provisions of this Section is not made, or in case any Decision of the Governor General in Council on any Appeal under this Section is not duly executed by the proper Provincial Authority in that Behalf, then and in every such Case, and as far only as the Circumstances of each Case require, the Parliament of Canada may make remedial Laws for the due Execution of the Provisions of this Section and of any Decision of the Governor General in Council Under this section. (43)

Article 93 clearly indicates that the diverse school systems established in the various geographical areas of the country would not be threatened by the newly established federal government. Indeed, any separate school rights acquired by a miniority group prior to 1867 were constitutionally guaranteed by the BNA. The Act also placed Canada in a unique category. Today, Canada is one of the few developed countries in which there is no national system of education.

What Patterns Did Canadian Education Develop from 1875 to 1918?

In 1875 Canada's population was primarily rural. Most schools were relatively small with most of them accurately representing the concept of the little red school house. The curriculum was simple and concentrated on the 3 Rs. However, as Canada approached the twentieth century the number of immigrants increased significantly while industrialization and urbanization also began to place additional strains on every province's education system. The basic education provided by existing schools was becoming inadequate for the needs of a society, which was slowly but certainly changing from a rural focus to an urban one. A result of this evolving demographic was a philosophical debate over the basic goals of education. Is the purpose of schools to help individuals to read the Bible, do simple mathematical calculations and write simple communications, or is the purpose to provide skilled workers who can meet the demands of commerce and industry?

While the roots of science and technical education can be traced back to the work of educators such as Sir John William Dawson, President of McGill University from 1855–1896, by the early twentieth century, science had become a significant component of provincial curricula. Technical education had also made significant inroads, and by 1918 it was available in most urban centres. However, while urban-area schools were successfully making the transition to a more scientifically and technologically based curriculum, rural areas were experiencing serious educational distress. The Federal Census of 1871 indicated that almost 88 percent of Canada's population resided in rural areas; however, the Federal Census of 1911 indicated that those living in rural areas constituted only 54 percent of the population. Additionally, urban areas paid teachers salaries that were often twice as high as those available in rural communities. This led to most of the best qualified teachers moving to, and remaining in, urban centres. Rural groups, composed mainly of farmers, began to make demands for a more relevant curriculum, better teachers, and better educational opportunities for their children.

By the early 1900s, the demand for teachers had grown dramatically. An increasing number of women entered the teaching field at this time, beginning a trend often referred to as the "feminization of teaching." Female teachers were given less respect from the community than their male predecessors, though they were still more highly regarded than women who worked in factories or in the domestic sphere. In addition, they were expected to be of high moral character. They were subjected to a level of public scrutiny hard to imagine today, as illustrated by the following Professional Reflection.

Professional Reflection — Reflecting on changes in the image of teachers

The following is a public school contract that teachers were required to sign in 1927. Analyze the contract and then write a one-paragraph description of the image of teachers and teaching reflected in the contract. How does this image differ from the current image of teachers and teaching?

Teacher Contract

I promise to take vital interest in all phases of Sunday-school work, donating of my time, service, and money without stint for the uplift and benefit of the community.

I promise to abstain from all dancing, immodest dressing, and any other conduct unbecoming a teacher and a lady.

I promise not to go out with any young men except in so far as it may be necessary to stimulate Sunday-school work.

I promise not to fall in love, to become engaged or secretly married.

I promise not to encourage or tolerate the least familiarity on the part of any of my boy pupils.

I promise to sleep at least eight hours a night, to eat carefully, and to take every precaution to keep in the best of health and spirits, in order that I may be better able to render efficient service to my pupils.

I promise to remember that I owe a duty to the townspeople who are paying me my wages, that I owe respect to the school board and the superintendent that hired me, and that I shall consider myself at all times the willing servant of the school board and the townspeople.

Source: Willard Waller, *The Sociology of Teaching*, N.Y.: John Wiley, 1932, p. 43. Copyright 1932 by John Wiley.

Attempts by educational officials to meet the demands of their rural citizens encountered varying degrees of success. Perhaps the most successful of these efforts was the consolidation of small rural school districts into larger ones, a process which, to some degree, is still taking place as Canada's rural population continues to shrink. Because of their larger student bodies, consolidated schools could provide greater opportunities for curriculum diversity. However, rural education still faced many challenges. The prairie provinces, for example, had been subject to a large influx of settlers from eastern and central Europe. Some of these settlers wanted their children to be at home working the land rather than at school. Others wanted their children educated in their native tongue but, as there were few teachers with the linguistic knowledge to provide such a service, English became the language of instruction.

At the conclusion of World War I in 1918, the Canadian educational system was taking on the basic elements of its present form. All provinces had developed centralized educational bureaucracies. Curricular issues around the preparation of students for an industrially, urban-focused life were being discussed and implemented, secondary schools were becoming more prevalent, normal schools for the preparation of teachers were becoming more common and, while some provinces had separate schools, these schools were publicly funded.

What Is the History of Schooling for First Nations Peoples?

From the beginning, settlers' efforts to indoctrinate First Nations children with European values through education was a shameful exercise, undertaken only to try to exterminate First Nations peoples by assimilation. The settlers and the clerics—first Roman Catholic, and later also Protestant—shared a common belief that the Native way of life was inferior in every way to their own.

However, as Barman, Hebert, and McCaskill point out in *Indian Education in Canada, Volume 1: The Legacy* (1986, 2–4) there was much that was admirable about the education provided by First Nations for their children. They taught their children about the unity of all life, honourable conduct, family responsibilities, individual responsibility, the importance of sharing, self-reliance, and survival skills. Their history was transmitted through stories, myths, and legends.

Unfortunately for First Nations peoples, the colonial clerical and other designated educators were primarily interested in "civilizing" Native peoples by converting them to Christianity. Because Native languages, culture, and political structures were different and non-Christian, they were deemed barbaric, and thus worthy of eradication. This belief in Native inferiority was institutionalized in the Treaty of Utrecht (which transferred Acadia from France to Britain) and was incorporated into the British North America act in 1867.

When Canada was created in 1867, by the British Parliament enacting the British North America Act, Section 91:24 placed the responsibility for "Indians and Indian Lands" firmly in the hands of the federal government. The later *Indian Act* of 1876 was enacted by Canada's Parliament to manage that responsibility, with the goal being—following exactly the British example—the complete assimilation of Native Peoples.

The Indian Act of 1876 included paternalistic provisions for how the government would manage band membership, education, Indian estates, and practically every social service. Native governments were also made subservient to the federal government.

Residential schools for Native children were first established in the 1840s. Like Indian day schools, residential schools were created to assimilate Native peoples. Children were forcibly taken from their families, locked up, forbidden to speak their own tongues, and often subjected to harsh, or even criminal acts. The stories of mental, physical, and sexual abuse to which they were subjected are deeply disturbing. Fortunately, the National Indian Brotherhood's (NIB) 1972 call for greater Native control of education was eventually heeded.

While the funding for First Nations schools is provided by the federal government, some control of education, primarily through federal–provincial agreements, is now in the hands of various bands. There are still difficulties, however. High dropout rates are an ongoing problem and they perpetuate the shortage of First Nation teachers and other professionals. School funding and equipment shortages also continue to exist.

On the positive side, educational challenges faced by First Nations children are now well-recognized, and First Nation leaders are working toward the creation of a fairer and more effective system of schools. Thus, the wrongs of the past are unlikely to be repeated. The rest of Canadian society watches with supportive hope as Canada's First Nations attempt the recreation of a first class educational system that was taken from them over the last 350 years.

"What is the History of Schooling for First Nations Peoples?" was collaboratively written by one of the authors and Mr. Daniel Paul, a First Nations author and former District Chief for the Shubenacadie Mi'kmaq Bands.

See Table 3.1 for Aboriginal populations of First Nations peoples by province and territory.

Table 3.1

Aboriginal populations

Name	Total population	Aboriginal population[1]	North American Indian	Metis	Inuit	Non-Aboriginal populalion
Canada	29 639 030	976 305	608 850	292 305	45 070	28 662 725
Newfoundland and Labrador	508 080	18 775	7040	5480	4560	489 300
Prince Edward Island	133 385	1345	1035	220	20	132 040
Nova Scotia	897 565	17 010	12 920	3135	350	880 560
New Brunswick	719 710	16 990	11 495	4290	155	702 725
Quebec	7 125 580	79 400	51 125	15 855	9530	7 046 180
Ontario	11 285 545	188 315	131 560	48 340	1375	11 097 235
Manitoba	1 103 700	150 045	90 340	56 800	340	953 655
Saskatchewan	963 155	130 185	83 745	43 695	235	832 960
Alberta	2 941 150	156 225	84 995	66 060	1090	2 784 925
British Columbia	3 868 875	170 025	118 295	44 265	800	3 698 850
Yukon Territory	28 520	6540	5600	535	140	21 975
Northwest Territories	37 100	18 730	10 615	3580	3910	18 370
Nunavut	26 665	22 720	95	55	22 560	3945

[1] Includes the Aboriginal groups (North American Indian, Métis and Inuit), multiple Aboriginal responses and Aboriginal responses not included elsewhere.

The Aboriginal identity population comprises those persons who reported identifying with at least one Aboriginal group, that is, North American Indian, Metis or Inuit, and/or who reported being a Treaty Indian or a Registered Indian, as defined by the *Indian Act* of Canada, and/or who reported being a member of an Indian Band or First Nation.

Source: Reproduced with permission from the Minister of Public Works and Government Services.

Recommended Resources

Paul, Daniel N. (1993). *We were not the savages*. Halifax, NS: Nimbus.
www.danielnpaul.com/Images.html
www.shannonthunderbird.com/indian_act.htm
www.siouxme.com/rainface.html
www.aboriginalconnections.com/

What Educational Advancements Took Place between the Great Wars (1918–1939)?

World War I made government officials recognize the need for technical and industrial education. War was becoming more automated and scientific. Soldiers with technical experience were becoming a necessity of modern warfare. As a consequence, through the *Technical Education Act of 1919* the federal government made funds for the development of technical/vocational schools and programs available to the provinces. While all areas of the country participated to greater or lesser degree in the establishment of vocationally-based programs, the exact nature of the programs they developed varied. Some added programs to existing schools, some established schools devoted exclusively to technical and vocational training, while others set up correspondence courses or summer schools.

The problems associated with the decline of rural populations continued throughout this period. Studies of these problems were conducted in provinces such as Ontario, New Brunswick, and Alberta. However, other than through the continued amalgamation of rural school districts into ever larger consolidated ones, little could be done to alleviate the rural school issue.

The period between the wars also saw a dramatic increase in the number of students who went on to a post-elementary education. A partial explanation for this may lie with the great depression, which started in 1929. Students who might have wanted to enter the labour force could not do so as there were no jobs for them. However, other factors were likely involved. Schools were becoming more appealing places, and there was a growing recognition that a good education was often the prerequisite for a good job. An additional factor almost certainly relates to the school-leaving age requirements that were starting to be introduced. For example, in 1922, Ontario had a law that every child must attend school, and it also required children to attend until they were sixteen years of age.

Curriculum and student discipline were subjects of great concern and much discussion during this period. What exactly should be taught? Should the emphasis be placed upon traditional academic courses, such as English and mathematics? Should there be technical and vocational courses? Should some courses be required for all students to take, while other could be electives? Should junior high schools be established, thus changing the model of eight years of elementary education followed by three or four years of secondary school? What types of disciplinary procedures should be established? Opinions on these and related topics varied from province to province. However, there was little agreement, and definitive answers would not be determined until after 1945.

Other, newer ideas and issues also made their appearance during this period. The theories of psychologists such as Edward Lee Thorndike started to receive attention, as did the concepts of progressive education espoused by John Dewey, one of the most noteworthy American philosophers of the twentieth century. Universities started to take an interest in teacher education and, as early as 1923, the University of British Columbia established a school of education for university graduates. Other universities followed this lead and, within the next 50 years, most of the traditional normal schools would cease to exist.

The period from 1918 to 1939 did not result in a great number of truly significant changes to the Canadian educational system. However, the ideas and forces which were to give our present-day system its final characteristics were now in place. The extended period of peace and prosperity which followed World War II would provide the ideal environment for the final evolution of Canada's present system of education.

What Are the Major Characteristics of Today's Canadian System of Education?

At the end of World War II Canadian education continued its evolution into the system as we know it today. The trend evident by 1945 would, for the most part, become well established by the end of the twentieth century. While each of the ten provinces and four territories has its own distinctive features, there are many commonalities.

Elementary

Education is compulsory for all children between the ages of six and sixteen although most provinces and territories have a Kindergarten (called Primary in some jurisdictions) for students who are five years of age. The length of the elementary program varies from five years in Saskatchewan to eight years in Ontario and Manitoba. Depending on the length of their elementary program, students next proceed to a middle school (normally Grades 6 to 8), a junior high (Grades 7 to 9), or a secondary school (in many areas Grades 9 to 12).

Secondary

Secondary schools (high schools) offer a variety of courses which are both academic and vocational in nature. High school students have compulsory courses in areas such as mathematics, languages, social studies, and the sciences. Elective courses, such as music, drama, and geology also form part of the high school curriculum. Most schools have programs which prepare students for admission to university or to a community college. In Quebec, the model is somewhat different. At the end of Grade 11, students can attend a *collège d'enseignement général et professional* (**CEGEP**) for either two years of preparatory study towards admission to a university, or three years of study in a technical/vocational program.

School Year

The lengths of both the **school year** and the school day are set by each province or territory's department of education. The Canadian average is 188 student days, with seven additional professional development days for teachers. However, Alberta, Saskatchewan, and Quebec have set the school year at 200 days. An additional factor in determining what constitutes a school year is the length of the school day. On average, this is 300 min of teacher-student contact time per day, but there are variations.

All Alberta students receive 950 h of instruction per year, while secondary students in Ontario receive 925 h, and elementary students only 850. By way of comparison with other countries, Canada's school year is in the middle. China has 251 days in its school year, Taiwan has 222 days, and the United Sates has 178 days. At 172 days, the school years of Portugal and Ireland are the shortest.

Separate Schools

Canada's publicly funded separate schools reflect the country's religious and linguistic diversity. Alberta, Saskatchewan, Ontario, Quebec, New Brunswick, and Newfoundland all have separate school systems based upon religious affiliation or language. While Nova Scotia does not have a separate school system, it does have schools whose students are almost exclusively French Acadians.

How Are Canadian Schools Funded?

It costs approximately $40 billion a year to finance Canada's 5.4 million elementary and secondary students, who attend one of the country's 15 500 public and separate schools. Teacher salaries consume an estimated 80 percent of the school budget, while the remainder goes for maintenance, student transportation, school supplies, and new construction. On average, it costs $6500 to $7000 to educate one student for one year.

As Figure 3.7 indicates, Canada's per student level of educational spending is one of the highest in the world. The actual money required for the operation of schools is raised through taxation at the territorial/provincial and municipal levels. One of the most recent pressures in education has been created by governments which want to balance their budgets through the reduction of their school-operation expenses.

Figure 3.7

International comparison of direct public spending on education.

Source: Organization for Economic Cooperation and Development, *Education at a glance: OECD indicators, 2000.*

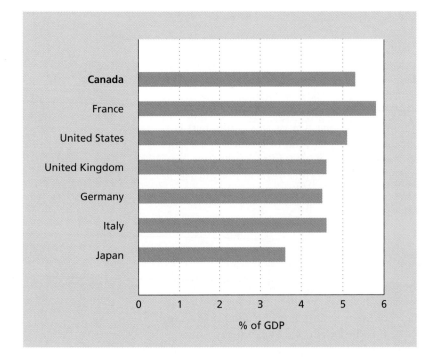

School Funding Formulas

School funding formulas are used to determine how much money is allocated to the operation of schools within a particular school district. While these formulas vary from one jurisdiction to another, the following constitutes a representative example.

Operating Formula for the Basic Costs of School Operation

- For every student in a school district the government gives the board a specified amount of money.
- A student is defined as someone who is under 21 years of age and listed on a class register as of September 30.

(Some provinces give schools half their funding for students enrolled on September 30, and the remainder for students enrolled as of May 30.)

■ Rural school districts receive a special allocation to cover the costs of student transportation.

■ Some students are more expensive than others to education. For example, a student who is deaf or blind might cost as much to educate as 2.2 students without such needs.

Maintenance Formula for the Upkeep and Repair of a School

■ Very similar to operating formulas but pertaining to buildings and equipment.

■ Boards are given a grant for each instruction area (classroom = 1.0) with adjustments made for laboratories (2.1) and gymnasium (4.5).

■ Telephone costs, paper costs, janitorial services, and other similar expenses are covered by this formula.

Capital Funding for Major Repairs or New Construction

■ A school board submits to its department of education a proposal for construction of a new school or major repairs to an existing school.

■ Department of education officials then review the proposal, compare it to other similar requests, and make a decision to accept or reject each on a case-by-case basis.

Local Funding

■ A municipality must pay a specified percentage of its board's operating expenses. Typically, this percentage can range from a low of 1 percent to as much as 20 percent. The municipality can, however, elect to allocate funds above the required percentage should it wish to do so.

■ Municipalities raise their required funding through the taxation of local property.

What Are Some Current Trends in Canadian Education?

While the tendency of territorial and provincial governments to reduce funding for the support of their schools is a concern, there are several other educational trends which have developed during the last ten years. Some of these have a very positive impact and reflect the vibrant nature of our collective public and separate school systems. Many of these topics will receive greater attention in later chapters.

Evaluation and Assessment

Most Canadians have a great interest in educational matters and are quick to express their concerns about curriculum issues and issues related to the quality of instruction their children receive. As a direct consequence of the criticism levelled at schools in these areas, there has been an increased emphasis placed upon the evaluation and assessment of the curriculum and the teachers who deliver it. The Council of Ministers of Education, Canada (CMEC) which meets regularly for the discussion of issues of common

Should school attendance beyond the elementary level become voluntary?

Should every child in Canada over twelve years old be required to attend high school? Should only those students who choose to be in school be permitted to attend? Should school attendance beyond the elementary level become voluntary?

Compulsory school attendance started to become a common feature of education in the early 20th century. By 1930 all provinces and territories had passed laws regarding this topic.

Over the years, individuals and groups dissatisfied with the schooling system in Canada have argued in favour of voluntary school attendance for a variety of reasons. Some believed that schools forced students to be too conforming and obedient. Others believed that compulsory attendance was simply a means of keeping disruptive adolescents off the streets. Today, many who home-school their children believe schools are unsafe, unhealthy, and poor settings for learning. On the other hand, opponents of voluntary school attendance say that the nation will be lost if citizens abdicate responsibility for the education of children over thirteen and release them to society with no further guidance. We would be giving up on them and limiting their futures, they say. Where do you stand on this issue? Should school attendance beyond the elementary level become voluntary?

In addition, many who oppose the idea of voluntary attendance believe strongly that the core of Canadian society is weakening, and lacking in such values of the past as honesty, perseverance, integrity, generosity, compassion, and service. Drugs, violence, sexual promiscuity, and the loss of ethics and morals have all taken their toll, they say, resulting in a society that is self-indulgent, irresponsible, and impatient for immediate gratification. Too many parents are unwilling to place demands on their children. In such a weakened society, is it wise to make school attendance after the age of twelve voluntary? Will parents choose the easy way out and let their children drop out of school when they are thirteen?

Furthermore, which children would remain in school if attendance were voluntary, the sons and daughters of the wealthy, or of the poor? Will the children who leave school when they are thirteen be short-changed in their career options? Will they be able to keep up with the expansion of technology and access to information? Will they acquire the knowledge and thinking skills necessary to make the important, complex decisions in their lives? Will they be able to negotiate as well in our increasingly complex society? Opponents to voluntary attendance after elementary school think not. They fear that the costs for those who leave, and for society as a whole, would be extensive and irreparable.

No, school attendance beyond elementary school should not become voluntary.

Opponents of voluntary school attendance believe that the original reason for requiring students to continue their schooling past the age of twelve remains valid today. Citizens need to be informed and able to think critically if democracy is to prevail. This necessity is especially important today because of the increasing complexity and diversity in society. As extensive immigration to Canada continues, new citizens and their children need to learn about the history, government, and values of their new land. In addition, the growing influence and sophistication of the news media requires an educated citizenry that can resist intellectual manipulation. Thus compulsory school attendance should be continued for the common good of the country.

Yes, school attendance beyond the elementary level should become voluntary.

"Education is wasted on the young!" say many people who return to college after being in the work world. they are more motivated to learn, bring more life experiences to their studies, use their time more efficiently, and earn higher grades after being out in the world for a while. Wouldn't adolescents discover the same thing if they weren't required to move on to middle or junior high school after elementary school? Instead of forcing thirteen-year-olds to stay in school, shouldn't we encourage them to travel, engage in meaningful service, or experience the work world before continuing their education? Their readiness to learn and their appreciation of the educational opportunities they were given would be greatly enhanced if that were the case, say those who favour voluntary school attendance.

The proponents also ask, "Do all adolescents benefit from having a secondary education?" Some students know exactly what they want to learn, but they are not able to find the instruction they desire in their high schools. Most secondary schools do not offer classes in such areas as paramedics, auto design, marketing, investments, computer graphics, song writing, art design, architecture, guitar playing, fashion design, script writing, film animation, flight training, river boat piloting, auto racing, skiing, broadcasting, scuba diving, parachuting, abnormal psychology, child development, and parenting. A resurgence of the apprenticeships of our colonial past may be the answer for some groups of today's young people.

Proponents of voluntary attendance argue that public schools would be more effective if they didn't have to deal with uncooperative students who wanted to leave but couldn't. These resistant students take teachers' and principals' time from the students who are there to learn. How much more productive schools would be if they were filled only with students motivated to learn! Educators, too, would find their work more rewarding, and teaching would become a more inviting profession. In addition, parent involvement in school would increase, because parents had chosen to have their children continue in school.

The tax money saved from having fewer students in school could enrich school offerings and extend students'

educational experiences. The extra money could even be spent on creative education and training alternatives that would appeal to and benefit those who chose to leave. Making school attendance voluntary after the age of twelve could result in a revitalized education system.

Where do you stand on this issue?

1. With which position do you agree and why?

2. What would you add to the list of subjects desired by students but not currently taught in secondary schools?

3. What do you think of the compromise position of giving people in Canada the option of having ten years of free education that they could take whenever they choose?

4. What other solutions can you suggest for helping students who don't want a traditional secondary education?

Recommended Sources

McGhan, B. (1997, Winter). Compulsory school attendance: an idea past its prime? *The Educational Forum.*

Noll, J. W. (Ed.). (1999). *Taking sides: clashing views on controversial educational issues,* 10th ed. Guilford, CT: McGraw-Hill.

---

interest, has advanced its School Achievement Indicators Program (SAIP) as one method for determining the effectiveness of provincial and territorial educational programs. Additionally, many school districts have created their own evaluation instruments to determine how well their schools are performing. While the CMEC, national teacher conferences, and other groups with an interest in education now share their practices regarding evaluation and assessment, they also deal with other topics as well. This mutual sharing of ideas has become one of the most valuable trends within Canadian education.

Students with Special Needs

The inclusive school movement has made significant gains in making schools more responsive to the needs of children with learning difficulties or physical disabilities. (Chapter 8 will deal with the complexities related to this topic.) The needs of groups such as the children of recent immigrants, members of our Aboriginal communities, and African-Canadian students are also being addressed. Indeed, many school districts now have departments or officials designated with the responsibility of meeting the needs of these minorities.

Ancillary Services

Canadian schools are responding to requests for additional services. Daycare facilities, for example, are now available in some secondary schools, as are programs in anger-management, peer mediation, peer drug-education, and respect-for differences. Schools are increasingly having their educational role intermixed with that of the family.

Technology

The advent of the internet and the need to prepare students for the world of information technology have led to increased funding for computers, data projectors, printers, scanners and other related pieces of hardware and software. Teachers now require increased professional development to deal with new teaching and learning methodologies which rely upon the new technology which confronts them. Persuading them to give up some of their more traditional teaching strategies is one of the many challenges facing the leaders of today's technology-enriched schools.

Curriculum Development

All departments of education now provide teachers with curriculum guides that contain lists of specific learning outcomes. There is an increased emphasis placed upon language development and use, mathematical skills and concepts, thinking skills, and the sciences. Teachers no longer have to develop a curriculum based upon some general guidelines for a particular subject at a specific grade level. The trend is now to give them a very specific curriculum to deliver along with concrete suggestions as to how they might deliver it effectively. On the one hand, this constitutes a reduction in teacher autonomy; on the other, it is a response to the criticisms of those who believe that teachers require more guidance to carry out their classroom responsibilities effectively.

Second Language Acquisition

Canada is a leader in the area of second language instruction. French as a second language is taught in most Canadian school districts and French Immersion (FI) programs are common in many areas. However, the shortage of qualified French Immersion teachers is generating concerns. While most FI programs start at some point in the lower elementary grades, the true difficulties arise at the secondary level where subjects such as physics, mathematics, and chemistry need to be taught in French. Finding a qualified English-speaking teacher for these subjects is already very difficult. Finding someone who can teach them in French is more difficult still.

There can be no doubt that Canadian schools are still in an evolutionary process. However, the independence of each province or territory, a characteristic which makes our educational system quite different from those of other countries, provides

Canadians with a great advantage. The provinces and territories are uniquely free to experiment with new educational practices without having to seek permission from a centralized federal bureaucracy. If a new practice is successful, the high degree of collaboration among the various Canadian units ensures that it may be instituted in other areas of the country. The cultural divisiveness and sectarian wrangling which characterized so much of Canada's educational history has actually been an exceptionally valuable gift. Rather than having a single, centralized bureaucracy within which a single bureaucrat might have the authority to stifle a good idea, Canada has fourteen independent departments of education. As a consequence, the possibilities for a novel educational practice to receive a valid field test are much higher here than in many other countries.

What Are Some Other Types of Canadian Schools?

While the large majority of Canadian students attend government-funded public or separate schools, there are several other options available to those parents who are unhappy with the education provided by these schools. While it is not possible to list all of these options, the following five examples provide a representative sample.

Independent Schools

Independent schools have existed from the earliest days of Canadian education. Often referred to as private schools (a term these schools dislike, because of its elitist connotation), these schools charge a tuition which can range from a low of $2000 per year to a high of over $25 000 per year. Most are religious in nature, or at least in origin, and often have a boarding school component. Parents who elect to send their children to independent schools do so for a variety of reasons. Some want the religious and/or social values of the home reinforced by the school, some believe the quality of the education delivered is better than in the public schools, while others believe that the characteristically small class sizes provide an environment in which their children are more likely to thrive.

In some provinces, such as Quebec and the western provinces, limited public funding is available under certain conditions. In all other areas the independent schools must provide their own funding. Overall, perhaps five to six percent of Canadian students attend independent schools.

Montessori Schools

Maria Montessori (1870–1952), an Italian physician who was influenced by Rousseau, believed that children's mental, physical, and spiritual development could be enhanced by providing them with developmentally-appropriate educational activities.

At Montessori's school for poor preschool-age children in Rome, teachers created learning environments based on students' levels of development and readiness to learn new material. According to the **Montessori method**, prescribed sets of materials and physical exercises are used to develop students' knowledge and skills, and students are allowed to use or not use the materials as they see fit. The materials arouse students' interest, and the interest motivates them to learn. Through highly individualized

Maria Montessori (1870–1952)

instruction, students develop self-discipline and self-confidence. Montessori's ideas spread throughout the world. While most Canadian Montessori schools are located in Ontario and British Columbia, there are a few in other provinces. (Webb, Metha, and Jordan 1999). Today, Montessorian materials and activities are a standard part of the early childhood and elementary curricula in public schools throughout the nation.

Hutterite Schools

The Hutterites are a unique group within Canadian society. For over 400 years, they have maintained unchanged their rural, communal way of life. Located primarily, but not exclusively, in western Canada, they are deeply religious and avoid excessive contact with the outside world. Most Hutterites now speak English as a first language, and **Hutterite schools** teach German as a second language.

A day in the life of a Hutterite student begins with a communal breakfast at 6:30 AM, followed immediately by instruction in German until 8:30 AM. English school begins at 8:50 AM and, after a school day of nine hours, the students are home for the daily 6:00 PM evening church service which is then followed by supper. Unlike other Canadian students, Hutterite children go to school six days per week.

Home-Schooling

While there are laws requiring that all children be educated, there is no legal requirement that parents send their children to a publicly or privately funded institution. It is perfectly valid for children to be educated at home. Fifteen years ago there were fewer than 2000 Canadian children who were being home-schooled. However, the situation has changed and there are now over 30 000 children being taught at home by one or both of their parents. The **home-schooling** movement is growing at such a rate that provincial and territorial departments of education are developing new rules, regulations, and procedures for those who wish to take advantage of the home-schooling practice. While there is little formal research which compares the later academic success of home-schooled children with that of children who had a more traditional educational experience, the initial indications suggest that home-schooled children do as well on standardized achievement tests as those who attend publicly or privately funded schools. When one home-schooled child was asked what she did not like about the practice, her only complaint was: "We don't get storm days off like the other kids."

Virtual Schools

New **virtual schools** are becoming popular in Canada, especially in British Colombia and Alberta. Virtual schools vary in significant ways from traditional schools. First, the courses are taken electronically via the internet rather than in-person within a regular classroom; and second, while some courses are scheduled for a particular time, others may be taken at the convenience of the student. In the model which has specifically scheduled class times, all students taking a particular class are expected to be online at the same time. They can take part in discussions, listen to a lecture, and send or receive information. In the model where a specific time is not scheduled, the student takes the course at such times as she or he decides. There is no "real-time" discussion as in the other model and communication with the instructor is via email or a dedicated listserv.

SUMMARY

What Determines Your Educational Philosophy?

- An educational philosophy is a set of beliefs about education—a set of principles to guide professional action.

- A teacher's educational philosophy is made up of personal beliefs about teaching and learning, students, knowledge, and what is worth knowing.

What Are the Branches of Philosophy?

- The branches of philosophy and the questions they address are (1) metaphysics (What is the nature of reality?), (2) epistemology (What is the nature of knowledge and is truth attainable?), (3) axiology (What values should one live by?), (4) ethics (What is good and evil, right and wrong?), (5) aesthetics (What is beautiful?), and (6) logic (What reasoning processes yield valid conclusions?).

What Are Five Modern Philosophical Orientations to Teaching?

- *Progressivism*—The aim of education should be based on the needs and interests of students.

- *Perennialism*—Students should acquire knowledge of enduring great ideas.

- *Essentialism*—Schools should teach students a core of "essential" knowledge and skills in a disciplined and systematic way.

- *Social reconstructionism*—In response to the significant social problems of the day, schools should take the lead in creating a new social order.

- *Existentialism*—In the face of an indifferent universe, students should acquire an education that will enable them to assign meaning to their lives.

What Psychological Orientations Have Influenced Teaching Philosophies?

- *Humanism*—Children are innately good, and education should focus on individual needs, personal freedom, and self-actualization.

- *Behaviourism*—By careful control of the educational environment and with appropriate reinforcement techniques, teachers can cause students to exhibit desired behaviours.

- *Constructivism*—Teachers should "understand students' understanding" and view learning as an active process in which learners construct meaning.

How Can You Develop Your Educational Philosophy?

- Instead of basing their teaching on only one educational philosophy, most teachers develop an eclectic educational philosophy.

- Professional teachers continually strive for a clearer, more comprehensive answer to basic philosophical questions.

What Cultural Traditions Have Led to the Development of the Canadian Education Landscape?

- Early Canadian education was founded upon the cultural traditions of France, England, Scotland, and the United States. The primary purpose of each tradition was the promotion of religion.

- The French tradition, in schools known as *petites écoles*, provided a rudimentary education. Instruction was provided by parish priests or their assistants. Boys and girls attended separate schools.

- The English tradition was primarily controlled by the Church of England with the quality of the education delivered being a function of class rather than merit. There were "public" schools for the wealthy and various other schools for the poor.

- The American tradition was originally modelled after the British tradition but the practicalities of frontier life led to its becoming increasing more practical.

- The Scottish tradition provided elementary and secondary education to students of both genders regardless of their social rank. Unlike the other traditions, the curriculum of Scottish schools also included subjects such as science and art.

What Were Teaching and Schools Like in Canada Prior to 1875?

- During this formative period of Canada's educational history, the school systems that evolved were a reflection of the cultural traditions that existed within Quebec, Atlantic Canada, Ontario, and the Northwest. In all areas, the struggle for state supported schools was the cause of much rancorous debate.

- In Quebec, during the period between its founding and fall (1608–1760), the school system was modelled after that of France. Later, with the arrival of English, Scottish, and Irish settlers tentative steps towards a more coherent school system took place. By 1875 Quebec had two schools systems: one for the English and one for the French. The government of Quebec paid for the support of the schools via taxation based upon local assessment.

- In Nova Scotia, Prince Edward Island, and New Brunswick, waves of settlers arrived from England, Scotland, and the United States. The school systems that evolved were state supported and operated. However, in Newfoundland and Labrador the schools eventually came to be supported by the state but operated by various religious denominations.

- In Ontario, where most of the settlers were either Loyalists or Americans who emigrated to that province, state supported and operated schools were firmly established by 1850.

- The Northwest was a thinly populated area during this period. However, by 1870 both Manitoba and British Columbia had state supported and operated schools. Alberta and Saskatchewan would later establish a system of state supported and operated separate schools based on religious lines.

- The British North America Act of 1867 established that education was to be a purely provincial responsibility.

What Patterns Did Canadian Education Develop from 1875 to 1918?

- In 1875 Canada's population was primarily rural; by 1918 it had become increasingly urban.
- All areas of the country developed centralized educational bureaucracies.
- Secondary schools became common and normal schools for the training of teachers became prevalent.

What Is the History of Schooling for First Nations Peoples?

- First Nations peoples used myths and legends to teach their children about the unity of all life, honourable conduct, individual and family responsibilities, and survival skills.
- Colonial clerical educators initially attempted to assimilate First Nations peoples by converting them to Christianity.
- Residential schools, established in the 1840s, were created to assimilate First Nations peoples into European culture. Children at these schools were forbidden to speak their native language and were often abused.
- Since the 1970s, control of education has been in the hands of various First Nations bands.

What Educational Advancements Took Place between the Great Wars (1918–1939)?

- Vocationally based education became common.
- Larger numbers of students went on to post-elementary education.
- Discussions about curricular and student discipline issues became common.
- The writings of educational psychologists and philosophers started to have an impact upon Canadian schools.

What Are the Major Characteristics of Today's Canadian System of Education?

- Education is compulsory for all children.
- Most provinces have an elementary component (Grades 1 to 6), a junior high component (Grades 7 to 9), and a high school program (Grades 10 to 12).
- The average school year in most provinces and territories is 188 days.
- Some jurisdictions have separate schools based upon either religion or language; others do not.

How Are Canadian Schools Funded?

- The costs of operating all of Canada's schools for one year is approximately $40 billion.

- Schools boards receive their operating, maintenance, and capital funding needs according to funding formulas, which differ from one province or territory to the next.

What Are Some Current Trends in Canadian Education?

- Evaluation and assessment are receiving increased attention.
- The inclusive school movement has led to students with special needs receiving increased attention and funding.
- Many Canadian schools now provide a variety of ancillary services such as day care and respect-for-differences programs.
- Information technology is now widely available in most schools.
- Curriculum guides with specific recommendations for teachers to follow are available in all school districts.
- French Immersion (FI) programs are available in all provinces and territories.

What Are Some Other Types of Canadian Schools?

- Independent schools, also known as private schools, charge tuition for the educational services they provide. Many of these schools have a religious affiliation. Some provide boarding facilities; other do not.
- Montessori schools, which base their curriculum upon the Montessori method, are most commonly found in Ontario and British Columbia.
- Some religious groups, such as the Hutterites of western Canada, operate their own schools.
- The home-schooling movement is becoming more popular. Departments of education are now developing regulations and procedures for those parents who wish to teach their children at home.
- Virtual schools are becoming more prevalent. Students "attend" class electronically via the internet.

KEY TERMS AND CONCEPTS

aesthetics, 83
American tradition, 92
axiology, 83
behaviourism, 89
British North America Act
   (BNA Act) 101
CEGEP, 107
cognitive science, 90
constructivism, 89
dame-schools, 92
educational philosophy, 79
English tradition, 92

epistemology, 82
essentialism, 85
ethics, 83
existentialism, 87
French tradition, 92
home-schooling, 114
humanism, 88
humanistic psychology, 88
Hutterite schools, 114
independent schools, 113
logic, 84
metaphysics, 82

Montessori method, 113
normal schools, 92
parochial schools, 92
perennialism, 84
petites écoles, 92
progressivism, 86
school year, 107
Scottish tradition, 93
separate schools, 98
social reconstructionism, 87
Socratic questioning, 84
virtual schools, 114

APPLICATIONS AND ACTIVITIES

Teacher's Journal

1. Imagine that you are a colleague of Claude, who was profiled in this chapter's opening scenario. Write a memo to him in which you react to his philosophical orientation to teaching.

2. Recall one of your favourite teachers in grades K–12. Which of the educational philosophies or psychological orientations to teaching described in this chapter best captures that teacher's approach to teaching? Write a descriptive sketch of that teacher in action.

3. Based on what you have read in this chapter, identify several broad or long-term trends in the development of Canadian education that continue even today. How are those trends reflected in educational policies and practices through the decade? How is this trend evident at different points in the past and now? How might this trend be manifested in the future?

4. Write a personal history of your experience as a student, focusing on the age or grade level of the students you plan to teach. Conclude with an analysis of how you expect your experience as a student will influence you as a teacher.

5. What does the history of textbooks tell us about education in Canada? What values and priorities do textbooks today seem to reflect in comparison to textbooks of the seventeenth, eighteenth, and nineteenth centuries?

6. Develop a proposal for researching the impact of the past on teaching today and record it in your teacher's journal. For suggestions on choosing a specific topic, locating information, and conducting the research, ask your instructor for Handout M 3.1, "Researching Impacts of the Past on Teaching Today."

Teacher's Database

1. Use your favourite internet search engine to go to the home page of Philosophy in Cyberspace, The History of Education Site, or another professional organization devoted to educational philosophy or history, and compile a list of online publications, associations, and reference materials that you could use in developing your educational philosophy further.

2. Explore encyclopedias, bibliographies, periodicals, news sources, and online reference works to research in greater detail the contributions of a pioneer in education or a historical development described in Chapter 3.

Observations and Interviews

1. Interview a teacher for the purpose of understanding his or her educational philosophy. Formulate your interview questions in light of the philosophical concepts discussed in this chapter. Discuss your findings with classmates.

2. Administer a philosophical inventory to a group of teachers at a local school. Analyze the results and compare your findings with classmates.

3. Observe the class of a teacher at the level in which you plan to teach. Which of the five philosophies or three psychological orientations to teaching discussed in this chapter most characterizes this teacher?

4. Visit a school and interview the principal about the school's educational philosophy. Ask him or her to comment on what is expected of teachers in regard to achieving the goals contained in the statement of philosophy.

5. Interview veteran teachers and administrators at a local school and ask them to comment on the changes in education that they have observed and experienced during their careers. What events do respondents identify as having had the greatest impact on their teaching? Tape record, videotape, or transcribe respondents' stories to share with classmates.

6. As a collaborative project with classmates, conduct on-site interviews and observations for the purpose of researching the history of a particular school and its culture or way of life. You might also collaborate with teachers and students of history or social studies at the school to help you in your investigation.

Professional Portfolio

1. Prepare a written (or videotaped) statement in which you describe a key element of your educational philosophy. To organize your thoughts, focus on *one* of the following dimensions of educational philosophy:

   - Beliefs about teaching and learning
   - Beliefs about students
   - Beliefs about knowledge
   - Beliefs about what is worth knowing
   - Personal beliefs about the six branches of philosophy

   Develop your statement of philosophy throughout the course, covering all dimensions. On completion of your teacher-education program, review your portfolio entry and make any appropriate revisions. Being able to articulate your philosophy of education and your teaching philosophy will be an important part of finding your first job as a teacher.

2. Prepare a video or audiotaped oral history of the school experiences of older members of the community. Focus on a topic or issue of special interest to you and prepare some questions and probes in advance. For instance, you might be interested in an aspect of curriculum or student relations. Analyze the oral histories in relation to the development of education in Canada and videotape or tape record your analysis.

Canadian School Governance and Law

The drastic reduction in the number of units of local government for education has been one of the most dramatic of all changes in Canada's pattern of government. And yet, it has occurred and is continuing with relatively little public concern or debate.

—Canadian Teachers' Federation as quoted in *Provincial Initiatives to Restructure Canadian School Governance in the 1990s*

focus questions

1. Who is involved in Canadian school governance?

2. What is the historical basis for the governance of Canadian schools?

3. What is the role of the federal government in Canadian education?

4. What is the role of the provincial government in Canadian education?

5. Why do we need school boards?

6. Why do you need a professional code of ethics?

7. What are your legal rights as a teacher?

8. What are your legal responsibilities as a teacher?

On entering the staff room during your preparation period, you can tell immediately that the four teachers in the room are having a heated discussion. "I don't see how you can say that teachers have much control over the schools," says Kim, a language arts teacher who came to the school three years ago. "It's all so political. The provincial Department of Education and the school boards —it's the politicians who really control the schools. We have minimal input into the design of the standardized tests our kids take. The scores of those tests seem to be the only thing people use to judge the schools' effectiveness. When the test scores are released, the politicians talk about making the education system more accountable; they're just exploiting the schools so they can get elected."

"If you want to know who *really* controls the schools," Serge, a mathematics teacher, says, "it's big business. The politicians are actually their pawns. Big business is concerned about international competition—so, they exert tremendous pressure on the politicians who, in turn, lean on the teachers. And then ... "

"Just a minute," says Frank, raising his hand to silence Serge. Frank is one of the school's lead teachers on several curriculum development teams. "Maybe that's the way things were in the past, but things *are* changing. I'm not saying that politics or big business didn't influence the schools, but we have a lot of influence over what we teach and how. Look at our various curriculum committees and all the school based program decisions our staff has made during the last two years—teaching teams, outcomes-based curriculum, integrated teaching approaches, and textbook and technology purchases."

"You're right, teaching really is changing," says Sharmila, a science teacher and multimedia coordinator for the school. She motions for you to have a seat at the table. Feeling a bit uncomfortable at the intensity of the discussion, but anxious to fit in with your new colleagues, you take a seat. "When I first started teaching ten years ago," Sharmila continues, "I never thought I'd see as many changes as I've seen in the last few years."

"Things are still top-down," counters Kim. "The Premier, the Minister of Education, the Department of Education, the school board, the superintendent, the principal—they all tell us what to do."

"Well, like Frank said, look at all the decisions our school-based committees have made," Sharmila answers. "Plus, just think about the professional development opportunities. We have a variety of ways to remain current in our practices. Some of us take university courses and others do workshops and attend conferences. There are more opportunities available now than when I started teaching. The Teachers' Union also takes part in collective bargaining on our behalf— that means we get to have a say in our salary, benefits, and working conditions."

"Exactly," says Frank. "Our last contract gave us a four percent increase in pay."

"Well, I don't quite share your optimism about how teachers have all this influence," says Kim. "Look at every provincial election—the politicians always try to exploit education. So, they talk about all the changes they'd make ... higher standards, more accountability for teachers, more input for parents, and so on. Politicians use education to build their political careers, and teachers are the ones who have to implement their utopian ideas."

"I agree to some extent," says Sharmila. "Politicians will always use education for their own ends. But that's just rhetoric; what's really happening, bit by bit, is that teachers are becoming much more influential."

"Let's just ask this new teacher here," says Frank as he smiles and nods in your direction.

"Don't you think teachers have a lot of influence over how schools are run? During the rest of your career, you'll be involved in school governance, won't you?"

Frank, Sharmila, Serge, and Kim look at you, awaiting your response. What do you say?

Who Is Involved in Canadian School Governance?

Understanding how power is shared in the area of school governance and being aware of the rights and responsibilities of today's educators is vital for beginning teachers. For example, the opening scenario for this chapter illustrates how teachers and various political interest groups seek to influence policies related to school governance. Clearly, teachers have much to gain from becoming involved in school curriculum and policy issues.

During the twenty-first century, many forces will continue to influence the governance of Canadian schools. Among the groups that will continue to influence the shaping of school policies follow:

1. *Parents*—Concerned with controlling local schools so that quality educational programs are available to their children.
2. *Students*—Concerned with policies related to freedom of expression, dress, behaviour, and curricular offerings.
3. *Teachers*—Concerned with their role in decision-making, improving working conditions, terms of employment, and other professional issues.
4. *Administrators*—Concerned with providing leadership so that various interest groups, including teachers, participate in the shared governance of schools and the development of quality educational programs.
5. *Taxpayers*—Concerned with proof that tax dollars are being spent on quality education programs.
6. *Politicians*—Concerned with the implementation of public school programs, guidelines, and legislative mandates related to the operation of schools while being ever mindful of public expectations.
7. *Minorities*—Concerned with the availability of equal educational opportunity for all.
8. *Educational theorists and researchers*—Concerned with using theoretical and research-based insights as the bases for improving schools at all levels.
9. *Businesses and corporations*—Concerned with receiving graduates who have the knowledge, skills, attitudes, and values to help an organization realize its goals.

The following sections examine the governance of Canadian schools and the degree to which various political forces influence schools.

What Is the Historical Basis for the Governance of Canadian Schools?

The defining moment in the governance of Canadian schools was the Confederation of Canada in 1867 with the passage of the British North America Act, later renamed the **Constitution Act of 1982**. The **British North America Act** established Canada as a nation and laid out a framework for public institutions. Section 93 of the British North America Act granted authority for education to the provinces in the following terms:

> In and for each province the Legislature may exclusively make laws in relation to education, subject, and according to the following provisions:

> Nothing in any law shall prejudicially affect any Right or Privilege with respect to Denominational Schools which any Class of Persons have by Law in the Province at the Union.

Under Section 4 of the Constitution Act of 1871, all constitutional power in extraprovincial territory (the Northwest Territories, Nunavut, and Yukon) is vested in the Parliament of Canada. However, most of this power has been delegated to the territorial legislatures. All three territories have departments of education that resemble their legislative counterparts and they perform similar functions (Bezeau 2002).

Apart from the limitations of the Constitution with respect to denominational and minority language educational rights, the provinces have the authority to enact legislation dealing with education and have assumed full legal responsibility for education. The systems that have been implemented are partly centralized and partly decentralized. Centralized functions were placed under the administration of provincial departments of education, while decentralized functions became the responsibility of locally appointed or elected school boards.

What Is the Role of the Federal Government in Canadian Education?

The granting of authority over education to the provinces meant that there would be no national or federal education office to direct or coordinate educational activities in the Canadian provinces and territories. This has influenced the shape and direction of school governance in Canada today.

Since there is no ministry of education, most relevant educational programs at the elementary and secondary school level come under the Secretary of State. The Secretary of State is involved in funding, but not delivering, such federal interest programs as official languages, Canadian studies, and multiculturalism (Bezeau 2002).

Although the primary responsibility for education rests with the Canadian provinces and territories, the federal government still plays an important role in education. At the national level, a number of federal departments intersect with education.

- Statistics Canada provides data and analysis about all aspects of education.
- Human Resources Development Canada (HRDC) conducts surveys, provides services and information, and does research in the areas of literacy, lifelong learning, and school-work transitions.
- Industry Canada (IC) offers services and links to Canadian schools and teachers through SchoolNet.
- Social Sciences and Humanities Research Council (SSHRC) funds educational research.

There are also several important national organizations that provide coordination and exchange of information; these include the Canadian Education Association (CEA); the Association of Canadian Community Colleges (ACCC); and the Association of Universities and Colleges of Canada (AUCC). (CERIS et al. n.d.)

In 1967, the **Council of Ministers of Education, Canada** (CMEC) was formed to act as the national voice of education in Canada. The CMEC acts as a forum for provincial and territorial ministers to meet and discuss matters that are of mutual interest. This organization is also the body that represents provincial and territorial interests in working with national education organizations, the federal government, foreign governments, and international organizations (education@canada n.d.).

The federal government also has responsibilities relating to the elementary and secondary education of Registered Indian children attending First Nations-administered or federal schools on reserves, or provincially-administered schools off reserves, and provides financial assistance to these students at the postsecondary level.

The nature and extent of federal involvement in education has been debated throughout the decades. However, federal involvement in elementary and secondary education in Canada ranks among the lowest of the industrialized world. Canada is one of the few countries without a federal office, department, or ministry of education. Although there have been calls for more federal input in the area of education, there is strong opposition to it by many groups and provinces (Bezeau).

Current educational trends at the national level include greater cooperation among organizations and provinces in matters of curriculum and general policy, sharing information and efforts to link research, policy, and practice (CERIS).

What Is the Role of the Provincial Government in Canadian Education?

Canadian systems of education in Canada begin at the provincial level. The provincial legislatures pass statutes that create an educational system and provide for its management and funding. Most provinces have one main statute called an **education act** or public schools act. Other statutes that relate directly to education include such matters as the creation of the ministry or **department of education**, private schools, teacher organizations, collective bargaining by teachers, and pension funds.

In most provinces, education at the elementary and secondary levels is the responsibility of a **minister of education**. The minister has formal responsibility for the department of education and its staff. The person directly below the minister in the hierarchy is the **deputy minister of education**, an appointed civil servant who manages the department on a day-to-day basis (Bezeau).

Although there are similarities among Canada's ten provinces and three territories, each is affected by the diversity of its own regional culture, history, and geography. Provincial departments of education use legislation on education and related regulations to exercise jurisdiction in the following areas:

- Curriculum content
- School funding
- Professional training and accreditation of teachers
- Student testing and assessment procedures
- School structures
- Development and publishing of curriculum guides
- Constitutions of school boards
- Choice and authorization of textbooks
- Selection and arrangements for the purchase of textbooks
- Determination of school district boundaries
- Development of criteria to open and close schools. (Fleming 1997)

In most provinces, the public education system begins with primary or Kindergarten, followed by elementary school for five to eight years. Education is compulsory from ages six or seven to age sixteen. Secondary schools usually continue from the end of elementary school to Grade 12. Many provinces include a junior high or middle school between the elementary and secondary levels; these usually last from two to three years.

In addition to public schools, there are publicly funded separate schools (Catholic schools and a small number of separate Protestant schools) in Newfoundland, Quebec, Ontario, Manitoba, Alberta, and Saskatchewan. Changes are taking place in the structures of these schools in some provinces.

Most provinces have minority-language schools; these are francophone in most cases and anglophone in Quebec. New Brunswick and Ontario have extensive French-language school programs. French immersion programs are available in most provinces (CERIS).

Local School Districts

Local school districts vary greatly in regard to demographics such as number of school-age children; educational, occupational, and income levels of parents; operating budget; number of teachers; economic resources; and number of school buildings.

At the local level, public education comes under the jurisdiction of **school boards**. These local school boards are also known in some provinces as school districts, school divisions, and in New Brunswick, as District Education Councils. The powers and duties of school boards are defined in provincial or territorial statutes and school board members are generally elected to office in public elections (education@canada).

The statutes that define the types of school boards and prescribe how they are created, dissolved, funded, and elected are among the most important type of education statutes. The powers of the school board are spelled out in detail and are the only powers that the boards have. All provinces have a system of grants to school boards administered by the Department of Education. These grants supplement money raised from local property tax in some provinces and provide virtually all of the funding for boards in others. Provincial grants are often accompanied by prescribed accounting and budgeting procedures and expenditure controls (Bezeau).

An example of a recent province–school board funding dispute occurred in the summer of 2002 in Ontario. Three school boards (Ottawa, Hamilton, and Toronto), defied a provincial law requiring school boards to pass balanced budgets. The Ontario government countered this by taking over the three boards and appointing their own supervisors (Bowman 2002).

Restructuring of School Districts

Since the early 1990s, many Canadian provinces have been involved in areas of school reform and have examined issues of educational governance. Efficiency, accountability, financial equity, parental and community involvement, and educational improvement are all reasons cited for governance restructuring (Saskatchewan School Trustees Association 1997).

The **Canadian School Board Association** identifies recent trends in school governance across Canada, including reductions in the number of school boards, a redefinition of roles and responsibilities, and an increased emphasis on student outcomes and responsibilities. This has resulted in changes in the roles and responsibilities of school boards, ministries and departments of education, parents, teachers, and administrators. There has been a move away from locally elected school board powers to more centralization of power at the provincial level. There has also been greater parent–community involvement through avenues such as mandated **school advisory councils**, delegations, petitions, study groups, and focus groups. Generally, provincial governments have taken greater control over financing, curriculum, and academic outcomes while encouraging parent and community members to become more involved in school level decision making through school councils (Pansengrau 1997).

Many provinces have reduced their number of school boards and have enlarged their size. Through the 1990s, the number of school boards in Canadian provinces went from 815 to 490 (CERIS).

A common feature of the restructuring initiatives across Canada was the top-down model of implementation that saw governments develop the models and processes used in the reorganization efforts. Generally, there was little response from the general public to the restructuring efforts of the various provinces. However, it was seen as a significant issue to school board members, administrators, and others working within the provincial systems. These groups were concerned with effects on jobs, displacement of administrators, and loss of local control over decision-making in the area of education (Fleming).

Dramatic Measures

In 1996, New Brunswick made the dramatic decision to eliminate elected school boards in the province and establish school-based, regional and provincial parent councils. This meant that the once community-elected school trustees were now replaced with parent chosen representatives at the school, regional, and provincial levels. This move was aimed at transferring more authority to parents in an effort to have them involved at the local level of education. New Brunswick's goals were improved accountability and more clearly defined school governance and administration.

In 1999, school governance became a significant provincial election issue with the opposition party promising reinstatement of locally elected governance structures. When they were elected, the new government undertook a consultation process that resulted in the reinstatement of locally elected education councils in 2000.

Why Do We Need School Boards?

In response to the school board restructuring of the 1990s, James A. Gunn, Superintendent of the Annapolis Valley Regional School Board in Nova Scotia, wrote the following November 1998 article, "Why Do We Need School Boards?"

> This question has been asked quite often over the past few years because of the school board amalgamations across Canada and beyond. During the debates about whether or not the amalgamations will be successful—it is too early to tell yet—I have come to my own conclusion about why we need school boards.
>
> This is not about the need for larger or smaller school systems or about administrative systems run by administrators. There will always be administrative systems, whether large or small. This is about the necessity of having school board members who are elected by the electors in electoral districts. New Brunswick has fairly large amalgamated school systems managed by administrators but there are no elected school boards. I believe the decision to eliminate elected representatives in New Brunswick was a mistake.
>
> I admit quite frankly that administrators who manage school systems would have things easier—and could have more freedom, depending on how much authority is delegated from the provincial government—if there were no school boards. But there would be something missing, something very important for students, the schools and the communities. That is governance, real governance carried out by citizens duly elected to represent the local communities served by the schools.

Yes, the provincial departments of education in Canada govern public education, so there is electoral representation at the higher level of government, but this is not sufficient in the case of public schools because schools are so close to our hearts and homes. There has to be a form of local governance dedicated solely to what schools are like and what happens in them and this has to be in the hands of individuals elected for a definite term of office. There is a certain reassurance in the fact that the important decisions will be made by a majority vote of a group of elected community members who are accountable to their electors.

Dr. James A. Gunn
Superintendent of the Annapolis
Valley Regional School Board
Nova Scotia

Reprinted by permission of Dr. James A. Gunn.

School Boards

Canadian provinces have the authority to enact laws governing their educational systems. Local school board power is that which is expressly granted to them by statute. In most communities, school board members are elected in general elections; this affords all citizens the opportunity to select their representatives and the opportunity to offer for office in this grassroots form of local government. In most provinces, school board elections are held in conjunction with and resemble municipal elections (Bezeau).

School boards are corporations and, as such, are legal persons that can enter into contracts, sue, and be sued. School boards benefit from limited liability. Taxpayers and board members acting in good faith are not liable for the obligations of the board (Bezeau).

Many school board meetings are open to the public; in fact, many communities even provide radio and television coverage. Open meetings allow parents and interested citizens an opportunity to express their concerns and to get more information about problems in the district.

Canada's largest school boards have greater enrolment than the total population of the three territories. Large boards are sometimes divided into families of schools and have sub-district offices for these families. The Toronto District School Board, Canada's largest school board, is responsible for educating more than 305 000 students, and contains 565 schools with over 30 000 employees. Peel District School Board, one of the largest and fastest-growing boards in Canada, has an annual budget of 654 million (Pansengrau).

The Canadian School Boards Association (CSBA) contends that in most communities, school boards rarely make front page news, but they do make a difference.

The CSBA outlines the following common functions of school boards:

- Hiring the district superintendent, who in turn hires school district staff on behalf of the school board
- Serving as a check to provincial powers
- Seeing that provincial education legislation and regulations are implemented at the local level
- Managing and controlling school property
- Setting annual budgets, hiring administrators, and teachers
- Making policy
- Operating schools
- Developing district education plans

The website of the Canadian Educational Policy and Administration Network features a cross-Canada chart with information on school boards, funding, and negotiation procedures in Canadian provinces and territories: www.cepan.ca/rrnew/sg/xcanchart.htm.

Superintendent of Schools

School board organization varies across Canada but most boards have a chief executive officer, its highest-ranking employee, who reports directly to the board. In most Canadian provinces this person is the superintendent of schools or **superintendent**. Though school boards operate very differently, the superintendent is invariably the key figure in determining a district's educational policy. The superintendent is the chief administrator of the school district, the person charged with the responsibility of seeing to it that schools operate in accord within provincial guidelines as well as policies set by the local school board. Though the school board delegates broad powers to the superintendent, his or her policies require board approval.

How the superintendent and his or her board work together appears to be related to the size of the school district, with superintendents and school boards in larger districts more likely to be in conflict. In large districts, the board's own divisiveness makes it less likely that the board will successfully oppose the superintendent (Wirt and Kirst 1997).

Superintendents must have great skill to respond appropriately to the many external political forces that demand their attention, and conflict is inevitable. It is a demanding position; effective superintendents demonstrate that they are able to play three roles simultaneously: politician, manager, and teacher (Hurwitz 1999).

The Role of Parents

Parents may not be involved legally in the governance of schools, but they do play an important role in education. One characteristic of successful schools is that they have developed close working relationships with parents. Additionally, children whose parents or guardians support and encourage school activities have a definite advantage in school.

Through participation on school advisory and site-based councils, parents are making important contributions to school efforts across the nation. In addition, groups such as the Parent-Teacher Association (PTA), Parent-Teacher Organization (PTO) or Parent Teacher Advisory Council (PTCA) give parents the opportunity to communicate with teachers on matters of interest and importance to them.

Through these groups, parents can become involved in the life of the school in a variety of ways—from making recommendations regarding school policies to providing much-needed volunteer services, or to initiating school-improvement activities such as fund-raising drives.

Many parents are also influencing the character of education through their involvement with the growing number of private schools. In addition, many parents are activists in promoting school choice and the home-schooling movement.

An example of a national parent organization that has influenced programs in public schools is **Canadian Parents for French** (CPF), a nation-wide voluntary organization with its head office in Ottawa. Established in 1977, the CPF promotes the teaching of French in Canadian schools. It is primarily Anglophone and is devoted to the teaching of French as a second language. Canadian Parents for French has a research and publishing program which provides information to parents interested in French instruction, particularly French Immersion, for their children. It lobbies at the federal, provincial, and school board levels (Bezeau).

School-Based Management

One of the most frequently used approaches to restructuring schools is **school-based management** (SBM). Most SBM programs have three components in common:

1. Power and decisions formerly made by the superintendent and school board are delegated to teachers, principals, parents, community members, and students at local schools. At SBM schools, teachers can become directly involved in making decisions about curriculum, textbooks, standards for student behaviour, staff development, promotion and retention policies, teacher evaluation, school budgets, and the selection of teachers and administrators.
2. At each school, a decision-making body (known as a board, cabinet, site-based team, or council)—made up of teachers, the principal, and parents—implements the SBM plan.
3. SBM programs operate with the whole-hearted endorsement of the superintendent of schools.

School Choice

In recent years, the **school choice** or "school of choice" issue in Canadian education has emerged as an issue in parts of the country. School boards across Canada are responding to public pressure for education choice. The Prince George School District in British Columbia, the Edmonton Public Schools in Alberta, and the province of Manitoba have all developed comprehensive school choice policies. Technology is providing Canadian educators the opportunity to offer choice not tied to a physical plant; virtual schools and distance education courses are becoming more common (Wagner 1998).

The debate continues about whether school choice programs will, in fact, promote equity and excellence. Advocates of school choice believe that giving parents more options will force public schools to adjust to free-market pressures—low-performing schools would have to improve or shut down. Moreover, they contend that parents whose children must now attend inferior, and sometimes dangerous, inner city schools would be able to send their children elsewhere.

On the other hand, opponents believe that school choice would have disastrous consequences for public schools and lead to students being sorted by race, income, and religion. School choice, they argue, would subsidize the wealthy by siphoning money away from the public schools and further widen the gap between rich and poor districts. Moreover, opponents point out that research does not indicate that school choice would improve education (Smith and Meier 1995), nor would it promote educational equity:

> Since poor parents lack the supplemental resources that rich people have for helping their children, it is foolish to argue that [school choice] would help to equalize educational opportunities. (For example, rich parents can afford the extra costs for transportation, clothing, and educational supplies when they send their children to a distant, private school; poor parents cannot) (Berliner and Biddle 1995, 175).

The Edmonton Public Schools: Choice and Accountability

Edmonton, Alberta, has virtually revolutionized its public school; every school is now an education enterprise led by a principal with the power to implement change and manage every aspect of the school. Throughout North America, Edmonton is viewed as a shining example of the benefits of school choice. The school district offers open enrolment and more kinds of schools than any other district on the continent. These options have resulted in almost half of all students attending schools outside of their neighbourhoods and achievement scores have risen across the board.

For more than 25 years, Edmonton Public Schools has combined school-site decision making with central-office responsibility for establishing policy, setting priorities, determining funding, and monitoring success. The district currently offers 30 alternative programs, many in multiple locations. More than 45 percent of elementary students, 50 percent of junior high students, and 60 percent of senior high students attend schools outside their designated attendance area.

Programs of choice fall into four major categories:

- *Language and culture*—Programs include French Immersion and bilingual programs in American Sign Language, Arabic, German, Hebrew, Mandarin, Spanish, and Ukrainian, as well as Aboriginal culture.
- *Subject matter*—Programs include academic alternatives (enrichment/acceleration, Advance Placement, International Baccalaureate), arts, hockey, science, dance, and visual and performing arts.
- *Instructional approach*—Schools offer thematic curriculum; teacher-directed instruction; distance learning; and a focus on research, science, and technology.
- *Religion*—Edmonton Christian School and Millwoods Christian School alternatives

Under Edmonton Public Schools' Diversification Framework, all district programs must follow board policies, teach the provincial curriculum, and receive funds in the same way. The district's program policy ensures that all programs are consistent with sound education theory and practice, have appropriate staff and instructional resources, and don't have a negative impact on current offerings (McBeath 2002, reprinted by permission).

Wagner (1998) cautions policymakers to examine the following questions in relation to the issue of school choice:

- Can choice increase opportunities for all children to learn successfully?
- Can choice increase parental involvement and support for students and schools?
- Can choice increase the overall accountability of the public education system?
- Can choice inform us about successful practice and what works?

Corporate–Education Partnerships

To develop additional sources of funding for equity and excellence, many local school districts have established partnerships with the private sector. These partnerships are sometimes referred to as P3s—**public–private partnerships**. Businesses may contribute funds or materials needed by a school, sponsor sports teams, award scholarships, provide cash grants for pilot projects and teacher development, and even construct school buildings.

In 1998, Toronto District School Board signed a deal with Cisco Systems, the US-based computer networking products giant, to introduce its own curriculum on networking fundamentals into selected high schools. One example of this corporate-education partnership is the Scarborough Academy for Technological, Environmental, and Computer Education (SATEC) in Ontario. The school joined the company's international Network of Cisco Networking Academies. The teachers, trained by Cisco, instruct the students on how to design, build and manage computer networks in courses over a two-year period. Upon passing and gaining their credits, they are qualified to take a test at an approved Cisco training centre in Toronto.

There are differing opinions about the trend towards corporate partnerships in Canadian schools. Those who are concerned about the trend fear that it will result in some schools obtaining better programs and facilities than others and that profit-driven companies will have too much influence on education. However, supporters of the initiative claim that it can provide schools with much needed funding and expertise (Weinberg 2003).

A Cautionary Note

The Canadian Teachers' Federation (2003) believes that materials intended for classroom use should be subjected to rigorous evaluation. They advise that successful partnerships are based on sound educational principles and are built on trust and mutual respect between the contracting parties.

As partnerships become more common, the following general principles should be considered:

- Children, families, and public education benefit when the private sector uses its influence to promote economic and social conditions that foster strong public institutions.
- The role of the private sector in shaping the goals of public policy and public education should not exceed that of any other sector or interest group.
- Establishing and maintaining an appropriate relationship between public education and the private sector is possible only when schools and systems are democratically governed and receive adequate funding.
- Ministers of Education, through consultation with teachers, parents, and the community should establish policies and regulations that address private sector involvement in education.
- Corporate donations of goods and services, including technology, should be distributed equitably (Canadian Teachers' Federation 2003).

Professional Reflection   School board budgeting simulation

In the following simulation, you are asked to assume the role of a rural school board member faced with budget cuts. As you work through this simulation exercise, reflect on the chapter issues surrounding the topic of school governance

School Board Budgeting Simulation

You are a member of a rural school board faced with this situation:

1. You are in the third year of a "period of restraint" and are faced with an overall 3 percent reduction in your budget.
2. Local ratepayers are unlikely to vote for any more increases in their basic tax rate.

3. The previous two years of restraint, each of which reduced revenues by 3 percent, have done away with any "fat" in the system. You have a barebones operation with large class sizes, overworked teachers and administrators, and have had to postpone many needed renovations to schools and equipment.

4. While teachers' salaries have been frozen, the costs of fuel, electricity, paper, etc., have all continued to rise at an average annual rate of four percent. An early retirement package for teachers has been vetoed by the teachers' union. Unless you can find some method for reducing costs even further, your board will have to start cutting programs.

Here are the basic facts with which you must deal:

1. Number of students in the school district is 9000. The average class size is in the 30 to 40 range (even at the elementary level), with some classes at the secondary level in the low forties.

2. Number of teachers in the school district is 350; of this number, 10 are probationary teachers who can be released without difficulty at an annual savings of $40 000 each. After this, you are down to teachers with "permanent contracts." These teachers can be released in reverse order of seniority but there is a problem. All of the probationary teachers, and almost all of those with limited seniority, are the "bright lights" in your system. The release of these teachers will leave your system with an aging, tired staff, most with no time or energy for extracurricular activities. In addition, many of these most recently hired teachers are in science, math, and information technology specialties at the secondary level. If they leave, there is no one to replace them and, while someone will have to take on their courses, the quality of instruction is certain to suffer. For any non-term teacher released you will save approximately $50 000.

3. Total Budget last Year: $31.2 million

4. Total Budget this year: $30 million

5. Salaries and benefits: $24 million

6. Transportation, fuel, maintenance, administration, paper, telephone, etc. consume $6 million but you have already made all the reductions possible in these areas. Otherwise, you will have to turn off the heat, lay off the few remaining secretaries, and do the janitorial work yourself.

Your choices would seem to come down to the following as you try to find some method for reducing your expenses by $1.2 million.

1. Reduce the number of teachers, thereby making class sizes even larger.

2. Reduce the number of programs you offer to your students. Programs that cannot be cut are "core" items such as math, English, French, social studies, and science. Anything else is "up for grabs."

3. Possibilities (with the saving potential for each area in parentheses) include:

   ■ Music, which will engender tremendous public outcry from parents and probably result in your not being re-elected. ($400 000)
   ■ Family Studies and Technology Education, which are the only courses keeping some of your students in school. ($400 000)
   ■ Guidance counselling services (already severely cut), which will have serious consequences for students with emotional problems, those needing help with career choices, university applications, and those with various types of special needs. ($250 000)

- Drama courses at the secondary level. ($75 000)
- Cafeteria services of one kind or another at all schools, which could result in various forms of nutritional problems for students. ($50 000)
- Bus service, which is necessary because most students are bussed to school in this rural area ($1 million)
- Secondary physical education teachers (already removed from elementary schools). ($250 000)
- Resource teachers who deal with the 10 to 20 percent of students who have various types of learning problems; most schools have only one. ($200 000)
- Trained librarians (already replaced by library technicians at the elementary
- level) at the secondary level. ($150 000)
- Information Technology teachers at all levels, which would place your students at a tremendous disadvantage with respect to other areas of the province. ($400 000)
- Art programs at the elementary level, already scaled back, could be cut entirely. ($150 000)
- Speech pathologist, who has a caseload of 100 students: ($50 000)
- Psychometrician, who coordinates all aspects of special education, and administers all the specialized tests for students with special needs. ($60 000)
- Vice-principals, many of whom now teach half-time. ($150 000)
- Central Office personnel have already been reduced to an accountant, a supervisor of personnel, a supervisor of operations, the superintendent, and a couple of secretaries. Cutting a supervisor will save you $80 000 and leave your system in disarray.

(Next year you have to find another $1.2 million—but that's another story.)

Instructions for "School Board" Members

- Reflect on the advantages and disadvantages associated with making cuts in each of the areas listed. Consider all social, economic, political, and educational aspects.
- Make a list of the cuts you eventually decide to make, giving the rationale that underlies each.
- Can you justify the final decisions you have made?
- Would your list change if you were looking at the problem from a teacher's perspective?

Ethical and Legal Questions

Closely related to issues of school governance are those that deal with ethical and legal questions. In this section of the chapter we examine significant ethical and legal issues that affect the rights and responsibilities of teachers, administrators, students, and parents. Teachers must act in accordance with a wide range of federal and provincial legislations and court decisions. As a teacher, you may need to deal with such legal issues as the teacher's responsibility for accidents, freedom of speech, and student rights. Without knowledge of the legal dimensions of such issues, you will be ill-equipped to protect your rights and the rights of your students.

Teachers [must] balance public obligations with their personal beliefs and purposes in teaching.

—David T. Hansen
The Call to Teach

Why Do You Need a Professional Code of Ethics?

The actions of professional teachers are determined not only by what is legally required of them, but also by what they know they *ought* to do. They do what is legally right, and they do the right thing. A specific set of values guides them. A deep and lasting commitment to professional practice characterizes their work. They have adopted a high standard of professional ethics and they model behaviours that are in accord with that code of ethics.

At present, the teaching profession does not have a uniform **code of ethics** similar to the Hippocratic oath, which all doctors are legally required to take when they begin practice. However, many provincial teachers' associations have developed a code of ethics for educators. The following British Columbia Teachers' Federation Code of Ethics offers an example:

Ethical Teaching Attitudes and Practices

Teaching is an ethical enterprise—that is, a teacher has an obligation to act ethically, to follow what he or she knows to be the most appropriate professional action to take. The best interests of students, not the teacher, provide the rule of thumb for determining what is ethical and what is not. Behaving ethically is more than a matter of following the rules or not breaking the law—it means acting in a way that promotes the learning and growth of students and helps them realize their potential.

Code of Ethics

British Columbia Teachers' Federation (BCTF)

The Code of Ethics states general rules for all members of the BCTF for maintaining high standards of professional service and conduct toward students, colleagues, and the professional union.

1. The teacher speaks and acts toward students with respect and dignity and deals judiciously with them, always mindful of their rights and sensibilities.
2. The teacher respects the confidential nature of information concerning students and may give it only to authorized persons or agencies directly concerned with their welfare.
3. The teacher recognizes that a privileged relationship with students exists and refrains from exploiting that relationship for material, ideological, or other advantage.
4. The teacher is willing to review with colleagues, students, and their parents/guardians the quality of service rendered by the teacher and the practices employed in discharging professional duties.
5. The teacher directs any criticism of the teaching performance and related work of a colleague to that colleague in private, and only then, after informing the colleague in writing of the intent to do so, may direct in confidence the criticism to appropriate individuals who are able to offer advice and assistance. (See note following #10 and procedure 31.B.12.)
6. The teacher acknowledges the authority and responsibilities of the BCTF and its locals and fulfills obligations arising from membership in his/her professional union.
7. The teacher adheres to the provisions of the collective agreement.
8. The teacher acts in a manner not prejudicial to job actions of other collective strategies of his/her professional union.
9. The teacher neither applies for nor accepts a position which is included in a Federation in-dispute declaration.
10. The teacher, as an individual or as a member of a group of teachers, does not make unauthorized representations to outside bodies in the name of the Federation or its locals.

Note: It shall not be considered a breach of Clause 5 of the Code of Ethics for a member to follow legal requirements or official protocols in reporting child protection issues.

Procedure 31.B.12

Advice on how to proceed with a concern respecting a colleague's teaching and related work may be sought from Federation staff and/or local officers in good faith. Such discussion will not constitute a breach of Clause 5. 'Appropriate individuals' in Clause 5 of the Code of Ethics shall mean those persons who are able to offer advice and assistance on questions of teaching performance and related work. The first emphasis should be at all times on exploring means of assisting, rehabilitating, and correcting.

(British Columbia Teachers' Federation 2003)

Unethical acts break the trust and respect on which good student–teacher relationships are based. An example of unethical conduct would be to talk publicly about students' problems and actions. Other examples would be using grades as a form of punishment, expressing rage in the classroom, or intentionally tricking students on tests. You could no doubt think of other examples from your own experience as a student.

Ethical Dilemmas in the Classroom and School

Teachers routinely encounter **ethical dilemmas** in the classroom and in the school. They often have to take action in situations in which all the facts are not known or for which no single course of action can be called right or wrong. At these times it can be quite difficult to decide what an ethical response might be. Dealing satisfactorily with ethical dilemmas in teaching often requires the ability to see beyond short-range consequences to consider long-range consequences.

Consider, for example, the following three questions based on actual case studies. On the basis of the information given, how would you respond to each situation?

1. Should the sponsor of the high school literary magazine refuse to print a well-written story by a budding writer if the piece appears to satirize a teacher and a student?
2. Is a reading teacher justified in trying to increase achievement for an entire class by separating two disruptive students and placing one in a reading group beneath his reading level?
3. Should a chemistry teacher punish a student (on the basis of circumstantial, inconclusive evidence) for a laboratory explosion if the example of decisive, swift punishment will likely prevent the recurrence of a similar event and thereby ensure the safety of all students?

As a student teacher, it is important that you begin your student teaching assignment with a knowledge of the legal aspects of teaching and a clear idea of your rights and responsibilities.

What Are Your Legal Rights As a Teacher?

It is frequently observed that with each freedom comes a corresponding responsibility to others and to the community in which we live. As long as there is more than one individual inhabiting this planet, there is a need for laws to clarify individual rights and responsibilities. This necessary balance between rights and responsibilities is perhaps more critical to teaching than to any other profession.

While schools do have limited power over teachers, teachers' rights to **due process** cannot be violated. Teachers, like all citizens, are protected from being treated arbitrarily by those in authority. A principal who disagrees with a teacher's methods cannot suddenly fire that teacher. A school board cannot ask a teacher to resign merely by claiming that the teacher's political activities outside of school are "disruptive" of the educational process. A teacher cannot be dismissed for "poor" performance without

Figure 4.1

Legal advice for student teachers

Source: Julie Mead and Julie Underwood, "A Legal Primer for Student Teachers." In Gloria Slick (Ed.), *Emerging Trends in Teacher Preparation: The Future of Field Experiences.* Thousand Oaks, CA: Corwin Press, Inc., 1995, pp. 49–50.

Legal Advice for Student Teachers

1. Read the teacher's handbook, if one is available, and discuss its contents with the cooperating teacher. Be sure you understand its requirements and prohibitions.

2. Thoroughly discuss school safety rules and regulations. Be certain you know what to do in case of emergency, before assuming complete control of the classroom.

3. Be aware of the potential hazards associated with any activity and act accordingly to protect children from those dangers.

4. Be certain you know what controls the district has placed on the curriculum you will be teaching. Are there specific texts and/or methodologies that district policy requires or prohibits?

5. Be certain that student records are used to enhance and inform your teaching. Make certain that strict confidentiality is respected.

6. Document any problems you have with students, or as a teacher, in case you are called upon to relate details at a later time.

Meg's Choice

What kinds of ethical issues might confront a student teacher? For an example, read the following case:

Meg Grant had really looked forward to the eight weeks she would spend as a student teacher in Mrs. Walker's high school English classes. Meg knew that Mrs. Walker was one of the best supervising teachers she might have been paired with, and she was anxious to do her best.

As part of an assignment for her English Methods course in university, Meg had been required to design an extended thematic unit for the grade level she would be teaching during her field experience. Meg had received high praise from her professor for the unit she had developed on "A Look to the Future." As part of the teaching materials, Meg had designed a number of learning experiences that centred around the Aldous Huxley classic, *Brave New World*. Meg and her professor agreed that this text would be appropriate for the senior English classes she would be teaching in her upcoming student teaching.

In Mrs. Walker's Grade 11 English class, Meg planned to teach *Brave New World* as the basis for a number of activities. When she outlined her plans to her cooperating teacher, Mrs. Walker pointed out to Meg that this book was controversial and some parents might object. She asked Meg to think about selecting an additional title that students could read if their parents objected to *Brave New World*. Meg, however, felt that Mrs. Walker was bowing to pressure from conservative parents, so she decided to go ahead and teach the book. Besides, her professor had enthusiastically endorsed the text as a good reading choice for this grade level.

Two weeks later Meg was called down to the principal's office where she was confronted by an angry father who said, "You have no right to be teaching my daughter this Communist trash; you're just a student teacher. Mrs. Walker would never have made such an inappropriate choice for her students."

Questions

1. What would be the most prudent action for Meg to take?

2. Does Meg have the same rights as a fully certified teacher? Is Mrs. Walker responsible in any way for what has happened?

3. Meg had received conflicting advice from her professor and her cooperating teacher about the suitability of the text. Which advice should she have followed? How could two professionals have such different views on teaching materials?

4. What other books might be problematic for teachers to teach in the classroom?

5. Find out what books are most frequently censored for use in the classroom.

6. Under what circumstances would you disregard the advice of your cooperating teacher?

highlights

What ethical and legal issues will you face regarding the use of media and technology in your classroom?

With the explosion of media and technology in schools, teachers face a new ethical and legal issue—adhering to **copyright laws**, which govern your use of media. Making an illegal copy of software on a computer hard drive, showing a video, or taping a television or radio program—in effect, stealing another person's "intellectual property"—is quite easy. It is therefore important that, as a teacher, you be an exemplar of ethical behaviour regarding copyrighted materials. Just as you would not allow students to plagiarize written material or submit work that was not their own, you should follow the same standard of behaviour regarding the use of media and technology.

Beginning teachers should be aware of the legalities of using resources in the classroom. It is tempting to want to use some of the valuable programming available on television and radio; however, Canadian copyright law contains very clear rules on taping and showing television and radio programs in the classroom. Copyright law in Canada, governed by the Copyright Act, is one of the principal means of protecting media and computer software in Canada.

The guide in showing media resources in the classroom is whether the program has been cleared for "public performance." Usually programs from school media centres have been cleared for public performance. What is taped from television or radio is another matter. Using taped programs in the classroom without permission can be an infringement of copyright. Similarly, the majority of films and videos rented from video stores are restricted to home viewing and may not be shown in schools without copyright clearance.

Imagine that during your first year of teaching, a colleague suggests showing a popular rental video to your combined classes that afternoon as a break from academic work. You will not be charging for the viewing and the group is under 50 students. What should you do in this case? How do you respond to your colleague's suggestion? What is the rationale for your response?

ample documentation that the performance was, in fact, poor and without sufficient time to meet clearly stated performance evaluation criteria.

Because board of education policies and regulations vary throughout the country, you should carefully read any available teacher handbook or school policy handbook.

Most provinces have **collective bargaining** laws that require them to negotiate contracts with teacher organizations. An important part of most collective bargaining agreements is the right of a teacher to file a **grievance**, a formal complaint against his or her employer. A teacher may not be dismissed for filing a grievance, and he or she is entitled to have the grievance heard by a neutral third party. Often, the teachers' union or professional association that negotiated the collective bargaining agreement will provide a teacher who has filed a grievance with free legal counsel.

Should schools require students to wear uniforms?

"When students trade in their unofficial uniforms of baggy pants, message T-shirts, backward baseball caps, and name-brand sneakers for a school-sanctioned outfit of white dress shirts, ties, and dark pants or skirts, do they behave better and take school more seriously?" Daniel Gursky (1996) asks the question and responds affirmatively. Observing that few teachers object, he quips: "Given rampant disorder among students, why criticize something that appears to make a difference?" Others disagree and regard adoption of school uniform policies as a simplistic response to a complex problem and a fad lacking in foundation.

Implemented into any proposed school uniform programs are "opt out" provisions, which allow students—with their parents' permission—to sidestep the uniform requirement. In addition, most programs include assistance for families unable to purchase the required uniforms.

Are school districts going in the right direction by encouraging school uniforms? Should schools require students to wear uniforms?

Schools should require students to wear uniforms.

Schools should require students to wear uniforms in an effort to improve school discipline, foster a better learning environment, and ensure appropriate clothing choices. Problems arise when some students cannot afford expensive designer clothing and sports wear. Theft and violence stemming from efforts by students to obtain the desired attire have led to serious school problems. Students whose parents cannot afford the "right" clothing and accessories may be bullied or harassed by others.

With a mandatory school uniform program, inciting attire would be forbidden. Safety would be enhanced in two ways: (1) gangs and other dissident groups would not be able to display their "colours" at school, and (2) outsiders not wearing uniforms would stand out on campus. With a glance, teachers, school officials, and campus security could spot strangers (and potential violence).

School learning would be enhanced in subtle ways. Just as clergy and university faculty in academic regalia move with a dignity absent when they wear casual clothes to wash cars or play sports, so too will students stand taller and conduct themselves more seriously when they dress up for school. Also, in uniforms, students look equal and thus are likely to receive more equitable attention and instruction. That, combined with a learning environment that feels safer, should raise students' academic achievements.

Schools should not require students to wear uniforms.

Schools should not require students to wear uniforms. To do so tramples students' rights of free expression and subjects them to a conformity that is unhealthy, interrupting the development of adolescents' identity and independence. Uniforms can also be personally demoralizing. With them, authorities send the message that the student cannot be trusted and needs to be controlled, much as prisoners do.

Mandatory uniform programs can also be degrading for students in families that cannot afford to purchase uniforms. Even though in most programs financial support is available to those in need, the stigma of receiving the assistance can be embarrassing, even humiliating.

Researchers question schools' claims that their uniform programs increase achievement, attendance, good discipline, and students' sense of safety. One contradiction to these claims is reported in *Education Week*: "Researchers David Brunsma and Kerry Rockquemore analyzed data on nearly 5000 Grade 10s who took part in a federal study that began in 1988. They found that Grade 10s in schools requiring uniforms were not less likely than their more casually dressed peers to fight, smoke, drink alcohol, take drugs, or otherwise get in trouble at school. And they were no more likely to attend school regularly or score higher on standardized tests. In fact, the data showed that achievement scores were slightly lower for students made to wear uniforms" (Viadero 1999, p. 23).

Noll reports Dennis L. Evans' argument that "the successful programs that have been cited are mostly in elementary schools where the problems that the uniforms will allegedly solve do not exist; among adolescent gangs, school uniforms will be cosmetic at best and will not change gang mentality" (Noll 1999, 307).

The lack of careful research and evaluation of the effectiveness of existing school uniform programs, the infringement on free expression, the curtailment of students' development of identity and independence, and the criticism that such programs are superficial, cause opponents to say no to requiring students to wear uniforms.

Recommended Sources

Guskey, D. (1996, March). 'Uniform' improvement? *Education Digest.*

Noll, J. W. (1999). *Clashing views on controversial educational issues,* 10th ed. Guilford, CT: McGraw-Hill.

Paliokas, K. L. and Rist, R. C. Do they reduce violence—or just make us feel better? *Education Week 61*(7), 46–9.

Portner, J. (1999, May 12). Schools ratchet up the rules on student clothing, threats. *Education Week.*

Viadero, D. (1999, January) *Education Week 10*(4), 23.

Where do you stand on this issue?

1. What is your experience with school uniforms?

2. Which position do you agree with and why?

3. Which arguments are most persuasive to you?

4. Propose a compromise position on this issue.

5. What other approaches could you develop to deter violence, promote discipline, and create a productive learning environment in schools?

What Are Your Legal Responsibilities As a Teacher?

Teachers are legally responsible for the safety and well-being of students assigned to them. Although it is not expected that a teacher be able to completely control the behaviour of young, energetic students, a teacher can be held liable for any injury to a student if it is shown that the teacher's negligence contributed to the injury.

Since it is the duty of teachers and school administrators to maintain a safe and orderly learning environment, it is important for you to have an understanding of the legal and regulatory frameworks that govern schools. These frameworks confer duties and powers and place constraints on the exercise of the power within the context of the school.

Legal Frameworks

The legal authority of schools in Canada is derived from the following areas of law:

- Federal and provincial statute law
- Common law
- Constitutional law

Additionally, federal statutes such as the **Youth Criminal Justice Act** (April, 2003) contain provisions relevant to school discipline.

Federal and Provincial Law

In Canadian provinces, the various School Acts impose the obligation on teachers and principals to maintain order and discipline in schools. For example, in Alberta, Section 15 of the School Act (1988) requires that a principal must "maintain order and discipline in the school and on the school grounds and during activities sponsored or approved by the board."

Although provincial laws have the most direct application to public education in Canada, there are federal statutes that influence responses to cases of serious student misconduct. One of most important of these is the *Youth Criminal Justice Act* (2003), a federal criminal statute applying to persons ages 12 to 17. Certain actions committed by students may not only violate school rules but also be considered criminal offences. These may include theft, assault, and possession of prohibited items such as weapons and drugs (Brien 2002).

Common Law

The interpretation of provincial and federal laws is the responsibility of the courts and judges, whose decisions are recorded and published for use in successive cases. This creates a body of jurisprudence known as common law. A key legal principle derived from common law has provided the foundation of teachers' disciplinary authority over their students for centuries. This principle holds that teachers stand *in loco parentis* ("in the place of parents") with respect to their students, and may thus exercise discipline consistent with that of a parent. This teacher–student relationship established under common law can be assumed to regulate teachers' disciplinary authority over their students except where expressly altered by statute or policy.

Constitutional Law

With the proclamation of the Charter of Rights and Freedoms in 1982, Canadian courts gained expanded authority to review provincial and federal legislation to ensure that it is consistent with constitutional principles. Since public schools are created under provincial statutory authority, the actions of school-based personnel exercising authority are subject to Charter scrutiny. Educators must ensure that decisions made on discipline matters are taken according to constitutional principles so that they respect students' Charter rights (Brien 2002, pp. 2–7).

The Influences of the Canadian Charter of Rights and Freedoms

In the school setting, the various Charter protections affect very different types of rights, such as the following:

- Students' freedom of expression, or mobility in the classroom;
- Discipline and criminal issues: these relate to protection against unreasonable detentions, searches, and procedural fairness issues;
- Discrimination and accommodation issues, religious practice, and student conduct (McCoubrey and Sitch 2001, 15).

School and School District Policies

School employees are also subject to policies established by schools and school boards according to their statutory authority; they are legally bound by policies set out by their school boards, superintendents, and school principals. District policies may, for example, regulate the procedures to be followed before suspending a student. These policies may be more restrictive than the statutory provisions (Brien, p. 7–8).

Legal Role and Status of Teachers

MacKay and Sutherland (1992) provide a clear framework from which to examine the legal roles and responsibilities of educators. Two of these major roles, "Teachers as Parents" and "Teachers as State Agents," are featured in the following sections:

Teachers As Parents: Negligence, Liability, Corporal Punishment

Negligence in the school setting is of importance to teachers who may worry about under what circumstances they can be sued. Negligence cases follow a three-step analysis:

1. What was the **duty of care** owed to the injured person?
   - Teachers must take reasonable steps to minimize the risk of injury.
   - Teachers are entrusted with large numbers of students and their duties of care extend inside and outside the classroom.
   - Teachers must take care to ensure that students are not exposed to any unnecessary risk of harm.

2. What is the **standard of care** required by the person?
   - Standard of care may vary depending on circumstances.
   - Courts attempt to establish what a "reasonable person" would do in similar circumstances: the question is one of good judgment.
   - Courts have determined that a teacher's standard of care is that of a "careful parent."
   - Some factors that are considered in determining appropriate conduct in a particular situation: age of student(s); nature of activity, amount of instruction given to student(s); school policies; foreseeable risk of danger; previous accidents in similar circumstances.

3. Was this standard of care breached?
   - The law expects teachers to act reasonably to minimize the occurrence of accidents.
   - Courts must consider if students contributed to their own misfortune.
   - What damages, if any, were suffered by the injured person?
   - The plaintiff must have suffered some ascertainable damage as recognized by law.

Negligence in School Settings: Tort Liability

A tort is a civil wrong done by one person to another. According to **tort liability** law, an individual who is negligent and at fault in the exercise of his or her legal duty may be required to pay monetary damages to the injured party. Teachers are held to a higher standard than ordinary citizens and certain teachers (eg., physical education and chemistry teachers) are held to an even higher standard because of the increased risk of injury involved in the classes they teach.

A Grade 8 science teacher in Louisiana left her class for a few moments to go to the school office to pick up some forms. While she was gone, her students continued to do some laboratory work that involved the use of alcohol-burning devices. Unfortunately,

one girl was injured when she tried to relight a defective burner. Could the teacher be held liable for the girl's injuries?

The events described above actually occurred in 1974 *(Station v. Travelers Insurance Co.)*. The court that heard the case determined that the teacher failed to provide adequate supervision while the students were exposed to dangerous conditions. Considerable care is required, the court observed, when students handle inherently dangerous objects, and the need for this care is magnified when students are exposed to dangers they don't appreciate.

Should this teacher/coach have any concerns about tort liability? How might this teacher reduce the risk of liability?

Specific Areas of Responsibility

The Classroom

- Teachers have the duty to supervise students in their classrooms.
- Reasons for absence, its duration, the type of accident, and nature of the class, are factors that would be considered in determining negligence.

Playgrounds and Outside

- Injuries outside schools are examined to determine if an adequate system of supervision was in place and if teachers adequately performed their tasks.
- Playground equipment is monitored for safety (loose boards, nails, broken glass, etc.).

Before and after School

- It is advisable for schools to establish clear hours of supervision for before and after school hours and to communicate this to parents.
- In the area of after school supervision, teachers have the responsibility to abide by parents' instructions and to be mindful of special circumstances such as early dismissal or emergencies such as snow storms.

Special Classrooms and Labs

- Classrooms where there are increased dangers such as special equipment, dangerous tools, open flames, or chemicals require a greater degree of supervision by school personnel, proper protection and adequate instructions, and precise warnings to students.
- Specialist teachers in industrial arts shops, science labs, gymnasiums, and home economics classes are held to a higher standard of care than regular classroom teachers.

Emergencies

- Teachers who take students on field trips or are in charge of high risk activities such as physical education classes may be directly confronted with emergency situations.
- Teachers are expected to take reasonable measures to cope with emergency situations.
- Basic first aid, life-saving techniques such as CPR, and proper training in emergency procedures are recommended for such teachers.
- Children who have severe anaphylactic reactions due to allergies from foods (peanuts, peanut butter) or bee stings, or who suffer from diabetes, seizures, or other serious medical conditions need special protection and monitoring. Teachers should make every effort to obtain such medical information from parents at the beginning of the school year. A plan for management should be devised with the parents; this may include storing and administering medication such as epinephrine.

Off School Property—Field Trips

- Protecting against legal liability is a must for field trips. Using proper risk management can help to reduce the possibility of a lawsuit occurring or succeeding due to accidents.
- Teachers should be aware of the need for waivers and parental permission forms, proper insurance, and safe practices.

    Appendix 4.2 provides a checklist to use when taking students off school property.

Liability for Corporal Punishment in Schools

Corporal punishment refers to the intentional use of physical force for an alleged offence or behaviour of a student.

- Touching without consent is a technical assault; in real terms, legal action is likely only when the touching results in some physical or emotional damage to the victim.
- Corporal punishment (use of strap) in schools has been largely abolished by school board policies that prohibit its use
- Criminal Code protections for teachers to use force by way of correction remain in existence in the form of Section 43:

    Every schoolteacher, parent or person standing in the place of a parent is justified in using force by way of correction toward a pupil or child, as the case may be, who is under his care, if the force does not exceed what is reasonable under the circumstances.

- In spite of Section 43, it is not recommended practice for teachers to resort to physical violence as a means of correction. (MacKay and Sutherland 1992)

The school board as employer is normally found liable for the acts of its employees. If teachers are found negligent, the finding of **liability** is usually found against the relevant school board under what is known as **vicarious liability**.

To protect students from harm and themselves from litigation, teachers should be vigilant about potentially harmful or dangerous situations. They are, for example, encouraged to be vigilant about seeking permission from a school administrator or the school board for trips off school property and should also ensure that they have adequate personal insurance coverage if they are transporting students in their own vehicles.

Teachers As Educational State Agents

Most provincial education acts provide some definition of the duties and roles of teachers in the framework of delivering educational services to students. These definitions describe the teachers' complex roles and responsibilities as **state agents**. Sections of the Charter of Rights and Freedoms of 1982 directly affect how teachers, as state agents, deal with and relate to students. The following sections will examine briefly how some of the various Charter rights apply to education:

Section 2: Fundamental Freedoms

Everyone has the following fundamental freedoms:

- Freedom of conscience and religion
- Freedom of thought, belief, opinion, and expression, including freedom of the press and other media of communication
- Freedom of peaceful assembly
- Freedom of association

Freedom of Conscience and Religion in the School Context

- Religious freedom is raised when there is a conflict between the school expectation and the practices of a particular religion.
- Examples include a religious requirement to wear a particular head covering, or to keep arms or legs covered, that may conflict with the school practice of banning hats inside school, or requiring that students wear specific gym attire.
- Court decisions have required schools to accommodate religious difference.

Freedom of Expression in the School Context

- Freedom of expression issues arise in the school whenever a student expresses a view that is contrary to the educational goals of the school.
- One example is the censoring of a school newspaper or the content in a school play.
- Canadian cases on freedom of expression issues, however, are scarce.

Freedom of Assembly and Association in the School Context

- Student protests of political or school activities can raise freedom of assembly issues when the protest occurs at the school or during school time.
- Examples include boycotting an event, or walking out of class.
- There is a lack of case law specific to students.
- Schools need to balance the rights of students to peaceful assembly with concerns for safety and order.

Section 8: The Right to Be Secure

Everyone has the right to be secure against unreasonable search or seizure:

- Searches are not uncommon in schools; they are seen as a means of maintaining rules and safety. Reasons for the objectives of the search can range from discovering a violation of classroom rules to possession of drugs.
- Examples range from the less intrusive (looking through desks for an annoying toy) to the more serious (such as school-wide locker inspections, strip searches, or emptying student's school bag).

■ Courts have given educators more latitude to maintain order in schools. A reasonable search in schools is subject to the following lower standard:

    a. The educator should reasonably believe a school rule has been broken.
    b. The educator should reasonably believe a search will reveal evidence of a breach.
    c. The educator is to consider all surrounding circumstances.
    d. The search is to be minimally intrusive.

Section 9: The Right Not to Be Arbitrarily Detained

Everyone has the right not to be arbitrarily detained or imprisoned.

■ Detentions in schools are routine and necessary for school safety.
■ Examples include students who pose threats to themselves or someone else until the situation can be diffused, or "after-school detentions" used for disciplinary purposes.
■ Educators should ensure that detentions are based on reasonable grounds and that the reason for the detention is communicated to the detained student.

Section 12: The Right Not to Be Subjected to Cruel or Unusual Punishment

Everyone has the right not to be subjected to any cruel or unusual treatment or punishment.

■ Educators exact punishment as a regular aspect of their job.
■ Examples include writing lines, extra homework, suspensions, letters home, and no recess.
■ Educators should consider punishment that focuses on meaningful consequences and rehabilitation.

Section 15: Equality before the Law

Every individual is equal before and under the law and has the right to equal protection and equal benefit of the law without discrimination based on race, national or ethnic origin, colour, religion, sex, age, or mental or physical disability.

■ There are a number of ways students can experience discrimination in the school setting.
■ Examples include non-accessibility for students with disabilities, negative stereotypes perpetuated by curriculum, insults directed at sexual orientation, and bullying.
■ Court decisions mean educators must give due regard to the requirement of accommodation regarding disability.
■ Proactive measures, such as preventing inappropriate and discriminatory language in school, taking steps to eliminate bullying, listening to concerns of students who feel discriminated against, and teaching students about the nature of, and laws with respect to, equality and respect are ways in which educators can model a system of justice.

(McCoubrey and Sitch 2001)

Reporting Child Abuse

Teachers, who are now *required* by law to report any suspected **child abuse**, are in positions to monitor and work against the physical, emotional, and sexual abuse and the neglect and exploitation of children. Teachers' professional journals and information from local, provincial, and federal child welfare agencies encourage teachers to be more

Table 4.1

Physical and behavioural indicators of child abuse and neglect

Type of Child Abuse/Neglect	Physical Indicators	Behavioural Indicators
Physical Abuse	Unexplained bruises and welts: ■ on face, lips, mouth ■ on torso, back, buttocks, thighs ■ in various stages of healing ■ clustered, forming regular patterns ■ reflecting shape of article used to inflict (electric cord, belt buckle) ■ on several different surface areas ■ regularly appear after absence, weekend, or vacation ■ human bite marks ■ bald spots Unexplained burns: ■ cigar, cigarette burns, especially on soles, palms, back, or buttocks ■ immersion burns (sock-like, glove-like, doughnut-shaped on buttocks or genitalia) ■ patterned like electric burner, iron, etc. ■ rope burns on arms, legs, neck, or torso Unexplained fractures: ■ to skull, nose, facial structure ■ in various stages of healing ■ broken arms or dislocated limbs ■ multiple or spiral fractures Unexplained lacerations or abrasions: ■ to mouth, lips, gums, eyes ■ to external genitalia Consistent hunger, poor hygiene, inappropriate dress	Wary of adult contacts Apprehensive when other children cry Behavioural extremes: ■ aggressiveness ■ withdrawal ■ overly compliant Afraid to go home: wants to stay after school "to help" Reports injury by parents Exhibits anxiety about normal activities, eg., napping Complains of soreness and moves awkwardly Destructive to self and others Early to school or stays late as if afraid to go home Accident prone Wears clothing that covers body when not appropriate Chronic runaway (especially adolescents) Cannot tolerate physical contact or touch
Physical Neglect	Consistent lack of supervision, especially in dangerous activities or long periods Unattended physical problems or medical needs Abandonment Lice Distended stomach, emaciated	Begging, stealing food Constant fatigue, listlessness, or falling asleep States there is no caregiver at home Frequent school absence or tardiness Destructive, pugnacious School dropout (adolescents) Early emancipation from family (adolescents)

observant of children's appearance and behaviour in order to detect symptoms of child abuse. Such sources often provide lists of physical and behavioural indicators of potential child abuse, similar to that shown in Table 4.1. Many communities, through their police departments or other public and private agencies, provide programs adapted for children to educate them about their rights in child-abuse situations and to show them how to obtain help.

Table 4.1 continued

Type of Child Abuse/Neglect	Physical Indicators	Behavioural Indicators
Sexual Abuse	Difficulty in walking or sitting ■ torn, stained, or bloody underclothing Pain or itching in genital area Bruises or bleeding in external genitalia, vaginal, or anal areas Venereal disease Frequent urinary or yeast infections Frequent unexplained sore throats	Unwilling to participate in certain physical activities Sudden drop in school performance Withdrawal, fantasy, or unusually infantile behaviour Crying with no provocation Bizarre, sophisticated, or unusual sexual behaviour or knowledge Anorexia (especially adolescents) Sexually provocative Poor peer relationships Reports sexual assault by caretaker Fear of or seductiveness toward males Suicide attempts (especially adolescents) Chronic runaway Early pregnancies
Emotional Maltreatment	Speech disorders such as stuttering Lags in physical development Failure to thrive (especially in infants) Asthma, severe allergies, or ulcers Substance abuse Inappropriate behaviour with adults	Habit disorders (sucking, biting, rocking, etc.) Conduct disorders (antisocial, destructive, etc.) Neurotic traits (sleep disorders, inhibition of play) Behavioural extremes: ■ compliant, passive ■ aggressive, demanding, overly adaptive behaviour: ■ inappropriately adult ■ inappropriately infantile Developmental lags (mental, emotional) Delinquent behaviour (especially adolescents)

Source: Adapted from Cynthia Crosson Tower, *The Role of Educators in the Prevention and Treatment of Child Abuse and Neglect,* The User Manual Series, 1992. Washington, DC: U.S. Department of Health and Human Services; and Derry Koralek, *Caregivers of Young Children: Preventing and Responding to Child Maltreatment,* The User Manual Series, 1992. Washington, DC: U.S. Department of Health and Human Services.

Schools usually have a specific process for dealing with suspected abuse cases, involving the school principal and counsellor as well as the reporting teacher. Because a child's physical welfare may be further endangered when abuse is reported, caution and sensitivity are required. Teachers are in a unique position to help students who are victims of child abuse, both because they have daily contact with them and because children learn to trust them.

Recommended Sources

Canadian Charter of Rights and Freedoms. (1982). Department of Justice Canada. Available at
  http://laws.justice.gc.ca/en/Charter/

Freeman, M. (1993). "Whither children: Protection, participation and autonomy?" *Manitoba Law
  Journal* (22), 307.

Proudfoot, A. & Hutchings, L. (1998). *Teacher beware: A legal primer for the classroom teacher.*
  Calgary: Detselig Enterprises Ltd.

Sussel, T. (1995). *Canada's legal revolution: Public education, the Charter and human rights.* Toronto:
  Emond Montgomery Ltd.

Best, C. *The best guide to Canadian legal research.* www.legalresearch.org/

Watkinson, A. (1999). *Education, students' rights and the Charter.* Saskatoon: Purich Publishing Ltd.

Five Cases: You Be the Judge!

The following five cases illustrate some of the principles discussed in this chapter. Judge the cases and then read the decisions of the courts provided after the case descriptions.

Legal Cases

Plumb Case

In a British Columbia case, the plaintiff, 15 years of age, was injured when struck by a ball thrown during a game of catch. The plaintiff had forgotten his glove that day and was not participating in the game. Instead he was lying on the grass to one side of the game. He was injured by a wild throw, which was missed by the intended catcher, bounced once on the grass, and struck the plaintiff. The one teacher on supervision had seen the game but did not believe that it posed any special risks. The school board and the child who had thrown the ball were named as plaintiffs.

Cropp Case

In this Saskatchewan case, the plaintiff was 14 years of age and wearing cowboy boots with five centimetre heels when he slipped, fell, and injured himself on a temporary walkway on the school grounds. He was required to take two classes in adjacent buildings and was moving between buildings one morning when the accident happened. This walkway was composed of coarse crushed rock held in place by board sidewalls supported by stakes.

Wiggins Case

In an early Ontario case, a board was sued for negligence when one of the students became crippled as a result of an unspecified disease. The student soaked her feet in freezing weather while moving between the school building and the outhouse. The court found that the board had landscaped the schoolyard in a manner that ensured proper drainage.

Simard Case

In a Quebec case, a child of eight years was injured in a fall while climbing down from a classroom window that she had closed. The classroom teacher had asked her to close the window, which required that she step on a chair, then on a radiator, and then on a small table located on the windowsill in order to reach the window. After closing the window she fell, striking the chair.

Road Pizza Case

In *Strong v. Moon*, the mother of an elementary school child suffered painful though minor injuries in an automobile accident that occurred just after she had let her daughter off at school. While the mother was lying on the road awaiting an ambulance, a school bus passed by, carrying children to the same school. Some children recognized the accident victim and later described the scene to her daughter, referring to the mother as "road pizza." Although the mother quickly recovered, the daughter suffered continuing psychological disturbances and eventually was forced to repeat her year. The plaintiff child and her mother sued the driver who had caused the mother's injuries for the suffering of the child.

Judicial Decisions

The five decisions below illustrate a variety of situations. The first involves a failure or alleged failure of supervision, whereas the second and third concern only occupiers' liability. The fourth case has elements of both, but was decided on the basis of supervision. The final case, although not a school case strictly speaking, has important implications for teachers.

Plumb Decision

The judge found no negligence on the part of any defendants. The level of supervision was adequate and the game of catch was not inherently dangerous. There had been no recklessness or intent to injure. The injury resulted from a purely accidental misthrow, which could not have been anticipated. A careful and prudent parent would reasonably allow teenaged children to play catch.

Cropp Decision

The school board was found to be negligent in failing to provide a safe walkway. The vice-chairman of the school board admitted during the cross-examination that he found the walkway to be unstable and that it did not measure up to the standard of safety that a school board should supply for its students. The student was not found to be contributorily negligent.

Wiggins Decision

The court concluded that three of the four conditions necessary for negligence had been established: a legal duty of care, a breach of that duty, and actual damage. The suit failed because the fourth condition, causal proximity, had not been demonstrated. There had been an epidemic in the area at the time, and the plaintiff had soaked her feet during cold weather while walking to and from school. The board's failure to maintain school grounds was not necessarily the cause of the child's disease.

Simard Decision

The teacher was found to be negligent and fully responsible in asking the child to close the window. She had not acted as would a good parent of a family. Because of the age of the child and the request of the teacher that the child close the window, the Quebec Superior Court found neither voluntary assumption of risk nor contributory negligence on the part of the child.

Road Pizza Decision

In the *Strong v. Moon* case, school officials had done everything they could to console and help the child and were not named as defendants. The driver who was responsible for the mother's injuries was not liable on grounds of excessive remoteness. The court held that the child's problems were not remote from the accident to be reasonably foreseeable by the offending driver. This case poses an obvious question for teachers: whether they can prevent the type of behaviour that caused the child's distress and, if so, how.

Source: © Lawrence M. Bezeau 2002.

SUMMARY

Who Is Involved in Canadian School Governance?

- Parents, students, teachers, administrators, taxpayers, politicians, minorities, educational theorists and researchers, and businesses and corporations are among the groups that exert influence on school policies in Canada.

- Schools reflect the society they serve and thus are influenced by out-of-school factors such as the mass media, demographic shifts, international events, and social issues.

What Is the Historical Basis for the Governance of Canadian Schools?

- The British North America Act of 1867 established Canada as a nation and laid out the frameworks for public institutions such as schools.

- Section 93 of the British North America Act granted authority for education to the provinces.

- Provinces have the authority to enact legislation dealing with education and have full legal responsibility for education.

What Is the Role of the Federal Government in Canadian Education?

- There is no national or federal education office to direct or coordinate educational activities in the Canadian provinces and territories; most relevant programs fall under the Secretary of State.

- At the national level, a number of federal departments and national organizations intersect with education.

What Is the Role of the Provincial Government in Canadian Education?

- Canadian systems of education begin at the provincial level with the passing of statutes that create the educational system and provide for its management and funding.

- Most Canadian provinces have an education act or public school act and an elected minister of education who is responsible for education at the elementary and secondary levels and an appointed deputy minister who manages the day-to-day operations of the department.

Why Do We Need School Boards?

- At the local level, public education comes under the jurisdiction of school boards.
- Local school districts, which vary greatly in size, locale, organizational structure, demographics, and wealth, are responsible for the management and operation of schools.
- Among the functions of school boards is the implementing of provincial education legislation and regulations at the local level, operating schools, making policy, setting annual budgets, and hiring administrators and teachers.
- The superintendent, the chief administrator of a local district, has a complex array of responsibilities and must work cooperatively with the school board and others in an environment that is often politically turbulent.
- Provinces fund school boards by a system of grants that supplement money raised from local property tax in some provinces and provide virtually all of the funding for boards in others.
- Local schools boards, whose members are usually elected, set educational policies for a district; however, many people believe that boards should be reformed to be more well informed and responsive.
- Through groups like the PTA or School Advisory Councils, some parents are involved in local school activities and reform efforts; others are involved with private schools; and some actively promote alternative approaches to education such as school choice and home-schooling.
- As part of restructuring in Canada, the number of school boards in most provinces has been reduced in recent years.

Why Do You Need a Professional Code of Ethics?

- Teaching requires ethical behaviour and many provincial teachers' associations have developed a code of ethics as a guide for their members.
- A professional code of ethics guides teachers' actions and enables them to build relationships with students based on trust and respect.
- A code of ethics helps teachers see beyond the short-range consequences of their actions to long-range consequences, and it helps them respond appropriately to ethical dilemmas in the classroom.

What Are Your Legal Rights As a Teacher?

- The right to due process protects teachers from arbitrary treatment by school districts and education officials regarding certification, nondiscrimination, contracts, tenure, dismissal, and academic freedom.
- Most provinces have collective bargaining laws that require them to negotiate contracts with teacher organizations and allow for teachers to file a grievance or formal complaint against employers.

What Are Your Legal Responsibilities As a Teacher?

- Teachers are responsible for meeting the terms of their teaching contracts, including providing for their students' safety and well-being.

- Student teachers should be aware that a potential for liability exists for them just as it does with licensed teachers, and they should clarify their rights and responsibilities prior to beginning student teaching.

- Legal authority of schools in Canada is derived from federal and provincial statute law, common law, and constitutional law.

- Legal roles and responsibilities of teachers include teacher as parent and teacher as educational state agent.

- The Charter of Rights and Freedoms directly affects how teachers deal with and relate to students.

- Among the legal responsibilities that concern teachers are: avoiding tort liability (specifically negligence), recognizing the physical and behavioural indicators of child abuse and then reporting suspected instances of such abuse, and observing copyright laws as they apply to photocopies, videotapes, computer software, and materials published on the internet.

KEY TERMS AND CONCEPTS

British North America
    Act, 125
Canadian Parents for
    French, 131
Canadian School Board
    Association, 128
child abuse, 149
code of ethics, 137
collective bargaining, 141
Constitution Act of
    1982, 125
copyright laws, 141
corporal
    punishment, 147

Council of Ministers of
    Education, Canada, 126
department of education,
    127
deputy minister of
    education, 127
due process, 139
duty of care, 145
education act, 127
ethical dilemmas, 139
grievance, 141
liability, 147
minister of education, 127
negligence, 145

public-private
    partnerships, 133
school advisory councils, 128
school-based
    management, 132
school boards, 128
school choice, 132
standard of care, 145
state agents, 148
superintendent, 131
tort liability, 145
vicarious liability, 147
Youth Criminal Justice
    Act, 143

APPLICATIONS AND ACTIVITIES

Teacher's Journal

1. Read the code of ethics for teachers in your province. Record in your journal examples of situations you observed or experienced in which you feel a teacher may have violated the principles. Conclude your analysis of these cases with a personal statement about your goals for ethical conduct as a teacher.

2. What limits do you believe should be placed on *what* teachers teach? on *how* they teach?

3. What is your position regarding corporal punishment? Are there circumstances under which its use is justified?

4. Imagine that you are given the choice to send your child to any school in your province. What factors would you consider in making your choice? Compare your list with the following list, most important coming first, from a recent survey of parents: quality of teaching staff, maintenance of school discipline, courses offered, size of classes, and test scores of students. What are the similarities and differences between the lists? What do the differences reveal about your view of education and schools?

5. Think of businesses and agencies in your community that might be good partners for a school. Select one of them and develop a proposal outlining the nature, activities, and benefits (to both) of the partnership you envision.

Teacher's Database

1. Conduct an internet search on one or more of the topics listed below or on another topic from Chapter 4. Narrow your search to issues and information relating to school law and the legal rights and responsibilities of school districts and schools, teachers and administrators, and students and parents. Include a search of news sources, such as Education Week on the Web, for summaries of recent court rulings pertaining to education and school law.

Topics on issues to search from Chapter 4:

- school uniforms
- free speech
- search and seizure
- collective bargaining
- copyright law
- corporal punishment
- professional ethics

2. Use the internet to gather information about the structure of education and school funding in your province. How many school boards are in your province? Which is the largest? What are enrolment figures, trends, and projections for your province? What are the figures for household income and poverty rate? Begin your data search at Statistics Canada and the provincial Department of Education.

Observations and Interviews

1. During an observation of a teacher's day, identify an ethical dilemma that the teacher confronts. Describe the dilemma and the teacher's response in a journal entry.

2. Visit a private school. Find out how teachers and other staff members are hired and how the school is organized and governed. How does the management and operation of this school differ from public schools?

3. Interview a school superintendent and ask him or her to comment on the role of the school board in that school district.

4. Interview a teacher and ask how the Department of Education affects the teacher's work. Would the teacher like to see the government more or less involved in education? Report your findings to the rest of the class.

5. Attend a meeting of a local school board and observe the communication and decision-making process at that meeting.

Professional Portfolio

Survey a group of students, teachers, and/or parents regarding a legal issue in education. Among the legal issues and questions you might address are the following:

- Under what circumstances should restrictions be placed on what teachers teach and how they teach?
- Should parents be allowed to provide home-schooling for their children?
- Are parents justified in filing educational malpractice suits if their children fail to achieve in school?
- Under what circumstances should restrictions be placed on students' freedom of expression?
- Should schools have the right to implement dress codes? guidelines for students' hairstyles? school uniforms?
- Should corporal punishment be banned? If not, under what circumstances should it be used?
- To combat drug abuse, should schools implement mandatory drug testing of students? of teachers?
- Should students have access to their educational records? should their parents or guardians?
- As part of an HIV/AIDS prevention program, should condoms be distributed to high school students? Should parental approval be required for participation?

The report summarizing the results of your survey should include demographic information such as the following for your sample of respondents: gender, age, whether they have children in school, level of education, and so on. When you analyze the results, look for differences related to these variables.

Appendix 4.1

- Check the school policy on travel; this includes transportation and insurance policies.
- Obtain approval from the school administration.
- Thoroughly prepare students and make them aware of what is acceptable behaviour. Class rules may need to be modified for the new learning situation. School bus rules should be emphasized.
- Discuss with the students the reason for going on the field trip and try to connect what they are learning in the classroom to what they will experience on the trip.
- Ensure that there are enough adults who have the required level of expertise and skills required for the safety of all students. It is a good idea to have an adult chaperone who has first aid training. Be mindful of adequate student : adult ratios.
- Have permission forms signed by parents of all students who are going on the trip. The forms should be accompanied by information notices that describe all the pertinent details of the trip. There should be specific pick up and drop off times stated in the information.
- Obtain knowledge of student allergies, medications, and have permission for emergency medical treatment. Ensure that you have medicare numbers and emergency numbers for students. Take along a first aid kit.
- Have a plan for what will happen if a student has to be sent home.
- Double check reservations, tickets, bookings before the trip. Know what method of payment is accepted if there are fees involved in the trip.
- Have a means of communicating with parents. This includes a cell phone, phone numbers of all parents, student information, and permission forms. Have a prearranged way to call all parents. A telephone tree is useful. A spare copy of these documents should be left at the school.

5

Social and Cultural
Realities Confronting
Today's Schools

*The educational system is part of
the common life and cannot escape
suffering the consequences that
flow from the conditions prevailing
outside the school building.*

—John Dewey "Introduction,"
The Use of Resources in Education

focus questions

1. What are the aims of education today?

2. How can schools be described?

3. What are schools like as social institutions?

4. How is cultural diversity represented in Canadian schools?

5. What is multicultural education?

6. How is gender a dimension of multicultural education?

7. What characteristics distinguish successful schools?

8. What social problems affect schools and place students at risk?

9. What are schools doing to address societal problems?

Jeff Banks, a history teacher at Lakeside High School, enters the faculty lunchroom and sees his friends, Sue Anderson, Nancy Watkins, and Bret Thomas, at their usual table in the corner. Lakeside is located in a medium-size city in Central Canada. The school, in the centre of a low- to middle-income area, has an enrolment of almost 1400 students. About 70 percent of these self-identify as Anglo-European Canadians, with the remaining 30 percent comprised of students from various ethnic and cultural groups. After English, the most common languages are Italian and East Indian. Lakeside has a reputation for being a "good" school—for the most part, students are respectful of their teachers. Parents, many of whom work in the several small businesses and industries found in the community generally support the school and are involved in school activities in spite of their heavy work schedules. The consensus among teachers is that most parents recognize that education is the key if their children are to "better themselves."

As soon as Jeff is within earshot of his friends, he knows they are talking about a tragic shooting at a Canadian high school. An unhappy student had brought a gun to school and shot a fellow student.

"It's so scary," Sue says, "Who knows, something like that could happen right here at Lakeside. We have no idea what kids have to deal with today."

"Yeah, we have no idea who might snap," says Bret. "With a lot of these school shootings lately, it seems to be a kid that no one would have expected. Quiet, polite, good student—you just never know."

"In some cases, that's true," Jeff says, placing his lunch tray on the table and then sitting down between Sue and Bret. "But a lot of times there are signs. A lot of these kids are loners and outcasts; they're into violent video games, cults, drugs, guns, you name it."

"What I want to know," says Sue, "is how we can prevent something like that from happening here? Since the Colorado shootings, there have been bomb scares, threats, guns confiscated at dozens of schools around the country."

"Well, I don't think metal detectors, more police in schools, and stiffer penalties for kids who bring guns to school are necessarily the answers," says Bret. "The question is, why are kids doing this?"

"Right, how can we prevent things like this?" says Jeff.

"If we're going to change things," says Sue, "we've got to figure out ways to identify and help kids who feel so desperate that they turn to violence."

"Well, that's all well and good," says Nancy with a sigh. "But I don't see where all of this is going to lead. Our responsibility as teachers is to educate our kids. We're not psychiatrists or social workers. We can't change society. Besides, we've got youth agencies, centres for families in crisis, and all kinds of social service agencies."

What is the role of schools at the start of the 21st century? Should teachers play a role in addressing social problems such as violence in our society? What would you say to a teacher who expresses views such as Nancy's?

The discussion among Jeff and his fellow teachers highlights the expectation of much of the public that schools (and teachers) have a responsibility to address problems that confront modern society. Those who agree with Nancy's point of view tend to believe that schools should teach only content to students. Others, however, believe that teachers have an obligation to address domestic social problems. Underlying both positions are conflicting views on the aims of education.

What Are the Aims of Education Today?

In Canada, people agree that the purpose of schools is to educate. Unlike other institutions in society, schools have been developed exclusively to carry out that very important purpose. That we are not always in agreement about what the **aims of education** should be, however, is illustrated by the fact that we disagree about what it means to be an educated person. Is a person with a college degree educated? Is the person who has overcome, with dignity and grace, extreme hardships in life educated?

Debate about the aims of education is not new. Fourth century BC philosopher Aristotle, for example, expressed the dilemma this way: "The existing practice [of education] is perplexing; no one knows on what principle we should proceed—should the useful in life, or should virtue, or should the higher knowledge, be the aim of our training; all three opinions have been entertained" (1941, 1306). Definitive answers to Aristotle's questions have not been achieved; instead, each generation has developed its own response to what the aims of education should be.

Education for Prosocial Values

Although there is widespread debate about what academic content the schools should teach, the public agrees that schools should teach **prosocial values** such as honesty, fairness, civility, and respect for the law. The well-being of any society requires support of such values; they enable people from diverse backgrounds to live together peacefully. Others we would add to this list include respect for others, industry or hard work, persistence or the ability to follow through, fairness in dealing with others, compassion for others, and civility and politeness (Elam, Rose, and Gallup 1994). The strong support for these prosocial values reflects the public's belief that the schools should play a key role in promoting the democratic ideal of equality for all.

Education for Socialization

Schools are places where the young become socialized—where they learn to participate intelligently and constructively in the Canadian society. Table 5.1 shows the percentage of the public in 1998 who believed that the practice of good citizenship was a "very important" measure of school effectiveness, even more important than going on to postsecondary education, getting a job, or scoring well on standardized tests.

Additionally, it is in our schools, more than any other institution within our society, that persons from various ethnic, racial, religious, and cultural backgrounds learn about Canadian values and customs. It is also through the schools that persons from such diverse backgrounds learn English or French, the nature of the Canadian parliamentary system, and the basic workings of our economic institutions.

Of the various aims that the schools have, achievement is the most universally agreed on. For most people, the primary purpose of schools is to impart to students the academic knowledge and skills that will prepare them either for additional schooling or for the world of work. Regardless of political ideology, religious beliefs, and cultural values, people want their schools to teach academic content.

Education for Personal Growth and Societal Improvement

Society places great value on the dignity and worth of the individual. Accordingly, one aim of schools is to enable the young to become all that they are capable of becoming. Unlike socialization or achievement, the emphasis on personal growth puts the individual first, society second. According to this view, the desired outcomes of education go beyond achievement to include the development of a positive self-concept and interpersonal skills, or what psychologist Daniel Goleman has termed "**emotional intelligence.**" According to Goleman (1997, 1998), schools should emphasize five

Table 5.1

What are the most important criteria for measuring school effectiveness?

	Very Important %	Somewhat Important %	Not Very Important %	Not at All Important %	Don't Know %
Percentage of students who graduate from high school	82	14	2	1	1
Percentage of high school graduates who practice good citizenship	79	15	3	1	2
Percentage of high school graduates who go on to college or junior college	71	24	3	1	1
Percentage who graduate from college or junior college	69	25	3	1	2
Percentage of graduates who get jobs after completing high school	63	28	5	2	2
Scores that students receive on standardized tests	50	34	9	3	4

Source: L. C. Rose and A. M. Gallup, "The 30th Annual Phi Delta Kappa/Gallup Poll of the Public's Attitudes toward the Public Schools," *Phi Delta Kappan,* September 1998, p. 48.

dimensions of emotional intelligence: self-awareness, handling emotions, motivation, empathy, and social skills. Emotional intelligence is essential for achievement in school, job success, marital happiness, and physical health; it enables students to live independently and to seek out the "good" life according to their own values, needs, and wants. The knowledge and skills students acquire at schools are seen as enabling them to achieve personal growth and self-actualization.

Schools also provide students with the knowledge and skills to improve society and the quality of life and to adapt to rapid social change. Naturally, there exists a wide range of opinions about how society might be improved. Some teachers, like Jeff, Sue, and Bret in this chapter's opening scenario, believe that one purpose of schooling is to address social problems such as violence in society; while other teachers, such as their friend, Nancy, believe schools should teach academic content and not try to change society. However, as James Banks (1999, 4) suggests, "Education within a pluralistic society should affirm and help students understand their home and community cultures. [To] create and maintain a civic community that works for the common good, education in a democratic society should help students acquire the knowledge, attitudes, and skills needed to participate in civic action to make society more equitable and just."

How Can Schools Be Described?

Given the wide variation in schools and their cultures, many models have been proposed for describing the distinguishing characteristics of schools. Schools can be categorized according to the focus of their curricula; for example, high schools might be college preparatory, vocational, or general. Another way to view schools is according to their organizational structure; for example, elementary (K–5), middle school (6–8), or high school (9–12).

Other models view schools metaphorically; that is, what is a school like? Some schools, for example, have been compared to factories; students enter the school as raw material, move through the curriculum in a systematic way, and exit the school as finished products. Terrence Deal and Kent Peterson (1999, 21) have suggested that exemplary schools "become like tribes or clans, with deep ties among people and with values and traditions that give meaning to everyday life." Others have suggested that schools are like banks, gardens, prisons, mental hospitals, homes, churches, families, and teams.

In the school-as-family metaphor, for example, the effective school is a caring community of adults who attend to the academic, emotional, social, and physical needs of the children and youth entrusted to their care.

Schools and Social Class

In spite of a general consensus that schools should promote social improvement and equal opportunity, some individuals believe that schools "reproduce" the existing society by presenting different curricula and educational experiences to students from different socio-economic classes. Students at a school in an affluent suburb, for example, may study chemistry in a well-equipped lab and take a field trip to a high-tech industry to see the latest application of chemical research, while students attending a school in another school district may learn chemistry from out-of-date texts, have no adequate lab in which to conduct experiments, and have limited opportunities for field trips because the school district has more limited funding. Schools, in effect, preserve the stratification within society and maintain the differences between the "haves" and the "have-nots." As Joel Spring puts it: "the affluent members of ... society can protect the educational advantages and, consequently, economic advantages, of their children by living in affluent school districts or by using private [independent] schools. Their children will attend the elite institutions of higher education, and their privileged educational background will make it easy for them to follow in the footsteps of their parents' financial success" (Spring 1999, 290–91).

What Are Schools Like As Social Institutions?

Schools are social institutions. An **institution** is an organization established by society to maintain and improve its way of life. Schools are the institutions our society has established for the purpose of educating the young. During the last 200 years, Canadian schools have developed complex structures, policies, and curricula to accomplish this mission. "The Institutional Structure of Education in Canada" is shown in Figure 5.1.

The School As a Reflection of Society

As you might expect, schools mirror the national, provincial/territorial culture and surrounding local culture and other special interests. Independent and parochial schools,

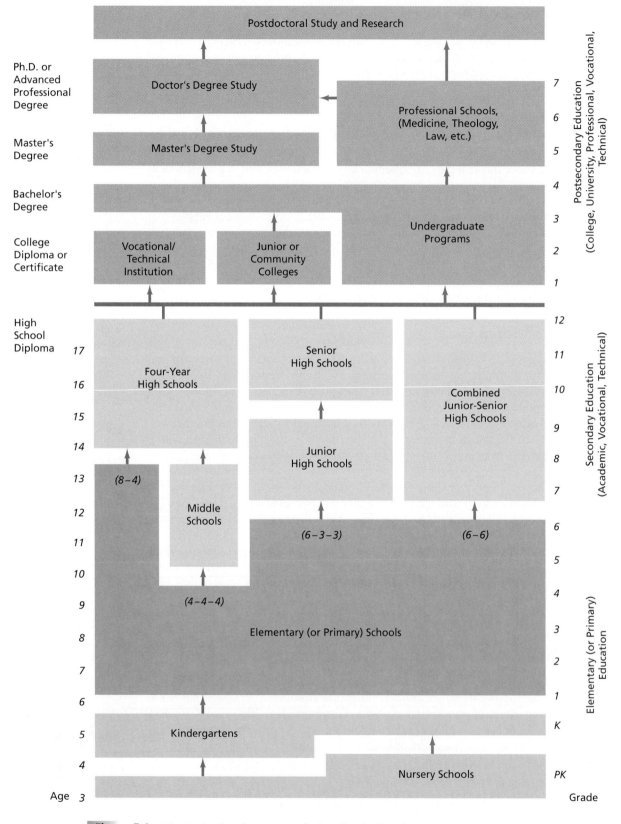

Figure 5.1 The institutional structure of education in Canada

for example, are often maintained by groups that see the school as a means of perpetuating their preferred way of life. Nevertheless, as Mary Henry (1993, 29) points out, "Schools are ... not simply puppets of the dominant mainstream society. They have their own unique concerns and their own 'poetry' of people and events. Whether public or private, all schools are not the same."

Rural, Suburban, and Urban Schools

Schools also reflect their location. Schools in rural, urban, and suburban settings often have significantly different cultures. Rural schools are often the focal point for community life and reflect values and beliefs that tend to be more conservative than those associated with urban and suburban schools. While the small size of a rural school may contribute to the development of a family-like culture, its small size may also make it difficult to provide students with an array of curricular experiences equal to that found at larger schools in more populated areas. In contrast, large suburban or urban schools may provide students with more varied learning experiences, but these schools may lack the cohesiveness and community focus of rural schools.

Schools and Community Environments

The differences among the environments that surround schools can be enormous. Urban schools, especially if located in less affluent districts, may reflect the social problems of the surrounding area. Middle-class families who can afford to, move away from such urban areas or place their children in independent schools. As a result, students in some urban school districts are increasingly from low-income backgrounds.

Though some communities may impact their schools in undesirable ways, many teachers at such schools find their work professionally stimulating and growth-enhancing. As one teacher said:

> In what ways do schools reflect their communities and the wider Canadian society? What difference might the community make for this school? for the students who attend it? for the teachers who work there?

I taught in two different environments — middle school in an inner city and high school in a more rural area. I think that combination was the experience that made me become a teacher. When I did my student teaching, I enjoyed it so much, and I realized I had a knack for it. When recruiters looked at my résumé, they were impressed that I had two different experiences I could draw from and elaborate on. I know that's how I got my job (Sallie Mae Corporation 1995, 8).

The Culture of the School

Although schools are very much alike, each school is unique. Each has a culture of its own—a network of beliefs, values and traditions, and ways of thinking and behaving that distinguishes it from other schools.

Much like a community, a school has a distinctive culture—a collective way of life. Terms that have been used to describe **school culture** include *climate, ethos, atmosphere,* and *character.* Some schools may be characterized as community-like places where there is a shared sense of purpose and commitment to providing the best education possible for all students. Other schools lack a unified sense of purpose or direction and drift, rudderless, from year to year. Still others are characterized by internal conflict and divisiveness and may even reflect what Deal and Peterson (1999) term a "toxic" school culture; students, teachers, administrators, and parents may feel that the school is not sufficiently meeting their needs.

The Physical Environment

The physical environment of the school both reflects and helps to create the school's overall culture. Displays of student art, trophy cabinets, bulletin boards with a sections for "Student of the Week" and newspaper clippings highlighting school activities or accomplishments all play in the creation of a school's culture. "Whether school buildings are squeezed between other buildings or located on sprawling campuses, their fenced-in area or other physical separation distinguishes them from the community-at-large" (Ballantine 1997, 210). Some schools are dreary places or, at best, aesthetically bland. The tile floors, concrete block walls, long, straight corridors, and rows of fluorescent lights often found in these schools contribute little to their inhabitants' sense of beauty, concern for others, or personal comfort.

Other schools are much more attractive. They are clean, pleasant, and inviting; and teachers and students take pride in their building. Overall, the physical environment has a positive impact on those who spend time in the school; it encourages learning and a spirit of cohesiveness.

Formal Practices of Schools

The formal practices of schools are well known to anyone who has been educated in Canadian schools. With some exceptions, students attend school from five or six years of age through sixteen at least, and usually to eighteen, Monday through Friday, September through June, for twelve or thirteen years. For the most part, students are assigned to a grade level on the basis of age rather than ability or interest. Assignment to individual classes or teachers at a given grade level, however, may be made on the basis of ability or interest.

Teachers and students are grouped in several ways in the elementary school and in one dominant pattern in junior and senior high school. At the elementary school level, the **self-contained classroom** is the most traditional and prevalent arrangement. In this type of classroom, one teacher teaches all or nearly all subjects to a group of about 25 children, with the teacher and students remaining in the same classroom for the entire day. Often art, music, physical education, and computer skills are taught in other parts of the school, so students may leave the classroom for scheduled periods. Individual students may also attend special classes for remedial or advanced instruction, speech therapy, or instrumental music and band lessons.

In **open-space schools**, students are free to move among various activities and learning centres. Instead of self-contained classrooms, open-space schools have large instructional areas with movable walls and furniture that can be rearranged easily. Grouping for instruction is much more fluid and varied. Students do much of their work independently, with a number of teachers providing individual guidance as needed.

In middle schools and junior and senior high schools, students frequently study four or five academic subjects taught by teachers who specialize in them. In this organizational arrangement, called **departmentalization**, students move from classroom to classroom for their lessons. High school teachers often share their classrooms with other teachers and use their rooms only during scheduled class periods.

School Traditions

School traditions are those elements of a school's culture that are handed down from year to year. The traditions of a school reflect what students, teachers, administrators, parents, and the surrounding community believe is important and valuable about the school. One school, for example, may have developed a tradition of excellence in academic programs; another school's traditions may emphasize the performing arts; and yet another may focus on athletic programs. Whatever a school's traditions, they are usually a source of pride for members of the school community.

Ideally, traditions are the glue that holds together the diverse elements of a school's culture. They combine to create a sense of community, identity, and trust among people affiliated with a school. Traditions are maintained through stories that are handed down, rituals and ceremonial activities, student productions, and trophies and artifacts that have been collected over the years.

The Culture of the Classroom

Just as schools develop their unique cultures, each classroom develops its own culture or way of life. The culture of a classroom is determined in large measure by the manner in which teacher and students participate in common activities. An additional factor is the variety of cultural, ethnic, and linguistic groups represented within some classrooms. In Canada's larger urban areas it is not uncommon for an individual school to have students from as many as 50 different cultural, ethnic, or linguistic groups. In addition, "the environment of the classroom and the inhabitants of that environment—students and teachers—are constantly interacting. Each aspect of the classroom affects all others. (Woolfolk, 1998, 440) Indeed, as any teacher can attest, the addition, or removal, of as few as one or two students from a class's roll can positively or negatively affect the classroom's culture.

The quality of teacher–student interactions is influenced by the physical characteristics of the setting (classroom, use of space, materials, resources, etc.) and the social dimensions of the group (norms, rules, expectations, cohesiveness, distribution of power and influence). These elements interact to shape **classroom culture**. Teachers who appreciate the importance of these salient elements of classroom culture are more likely to create environments that they and their students find satisfying and growth-promoting. For example, during the second month of student teaching in Grade 2, "Miss Martin" reflects on her efforts to create classroom culture characterized by positive teacher–student interactions:

I started off with a big mistake. I tried to be their friend. I tried joining with them in all the jokes and laughter that cut into instruction time. When this didn't work, I overcompensated by yelling at them when I needed them to quiet down and get to work. I wasn't comfortable with this situation. I did not think it was like me to raise my voice at a child. I knew I needed to consider how they felt. I realized that if I were them, I'd hate me, I really would. In desperation, I turned to my education textbooks for advice.

This was a huge help to me, but a book can only guide you. It can't establish a personality for you or even manage your classroom for you. You have to do that yourself and as lovingly and effectively as possible. But I had so much trouble finding a middle ground: love them, guide them, talk to them, manage them, but don't control them (Rand and Shelton-Colangelo 1999, 8–9).

Similarly, a beginning teacher at an experimental school describes the classroom culture she wants to create: "What I'm trying to get to in my classroom is that they have power. I'm trying to allow students to have power—to know what their knowledge is and to learn to create their own ideas as opposed to my being the one who is the only holder of ideas in the universe. I want to transfer the authority back to them" (Dollase 1992, 101). The efforts of this teacher to create an empowering classroom culture were supported by the culture of the school itself: "Because her comments reflect the prevailing view of this small, neo-progressive public school, she is able to implement her philosophy in her upper-level middle school classroom. [T]he structure of the school and the organization of the school day, which permits more personalization and more time with each class, are school variables that allow her a chance to succeed in redefining the authority relationships in her class" (Dollase 1992, 101).

How Is Cultural Diversity Represented in Canadian Schools?

The percentage of ethnic minorities in Canadian schools has been growing steadily since the end of World War II. According to Statistics Canada's report on the census of 2001, 18.4 percent of Canada's population was born in other countries, the highest percentage of any country except for Australia. Statistics Canada also reports that 94 percent of these new citizens settled in large urban areas, with Montreal, Toronto, and Vancouver accounting for 73 percent of the total (Statistics Canada 2001b). (Table 5.2 provides a list of the most common ethnic origins.)

Clearly, the increasing **diversity** of Canadian society has extensive implications for schools. There is, for example, an increased demand for English as a Second Language (ESL) programs and teachers. All but a few school districts face a critical shortage of minority teachers. As well, there is a need to develop curricula and strategies that address the needs and backgrounds of all students—regardless of their social class, gender, sexual orientation, or ethnic, racial, or cultural identity.

The Meaning of Culture

Culture is *the way of life* common to a group of people. It consists of the values, attitudes, and beliefs that influence their traditions and behaviour. It is also a way of interacting with and looking at the world. Though at one time it was believed that Canada was a "melting pot" in which ethnic cultures would melt into one, ethnic and cultural differences have remained very much a part of life in Canada. A "salad-bowl"

Table 5.2

Population by selected ethnic origins, Canada

Definitions and notes	2001		
	Total responses	Single responses	Multiple responses
	Number	Number	Number
Total population Ethnic origin	**29 639 035**	**18 307 545**	**11 331 490**
Canadian	11 682 680	6 748 135	4 934 545
English	5 978 875	1 479 525	4 499 355
French	4 668 410	1 060 760	3 607 655
Scottish	4 157 210	607 235	3 549 975
Irish	3 822 660	496 865	3 325 795
German	2 742 765	705 600	2 037 170
Italian	1 270 370	726 275	544 090
Chinese	1 094 700	936 210	158 490
Ukrainian	1 071 060	326 195	744 860
North American Indian	1 000 890	455 805	545 085
Dutch (Netherlands)	923 310	316 220	607 090
Polish	817 085	260 415	556 665
East Indian	713 330	581 665	131 665
Norwegian	363 760	47 230	316 530
Portuguese	357 690	252 835	104 855
Welsh	350 365	28 445	321 920
Jewish	348 605	186 475	162 130
Russian	337 960	70 895	267 070
Filipino	327 550	266 140	61 405
Metis	307 845	72 210	235 635
Swedish	282 760	30 440	252 325
Hungarian (Magyar)	267 255	91 800	175 455
American (USA)	250 005	25 205	224 805
Greek	215 105	143 785	71 325
Spanish	213 105	66 545	146 555
Jamaican	211 720	138 180	73 545
Danish	170 780	33 795	136 985
Vietnamese	151 410	119 120	32 290

Source: Statistics Canada: Census 2001. Retrieved April 10, 2003 from www.statcan.ca/english/Pgdb/demo28a.htm. Reproduced with the permission of the Minister of Public Works and Services.

analogy more accurately captures the multicultural diversity of Canadian society. That is, the distinguishing characteristics of cultures tend be preserved and valued rather than blended into a single monoculture. An **ethnic group** is made up of individuals within a larger culture who share a self-defined racial or cultural identity and a set of beliefs, attitudes, and values. Members of an ethnic group distinguish themselves from others in the society by physical and social attributes. In addition, you should be aware that the composition of ethnic groups can change over time and there is often as much variability within groups as between them. The biological concept of **race** suggests that there are natural, physical variations among humans that are hereditary, reflected in body shape and/or skin coloration, and identifiable by terms such as Negroid, Caucasoid, and Mongoloid. While most individuals have a personal concept of what constitutes race, this issue is a complicated one that goes far beyond the scope of this text.

Dimensions of Culture

Within Canada, we find cultural groups that differ according to other distinguishing factors, such as religion, politics, economics, and geographic region. The regional culture of Newfoundland, for example, is quite different from that of Alberta. Similarly, British Columbians are culturally different from *les québécois*. However, everyone in Canada does share some common dimensions of culture. James Banks, an authority on multicultural education, has termed this shared culture the "national macro-culture" (Banks 1999). In addition to being members of the national macro-culture, people in Canada are often members of specific ethnic groups.

Students in today's classrooms have diverse cultural identities. As a teacher, what steps will you take to integrate *all* students into the classroom?

Cultural Identity

In addition to membership in the Canadian macro-culture, each individual participates in an array of subcultures, each with its customs and beliefs. Collectively, these subcultures determine an individual's **cultural identity**, an overall sense of who one is. Other possible elements that might shape a person's cultural identity include age, racial identity, exceptionalities, language, gender, sexual orientation, income level, and beliefs and values. These elements have different significances for different people. For example, the cultural identity of some people is most strongly determined by their occupations; for others by their ethnicity; and for others by their religious beliefs.

Remember that your future students will have their own complex cultural identities, which are no less valid for being different. For some of them, these identities may make them feel "disconnected" from the attitudes, expectations, and values conveyed by the school. For example:

Students who come from homes where languages other than English are the medium of communication, who share customs and beliefs unique to their cultural community and/or home countries, or who face the range of challenges posed by economic insecurity will not often find much of their family, community, or national existence reflected in the school setting. Often these students feel that school is itself foreign, alienating, and unrelated to their beliefs and concerns (Rice and Walsh 1996, 9).

As a teacher, you will be challenged to understand the subtle differences in cultural identities among your students and to create a learning environment that enables all students to feel comfortable in school and "connected to" their school experiences.

Language and Culture

Culture is embedded in language, a fact that has sometimes resulted in historical conflicts between the English and French-speaking groups in our society. While Canadians generally support the preservation of ethnic cultures, most believe that new immigrants should learn one of the two official languages, English and French, if they are to function effectively within Canadian society. While the types of English as a Second Language (ESL) programs vary from one jurisdiction to another, Figure 5.2 contains most of the variants. Interestingly, Statistics Canada reports in its 2001 article, "Census: Ethnocultural portrait: Canada," that its Longitudinal Survey of Children and Youth indicates that, over time, children with immigrant parents "caught up to, and sometimes surpassed, the academic performance of their classmates with Canadian-born parents."

Advice for Monolingual Teachers

Teachers must continue to meet the needs of language-minority students. These needs are best met by teachers who speak their native language as well as English. However, this is often not possible, and monolingual teachers, particularly those in large urban areas, will find increasing numbers of such students in their classrooms.

Four Types of Bilingual Education Programs

Immersion programs: Students learn English and other subjects in classrooms where only English is spoken. Aides who speak the first language of students are sometimes available, or students may also listen to equivalent audiotaped lessons in their first language.

Transition programs: Students receive reading lessons in their first language and lessons in English as a Second Language (ESL). Once they sufficiently master English, students are placed in classrooms where English is spoken and their first language is discontinued.

Pull-out programs: On a regular basis, students are separated from English-speaking students so that they may receive lessons in English or reading lessons in their first language. These are sometimes called sheltered English programs.

Maintenance programs: To maintain the student's native language and culture, instruction in English and instruction in the native language are provided from Kindergarten through Grade 12. Students become literate.

Figure 5.2

Four types of bilingual education programs

The Concept of Multiculturalism

Multiculturalism is a set of beliefs based on the importance of seeing the world from different cultural frames of reference and on recognizing and valuing the rich array of cultures within a nation and within the global community. For teachers, multiculturalism affirms the need to create schools where differences related to race, ethnicity, gender, disability, and social class are acknowledged and all students are viewed as valuable members and as human resources for enriching the teaching–learning process. Furthermore, a central purpose of teaching, according to the multiculturalist view, is to prepare students to live in a culturally pluralistic world—a world that "contrasts sharply with cultural assimilation, or 'melting pot' images, where ethnic minorities are expected to give up their traditions and blend in or be absorbed by the mainstream society or predominant culture" (Bennett 1999, 11).

Stereotyping and Racism

Although teachers should expand their knowledge of and appreciation for the diverse cultural backgrounds of their students, they should also guard against forming stereotypes or overgeneralizations about those cultures. **Stereotyping** is the process of attributing behavioural characteristics to all members of a group. In some cases, stereotypes are formed on the basis of limited experiences with and information about the group being stereotyped, and the validity of these stereotypes is not questioned.

Within any cultural group that shares a broad cultural heritage, however, considerable diversity exists. For example, two Asian-Canadian children who live in the same community and attend the same school may appear alike to their teachers when, in reality, they are very different. One may come from a home where Mandarin is spoken and Chinese holidays are observed; the other may be Vietnamese, speak no language but English, and observe only Canada's official holidays.

To help immigrant students adjust to Canadian culture, Qiu Liang offers teachers the following advice based on his school experiences as a Chinese immigrant:

> They [teachers] should be more patient [with an immigrant child] because it is very difficult for a person to be in a new country and learn a new language. Have patience.

> If the teacher feels there is no hope in an immigrant child, then the child will think, "Well, if the teacher who's helping me thinks that I can't go anywhere, then I might as well give up myself" (Igoa 1995, 99–100).

Similarly, Dung Yoong offers these recommendations based on her educational experiences as a Vietnamese immigrant:

> Try to get them to talk to you. Not just everyday conversation, but what they feel inside. Try to get them to get that out, because it's hard for kids. They don't trust—I had a hard time trusting and I was really insecure because of that.

> [P]utting an immigrant child who doesn't speak English into a classroom, a regular classroom with Canadian students, is not very good. It scares [them] because it is so different. [Teachers] should start [them] slowly and have special classes where the child could adapt and learn a little bit about Canadian society and customs (Igoa 1995, 103).

In addition to being alert for stereotypes they and others may hold, teachers should learn to recognize **individual racism**, the prejudicial belief that one's ethnic or racial group is superior to others, and **institutional racism**, "established laws, customs, and practices which systematically reflect and produce racial inequalities in Canadian society ... whether or not the individuals maintaining those practices have racist intentions" (Jones 1981, 118).

As a teacher, you will not be able to eliminate stereotypic thinking or racism in society. However, you have an obligation to all your students to see that your curriculum and instruction are free of any forms of stereotyping or racism. To provide equal educational opportunity to all students means that teachers and schools promote the full development of students as individuals, without regard for race, ethnicity, gender, sexual orientation, socio-economic status, abilities, or disabilities. More specifically, educators fulfill this important mission by continually evaluating the appropriateness of the curricular and instructional experiences they provide to each student. The following Professional Reflection will help you examine, and possibly reassess, your cultural attitudes and values and determine whether you have stereotypes about other cultural groups.

Professional Reflection   Reflecting on your cultural identity

In a Teacher's Journal entry, describe your cultural identity. Who are you? What beliefs, customs, and attitudes are part of your culture? Which of these are most important to your cultural identity?

Next, think of the ethnic and cultural groups in Canada with which you are unfamiliar. When you become a teacher, some of your students may be from these groups. What are some stereotypes about these groups that you tend to believe? How might these stereotypes influence your teaching and teaching effectiveness? How will you test or change your beliefs as part of the process of becoming a teacher?

What Is Multicultural Education?

Multicultural education is committed to the goal of providing all students—regardless of socioeconomic status, gender, sexual orientation or ethnic, racial, or cultural backgrounds—with equal opportunities to learn in school. Multicultural education is also based on the fact that students do not learn in a vacuum—their culture predisposes them to learn in certain ways. And finally, multicultural education recognizes that current school practices have provided, and continue to provide, some students with greater opportunities for learning than students who belong to other groups.

Dimensions of Multicultural Education

According to James A. Banks, "Multicultural education is a complex and multidimensional concept" (Banks 1999, 13). More specifically, Banks suggests that multicultural education may be conceptualized as consisting of five dimensions: (1) content integration, (2) knowledge construction, (3) prejudice reduction, (4) an equity pedagogy, and

(5) an empowering school culture (see Figure 5.3). As you progress through your teacher education program and eventually begin to prepare curriculum materials and instructional strategies for your multicultural classroom, remember that integrating content from a variety of cultural groups is just one dimension of multicultural education. Multicultural education is not "something that is done at a certain time slot in the school day where children eat with chopsticks or listen to Peruvian music ... [it is] something that is infused throughout the school culture and practiced daily" (Henry 1996, 108).

Multicultural education promotes students' positive self-identity and pride in their heritage, acceptance of people from diverse backgrounds, and critical self-assessment. In addition, multicultural education can prompt students, perhaps with guidance from their teachers, to take action against prejudice and discrimination within their school. Indeed, as Joel Spring says, "multicultural education should create a spirit of tolerance and activism in students. An understanding of other cultures and of differing cultural frames of reference will ... spark students to actively work for social justice" (Spring 1998, 163). For example, students might reduce the marginalization of minority-group students in their school by inviting them to participate in extracurricular and after-school activities.

Figure 5.3

Banks' dimensions of multicultural education

Source: From James A. Banks, and Cherry A. McGee Banks. *Multicultural Education: Issues and Perspectives,* 3rd ed. Copyright © 1997 by Allyn & Bacon. Reprinted by permission, p. 24.

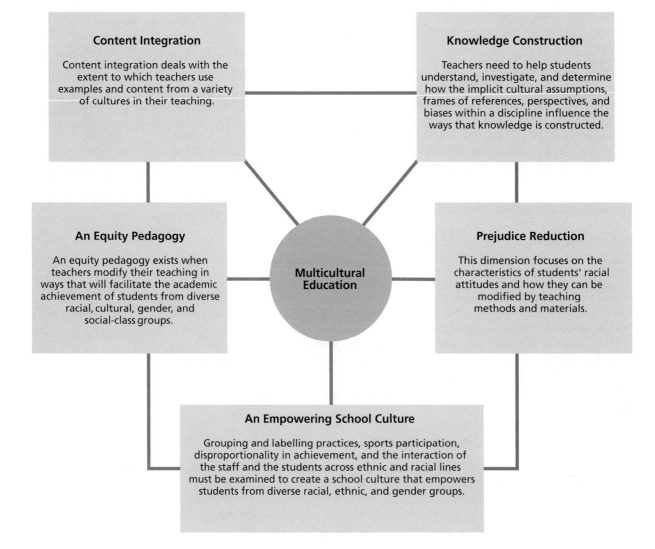

Teaching for Excellence

Prime Minister's Award for Teaching Excellence Recipients: Marie Louise Mastromonaco and Sharon Davis

Marie Louise Mastromonaco
Bishop Grandin High School, Calgary, Alberta
Subjects taught: Grades 10 to 12,
English as a Second Language (ESL)

Mrs. Mastromonaco created partnership programs that allow ESL students to work together and with community organizations to enhance their learning and discover opportunities for their future lives. More than 55 percent of ESL students now take part in these programs.

She developed adjunct classes tailored to help ESL students in mainstream English and social studies courses. Beginning with six students in 1999–2000, the program has already more than doubled in size, and participants have shown a marked improvement in their grades.

The Volunteer Host and Tutor program has had the same enthusiastic response. In the first semester of 2001–2002, 24 ESL students were paired with 28 tutors.

Mrs. Mastromonaco created special teaching units to help ESL students understand Canadian history and culture, including *Immigrants All*, *Spirit of the West* (in which she took part in a five-day cattle drive) and *Along the River's Edge* (an interactive unit on Calgary's early history).

> I have never met a teacher with such passion for teaching and caring for students until I met you.
> —*Former student*

> A lifelong commitment to improving each child's destiny is a major accomplishment by any measure. Mrs. Mastromonaco's outstanding contributions live on in her students who now call Canada home.
> —*Department head*

Sharon Davis
Jack Hulland Elementary School, Whitehorse, Yukon
Subjects taught: Counsellor, Kindergarten to Grade 7

Because Mrs. Davis has worked so long in the community, she has built a legacy of trust that enables her to bridge relations, particularly in the First Nations community, and provide a valuable historical perspective on conflicts in the school. She has done the following:

- Developed class meetings in which students raise problems and concerns. Students learn appropriate communications, conflict resolution and problem-solving skills, among others.
- Introduced Family Group Conferencing, a restorative justice program used as an alternative to suspension if parents wish, and as a vehicle for solving interpersonal conflict and dealing with bullying.
- Interaction problems needing to be referred to the office have declined during her tenure, and fights and incidents of bullying are almost non-existent.
- Students solve their own problems. Recently, a group of students asked Mrs. Davis to help them sort out a conflict. As they sat down in her office, one said, "You know what Mrs. Davis? I think we can solve this on our own."

> "What distinguishes Sharon from others "just doing their job" is her tireless dedication to her school community and that she genuinely cares."
> —*School Council member*

> "Mrs. Davis is the nicest person I have ever met. She makes us feel better and helps us all at work. She is there when we are sad and she helps us separate fights."
> —*Student*

Source: Government of Canada (2001). Prime Minister's awards for teaching excellence: Exemplary practices. Retrieved October 3, 2003 from http://pma-ppm.ic.gc.ca/bio01-e.asp?prov=al

Multicultural Curricula

As a teacher you will teach students who historically have not received full educational opportunity—students from the many racial and ethnic minority groups in Canada, students from low-income families or communities, students with exceptional abilities or disabilities, students who are gay or lesbian, and students who are male or female.

You will face the challenge of reaching out to all students and teaching them that they are persons of worth who can learn.

In your diverse classroom your aim is not to develop a different curriculum for each group of students—that would be impossible and would place undue emphasis on differences among students. Rather, your curriculum should help increase students' awareness and appreciation of the rich diversity in Canadian culture. A **multicultural curriculum** addresses the needs and backgrounds of all students regardless of their cultural identity. As Banks suggests, the multicultural curriculum "enable[s] students to derive valid generalizations and theories about the characteristics of ethnic groups and to learn how they are alike and different, in both their past and present experiences.... [It] focus[es] on a range of groups that *differ* in their racial characteristics, cultural experiences, languages, histories, values, and current problems" (Banks 1997, 15). Teachers who provide multicultural education recognize the importance of asking questions such as those posed by Valerie Ooka Pang: "Why is a child's home language important to keep? What strengths does culture give children? What impact does culture have on learning? What does racism, sexism, or classism look like in schools?" (Pang 1994, 292).

In developing a multicultural curriculum, you should be sensitive to how your instructional materials and strategies can be made more inclusive so that they reflect cultural perspectives, or "voices," that previously have been silent or marginalized in discussions about what should be taught in schools and how it should be taught. "Non-dominant groups representing diversity in the school whose voices traditionally have not been heard include those defined by race, language, gender, sexual orientation, alternative family structures, social class, disability, bilingualism, and those with alien or refugee status" (Henry 1996, 108). Effective teachers attend to these previously unheard voices not as an act of tokenism but with a genuine desire to make the curriculum more inclusive and to "create space for alternative voices, not just on the periphery but in the center" (Singer 1994, 286).

Multicultural Instructional Materials and Strategies

To create classrooms that are truly multicultural, teachers must select instructional materials that are sensitive, accurately portray the contributions of ethnic groups, and reflect diverse points of view. Teachers must also recognize that "[s]ome of the books and other materials on ethnic groups published each year are insensitive, inaccurate, and written from mainstream and insensitive perspectives and points of view" (Banks 1997, 124). Some guidelines for selecting multicultural instructional materials follow.

- Books and other materials should accurately portray the perspectives, attitudes, and feelings of ethnic groups.
- Fictional works should have strong ethnic characters.
- Books should describe settings and experiences with which all students can identify and yet should accurately reflect ethnic cultures and lifestyles.
- The protagonists in books with ethnic themes should have ethnic characteristics but should face conflicts and problems universal to all cultures and groups.
- The illustrations in books should be accurate, ethnically sensitive, and technically well done.
- Ethnic materials should not contain racist concepts, clichés, phrases, or words.
- Factual materials should be historically accurate.

- Multiethnic resources and basal textbooks should discuss major events and documents related to ethnic history (Banks 1997, 125–26).

Yvonne Wilson, an elementary teacher from our aboriginal community, points out that a teacher's willingness to learn about other cultures is very important to students and their parents:

> People in the community know if you are trying to understand their culture. Students also see it. Becoming involved—going to a powwow or participating in other cultural events—shows people that here is a teacher who is trying to learn about our culture.

Participating wholeheartedly in cross-cultural experiences will help you to grow in the eight areas outlined in Figure 5.4 as essential for successful teaching in a diverse society.

Figure 5.4

Essential knowledge and skills for successful teaching in a diverse society

Source: Adapted from Forrest W. Parkay and Henry T. Fillmer, "Improving Teachers' Attitudes toward Minority-Group Students: An Experiential Approach to Multicultural Inservice," *New Horizons Journal of Education* (November 1984), pp. 178–79.

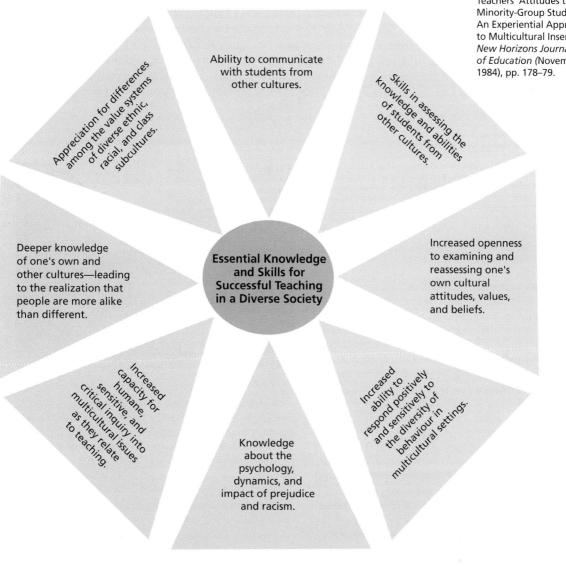

Ability to communicate with students from other cultures.

Skills in assessing the knowledge and abilities of students from other cultures.

Appreciation for differences among the value systems of diverse ethnic, racial, and class subcultures.

Essential Knowledge and Skills for Successful Teaching in a Diverse Society

Increased openness to examining and reassessing one's own cultural attitudes, values, and beliefs.

Deeper knowledge of one's own and other cultures—leading to the realization that people are more alike than different.

Increased capacity for humane, sensitive, and critical inquiry into multicultural issues as they relate to teaching.

Knowledge about the psychology, dynamics, and impact of prejudice and racism.

Increased ability to respond positively and sensitively to the diversity of behaviour in multicultural settings.

How Is Gender a Dimension of Multicultural Education?

Though it may be evident that gender affects students' learning in many ways, it may not be evident that gender is an important dimension of multicultural education. However, as Tozer, Violas, and Senese point out:

> Traditional definitions of culture have centered around the formal expression of a people's common existence—language, art, music, and so forth. If culture is more broadly defined to include such things as ways of knowing, ways of relating to others, ways of negotiating rights and privileges, and modes of conduct, thought, and expression, then the term "culture" applies not only to ethnic groups but to people grouped on the basis of gender. [G]ender entails cultural as well as physiological dimensions (Tozer, Violas, and Senese 1993, 310).

Gender Differences

Cultural differences between males and females are partially shaped by society's traditional expectations of them. Through **sex role stereotyping**, families, the media, the schools, and other powerful social forces condition boys and girls to act in certain ways regardless of abilities or interests. As we mentioned previously, one of the aims of schools is to socialize students to participate in society. One dimension of the **sex role socialization** process sometimes conveys to students certain expectations about the way boys and girls are "supposed" to act. We used to suggest that girls are supposed to

 technology

highlights

Does gender equity exist in the use of educational technology?

Considerable evidence indicates that boys tend to have more experience with and positive attitudes toward computer technology than girls (Bitter and Pierson 1999; Comber et al 1997; Hammett 1997; Valenza 1997; Whitley 1997). In addition, boys participate in more elective technology courses and activities than girls. A partial explanation for this difference may stem from the fact that "Software generally tends to emphasize male-dominated activities. Games often include violence and competition as motivation. These software characteristics tend to attract males" (Bitter and Pierson 1999, 240). Also, some computer software and online advertisements promote gender stereotypes (Knupfer 1998). In addition, Cornelia Brunner and Dorothy Bennett (1997) suggest that the attitude of girls toward technology might reflect a tendency in schools to celebrate the speed and power of the machine (the "masculine view") rather than the social function of technology (the "feminine view").

In any case, as the use of technologies continues to become more widespread in society and schools, teachers must make a special effort to ensure that girls have equal access to technology and that their technology-related experiences are positive and growth-enhancing. What steps will you take to ensure that your use of technology reflects gender equity? How will you encourage your students, regardless of gender, to acquire additional knowledge and skills with computers?

play with dolls, boys with trucks. It was also believed that girls are supposed to be passive, boys active. Girls are supposed to express their feelings and emotions when in pain, boys to repress their feelings and deny pain.

Students may be socialized into particular gender-specific roles as a result of the curriculum materials they use at school. By portraying males in more dominant, assertive ways and portraying females in ways that suggest that they are passive and helpless, textbooks can subtly reinforce expectations about the way girls and boys "should" behave. Within the last few decades, though, publishers of curriculum materials have become more vigilant about avoiding these stereotypes.

In the mid-1990s, however, some gender equity studies had more mixed findings. In their analysis of data on achievement and engagement of 9000 Grade 8 boys and girls, researchers Valerie Lee, Xianglei Chen, and Becky A. Smerdon concluded that "the pattern of gender differences is inconsistent. In some cases, females are favored; in others males are favored" (Lee, Chen, and Smerdon 1996). Similarly, Larry Hedges and Amy Nowell found in their study of 32 years of mental tests given to boys and girls that, while boys do better than girls in science and mathematics, they were "at a rather profound disadvantage" in writing and scored below girls in reading comprehension (Hedges 1996, 3).

Why and in what ways does gender bias persist in many Canadian classrooms and schools?

Additional research and closer analyses of earlier reports on gender bias in education were beginning to suggest that boys, not girls, were most "shortchanged" by the schools (Sommers, 1996). Numerous articles as well as a 1999 PBS series that began with a program titled "The War on Boys" challenged the conclusions of the earlier AAUW report, *How Schools Shortchange Girls*. Other commentary discounted gender bias in the schools as a fabrication of radical feminism; among the first to put forth this view was Christina Hoff Sommers' (1994) controversial book, *Who Stole Feminism? How Women Have Betrayed Women*; and, more recently, Judith Kleinfeld's (1998) *The Myth That Schools Shortchange Girls: Social Science in the Service of Deception* and Cathy Young's (1999) *Ceasefire!*

To examine gender issues in the public schools, and to shed light on gender differences in academic achievement, Warren Willingham and Nancy Cole (1997) conducted a seminal study of the scores of 15 million United States students in the fourth, eighth, and twelfth grades on hundreds of standardized exams used by schools and college placement exams such as the SAT. Contrary to long-standing assumptions that there are pronounced differences between the performance of males and females on standardized tests, their study found that "There is not a dominant picture of one gender excelling over the other and, in fact, the average performance difference across all subjects is essentially zero." Boys and girls, Willingham and Cole found, were fairly evenly matched in verbal and abstract reasoning, math computation, and the social sciences. The superiority of boys in math and science was found to be surprisingly slight and "significantly smaller than 30 years ago." Boys were found to have a clear advantage in mechanical and electronic ability and knowledge of economics and history, while girls had a clear advantage in language skills, especially writing, and a "moderate edge" in short-term memory and perceptual speed. Furthermore, the authors concluded that gender differences in test scores are not the result of bias in the exams; instead, the differences are genuine and would be reflected also in more carefully designed tests.

However, in 2002 the Council of Ministers of Education, Canada (CMEC), as part of its School Achievement Indicators Program (SAIP), released the following data regarding the writing skills of Canadian 13- and 16-year-old students. These results indicate that a gender gap in the relative writing skills of boys and girls appears to be developing. The assessment was administered to approximately 24 000 students in all provinces and territories except Nunavut. Performance is reported on a five-point scale, with one being the lowest and five the highest.

Some major findings of the SAIP test:

1. More than 80 percent of 13-year-olds reached level 2 and above. According to the test designers, level 2 is the level that most 13-year-olds should reach. Over 40 percent reached level 3 and above.
2. Over 60 percent of 16-year-olds reached level 3 or above. Level 3 is the level most 16-year-olds should reach, according to test designers.
3. Significantly more girls in both age groups performed at higher levels than boys. This gender gap is consistent with current trends in Language Arts assessment as confirmed in the Programme for International Student Assessment (PISA) 2000 reading assessment.
4. Among francophones, students in Quebec outperformed francophone students in minority-language settings for both age groups.

Gender-Fair Classrooms and Curricula

Although research and debate about the bias boys and girls encounter in school will no doubt continue, it is clear that teachers must encourage girls and boys to develop to the full extent of their capabilities and provide them an education that is free from **gender bias**—subtle favouritism or discrimination on the basis of gender. In her article "The Quality Teacher" (1993, 6) Kimberley Burstall reports the results of a survey she administered to a gender-balanced group of 300 Nova Scotia students from Grades 5, 8, and 11. The survey asked the students to select, from an extensive list of options, the three characteristics they considered most important for a "good teacher." In first place, with a score of 200, was "Treats boys and girls equally." As it is through language that gender fairness is most easily observed, it is important for teachers to be very careful in the selection of words they use when interacting with students. To check your own sensitivity to gender-fair language, we suggest you complete the Gender-Neutral Questionnaire located in Appendix 5.1.

Following is a list of basic guidelines for creating a **gender-fair classroom**. Adherence to these guidelines will help teachers "address the inequities institutionalized in the organizational structure of schools, the curriculum selected to be taught, the learning strategies employed, and their ongoing instructional and informal interactions with students" (Stanford 1992, 88).

- Become aware of differences in interactions with girls and boys.
- Promote boys' achievement in reading and writing and girls' achievement in mathematics and science.
- Reduce young children's self-imposed sexism.
- Teach about sexism and sex role stereotyping.
- Foster an atmosphere of collaboration between girls and boys.

Sexual Orientation

In addition to gender bias, some students experience discrimination on the basis of their sexual orientation. To help all students realize their full potential, teachers should acknowledge the special needs of gay, lesbian, and bisexual students for "there is an invisible gay and lesbian minority in every school, and the needs of these students [a]re often unknown and unmet" (Besner and Spungin 1995, xi). One study of 120 gay and lesbian students ages 14 to 21 found that only one-fourth said they were able to discuss their sexual orientation with school counsellors, and less than one in five said they could identify someone who had been supportive of them (Tellijohann and Price 1993). Moreover, a similar study of lesbian and gay youth reported that 80 percent of participants believed their teachers had negative attitudes about homosexuality (Sears 1991).

Based on estimates that as much as 10 percent of society may be homosexual, a high school with an enrolment of 1500 might have as many as 150 gay, lesbian, and bisexual students (Besner and Spungin 1995; Stover 1992). Several professional organizations have passed resolutions urging members and school districts to acknowledge the special needs of these students.

Homosexual students can experience school-related problems and safety risks. The hostility which gay, lesbian, and bisexual youth can encounter may cause them to feel confused, isolated, and self-destructive (Alexander 1998; Jordan, Vaughan, and Woodworth 1997; Edwards 1997; Anderson, 1997). Teachers and other school personnel can provide much-needed support. Informed, sensitive, and caring teachers can play an important role in helping all students develop to their full potential. Such teachers realize the importance of recognizing diverse perspectives, and they create inclusive classroom environments that encourage students to respect differences among themselves and others and to see the contributions that persons from all groups have made to society.

What Characteristics Distinguish Successful Schools?

At this point in your professional education you may, because of the very diverse nature of today's school populations, be uncertain of your ability to develop a positive classroom climate within your classroom. However, a great many schools in all settings and with all kinds of students are highly successful, including inner city and isolated rural schools and schools that serve pupils of all socio-economic, racial, and ethnic backgrounds. What are the characteristics of these schools? Do they have commonalities that account for their success?

Measures of Success

First, we must define what we mean by a **successful school**. One measure of success, naturally, is that students at these schools achieve at a high level and complete requirements for graduation. Whether reflected in scores on standardized tests or other documentation of academic learning gains, students at these schools are learning. They are achieving literacy in reading, writing, computation, and computer skills. They are learning to solve problems, think creatively and analytically, and, most importantly, they are learning to learn.

Another valid measure of success for a school is that it achieves results that surpass those expected from comparable schools in comparable settings. The achievement of students goes beyond what one would expect. In spite of surrounding social, economic, and political forces that impede the educative process at other schools, these schools are achieving results.

Finally, successful schools are those that are improving, rather than getting worse. School improvement is a slow process, and schools that are improving—moving in the right direction rather than declining—are also successful.

Research on School Effectiveness

During the 1980s and early 1990s, much research was conducted to identify the characteristics of successful (or effective) schools. The characteristics of successful schools were described in different ways in several research projects. The following list is a synthesis of these findings.

- *Strong leadership*—Successful schools have strong leaders—individuals who value education and see themselves as educational leaders, not just as managers or bureaucrats. They monitor the performance of everyone at the school—teachers, staff, students, and themselves. These leaders have a vision of the school as a more effective learning environment, and they take decisive steps to bring that about.
- *High expectations*—Teachers at successful schools have high expectations of students. These teachers believe that all students, rich or poor, can learn, and they communicate this to students through realistic, yet high, expectations.
- *Emphasis on basic skills*—Teachers at successful schools emphasize student achievement in the basic skills of reading, writing, and mathematical computation.
- *Orderly school environment*—The environments of successful schools are orderly, safe, and conducive to learning. Discipline problems are at a minimum, and teachers are able to devote greater amounts of time to teaching.
- *Frequent, systematic evaluation of student learning*—The learning of students in successful schools is monitored closely. When difficulties are noticed, appropriate remediation is provided quickly.
- *Sense of purpose*—Those who teach and those who learn at successful schools have a strong sense of purpose. From the principal to the students, everyone at the school is guided by a vision of excellence.
- *Collegiality and a sense of community*—Teachers, administrators, and staff at successful schools work well together. They are dedicated to creating an environment that promotes not only student learning but also their own professional growth and development.
- *Strategies for effective schools*—Research has also focused on strategies for making schools more effective. A synthesis of research (Newmann and Wehlage 1995) conducted between 1990 and 1995 on school improvement identified four characteristics of successful schools:
- *Focus on student learning*—Planning, implementation, and evaluation focus on enhancing the intellectual quality of student learning. All students are expected to achieve academic excellence.
- *Emphasis on authentic pedagogy*—Students are required to think, to develop in-depth understanding, and to apply academic learning to important, realistic problems. Students might, for example, conduct a survey on an issue of local concern, analyze the results, and then present their findings at a town council meeting.
- *Greater school organizational capacity*—The ability of the school to strive for continuous improvement through professional collaboration is enhanced. For example, teachers exchange ideas to improve their teaching; they seek feedback from students, parents, and community members; and they attend conferences and workshops to acquire new materials and strategies.
- *Greater external support*—The school receives critical financial, technical, and political support from outside sources.

In short, the cultures of effective schools encourage teachers to grow and develop in the practice of their profession. As the Secondary Schools in Canada: The National Report of the Exemplary Schools Project, (Gaskell 1995, 278) states: "School success is a complex and constantly evolving concept; different communities place emphasis on different elements. Success is a fragile quality that always involves a balance among different demands and pressures. It needs to be constantly reevaluated as conditions change. Successful schools are consciously trying to improve themselves by continuing inquiry and deliberative change."

What Social Problems Affect Schools and Place Students at Risk?

A complex and varied array of social issues impact schools. These problems often detract from the ability of schools to educate students according to the seven aims discussed at the beginning of this chapter: educational goals, prosocial values, socialization, achievement, personal growth, social change, and equal opportunity. Furthermore, schools are often charged with the difficult (if not impossible) task of providing a front-line defense against such problems.

One of the most vocal advocates of the role of schools in solving social problems was George S. Counts, who said in his 1932 book, *Dare the School Build a New Social Order?* that "If schools are to be really effective, they must become centers for the building, and not merely the contemplation, of our civilization" (p. 12). Many people, however, believe that schools should not try to build a new social order. They should be concerned only with the academic and social development of students—not with solving society's problems. Nevertheless, the debate over the role of schools in regard to social problems will continue to be vigorous. For some time, schools have served in the battle against social problems by offering an array of health, education, and social service programs. Schools provide breakfasts, nutritional counselling, diagnostic services related to health and family planning, after-school child care, job placement, and sex and drug education, to name a few. In the following sections we examine several societal problems that directly influence schools, teachers, and students.

Identifying Students at Risk

An increasing number of young people live under conditions characterized by extreme stress, chronic poverty, crime, and lack of adult guidance. As James Garbarino (1999, 12) points out: "In almost every community ... growing numbers of kids live in a socially toxic environment." Frustrated, lonely, and feeling powerless, many youths escape into music with violence-oriented and/or obscene lyrics, violent video games, cults, movies, and television programs that celebrate gratuitous violence and sex, and cruising shopping malls or "hanging out" on the street. Others turn also to crime, gang violence, promiscuous sex, or substance abuse. Not surprisingly, these activities place many young people at risk of dropping out of school. **Students at risk** of dropping out tend to get low grades, perform below grade level academically, are older than the average student at their grade level because of previous retention, and have behaviour problems at school. It is estimated that the following percentages of 14-year-olds are likely to exhibit one or more at-risk behaviours (substance abuse, sexual behaviour, violence, depression, or school failure) and to experience serious negative outcomes as a result: 10 percent at very high risk, 25 percent at high risk, 25 percent at moderate risk, 20 percent at low risk, and 20 percent at no risk (Dryfoos 1998).

Many Canadian children live in families that help them grow up healthy, confident, and skilled, but many do not. Instead, their life settings are characterized by problems of alcoholism or other substance abuse, family violence, unemployment, poverty, poor nutrition, teenage parenthood, and a history of school failure. Such children live in communities and families that have many problems and frequently become dysfunctional, unable to provide their children with the support and guidance they need. Children who experience the negative effects of poverty are from families of all ethnic and racial groups.

The life experiences of students who are at risk of dropping out can be difficult for teachers to imagine; and, as the following comments by a student teacher in a Grade 3 classroom illustrate, encountering the realities of poverty for the first time can be upsetting.

> [Some] students came in wearing the same clothes for a week. Others would come in without socks on. No pencils, crayons, scissors, or glue. Some without breakfast, lunch, or a snack. My heart bled every day. I found myself becoming upset about their lives. I even found myself thinking about them at night and over the weekend. [I] noticed that they were extremely bright students, but their home life and economic status hindered them from working to their potential. Some of my students couldn't even complete their homework because they had no glue, scissors, or crayons at home (Molino 1999, 55).

Although Canada is one of the richest countries in the world, it has by no means achieved an enviable record in regard to poverty among children. According to Statistics Canada, 20 percent of children under eighteen years of age live in families below the poverty line.

Family Stress

The stress placed on families in a complex society is extensive and not easily handled. For some families, such stress can be overwhelming. The structure of families who are experiencing the effects of financial problems, substance abuse, or violence, for example, can easily begin to crumble. Health challenges where a family member has developed cancer or other serious disease can also lead to significantly increased levels of stress.

Stress within the family can have a significant negative effect on students and their ability to focus on learning while at school. Such stress is often associated with health and emotional problems, failure to achieve, behavioural problems at school, and dropping out of school.

With the high rise in divorce and women's entry into the workforce, family constellations have changed dramatically. No longer is a working father, a mother who stays at home, and two or three children the only kind of family in Canada. The number of single-parent families, stepparent families, blended families, and extended families has increased dramatically during the last decade. In 1996, Statistics Canada released Growing Up In Canada: The National Longitudinal Survey of [22 000] Canadian Children and Youth. This report indicated that:

- 14.6 percent of children under age 12 lived in a lone-parent family headed by a woman. One in six (17 percent) of these children had some form of conduct disorder; one in nine (11 percent) had repeated a grade at school.

- 41 percent of children in female single-parent families had at least one kind of problem as compared with 26 percent of children in all families.
- A child with a single-parent mother was almost twice as likely to face academic or behavioural problems as were children in a two-parent family.

Just as there is diversity in the composition of today's families, so, too, there is diversity in the styles with which children are raised in families. Because of the number of working women and single-parent homes, an alarming number of **latchkey children** are unsupervised during much of the day. To meet the needs of these children, some schools offer before- and after-school programs.

In addition, many middle-class couples are waiting longer to have children. Although children of such couples may have more material advantages, they may be somewhat "impoverished" in regard to the reduced time they spend with their parents. To maintain their lifestyle, these parents are often driven to spend more time developing their careers. As a result, the care and guidance their children receive is inadequate, and "Sustained bad care eventually leads to a deep-seated inner sense of insecurity and inadequacy, emotional pain, and a troublesome sense of self" (Comer 1997, 83). To fill the parenting void that characterizes the lives of an increasing number of children from all economic classes, schools and teachers are being called on to play an increased role in the socialization of young people.

Substance Abuse

One of the most pressing social problems confronting today's schools is the abuse of illegal drugs, tobacco, and alcohol. The use of drugs among young people varies from community to community and from year to year, but overall it is disturbingly high. Mind-altering substances used by young people include the easily acquired glue, white correction fluid, and felt marker, as well as marijuana, amphetamines, and cocaine. The abuse of drugs not only poses the risks of addiction and overdosing, but is also related to problems such as HIV/AIDS, teenage pregnancy, depression, suicide, automobile accidents, criminal activity, and dropping out of school. For an alarming number of young people, drugs are seen as a way of coping with life's problems.

Violence and Crime

While Canada experienced a decline in serious violent crimes during the 1990s, crime rates among adolescents has remained relatively constant. Statistics Canada reports in *Crime Statistics 2001* the following:

- The youth crime rate, as measured by the rate of youths aged 12 to 17 formally charged by police, rose a slight 1 percent for the second straight year, after decreasing from 1991 to 1999.
- The violent crime rate for youths increased 2 percent, its second consecutive gain, but the youth property crime rate continued to drop, falling 3 percent. Police-reported data show that 16 is the peak age of offending among all youths and adults for both violent and property crimes.
- There were 30 youths accused of homicide in 2001—the lowest level in over 30 years and 18 fewer than the average of 48 over the past decade.
- The rate of youths charged with robbery climbed 10 percent in 2001, and youths charged with motor vehicle theft rose 7 percent. The rate of young people charged with breaking and entering fell 6 percent, the tenth consecutive decline.

Figure 5.5

Security measures

Source: Indicators of School Crime and Safety, 1998. Washington, DC: National Center for Education Statistics.

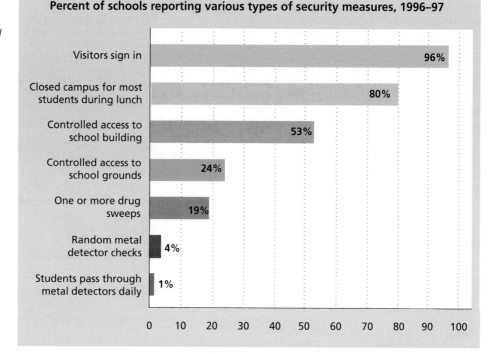

Percent of schools reporting various types of security measures, 1996–97

Visitors sign in — 96%
Closed campus for most students during lunch — 80%
Controlled access to school building — 53%
Controlled access to school grounds — 24%
One or more drug sweeps — 19%
Random metal detector checks — 4%
Students pass through metal detectors daily — 1%

Canadian concern about school crime and safety heightened as a result of a string of American and Canadian school shootings between 1996 and 1999. Among the communities that had to cope with such tragic incidents were Moses Lake, Washington (1996); Pearl, Mississippi (1997); West Paducah, Kentucky (1997); Jonesboro, Arkansas (1998); Springfield, Oregon (1998); Littleton, Colorado (1999), and Taber, Alberta (1999). As a consequence, Canadian school officials have become much more concerned student safety and have started to initiate safety measures similar to those already common in many United States' schools. (See Figure 5.5.)

The American Psychological Association reviewed research studies and concluded that television violence *alone* is responsible for up to 15 percent of all aggressive behaviour by children and youth (Garbarino 1999). Lastly, David Grossman, a military psychologist, and his colleague pointed out that violent point-and-shoot video games are similar to those used to "desensitize" soldiers to shoot at human figures (Grossman and Siddle 1999).

As a result of the school shootings listed earlier and the public's concern with school crime and violence, many schools developed crisis management plans to cope with violent incidents on campus. Schools also reviewed their ability to provide students, faculty, and staff with a safe environment for learning. The following "School Safety Checklist" excerpted from the National Education Association's *School Safety Check Book* presents a starting point for evaluating school safety.

School Safety Checklist

Give your school a thorough crime prevention inspection now. Use this checklist as a guideline to determine your school's strengths and weaknesses.

1. Is there a policy for dealing with violence and vandalism in your school? (The reporting policy must be realistic and strictly adhered to.)
2. Is there an incident reporting system?
3. Is the incident reporting system available to all staff?
4. Is there statistical information available as to the scope of the problems at your school and in the community?
5. Have the school, school board and administrators taken steps or anticipated any problems through dialogue?
6. Does security fit into the organization of the school? (Security must be designed to fit the needs of the administration and made part of the site.)
7. Are the teachers and administrators aware of laws that pertain to them? To their rights? To students' rights? Of their responsibility as to enforcement of and respect for rules, regulations, policies, and the law?
8. Is there a working relationship with your local law enforcement agency?
9. Are students and parents aware of expectations and school discipline codes?
10. Are there any actual or contingency action plans developed to deal with student disruptions and vandalism?
11. Is there a policy as to restitution or prosecution of perpetrators of violence and vandalism?
12. Is there any in-service training available for teachers and staff in the areas of violence and vandalism and other required reporting procedures?
13. Is there a policy for consistent monitoring and evaluation of incident reports?
14. Is the staff trained in standard crime prevention behaviour?

Source: Excerpted from *The School Safety Check Book* by the National School Safety Center, 141 Duesenberg Dr., Suite 16, Westlake Village, CA, 91362, www.nssc1.org.

Now that you have completed the School Safety Checklist, consider the following excerpt that describes a program called "Peaceful Schools International." As explained below by V. Lois Ross, principal of Meadows School in Manitoba, the mandate of this program is to foster safe and peaceful school environments.

Peaceful Schools International

Imagine a school of about 350 students from Kindergarten to Grade 6 which is nestled on the outskirts of a mid sized city. Many of the educators and the principal have long standing experience at this school. Historically, this student body has been described as a rural and urban mixture from relatively stable, white, middle class families.

Now, imagine this same school which, over a period of three years, has been transformed to include nearly 500 students from Kindergarten to Grade 8. A number of educators have transferred into this school to teach at the new levels and a new principal has been assigned. Due to the opening of a large pork processing facility in the city, several families have moved into a high-density apartment residence located in the area, and as a result the student body now reflects much more diversity and transience. The school is now operating over capacity and space has become an issue.

Although the situation described above reflects challenges, it also poses opportunities for the staff, students and parent body to collaborate and implement a number of positive initiatives to foster the development of a healthy K to 8 learning community; one that attempts to negate the traumas of misbehaviour including bullying and other social concerns. One such initiative included the application for, and adoption of, Peaceful Schools International.

The appeal of this program comes from its mandate to support schools in their quest to establish and maintain a peaceful, caring and safe atmosphere. Acceptance into this organization is based on an application process which includes, for example, documentation of collaborative decision-making, multi-disciplinary approaches and overall commitment from all stakeholders at the school. Participants are challenged to generate creative, grassroots ideas, so instead of a "canned program," each school develops approaches which are uniquely tailored to its own setting.

Poetry, songs, drama, class challenges, community service and art are all being utilized, to date, to energize our focus of a safe, respectful, caring, peaceful K-8 learning community. Both staff and students are now strongly engaged in this focus. Just imagine the possibilities now!

Source: Reprinted by permission of V. Lois Ross.

Teen Pregnancy

Each year thousands of Canadian teenage women (one in every 20) between the ages of 15 and 19 will become pregnant, and about 85 percent of these pregnancies are unintended. Indeed, most teachers of adolescents today may expect to have at least some students who are, or have been, pregnant.

Since peaking in 1990, the teenage pregnancy, birth, and abortion rates have declined. About 20 percent of this decrease has been the result of decreased sexual activity and 80 percent the result of more effective contraceptive practices among sexually active teenagers (Alan Guttmacher Institute 1999). Nevertheless, teen pregnancies remain a serious problem in society. Because the physical development of girls in adolescence may not be complete, complications can occur during pregnancy and in the birthing process. Also, adolescents are less likely to receive prenatal care in the crucial first trimester; they tend not to eat well-balanced diets; and are not free of harmful substances such as alcohol, tobacco, and drugs, which are known to be detrimental to a baby's development. These young mothers "are at risk for chronic educational, occupational, and financial difficulties, and their offspring are also at risk for medical, educational, and behavioural problems" (Durlak 1995, 66). Because many teen mothers drop out of school, forfeiting their high school diplomas and limiting their access to decent, higher-paying job opportunities, they and their children tend to remain at the bottom of the economic ladder.

Suicide among Children and Youths

The increase in individual and multiple suicides is alarming for, in any given year, approximately 500 Canadian youths and adolescents will take their own lives. Among teenagers it is the third leading cause of death. Additionally, it is estimated that there are 8 to 25 attempted suicides for one completion. According to the Centers for Disease Control and Prevention (1998b), about 21 percent of high school students seriously considered committing suicide in 1997; about 16 percent made a specific suicide plan; about 8 percent actually attempted suicide; and about 3 percent required medical attention as a result of their suicide attempt.

Although female students are almost two times more likely than male students to have seriously considered attempting suicide during the preceding twelve months, about six times as many male students as females actually commit suicide. Also, lesbian and gay youth are two to three times more likely to attempt suicide than their heterosexual peers, and they account for up to 30 percent of all completed suicides among youth (Besner and Spungin 1995).

Should metal detectors be installed in schools?

Violence by or against students occurs in schools in many developed countries. Canada and the United states have had their own unfortunate occurrences—but so have others. In Dunblane, Scotland, a madman burst into a school and killed a teacher and 16 Kindergarten students. In Japan a middle school student was recently convicted of beheading another student, and other nations have experienced other horrific events. The question then becomes: How should schools react to this increased rate of violence?

In Canada, one popular response has been the Alberta Teachers' Association's Safe and Caring Schools program (SACS) (www.teachers.ab.ca/safe/Recognition.htm), which has, as its primary focus, the provision of advice and assistance required to communities wanting to develop the skills and knowledge essential for the provision of safe and caring schools. Supporters of the SACS program can now be found in British Columbia, Alberta, Saskatchewan, Ontario, and the Maritimes. The Ottawa–Carlton Board of Education has, for example, adapted the SACS curriculum outcomes to reflect the Ontario curriculum. In addition to the SACS program, the Lions Quest and the Peaceful Schools International are dedicated to the same objective of making schools safe for students. Unfortunately, it takes time to make all schools safe and caring places and some feel that other approaches should be taken.

In the United States, within ten days of the Columbine High School 1999 shooting spree, an event that that took the lives of fourteen students and a teacher while wounding over 20 others, the U.S. Secretary of Education, Richard Riley, sought to make sense of the tragedy. Speaking at Walt Whitman High School in Bethesda, Maryland, he told his audience, "We have always had schoolyard fights, but now there is a new level of fear because of these weapons of deadly violence." Crime statistics at the time indicated an actual decline in the juvenile violence rate, but lethality had increased, mainly due to guns.

"Guns and youth are a particularly deadly combination," observed a report by the Center for the Study and Prevention of Violence at the University of Colorado at Boulder. "Guns give youth the feeling of power, and during adolescence, abstract reasoning about the consequences of gun use and the capacity to read social cues are incomplete." The need to separate the two is obvious. But the way to do that is a challenge. Should metal detectors be installed in schools? Are there less ominous ways to handle the problem? Can schools be kept safe without becoming fortresses?

Metal detectors should be installed in schools.

A shooting in a school is like an earthquake in a city: It shakes the very foundation of what was thought to be solid, secure, and safe. Children and youth need to feel confident that their school is a safe and secure place. The thought of requiring students to spend their days in environments that make them vulnerable to violence is abhorrent. Expecting students to tackle their studies and find learning engaging when they are fearful for their lives is ludicrous. And yet that is exactly what we are doing if we fail to install metal detectors in schools.

After bombings occurred in air travel, metal detectors were installed in airports in order to protect passengers. Few complained, realizing that the personal inconvenience assured them of greater protection and peace of mind. They accepted the need to lose a liberty for the good of all. If adults are granted such protection from the violence in our society, should we not provide the same for our children and youth?

Metal detectors and similar devices are technological advances that help reduce crime in a variety of settings. In addition to the security they provide in airports, they prevent people from taking library books they haven't checked out and protect stores from shoplifters. Just as we have learned to accept metal detectors in libraries, airports, and stores, so their presence in schools would soon be hardly noticed.

Model programs that have decreased student weapon violations by 70 to 86 percent include weapon scanning with metal detectors along with random searches conducted by police. Other features of such model programs include eliminating building areas that cannot be viewed by surveillance cameras and training school security officers by local police forces. These model programs also call for teachers and students to be trained in how to handle dangerous situations and ways to avoid them. The installation of metal detectors is clearly where protection from school violence must begin.

Metal detectors should not be installed in schools.

Using metal detectors to prevent school violence is like putting an adhesive bandage on an infected wound. Not only will it not remedy the problem, but it could also make it even worse. Students who have not considered bringing a weapon to school might decide to do so simply to challenge the system. Like gang members who write graffiti on dangerous highway overpasses, similar minds will be motivated to find ways to bypass the metal detector. Metal detectors also present a foreboding welcome to a school campus and convey to students the messages "We have problems here" and "We don't trust you."

Instead, the way to prevent school violence is to get to the heart of students' problems. What causes the anger and alienation that eventually explodes in destructive, and sometimes deadly, acts? Teaching students how to solve their problems, handle disappointments, and seek help when it's needed are ways in which some schools have tried to reduce violence. Conflict management, peace building, using literature to teach empathy, forbidding teasing, and anti-bullying programs are other approaches.

In his speech at Walt Whitman High, Secretary Riley urged community members, parents, and students themselves to play active roles in reversing the trend toward greater violence. "I ask all Americans to believe as I do in this generation of young people.... We must send ... a powerful message of hope and security. We will do everything we can to protect you, to listen to you, and to reach out to you so that you feel connected.... This is why I ask parents again and again to slow down your lives." He told students to speak to adults when they believe something violent is about to happen. He never mentioned metal detectors, and rightly so. Finding ways to reduce alienation and create community in our schools is a better approach to promoting school safety.

Where do you stand on this issue?

1. With which position do you agree? Why?
2. What are "zero tolerance" policies and should they be used?
3. How can teachers help prevent violence in schools?
4. How do schools and airports compare in their needs for metal detectors?
5. What compromise position can you suggest?

Recommended Sources

Center for the Study and Prevention of Violence, University of Colorado at Boulder (1991, April 21). Response to the Columbine school incident.

Department of Education (1999, April 30). Safe schools, healthy schools: remarks as prepared for delivery by U.S. Secretary of Education Richard W. Riley

Walters, L. S. (1999, January/February). What makes a good school violence prevention program? *Harvard Education Letter.*

Alberta Teachers' Association. Safe and Caring Schools program www.teachers.ab.ca/safe/Recognition.htm

What Are Schools Doing to Address Societal Problems?

Responding to the needs of at-risk students will be a crucial challenge for schools, families, and communities during the twenty-first century. Since most children attend school, it is logical that this pre-existing system be used for reaching large numbers of at-risk children (and through them, their families). During the last decade, many school districts have taken innovative steps to address societal problems that impact students' lives.

Though programs that address social problems are costly, the public believes that schools should be used for the delivery of health and social services to students and their families. However, there is some disagreement about the extent to which school facilities should be used for anything but meeting students' educational needs. For example, in a publication titled *Putting Learning First,* the Committee for Economic

Development (1994, 1) stated, "Schools are not social service institutions; they should not be asked to solve all our nation's social ills and cultural conflicts." In isolated instances, community groups and school boards have resisted school-based services such as family planning clinics and mental health services.

Intervention Programs

Under pressure to find solutions to increasing social problems among children and adolescents, educators have developed an array of intervention programs. In general, the aim of these programs is to address the behavioural, social, and academic adjustment of at-risk children and adolescents so they can receive maximum benefit from their school experiences.

In the following sections, we briefly review several comprehensive strategies that have proven effective in addressing academic, social, and behavioural problems among children and adolescents; these approaches to intervention are peer counselling, and school-based interprofessional case management. Chapter 5 presents additional information about recent, innovative steps schools are taking for the *prevention* of the effects of social problems on students. Also see Appendix 5.2 for "Selected Resources for Meeting Needs of Students Placed at Risk"—a list of publications, organizations, and online locations that are good sources of information on the problems children and youth may encounter.

Peer Counselling

To address the social problems that affect students, some schools have initiated student-to-student **peer counselling** programs—usually monitored by a school counsellor or other specially trained adult. In peer counselling programs, students can address problems and issues such as low academic achievement, interpersonal problems at home and at school, substance abuse, and career planning. Evidence indicates that both peer counsellors and students experience increased self-esteem and greater ability to deal with problems.

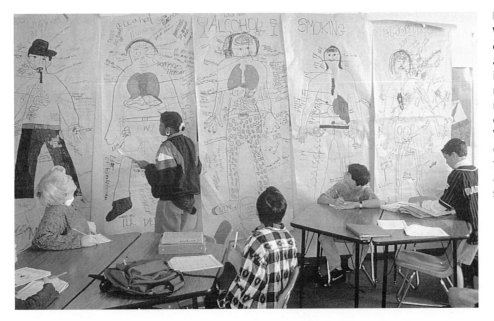

What approach to the education of students at risk does the scene in this photograph represent? What other risk factors affect children and youths? What are some other effective approaches for helping students at risk to succeed in school?

When peer counselling is combined with cross-age tutoring, younger students can learn about drugs, alcohol, premarital pregnancy, delinquency, dropping out, HIV/AIDS, suicide, and other relevant issues. Here the groups are often college-age students meeting with those in high school, or high school students meeting with those in junior high school or middle school. In these preventative programs, older students sometimes perform dramatic episodes that portray students confronting problems and model strategies for handling the situations presented.

School-Based Interprofessional Case Management

In responding to the needs of at-risk students, it has been suggested that schools "will need to reconceptualize the networks of community organizations and public services that might assist, and they will need to draw on those community resources" (Edwards and Young 1992, 78). One such approach to forming new home/school/community partnerships is known as **school-based interprofessional case management.** The approach uses professionally trained case managers who work directly with teachers, the community, and the family to coordinate and deliver appropriate services to at-risk students and their families. The case management approach is based on a comprehensive service delivery network of teachers, social agencies, and health service agencies.

Alternative Schools and Curricula

To meet the needs of students whom social problems place at risk, many school districts have developed alternative schools and curricula. Usually, an **alternative school** is a small, highly individualized school separate from the regular school; in other cases, the alternative school is organized as a **school-within-a-school.** Alternative school programs usually provide remedial instruction, some vocational training, and individualized counselling. Since they usually have much smaller class sizes, alternative school teachers can monitor students' progress more closely and, when problems do arise, respond more quickly and with greater understanding of student needs.

To reach students who are not successful at regular schools, alternative schools offer a program of individualized instruction, small class sizes, and various enrichment programs delivered in what school staff describe as a "supportive, non-coercive, nontraditional setting." Most students are expected to return to their regular schools after a minimum of four weeks.

While they don't work in alternative school settings, many highly effective regular teachers have developed alternative curricula to meet the unique learning needs of students at risk. Many teachers, for example, link students' learning to the business, civic, cultural, and political segments of their communities. The rationale is that connecting at-risk students to the world beyond their schools will enable them to see the relevance of education.

SUMMARY

What Are the Aims of Education Today?

- Though debate about the aims of education continues, the public believes that schools have a responsibility to address problems confronting Canadian society.

- Agreement exists regarding six additional broad educational aims—education for prosocial values, socialization, achievement, personal growth, social change, and equal opportunity.

How Can Schools Be Described?

- Schools can be categorized according to the focus of their curricula and according to their organizational structures.

- Metaphors for schools have suggested that schools are like families, tribes or clans, banks, gardens, prisons, and so on, with the school-as-family metaphor often describing schools that are successful.

- Some people believe that schools reproduce the existing social class structure, that they maintain the differences between the "haves" and "have-nots."

What Are Schools Like As Social Institutions?

- As social institutions that contribute to the maintenance and improvement of society, schools mirror Canadian culture and the surrounding local culture.

- Schools develop their own unique cultures, and the community environment that surrounds a school can impact it positively or negatively.

- Elements of a school's physical environment such as self-contained classrooms, open-space arrangements, and departmentalization contribute to a school's character and culture. Similarly, each classroom develops its own culture, which is influenced by the physical setting and the social dimensions of the group.

How Is Cultural Diversity Represented in Canadian Schools?

- The percentage of ethnic **minorities** in Canadian schools has been growing steadily since the end of World War II. According to Statistics Canada's report on the census of 2001, 18.4 percent of Canada's population was born in other countries, the highest percentage of any country except for Australia. Statistics Canada also reports that 94 percent of these new citizens settled in large urban areas with Montreal, Toronto, and Vancouver accounting for 73 percent of the total.

- Culture is defined as the way of life common to a group of people, including beliefs, attitudes, habits, values, and practices.

- Dimensions of cultural identity include beliefs, attitudes, and values; racial identity; exceptionalities; language; gender; ethnicity; income level; and occupation.

- **Ethnicity** refers to a commonly shared racial or cultural identity and a set of beliefs, values, and attitudes. The concept of race is used to distinguish among people on the basis of biological traits and characteristics. A minority group is a group of people who share certain characteristics and are fewer in number than the majority of a population.

- Stereotyping is the process of attributing certain behavioural characteristics to all members of a group, often on the basis of limited experiences with and information about the group being stereotyped. Individual racism is the prejudicial belief that one's own ethnic or racial group is superior to others, and institutional racism refers to laws, customs, and practices that lead to racial inequalities.

What Is Multicultural Education?

- Five dimensions of multicultural education have been suggested: content integration, knowledge construction, prejudice reduction, an equity pedagogy, and an empowering school culture.

- A multicultural curriculum addresses the needs and backgrounds of all students—regardless of their cultural identity—and expands students' appreciation for diversity. Effective multicultural materials and instructional strategies include the contributions of ethnic groups and reflect diverse points of view or "voices" that previously may have been silenced or marginalized in society.

How Is Gender a Dimension of Multicultural Education?

- Gender includes ways of knowing and "modes of conduct, thought, and expression;" these are dimensions of culture.

- Both boys and girls experience inequities in the classroom; teachers, however, can provide both sexes with an education free of *gender bias* by creating gender-fair classrooms and curricula.

- Teachers should acknowledge the special needs of students who are gay, lesbian, or bisexual, and provide them with safe, supportive learning environments.

What Characteristics Distinguish Successful Schools?

- Three aspects of successful schools have been suggested: (1) their students manifest a high level of learning; (2) their results surpass those for comparable schools; and (3) they are improving rather than getting worse.

- Research has identified seven characteristics of effective schools: strong leadership, high expectations, emphasis on basic skills, orderly school environment, frequent and systematic evaluation of student learning, sense of purpose, and collegiality and a sense of community.

- Research indicates that successfully restructured schools emphasize student learning, authentic pedagogy, building organizational capacity, and external support.

What Social Problems Affect Schools and Place Students at Risk?

- Among the many social problems that impact the school's ability to educate students are poverty, family stress, substance abuse, violence and crime, teen pregnancy, HIV/AIDS, and suicide.

- Children at risk, who represent all ethnic and racial groups and all socio-economic levels, tend to get low grades, underachieve, be older than other students at the same grade level, and have behaviour problems at school.

What Are Schools Doing to Address Societal Problems?

- Schools have developed intervention and prevention programs to address social problems. Three effective intervention programs are peer counselling, and school-based interprofessional case management.

■ Many school districts have developed alternative schools or schools-within-a-school that provide highly individualized instructional and support services for students who have not been successful in regular schools. Also, highly effective teachers modify their techniques and develop alternative curricula to meet the needs of students at risk.

KEY TERMS AND CONCEPTS

aims of education, 162
alternative school, 194
classroom culture, 169
cultural identity, 172
culture, 170
departmentalization, 169
diversity, 170
emotional intelligence, 163
ethnic group, 172
ethnicity, 195
gender bias, 182
gender-fair classroom, 182
individual racism, 174

institution, 165
institutional racism, 174
latchkey children, 187
minorities, 195
multicultural
    curriculum, 178
multicultural
    education, 175
multiculturalism, 174
open-space schools, 169
peer counselling, 193
prosocial values, 163
race, 172

school-based
    interprofessional case
    management, 194
school culture, 168
school traditions, 169
school-within-a-school, 194
self-contained classroom,
    168
sex role socialization, 180
sex role stereotyping, 180
stereotyping, 174
students at risk, 185
successful school, 183

APPLICATIONS AND ACTIVITIES

Teacher's Journal

1. Collect and summarize several newspaper and magazine articles that contain references to the public's expectations of education and the schools. To what extent do the articles address the four aims discussed in this chapter? To what extent do they identify social problems that schools are expected to address?

2. Identify and then defend your choice of school improvements that you consider most important for improving the quality of education in Canada. What aims of education do your choices reflect?

3. Reflect on your experiences with the impact of social problems on teaching and learning at the elementary, middle, or high school levels. Select one of the social issues or problems discussed in this chapter and describe its influences on you or your peers.

4. Reflecting on your experiences in schools and the five dimensions of multicultural education (see Figure 5.5 on page 190), describe the steps your teachers took to create an empowering school culture and social climate.

5. During your school years, did you ever experience discrimination as a member of a "different" group? Write about one outstanding incident that you feel affected your performance as a student.

6. As a teacher, what activities and materials might you use in a specific learning context to reduce the prejudices of students toward groups different from theirs?

7. Describe an example of sex-role stereotyping or gender bias that you experienced or observed in a school setting and how you felt about it.

1. Join or start an interactive online discussion on one or more of the following topics discussed in this chapter. You might join a newsgroup already in progress or request discussion partners via an email mailing list or via any one of the message board opportunities that are offered at many of the sites you have already explored. You might also establish a communication link among your classmates or with students in other schools who are taking a similar course.

teen pregnancies	effective schools
at-risk students	family stress
gender equity	English as a Second Language (ESL)
cultural diversity	multicultural education
substance abuse	latchkey children
crime and violence in schools	youth suicide
school improvement	school-based clinics
children in poverty	alternative schools

2. Formulate a research question concerning demographic aspects of students and their families, and go online to gather current national and provincial statistics on topics related to your question. For example, your question might relate to one or more of the above topics.

3. Develop a collaborative project with classmates to investigate and report on issues in drug abuse prevention, at-risk intervention, or violence prevention. Begin by exploring web sites such as Children, Youth and Families Education and Research Network (CYFERNet); and Children, Youth, and Families at Risk (CYFAR). Both sites have extensive resources, databases, and services for at-risk children, youth, and their families.

1. Visit a school in your community recognized as successful or effective. What evidence do you find of the characteristics of successful schools (or successfully restructured schools) discussed in this chapter? Are there other characteristics you would add to the list based on your observations?

2. Reflect on your experiences relating to social problems at the elementary, middle, or high school levels. Then gather statistics and information about how a local school or local school district is responding to the social problems discussed in this chapter.

3. Obtain at least one statement of philosophy, or mission statement, from a school with which you are familiar. Analyze the statement(s), identifying and highlighting portions that refer to the major aims of education discussed in this chapter (educational goals, prosocial values, socialization, achievement, cultural and ethnic groups, personal growth, social change, and equal educational opportunity).

4. If possible, visit a school that has an enrolment of students whose cultural or socioeconomic backgrounds differ from your own. What feelings and questions about these students emerge as a result of your observations? How might your feelings affect your teaching and teaching effectiveness? How might you go about finding answers to your questions?

5. Interview a teacher at the school identified in the above activity. What special satisfactions does he or she experience from teaching at the school? What significant problems relating to diversity does he or she encounter, and how are they dealt with?

Professional Portfolio

1. Analyze a school as a social institution. How is the school organized in terms of roles and statuses? How does the school's organization and functioning reflect the wider society as well as the community in which it is located? What characteristics of the school and its people relate to the urban, rural, or suburban nature of the school environment?

2. Develop a case study of a school's culture. Visit a local school or base your study on a school you have attended. Organize your case in terms of the following categories of information:

   - *Environment*—How would you describe the school facility or physical plant and its material and human resources? How is space organized? What is the climate of the school?
   - *Formal Practices*—What grades are included at the school? How is the school year organized? How is time structured? How are students and teachers grouped for instruction?
   - *Traditions*—What events and activities and products seem important to students, teachers, and administrators? What symbols, slogans, and ceremonies identify membership in the school? How do community members view and relate to the school?

   Draw conclusions from your case study: What aspects of the school culture seem to support learning and academic achievement? On the basis of your case study, draft a position statement on the kind of culture you would like to create or promote in your classroom.

3. Prepare an annotated directory of local resources for teaching students about diversity, implementing multicultural curricula, and promoting harmony or equity among diverse groups. For each entry, include an annotation—that is, a brief description of the resource materials and their availability.

   - Resources for your personalized directory should be available through local sources such as your university library, public library, community agencies, and so on. Among the types of resources you might include are the following:
   - Films, videos, audio tapes, books, and journal articles
   - Simulation games designed to improve participants' attitudes toward diversity
   - Motivational guest speakers from the community
   - Ethnic museums and cultural centres
   - Community groups and agencies dedicated to promoting understanding among diverse groups
   - Training and workshops in the area of diversity

Appendix 5.1

The following questions are designed to determine how gender-neutral you are with respect to your normal speech patterns. When you respond to these questions, please answer honestly. Do not respond with what you consider to be the "correct" answer; rather, respond with an answer which truly reflects how you speak in the situations described.

	Yes	No
1. Would you refer to the boy who delivers your daily newspaper as the "paperboy"?	_____	_____
2. Would you refer to a member of your local fire department as a "fireman"?	_____	_____
3. Would you refer to a woman who works for your police department as a "policewoman"?	_____	_____
4. Would you refer to the man who delivers your mail as the "mailman"?	_____	_____
5. Do you almost invariably say "his and hers" as opposed to "hers and his"?	_____	_____
6. Do you, or would you, use phrases such as the following: "Don't rag me" or "She ragged him out"?	_____	_____
7. Do you comment on the dress or physical appearance of women far more often than you do of men?	_____	_____
8. In your normal speech do you ever use the term "mankind" or "man" when referring to the human race?	_____	_____
9. When referring to native peoples and early European settlers would you ever use the term "the white man"?	_____	_____
10. When referring to people who fish do you call them "fishermen"?	_____	_____
11. When referring to a clerk who has waited on you, would you ever use such a phrase as "the lady who works at the clothing store"?	_____	_____
12. When talking of the woman who cleans your house or apartment would you refer to her as the "cleaning lady"?	_____	_____
13. When speaking of artificial or synthetic products do you ever use the term "manmade" to describe such products?	_____	_____
14. Would you use the word "guys" when speaking to, or about, a group comprised of females and males?	_____	_____
15. If you were writing a formal paper and used the following quotation: "Every bank manager must watch his staff with care," would you fail to make an editorial insertion so the quotation read: "Every bank manager must watch his [or her] staff with care"?	_____	_____
16. Would you ever refer to a medical doctor who treated you as a "woman doctor" or, in the case of a man who is a nurse, as a "male nurse"?	_____	_____
17. Would you ever refer to a woman who was bothering you in some way as "a bitch"?	_____	_____
18. Do you often use the pronouns "he" or "his" when referring to someone whose sex is unknown to you? eg., "I would like to speak to the manager if he's in"?	_____	_____
19. Do you ever refer to the person who attends you on an airplane as the "stewardess"?	_____	_____
20. To the best of your knowledge has anyone—within the last month—ever corrected you for what she or he considered to be your use of sexist language?	_____	_____

Totals: _____ _____

Appendix 5.1 *(continued)*

Rating scale is based upon the number of "Yes" responses. If you do not know why a specific "Yes" response is considered inappropriate, you might visit one of the numerous "gender-neutral language" web sites.

16–20   *Watch your tongue or it may hurt you.*
Many of those involved in hiring teachers are language sensitive, will notice your speech patterns, and select someone else.

11–15   *Fair.*
You're trying, but you've still have a long way to go.

6–10   *Good.*
This probably puts you in the top 10 percent of the population with respect to gender-neutral language.

0– 5   *Very impressive.*

Explanations as to why "Yes" answers are inappropriate can be found on the pages which follow.

Appendix 5.1 *(continued)*

Languages tend to reflect the prejudices of the society from which they have evolved. English, which developed within a male-centred, patriarchal society, traditionally assigned the masculine gender to terms or individuals which might have been neutral or feminine in nature. A book title such as *The History of Western Man* provides a perfect example of this practice.

As our language continues to evolve it is appropriate for everyone, and educators in particular, to assist our language's progress towards a more inclusive model. Language which is exclusionary can alienate our readers or listeners who may feel personally diminished or—and this is the critical point for teachers—reject our message because they perceive us as sexist or insensitive to their existence.

A common reaction among those who take this test and score poorly on it is to say: "There is no need for me to become politically correct." This response suggests an insensitivity to the realities of today's society. The issue is not one of political correctness; rather, it is one of fairness and clarity. To speak of the "guys" when referring to a group that contains both male and female students is definitely misleading. Similarly, to speak about the "firemen" hosing down your burning house, several of whom are women, is both unfair and confusing.

The "Yes" answers within the *Gender-Neutral Language Test* are regarded as inappropriate. The explanations, and suggested gender-neutral alternative uses, follow.

1. Paperboy: Genderist. Some girls also deliver newspapers—as do many adult men and women. Newspaper publishers refer to all such individuals as "paper carriers."
2. Fireman: Genderist. Both men and women work for fire departments and all refer to themselves with the accurate and gender-neutral term of "firefighter."
3. Policewoman: Genderist. Both men and women work for police departments. All of them refer to themselves as "police officers."
4. Mailman: Genderist. Both men and women deliver mail to homes; both refer to themselves as "postal carriers."
5. His/Hers; Hers/His. To always place the masculine "his" first is regarded by many as insensitive. The recommendation is to alternate the use of his/hers with hers/his.

6. Don't rag me: Sexist and insulting. It is a reference to premenstrual syndrome (PMS) and women's use of sanitary napkins during menstruation.
7. Women's dress/appearance. If you comment equally about the dress and/or appearance of both men and women, there is little problem. However, if you single out women for special comment you are being sexist, whether you are a man or a woman.
8. Man/Mankind: Sexist. These usages, when referring to both men and women, are exclusionary. Use "humans," "humanity," "people," or another word or phrase that does not involve a particular gender.
9. White Man: Genderist. This suggests that all early settlers were white males. This is certainly erroneous on a number of levels. Use "Europeans" or, simply, "early settlers."
10. Fishermen: Genderist. There are many women who fish. If speaking about inshore people who fish, use the term "anglers" or "fishers;" if speaking about offshore people who fish, use "fishers."
11. Lady: Stereotypical. It is perfectly acceptable to say "Ladies and gentlemen" for this is a parallel use of masculine and feminine terms. However, to use lady as a generic synonym for a woman is inappropriate. A lady is a woman who acts and behaves in a socially prescribed manner. Using lady as the reference to a woman about whom you know little tends to suggest that (a) she is not necessarily viewed as a mature and responsible individual and (b) that she should act in a manner that befits a lady.
12. Cleaning lady: Genderist. (See #11 above). Men also clean houses. Use "cleaner."
13. Manmade: Genderist. Women also make things. Use "artificial," synthetic," or "manufactured."
14. Guys: Genderist. Guys are males. Using this word as a collective noun for a group of males and females is inappropriate; using it as a reference to a group comprised exclusively of females is even more inappropriate.
15. Editorial insertions: These are usually placed within material directly cited from another writer. To indicate to your readers that you are sensitive to language gender issues you should make such editorial insertions whenever the need arises.

16. Woman Doctor: Genderist. Expressions such as "woman doctor" or "male nurse" imply that the occupation in question normally "belongs" to a man or to a woman. Make women part of the rule, not the exception.
17. Bitch: Sexist and insulting. A bitch is a female dog with a perceived bad temper. To refer to a woman as a bitch is highly inappropriate.
18. He: Genderist. If a person's gender is unknown to you, do not automatically refer to that person with a masculine pronoun. Use any gender-neutral term such as: owner, manager, superior, etc.
19. Stewardess: Genderist. It has been 25 years since any flight attendant, male or female, used such a term. Although the term actress lives on, most words with the feminine *-ess* ending are being dropped from use.
20. Your use of sexist language. If someone has corrected you for such use, or if you scored poorly on the *Gender-Neutral Language Test*, perhaps you should visit one of the websites listed above.

Gender-Neutral Language Websites

www.ucc.ie/ucc/equalcom/language.html#Page4

www.otago.ac.nz/personnelservices/Policies/NonSexistLang Guide.html

http://langue.lc.chubu.ac.jp/jalt/pub/tlt/98/may/beebe.html

http://coral.wcupa.edu/stupaper/01gems.htm

Appendix 5.2

Selected Books for Meeting Needs of Students Placed at Risk

101 Ways to Develop Student Self-Esteem and Responsibility. Jack Canfield and Frank Siccone. Boston: Allyn and Bacon, 1994.

Against The Odds: How "At-risk" Children Exceed Expectations. Janie Bempechat. San Francisco: Jossey-Bass, 1998.

Assessment and Instruction of Culturally and Linguistically Diverse Students with or At-risk of Learning Problems: From Research to Practice. Virginia Gonzalez, Rita Brusca-Vega, and Thomas Yawkey. Boston: Allyn and Bacon, 1997.

At-risk Students: Tools for Teaching in Problem Settings. Susan L. Peterson. San Francisco: International Scholars Publications, 1998.

Beyond Discipline: From Compliance to Community. Alfie Kohn. Alexandria, VA: Association for Supervision and Curriculum Development, 1996.

Get to School Safely! Washington, DC: National Institute on the Education of At-Risk Students.

Hope at Last for At-Risk Youth. R.D. Barr and W.H. Parrett. Boston: Allyn and Bacon, 1995.

Last Chance High: How Girls and Boys Drop In and Out of Alternative Schools. Deirdre Kelly. New Haven, CT: Yale University Press, 1993.

Mentoring Students at Risk: An Underutilized Alternative Education Strategy for K-12 Teachers. Gary Reglen. Springfield, IL: Charles C. Thomas Publishers, 1998.

The New Circles of Learning: Cooperation in the Classroom and School. David W. Johnson, Roger T. Johnson, and Edythe J. Holubec. Alexandria, VA: Association for Supervision and Curriculum Development, 1994.

Open Lives, Safe Schools. Donovan R. Walling (Ed.). Bloomington, IN: Phi Delta Kappa Educational Foundation, 1996.

Reducing School Violence through Conflict Resolution. David W. Johnson and Roger T. Johnson. Alexandria, VA: Association for Supervision and Curriculum Development, 1995.

Resiliency in Schools: Making It Happen for Students and Educators. Nan Henderson and Mike M. Milstein. Thousand Oaks, CA: Corwin Press, 1996.

Safe Passage: Making It Through Adolescence in a Risky Society. Joy G. Dryfoos. New York: Oxford University Press, 1998.

A School for Healing: Alternative Strategies for Teaching At-risk Students. Rosa L. Kennedy and Jerome H. Morton. New York: P. Lang, 1999.

The School Safety Handbook: Taking Action for Student and Staff Protection. Kenneth Lane, Michael D. Richardson, and Dennis W. Van Berkum (Eds.). Lancaster, PA: Technomic Publishing Company, 1996.

Students at Risk. H. Lee Manning and Leroy G. Baruth. Boston: Allyn and Bacon, 1995.

Talk It Out: Conflict Resolution in the Elementary Classroom. Barbara Porro. Alexandria, VA: Association for Supervision and Curriculum Development, 1996.

Teaching Mainstreamed, Diverse, and At-risk Students in the General Education Classroom. Sharon Vaughn, Candace S. Bos, and Jeanne S. Schumm. Boston: Allyn and Bacon, 1997.

Teaching Social Competence: A Practical Approach for Improving Social Skills in Students At-risk. Dennis R. Knapczyk and Paul Rodes. Pacific Grove, CA: Brooks/Cole, Pub. Co., 1996.

Toward Resiliency: At-risk Students Who Make It to College. Laura J. Horn, Xianglei Chen, and Clifford Adelman. Washington, DC: U.S. Department of Education.

Treating Adolescent Substance Abuse: Understanding the Fundamental Elements. George R. Ross. Boston: Allyn and Bacon, 1994.

Using Educational Technology with At-risk Students: A Guide for Library Media Specialists and Teachers. Roxanne B. Mendrinos. Westport, CT: Greenwood Press, 1997.

Waiting for a Miracle: Why Schools Can't Solve Our Problems—And How We Can. James P. Comer. New York: Dutton, 1997.

part three

The Art of Teaching

dear mentor

On Becoming a Master Teacher

Dear Mentor,

I have been a university student for two years. I would like to find out how to become a master teacher. What is the profile of a master teacher?

Sincerely,

Darryl Hampton

D
ear Darryl,

Congratulations on being a second-year university student with the goal of becoming a teacher. Teaching is a valuable profession and one that will require your heart, talent, and energy.

Regarding how to become a master teacher, I think you've taken an important first step by asking the question. Look for master teachers and observe them. Keep in mind what good teaching looks like. Seek a mentor and make time for the relationship.

As you begin your career, it is important that you know and use the academic standards for your subject area—whether it is elementary education, middle school math, or high school English. Your lesson plans should show how you will teach students the learning strategies they will need to meet those standards. Join the academic professional organization in your subject area. The members can become an expert support group.

Also, take time to observe and learn about your school's culture. Seek to understand the school's community. From there, decide how you can be a positive contributor to both your school and community.

Believe in your ability to teach. When a challenge faces you, use your problem-solving skills. For example, in your class there could be a student who is reading below grade level. Use a variety of instructional methods to engage the student, and continue to explore other approaches to teaching reading skills. Read articles, attend professional development classes, or consult with your school district's or university's reading specialists. For, you see, as a teacher, your learning is ever-growing.

But most important of all, believe in your students' desire to learn. That has become my driving force. My students motivate and inspire me to become a better teacher for them. As the professional in the classroom, a teacher must provide a safe and caring environment that encourages learning and effort. It is not enough to instill high dreams. We must equip our students with academic skills so that they have the tools to reach those dreams.

Incorporate your talents and interests into your teaching. That's one way to show your students a connection between what they learn in school and the real world.

In closing, I want to share with you some advice for new teaches that my second and third graders gave: "I would suggest patience and thoughtfulness, and make them laugh a little." "If a student needs help don't tell them the answer; just help them with the problem." So Darryl, you see, students really want a teacher's help.

Above all, remember to celebrate successes, because encouragement is never wasted.

Sincerely,

Janice James

6

Addressing Learners' Individual Needs

I was ... fortunate that I chose theoretical physics, because it is all in the mind. So my disability has not been a serious handicap.

—Stephen W. Hawking
In *A Brief History of Time: From the Big Bang to Black Holes*

focus questions

1. How do students' needs change as they develop?

2. How do students vary in intelligence?

3. How do students vary in ability and disability?

4. What are special education, mainstreaming, and inclusion?

5. How can you teach all learners in your inclusive classroom?

It's late Friday afternoon, the end of the fourth week of school, and you've just finished arranging your classroom for the cooperative learning groups you're starting on Monday. Leaning back in the chair at your desk, you survey the room and imagine how things will go on Monday. Your mental image is positive, with one possible exception—eleven-year-old Rick. Since the first day of school, he's been very disruptive. His teacher last year described him as "loud, aggressive, and obnoxious."

Since school began, Rick has been belligerent and noncompliant. For the most part, he does what he wants, when he wants. As far as you know, he has no close friends; he teases the other kids constantly and occasionally gets into fights.

Rick's parents divorced when he was in the second grade. His father was given custody of Rick and his younger sister. Two years later, Rick's father married a woman with three children of her own. You've heard that Rick's two new half-brothers, 13 and 15 years old, are "out of control," and the family has been receiving counselling services from the local mental health clinic.

Rick's school records indicate that other teachers have had trouble with him in the past. Academically, he's below his classmates in all subjects except physical education and art. Comments from two of his previous teachers suggest Rick has a flair for artwork. Last year, Rick was diagnosed with mild learning and behaviour disorders.

Mr. Macdonald, the school guidance counsellor, and Ms Tamashiro, the school's special educator, have been working with you on developing an individualized education program (IEP) for Rick. In fact, before school on Monday, you're meeting with Ms Tamashiro to discuss how to involve Rick in the cooperative learning groups. You're anxious to get her suggestions, and you're confident that with her help and Mr Mac-Donald's you can meet Rick's learning needs.

As the preceding scenario about Rick suggests, teachers must understand and appreciate students' unique learning and developmental needs. They must be willing to learn about students' abilities and disabilities and to explore the special issues and concerns of students at three broad developmental levels—childhood, early adolescence, and late adolescence. The need to learn about the intellectual and psychological growth of students at the age level you plan to teach is obvious. In addition, understanding how their interests, questions, and problems will change throughout their school years will better equip you to serve them in the present. In this chapter, we look at how students' needs change as they develop and how their needs reflect various intelligences, abilities, and disabilities.

How Do Students' Needs Change As They Develop?

Development refers to the predictable changes that all human beings undergo as they progress through the life span—from conception to death. Although developmental changes "appear in orderly ways and remain for a reasonably long period of time" (Woolfolk 1998, 24), it is important to remember that students develop at different rates. Within a given classroom, for example, some students will be larger and physically more mature than others; some will be socially more sophisticated; and some will be able to think at a higher level of abstraction.

As humans progress through different **stages of development**, they mature and learn to perform the tasks that are a necessary part of daily living. There are several different types of human development. For example, as children develop physically, their bodies undergo numerous changes. As they develop cognitively, their mental capabilities expand so that they can use language and other symbol systems to solve problems. As they develop socially, they learn to interact more effectively with other people—as individuals and in groups. And, as they develop morally, their actions come to reflect a greater appreciation of principles such as equity, justice, fairness, and altruism.

Because no two students progress through the stages of cognitive, social, and moral development in quite the same way, teachers need perspectives on these three types of development that are flexible, dynamic, and, above all, useful. By becoming familiar with models of cognitive, social, and moral development, teachers at all levels, from preschool through college, can better serve their students. Three such models are Piaget's theory of **cognitive development**, Erikson's stages of **psychosocial development**, and Kohlberg's stages of **moral reasoning.**

Piaget's Model of Cognitive Development

Jean Piaget (1896–1980), the noted Swiss biologist and epistemologist, made extensive observational studies of children. He concluded that children reason differently from adults and even have different perceptions of the world. Piaget surmised that children learn through actively interacting with their environments, much as scientists do, and proposed that a child's thinking progresses through a sequence of four cognitive stages (see Figure 6.1). According to Piaget's theory of cognitive development, the rate of progress through the four stages varies from individual to individual. During the school years, students move through the **preoperational stage**, the **concrete operations stage**, and the **formal operations stage**; yet because of individual interaction with the total environment, each student's perceptions and learning will be unique. According to Piaget:

Jean Piaget
(1896–1980)

> The principal goal of education is to create [learners] who are capable of doing new things, not simply repeating what other generations have done—[learners] who are creative, inventive, and discoverers. [We] need pupils who are active, who learn early to find out by themselves, partly by their own spontaneous activity and partly through material we set up for them; who learn early to tell what is verifiable and what is simply the first idea to come to them (quoted in Ripple and Rockcastle 1964, 5).

Figure 6.2 presents guidelines for teaching children at the preoperational stage, the concrete operations stage, and the formal operations stage.

Erikson's Model of Psychosocial Development

Erik Erikson's model of psychosocial development delineates eight stages, from infancy to old age (see Table 6.1). For each stage a **psychosocial crisis** is central in the individual's emotional and social growth. Erikson expresses these crises in polar terms; for instance, in the first stage, that of infancy, the psychosocial crisis is trust versus mistrust. Erikson explains that the major psychosocial task for the infant is to develop a sense of trust in the world but not to give up totally a sense of distrust. In the tension between the poles of trust and mistrust, a greater pull toward the more positive pole is considered healthy and is accompanied by a virtue. In this case, if trust prevails, the virtue is hope. Shortly before his death in 1994 at the age of 91, Erikson postulated a ninth stage in the human life cycle, *gerotranscendence*, during which some people mentally transcend the reality of their deteriorating bodies and faculties. In the final chapter of an extended version of Erikson's *The Life Cycle Completed*, first published in 1982, his wife and lifelong colleague, Joan M. Erikson (1901–1997), described the challenge of the ninth stage:

Erik Erikson
(1902–1994)

> Despair, which haunts the eighth stage, is a close companion in the ninth, because it is almost impossible to know what emergencies and losses of physical ability are imminent. As independence and control are challenged, self-esteem and confidence weaken. Hope and trust, which once provided firm support, are no longer the sturdy props of former days. To face down despair with faith and appropriate humility is perhaps the wisest course (Erikson 1997, 105–6).

When we examine the issues and concerns of students in childhood and early and late adolescence later in this chapter, we will return to Erikson's model of psychosocial development. For further information on this significant and useful theory of development, we recommend that you read Erikson's first book, *Childhood and Society* (1963).

1. **Sensorimotor Intelligence (birth to 2 years):**
Behaviour is primarily sensory and motor. The child does not yet "think" conceptually; however, "cognitive" development can be observed.

2. **Preoperational Thought (2–7 years):**
Development of language and rapid conceptual development are evident. Children begin to use symbols to think of objects and people outside of their immediate environment. Fantasy and imaginative play are natural modes of thinking.

3. **Concrete Operations (7–11 years):**
Children develop ability to use logical thought to solve concrete problems. Basic concepts of objects, number, time, space, and causality are explored and mastered. Through use of concrete objects to manipulate, children are able to draw conclusions.

4. **Formal Operations (11–15 years):**
Cognitive abilities reach their highest level of development. Children can make predictions, think about hypothetical situations, think about thinking, and appreciate the structure of language as well as use it to communicate. Sarcasm, puns, argumentation, and slang are aspects of adolescents' speech that reflect their ability to think abstractly about language.

Figure 6.1

Piaget's stages of cognitive growth

Kohlberg's Model of Moral Development

According to Lawrence Kohlberg (1927–1987), the reasoning process people use to decide what is right and wrong evolves through three levels of development. Within each level, Kohlberg has identified two stages. Table 6.2 on page 215 shows that at Level I, the preconventional level, the individual decides what is right on the basis of personal needs and rules developed by others. At Level II, the conventional level, moral decisions reflect a desire for the approval of others and a willingness to conform to the expectations of family, community, and country. At Level III, the postconventional level, the individual has developed values and principles that are based on rational, personal choices that can be separated from conventional values.

Figure 6.2

Guidelines for Teaching School-Age Children at Piaget's Three Stages of Cognitive Growth

Guidelines for teaching school-age children at Piaget's three stages of cognitive growth

Source: Excerpted from Anita E. Woolfolk, *Educational Psychology,* 7th ed. Boston: Allyn and Bacon, 1998, pp. 33, 36, 39. Copyright © 1998 by Allyn and Bacon. Reprinted by permission.

Teaching the Child at the Preoperational Stage

1. Use concrete props and visual aids whenever possible.
2. Make instruction relatively short, using actions as well as words.
3. Don't expect the students to be consistent in their ability to see the world from someone else's point of view.
4. Be sensitive to the possibility that students may have different meanings for the same word or different words for the same meaning. Students may also expect everyone to understand words they have invented.
5. Give children a great deal of hands-on practice with the skills that serve as building blocks for more complex skills such as reading comprehension.
6. Provide a wide range of experiences in order to build a foundation for concept learning and language.

Teaching the Child at the Concrete-Operational Stage

1. Continue to use concrete props and visual aids, especially when dealing with sophisticated material.
2. Continue to give students a chance to manipulate and test objects.
3. Make sure presentation and readings are brief and well organized.
4. Use familiar examples to explain more complex ideas.
5. Give opportunities to classify and group objects and ideas on increasingly complex levels.
6. Present problems that require logical, analytical thinking.

Teaching the Child at the Formal Operations Stage

1. Continue to use concrete-operational teaching strategies and materials.
2. Give students the opportunity to explore many hypothetical questions.
3. Give students opportunities to solve problems and reason scientifically.
4. Whenever possible, teach broad concepts, not just facts, using materials and ideas relevant to the students' lives.

Kohlberg suggests that "over 50 percent of late adolescents and adults are capable of full formal reasoning [ie., they can use their intelligence to reason abstractly, form hypotheses, and test these hypotheses against reality], but only 10 percent of these adults display principled (Stages 5 and 6) moral reasoning" (2000, 138–39). In addition, Kohlberg found that maturity of moral judgment is not highly related to IQ or verbal intelligence.

Some individuals have criticized Kohlberg's model as being too systematic and sequential, limited because it focuses on moral reasoning rather than actual behaviour, or biased because it tends to look at moral development from a male perspective (Bracey 1993). Carol Gilligan, for example, suggests that male moral reasoning tends to address the rights of the individual while female moral reasoning addresses the individual's responsibility to other people. In her book, *In a Different Voice: Psychological Theory and Women's Development* (1993), Gilligan refers to women's principal moral voice as the "ethics of care," which emphasizes care of others over the more male-oriented "ethics of justice." Thus, when confronted with a moral dilemma, females tend to suggest solutions based more on altruism and self-sacrifice than on rights and rules (Gilligan 1993).

Lawrence Kohlberg
(1927–1987)

Table 6.1

Erikson's eight stages of psychological development

Stage	Psychosocial Crisis	Approximate Age	Important Event	Description
1. Infancy	Basic trust versus basic mistrust	Birth to 12–18 months	Feeding	The infant must form a first loving, trusting relationship with the caregiver or develop a sense of mistrust.
2. Early Childhood	Autonomy versus shame/doubt	18 months to 3 years	Toilet training	The child's energies are directed toward the development of physical skills, including walking, grasping, controlling the sphincter.
3. Play Age	Initiative versus guilt	3 to 6 years	Independence	The child learns control but may develop shame and doubt if not handled well.
4. School Age	Industry versus inferiority	6 to 12 years	School	The child continues to become more assertive and to take more initiative but may be too forceful, which can lead to guilt feelings.
5. Adolescence	Identity versus role confusion	Adolescence	Peer relationships	The child must deal with demands to learn new skills or risk a sense of inferiority, failure, and incompetence.
6. Young Adult	Intimacy versus isolation	Young adulthood	Love relationships	The teenager must achieve identity in occupation, gender roles, politics, and religion.
7. Adulthood	Generativity versus stagnation	Middle adulthood	Parenting/Mentoring	The young adult must develop intimate relationships or suffer feelings of isolation. Each adult must find some way to satisfy and support the next generation.
8. Mature Love	Ego integrity versus despair	Late adulthood	Reflection on and acceptance of one's life	The culmination is a sense of acceptance of oneself as one is and a sense of fulfillment.

Source: Adapted from Lester A. Lefton, *Psychology*, 7th ed. Boston: Allyn and Bacon, 1999. Copyright © 1999 by Allyn and Bacon. Reprinted by permission.

The question remains, can moral reasoning be taught? Can teachers help students develop so that they live according to principles of equity, justice, caring, and empathy? Kohlberg suggests that the following three conditions can help children internalize moral principles:

1. Exposure to the next higher stage of reasoning
2. Exposure to situations posing problems and contradictions for the child's current moral structure, leading to dissatisfaction with his [her] current level
3. An atmosphere of interchange and dialogue combining the first two conditions, in which conflicting moral views are compared in an open manner (Kohlberg 2000, 144)

One approach to teaching values and moral reasoning is known as **character education,** a movement that stresses the development of students' "good character." *Character Education,* a 2001 report by the Calgary Board of Education, is one of many examples that makes clear the need for character education to make a "comeback" in

Table 6.2

Kohlberg's theory of moral reasoning

I. Preconventional Level of Moral Reasoning

Child is responsive to cultural rules and labels of good and bad, right or wrong, but interprets these in terms of consequences of action (punishment, reward, exchanges of favours).

Stage 1: Punishment-and-obedience orientation
Physical consequences of action determine its goodness or badness. Avoidance of punishment and deference to power are valued.

Stage 2: The instrumental-relativist orientation
Right action consists of that which satisfies one's own needs and occasionally the needs of others. Reciprocity is a matter of "You scratch my back and I'll scratch yours."

II . Conventional Level of Moral Reasoning

Maintaining the expectations of the individual's family, group, or nation is perceived as valuable, regardless of consequences.

Stage 3: The interpersonal concordance or "good boy–nice girl" orientation
Good behaviour is that which pleases or helps others and is approved by them.

Stage 4: The "law and order" orientation
Orientation toward fixed rules and the maintenance of the social order. Right behaviour consists of doing one's duty and showing respect for authority.

III. Postconventional, Autonomous, or Principled Level of Moral Reasoning

Effort to define moral principles that have validity and application apart from the authority of groups.

Stage 5: The social-contract, legalistic orientation
Right action defined in terms of rights and standards that have been agreed on by the whole society. This is the "official" morality of the American government and Constitution.

Stage 6: The universal-ethical-principle orientation
Right is defined by conscience in accord with self-chosen *ethical principles* appealing to logic and universality.

Source: Adapted from Lawrence Kohlberg, "*The Cognitive-Developmental Approach to Moral Education*," in *Curriculum Planning: A Contemporary Approach*, 7th ed., Forrest W. Parkay and Glen Hass (eds.). Boston: Allyn and Bacon, 2000, p.137. The original version appeared in *Journal of Philosophy*, *70*(18), 1973, pp. 631–32.

our society (Jeary 2001). This report, which draws heavily upon the work of Piaget, Kohlberg, Kohn and other primarily American sources for its recommendations, strongly suggests that a movement grounded primarily within the United States has crossed the border and taken root in Canada. Books and resources for Canadian teachers who might wish to introduce character education into their classrooms are becoming more readily available, and most provincial departments of education are giving varying degrees of attention to the topic. Even service organizations are becoming involved. The Lions Club of Canada now offers its Lions-Quest life skills program to students and teachers. "Lions-Quest programs teach youth to accept responsibility, communicate effectively, set goals, make healthy decisions, and resist pressure to use alcohol and drugs. Lions clubs, districts and multiple districts support Lions-Quest through funding, coordination of teacher training, and in other ways." In addition, Figure 6.3 illustrates twelve strategies teachers can use to create moral classroom communities.

Figure 6.3

A comprehensive approach to values and character education

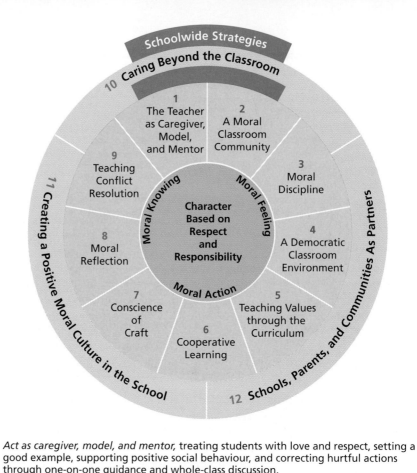

1. *Act as caregiver, model, and mentor,* treating students with love and respect, setting a good example, supporting positive social behaviour, and correcting hurtful actions through one-on-one guidance and whole-class discussion.

2. *Create a moral community,* helping students know one another as persons, respect and care about one another, and feel valued membership in, and responsibility to, the group.

3. *Practice moral discipline,* using the creation and enforcement of rules as opportunities to foster moral reasoning, voluntary compliance with rules, and a respect for others.

4. *Create a democratic classroom environment,* involving students in decision making and the responsibility for making the classroom a good place to be and learn.

5. *Teach values through the curriculum,* using the ethically rich content of academic subjects (such as literature, history, and science) as vehicles for teaching values and examining moral questions.

6. *Use cooperative learning* to develop students' appreciation of others, perspective taking, and the ability to work with others toward common goals.

7. *Develop the "conscience of craft"* by fostering students' appreciation of learning, capacity for hard work, commitment to excellence, and sense of work as affecting the lives of others.

8. *Encourage moral reflection* through reading, research, essay writing, journal keeping, discussion, and debate.

9. *Teach conflict resolution,* so that students acquire the essential moral skills of solving conflicts fairly and without force.

10. *Foster caring beyond the classroom,* using positive role models to inspire altruistic behaviour and providing opportunities at every grade level to perform school and community service.

11. *Create a positive moral culture in the school,* developing a schoolwide ethos that supports and amplifies the values taught in classrooms.

12. *Recruit parents and the community as partners in character education,* letting parents know that the school considers them their child's first and most important moral teacher.

Is character education an effective way to improve society?

Character education and the teaching of moral values have been part of provincial educational systems from their inception. The main reason schools were created was to see that children learned to read the Bible so they could lead good lives and find salvation Over the years, and with the exception of Canada's parochial schools, the ties to religion in education weakened. They have been replaced with an emphasis on acquiring knowledge for an informed citizenship, first, on knowledge for occupational purposes; and later, in the 1960s and 1970s, knowledge for individual growth and self-fulfillment. Today, with the perceived increases in racism, hate crimes, gang activity, random violence and a general erosion of ethical behaviour and common decency, many people call for a return to teaching values and morals in schools. As a consequence, all Canadian provinces and territories now have some form of character education in their public schools. Independent (private) schools, many of which have roots within one denomination or another, have continued to deliver character or moral education. Indeed, these schools use their provision of a character building environment as a major reason for parents to enroll their children with them.

Proponents regard character education as a necessary and effective way to improve society. Opponents disagree, believing that character education is too authoritarian in its implementation, narrow in its perspective, and intrusive into family matters. Where do you stand on this issue? Do you think character education will improve society?

Today's proponents observe that educators do teach values in school whether they do so intentionally or not. The way teachers do things in school—often referred to as the hidden curriculum—can teach students that people are not equal, working independently is better than helping others (the latter is "cheating"), external rewards should be sought, competition is good, obedience should be paid to authorities, one should take care of "Number one," and winning is everything. The proponents argue that since educators are teaching values anyway—even some values we wish they weren't teaching—they should do so consciously and deliberately with a formal program.

They also point out that today's students come from a different family and social environment than their predecessors did. The increased number of single-parent families and families with both parents working outside the home and the decrease in extended families living together combine to empty homes of adults that could guide students in their moral development. Schools must pick up the slack and give students the moral direction and tools they need to negotiate today's increasingly complex and morally challenging society. These proponents suggest that schools plan their programs with the assistance of parents, determining together the goals to pursue and the values to emphasize. They argue that to fail to offer character education in schools and instead leave it to parents already stressed by finances and overwork is to place at risk a safe and healthy future for the nation's children and youth.

Character education is an effective way to improve society.

Proponents of character education believe that morals and ethics are inherent and necessary aspects of education. Many Canadians would agree that educating a person in mind but not in morals is to educate a menace to society. Ernest Boyer, the late president of the Carnegie Foundation for the Advancement of Teaching wrote, "Education unguided by an ethical compass is potentially more dangerous than ignorance itself." In his book *The Basic School,* Boyer (1995) stressed that schools should not concern themselves only with teaching and instruction but also with giving students an appreciation for the dignity of human life and empowering them to make a difference in society.

Character education is not an effective way to improve society.

In his book *Answering the "Virtuecrats": A Moral Conversation on Character Education,* Robert Nash writes, "In the extreme, much character education is unnecessarily apocalyptic and narrow in its cultural criticism, inherently authoritarian in its convictions, excessively nostalgic and premodern in its understanding of virtue, too closely aligned with a reactionary (or a radical) politics, anti-intellectual in its curricular initiatives, hyperbolic in its moral claims, dangerously antidemocratic, and overly simplistic in its contention that training and imitation alone are sufficient for instilling moral character" (1997, 10). He critiques the works of authors in three schools of moral education—conservative, liberal, and libertarian—and proposes his own approach, the cultivation of a "democratic character," a pragmatic means of coping with conflicting perspectives and the potential of "unruly disagreements" in a pluralistic society.

The loudest cry of opponents is that moral development is a family matter and not the school's. They complain that schools already infringe on families more than they should and that teachers should not take time away from academics to teach moral values. Many parents worry that their children will be taught values that contradict their religious beliefs. Others ask the question, "Whose values will be taught?"

Alfie Kohn, in an article entitled "How Not to Teach Values," asks a related question: "Which values will be taught?" (1997). He believes that most character education programs are based on a conservative perspective and require obedience to authority. He describes the typical method of instruction in character education programs as "tantamount to indoctrination. The point is to drill students in specific behaviours rather than to engage them in deep, critical reflection about certain ways of being." He asks his readers to speculate on "the concrete differences between a school dedicated to turning out students who are empathic and skeptical and a school dedicated to turning out students who are loyal, patriotic, obedient, and so on." Kohn proposes that the better way to teach values is to lead students to ask themselves "what kind of person one ought to be, which traditions are worth keeping, and how to proceed when two basic values seem to be in conflict." Such discussions, character education opponents argue, should take place in the family and places of worship, not in schools.

Recommended Sources

Allan, R. (2001) In my world: A citizenship initiative and a progressive account of teacher change. *Research Connections Canada, (VII)*, 105–115. Canadian Childcare Federation.

Covell, K. & Howe, R. B. (2000). Moral education through the 3r's: rights, respect, and responsibility. *Journal of Moral Education, 30 (1)*, 31–43.

Kohn, A. (1997, February). How not to teach values: A critical look at character education, *Phi Delta Kappan*, 428–39.

Lickona, T. (1993). The return of character education, *Educational Leadership, 51 (3)*, 6–11.

Nash, R. J. (1997). *Answering the "virtuecrats": A moral conversation on character education.* New York: Teachers College Press.

Related Resources

Building Character with Literacy. (Available from Young People's Press. 1731 Kettner Blvd., San Diego, CA 92101. 1-800-231-9774.)

The Moral Intelligence of Children. (1998). Robert Coles. (Available from Penguin.)

The Giraffe Project. (Available from P.O. Box 759, Langley, WA 98260. 360-221-7989. email: medlock@giraffe.org. Also see www.giraffe.org/projectinfo.html).

Eleven Principles of Effective Character Education. Thomas Lickona and Catherine Lewis. Video commissioned by the Character Education Partnership. (Available from National Professional Resources, 25 South Regent Street; Port Chester, NY 10573. 1-800-453-7461.)

Building Character in Schools: Practical Ways to Bring Moral Instruction to Life. Kevin Ryan and Karen E. Bohlin. (Available from Jossey-Bass, a Wiley company.)

Related Websites

Visit the websites of the following resources:

A New Zealand Values Education Initiative.www.cornerstonevalues.org/education.htm

Character Education Network www.character.net/main/traits.asp

Centre for the Advancement of Ethics and Character www.bu.edu/education/caec/

Where do you stand on this issue?

1. Which position best reflects your own?

2. Which values, if any, would you like to see emphasized in schools today?

3. List several values that have a religious basis and several that apply to all people.

4. What methods could be used to teach character education through critical thinking?

5. Distinguish between indoctrination, instruction, and learning in a character education program.

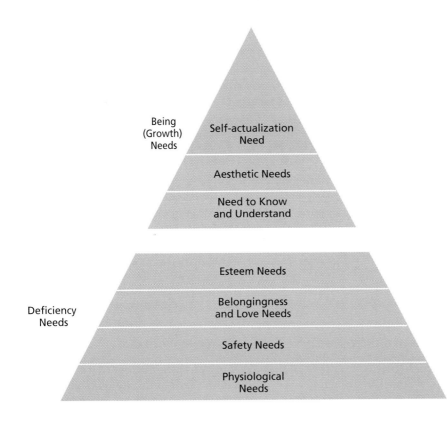

Figure 6.4

Maslow's hierarchy of needs.

Note: The four lower-level needs are called deficiency needs because the motivation to satisfy them decreases when they are met. On the other hand, when being (growth) needs are met, motivation to fulfill them increases.

Source: Based on Abraham H. Maslow, *Toward a Psychology of Being,* 3rd ed. New York: John Wiley & Sons, 1999; and *Motivation and Personality,* 3rd ed. Addison-Wesley Publishing Company, 1987.

Maslow's Model of Hierarchy of Needs

Students' developmental levels also vary according to how well their biological and psychological needs have been satisfied. Psychologist Abraham Maslow (1908–1970) formulated a model of a **hierarchy of needs** (see Figure 6.4) that suggests that people are motivated by basic needs for survival and safety first. When these basic needs have been met sufficiently, people naturally seek to satisfy higher needs, the highest of which is self-actualization—the desire to use one's talents, abilities, and potentialities to the fullest. Students whose needs for safety have been fairly well satisfied will discover strong needs for friendship, affection, and love, for example. If efforts to satisfy the various needs are thwarted, the result can be maladjustment and interruption or delay in the individual's full and healthy development.

The hierarchy of needs model has particular relevance for teachers because students differ markedly in terms of where they are on Maslow's hierarchy of needs. Many families lack the resources to provide adequately for children's basic needs. Children from families that are concerned with day-to-day survival may not receive the support that could help them succeed in school. They come to school tired and hungry and may have trouble paying attention in class. Others may be well fed and clothed but feel unsafe, alien, or unloved; they may seek to protect themselves by withdrawing emotionally from activities around them.

Developmental Stresses and Tasks of Childhood

During Erikson's school-age stage, children strive for a sense of industry and struggle against feelings of inferiority. If successful, they gain the virtue of competence, believing in their abilities to do things. If children find evidence that they are inferior to others, if they experience failure when they try new tasks, and if they struggle without ever gaining a sense of mastery, then they feel incompetent.

Children gain the sense of industry needed at this age by playing seriously, mastering new skills, producing products, and being workers. When they first go to school they are oriented toward accomplishing new things (some kindergartners expect to learn to read on their first day of school and are disappointed when they don't). For young schoolchildren, the idea of work is attractive; it means that they are doing something grown-up.

Is childhood a time of carefree play or a period of stress? Certainly the answer depends on the life circumstances and personality of the individual child. In a study of stressful events in the lives of more than 1700 children in Grades 2 to 9 in six countries, Karou Yamamoto and his associates found that the most stressful events "threaten[ed] one's sense of security and occasion[ed] personal denigration and embarrassment" (Yamamoto et al. 1996, 139). Other studies have shown that serious stress is experienced by latchkey children, for example, who are left on their own or in each others' care for part or all of the day.

Developmental Stresses and Tasks of Adolescence

Many psychologists believe that adolescence contains two distinct stages: an early period covering the ages of ten to twelve through the ages of fourteen to sixteen, and a late period from approximately fifteen to sixteen through nineteen. Although a continuity exists in each individual's life, the psychosocial issues of adolescence—coping with change and seeking identity—vary in form and importance as individuals progress through the transition from childhood to adulthood.

In Erik Erikson's model of the eight stages of humans, identity versus role diffusion is the psychosocial crisis for the adolescent years. Although the quest for identity is a key psychosocial issue for both early and late adolescence, many believe that Erikson's identity-versus-role diffusion stage fits best for early adolescence. During this time, young adolescents, using their new thinking abilities, begin integrating a clearer sense of personal identity. Erikson's role diffusion refers to the variety of roles that adolescents have available to them.

According to Erikson's theory, when adolescents identify themselves with a peer group, with a school, or with a cause, their sense of fidelity—the "virtue" of this stage—is clear and strong. At this stage adolescents are loyal and committed, sometimes to people or ideas that may dismay or alarm their parents, sometimes to high ideals and dreams.

What needs must this child satisfy for healthy development? What childhood stresses does she face? What developmental tasks must she accomplish in her psychosocial development? What needs, stresses, and developmental tasks will affect this child as an adolescent? Why is information about development important to teachers?

In late adolescence, the quest for identity shifts from relying on others to self-reliance. Young people continue to work on strengthening their sense of identity in late adolescence, but as they do so they draw less on the reactions of their peers and more on their own regard for what matters. Although late adolescents possess an array of interests, talents, and goals in life, they share a desire to achieve independence. More like adults than children, late adolescents are anxious to use newly acquired strengths, skills, and knowledge to achieve their own purposes, whether through marriage, parenthood, full-time employment, education beyond high school, a career, or military service.

The vulnerability of today's adolescents is portrayed graphically in *Great Transitions: Preparing Adolescents for a New Century*, a report by the Carnegie Council on Adolescent Development: "Altogether, nearly half of American adolescents are at high or moderate risk of seriously damaging their life chances. The damage may be near-term and vivid, or it may be delayed, like a time bomb set in youth" (Carnegie Council on Adolescent Development 1995). While there is little data to support a contention that an exactly similar situation exists in Canada, Canadian students do face an alarming number of risks. Foremost among these are fears of academic failure and retention, anorexia, bullying, criminal activity, cultism, depression, discipline problems, dropouts, drug abuse, homicides, incest, prostitution, runaways, school absenteeism, suicide, teenage pregnancy, vandalism, and the contraction of sexually transmitted diseases.

What can teachers do to help children and adolescents develop to their full potential? To help prevent the problems that place them at risk, an energetic, creative, and multifaceted approach is necessary. Figure 6.5 presents several strategies for helping students develop competence, positive self-concepts, and high esteem and for intervening to prevent or address problems that place them at risk.

Figure 6.5

What teachers can do to help children and adolescents develop

1. **Provide Opportunities and Encouragement for Students to Develop Competence.**

   - Provide a learning environment in which students can risk making mistakes.
   - Assign work that students can perform successfully and still be challenged.
   - Have realistic but high expectations for students.
   - Express belief in students' ability to succeed.
   - Encourage industry by letting students work on goals or projects of their choosing.
   - Provide opportunities for students to take special responsibility.
   - Assign older students to work with younger ones.
   - Reward industry and competence.

2. **Promote the Development of Positive Self-concept and High Self-esteem.**

   - Give praise more than criticism.
   - Take students and their work seriously.
   - Respect students' dignity.
   - Plan individual and group activities that boost morale.
   - Provide opportunities for students to interact and work cooperatively.
   - Teach and model acceptance of human diversity and individuality.
   - Develop systems for the recognition and reward of individual and group achievement.
   - Support students' efforts to achieve and appropriately express independence.

3. **Intervene to Prevent or Address Problems That Place Students at Risk.**

   - Provide a safe and structured learning environment where students feel secure.
   - Practice effective leadership and classroom management.
   - Provide opportunities to discuss preferences, values, morals, goals, and consequences.
   - Teach and model critical thinking, decision making, and problem solving.
   - Teach and model prosocial attitudes and behaviours and conflict resolution strategies.
   - Provide information on subjects of special concern to students and parents.
   - Cultivate family involvement.
   - Collaborate, consult, network, and refer on behalf of students.

How Do Students Vary in Intelligence?

In addition to developmental differences, students differ in terms of their intellectual capacity. Unfortunately, test scores, and sometimes intelligence quotient (IQ) scores, are treated as accurate measurements of students' intellectual ability because of their convenience and long-time use. What is intelligence and how has it been redefined to account for the many ways in which it is expressed? Though many definitions of intelligence have been proposed, the term has yet to be completely defined. One view is that **intelligence** is the ability to learn. As David Wechsler, the developer of the most widely used intelligence scales for children and adults, said: "Intelligence, operationally defined, is the aggregate or global capacity to act purposefully, to think rationally, and to deal effectively with the environment" (Wechsler 1958, 7). Other definitions of intelligence that have been proposed are the following:

- Goal-directed adaptive behaviour
- Ability to solve novel problems
- Ability to acquire and think with new conceptual systems
- Problem-solving ability
- Planning and other metacognitive skills
- Memory access speed
- What people think intelligence is
- What IQ tests measure
- The ability to learn from bad teaching (Woolfolk 1998, 109)

Intelligence Testing

The intelligence tests that we now use can be traced to the 1905 Metrical Scale of Intelligence designed by French psychologists Alfred Binet and Theodore Simon, who were part of a Paris-based commission that wanted a way to identify children who would need special help with their learning. Binet revised the scale in 1908, which was adapted for American children in 1916 by Lewis Terman, a psychologist at Stanford University. Terman's test was, in turn, further adapted, especially by the US Army, which transformed it into a paper-and-pencil test that could be administered to large groups. The use of such intelligence tests has continued throughout the years. Approximately 67 percent of the population have an IQ between 85 and 115—the range of normal intelligence. "Gifted" individuals have an IQ of 130+ while those at the genius level have an IQ of 140 or better.

Individual intelligence tests are presently valued by psychologists and those in the field of special education because they can be helpful in diagnosing a student's strengths and weaknesses. However, group intelligence tests given for the purpose of classifying students into like-score groups have received an increasing amount of criticism and have been greatly reduced in scope. Most Canadian school districts have policies similar to this example from the Ottawa–Carlton District School Board (2000).

> Commercial standardized tests in the schools of the Ottawa-Carleton district should be used sparingly, as one method of providing information concerning student strengths and weaknesses and as one of the bases for program adjustment or improvement. Commercial standardized tests should be considered in conjunction with additional data derived from the following methods:
>
> 1. Classroom observation, teacher-made tests and assignments, and student portfolios
> 2. Conferences with parents

3. Locally developed (district) testing
4. Results and recommendations by Special Education/Student Services staff based on individual assessment(s)

The most significant and dramatic criticism of group IQ tests has been that test items and tasks are culturally biased, drawn mostly from white middle-class experience. Thus the tests are more assessments of how informed students are about features in a specific class or culture than of how intelligent students are in general. Although the criticism continues, a number of psychometricians are seeking other solutions by attempting to design culture-free intelligence tests.

Multiple Intelligences

Many theorists believe that intelligence is a basic ability that enables one to perform mental operations in the following areas: logical reasoning, spatial reasoning, number ability, and verbal meaning. However, "the weight of the evidence at the present time is that intelligence is multidimensional, and that the full range of these dimensions is not completely captured by any single general ability" (Sternberg 1996, 11). Howard Gardner, for example, believes that human beings possess at least eight separate forms of intelligence; "each intelligence reflects the potential to solve problems or to fashion products that are valued in one or more cultural settings. [Each] features its own distinctive form of mental representation" (Gardner 1999, 71–72). Drawing on the theories of others and research findings on savants, prodigies, and other exceptional individuals, Gardner originally suggested in *Frames of Mind* (1983) that human beings possessed seven human intelligences: logical-mathematical, linguistic, musical, spatial, bodily-kinesthetic, interpersonal, and intrapersonal. In the mid-1990s, he identified an eighth intelligence, that of the naturalist; and in his most recent book, *The Disciplined Mind*, he suggests that "it is possible that human beings also exhibit a ninth, existential intelligence—the proclivity to pose (and ponder) questions about life, death, and ultimate realities" (Gardner 1999, 72). According to Gardner, every person possesses the eight intelligences (see Figure 6.6), yet each person has his or her particular blend of the intelligences.

Gardner's theory of **multiple intelligences** is valuable for teachers. As Robert Slavin suggests, "Teachers must avoid thinking about children as smart or not smart because there are many ways to be smart (Slavin 2000, 130). Some students are talented in terms of their interpersonal relations and exhibit natural leadership abilities. Others seem to have a high degree of what Peter Salovey and David Sluyter (1997) term *emotional intelligence*—awareness of and ability to manage their feelings. Differences in musical, athletic, and mechanical abilities can be recognized by even the minimally informed observer. Because these intelligences are not tested or highlighted, they may go unnoticed and possibly wasted.

However, keep in mind Gardner's "reflections" twelve years after the publication of *Frames of Mind* (Gardner 1995, 206):

> MI [multiple intelligence] theory is in no way an educational prescription. [E]ducators are in the best position to determine the uses to which MI theory should be put …

Learning Styles

Students vary greatly in regard to **learning styles**, the approaches to learning that work best for them. These differences, also known as *learning style preferences* or *cognitive styles* (Woolfolk 1998), lead students to interact with their environments in

Figure 6.6

The eight intelligences

Source: Project SUMIT (Schools Using Multiple Intelligence Theory), "Theory of Multiple Intelligences."

The Eight Intelligences

Linguistic intelligence allows individuals to communicate and make sense of the world through language. Poets exemplify this intelligence in its mature form. Students who enjoy playing with rhymes, who pun, who always have a story to tell, who quickly acquire other languages—including sign language— all exhibit linguistic intelligence.

Musical intelligence allows people to create, communicate, and understand meanings made out of sound. While composers and instrumentalists clearly exhibit this intelligence, so do the students who seem particularly attracted by the birds singing outside the classroom window or who constantly tap out intricate rhythms on the desk with their pencils.

Logical-mathematical intelligence enables individuals to use and appreciate abstract relations. Scientists, mathematicians, and philosophers all rely on this intelligence. So do the students who "live" baseball statistics or who carefully analyze the components of problems—either personal or school-related—before systematically testing solutions.

Spatial intelligence makes it possible for people to perceive visual or spatial information, to transform this information, and to recreate visual images from memory. Well-developed spatial capacities are needed for the work of architects, sculptors, and engineers. The students who turn first to the graphs, charts, and pictures in their textbooks, who like to "web" their ideas before writing a paper, and who fill the blank space around their notes with intricate patterns are also using their spatial intelligence.

Bodily-kinesthetic intelligence allows individuals to use all or part of the body to create products or solve problems. Athletes, surgeons, dancers, choreographers, and craftspeople all use bodily-kinesthetic intelligence. The capacity is also evident in students who relish gym class and school dances, who prefer to carry out class projects by making models rather than writing reports, and who toss crumpled paper with frequency and accuracy into wastebaskets across the room.

Interpersonal intelligence enables individuals to recognize and make distinctions about others' feelings and intentions. Teachers, parents, politicians, psychologists, and salespeople rely on interpersonal intelligence. Students exhibit this intelligence when they thrive on small-group work, when they notice and react to the moods of their friends and classmates, and when they tactfully convince the teacher of their need for extra time to complete the homework assignment.

Intrapersonal intelligence helps individuals to distinguish among their own feelings, to build accurate mental models of themselves, and to draw on these models to make decisions about their lives. Although it is difficult to assess who has this capacity and to what degree, evidence can be sought in students' uses of their other intelligences—how well they seem to be capitalizing on their strengths, how cognizant they are of their weaknesses, and how thoughtful they are about the decisions and choices they make.

Naturalist intelligence allows people to distinguish among, classify, and use features of the environment. Farmers, gardeners, botanists, geologists, florists, and archaeologists all exhibit this intelligence, as do students who can name and describe the features of every make of car around them.

dissimilar ways. Some, for example, might prefer a highly structured approach to learning; while others might have a preference for a learning environment which is less structured and less predictable.

Students' learning styles are determined by a combination of hereditary and environmental influences. Some more quickly learn things they hear; others learn faster when they see material in writing. Some need a lot of structure; others learn best when they can be independent and follow their desires. Some learn best in formal settings; others learn best in informal, relaxed environments. Some need almost total silence to concentrate; others learn well in noisy, active environments. Some are intuitive learners; some prefer to learn by following logical, sequential steps.

There is no one "correct" view of learning styles to guide teachers in their daily decision making. Culture-based differences in learning styles are subtle, variable, and difficult to describe; and learning styles change as the individual matures. Moreover, critics maintain that there is little evidence to support the validity of dozens of conceptual models for learning styles and accompanying assessment instruments. Nevertheless, you should be aware of the concept of learning styles and realize that any given classroom activity may be more effective for some students than for others. Knowledge of your own and your students' learning styles will help you to individualize instruction and motivate your students.

Professional Reflection   Identify your learning style preferences

Describe your preferred learning environment. Where, when, and how do you learn best? Does certain lighting, food, or music seem to enhance your learning? Think about how you acquire new information—do you prefer being analytical and abstract or commonsensical and concrete? Do you prefer thinking about things or doing things? Do you prefer to learn alone, in a small group, or in a large group? When given an assignment, do you prefer a lot of structure and details, or do you prefer more unstructured or open-ended assignments?

How Do Students Vary in Ability and Disability?

Students also differ according to their special needs and talents. Some enter the world with exceptional abilities or disabilities; others encounter life experiences that change their capabilities significantly, and still others struggle with conditions that medical scientists have yet to understand. Where possible, all children and youth with exceptionalities are given a public education in provincial and territorial schools.

Exceptional Learners

Children "who require special education and related services if they are to realize their full human potential" (Hallahan and Kauffman 2000, 7) are referred to as **exceptional learners.** They are taught by special education teachers and by regular teachers into whose classrooms they have been integrated or *included.* Among the many exceptional children that teachers may encounter in the classroom are students who have physical, mental, or emotional disabilities and students who are gifted or talented.

Special-needs students are often referred to synonymously as *handicapped* or *disabled.* However, it is important for teachers to understand the following distinction between a disability and a handicap:

A disability ... results from a loss of physical functioning (e.g., loss of sight, hearing, or mobility) or from difficulty in learning and social adjustment that significantly interferes with normal growth and development. A handicap is a limitation imposed on the individual by environmental demands and is related to the individual's ability to adapt or adjust to those demands (Hardman, Drew, and Egan 1999, 3).

For example, Stephen W. Hawking, the gifted physicist who provides the epigraph for this chapter, has amyotrophic lateral sclerosis (also known as Lou Gehrig's disease), which requires him to use a wheelchair for mobility and a speech synthesizer to communicate. If Hawking had to enter a building accessible only by stairs, or if a computer virus infected his speech synthesizer program, his disability would then become a handicap.

In addition, teachers should know that current language use emphasizes the concept of "people first." In other words, a disabling condition should not be used as an adjective to describe a person. Thus, one should say "a child with a visual impairment," not a "blind child" or even a "visually impaired child."

Teachers should also realize that the definitions for disabilities are generalized, open to change, and significantly influenced by the current cultural perception of normality. During the last half century the definition of mental retardation has gone through several evolutions to reflect shifting views of people with cognitive disabilities.

Cautions about labelling should also apply to gifted and talented students. Unfortunately, people commonly have a negative view of gifted and talented youngsters. Like many ethnic groups, gifted students are "different" and thus have been the target of many myths and stereotypes. However, a landmark study of 1528 gifted males and females begun by Lewis Terman (Terman, Baldwin, and Bronson 1925; Terman and Oden 1947, 1959) in 1926 and to continue until 2010 has "exploded the myth that high-IQ individuals [are] brainy but physically and socially inept. In fact, Terman found that children with outstanding IQs were larger, stronger, and better coordinated than other children and became better adjusted and more emotionally stable adults" (Slavin 2000, 428).

Students with Disabilities

In December of 2001 the Ontario Human Rights Commission (OHRC) stated that "there is a lack of reliable, current information on children with disabilities in Canada." Additionally, determining what to consider as a disability is an exceptionally difficult problem. The following data must therefore be regarded as approximations of the **students with disabilities** situation in Canada.

1. The Canadian Council on Social Development (CCSD), using information gathered since 1994 by the National Longitudinal Survey of Children and Youth in Canada, estimates that 13 percent of children aged 11 or younger have a chronic or activity limitation—excluding allergies, "emotional problems," and learning disabilities. If children with allergies are added in, the figure rises to 23 percent, and if those with emotional problems and learning disabilities are also included, the number rises to over 30 percent. To order the publication, see *Children and Youth with Special Needs (November 2001)* online at www.ccsd.ca (Hanvey 2001).
2. Research from the National Population Health Survey found that 14.6 percent of children aged six to eleven had a disability related to limited physical activity, emotional problems, or learning disabilities (Statistics Canada 2001a).

3. The Roehr Institute, in *Count Us In: A Demographic Overview of Childhood and Disability in Canada* (2000), states that between 5 and 20 percent of Canadian families have children with disabilities. In 15 percent of cases the disability is moderate to severe.

4. The OHRC reports that in the fall of 2000 approximately 260 000, 12.5 percent of the entire student population, were having special education programs and services delivered to them. Results from other provinces and territories are comparable.

5. A reasonable estimate regarding the number of students with a special need that requires some form of intervention by educators would be 10 to 15 percent. Table 6.3 gives a brief definitional overview of the various types of disabilities students may experience.

Since the term **learning disability (LD)** was first introduced in the early 1960s, there has been no universally accepted definition. However, the following statement, adopted by the Learning Disabilities Association of Canada on January 30, 2002, provides an excellent overview of how broadly defined this specialized area has become.

"Learning Disabilities" refer to a number of disorders which may affect the acquisition, organization, retention, understanding or use of verbal or nonverbal information. These disorders affect learning in individuals who otherwise demonstrate at least average abilities essential for thinking and/or reasoning. As such, learning disabilities are distinct from global intellectual deficiency.

Learning disabilities result from impairments in one or more processes related to perceiving, thinking, remembering or learning. These include, but are not limited to: language processing; phonological processing; visual spatial processing; processing speed; memory and attention; and executive functions (eg. planning and decision-making).

Table 6.3

Types of disability

1. *Specific learning disabilities (LD)*—Learning is significantly hindered by difficulty in listening, speaking, reading, writing, reasoning, or computing

2. *Speech or language impairments*—Significant difficulty in communicating with others as a result of speech or language disorders

3. *Mental retardation*—Significant limitations in cognitive ability

4. *Serious emotional disturbance (SED)*—Social and/or emotional maladjustment that significantly reduces the ability to learn

5. *Hearing impairments*—Permanent or fluctuating mild to profound hearing loss in one or both ears

6. *Orthopedic impairments*—Physically disabling conditions that affect locomotion or motor functions

7. *Other health impairments*—Limited strength, vitality, or alertness caused by chronic or acute health problems

8. *Visual impairments*—Vision loss that significantly inhibits learning

9. *Multiple disabilities*—Two or more interrelated disabilities

10. *Deaf-blindness*—Vision and hearing disability that severely limits communication

11. *Autism and other*—Significantly impaired communication, learning, and reciprocal social interactions

Learning disabilities range in severity and may interfere with the acquisition and use of one or more of the following:

- Oral language (eg. listening, speaking, understanding)
- Reading (eg. decoding, phonetic knowledge, word recognition, comprehension)
- Written language (eg. spelling and written expression); and
- Mathematics (eg. computation, problem solving)

Learning disabilities may also involve difficulties with organizational skills, social perception, social interaction and perspective taking.

Learning disabilities are lifelong. The way in which they are expressed may vary over an individual's lifetime, depending on the interaction between the demands of the environment and the individual's strengths and needs. Learning disabilities are suggested by unexpected academic under-achievement or achievement which is maintained only by unusually high levels of effort and support.

Learning disabilities are due to genetic and/or neurobiological factors or injury that alters brain functioning in a manner which affects one or more processes related to learning. These disorders are not due primarily to hearing and/or vision problems, socio-economic factors, cultural or linguistic differences, lack of motivation or ineffective teaching, although these factors may further complicate the challenges faced by individuals with learning disabilities. Learning disabilities may co-exist with various conditions including attentional, behavioural and emotional disorders, sensory impairments or other medical conditions.

For success, individuals with learning disabilities require early identification and timely specialized assessments and interventions involving home, school, community and workplace settings. The interventions need to be appropriate for each individual's learning disability subtype and, at a minimum, include the provision of: specific skill instruction; accommodations; compensatory strategies; and self-advocacy skills.

Source: Official Definition of Learning Disabilities. (2002, January). Reprinted by permission of the Learning Disabilities Association of Canada. Retrieved October 3, 2003 from www.ldac-taac.ca/english/defined/definew.htm

Now imagine that you are concerned about two of your new students—Mary and Beomjoon. Mary has an adequate vocabulary and doesn't hesitate to express herself, but her achievement in reading and mathematics doesn't add up to what you believe she can do. Often, when you give the class instructions, Mary seems to get confused about what to do. In working with her one-on-one, you've noticed that she often reverses letters and numbers the way much younger children do—she sees a *b* for a *d* or a *6* for a *9*. Mary may have a learning disability, causing problems in taking in, organizing, remembering, and expressing information. Like Mary, students with learning disabilities often show a significant difference between their estimated intelligence and their actual achievement in the classroom.

Beomjoon presents you with a different set of challenges. He is obviously bright, but he frequently seems to be "out of sync" with classroom activities. He gets frustrated when he has to wait for his turn. He sometimes blurts out answers before you've even asked a question. He can't seem to stop wiggling his toes and tapping his pencil, and he often comes to school without his backpack and homework. Beomjoon may have **attention deficit hyperactivity disorder (ADHD)**, one of the most commonly diagnosed disabilities among children. Students with ADHD have difficulty remaining still so they can concentrate. Students with an **attention deficit disorder (ADD)** have difficulty focusing their attention long enough to learn well.

Treatment for students with ADD/ADHD includes behaviour modification and medication. Since the early 1980s, Ritalin has become the most commonly prescribed drug for ADD/ADHD, and thousands of Canadian children are currently estimated to take Ritalin to increase their impulse control and attention span.

By being alert for students who exhibit several of the following characteristics, teachers can help in the early identification of students with learning disabilities so they can receive the instructional adaptations or special education services they need.

- Significant discrepancy between potential and academic achievement
- Distractibility or inability to pay attention for as long as peers do
- Hyperactive behaviour, exhibited through excessive movement
- Inattentiveness during lectures or class discussions
- Impulsiveness
- Poor motor coordination and spatial relation skills
- Inability to solve problems
- Poor motivation and little active involvement in learning tasks
- Over-reliance on teacher and peers for class assignments
- Evidence of poor language and/or cognitive development
- Immature social skills
- Disorganized approach to learning
- Substantial delays in academic achievement (Smith 1998, 139)

Students Who Are Gifted and Talented

You are concerned about the poor performance of Paul, a student in your eighth-period high school class. Paul is undeniably bright. When he was ten, he had an IQ of 145 on the Stanford-Binet. Last year, when he was sixteen, he scored 142. Paul's father is a physician, and his mother is a professor. Both parents clearly value learning and are willing to give Paul any needed encouragement and help.

Throughout elementary school, Paul had an outstanding record. His teachers reported that he was brilliant and very meticulous in completing his assignments. He entered high school amid expectations by his parents and teachers that he would continue his outstanding performance. Throughout his first two years of high school, Paul never seemed to live up to his promise. Now, halfway through his junior year, Paul is failing English and geometry. Paul seems to be well adjusted to the social side of school. He has a lot of friends and says he likes school. Paul explains his steadily declining grades by saying that he doesn't like to study.

Paul may be gifted. **Gifted and talented** students, those who have demonstrated a high level of attainment in intellectual ability, academic achievement, creativity, or visual and performing arts, are evenly distributed across all ethnic and cultural groups and socio-economic classes. Although you might think it is easy to meet the needs of gifted and talented students, you will find that this is not always the case. "Students with special gifts or talents often challenge the system of school, and they can be verbally caustic. Their superior abilities and unusual or advanced interests demand teachers who are highly intelligent, creative, and motivated" (Hallahan and Kauffman 2000, 497). The ability of such students to challenge the system is reflected in a recent US Department of Education study that found that gifted and talented elementary schoolchildren have mastered 35 percent to 50 percent of the grade curriculum in five basic subject areas *before* starting the school year. The situation in Canada is likely similar.

Gifted and talented students benefit from accelerated and enriched learning experiences. What are some forms of acceleration and enrichment that you will offer your students?

There are many forms that giftedness may take; Joseph S. Renzulli (1998), Director of the National Research Center on the Gifted and Talented at the University of Connecticut, for example, suggests two kinds of giftedness: "schoolhouse giftedness [which] might also be called test-taking or lesson-learning giftedness" and "creative-productive giftedness." The trend during the last few decades has been to broaden our view of what characterizes giftedness.

Drawing from the work of Renzulli and his colleagues, Woolfolk (1998) defines *giftedness* "as a combination of three basic characteristics: above-average general ability, a high level of creativity, and a high level of task commitment or motivation to achieve in certain areas. Truly gifted children are not the students who simply learn quickly with little effort. The work of gifted students is original, extremely advanced for their age, and potentially of lasting importance" (Woolfolk 1998, 126). Depending on the criteria used, estimates of the number of gifted and talented students range from 3 to 5 percent of the total population.

Strategies for teaching students who are gifted and talented begin with effective teachers. Educational psychologist Anita Woolfolk suggests that "Teaching methods for gifted students should encourage abstract thinking (formal-operational thought), creativity, and independence, not just the learning of greater quantities of facts. In working with gifted and talented students, a teacher must be imaginative, flexible, and unthreatened by the capabilities of these students. The teacher must ask, What does this child need most? What is she or he ready to learn? Who can help me to challenge them?" (Woolfolk 1998, 129).

Research indicates that effective teachers of the gifted and talented have many of the same characteristics as their students (Davis and Rimm 1998; Piirto 1999). In fact, Feldhusen (1997) suggests that teachers of gifted students should be gifted themselves and should possess the following characteristics:

- Be highly intelligent
- Have cultural and intellectual interests
- Strive for excellence and high achievement
- Be enthusiastic about talent
- Relate well to talented people
- Have broad general knowledge

Several innovative approaches exist for meeting the educational needs of gifted students.

- *Acceleration*—Accelerated programs for intellectually precocious students have proven successful. For example, an analysis of 314 studies of the academic, psychological, and social effects of acceleration practices at the elementary and secondary levels found "generally positive academic effects for most forms of acceleration" and no negative effects on socialization or psychological adjustment (Rogers 1991). In addition, the analysis identified the following acceleration options as the most beneficial at different grade levels:

- *Elementary school*—early entrance, grade-skipping, non-graded classes, and curriculum compacting (modifying the curriculum to present it at a faster pace).
- *Junior high school*—grade-skipping, grade telescoping (shortening the amount of time to complete a grade level), concurrent enrollment in a high school or college, subject acceleration, and curriculum compacting.
- *Senior high school*—concurrent enrollment, subject acceleration, advanced placement (AP) classes, mentorships, credit by examination, and early admission to college.
- *Self-directed or independent study*—For some time, self-directed or independent study has been recognized as an appropriate way for teachers to maintain the interest of gifted students in their classes. Gifted students usually have the academic backgrounds and motivation to do well without constant supervision and the threat or reward of grades.
- *Individual education programs*—Because all Canadian provinces and territories have some version of Individual Education Programs (IEPs) for special education students, IEPs have been promoted as an appropriate means for educating gifted students. Most IEPs for gifted students involve various enrichment experiences, self-directed study, and special, concentrated instruction given to individuals or small groups in pull-out programs.

What Are Special Education, Mainstreaming, and Inclusion?

Prior to the twentieth century, children with disabilities were usually segregated from regular classrooms and taught by teachers in provincially or privately operated schools. Today, an array of programs and services in general and special education classrooms is aimed at developing the potential of exceptional students. Three critical concepts to promote the growth, talents, and productivity of exceptional students are special education, mainstreaming, and inclusion.

Special education refers to "specially designed instruction that meets the unusual needs of an exceptional student" (Hallahan and Kauffman 2000, 12). Teachers who are trained in special education become familiar with special materials, techniques, and equipment and facilities for students with disabilities. For example, children with visual impairment may require reading materials in large print or Braille; students with hearing impairment may require hearing aids and/or instruction in sign language; those with physical disabilities may need special equipment; those with emotional disturbances may need smaller and more highly structured classes; and children with special gifts or talents may require access to working professionals. "Related services—special transportation, psychological assessment, physical and occupational therapy, medical treatment, and counselling—may be necessary if special education is to be effective" (Hallahan and Kauffman 1997, 14).

Special Education Laws

Prior to 1980 the needs of students with disabilities were primarily met through self-contained special education classes within regular schools. However, within the last 25 years this situation has changed dramatically. The self-contained special education class has disappeared from most school districts and a more inclusive educational philosophy, based upon an increased concern for human rights, has taken hold. Students who would previously have been placed in segregated classrooms are now placed within regular classrooms. Additionally, all provinces and territories now have laws, regulations, or policies which support this practice. While the exact nature of how inclusion is accomplished varies from one jurisdiction to another, as does the degree to which the various laws, policies and regulations are enforced, the advocates of children with special needs have achieved a remarkable degree of success. Of particular assistance to these advocates has been the **Canadian Charter of Rights and Freedoms**. Because only Quebec and Saskatchewan have human rights codes which guarantee every citizen the right to an education, the Charter has been increasingly used to support the rights of students with special needs.

Individualized education plan—A student with a disability of sufficient severity is given a written **Individualized Education Plan (IEP)** or Individualized Program Plan (IPP) that meets the child's needs and specifies educational goals, methods for achieving those goals, and the number and quality of special educational services to be provided. The IEP is regularly reviewed by five parties: (1) a parent or guardian, (2) the child, (3) a teacher, (4) a professional who has recently evaluated the child, and (5) others, usually the principal or a special-education resource person from the school district. When appropriate, IEPs sometimes have related agreements to ensure that students with disabilities receive any necessary services such as special transportation arrangements or other supportive services as may be required to assist a child with a disability to benefit from special education. (See Appendixes 6.1 and 6.2.)

Confidentiality of records— Protocols ensure that records on a child are kept confidential. In some provinces parental permission is required before any official may look at a child's records. Moreover, parents can amend a child's records if they feel information in it is misleading, inaccurate, or violates the child's rights.

Figure 6.7

Landmark Special Education Decision

Landmark Special Education Decision

Eaton v. Brant county board of Education (February 15, 1995) Toronto, O.J. No. 315/No. C19214 (Ont. CA)

In a decision long fought for by advocates for the disabled and dreaded by school authorities, The Ontario Court of Appeal held that the Canadian Charter of Rights and Freedoms did indeed create a presumption, and a very strong presumption, in favour of the integration of handicapped persons into the mainstream of the community, and particularly the integration of disabled students into the regular classroom. The Court held that to rebut this presumption, school authorities would bear the onus of proving not only that integration in the regular school was not appropriate in a given circumstance, but also that placement in a segregated setting would be the only appropriate alternative. Further, the Court rewrote the legislative scheme for special education in Ontario, a scheme that sought to provide disabled students with procedural fairness in seeking a reasonable educational program. It held that the legislation must ensure that when a parent, acting on behalf of the disabled student, refuses to consent to a segregated educational placement for the student, school authorities must comply with the wishes of the parent "unless alternatives are proven inadequate."

Source: Reprinted from *Education Law Reporter: Elementary and Secondary Schools*, (6) 49.

Due process—Parents have the right to disagree with an IEP or an evaluation of their child's abilities. If a disagreement arises, in most boards it is settled through an impartial hearing where due process is followed. At the hearing, parents may be represented by a lawyer, give evidence, and cross-examine the school personnel involved. If the parents or guardians of a child disagree with the outcome they may appeal the decision to the provincial department of education. If still dissatisfied with the outcome the case may then be taken to the civil courts.

Canadian educators recognize that children with disabilities should be educated in the **least restrictive environment**. In other words, a student must be placed within a general education classroom whenever such inclusion is feasible and appropriate and the child would receive educational benefit from such placement. Figure 6.8 shows the educational service options for students with disabilities, from the most inclusive to the most restrictive.

Meeting the Challenge of Inclusion

To help teachers satisfy the requirements of the new inclusive paradigm, school districts across the nation have developed in-service programs designed to acquaint classroom teachers with the unique needs of students with disabilities. In addition, colleges and universities with preservice programs for educators have added courses on teaching students with special educational needs.

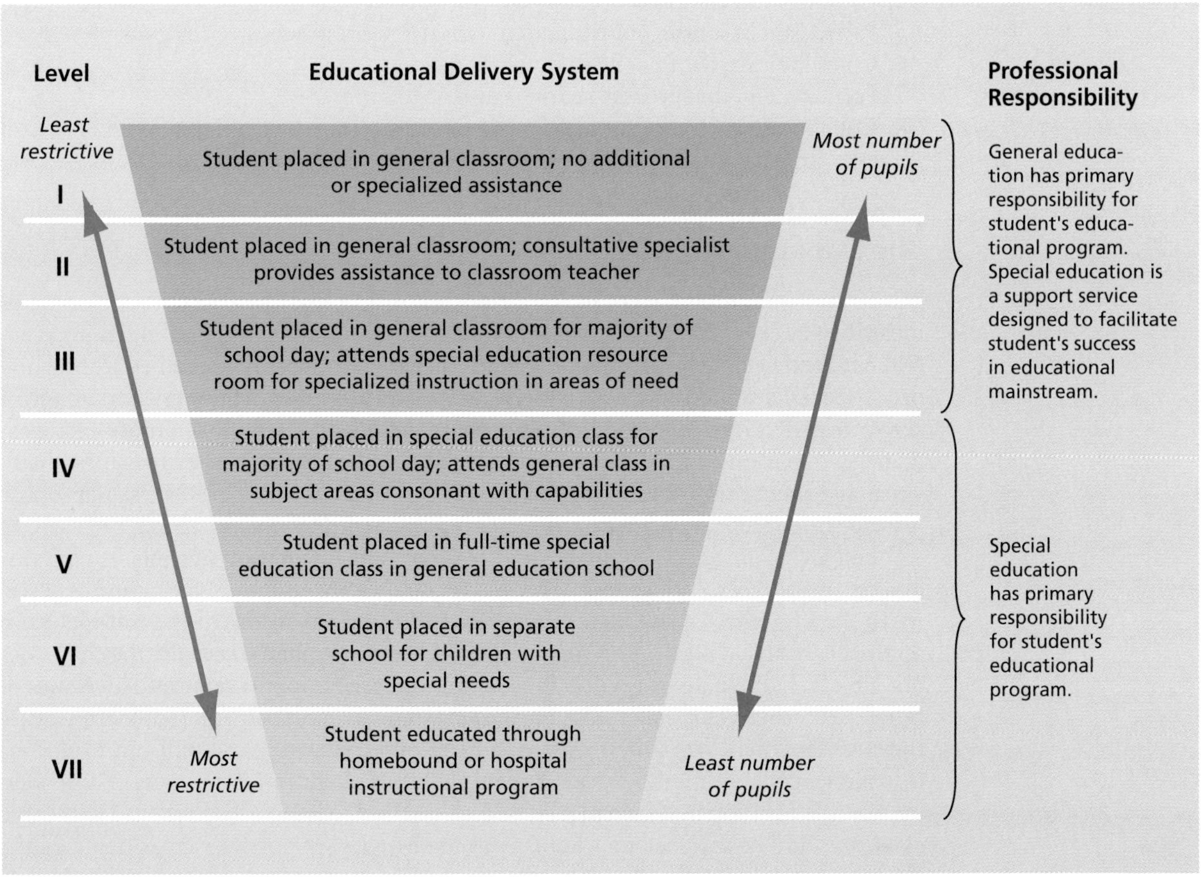

Figure 6.8

Educational service options for students with disabilities

Source: Michael L. Hardman, Clifford J. Drew, and M. Winston Egan, *Human Exceptionality: Society, School and Family,* 6th ed. Boston: Allyn and Bacon, 1999, p. 28. Copyright © 1999 by Allyn and Bacon. Reprinted by permission.

Level	Educational Delivery System	Professional Responsibility
I *Least restrictive*	Student placed in general classroom; no additional or specialized assistance *Most number of pupils*	General education has primary responsibility for student's educational program. Special education is a support service designed to facilitate student's success in educational mainstream.
II	Student placed in general classroom; consultative specialist provides assistance to classroom teacher	
III	Student placed in general classroom for majority of school day; attends special education resource room for specialized instruction in areas of need	
IV	Student placed in special education class for majority of school day; attends general class in subject areas consonant with capabilities	Special education has primary responsibility for student's educational program.
V	Student placed in full-time special education class in general education school	
VI	Student placed in separate school for children with special needs	
VII *Most restrictive*	Student educated through homebound or hospital instructional program *Least number of pupils*	

The new guidelines require that schools must make a significant effort to include *all* children in the classroom. However, it is not clear how far schools must go to meet the requirement. For example, should children with severe disabilities be included in general education classrooms if they are unable to do the academic work? Recent court cases have ruled that students with severe disabilities must be included if there is a potential benefit for the child, if the class would stimulate the child's language development, or if other students could act as appropriate role models for the child. School districts, departments of education, and the Canadian judicial system are presently in an extended process of determining the answers to such questions.

To meet the challenges of inclusion, teachers must have knowledge of various disabilities and the teaching methods and materials appropriate for each. Since teachers with negative attitudes toward students with special needs can convey these feelings to all students in a class and thereby reduce the effectiveness of inclusion (Lewis and Doorlag 1999), general education teachers must have positive attitudes toward students with special needs. An accepting, supportive climate can significantly enhance the self-confidence of students with disabilities.

In addition, Hallahan and Kauffman suggest that all teachers should be prepared to participate in the education of exceptional learners. Teachers should be willing to do the following:

1. Make maximum effort to accommodate individual students' needs.
2. Evaluate academic abilities and disabilities.
3. Refer [students] for evaluation [as appropriate].
4. Participate in eligibility conferences [for special education].
5. Participate in writing individualized education programs.
6. Communicate with parents or guardians.
7. Participate in due process hearings and negotiations.
8. Collaborate with other professionals in identifying and making maximum use of exceptional students' abilities (Hallahan and Kauffman 2000, 20–22).

The Debate over Inclusion

While **mainstreaming** refers to the provision of the least restrictive environment, **inclusion** goes beyond mainstreaming to integrate all students with disabilities into general education classes and school life with the active support of special educators and other specialists and service providers, as well as **assistive technology** and adaptive software. Advocates of inclusion believe that "if students cannot meet traditional academic expectations, then those expectations should be changed. They reject the mainstreaming assumption that settings dictate the type and intensity of services and propose instead the concept of inclusion" (Friend and Bursuck 1999, 4).

Full inclusion goes even further and calls for "the integration of students with disabilities in the general education classrooms at all times regardless of the nature or severity of the disability" (Friend and Bursuck 1999, 4). According to the full-inclusion approach, if a child needs support services, these are brought *to the child;* the child does not have to participate in a pull-out program to receive support services. Advocates of full inclusion maintain that pull-out programs stigmatize participating students because they are separated from their general-education classmates, and pull-out programs discourage collaboration between general and special education teachers. Those who oppose full inclusion maintain that classroom teachers, who may be burdened with large class sizes and be assigned to schools with inadequate support services, often lack the training and instructional materials to meet the needs of all exceptional students. However, while support for full inclusion varies, the trend towards it continues.

How do classroom teachers feel about inclusion? These comments by two junior high teachers suggest the concerns general education teachers may have about the availability of resources to help them be successful in inclusive classrooms.

> At first I was worried that it would all be my responsibility. But after meeting with the special education teacher, I realized that we would work together and I would have additional resources if I needed them (Vaughn, Bos, and Schumm 1997, 18).

> At first I was nervous about having students with disabilities in my class. One of the students has a learning disability, one student has serious motor problems and is in a wheelchair, and the third student has vision problems. Now I have to say the adaptations I make to meet their special learning needs actually help all of the students in my class. I think that I am a better teacher because I think about accommodations now (Vaughn, Bos, and Schumm 1997, 18).

Equal Opportunity for Exceptional Learners

Like many groups in our society, exceptional learners have often not received the kind of education that most effectively meets their needs. Approximately 10 percent of the population aged three to twenty-one is classified as exceptional; that is, "they require special education because they are markedly different from most children in one or more of the following ways: They may have ... learning disabilities, emotional or behavioral disorders, physical disabilities, disorders of communication, autism, traumatic brain injury, impaired hearing, impaired sight, or special gifts or talents" (Hallahan and Kauffman 2000, 7).

Just as there are no easy answers for how teachers should meet the needs of students from diverse cultural backgrounds, there is no single strategy for teachers to follow to ensure that all exceptional students receive an appropriate education. The key, however, lies in not losing sight of the fact that *the most important characteristics of exceptional children are their abilities*" (Hallahan and Kauffman 2000, 6).

To build on students' strengths, classroom teachers must work cooperatively and collaboratively with special education teachers, and students in special education programs must not become isolated from their peers. In addition, teachers must understand how some people can be perceived as "different" and presumed to be "handicapped" because of their appearance or physical condition. Evidence suggests, for example, that people who are short, obese, or unattractive are often victims of discrimination, as are people with conditions such as AIDS, cancer, multiple sclerosis, or epilepsy. Significantly, many individuals with clinically diagnosable and classifiable impairments or disabilities do not perceive themselves as *handicapped*. The term itself means permanently unable to be treated equally.

Officially labelling students has become a necessity with the passage of the laws that provide education and related services for exceptional students. The classification labels help determine which students qualify for the special services, educational programs, and individualized instruction provided by the laws, and they bring to educators' attention many exceptional children and youth whose educational needs could be overlooked, neglected, or inadequately served otherwise. Detrimental aspects include the fact that classification systems are imperfect and have arbitrary cutoff points that sometimes lead to injustices. Also, labels tend to evoke negative expectations, which can cause teachers to avoid and underteach these students, and their peers to isolate or reject them, thereby stigmatizing individuals, sometimes permanently. The most serious detriment, however, is that students so labelled are taught to feel inadequate, inferior, and limited in terms of their options for growth.

Help! Tell Me about This Kid!

DonnaLee Brown, M.A., is an elementary school counsellor with twenty-three years of experience. She compiled this case on the basis of her work with several children in recent years.

Mary Stone, a second grade teacher, had "inherited" Linda on the third day of school. She had heard rumours about the child's difficulties the previous year. She also knew about the special education assessment that was under way and the private ADHD diagnosis she had received. Mary stuck her head in my office with a frantic, "What can you tell me about this kid Linda?"

"Linda? Linda who?"

Mary said plaintively, "All I need is another messed up kid! I've already got Beth, Mario, and Jonathan. And I heard Linda can't even read or write! How can I be expected to include her in group work? And I can't work one-on-one with her all the time!"

Several days later, Mary's calls to me came on a regular basis. "Please come as soon as you can and get Linda! She is wet and smells of urine, and the kids are saying things." And, "Please come. Linda won't do what I tell her to do. She is unteachable!" And, "Linda refuses to talk to me. I ask her a question and she's totally silent. Help!"

When Linda's test results came in, they indicated that her IQ score was above average. They also showed that she had a lot of difficulty with sound/symbol associations but no difficulty reproducing written symbols and doing sequencing of all kinds. She appeared to be disturbed in the area of emotional attachment, and she exhibited oppositional behaviour. The last we knew!

I also had regular contact with Linda since she came daily to my office for her dry clothes. While there she would show me magic tricks with Pokémon cards and visit. She described her class as boring, her teacher as stupid, and the work as never-ending.

How Can You Teach All Learners in Your Inclusive Classroom?

Teachers have a responsibility to address all students' developmental, individual, and exceptional learning needs. Although addressing the range of student differences in the inclusive classroom is challenging, it can also be very rewarding. Consider the comments of three first-year teachers who reflect on their successes with diverse learners:

> I taught a boy with ADD. His first-grade teacher segregated him from other students, but I had him stay with his peer group. Soon, I heard from other teachers that he was not being a troublemaker anymore. By year's end, he had published his own booklet for a writing project.

She complained that she had no chance of earning recess, so she decided not to do anything, not even to talk. When Ms Stone asked her something, she would not answer. Her teacher would then get red in the face and lean really close to her—and that made all the kids laugh. She added, "The kids really like me!"

Working with the class and incorporating several suggestions from me, Mary gradually fit Linda into group work with a peer partner and an agreement from the group about their expectations of Linda: She was to contribute ideas when inspired and was not to be expected to write for the group unless she volunteered. Mary and Linda also agreed that Linda could use head-nodding to signal "yes" or "no" whenever Mary questioned her or gave her directives in class. Linda agreed to accept a "reminder signal" from her peer partner for two bathroom trips a day (before recess and before math).

While all was not perfect, the number of Linda's trips to my office for clean clothes diminished, and Mary's calls for help stopped completely. When Mary did drop by my office, it was more often to share a laugh, celebrate a success, or discuss a new behaviour management strategy. I knew Linda was in good hands when Mary began telling *me* about "this kid."

Questions

1. Why do you think Linda prefers to use head-nodding rather than verbal answers?

2. How did Mary involve others in integrating Linda into the class?

3. What accommodations did Mary need to make to work effectively with Linda?

4. How can counsellor intervention assist teachers and students like Mary and Linda?

5. What does Linda gain or lose by being included in Mary Stone's class?

I had a troubled student who dropped out of school mid-year after I had spent a considerable amount of time working with him. He went to court over a trespassing charge, so I went to court with him. His mother wrote me a letter saying I had been such a positive influence on him and she was very grateful. It was the relationships I was able to establish with these kids that meant so much to me. The opportunity to take kids with disciplinary problems and make them your kids—to get them to trust you and do what they need to do—is the most rewarding part of teaching.

One little girl in my Kindergarten class had neurological problems, but all the children joined together in helping her. By the end of the year, she was kicking and screaming, not because she had to come to school, but because she had to leave! (Sallie Mae Corporation 1994, 5, 11).

Though it is beyond the scope of this book to present in-depth instructional strategies to address students' diverse learning needs, Appendix 6.3 presents "Examples of Instructional Strategies for Teaching All Learners." In addition, attention to three key areas will enable you to create a truly inclusive classroom: collaborative consultation, partnerships with parents, and assistive technology for special learners.

Collaborative Consultation with Other Professionals

One approach to meeting the needs of all students is known as **collaborative consultation,** an approach in which a classroom teacher meets with one or more other professionals (a special educator, school psychologist, or resource teacher, for example) to focus on the learning needs of one or more students. The following first-year teacher describes how collaborative consultation enabled her to meet the needs of a special student.

> I taught a child with Down's Syndrome who was very frustrated. I convened a meeting that included school district experts, his parents, and a resource teacher, suggesting a change in educational strategy. All agreed to pilot the plan, and things have worked more smoothly ever since. It was a very rewarding experience (Sallie Mae Corporation 1995, 11).

Collaborative consultation is based on mutuality and reciprocity (Hallahan and Kauffman 1994), and participants assume equal responsibility for meeting students' needs. Friend and Bursuck (1999) make the following suggestions for working with a consultant:

1. Do your homework. Working with a consultant should be an intervention you seek only after you have attempted to identify and resolve the problem by analyzing the situation yourself, talking about it with parents, presenting it at a grade-level meeting, and so on.
2. Demonstrate your concern with documentation. At your initial meeting with a consultant, bring samples of student work, notes recounting specific incidents in the classroom, records of correspondence with parents, and other concrete information.
3. Participate actively. If you clearly describe the problem, contribute specific information about your expectations for how the situation should change, offer your ideas on how best to intervene to resolve the problem, implement the selected strategy carefully, and provide your perception of the effectiveness of the strategy, you will find consultation very helpful.
4. Carry out the consultant's suggestions carefully and systematically.
5. Contact the consultant if problems occur (Friend and Bursuck 1996, 96).
   To enhance the educational experiences of their students with disabilities, general education teachers are often assisted by special educators and other support professionals. The following professionals are among those who consult and/or collaborate with general education teachers:

Consulting teacher—A special educator who provides technical assistance such as arranging the physical setting, helping to plan for instruction, or developing approaches for assessing students' learning

Resource-room teacher—A special educator who provides instruction in a resource room for students with disabilities

School psychologist—Consults with the general education teacher and arranges for the administration of appropriate psychological, educational, and behavioural assessment instruments; may observe a student's behaviour in the classroom

Speech and language specialist—Assesses students' communication abilities and works with general education teachers to develop educational programs for students with speech and/or language disorders

Physical therapist—Provides physical therapy for students with physical disabilities

Occupational therapist—Instructs students with disabilities to prepare them for everyday living and work-related activities

Working with Parents

In addition to working with education professionals to meet the learning needs of all students, effective teachers develop good working relationships with parents. Parents of exceptional children can be a source of valuable information about the characteristics, abilities, and needs of their children; they can be helpful in securing necessary services for their children; and they can assist you by reviewing skills at home and praising their children for their learning. Some school districts, such as the Toronto District School Board, require that all teachers contact all their students' parents/guardians on a regular basis. While this adds one more task to each teacher's workload, boards that have such policies obviously recognize the importance of their schools having a strong relationship with their students' homes.

Assistive Technology for Special Learners

The ability of teachers to create inclusive classrooms has increased dramatically as a result of many technological advances that now make it easier for exceptional students to learn and communicate. For example, computer-based word processing and math tutorials can greatly assist students with learning disabilities in acquiring literacy and computational skills. Students with hearing impairments can communicate with other students by using telecommunications equipment, and students with physical disabilities can operate computers through voice commands or with a single switch or key. Among the recent developments in assistive technology are the following:

1. Talking word processor
2. Speech synthesizer
3. Touch-sensitive computer screens
4. Computer screen image enlarger
5. Teletypewriter (TTY) (connects to telephone and types a spoken message to another TTY)
6. Customized computer keyboards
7. Ultrasonic head controls for computers
8. Voice-recognition computers
9. Television closed captioning
10. Kurzweil reading machine (scans print and reads it aloud)

The IEP for this student with multiple disabilities provides for assistive technology, which enables her to create and respond to language.

highlights

How can word prediction software enhance the writing abilities of students with disabilities?

"What should I write?" "What words will best express what I want to say?" Although most people find these questions at least somewhat difficult to answer, students with disabilities may confront unique challenges when they write. Students with learning disabilities may not be able to retain ideas in their memory long enough to express them in writing; others may have difficulty with spelling; and students with motor disabilities may be challenged when forming letters with pen or pencil or making repetitive keystrokes on a word processor.

Students with disabilities that affect their ability to write can be assisted by word prediction software that reduces the number of keystrokes needed to type words. When writing with word prediction software, a student types the first letter of a word, and then a numbered list of words beginning with that letter appears on the computer screen. If the desired word is on the list, the student enters the number and the word is typed automatically. For example, assume a student wants to write the word *tonight* to complete the sentence "I will watch TV *tonight.*" First, she enters a "t" and the list of common "t" words shown in screen # 1 appears. Since the word *tonight* is not on this list, she types an "o" and screen #2 appears. Since *tonight* is on this list, she types a number "3" and the word is entered automatically. Thus, the seven keystrokes needed to write *tonight* has been reduced to three.

The following list describes additional features of various word prediction software programs.

1. *Synthesized speech output*
2. *Prediction methods*—Some programs predict on the basis of spelling only, while others consider the words that have come before in the sentence; for example only nouns are listed after the word a or an.
3. *List updating*—After "learning" a student's vocabulary, the word prediction program tailors the word prediction lists to the student's usage. Some programs update automatically, while others allow the user to decide when to update.
4. *Prediction window customizing*
5. *Keyboard sensitivity adjustment*—Keyboard sensitivity can be adjusted to prevent repetition if keys are not quickly released.

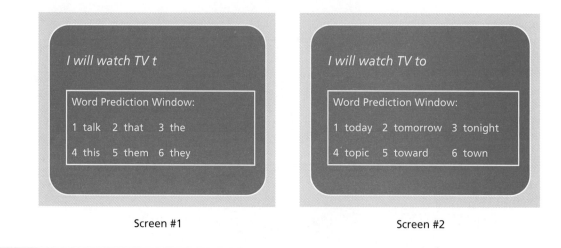

I will watch TV t

Word Prediction Window:

1 talk   2 that   3 the

4 this   5 them   6 they

Screen #1

I will watch TV to

Word Prediction Window:

1 today   2 tomorrow   3 tonight

4 topic   5 toward   6 town

Screen #2

In addition, assistive technology includes devices to enhance the mobility and everyday activities of people with disabilities (wheelchairs, lifts, adaptive driving controls, scooters, laser canes, feeders).

Many technology-related special education resources and curriculum materials are available on the internet. One of these sites, The National Center to Improve Practice in Special Education through Technology, Media, and Materials, also maintains discussion forums for teachers of students with disabilities. Clearly, the dazzling revolution in microelectronics will continue to yield new devices to enhance the learning of all students.

SUMMARY

How Do Students' Needs Change As They Develop?

- People move through different stages of cognitive, psychosocial, and moral development throughout their life spans.

- Piaget maintains that children, who reason differently from adults, pass through four stages of cognitive development as they mature. Effective teachers are aware of the characteristics of school-age children's thinking during three of these stages: the preoperational stage, the concrete operations stage, and the formal operations stage.

- According to Erikson's model of psychosocial development, people pass through eight stages of emotional and social development throughout their lives. Each stage is characterized by a "crisis" with a positive and negative pole. Healthy development depends upon a satisfactory, positive resolution of each crisis.

- Kohlberg believes that moral development, the reasoning people use to decide between right and wrong, evolves through three levels. Evidence suggests that males may base their moral reasoning on rights and rules, and females on altruism and self-sacrifice. Many teachers and schools emphasize character education to "teach" moral reasoning and values.

- Maslow suggests that human growth and development depends on how well the individual's biological and psychological needs have been met. According to his hierarchy of needs model, people must satisfy their survival and safety needs before addressing "higher" needs such as self-actualization.

- Teachers must be aware of the developmental stresses and tasks students encounter during childhood and early and late adolescence.

How Do Students Vary in Intelligence?

- There are conflicting definitions of *intelligence*; they range from "what IQ tests measure" to "goal-directed adaptive behaviour." Some theorists believe intelligence is a single, basic ability, though recent research suggests that there are many forms of intelligence.

- According to Howard Gardner's theory of multiple intelligences, there are at least eight human intelligences.

- Students differ in their learning styles—the patterns of behaviour they prefer to use while learning. Although there is conflict about the concept of learning styles, effective teachers are aware of differences among students regarding their preferences for learning activities.

How Do Students Vary in Ability and Disability?

■ Some students are "exceptional" because they have abilities or disabilities that distinguish them from other students. Students with physical, cognitive, or emotional disabilities and students who are gifted and talented have unique learning needs.

■ There is a lack of agreement regarding the definition of *learning disability (LD)*. Teachers can identify students with learning disabilities by noting difficulties students have acquiring and processing new information. Learning disabilities are the most common disability among students, with attention deficit hyperactivity disorder (ADHD) and attention deficit disorder (ADD) the most common learning disabilities.

■ There are many forms of giftedness. Among the approaches used to meet the learning needs of gifted students are acceleration, self-directed or independent study, individual education programs, special or magnet schools, and weekend and summer programs.

What Are Special Education and Inclusion?

■ Special education includes a variety of educational services to meet the needs of exceptional students. Provincial and territorial laws, regulations, and policies support features such as the least restrictive environment, individualized education program (IEP), confidentiality of records, and due process.

■ *Mainstreaming* is the process of integrating students with disabilities into regular classrooms.

■ *Inclusion* integrates all students with disabilities into regular classrooms, with the support of special education services as necessary. *Full inclusion* is the integration of students with disabilities in general education classrooms at all times regardless of the severity of the disability.

How Can You Teach All Learners in Your Inclusive Classroom?

■ Though challenging, teachers have a responsibility to create inclusive classrooms that address the developmental, individual, and exceptional learning needs of all students.

■ Through collaborative consultation, an arrangement whereby the regular classroom teacher collaborates with other education professionals, teachers can meet the needs of exceptional students. Collaborative consultation is based on mutuality and reciprocity, and all participants assume responsibility for meeting students' needs.

■ By developing effective relationships with parents of exceptional students, teachers acquire valuable information and support.

■ An array of assistive technologies and resources is available to help exceptional students learn and communicate in inclusive classrooms.

assistive technology, 234
attention deficit disorder (ADD), 228
attention deficit hyperactivity disorder (ADHD), 228
Canadian Charter of Rights and Freedoms, 232
character education, 214
cognitive development, 210
collaborative consultation, 238

concrete operations stage, 211
exceptional learners, 225
formal operations stage, 211
full inclusion, 234
gifted and talented, 229
hierarchy of needs, 219
inclusion, 234
individualized education plan (IEP), 232
intelligence, 222
learning disability (LD), 227
learning styles, 223

least restrictive environment, 223
mainstreaming, 234
moral reasoning, 210
multiple intelligences, 223
preoperational stage, 211
psychosocial crisis, 211
psychosocial development, 210
special education, 231
stages of development, 210
students with disabilities, 226

APPLICATIONS AND ACTIVITIES

Teacher's Journal

1. Through a series of vignettes, relate Erikson's stages of psychosocial development to your own experiences as a child and as an adolescent. How did sources of stress, psychosocial crises, and your resolution of them affect your learning in school?

2. Do you know your IQ or recall participating in an IQ test? How do you regard yourself in terms of intelligence and how did you come by your beliefs about your intelligence? Do you think these beliefs influenced your motivation, choices, and achievement as a student? Do you think they influenced your school or class placements? Do you think they influenced the way your teachers and peers responded to you? What criteria would you use now to evaluate the fairness of IQ testing and the appropriateness of the use of IQ scores?

3. Recount an experience you had as an exceptional student or one that involved a person with disabilities. What did you learn from this experience or from your reflection on it that could help you as a teacher?

Teacher's Database

1. Investigate sources of information on students with disabilities or exceptional learners such as SchoolNet, www.schoolnet.ca/sne/, or the following URL, which has links to numerous sites that deal with special education topics. www.schdist42.bc.ca/ProjectInfo/CanSpEd.html

2. "Observe" children online by locating chat rooms by and for children and youth. As an adult you may not be allowed to participate, but in many cases you will be invited to visit (called "lurking" in internet jargon). What educational interests,

needs, and concerns do students share with one another? How might visiting students' sites online be viewed as an extension of your field experiences as an education student or as a student teacher? What teacher observation techniques and protocols could you use in this situation? What are some ethical concerns about this practice? How might any new knowledge of students gained in this way help to make you a more effective teacher?

Observations and Interviews

1. Observe in a classroom that has exceptional students. What steps does the teacher take to meet the needs of these students? Interview the teacher to determine what he or she sees as the challenges and rewards of teaching exceptional students.

2. Observe and interview a student in the age group you wish to teach to conduct a brief case study that focuses on common developmental tasks for that age group and the areas of individual differences highlighted in this chapter. Then prepare a written portrait of the student.

3. Visit a school at the level you plan to teach. Interview the counsellor, asking questions about the problems that bring students to the counsellor most often. If possible, shadow the school counsellor for a day.

4. Attend an extracurricular event such as a high school basketball game or Little League soccer game. Observe the students on the field as well as any students watching the players. Notice the differences among the students in terms of their physical appearance, clothing and hairstyles, athletic abilities, social skills, and evidence of personal interests and confidence. Share your observations in class.

Professional Portfolio

For the grade level and content area you are preparing to teach, identify learning activities that address each of the eight multiple intelligences identified by Gardner. For example, you might plan activities such as the following. For one activity in each category, list the preparations you would need to make and/or the materials you would need to gather, and add this information to your portfolio.

Logical-Mathematical
- Design an experiment on ...
- Describe the rules for a new board game called ...

Linguistic
- Write a short story about ...
- Write a biographical sketch of ...

Musical
- Write song lyrics for ...
- Locate music that sounds like ...

Spatial
- Draw, paint, or sculpt a ...
- Create an advertisement for ...

Bodily-Kinesthetic

- Do a dance that shows ...
- Role play a person who is

Intrapersonal

- Assess your ability to ...
- Describe how you feel about ...

Interpersonal

- Show one or more of your classmates how to ...
- In a small group, construct a ...

Naturalist

- Identify the trees found in ...
- Classify the rocks found in ...

Appendix 6.1

Policy 2.2

Each school board is responsible for establishing a process of identification, assessment, program planning and evaluation for students with special needs.

2.2 Guidelines

The school board is responsible for the implementation of this process; therefore, each procedural step should be documented in the school board's special education policy manual. School boards are encouraged to refer to the appropriate sections of the Department of Education and Culture's Special Education Policy Manual.

2.2 Sample Procedure

On the following pages is a sample outline, in graphic and written form, of how a program planning process might be implemented. It is not intended as a prescribed approach, but rather as an illustration.

Identification, Assessment, and Program Planning Process

Stage 1—Screening and Identification

This stage may be initiated by a variety of people. Some children and students may come to school with a myriad of assessments and programming information from other agencies or from another school. Some students may have been in school for a number of years and their special needs may be identified at a later stage by the classroom teacher who regularly observes students in the learning situation. The planning process can be initiated at any time based on student need.

If a student has been identified as needing an individual program plan before entry to school, the team may wish to start the process at step 3, "Referral to Program Planning Team," to avoid delay.

Parents are expected to be involved at the beginning of the process. Classroom teachers, parents, students, and outside agency personnel and resource teachers are all possible initiators at this stage. The principal should be aware of any communication concerning students at this stage.

Stage 2—Exploration of Instructional Strategies

After a student has been identified as requiring additional planning to meet his/her needs, the classroom teacher

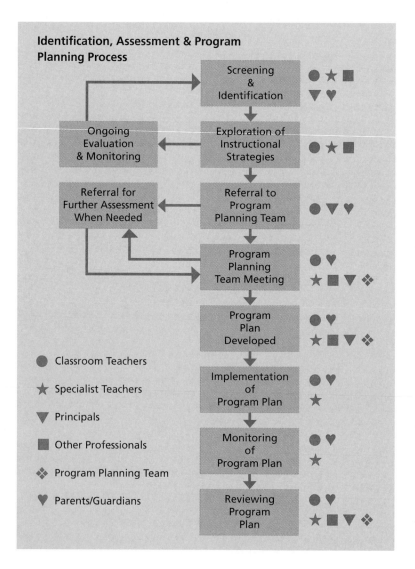

Identification, Assessment & Program Planning Process

- ● Classroom Teachers
- ★ Specialist Teachers
- ▼ Principals
- ■ Other Professionals
- ❖ Program Planning Team
- ♥ Parents/Guardians

uses available material and human resources to explore a variety of strategies in the learning process. In all schools there is a wealth of experience to draw upon. In exploring alternative methods of working with students, teachers may also wish to consult supervisors, school psychologists, or other available personnel. The key at this stage is to be as creative as possible in determining a wide variety of behavioural and/or curriculum strategies to meet student needs while ensuring accurate record keeping in terms of the outcome of utilizing these approaches. Determining why a method doesn't produce the desired outcome can yield as much information as one that does. Cooperation and collaboration among professionals and parents are essential at this stage.

The identification, assessment, and program planning process may not go beyond this stage for many students as their needs may be met through ongoing evaluation and monitoring in the classroom (Policy 2.4).

Stage 3—Referral to Program Planning Team

If the classroom teacher requires further support to meet the needs of a student, he/she may wish to refer to the program planning team.

The format of the referral depends on school and district/regional procedures. In some cases the initiator of the referral may be required to have certain types of information available for the principal in order to make an informed decision whether or not to select team members and set a date for the program planning team meeting. Information required may include anecdotal information, observation records, informal assessment, interviews with the student and involved agencies, school records or any other information available that may be of help in program planning. Care should be taken not to use outdated or irrelevant assessment data.

Stage 4—Program Planning Team Meeting

The program planning team must ensure that the problem or difficulty facing the student and/or teachers and parents is clarified before proceeding with planning. The reason for referral does not always match the team's clarification of the problem and careful problem solving at this stage can prevent unnecessary or inappropriate steps being taken.

Team members should be those who have responsibility for the student's learning. The team should always include the principal or vice-principal, teachers involved, and parents/guardians. (See policy 2.4). These members form the core of the team. The selection of additional members depends on the needs of the student and on the personnel resources of the school district and community. In cases where there are many teachers involved, as in high school, reports can be gathered from teachers for

presentation at the team meeting; however, key personnel should be present. In some cases this may include the student, especially at a high school level when career/transitional decisions are being discussed. Every attempt should be made to encourage parents to feel comfortable in presenting their view of the student's strengths and needs.

The team meeting provides an opportunity for members to come together to clarify, given all available information, the student's strengths and needs and to decide on future actions to be taking in terms of program planning. The meeting should not be a forum for teachers, administrators, and other agency personnel to present a completed program to the parents. If this is done, the parents become outsiders to the process and do not have the opportunity to affect decision making in any meaningful way. Together, the members should discuss the information as observed and collected by each member. Concerns should be expressed openly and information presented, without judgment rebuttal. However, in cases where differences of opinion occur, the chairperson would act as mediator in the process.

The team decides whether or not to proceed with development of an individualized program plan (IPP). The meeting may highlight the need for a change in instructional strategies or evaluation methods while maintaining the objectives of a prescribed course. When this occurs, a statement outlining adaptation of strategies, evaluation methods and support services required should be recorded in the student's cumulative file. However, when the objectives of provincially approved curriculum must be changed to meet the needs of the student, an IPP becomes necessary. An IPP may focus on behavioural as well as curriculum outcomes to address student behaviours which may inhibit learning. At this point, the chairperson designates responsibility areas to the team members to develop the individualized program plan according to the priorities, goals, and approaches set at the meeting, or to collect further information if necessary.

Stage 5—Program Plan Developed

The program planning team uses information gathered to write the program plan. Those that have responsibility for implementation of parts of the plan should be involved in developing the objectives, deciding on strategies, and evaluation procedures. The individual program plan should include the following components (Policy 2.6):

- a summary of student strengths and needs
- annual individualized outcomes (goals)
- specific individualized outcomes (objectives)
- recommended services
- responsibility areas
- review dates
- signatures

Stage 6—Implementation of Program Plan

Team members are assigned responsibility areas and monitor student progress. The teacher responsible for teaching the student is also responsible for evaluating the student's progress in that curriculum area (Policies 2.5 and 2.6).

Stage 7—Monitoring

Teachers and designated team members are required to evaluate individual program plans in order to assess student progress continually.

Stage 8—Review of Program Plan

The program planning team is responsible for reviewing the student's progress in the plan and meeting to discuss changes when necessary. The program plan should be reviewed at least twice annually.

Source: Reprinted from the Special Education Policy Manual. (1996). Nova Scotia Department of Education and Culture, pp. 36-41

Appendix 6.2

Student's Primary Classification: Serious Emotional Disturbance

Secondary Classification: None

Student Name *Diane*

Date of Birth *5-3-91*

Primary Language:

HOME *English*   Student *English*

Date of IEP Meeting *March, 27, 2004*

Entry Date to Program *March, 27, 2004*

Projected Duration of Services *One school year*

Services Required *Specify amount of time in educational and/or related services per day or week*

General Education Class *4—5 h/day*

Resource Room *1—2 h/day*

Special Ed Consultation in General Ed Classroom
Co-teaching and consultation with general education teacher in the areas of academic and adaptive skills as indicated in annual goals and short-term objectives.

Self-Contained *none*

Related Services *Group counselling sessions twice weekly with guidance counsellor. Counselling to focus on adaptive skill development as described in annual goals and short-term objectives*

RE. Program *45 min. daily in general ed PE class with support from adapted PE teacher as necessary*

Assessment

Intellectual *WISC-R*

Educational *Key Math Woodcock Reading*

Behavioural/Adaptive *Burks*

Speech/Language

Other

Vision *Within normal limits*

Hearing *Within normal limits*

Classroom Observation Done

Dates *1/15—2/25/03*

Personnel Conducting Observation *School Psychologist, Special Education Teacher, General Education Teacher*

Present Level of Performance Strengths:
1) *Polite to teachers and peers*
2) *Helpful and cooperative in the classroom*
3) *Good grooming skills*
4) *Good in sports activities*

Access to General Education Curriculum
Diane will participate in all content areas within the general education curriculum. Special education supports and services will be provided in the areas of math and reading.

Effect of Disability on Access to General Education Curriculum
Emotional disabilities make it difficult for Diane to achieve at expected grade level performance in general education curriculum in the areas of reading and math. It is expected that this will further impact her access to the general education curriculum in other content areas (such as history, biology, English) as she enters junior high school.

Participation in Provincial Assessments
Diane will participate in all province wide assessments of achievement. No adaptations or modifications required for participation.

Justification for Removal from General Education Classroom:
Diane's objectives require that she be placed in a general education classroom with support from a special education teacher for the majority of the school day. Based on adaptive behaviour assessment and observations, Diane will receive instruction in a resource room for approximately one to two hours per day in the areas of social skill development.

Reports to Parents on Progress Toward Annual Goals:
Parents will be informed of Diane's progress through weekly reports of progress on short-term goals, monthly phone calls from general ed teachers, special education teachers, and school psychologist, and regularly scheduled report cards at the end of each term.

Appendix 6.2 *(continued)*

Areas Needing Specialized Instruction and Support

1. Adaptive Skills
   - Limited interaction skills with peers and adults
   - Excessive facial tics and grimaces
   - Difficulty staying on task in content subjects, especially reading and math.
   - Difficulty expressing feelings, needs, and interests

2. Academic Skills
   - Significantly below grade level in math—3.9
   - Significantly below grade level in reading—4.3

Annual Review: Date: _____

Comments/Recommendations

_____
_____
_____
_____
_____

Team Signatures   IEP Review Date _____

LEA Rep. _____

Parent _____

Sp Ed Teacher _____

Gen Ed Teacher _____

School Psych _____

Student (as appropriate) _____

Related Services Personnel (as appropriate) _____

Objective Criteria and Evaluation Procedures _____

IEP—Annual Goals and Short-Term Objectives	Persons Responsible	Objective Criteria and Evaluation Procedures
#1 ANNUAL GOAL: Diane will improve her interaction skills with peers and adults.	General education teacher and special ed teacher (resource room)	Classroom observations and documented data on target behaviour
S.T. OBJ. Diane will initiate conversation with peers during an unstructured setting twice daily.	School psychologist consultation	
S.T. OBJ. When in need of assistance, Diane will raise her hand and verbalize her needs to teachers or peers without prompting 80% of the time.		
#2 ANNUAL GOAL: Diane will increase her ability to control hand and facial movements.	General education teacher and special ed teacher (resource room)	Classroom observations and documented data on target behaviour
S.T. OBJ. During academic work, Diane will keep her hands in an appropriate place and use writing materials correctly 80% of the time.	School psychologist consultation	
S.T. OBJ. Diane will maintain a relaxed facial expression with teacher prompt 80% of the time. Teacher prompt will be faded over time.		
#3 ANNUAL GOAL: Diane will improve her ability to remain on task during academic work.	General education teacher and special ed teacher (resource room)	Classroom observations and documented data on target behaviour
S.T. OBJ. Diane will work independently on an assigned task with teacher prompt 80% of the time.	School psychologist consultation	
S.T. OBJ. Diane will complete academic work as assigned 90% of the time.		

Appendix 6.2 *(continued)*

IEP—Annual Goals and Short-Term Objectives	Persons Responsible	Objective Criteria and Evaluation Procedures
#4 ANNUAL GOAL: Diane will improve her ability to express her feelings. **S.T. OBJ.** When asked how she feels, Diane will give an adequate verbal description of her feelings or moods with teacher prompting at least 80% of the time. **S.T. OBJ.** Given a conflict or problem situation, Diane will state her feelings to teachers and peers 80% of the time.	General education teacher and special ed teacher (resource room) School psychologist consultation	Classroom observations and documented data on target behaviour
#5 ANNUAL GOAL: Diane will improve math skills one grade level. **S.T. OBJ.** Diane will improve rate and accuracy in oral 1- and 2-digit division facts to 50 problems per minute without errors. **S.T. OBJ.** Diane will improve her ability to solve word problems involving t—x—v.	Collaboration of general education teacher and special education teacher through co-teaching and consultation	Precision teaching Addison Wesley Math Program Scope and Sequence Districtwide Assessment of Academic Achievement
#6 ANNUAL GOAL: Diane will improve reading skills one grade level. **S.T. OBJ.** Diane will answer progressively more difficult comprehension questions in designated reading skills program. **S.T. OBJ.** Diane will increase her rate and accuracy of vocabulary words to 80 wpm without errors.	Collaboration of general education teacher and special education teacher through co-teaching and consultation	Precision teaching Barnell & Loft Scope and Sequence District wide Assessment of Academic Achievement

Source: Michael L. Hardman, Clifford J. Drew, and M. Winston Egan, *Human Exceptionality: Society, School, and Family,* 6th ed. Boston: Allyn and Bacon, 1999, pp. 123–25. Copyright © 1999 by Allyn and Bacon. Used with permission.

Appendix 6.3

1. Present material on tape for students who cannot read successfully. School volunteers, older students, or parents can be asked to make recordings of assigned material.

2. Allow students to tape record answers if writing is difficult or their handwriting is illegible.

3. Provide lots of visual reminders (pictures, maps, charts, graphs) for students who have trouble listening or attending.

4. Present handouts that are clear, legible, and uncrowded. Blurred copies [can be] very hard for [students with disabilities] to read.

5. Break directions and assignments into small steps. Completion of each step is an accomplishment—reward it.

6. Give tests orally if the child has trouble with reading, spelling, or writing. Testing that demonstrates what the student knows rather than language skills gives you a clearer picture of the student's abilities. The student demonstrates abilities, not disabilities.

7. Emphasize quality rather than quantity of writing.

8. Be consistent with directions, rules, discipline, and organization.

9. Arrange the class schedule so that the exceptional student does not miss important activities when he or she goes to the resource room.

10. Dispense encouragement freely but fairly. If students make errors, help them find the correct answers, and then reward them.

11. Discover the exceptional student's strengths and special interests. Capitalize on them in the regular classroom.

12. Carefully establish routines so that the student does not become further handicapped by the confusion of unclear expectations.

13. Arrange desks, tables, and chairs so every person can be easily seen and every word easily heard. Remember, students with hearing impairments need to see your face as you speak.

14. If possible, schedule difficult subjects when there are no outside noises, such as a class at recess.

15. Provide carrels or screens—an "office"—for students who are easily distracted.

16. When checking students' work, check correct answers rather than incorrect answers. The student is still informed of mistakes, but sees his or her successes emphasized.

17. Allow the exceptional student to tape lectures or arrange for a classmate who writes neatly to use carbon paper. Either the carbon copy or a copy of the teacher's notes can be given to the exceptional student.

18. Correct deficient lighting, glare from windows, and light-blocking partitions. Small light problems can be distractions for some exceptional students.

19. Fit the furniture to the child. Discomfort leads to distraction and restlessness.

20. Generally, become sensitive to the obstacles which prevent the exceptional student from exercising his or her abilities.

Source: Pamela Maniet-Bellerman, *Mainstreaming Children with Disabilities: A Guide to Accompany "L.D." Does NOT Mean Learning Dumb!* Pittsburgh: Upward Bound Press; as presented in R. R. McCown and Peter Roop, *Educational Psychology and Classroom Practice: A Partnership*, Boston: Allyn and Bacon, 1992, pp. 424–425.

7

Creating a Community of Learners

Teacher-oriented, passive-student approaches to instruction are outdated ... we cannot effectively conduct our classes as if students were sponges who sit passively and absorb attentively.

—A middle school mathematics teacher, quoted in Burden and Byrd (1999, 103)

focus questions

1. What determines the culture of the classroom?
2. How can you create a positive learning environment?
3. What are the keys to successful classroom management?
4. What teaching methods do effective teachers use?
5. What are some characteristics of effective teaching?

September 26

I set up a classroom library. We don't use the reading textbook. What for? Grown-ups don't read textbooks unless they're forced. I told them we could read real books so long as they don't steal any. I make a big show of counting the books at the end of the day. The kids sigh audibly when they're all there. They look beautiful, like a bookstore, facing out in a big wooden display my uncle made for me. Plus, it covers the bullet-riddled window that never was repaired.

We don't call the subjects the old-fashioned names in Room 211. Math is "Puzzling," science is "Mad Scientist Time," social studies is "T.T.W.E." which stands for "Time Travel and World Exploring," language arts is "Art of Language," and reading is "Free Reading Time." I did this because I figured kids at this age come to me with preconceived notions of what they are good at. This way, a kid who thinks she's no good in math might turn out to be good at Puzzling, and so on.

In the morning, three things happen religiously. I say good morning, real chipper, to every single child and make sure they say good morning back. Then I collect "troubles" in a "Trouble Basket," a big green basket into which the children pantomime unburdening their home worries so they can concentrate on school. Sometimes a kid has no troubles. Sometimes a kid piles it in, and I in turn pantomime bearing the burden. This way, too, I can see what disposition the child is in when he or she enters. Finally, before they can come in, they must give me a word, which I print on a piece of tagboard and they keep in an envelope. It can be any word, but preferably one that they heard and don't really know or one that is personally meaningful. A lot of times the kids ask for *Mississippi,* just to make me spell it. We go over the words when we do our private reading conferences. I learned this from reading *Teacher* by Sylvia Ashton-Warner, who taught underprivileged Maori children in New Zealand. She says language should be an organic experience. I love her approach.

It takes a long time to get in the door this way, but by the time we are in, I know every kid has had and given a kind greeting, has had an opportunity to learn something, and has tried to leave his or her worries on the doorstep. Some kids from other classrooms sneak into our line to use the Trouble Basket or to get a word card.

Then the national anthem blares over the intercom. The kids sing with more gusto now that we shout "Play ball!" at the end. We do Puzzling until 10:30, then we alternate Mad Sciencing with T.T.W.E., lunch, reading aloud, Free Reading and journaling, and Art of Language.

At the end of the day, as the kids exit, they fill in the blanks as I call out, "See you in the [morning!]." "Watch out for the [cars!]." "Don't say [shut up!]." "I love [you!]." This is a game I played with my father at bedtime growing up. It gives the day a nice closure (Codell 1999, 29–31).

The opening scenario for this chapter, taken from *Educating Esmé: Diary of a Teacher's First Year,* by Esmé Raji Codell, a Grade 5 teacher, illustrates how one teacher organized her classroom to create a positive learning environment. Sensitivity to the elements that combine to give a day in the classroom a "nice closure" is the hallmark of a professional, reflective teacher. For teacher education students such as you, making the transition between the study of teaching and actual teaching can be a challenge. The more you understand how "the classroom learning environment develops gradually, in response to the teacher's communication of expectations, modelling of behaviour, and approach to classroom management" (Good and Brophy 1997, 129), the better prepared you will be to make the transition smoothly.

What Determines the Culture of the Classroom?

As you learned in Chapter 5, one definition of *culture* is the way of life common to a group of people. In much the same way, each classroom develops its own culture. The culture of a classroom is determined by the manner in which teachers and students participate in common activities.

The activities that teachers and students engage in are influenced by several factors. As a teacher, you will make countless decisions that will shape the physical and social milieus of your classroom. From seating arrangement, to classroom rules and procedures, to the content and relevance of the curriculum, you will have a strong influence on the culture that emerges in your classroom. You will have many methodological choices to make—when to shift from one activity to another, when to use discussion rather than lecture, or whether to make one requirement rather than another.

Classrom Climate

Part of the environment of the classroom is **classroom climate**—the atmosphere or quality of life in a classroom. The climate of your classroom will be determined by how you interact with your students and "by the manner and degree to which you exercise authority, show warmth and support, encourage competitiveness or cooperation, and allow for independent judgment and choice" (Borich 1996, 470).

Classroom climates are complex and multidimensional; their character is determined by a wide array of variables, many of which are beyond the teacher's control. Nevertheless, our observations of high-performing teachers have confirmed that they take specific steps to create classroom climates with the following eight characteristics:

- A productive, task-oriented focus
- Group cohesiveness
- Open, warm relationships between teacher and students
- Cooperative, respectful interactions among students
- Low levels of tension, anxiety, and conflict
- Humour
- High expectations
- Frequent opportunities for student input regarding classroom activities

These dimensions of classroom climates are within teachers' spheres of influence and are promoted, consciously or unconsciously, by their styles of communicating and treating students. As the following reflections by a student teacher indicate, creating a classroom climate characterized by these eight dimensions is not easy; teachers must make moment-to-moment judgments about what actions will enhance students' motivation to learn.

> The next day, as I was going over the instructions for a science experiment I noticed Sheila and Devon leaning over and whispering. I immediately stopped my presentation and said, "Sheila and Devon, you need to turn around in your seats and stop whispering while I am talking." Both girls rolled their eyes and slowly turned their bodies around in their seats. Neither of them made eye contact with me as I continued the lesson. Although the class was now quiet, I felt uncomfortable myself. As the students gathered the science materials they needed to carry out the experiment in their cooperative learning groups, I noticed that Theresa was passing a note to Sheila. Trying to hide my anger and frustration, I said, "Theresa, you need to get rid of that note now. You can come up and put it in the wastebasket. It is time to be working on science, not note passing." Although singling out the girls worked in the short term, to tell the truth I did not feel comfortable dealing with the situation as I did.

> I didn't want to feel as if I was spending half the time handling misbehaviour, but that's just what I was doing. I had learned in school to reach for student strengths, so I am trying to practice the strategy of giving the students a better attitude

about themselves through praise. I explained to them that by correcting their behaviour I was just trying to create a climate in which they could learn. I am trying to be a supportive teacher who still corrects misbehaviour—always with the goal of redirecting students toward meaningful classroom work.

That same afternoon, I began to gather the students together for literature circles. I had four groups reading different novels. Today I was planning to have the students discuss their reactions to the first chapter and make predictions about the rest of the book. For the first five minutes or so, the groups were very productive, and I felt a surge of hope that all would go well. Just then, I noticed Devon lean back in her chair to pass a note to Theresa, who was in a different group. I wanted to shout across the room at them, but I kept my calm and tried to figure out what I should do now (Rand and Shelton-Colangelo 1999, 10–11).

How would you describe this classroom climate using the eight dimensions listed earlier? What changes in the student teacher's behaviour could transform the overall climate?

Although teachers influence the classroom climate by the way they regard and treat students, they also shape it by their instructional decisions. David Johnson and Roger Johnson, two researchers in the area of classroom communication and dynamics, delineate three types of interactions promoted by instructional decisions: cooperative or positive interdependence, competitive or negative interdependence, and individualistic or no interdependence (Johnson and Johnson 1999). To illustrate the three types, Johnson and Johnson suggest that a group project to measure classroom furniture would promote cooperative interdependence; a race to be the first student to measure the furniture would call for competitive interdependence; and having a student measure the furniture independently would be an example of no interdependence. Johnson and Johnson believe that teachers should use strategies that foster all three forms of interactions, depending on their instructional goals, but that, ideally, the emphasis should be on furthering cooperative interdependence.

What words would you use to describe the apparent climate of this classroom? In what ways does this classroom appear to be an effective learning environment? What would you look for to determine if this is a caring classroom?

Classroom Dynamics

Interactions between teachers and students are the very core of teaching. The quality of these interactions reveals to students how the teacher feels about them. Teachers who empathize with students, genuinely respect them, and expect them to learn are more likely to develop a classroom climate free of management problems. In classrooms with positive group dynamics, teachers and students work toward a common goal—learning. In classrooms with negative interactions, the energy of teachers and students may be channeled into conflict rather than into learning.

There is no precise formula to guarantee success in the classroom; however, educational psychologist Anita Woolfolk (1998, 427) suggests four "necessary conditions" to increase student learning through positive interactions:

1. The classroom must be relatively organized and free from constant interruptions and disruptions.
2. The teacher must be a patient, supportive person who never embarrasses students for mistakes.
3. The work must be challenging but reasonable.
4. The learning tasks must be authentic.

Teacher Communication

Successful teachers possess effective communication skills. They express themselves verbally and nonverbally (and in writing) in a manner that is clear, concise, and interesting. They "are able to communicate clearly and directly to their students without wandering, speaking above students' levels of comprehension, or using speech patterns that impair the clarity of what is being presented" (Borich 1996, 11). In addition, they are good listeners. Their students feel that not only are they heard, they are understood.

Effective teachers relish the live, thinking-on-your-feet dimensions of classroom communication. Their communication skills enable them to respond appropriately to events that could sabotage the plans of less effective teachers: a student's clowning, announcements on the public address system, interruptions by other teachers or parents, students' private arguments or romances, or simply the mood of the class at that particular time.

Student Interaction

In addition to engaging in positive, success-oriented interactions with their students, effective teachers foster positive, cooperative interactions among students. As a result, students feel supported by their peers and free to devote their attention to learning. Richard Schmuck and Patricia Schmuck (1997) describe the climate of such classrooms as "mature" and "self-renewing." Their research on classroom group processes has led them to identify the four sequential stages of group development portrayed in Figure 7.1.

Figure 7.1

Characteristics of groups at four stages of development

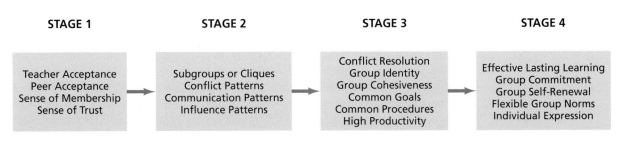

STAGE 1	STAGE 2	STAGE 3	STAGE 4
Teacher Acceptance Peer Acceptance Sense of Membership Sense of Trust	Subgroups or Cliques Conflict Patterns Communication Patterns Influence Patterns	Conflict Resolution Group Identity Group Cohesiveness Common Goals Common Procedures High Productivity	Effective Lasting Learning Group Commitment Group Self-Renewal Flexible Group Norms Individual Expression

During Stage 1 of a class's group development, students are on their best behaviour. Teachers who are aware of this "honeymoon period" use it to their advantage; they discuss and teach classroom rules and procedures, outline their goals, and deliberately set the classroom tone and standards they want. During Stage 2, teachers seeking to promote group development are advised to encourage student participation and communication and to discourage the formation of cliques.

Groups that have met the requirements of the preceding stages move into Stage 3, which lasts for the majority of the expected life of the group (in other words, the semester or the school year). This stage is characterized by the group's willingness to set clear goals, share tasks, and agree on deadlines. At Stage 4, the final stage, group members fully accept responsibility for the group's quality of life, and they continuously strive to improve it.

In addition, teachers who effectively orchestrate group processes in their classrooms recognize that, for good or ill, students as well as teachers exert leadership in classrooms. Wise teachers quickly identify student leaders and develop ways to focus their leadership abilities on the attainment of goals that benefit the entire class. Teachers should also encourage their students to develop leadership skills.

How Can You Create a Positive Learning Environment?

A positive classroom climate and positive classroom dynamics are prerequisites for a good learning environment. Creating and then maintaining a positive learning environment is a multidimensional challenge. While no single set of strategies will ensure success in all situations, educational researchers have identified teacher behaviours that tend to be associated with high levels of student learning. Effective teachers also know how to use these behaviours and *for what purposes* they are best suited. The following sections address three important dimensions of positive learning environments: the caring classroom, the physical classroom environment, and classroom organization, including procedures for grouping students for instruction and managing time.

The Caring Classroom

At this point in your preparation to become a teacher, you may feel uncertain of your ability to create a positive classroom climate and to orchestrate the complex dynamics of the classroom so that you and your students become a cohesive, productive, and mutually supportive group. In your quest to achieve these aims, it will help to remember that an authentic spirit of caring is at the heart of an effective learning environment. "[C]aring interactions between teachers, students, and parents often make the difference between positive school experiences and frustration or alienation" (Chaskin and Rauner 1995, 667–68).

How do teachers establish a **caring classroom**? First, teachers demonstrate caring through their efforts to help all students learn to their fullest potential. "Teachers display genuine caring for students when they find out about students' abilities and motivations. They continue this pervasive caring by providing all their students with the appropriate amount of support, structure, and expectations they need in order to be self-directed, responsible learners" (Zehm and Kottler 1993, 54). In addition, teachers realize that how they speak and listen to students determines the extent to which students believe their teachers care about them. In a synthesis of research on classroom environments that enhance students' learning, Herbert Walberg and Rebecca Greenberg (1997, 46) found that "students learn more when their classes are satisfying, challenging, and friendly and they have a voice in decision making. [When] classes are unfriendly, cliquish, and fragmented, they leave students feeling rejected and therefore impede learning." Table 7.1, based on Walberg and Greenberg's work, presents fifteen dimensions of classroom life and how each influences students' learning at the junior and senior high levels.

While students learn best in caring classrooms, Nel Noddings has suggested that students also must learn to care for others. Toward this end, she recommends reorganizing the school curriculum around "themes of care" and points out that "educators must recognize that caring for students is fundamental in teaching and that developing people with a strong capacity for care is a major objective of responsible education" (Noddings 1995, 678).

Table 7.1

Fifteen dimensions of classroom environment

Dimension	Percent Positive Influence on Learning		Description
Satisfaction	100	(17)	Students enjoy classroom work and find it satisfying.
Challenge	87	(16)	Students find the work difficult and challenging.
Cohesiveness	86	(17)	Students know one another well and are helpful and friendly toward one another.
Physical Environment	85	(15)	Adequate books, equipment, space, and lighting are available.
Democracy	85	(14)	Students share equally in making decisions that affect the entire class.
Goal Direction	73	(15)	Learning goals are clear.
Competition	67	(9)	Competition among students is minimized.
Formality	65	(17)	Class is informal, with few formal rules to guide behaviour.
Speed	54	(14)	Students have sufficient time to finish their work.
Diversity	31	(14)	Students' interests differ and are provided for.
Apathy	14	(15)	Students don't care about what the class does.
Favouritism	10	(13)	All students do not enjoy the same privileges; the teacher has favourites.
Cliquishness	8	(13)	Certain students work only with close friends and refuse to interact with others.
Disorganization	6	(17)	Activities are disorganized and confusing, rather than well organized and efficient.
Friction	0	(17)	Tension and quarreling among students characterize the classroom.

Note: Percent indicates the percentage of research studies that reported a positive influence on learning for that dimension; number in parenthesis indicates number of research studies that investigated that dimension.

Source: Adapted from Herbert J. Walberg and Rebecca C. Greenberg, "Using the Learning Environment Inventory," *Educational Leadership,* May 1997, p. 47.

The Classroom As a Physical Environment

When you become a teacher, the physical environment you work in will probably be similar to that of schools you attended. However, we encourage you, with the help of your students, to make your surroundings as safe, pleasant, and convenient as possible. Fresh air; plants; clean, painted walls; displays of students' work; a comfortable reading or resource area; and a few prints or posters can enhance the quality of teacher–student relationships. Seating arrangements and the placement of other classroom furniture also do much to shape the classroom environment. Although seating by rows may be very appropriate for whole-group instruction or examinations, other arrangements may be more beneficial for other activities. For example, you can enhance small-group activities by moving desks into small clusters in different parts of the room. Figure 7.2 shows the arrangement of a classroom at an exemplary elementary school. The room is designed to encourage students to learn through discovery at learning centres located around the room.

Figure 7.2

Learning centres in an elementary classroom

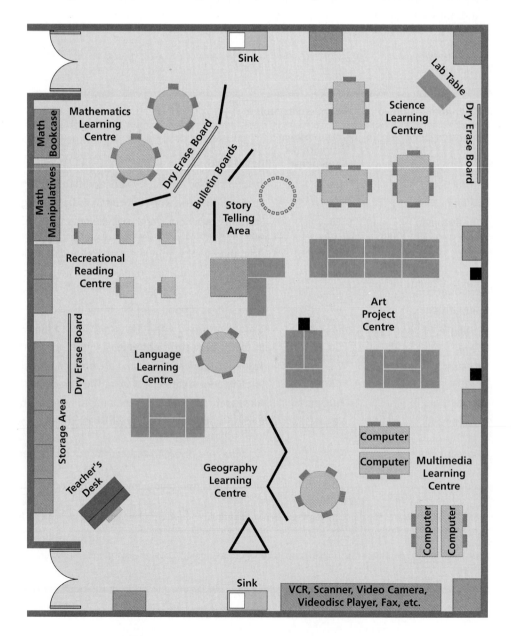

However you design your classroom, take care to ensure that seating arrangements do not reduce the opportunity of some students to learn. For example, students in some classrooms receive more attention if they are seated in the "action zone," the middle front-row seats and seats on the middle aisle. Teachers often stand near this area and unknowingly give students seated there more opportunities to speak.

Classroom Organization

A factor in positive learning environments is **classroom organization**—the way teachers and students are grouped for instruction, the way learning tasks are structured, and other resources used. The following sections focus on these aspects of classroom organization.

Grouping Students by Ability

Two common approaches for grouping students on the basis of shared characteristics are between-class ability grouping, often called tracking, and within-class ability grouping. Students who attend schools where **between-class ability grouping** is practiced are assigned to classes on the basis of ability or achievement. This practice is not common in Canadian schools. Another form of between-class ability grouping, especially at the high school level, is based on students' goals after graduation. Many high schools, for example, offer honours classes or French Immersion programs.

Research suggests that, for the most part, between-class ability grouping does not contribute to greater achievement (Good and Brophy 2000). Supporters nevertheless claim that teachers are better able to meet the needs of students in homogeneous groupings. Among the alternatives to between-class ability grouping are heterogeneous (or mixed-ability) grouping, regrouping by subject area, the Joplin Plan (regrouping students for reading instruction by ability across grade levels), and cooperative learning.

Within-class ability grouping often is used for instruction in reading and mathematics within a class, where a teacher instructs students in homogeneous, small groups. Within-class grouping is used widely in elementary classrooms. Perhaps you can recall learning to read in a small group with a name such as the Sparrows, the Robins, or the Bluejays. Like tracking, within-class ability grouping can heighten preexisting differences in achievement between groups of students, especially if teachers give high-achieving groups more attention. Also, once students are grouped, they tend not to be regrouped, even when differences in achievement are reduced.

At best, evidence to support student groupings is mixed. Whether students are grouped on the basis of ability, curricular interests, or disabling condition, there is a danger that some group labels can evoke negative expectations, causing teachers to "underteach" certain students, and their peers to isolate or reject them. The most serious consequence, of course, is that students so labelled are taught to feel inadequate, inferior, and limited in their options for growth.

Grouping Students for Cooperative Learning

Cooperative learning is an approach to teaching in which students work in small groups, or teams, sharing the work and helping one another complete assignments. Student-Team-Learning, for example, is a cooperative approach teachers use to increase the basic skills achievement of at-risk students. In cooperative learning arrangements, students are motivated to learn in small groups through rewards that are made available to the group as a whole and to individual members of the group. Cooperative learning includes the following key elements:

- Small groups (four to six students) work together on learning activities.
- Assignments require that students help one another while working on a group project.

Prime Minister's Award for Teaching Excellence Recipient: Sharon Davis

Jack Hulland
Elementary School, Whitehorse, Yukon

Teachers are in the best position to listen to fears and worries that parents express and tie these to educational objectives. Sharon Davis, the school counsellor at Jack Hulland Elementary School in Whitehorse, Yukon cites an interesting example. Parents came to her because they were concerned about the number of fights on the playground. Because of her training as a teacher-counsellor, Davis recognized that the fights were occurring because children did not know how to play.

"Today's children spend so much time in structured activities that they are unable to play without a referee or coach overseeing them. Anytime something goes wrong, and there is no authority to refer to, a fight breaks out. A group of parents got together and started a group called POPs (Peace on the Playground). The parents trained some Grade 7 students who then showed the younger children ways to resolve problems when playing games."

This effective program was born when parents and a teacher, Davis, had a chance to actually talk with and listen to one another. These exchanges have become a regular part of school life at Jack Hulland Elementary. Groups meet regularly so that parents can share their concerns.

It is important to recognize parents who make the effort and take time out of their busy days to volunteer at school. Every year, Jack Hulland Elementary has a volunteer tea to show appreciation to those individuals, and each volunteer gets a certificate. Davis points out that when children see themselves as part of a community that includes both their teachers and their parents, it changes the way they make decisions that have lifelong consequences.

Source: Reproduced with the permission of the Minister of Public Works and Government Services, 2003. Prime Minister's awards for teaching excellence: Exemplary practices. *Beyond the Classroom Walls*. Retrieved 22 January 2003, from pma-ppm.ic.gc.ca/exemplary/1999/Beyond.html

- In competitive arrangements, groups may compete against one another.
- Group members contribute to group goals according to their talents, interests, and abilities.

In addition, cooperative learning is an instructional method that can strengthen students' interpersonal skills. When students from different racial, ethnic, and cultural backgrounds and mainstreamed special-needs students all contribute to a common group goal, friendships increase and group members tend to view one another as more equal in status and worth.

Cooperative learning also enables students to learn a variety of roles and responsibilities, as the following comments by a Grade 5 science teacher indicate:

I have the class divided into groups of five students and each group works as a team. The job duties are as follows: principal investigator (PI), materials manager (MM), reader, recorder, and reporter. The PI is the leader of the group and helps mediate when problems occur. The PI is the only student who can come to me with questions during the actual procedure. This rule enables me to monitor the groups and also teaches the group to work independently.

Students change job duties within their group [for] each activity and every six weeks students change groups. This plan gives each student the experience of working with different classmates as well as learning the responsibility of group participation through performing the different job duties.

Delivering Instruction

The delivery of instruction is a key element in creating positive learning environments. What the teacher does and what students do have powerful influences on learning and on the quality of classroom life. A common activity format in elementary schools consists of students doing seatwork on their own or listening to their teachers and participating in whole-class recitations. In addition, students participate in reading groups, games, and discussions; take tests; check work; view films; give reports; help clean up the classroom; and go on field trips.

A teacher must answer the question, "What activity will enable me to accomplish my instructional goals?" Teachers also must realize that learning activities should meet *students'* goals; that is, the activities must be meaningful and authentic for students. **Authentic learning tasks** enable students to see the connections between classroom learning and the world beyond the classroom—both now and in the future. To understand how authentic learning tasks can motivate students to learn, reflect upon your own school experiences. Do you recall memorizing facts only because they would appear on a test? Did you ever wonder why a teacher asked you to complete a learning task? Did you ever feel that a teacher asked you to do "busywork"? What kinds of learning tasks motivated you the most?

Herbert A. Thelen (1981, 86) contends that authenticity is "the first criterion all educational activity must meet." According to Thelen, an activity is authentic for a person if he or she "feels emotionally 'involved' and mentally stimulated ... is aware of choices and enjoys the challenge of making decisions," and feels he or she "has something to bring to the activity and that its outcome will be important" (Thelen 1981, 86). A comprehensive nationwide study of successfully restructured schools reported that "authentic pedagogy" helps students to (1) "construct knowledge" through the use of higher-order thinking, (2) acquire "deep knowledge" (relatively complex understandings of subject matter), (3) engage in "substantive conversations" with teachers and peers, and (4) make connections between substantive knowledge and the world beyond the classroom (Newmann and Wehlage 1995; Newmann et al. 1996). In addition, as Figure 7.3 shows, high authentic pedagogy classes boost achievement for students at all grade levels. The following Professional Reflection illustrates the differences between high and low authentic pedagogy.

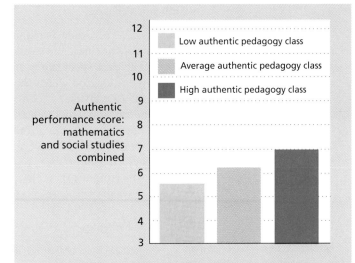

Note: The analysis included 2,100 students in 125 classrooms in 23 schools. Most students had either a mathematics or social studies score, and the two subjects were scored on the same 12-point scale. There were no major differences in the effect of authentic pedagogy on achievement between the two subjects.

Figure 7.3

Level of authentic student performance for students who experience low, average, and high authentic pedagogy in restructuring elementary, middle, and high schools.

Source: Fred M. Newmann and Gary G. Wehlage, *Successful School Restructuring: A Report to the Public and Educators by the Center on Organization and Restructuring of Schools.* University of Wisconsin-Madison: Center on Organization and Restructuring of Schools, 1995, pp. 21, 55.

Professional Reflection — How do low and high authentic pedagogy differ?

Read the following descriptions of low and high authentic pedagogy classes in social studies. What differences do you notice between the two classes? What do you think Mrs. Allen's students thought about the learning tasks they were asked to complete? Ms States' students? When you were a Grade 5 or 6 student, which teacher would you have preferred? Why?

Low Authentic Pedagogy

The task for a class of Grade 5s required them to copy a set of questions about famous explorers from a worksheet and to add the correct short-answer responses in the appropriate spots. The class spent thirty minutes on this exercise, which was part of a larger unit on exploration and which the teacher, Mrs. Allen, described as very consistent with the typical assessment.

During the four times that [researchers] observed Allen's hour-long classes, students read aloud from the textbook, a routine occasionally punctuated with Allen's asking them factual recall questions. During one class, students copied a chart from the board organizing the facts from the reading into categories. After finding more facts to fill up the chart, the students then completed a worksheet crossword puzzle built from the vocabulary words of the lesson (Marks, Newmann, and Gamoran 1996, 59–60).

High Authentic Pedagogy

As an assessment of their learning, Ms States had her class of 5s and 6s research and write a paper on ecology, an assignment that occupied forty hours of class time during the twelve-week grading period. Each student produced several drafts of the paper and met individually with the teacher several times to discuss the drafts. Before they began the project, students received eleven pages of written directions on how to research, organize, and write the paper, including a step-by-step checklist for completing the assignment, a sample outline, and sample bibliography entries. The paper counted for 75 percent of the student's grade for the twelve-week period (Marks, Newmann, and Gamoran, 1996, 60).

Structuring the Use of Time

How teachers use time affects student learning. **Allocated time** is the time teachers allocate for instruction in various areas of the curriculum. Teachers vary widely in their instructional use of time. Educational researchers Tom Good and Jere Brophy report, for example, that "some students [may receive] as much as four times more instructional time in a given subject than other students in the same grade" (Good and Brophy 1997, 29–30).

Researchers have shown that **time on task**—the amount of time students are actively engaged in learning activities—is directly related to learning. As anyone who has ever daydreamed while appearing to pay attention can confirm, time on task is difficult to measure. In response to this difficulty, researchers have introduced the concept of **academic learning time**—the amount of time a student spends working on academic tasks with a high level of success (80 percent or higher) Not surprisingly, learning time, like allocated time, varies greatly from classroom to classroom.

An additional concept that is proving useful in understanding teachers' use of time in the classroom is known as **opportunity to learn** (OTL). OTL is based on the premise that teachers should use time to provide all students with challenging content through appropriate instruction.

In some Canadian provinces, the Departments of Education are making specific minimum daily guidelines regarding how time should be used in classrooms. For example, in 2002, the Nova Scotia Education Department specified how much time elementary students should spend learning the basics. The minimum daily guidelines are:

Grades Primary to 2—Language arts, 90 min; math, 45 min

Grade 3—Language arts, 1 h, 55 min; math, 60 min

Grades 4 to 6—Language arts, 90 min; math, 60 min
Similar time standards are expected to be introduced in junior high schools in 2003. (*Halifax Herald* 2003).

To increase the time available for active learning, many high schools have implemented block scheduling arrangements. **Block scheduling** uses longer blocks of time each class period, with fewer periods each day. Longer blocks of time allow more in-depth coverage of subject matter and lead to deeper understanding and higher-level applications. Block scheduling also gives teachers more time to present complex concepts and students more time to practice applying those concepts to authentic problems.

What Are the Keys to Successful Classroom Management?

For most new teachers, classroom management is a primary concern. How can you prevent discipline problems from arising and keep students productively engaged in learning activities? While effective **classroom management** cannot be reduced to a cookbook recipe, there are definite steps you can take to create an effective learning environment in your classroom. First, it is important to understand that classroom management refers to how teachers structure their learning environments to prevent, or minimize, behaviour problems; *discipline* refers to the methods teachers use *after* students misbehave. *Classroom management* is prevention-oriented, while *discipline* is control-oriented. Second, it is important to recognize that "the key to good management is use of techniques that elicit student cooperation and involvement in activities and thus *prevent* problems from emerging in the first place" (Good and Brophy 1997, 129). In addition, sound classroom management techniques are based on the guidelines for creating an effective learning environment presented previously in this chapter—in other words, (1) creating a caring classroom, (2) organizing the physical classroom environment, (3) grouping students for instruction, (4) providing authentic learning tasks, and (5) structuring the use of time to maximize students' learning. Positive leadership and preventive planning thus are central to effective classroom management.

The Democratic Classroom

Research findings suggest that teachers who allow students to participate in making decisions about the physical classroom environment, classroom rules and procedures, modifications to the curriculum, and options for learning activities also have fewer discipline problems. Students in **democratic classrooms** have both more power and more responsibility than students in conventional classrooms. On the premise that if students are to live in a democracy, they must learn to manage freedom responsibly, teachers model democracy by giving their students some choices and some control over classroom activities. William Glasser, well-known psychiatrist and author of *Quality School* (1998a), *The Quality School Teacher* (1998b), *Choice Theory* (1998c), and (with Karen Dotson) *Choice Theory in the Classroom* (1998), recommends that teachers develop "quality" classrooms based on democratic principles. According to Glasser, many teachers struggle with classroom management because their actions are guided by stimulus–response theory; that is, they try to coerce students through rewards or punishment, or what many teachers term "logical consequences." Instead, Glasser maintains that teachers should establish "quality" environments in the classroom by following **choice theory**—that is, recognizing that human beings make choices that enable them to create "quality worlds" that satisfy four needs: the need to belong, the need for power, the need for freedom, and the need for fun. From a *choice theory* perspective, misbehaviour in the classroom arises when students' learning experiences do not enable them to create quality worlds for themselves. Therefore, teachers "must give up bossing and turn to 'leading'" (Glasser 1997, 600). We follow leaders, Glasser says, because we believe they are concerned about our welfare. To persuade students to do quality schoolwork, teachers must establish warm, noncoercive relationships with students; teach students meaningful skills rather than ask them to memorize information; enable them to experience satisfaction and excitement by working in small teams; and move from teacher evaluation to student self-evaluation.

Preventive Planning

In what other ways can teachers prevent discipline problems from occurring? The key to prevention is excellent planning and an understanding of life in classrooms. In addition, teachers who have mastered the essential teaching skills have fewer discipline problems because students recognize that such teachers are prepared, well organized, and have a sense of purpose. They are confident of their ability to teach all students, and their task-oriented manner tends to discourage misbehaviour.

In a seminal study of how teachers prevent discipline problems, Jacob Kounin looked at two sets of teachers: those who managed their classrooms smoothly and productively with few disruptions and those who seemed to be plagued with discipline problems and chaotic working conditions. He found that the teachers who managed their classrooms successfully had certain teaching behaviours in common: (1) they displayed the proverbial eyes-in-the-back-of-the-head, a quality of alertness Kounin referred to as *withitness*, (2) they used individual students and incidences as models to communicate to the rest of the class their expectations for student conduct—Kounin's *ripple effect*, (3) they supervised several situations at once effectively, and (4) they were adept at handling transitions smoothly (Kounin 1970). In addition to the principles of effective classroom management that emerge from Kounin's study, two key elements of preventive planning are establishing rules and procedures and organizing and planning for instruction.

Establishing Rules and Procedures

Educational researchers have found that effective classroom managers have carefully planned rules and procedures, which they teach early in the year using clear explanations, examples, and practice (Evertson et al. 1997; Good and Brophy 1997). Your classroom rules should be clear, concise, reasonable, and few in number. For example, five general rules for elementary-age students might include: (1) be polite and helpful; (2) respect other people's property; (3) listen quietly while others are speaking; (4) do not hit, shove, or hurt others; and (5) obey all school rules. Rules for the secondary level might stipulate the following: (1) bring all needed materials to class; (2) be in your seat and ready to work when the bell rings; (3) respect and be polite to everyone; (4) respect other people's property; (5) listen and stay seated while someone else is speaking; and (6) obey all school rules (Evertson et al. 1997).

It is important to enforce classroom rules consistently and fairly. "Consistency is a key reason why some rules are effective while others are not. Rules that are not enforced or that are not applied evenly and consistently over time result in a loss of prestige and respect for the person who has created the rules and has the responsibility for carrying them out" (Borich 1996, 364).

Procedures—the routines your students will follow as they participate in learning activities—also are essential for smooth classroom functioning and minimizing opportunities for misbehaviour. How will homework be collected? How will supplies be distributed? How will housekeeping chores be completed? How will attendance be taken? How do students obtain permission to leave the classroom? Part of developing classroom rules and procedures is to decide what to do when students do not follow them. Students must be made aware of the consequences for failing to follow rules or procedures. For example, consequences for rule infractions can range from an expression of teacher disapproval to penalties such as loss of privileges, detention after school, disciplinary conference with a parent or guardian, or temporary separation from the group.

Organizing and Planning for Instruction

The ability to organize instructional time, materials, and activities so that classes run smoothly are skills that will enable you to keep your students engaged in learning, thereby reducing the need for discipline. Time spent planning authentic learning activities that are appropriate to students' needs, interests, and abilities will enable you to enjoy the professional satisfaction that comes from having a well-managed classroom.

In the following, a remedial algebra teacher in an urban school tells how organization and planning helped her effectively teach a class of 27 students, Grades 9 through 12, who enrolled in the class "for a myriad of reasons, [including] absenteeism, learning disabilities, course failure, unwillingness to do required course work, personal problems, nonconformity, and a need for credits":

> I am consistently rewarded by the creative thinking and quickness of these students when they are asked to do something other than listen to my thinking, take notes, and copy examples from the board. I have learned that planning meaningful activities, choosing engaging tasks, organizing small groups and pair problem-solving experiences, valuing thinking, and carefully assessing understanding promote an improved classroom atmosphere where learning is the objective for everyone (Schifter 1996, 75–76).

Effective Responses to Student Behaviour

When student misbehaviour does occur, effective teachers draw from a repertoire of problem-solving strategies. These strategies are based on their experience and common sense, their knowledge of students and the teaching-learning process, and their knowledge of human psychology. There are many structured approaches to classroom management; some are based on psychological theories of human motivation and behaviour, while others reflect various philosophical views regarding the purposes of education. None of these approaches, however, is appropriate for all situations or for all teachers or for all students, and the usefulness of a given method depends, in part, on the teacher's individual personality and leadership style and ability to analyze the complex dynamics of classroom life. In addition, what works should not be the only criterion for evaluating structured or "packaged" approaches to discipline; what they teach students about their self-worth, acting responsibly, and solving problems is also important (Curwin and Mendler 1988, 1989).

Severity of Misbehaviour

Your response to student misbehaviour will depend, in part, on whether an infraction is mild, moderate, or severe and whether it is occurring for the first time or is part of a pattern of chronic misbehaviours. For example, a student who throws a wad of paper at another student might receive a warning for the first infraction, while another student who repeatedly throws objects at other students might receive an after-school detention. Definitions of the severity of misbehaviour vary from school to school and from province to province. Table 7.2 presents one classification of examples of mild, moderate, and severe misbehaviours and several alternative responses.

Table 7.2

Mild, moderate, and severe misbehaviours and some alternative responses

Misbehaviours	Alternative Responses
Mild misbehaviours	**Mild responses**
Minor defacing of school property or property of others	Warning
Acting out (horseplaying or scuffling)	Feedback to student
Talking back	Time out
Talking without raising hand	Change of seat assignment
Getting out of seat	Withdrawal of privileges
Disrupting others	After-school detention
Sleeping in class	Telephone/note to parents
Tardiness	
Throwing objects	
Exhibiting inappropriate familiarity (kissing, hugging)	
Gambling	
Eating in class	
Moderate misbehaviours	**Moderate responses**
Unauthorized leaving of class	Detention
Abusive conduct toward others	Behaviour contract
Noncompliant	Withdrawal of privileges
Smoking or using tobacco in class	Telephone/note to parents
Cutting class	Parent conference
Cheating, plagiarizing, or lying	In-school suspension
Using profanity, vulgar language, or obscene gestures	Restitution of damages
Fighting	Alternative school service (eg., clean up, tutoring)
Severe misbehaviours	**Severe responses**
Defacing or damaging school property or property of others	Detention
Theft, possession, or sale of another's property	Telephone/note to parents
Truancy	Parent conference
Being under the influence of alcohol or narcotics	In-school suspension
Selling, giving, or delivering to another person alcohol, narcotics, or weapons	Removal from school or alternative school placement
Teacher assault or verbal abuse	
Incorrigible conduct, noncompliance	

Source: Gary Bovich, *Effective Teaching Methods,* 3rd ed. Englewood Cliffs, NJ: Merrill, 1996, p. 527. © 1996. Reprinted by permission of Prentice-Hall, Inc., Upper Saddle River, NJ.

Constructive Assertiveness

The effectiveness of your responses to students' misbehaviour will depend, in part, on your ability to use "constructive assertiveness" (Evertson et al. 1997). Constructive assertiveness "lies on a continuum of social response between aggressive, overbearing pushiness and timid, ineffectual, or submissive responses that allow some students to trample on the teacher's and other students' rights. Assertiveness skills allow you to communicate to students that you are serious about teaching and about maintaining a classroom in which everyone's rights are respected" (Evertson et al, 1997 139). Communication based on constructive assertiveness is neither hostile, sarcastic, defensive, nor vindictive; it is clear, firm, and concise.

Evertson and colleagues (1997) suggest that constructive assertiveness has three basic elements:

- A clear statement of the problem or concern
- Body language that is unambiguous (eg., eye contact with student, erect posture, facial expressions that match the content and tone of corrective statements)
- Firm, unwavering insistence on appropriate behaviour

Lee Cantor developed an approach to discipline based on teacher assertiveness. The approach calls on teachers to establish firm, clear guidelines for student behaviour and to follow through with consequences for misbehaviour. Cantor (1989, 58) comments on how he arrived at the ideas behind assertive discipline: "I found that, above all, the master teachers were assertive; that is, they *taught* students how to behave. They established clear rules for the classroom, they communicated those rules to the students, and they taught students how to follow them." **Assertive discipline** requires teachers to do the following:

1. Make clear that they will not tolerate anyone preventing them from teaching, stopping learning, or doing anything else that is not in the best interest of the class, the individual, or the teacher.
2. Instruct students clearly and in specific terms about what behaviours are desired and what behaviours are not tolerated.
3. Plan positive and negative consequences for predetermined acceptable or unacceptable behaviours.
4. Plan positive reinforcement for compliance. Reinforcement includes verbal acknowledgment, notes, free time for talking, and, of course, tokens that can be exchanged for appropriate rewards.
5. Plan a sequence of steps to punish noncompliance. These range from writing a youngster's name on the board to sending the student to the principal's office (MacNaughton and Johns 1991, 53).

Teacher Problem Solving

When a teacher's efforts to get a student to stop misbehaving are unsuccessful, a problem-solving conference with the student is warranted. A problem-solving conference may give the teacher additional understanding of the situation, thus paving the way for a solution. A conference also helps teacher and student understand the other's perceptions better and begin to build a more positive relationship.

The goal of a problem-solving conference is for the student to accept responsibility for his or her behaviour and make a commitment to change it. While there is no "right way" to conduct a problem-solving conference, Glasser's choice theory lends itself to a conferencing procedure that is flexible and appropriate for most situations.

Students will usually make good choices (ie., behave in an acceptable manner) if they experience success and know that teachers care about them. The following steps are designed to help misbehaving students see that the choices they make may not lead to the results they want.

1. Have the misbehaving student evaluate and take responsibility for his or her behaviour. Often, a good first step is for the teacher to ask, "What are you doing?" and then, "Is it helping you?"
2. Have the student make a plan for a more acceptable way of behaving. If necessary, the student and the teacher brainstorm solutions. Agreement is reached on how the student will behave in the future and the consequences for failure to follow through.
3. Require the student to make a commitment to follow the plan.
4. Don't accept excuses for failure to follow the plan.
5. Don't use punishment or react to a misbehaving student in a punitive manner. Instead, point out to the student that there are logical consequences for failure to follow the plan.
6. Don't give up on the student. If necessary, remind the student of his or her commitment to desirable behaviour. Periodically ask, "How are things going?"

Developing Your Own Approach to Classroom Management

No approach to classroom management is effective with all students at all times. How you respond to misbehaviour in your classroom will depend on your personality, value system, and beliefs about children and will range along a continuum from the "minimum power" of giving students nonverbal cues to the "maximum power" of physical intervention.

Classroom management expert Charles Wolfgang points out that teachers usually present one of three "faces" (or attitudes) to students who misbehave:

1. The *relationship-listening* "face" involves the use of minimum power. This reflects a view that the student has the capabilities to change his or her own behaviour, and that if the student is misbehaving, it is because of inner emotional turmoil, flooded behaviour, or feelings of inner inadequacy.
2. The *confronting-contracting* "face" is one of "I am the adult. I know misbehaviour when I see it and will confront the student to stop this behaviour. I will grant the student the power to decide how he or she will change, and encourage and contract with the student to live up a mutual agreement for behavioural change."
3. The *rules and consequences* "face" is one that communicates an attitude of "This is the rule and behaviour that I want and I will set out assertively to get this action" (Wolfgang 1999, 5–6).

In your journey toward becoming a professional teacher, you will develop a repertoire of strategies for classroom management; then, when you encounter a discipline problem in the classroom, you can analyze the situation and respond with an effective strategy. The ability to do so will give you confidence, like the following beginning teacher:

> I went into the classroom with some confidence and left with lots of confidence. I felt good about what was going on. I established a comfortable rapport with the kids and was more relaxed. Each week I grew more confident. When you first go in you are not sure how you'll do. When you know you are doing OK, your confidence improves.

What Teaching Methods Do Effective Teachers Use?

As we pointed out in our discussion of educational philosophy in Chapter 3, beliefs about teaching and learning, students, knowledge, and what is worth knowing influence the instructional methods a teacher uses. In addition, instruction is influenced by variables such as the teacher's style, learners' characteristics, the culture of the school and surrounding community, and the resources available. All of these components contribute to the "model" of teaching the teacher uses in the classroom. A model of teaching provides the teacher with rules of thumb to follow to create a particular kind of learning environment, or, as Bruce Joyce, Marsha Weil, and Emily Calhoun point out in *Models of Teaching* (2000, 13), a model of teaching is "a description of a learning environment." Table 7.3 presents brief descriptions of four widely used models of teaching.

Table 7.3

Four instructional models

	Goals and Rationale	Methods
Cooperative Learning	Students can be motivated to learn by working cooperatively in small groups if rewards are made available to the group as a whole and to individual members of the group.	■ Small groups (four to six students) work together on learning activities. ■ Assignments require that students help one another while working on a group project. ■ In competitive arrangements, groups may compete against one another. ■ Group members contribute to group goals according to their talents, interests, and abilities.
Theory into Practice	Teachers make decisions in three primary areas: content to be taught, how students will learn, and the behaviours the teacher will use in the classroom. The effectiveness of teaching is related to the quality of decisions the teacher makes in these areas.	The teacher follows seven steps in the classroom: 1. Orients students to material to be learned 2. Tells students what they will learn and why it is important 3. Presents new material that consists of knowledge, skills, or processes students are to learn 4. Models what students are expected to do 5. Checks for student understanding 6. Gives students opportunity for practice under the teacher's guidance 7. Makes assignments that give students opportunity to practice what they have learned on their own
Behaviour Modification	Teachers can shape student learning by using various forms of enforcement. Human behaviour is learned, and behaviours that are positively reinforced (rewarded) tend to increase and those that are not reinforced tend to decrease.	■ Teacher begins by presenting stimulus in the form of new material. ■ The behaviour of students is observed by the teacher. ■ Appropriate behaviours are reinforced by the teacher as quickly as possible.
Nondirective Teaching	Learning can be facilitated if teachers focus on personal development of students and create opportunities for students to increase their self-understanding and self-concepts. The key to effective teaching is the teacher's ability to understand students and to involve them in a teaching–learning partnership.	■ Teacher acts as a facilitator of learning. ■ Teacher creates learning environments that support personal growth and development. ■ Teacher acts in the role of a counsellor who helps students to understand themselves, clarify their goals, and accept responsibility for their behaviour.

Effective teachers use a repertoire of teaching models and assessment strategies, depending upon their situations and the goals and objectives they wish to attain. Your teaching strategies in the classroom will most likely be eclectic, that is, a combination of several models and assessment techniques. Also, as you gain classroom experience and acquire new skills and understanding, your personal model of teaching will evolve, enabling you to respond appropriately to a wider range of teaching situations.

Methods Based on Learning New Behaviours

Many teachers use instructional methods that have emerged from our greater understanding of how people acquire or change their behaviours. **Direct instruction,** for example, is a systematic instructional method that focuses on the transmission of knowledge and skills from the teacher (and the curriculum) to the student. Direct instruction is organized on the basis of observable learning behaviours and the actual products of learning. Generally, direct instruction is most appropriate for step-by-step knowledge acquisition and basic skill development but not appropriate for teaching less structured, higher-order skills such as writing, the analysis of social issues, and problem solving.

Extensive research was conducted in the 1970s and 1980s on the effectiveness of direct instruction (Gagné, 1974, 1977; Good and Grouws, 1979; Rosenshine, 1988; Rosenshine and Stevens, 1986). The following eight steps are a synthesis of research on direct instruction and may be used with students ranging in age from elementary to senior high school.

1. Orient students to the lesson by telling them what they will learn.
2. Review previously learned skills and concepts related to the new material.
3. Present new material, using examples and demonstrations.
4. Assess students' understanding by asking questions; correct misunderstandings.
5. Allow students to practice new skills or apply new information.
6. Provide feedback and corrections as students practice.
7. Include newly learned material in homework.
8. Review material periodically.

A direct instruction method called **mastery learning** is based on two assumptions about learning: (1) virtually all students can learn material if given enough time and taught appropriately and (2) students learn best when they participate in a structured, systematic program of learning that enables them to progress in small, sequenced steps (Carroll 1963; Bloom 1981):

1. Set objectives and standards for mastery.
2. Teach content directly to students.
3. Provide corrective feedback to students on their learning.
4. Provide additional time and help in correcting errors.
5. Follow a cycle of teaching, testing, reteaching, and retesting.

In mastery learning, students take diagnostic tests and then are guided to do corrective exercises or activities to improve their learning. These may take the form of programmed instruction, workbooks, computer drill and practice, or educational games. After the corrective lessons, students are given another test and are more likely to achieve mastery.

Methods Based on Child Development

As you learned in Chapter 6, children move through stages of cognitive, psychosocial, and moral development. Effective instruction includes methods that are developmentally appropriate, meet students' diverse learning needs, and recognize the importance of learning that occurs in social contexts. For example, one way that students reach higher levels of development is to observe and then imitate their parents, teachers, and peers, who act as models. As Woolfolk (1998, 229) points out:

> Modeling has long been used, of course, to teach dance, sports, and crafts, as well as skills in subjects such as home economics, chemistry, and shop. Modeling can also be applied deliberately in the classroom to teach mental skills and to broaden horizons—to teach new ways of thinking. Teachers serve as models for a vast range of behaviors, from pronouncing vocabulary words, to reacting to the seizure of an epileptic student, to being enthusiastic about learning.

Effective teachers also use **modelling** by "thinking out loud" and following three basic steps of "mental modelling" (Duffy and Roehler 1989):

1. Showing students the reasoning involved
2. Making students conscious of the reasoning involved
3. Focusing students on applying the reasoning

In this way, teachers can help students become aware of their learning processes and enhance their ability to learn.

Since the mid-1980s, several educational researchers have examined how learners *construct* understanding of new material. "Constructivist views of learning, therefore, focus on how learners make sense of new information—how they construct meaning based on what they already know" (Parkay and Hass 2000, 168). Teachers with this constructivist view of learning focus on students' thinking about the material being learned and, through carefully orchestrated cues, prompts, and questions, help students arrive at a deeper understanding of the material. The common elements of **constructivist teaching** include the following:

- The teacher elicits students' prior knowledge of the material and uses this as the starting point for instruction.
- The teacher not only presents material to students, but he or she also responds to students' efforts to learn the material. While teaching, the teacher must *learn about students' learning*.
- Students not only absorb information, but they also actively use that information to construct meaning.
- The teacher creates a social milieu within the classroom, a community of learners, that allows students to reflect and talk with one another as they construct meaning and solve problems.

Constructivist teachers provide students with support, or "scaffolding," as they learn new material. By observing the child and listening carefully to what he or she says, the teacher provides **scaffolding** in the form of clues, encouragement, suggestions, or other assistance to guide students' learning efforts. The teacher varies the amount of support given on the basis of the student's understanding—if the student understands little, the teacher gives more support; conversely, the teacher gives progressively less support as the student's understanding becomes more evident. Overall, the teacher provides just enough scaffolding to enable the student to "discover" the material on his or her own.

The concept of scaffolding is based on the work of L. S. Vygotsky, a well-known Soviet psychologist. Vygotsky (1978, 1980) coined the term *zone of proximal development* to refer to the point at which students need assistance in order to continue learning. The effective teacher is sensitive to the student's zone of development and ensures that instruction neither exceeds the student's current level of understanding nor underestimates the student's ability.

Methods Based on the Thinking Process

Some instructional methods are derived from the mental processes involved in learning, thinking, remembering, problem solving, and creativity. **Information processing,** for example, is a branch of cognitive science concerned with how people use their long- and short-term memory to access information and solve problems. The computer is often used as an analogy for information processing views of learning:

> Like the computer, the human mind takes in information, performs operations on it to change its form and content, stores the information, retrieves it when needed, and generates responses to it. Thus, processing involves gathering and representing information, or *encoding*; holding information, or *storage*; and getting at the information when needed, or *retrieval*. The whole system is guided by *control processes* that determine how and when information will flow through the system (Woolfolk 1998, 249-50).

Although several systematic approaches to instruction are based on information processing—teaching students how to memorize, think inductively or deductively, acquire concepts, or use the scientific method, for example—they all focus on how people acquire and use information. Table 7.4 presents general teaching guidelines based on ideas from information processing.

In **inquiry learning** and **discovery learning** students are given opportunities to inquire into subjects so that they "discover" knowledge for themselves. When teachers ask students to go beyond information in a text to make inferences, draw conclusions, or form generalizations; and when teachers do not answer students' questions, preferring instead to have students develop their own answers, they are using methods based on inquiry and discovery learning. These methods are best suited for teaching

---

Table 7.4

Using information processing ideas in the classroom

- Make sure you have the students' attention. For example, begin a lesson by asking a question that stimulates interest in the topic.
- Help students separate essential from nonessential details and focus on the most important information as it relates to instructional objectives.
- Help students make connections between new information and what they already know.
- Provide for repetition and review of information and the practice of skills.
- Present material in a clear, organized, concrete way. For example, give students a brief outline to follow and summarize lessons.
- Focus on meaning, not memorization.

Source: Adapted from Anita E. Woolfolk, *Educational Psychology,* 7th ed. Boston: Allyn and Bacon, 1998, p. 265–68.

concepts, relationships, and theoretical abstractions, and for having students formulate and test hypotheses. The following example shows how inquiry and discovery learning in a Grade 1 classroom fostered a high level of student involvement and thinking.

> The children are gathered around a table on which a candle and jar have been placed. The teacher, Jackie Wiseman, lights the candle and, after it has burned brightly for a minute or two, covers it carefully with the jar. The candle grows dim, flickers, and goes out. Then she produces another candle and a larger jar, and the exercise is repeated. The candle goes out, but more slowly. Jackie produces two more candles and jars of different sizes, and the children light the candles, place the jars over them, and the flames slowly go out. "Now we're going to develop some ideas about what has just happened," she says. "I want you to ask me questions about those candles and jars and what you just observed" (Joyce, Weil, and Calhoun 2000, 3).

Methods Based on Peer-Mediated Instruction

Student peer groups can be a deterrent to academic performance (Steinberg et al. 1996), but they can also motivate students to excel. Because school learning occurs in a social setting, **peer-mediated instruction** provides teachers with options for increasing students' learning. Cooperative learning, described earlier in this chapter, is an example of peer-mediated instruction. Another example is **group investigation,** in which the teacher's role is to create an environment that allows students to determine what they will study and how. Students are presented with a situation to which they "react and discover basic conflicts among their attitudes, ideas, and modes of perception. On the basis of this information, they identify the problem to be investigated, analyze the roles required to solve it, organize themselves to take these roles, act, report, and evaluate these results" (Thelen 1960, 82).

The teacher's role in group investigation is multifaceted; he or she is an organizer, guide, resource person, counsellor, and evaluator. The method is very effective in increasing student achievement (Sharan and Sharan 1989/90, 17–21), positive attitudes toward learning, and the cohesiveness of the classroom group. The model also allows students to inquire into problems that interest them and enables each student to make a meaningful, authentic contribution to the group's effort based on his or her experiences, interests, knowledge, and skills.

Other common forms of peer-mediated instruction include peer tutoring and cross-age tutoring. In **peer-tutoring** arrangements, students are tutored by other pupils in the same class or the same grade. **Cross-age tutoring** involves, for example, Grade 6 students tutoring Grade 2 students in reading. Research clearly shows that with proper orientation and training, cross-age tutoring can greatly benefit both "teacher" and learner (Henriques 1997; Schneider and Barone 1997; Utay and Utay 1997; Zukowski 1997). Pilot programs pairing students at risk of dropping out of school with younger children and with special-needs students have proved especially successful.

What Are Some Characteristics of Effective Teaching?

The *outcomes* of effective teaching are relatively easy to enumerate: (1) students acquire an understanding of the subject at hand; (2) they can apply what they have learned to new situations; and (3) they have a desire to continue learning. However, if we wish to identify the *characteristics* of effective teaching, we find ourselves confronted with a more difficult task.

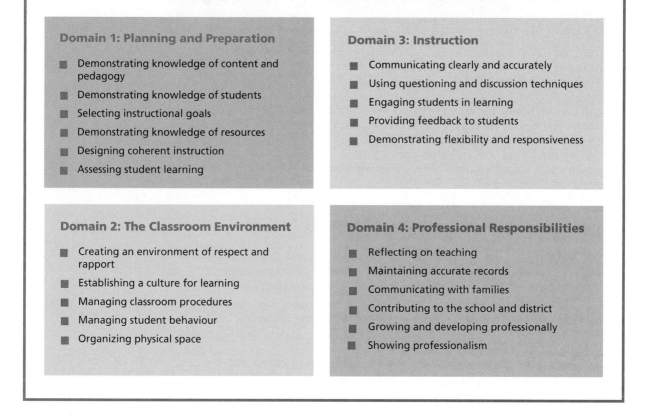

Domain 1: Planning and Preparation

- Demonstrating knowledge of content and pedagogy
- Demonstrating knowledge of students
- Selecting instructional goals
- Demonstrating knowledge of resources
- Designing coherent instruction
- Assessing student learning

Domain 3: Instruction

- Communicating clearly and accurately
- Using questioning and discussion techniques
- Engaging students in learning
- Providing feedback to students
- Demonstrating flexibility and responsiveness

Domain 2: The Classroom Environment

- Creating an environment of respect and rapport
- Establishing a culture for learning
- Managing classroom procedures
- Managing student behaviour
- Organizing physical space

Domain 4: Professional Responsibilities

- Reflecting on teaching
- Maintaining accurate records
- Communicating with families
- Contributing to the school and district
- Growing and developing professionally
- Showing professionalism

Figure 7.4

The Praxis framework for teaching

Source: Charlotte Danielson, *Enhancing Professional Practice: A Framework for Teaching.* Alexandria, VA: Association for Supervision and Curriculum Development, 1996.

What do effective teachers do when they are teaching? How do they communicate with students? How do they manage classroom activities? What models of teaching do they use? As the previous discussions of classroom cultures, learning environments, classroom management, and teaching methods suggest, answers to questions such as these are not easy to formulate. However, one broad helpful view of the characteristics that underlie all effective teaching is the "Framework for Teaching," developed as part of the Praxis Series: Professional Assessments for Beginning Teachers. According to the Praxis framework, teachers must be proficient in four domains: planning and preparation, structuring classroom environment, instruction, and professional responsibilities. Teachers must be effective within these domains while taking into account individual, developmental, and cultural differences among students and differences among subjects. Figure 7.4 shows the tasks teachers should be able to perform within the four domains.

Establishing Goals

One characteristic of successful teachers is that they focus on the outcomes—the results or consequences of their teaching. Regardless of the instructional method used, with clear goals to provide guidance, teachers can make good decisions about classroom activities to select or develop.

Goals are general statements of purpose that guide schools and teachers as they develop instructional programs. **Instructional goals** can be derived from the curriculum or

From this photo, what can you tell about this teacher's proficiency in planning and preparation, structuring classroom environment, instruction, and professional responsibilities?

content being taught; or, as you saw in Chapter 3, they can be derived from various educational philosophies. Goals range from very broad statements of purpose that apply to a large number of students to those that apply to students in a particular classroom. In addition, teachers evaluate their teaching by how well students master certain objectives. **Learning objectives** are specific, measurable outcomes of learning that students are to demonstrate. For example, "Students will identify the structural elements of cells and explain their functions" might be a specific objective toward a larger goal of "understanding biological concepts and principles."

Successful teachers also realize that the quality of their teaching depends on what students can *do*, not only on what they *know*. To evaluate their effectiveness in this area, teachers assess students' mastery of performance tasks in which they apply their learning to a new problem. Figure 7.5 illustrates two different approaches to lesson planning that take into account targeted goals, objectives, and performance tasks.

Appendix 7.1 provides guidelines for teachers in providing students with Study Skills information, which can be incorporated into lessons for effective instruction.

Linking Assessment with Instruction

In assessing students' learning, teachers make judgments about the performance of students and about their own performance as teachers. Successful teachers use **assessment** to evaluate the effectiveness of their teaching because they recognize that how well students learn depends on how well they teach.

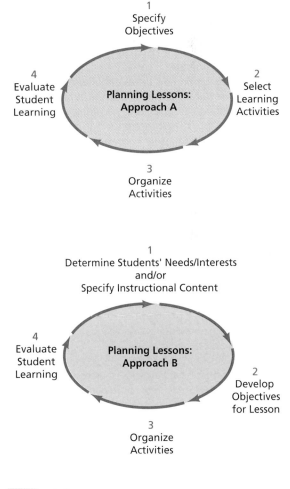

Figure 7.5

Two approaches to planning lessons

Should the use of standardized testing be increased?

Assessment of student learning is essential: students, teachers, school administrators, parents, and the public need to know how schools and students are doing. Not knowing is like shooting arrows at a target out of your line of vision and never being told how close you are to the bull's-eye. Simply to be told "Shoot another one, shoot another one" will not help you get closer to the target. Madeline Hunter, UCLA teacher educator and author of *Enhancing Teaching* (1994), used that illustration to emphasize the importance of feedback. Although most educators agree with Hunter in general principle, they disagree as to which type of assessment is best and how extensive it should be.

Canada is beginning to take the lead of the United States, Great Britain, and New Zealand in instituting standardized testing. Testing has been an integral part of Canadian schools since their inception and all provinces engage in some form of large-scale assessment. Under the Constitution, individual Canadian provinces are responsible for education. Provincially, testing varies with some provinces assessing Grades 3, 6, and 9, or 4, 7, 10 and Grade 12. A number of Canadian provinces also participate in international assessment programs such as the Third International Math and Science Study (TIMSS).

The Canadian Council of Ministers of Education (CMEC) developed the school Achievement Indicators Program (SAIP) in 1993 to provide information to the Canadian public on how well their education systems were meeting the needs of students and society. The SAIP is a cyclical program of pan-Canadian assessment of student achievement in math, reading and writing, and science (Council of Ministers of Education, Canada).

Opponents of increasing the use of standardized testing note that alternative forms of assessment—teacher-constructed tests, student portfolios, evaluations of student performances, and teacher judgments—are better ways to determine how well students are learning. They fear that mandating more standardized testing will discriminate against schools with greater populations of language-minority students and students from lower socio-economic groups. They also warn that curricula will be narrowed by teaching to the test and express concern that the consequences of poor test results can negatively affect the lives of students and teachers.

Where do you stand on this issue? Should the use of standardized testing be increased?

Yes, the use of standardized testing should be increased.

Educators must be held accountable for student learning. Parents entrust their children to schools to educate them well. The community invests in school buildings, teachers' salaries, and curricular resources, and thus people have a right to know how well the schools are doing. For schools to expect to proceed without any accountability is unreasonable and irresponsible.

Educators themselves also need to know how they are doing. As in Madeline Hunter's archery illustration, if educators do not know whether they are on target, they are unable to improve their performance. Teachers should be continually evaluating their strategies and education programs in terms of the programs' effectiveness in promoting students' learning. If teachers do not do this, students, who are the centre of the education enterprise, are the losers. The portion of their lives that students spend in school can be a waste rather than a life-changing boon. For teachers not to take care in assessing their own effectiveness is to risk short-changing children and youth.

Canada spends proportionally more money on education than most other industrialized countries. Tests such as the Canadian SAIP can provide Canada-wide data on the achievement levels of 13 and 16 year old students; the results are used to assess whether students know more or less than expected and to assist provincial departments of education with future curriculum decisions (Osborne 1999). A recent study commissioned for the Advancement of Excellence in Education, Student Assessment in Canada, calls for a broad level of testing in all provinces in order to measure and improve school and student performance (Smythe 2001).

No, the use of standardized testing should not be increased.

The arguments against using more standardized testing are summarized succinctly and dramatically by George

Madaus, Boston College Professor of Education and Director of the Center for the Study of Testing:

The tests can become the ferocious master of the educational process, not the compliant servant they should be. Measurement-driven instruction invariably leads to cramming; narrows the curriculum; concentrates attention on those skills most amenable to testing (and today this means skills amenable to the multiple-choice format); constrains creativity and spontaneity of teachers and students; and, finally, demeans the professional judgment of teachers. (Madaus 1999)

Other opponents are especially concerned about the misuse of the resulting scores. W. James Popham, author of *Testing! Testing! What Every Parent Should Know about School Tests* (1999), points out that "even the standardized test items that actually measure knowledge and skills that might be taught in school will often fail to coincide with the content stressed in a specific school." When that is the case, the school rates poorly in comparison to other schools even though it may have been doing a superior job teaching the content it deems important.

Some districts evaluate teachers in terms of how well their students score on standardized tests, ignoring the fact that the tests are more reflective of "what children bring to school, not what they learn there," Popham argues. He urges teachers to "become thoroughly familiar with the innards of any standardized test being used in their setting. These tests are not sacrosanct instruments." Teachers should investigate a test's history, development, current use, norming population, fit with the school's curriculum and goals, and the number of questions in each skill area. Such knowledge is essential for interpreting the results to children, parents, principals, district administrators—and the news media. The last group can unfairly damage a school's reputation, a realistic fear that drives some administrators to overstress test scores, promoting teaching to the test and narrowing curriculum in the process.

Most important is the impact the scores of questionable standardized tests can have on the education and lives of children and young people. An overreliance on standardized test scores can lead to inappropriate assignments to remediation programs, unjustified retentions of students, increases in dropout rates, and reduced career opportunities for students. Adriana Steinberg, in a 1999 *Harvard Education Letter,* provides one illustration of the human dimension of the problem:

Standardized test scores do not differentiate between a newly mainstreamed bilingual student who rewrites each paper four or five times and meets twice a week after school with a math tutor, but who does not yet know enough academic English to decipher arcane test items, and a student whose disengage-ment from school and low estimation of his own academic abilities cause him to give up midway through the first section of the test and leave much of the rest blank.

The Canadian Teachers Federation has written extensively against the rising tide of standardized testing. In their *Standardized Testing: Undermining Equity in Education*, they argue that standardized tests are inadequate in assessing complex student learning and development. The publication examines the effects of standardized testing on educational equity with particular emphasis on the impact of testing bias and the misuse of test data (Froese-Germain 1999).

Teachers know better than developers of tests how *their* students are doing, why they are doing well or poorly, and how to assist them individually. Their opinions matter much more than scores on standardized tests taken in an artificial setting on one or two days of the entire school year. Their judgments deserve the public's trust. Standardized testing should not be increased, because teachers need all the time they can get to do their most important work—teaching.

Where do you stand on this issue?

1. What is your position on increasing standardized testing? Why do you hold this position?

2. Which form of assessment has been most helpful to you as a student? How can you tell?

3. Propose a compromise position regarding standardized testing.

4. How would you interpret children's standardized test scores for their parents?

5. Find two examples of standardized tests and evaluate the aspects of tests that Popham cites.

Recommended Sources

Alberta Teachers Association. (2001). The Learning Team, "Teachers and Parents Need to Fight Standardized Testing," Volume 3, April 3, 2001. Retrieved October 24, 2003 from: www.teachers.ab.ca/resources/ata.learningteam/index.cfm?p_ID=1809&Volume=4&Issue=3

British Columbia Teachers' Federation. (1997). *Opportunities to learn: Accountability in education in British Columbia.* A Brief to the Minister of Education, Skills, and Training for the British Columbia Teachers' Federation. Retrieved October 24, 2003 from www.bctf.ca/publications/briefs/ocg/

Canadian Teachers Federation. (2000). *Assessment and eval-uation: National Testing.* Retrieved October 24, 2003 from: www.ctf-fce.ca/en/default.htm

Earl, L.M. (1999). Assessment and accountability in educa-tion: improvement or surveillance" Education Canada. 39 (3). 4-6.

Madaus, G. F. (1999). *The influence of testing on the curricu-lum.* In Margaret J. Early and Kenneth J. Rehage (Eds.). *Issues in curriculum: A selection of chapters from past NSSE yearbooks: Ninety-eighth yearbook of the national society for the study of education, Part II.* Chicago: Uni-versity of Chicago Press.

Osborne, K. (1999). *Education: A guide to the Canadian school debate—or, who want what and why?* Montreal: Penguin/McGill Institute.

Popham, W. J. (1999, May 12). Commentary: assessment apa-thy. *Education Week.*

Rose, L. C. and Gallup, A. M. (1998, September). The 30th annual Phi Delta Kappa/Gallup poll of the public's atti-tudes toward the public schools. *Phi Delta Kappan.*

Steinberg, A. (1999, March/April). The human cost of over-reliance on tests. *Harvard Education Letter.*

To assess students' learning, teachers use measurement and evaluation techniques. **Measurement** is the gathering of quantitative data related to the knowledge and skills students have acquired. Measurement yields scores, rankings, or ratings that teachers can use to compare students. **Evaluation** involves making judgments about or assign-ing a value to those measurements. **Formative evaluation** occurs when the teacher measures students' learning for instruction. **Summative evaluation** is used by teachers to determine grades at the end of a unit, semester, or year and to decide whether stu-dents are ready to proceed to the next phase of their education.

Authentic assessments (sometimes called *alternative assessments*) require students to use higher-level thinking skills to perform, create, or solve real-life problems—not just choose one of several designated responses as on a multiple-choice test. The authen-tic assessments a teacher might use include evaluating the quality of individual and small-group projects, videotaped demonstrations of skills, or participation in com-munity-based activities. In science, for example, students might design and conduct an experiment; in mathematics, they might explain in writing how they solved a problem. Authentic assessments require students to solve problems or to work on tasks that approximate as much as possible those they will encounter beyond the classroom. **Portfolio assessment** is based on a collection of student work that "tell[s] a story of a learner's growth in proficiency, long-term achievement, and significant accomplish-ments in a given academic area" (Tombari and Borich 1999, 164). For students, an important part of portfolio assessment is clarifying the criteria used to select work to be included in the portfolio. **Performance assessment** is used to determine what stu-dents can do as well as what they know. In some cases, the teacher observes and then evaluates an actual performance or application of a skill; in others, the teacher eval-uates a product created by the student.

Examples of Effective Teachers

This chapter concludes with comments by several effective teachers in which they describe strategies that help them create communities of learners. As you read the teach-ers' comments, identify how each has put into practice many of the concepts dis-cussed in this chapter. In addition, reflect on the degree to which that teacher's approach would "fit" your personality and value system.

highlights

How do effective teachers use technology to enhance their instruction?

Effective teachers recognize that educational technologies should be used to enhance students' inquiry, reflection, and problem solving rather than merely "grafted" onto existing practices. They also recognize that "schools need not be technology rich to be 'information age.' Rather, the phrase 'information age' signals that the schools focus on developing students' critical habits of mind with regard to ideas and evidence—the ability to use their minds well" (Brunner and Tally 1999, 32).

In the following excerpt, a teacher from Newfoundland describes in her own words how she effectively integrated technology into her Grade 9 curriculum.

Anna Gosse,
Middle School Science Teacher, Newfoundland

The challenge for teachers is to actively involve students in curriculum that is enhanced by the use of technology and that illustrates how the technological skills that they possess can be used for practical purposes.

This is my fourth year teaching and the internet was really just coming onto the scene in educational terms when I was in university. The integration of technology into the classroom has been my most recent personal objective.

Technology can and should be used in more meaningful ways other than typing up assignments and finding information. I have created several lessons and assignments around the use of technology. Being a science teacher, the use of technology extends beyond the regular computer image to include graphical analysis, electronic probes, and monitoring devices of unlimited sources. One of my favourite lessons in the Grade 9 science curriculum is on dichotomous keys. The students research five organisms from the same family and create a dichotomous key web page to properly identify the organisms by scientific names. Each project requires about 10 web pages with limited information contained on each page, so that means lots of links. For example, each question leads to a link, which takes you either to the correct identification of an organism or the next question until you have identified the organism. The students really enjoy it. I have only one student who did not complete the assignment this year and that was due to absenteeism. Generally, the submissions of high quality assignments of a non-technology nature are much lower. A sample can be viewed at the following website. www.k12.nf.ca/lms/keyweb/. I recommend the Penguin or Whale page.

This was my first time giving this assignment which was prepared with Composer. Since then, upon evaluation, changes have been made and this year we are now using FrontPage to create some awesome projects soon to be online.

James Turner, Teacher in an Alternative High School, Southwest Regional School Board, Nova Scotia

Teaching in an alternate school, everything we do is somehow "altered" to give personal meaning to the students within the context of their lives. Their lives in so far as school is concerned, have not been positive experiences to date. Often this negative experience stretches into nearly all aspects of their lives.

Each day we begin with a meeting called a "round up." Information is exchanged, the day is defined or redefined as needed, issues from the previous days are addressed, students may address things they want to talk about concerning school, their classes, their classmates, etc. The day ends the same way and this meeting is often quite long as we address whatever has happened that may be a "teachable moment."

We also concern ourselves with the students' lives outside of school. In the end what we change the most is the fact that they are not just one of the herd; they are one of the family and we care what they do and what happens to them. Daily!

Marie Church, Grade 1 Teacher, Inner City School, Rothesay, New Brunswick

Four years ago, I was teaching in an inner city school with 99 percent minority enrollment. From the beginning, I was convinced that all these children could learn. My goal each day was to provide material and present in such a way that ensured every student would experience some degree of success. I will never forget one particular series of lessons.

As part of the primary language arts curriculum children spend a great deal of time building a reading vocabulary. Our newest program includes wonderful stories, poems, and songs as well as important emphasis on phonemic awareness. To provide personal meaning for each child, regardless of social background or culture, we also write experience stories (one of their favourite activities) where each child composes sentences about himself/herself in relation to the current theme. They write about personal preferences, experiences, family, friends, or pets and later share them with their families at home, as well as their classmates. As young children read and write about themselves and others within their immediate social world, it gives true meaning and relevancy to curriculum, while sparking interest and motivation.

Rona Howald, Grade 4 Teacher, Quispamsis, New Brunswick

Saint John's Cherry Brook Zoo is used by our students as a learning resource and features many endangered species and models of extinct animals. The city has eliminated its funding to the zoo and in order to remain in the area, it has undertaken an appeal for funds from the local community. In the past, we have had a day at the zoo for our entire school population of 450 students but in winter this is impractical and the zoo is only open on the weekends.

Instead of holding our usual Valentine's Day activities in February, we decided to put our "Hearts into the Zoo"! We asked that funds normally devoted to cards and treats be made available to students to help support the animals. We did not just ask for donations, we provided activities in return for their support. We had Frances Helyar, a local storyteller and song writer, entertain us with animal stories. Other features of the week before Valentine's Day were face painting, photos with school mascots (the "pride of Lakefield lions"), guessing games, raffles, a heart tree, and class cheers. Students were encouraged to bring their favourite stuffed animal to school for a parade. We integrated our language arts, math, art, and music to include our theme. The students and staff had an enjoyable week and we raised over $2400 for the zoo.

This showed everyone that curriculum can be integrated and expanded beyond the classroom walls and that students can learn valuable lessons about caring for the world around them while still having fun.

Source: Contributions in this section are reproduced with permission from the teachers themselves.

SUMMARY

What Determines the Culture of the Classroom?

- From seating arrangements, to classroom rules and procedures, to the content and relevance of the curriculum, teachers make many decisions that influence the culture of the classroom.

- Classroom climate refers to the atmosphere or quality of life in a classroom. The climates established by high-performing teachers are characterized by a productive, task-oriented focus; group cohesiveness; open, warm relationships between teacher and students; cooperative, respectful interactions among students; low levels of tension, anxiety, and conflict; humour; high expectations; and frequent opportunities for student input regarding classroom activities.

How Can You Create a Positive Learning Environment?

- An important element of a positive learning environment is a caring classroom climate. Teachers show care for students by providing support, structure, and appropriate expectations.

- The physical environment of a classroom—seating arrangements and the placement of other classroom furniture, for example—can make a positive contribution to students' learning.

- Classroom organization, how students are grouped for instruction and how time is used, is an important element of the effective learning environment. Among the patterns for organizing classrooms are grouping students by ability, grouping students for cooperative learning, using activity formats based on authentic learning tasks, and using time to maximize students' learning.

What Are the Keys to Successful Classroom Management?

- The key to successful classroom management is preventing problems before they occur. Teachers who prevent problems foster effective, harmonious interpersonal interactions; understand how their leadership style influences students; and facilitate the development of the classroom group so that it becomes more cohesive and supportive.

- Teachers who establish a democratic classroom climate that allows students to participate in making decisions about the classroom environment, rules and procedures, curriculum materials, and learning activities have fewer discipline problems.

- When management problems occur, effective teachers use a repertoire of problem-solving skills based on experience, common sense, and understanding of the teaching–learning process. Regardless of the management strategy used, effective teachers base their response to problems on three elements of "constructive assertiveness": a clear statement of the problem or concern; unambiguous body language; and a firm, unwavering insistence on appropriate behaviour.

What Teaching Methods Do Effective Teachers Use?

- Although it is difficult to identify all the skills teachers need, research indicates that effective teachers use a repertoire of models of teaching based on students' learning behaviours, child development, the thinking process, and peer mediation.

- Direct instruction and mastery learning are based on the view that learning is the acquisition of new behaviours.

- Modelling, constructivism, and scaffolding are based primarily on an understanding of how students construct meaning as they learn new material.

- Information processing, inquiry learning, and discovery learning are based on our understanding of the cognitive processes involved in learning.

- Peer-mediated instruction, which views learning as taking place in social situations, includes cooperative learning, group investigation, and peer- and cross-age tutoring.

What Are Some Characteristics of Effective Teaching?

- Effective teaching focuses on outcomes—the results or consequences of teaching. Outcomes include clear goals, objectives, and performance tasks that students are to master.

- Successful teachers modify their instruction based on assessments of students' understanding.

- Measurement refers to gathering data related to students' knowledge and skills, while evaluation involves making judgments about or assigning value to those judgments. In addition to traditional tests, teachers can use authentic assessments, portfolio assessments, and performance assessments to measure and evaluate students' learning.

KEY TERMS AND CONCEPTS

academic learning
   time, 266
allocated time, 266
assertive discipline, 271
assessment, 279
authentic assessments, 282
authentic learning
   tasks, 265
between-class ability
   grouping, 263
block scheduling, 267
caring classroom, 260
choice theory, 267
classroom climate, 257
classroom management, 267

classroom organization, 263
constructivist teaching, 275
cooperative learning, 263
cross-age tutoring, 277
democratic classrooms, 267
direct instruction, 274
discovery learning, 276
evaluation, 282
formative evaluation, 282
group investigation, 277
information processing, 276
inquiry learning, 276
instructional goals, 278
learning objectives, 279
mastery learning, 274

measurement, 282
modelling, 275
opportunity to learn
   (OTL), 266
peer-mediated
   instruction, 277
peer-tutoring, 277
performance
   assessment, 282
portfolio assessment, 282
scaffolding, 275
summative evaluation, 282
time on task, 266
within-class ability
   grouping, 263

APPLICATIONS AND ACTIVITIES

Teacher's Journal

1. Recall the teachers and classmates you had during your school career. Select one class and analyze its group processes in terms of the stages of group development discussed in this chapter. At what stage of development was the group near the end of the school year? What conditions facilitated or impeded the development of this group?

2. Describe the "ideal" physical classroom environment for you. How would the seating arrangement facilitate the attainment of your instructional goals and objectives? How would you involve students in arranging the classroom?

3. Describe your leadership style as it relates to classroom management. In which aspects of leadership and classroom management do you feel most and least confident? What might you do, or what skills might you acquire, to strengthen your effectiveness in areas you feel you lack confidence? Develop your ideas into a statement of professional goals.

Teacher's Database

1. Visit the home pages of three or more of the following research publications on the web. These journals focus on educational research, learning theories, student and teacher attitudes and behaviours, and the effectiveness of teaching methods. Some journals especially emphasize the implications of educational psychology theory and research for educational policy and applications to teaching practice. Note the kinds of studies and research topics each selected journal reports. How might articles in these journals help you as an education major? as a classroom teacher? as a teaching professional?

   Cognition and Instruction
   Contemporary Educational Psychology
   Educational Psychologist
   Educational Psychology Review
   Educational Researcher
   Journal of Educational Psychology
   Review of Research in Education
   Journal of Teaching and Teacher Education
   Social Psychology of Education
   Review of Educational Research

2. What resources are available on the internet for developments in educational assessment? Begin in the ERIC Clearinghouse on Assessment and Evaluation. This clearinghouse contains the Test Locator service, searchable testing databases, tips on how to best evaluate a test, and information on fair testing practices.

Observations and Interviews

1. Observe several teachers at the level for which you are preparing to teach and try to identify the teaching methods they are using as part of their instructional repertoires.
2. Interview a classroom teacher about the assessment of students' learning. How do the assessment methods used by this teacher relate to his or her goals and objectives? To what extent does the teacher use authentic assessments?

Professional Portfolio

1. Prepare a poster depicting a classroom arrangement appropriate for the subject area and grade level for which you are preparing to teach. The poster should indicate the seating arrangement and location of other classroom furniture. In addition, make a list of classroom rules that will be posted in the room. You may wish to organize the rules according to the following categories.

- Rules related to academic work
- Rules related to classroom conduct
- Rules that must be communicated on your first teaching day
- Rules that can be communicated later

2. Last, prepare a flow chart depicting routine activities for a typical day. This chart could include procedures for the following:

- Handling attendance, tardy slips, and excuses
- Distributing materials
- Turning in homework
- Doing seatwork or various in-class assignments
- Forming small groups for cooperative learning activities
- Returning materials and supplies at the end of class

Appendix 7.1

While what follows are technically study skills, an effective teacher can take advantage of the principles and incorporate them into her/his instructional lessons.

A. The more senses involved in learning a fact, concept, generalization or skill, the greater the likelihood that it will be remembered.

1. Assume you are learning the steps required for proper use of a word processor. Here is the probability of your recalling all of the instructions you received 24 h later under various learning conditions.

	Percent probability of recall
– hear instructions only	15
– hear/read instructions	30
– hear/read/say aloud	45
– hear/read/say/write	60
– hear/read/say/write/do	75
– add one rehearsal	90

   (Obviously, these percentages are only approximate and will vary widely from one individual to another.)

2. In general, students should be taught to use the following practices for use when studying.
   - write down key words or phrases
   - use a highlighter to mark key words or phrases
   - underline key words or phrases (not as good as highlighting)
   - say important things aloud
   - make mental pictures of things to be remembered

B. The importance of scheduled review: Retaining studied material

1. Student reviews classroom material that evening .... 5 min
2. Student reviews same material the next day .... 4 ”
3. Student reviews same material one week later .... 3 ”
4. Student reviews same material one month later .... 3 ”
5. Six months later the student has probably still remembered the material. A further three-minute review at the six-month point would likely result in retention of the learned material for life.

C. The importance of interrupted study

Because it is necessary for the mind to rest, and because there is a greater tendency for items to be transferred from short-term to long-term memory with repeated exposures, the following two study habits should be adopted by students. If studying for a two-hour period, breaks should be taken at increasingly shorter periods. Perhaps the first might be taken after 30 to 40 min and the final break after only 20 min or so. The length of the break should be 10 min; anything less hurts study effectiveness and anything longer has been demonstrated to be unnecessary. Two hours of study with breaks will lead to a greater degree of learning than two hours of non-stop study.

D. If faced with a choice between going over test material once during a two-hour study session, or going over it two times (but somewhat less thoroughly) the second of these methods will usually lead to a higher mark.

When students study and immediately go to sleep, there is an approximate 5 percent loss of learned material. Since the loss when awake is roughly the same rate per hour, the most effective time to study for a test is just before bedtime—especially if the material is being learned for the first time.

E. Music can increase or decrease the effectiveness of the study process. Certain types of music, such as classical Baroque, have the same rhythm as the brain's delta waves. Since we learn best when our delta waves are operating smoothly, and since some music can encourage their appearance (delta waves disappear when we are upset or listening to discordant music) selective use of some softly-played background music may help the study process.

F. Visualization can be a powerful tool for learning new material. Not only does it make learning easier for most people, it greatly encourages the retention of the learned material. Teachers who can bring a strong visualization component to their teaching will increase the learning that their students experience.

Appendix 7.1 *(continued)*

G. Mnemonic devices can be useful devices for learning certain specialized types of information, eg., HOMES, which stands for the Great Lakes: Huron, Ontario, Michigan, Erie, Superior.

H. Reductionism can also be helpful. For example, reduce an entire course to a point outline format with all important topics/phrases/concepts listed.

I. Writing tests or examinations:
   (a) Read the test or exam over before starting to write. This allows the subconscious to bring forth information which may have already been forgotten. It also allows the student to write down a few notes on topics which he/she may forget before the test ends.
   (b) After completing the writing of a test, read the question sheet over to be certain all questions have been answered.

Source: Based on information from *Accelerated Learning* by Colin Rose (1987). Dell Publishing: New York.

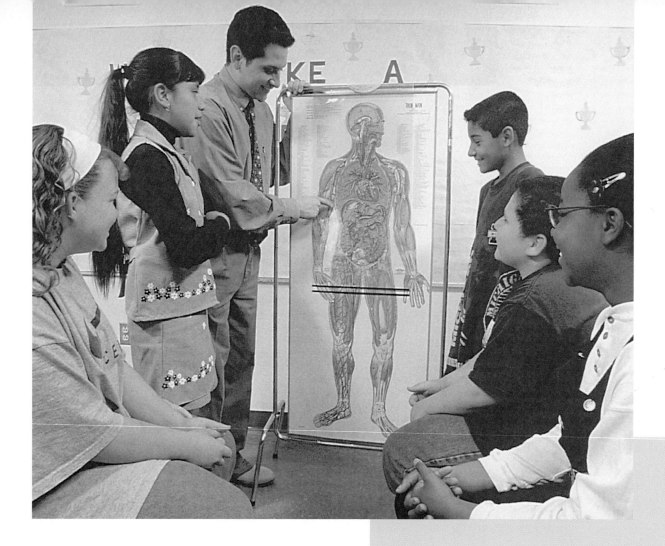

Developing and Implementing the Curriculum

An educator is entrusted with the most serious work that confronts humankind: the development of curricula that enable new generations to contribute to the growth of human beings and society.

—William H. Schubert,
Curriculum: Perspective, Paradigm, and Possibility

focus questions

1. What is taught in schools?
2. How is the school curriculum developed?
3. What reform efforts have affected the curriculum?
4. What are some current subject-area trends?

As a beginning teacher, you are attending your school's open house held one evening during the early fall. From 7:30 to 9:00 PM, teachers stay in their classrooms and visit with parents as they drop by. Several parents have already visited your classroom and heard you explain your curriculum. Judging by their comments and questions, you think they appear to be pleased with what their children are learning.

Shortly before 9:00 PM, the parents of one of your students enter the room. After greeting them, you start to outline the goals and objectives of your curriculum. They listen attentively; the father even jots down a few notes on the cover of the open house program he was given at the orientation session in the auditorium.

"My curriculum is organized around an integrated, thematic approach," you say. "Each theme addresses a key concept—how animals have influenced the lives of human beings on earth, for example. As kids explore each theme, they learn relevant skills from areas such as language, reading, mathematics, science, art, and music."

To illustrate the thematic approach, you direct the parents' attention to a nearby bulletin board display titled "How Do Animals Influence Our Lives?" The bulletin board features children's drawings that are clustered into categories such as "Companionship," "Transportation," "Food," "Work," and "Recreation."

After a brief pause, you continue. "Overall, one of the main goals of my curriculum is for students to go beyond the basics. I want them to know how to use the material they learn, how to solve problems. The curriculum should be a unified whole, rather than separate, disconnected parts."

At this point, your student's mother says, "I'm not sure I agree. The purpose of the curriculum should be to learn the basics. We want our child to do well on the provincial test of basic skills. If the curriculum is organized around themes, how can we be sure the kids master the basics?"

"Right," her husband says. "If kids don't do well on the test, they're less likely to continue their education. To focus on anything other than the basics is to emphasize needless frills. That may sound harsh, but that's the way I feel."

How do you justify your curriculum to these parents?

Think back to your experiences as a student at the elementary, middle, junior, and secondary schools you attended. What things did you learn? Certainly, the curriculum you experienced included reading, computation, handwriting, spelling, geography, and history. In addition to these topics, though, did you learn something about cooperation, competition, stress, physical fitness, video games, computers, popularity, and the opposite sex? Or, perhaps, did you learn to love chemistry and to hate English grammar?

What Is Taught in Schools?

The countless things you learned in school make up the curriculum that you experienced. Curriculum theorists and researchers have suggested several different definitions for **curriculum**, with no one definition universally accepted. Here are some definitions in current use.

1. A course of study, derived from the Latin *currere*, meaning "to run a course"
2. Course content, the information or knowledge that students are to learn
3. Planned learning experiences
4. Intended learning outcomes, the *results* of instruction as distinguished from the *means* (activities, materials, etc.) of instruction
5. All the experiences that students have while at school

No one of these five is in any sense the "right" definition. The way we define curriculum depends on our purposes and the situation we find ourselves in. If, for example, we were advising a high school student on the courses he or she needed to take in order to prepare for college, our operational definition of curriculum would most likely be "a course of study." However, if we were interviewing Grade 6 students for their views on the K–6 elementary school they had just graduated from, we would probably want to view curriculum as "all the experiences that students have while at school." Let us posit an additional definition of curriculum: *Curriculum refers to the experiences, both planned and unplanned, that enhance (and sometimes impede) the education and growth of students.*

Kinds of Curriculum

Elliot Eisner, a noted educational researcher, has said that "schools teach much more— and much less—than they intend to teach. Although much of what is taught is explicit and public, a great deal is not" (1994, 87). For this reason, we need to look at the four curricula that all students experience. The more we understand these curricula and how they influence students, the better we will be able to develop educational programs that do, in fact, educate.

Explicit Curriculum

The explicit, or overt, curriculum refers to what a school intends to teach students. This curriculum is made up of several components: (1) the goals, aims, and learning objectives the school has for all students, (2) the actual courses that make up each student's course of study, and (3) the specific knowledge, skills, and attitudes that teachers want students to acquire. If we asked a principal to describe the educational program at his or her school, our inquiry would be in reference to the explicit curriculum. Similarly, if we asked a teacher to describe what he or she wished to accomplish with a particular class, we would be given a description of the explicit curriculum.

In short, the **explicit curriculum** represents the publicly announced expectations the school has for its students. These expectations range from learning how to read, write, and compute to learning to appreciate music, art, and cultures other than one's own. In most instances, the explicit curriculum takes the form of written plans or guides for the education of students. Examples of such written documents are course descriptions, curriculum guides that set forth the goals and learning objectives for a school or district, texts and other commercially prepared learning materials, and teachers' lesson plans. Through the instructional program of a school, then, these curricular materials are brought to life.

Hidden Curriculum

The hidden, or implicit, curriculum refers to the behaviours, attitudes, and knowledge the culture of the school unintentionally teaches students (Parkay and Hass 2000). In addition, the **hidden curriculum** addresses "aspects of schooling that are recognized only occasionally and remain largely unexamined, particularly the schools' pedagogical, organizational, and social environments, and their interrelations" (Cornbleth 1990, 48). For example, one study of an "effective" inner city elementary school revealed that students had "learned" that grades depended as much or more on their attitudes and behaviour as on their academic ability. When asked, "How do you earn grades for your report card?" the responses of Grade 5 and 6 students included the following (Felsenthal 1982, 10):

> If you want to earn good grades you got to hand in your work on time. You got to sit up straight and don't talk to no one.

> You have to be quiet, be a nice student and know how to write and read and stuff.

As a result of the hidden curriculum of schools, students learn more than their teachers imagine. Although teachers cannot directly control what students learn through the hidden curriculum, they can increase the likelihood that what it teaches will be positive. By allowing students to help determine the content of the explicit curriculum, by inviting them to help establish classroom rules, and by providing them with challenges appropriate for their stage of development, teachers can ensure that the outcomes of the hidden curriculum are more positive than negative.

Null Curriculum

Discussing a curriculum that cannot be observed directly is like talking about dark matter or black holes, unseen phenomena in the universe whose existence must be inferred because their incredible denseness and gravitational fields do not allow light to escape. In much the same way, we can consider the curriculum that we *do not* find in the schools; it may be as important as what we *do* find. Elliot Eisner has labelled the intellectual processes and content that schools do not teach "the **null curriculum**—the options students are not afforded, the perspectives they may never know about, much less be able to use, the concepts and skills that are not a part of their intellectual repertoire" (1994, 106–7).

For example, the kind of thinking that schools foster among students is largely based on manipulations of words and numbers. Thinking that is imaginative, subjective, and poetic is stressed only incidentally. Also, students are seldom taught anthropology, sociology, psychology, law, economics, filmmaking, or architecture.

Eisner points out that "certain subject matters have been traditionally taught in schools not because of a careful analysis of the range of other alternatives that could be offered but rather because they have traditionally been taught. We teach what we teach largely out of habit, and in the process neglect areas of study that could prove to be exceedingly useful to students" (1994, 103).

Professional Reflection   Identifying kinds of curriculum

Reflect on your experiences with the curriculum as an elementary, middle, or high school student. Then, focusing on one part of the explicit curriculum that you experienced—a particular subject or a particular class—identify possible aspects of the hidden curriculum and possible areas of null curriculum. What conclusions might you draw about beliefs and values concerning the curriculum held by educators? local communities? the wider society? How did those beliefs and values affect you and your education?

Extracurricular/Cocurricular Programs

The curriculum includes school-sponsored activities—music, drama, special interest clubs, sports, and student council, to name a few—that students may pursue in addition to their studies in academic subject areas. When such activities are perceived as additions to the academic curriculum, they are termed *extracurricular*. When these activities are seen as having important educational goals—and not merely as extras added to the academic curriculum—they are termed *cocurricular*. To reflect the fact that these two labels are commonly used for the same activities, we use the term *extracurricular/cocurricular* activities.

Though **extracurricular/cocurricular programs** are most extensive on the secondary level, many schools at the elementary, middle, and junior high levels also provide their students with a broad assortment of extracurricular/cocurricular activities. For those students who choose to participate, such activities provide an opportunity to use social and academic skills in many different contexts.

Research shows that the larger a school is, the less likely it is that a student will take part in extracurricular/cocurricular activities. At the same time, those who do participate tend to have higher self-concepts than those who do not (Coladarci and Cobb 1996). The actual effects that extracurricular/cocurricular activities have on students' development, however, are not entirely clear. Although it is known that students who participate in extracurricular/cocurricular activities tend to receive higher grades than nonparticipants and are more frequently identified as gifted (Jordan and Nettles 1999; Modi, Konstantopoulos, and Hedges 1998; Gerber 1996), it is not known whether participation influences achievement, or whether achievement influences participation. However, research has shown that participation has a positive influence on the decision to remain in school (Mahoney and Cairns 1997), educational aspirations (Modi, Konstantopoulos, and Hedges 1998), and the occupation one aspires to and eventually attains (Holland and Andre 1987; Brown, Kohrs, and Lanzamo 1991). Furthermore, students themselves tend to identify extracurricular/cocurricular activities as a high point in their school careers.

It is also clear that students who might benefit the most from participating in extracurricular/cocurricular activities—those below the norm in academic achievement and students at risk—tend not to participate. Results from a national survey comparing school leavers and high school graduates 18 to 20 years of age conducted in September of 1993 and the School Leavers Follow-Up Survey of 1995 indicate that one of the characteristics of high school dropouts is that they do not participate in extracurricular actitivities.

Curriculum Content

Like the parents featured in this chapter's opening scenario, many Canadians believe that the "basics" of reading, writing, and mathematics plus the development of good work habits should be the heart of the curriculum. However, there are also many who feel that the school curriculum should also emphasize social and life skills. Many schools have introduced curriculum aimed at combating such social problems as violence and racism.

The Canadian Teachers' Federation (CTF), as part of its National Issues in Education Initiative, raises the following questions about what should be taught in schools:

1. Should students be taught basic life skills that build self-esteem and prepare them to deal with conflict at work and in their daily lives?
2. Are schools the right place to offer AIDS education, suicide prevention, alcohol and drug abuse counselling, and early intervention for disadvantaged children and their families?
3. Should the public school curriculum include perspectives on cross-cultural awareness, racism, sexism and violence, designed to make our society a safer and more democratic place to live?
4. Is the public school system focusing on "extras" at the expense of core subjects like math, science, and reading?

The CTF makes the following points:

- Many education critics believe that self-esteem and life skills are far less important for students than core curriculum that will prepare them for the world of work.

But business leaders are keenly interested in hiring graduates who have the ability to think creatively, work cooperatively, and settle conflicts rather than letting them escalate. Many students will not acquire these skills if they are not taught in schools.

- Field trips, cultural activities, and outdoor education curricula are often dismissed as unnecessary frills. But these programs give students valuable experience of the world outside the classroom that would be virtually impossible to replicate in school.

- In 1990, the Ontario Advisory Committee on Children's Services identified the public school system as the logical hub for a range of health, recreation, and social services for children and their families. The committee's report, *Children First*, called for greater integration of child and family service programs, with schools as the key point of delivery.

How Is the School Curriculum Developed?

Although there is no easy-to-follow set of procedures for developing curriculum, Ralph Tyler has provided four fundamental questions that must be answered in developing any curriculum or plan of instruction. These four questions, known as the **Tyler rationale**, are as follows (Tyler 1949, 1):

1. What educational purposes should the school seek to attain?
2. What educational experiences can be provided that are likely to attain these purposes?
3. How can these educational experiences be effectively organized?
4. How can we determine whether these purposes are being attained?

Tyler's classic work has been used by a great number of school systems to bring some degree of order and focus to the curriculum development process.

The Focus of Curriculum Planning

In discussing curriculum development, it is helpful to clarify the focus of curriculum planning. Figure 8.1 illustrates two dimensions of this planning process: the target and the time orientation. The target of curriculum planning may be at the macro- or the micro-level. At the macro-level, decisions about the content of the curriculum apply to large groups of students. The national goals for education and provincial-level curriculum guidelines are examples of macro-level curricular decisions. At the micro-level, curriculum decisions are made that apply to groups of students in a particular school or classroom. To some extent, all teachers are micro-level curriculum developers—that is, they make numerous decisions about the curricular experiences they provide students in their classrooms.

Another dimension of curriculum planning is the time orientation—does the planning focus on the present or the future? In addition to the national goals and provincial-level curriculum guidelines, the semester-long or monthly plans or unit plans that teachers make are examples of future-oriented curriculum planning. Present-oriented curriculum planning usually occurs at the classroom level and is influenced by the unique needs of specific groups of students. The daily or weekly curriculum decisions and lesson plans that teachers make are examples of present-oriented curriculum planning.

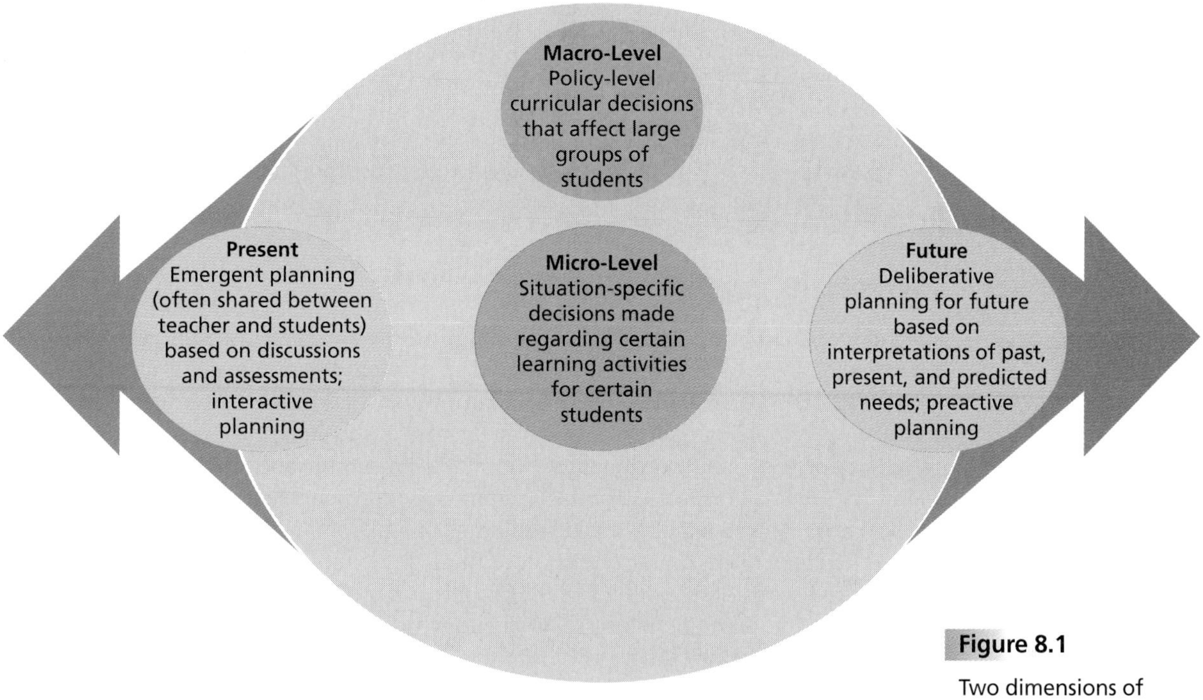

Figure 8.1

Two dimensions of curriculum planning

Student-Centred versus Subject-Centred Curricula

A key concern in curriculum development is whether greater emphasis should be given to the requirements of the subject area or to the needs of the students. It is helpful to imagine where a school curriculum might be placed on the following continuum.

Student-Centred ←——————→ Subject-Centred
Curriculum   Curriculum

Although no course is entirely subject- or student-centred, curricula vary considerably in the degree to which they emphasize one or the other. The **subject-centred curriculum** places primary emphasis on the logical order of the discipline students are to study. The teacher of such a curriculum is a subject-matter expert and is primarily concerned with helping students understand the facts, laws, and principles of the discipline. Subject-centred curricula are more typical of high school education.

Some teachers develop curricula that reflect greater concern for students and their needs. Though teachers of the **student-centred curriculum** also teach content, they emphasize the growth and development of students. This emphasis is generally more typical of elementary school curricula.

The Integrated Curriculum

The opening scenario for this chapter is based on the integrated approach to developing the school curriculum. Used most frequently with elementary-age students, the **integrated curriculum** draws from several different subject areas and focuses on a theme or concept rather than on a single subject. Early childhood education expert Suzanne Krogh (2000, 340) suggests that an integrated approach based on thematic "webs" is a more "natural" way for children to learn:

[Children] do not naturally learn through isolating specific subjects. These have been determined by adult definition. Children's natural learning is more likely to take place across a theme of interest: building a fort, exploring a sandbox, interacting with the first snow of winter. Teachers can create a good deal of their curriculum by building webs made up of these themes of interest. Done with knowledge and care, a web can be created that incorporates most, or even all, of the required and desired curriculum.

Who Plans the Curriculum?

Various agencies and people outside the school are involved in curriculum planning. Textbook publishers, for example, influence what is taught because many teachers use textbooks as curriculum guides. The Canadian Council of Ministers of Education and the Canadian School Boards Association contribute to curriculum planning by setting national education goals, and individual provincial departments of education develop both broad aims for school curricula and specific minimum competencies for students to master.

Within a given school, the curriculum-planning team and the classroom teacher plan the curriculum that students actually experience. As a teacher you will draw from a reservoir of curriculum plans prepared by others, thus playing a vital role in the curriculum-planning process. Whenever you make decisions about what material to include in your teaching, how to sequence content, and how much time to spend teaching certain material, you are planning the curriculum.

What Influences Curricular Decisions?

From the earliest colonial schools to schools of the twenty-first century, curricula have been broadly influenced by a variety of religious, political, and utilitarian agendas. Figure 8.2 illustrates the influence of community pressures, court decisions, students' life situations, testing results, teachers' professional organizations, research results, and other factors. The inner circle of the figure represents factors that have a more direct influence on curriculum development (such as students' needs and school district policies). The outer circle represents factors that are more removed from the school setting or have less obvious effects on the curriculum. Individual schools respond to all these influences differently, which further affects their curricula. Let us examine some of these influences in greater detail.

Social Issues and Changing Values

Values that affect curriculum planning include prevailing educational theories and teachers' educational philosophies. In addition, curriculum planners respond to social issues and changing values in the wider society. As a result, current social concerns find their way into textbooks, teaching aids, and lesson plans. Often curriculum changes are made in the hope that changing what students learn will help solve social problems or achieve local, province-wide, or national goals.

As Canada's population has become more culturally diverse, curriculum changes have been made to reflect divergent interests and values. This divergence has lead to controversies over curriculum content and conflicting calls for reform. Additional curriculum controversies have arisen over calls for the elimination of all activities or symbols that have their origins in organized religion, including even secularized or commercialized ones such as Halloween and the Easter bunny. Curriculum changes to promote greater social integration or equity among racial or ethnic groups may draw complaints of irrelevancy or reverse discrimination. Traditionalists may object to curriculum changes that reflect feminist views.

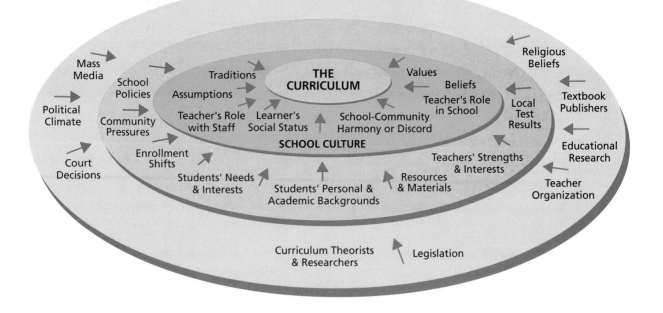

Figure 8.2

Influences on the school curriculum

As you can imagine, consensus on many curriculum reform issues is never achieved. However, because of their public accountability, schools must consider how to respond to those issues. In the end, the creative and evaluative tasks of choosing and developing curriculum materials are a source of both empowerment and frustration for teachers. Budget constraints, social and legal issues, and provincial and local curriculum mandates often determine curriculum choices.

The Canadian Teachers' Federation believes that education must be provided on an equitable basis to all students, through elementary and secondary school programs that do the following:

- Develop the intellectual, aesthetic, physical, emotional, and ethical capacities of each student.
- Prepare students to become responsible and productive members of society.
- Provide opportunities for students to learn about Canadian history, literature, culture, government, and heritage.
- Enable students to learn about the global community, and about Canada's place in that community.

The Canadian School Boards Association issued a statement of national educational goals in 1992. The statement stressed the importance of equal access to quality programs for all school age children, and suggested that school choice should take the form of a range of public school programs, designed to address diverse learning needs and interests (Canadian Teachers' Federation).

Textbook Publishing

Textbooks greatly influence the curriculum. According to one study, "with nearly 95 percent of classroom instruction in Grades K–8 and 90 percent of homework time derived from printed materials, textbooks predominate the school day" (Vanes 1992, 444). In addition, textbook publishers influence school curricula by providing teaching objectives, learning activities, tests, audiovisual aids, and other supplements to assist their customers.

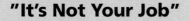
"It's Not Your Job"

The Prince William Consolidated Senior High School is in a rural area in a Canadian province. The school's community is not culturally diverse, and most of the students come from traditional, conservative homes. The largest industry in the area is farming and most of the families are fourth and fifth generation Canadians. The students come from largely middle class homes and most of them have not travelled much outside of the province. The predominant religion is Christianity.

The Grade 11 classes of Prince William Consolidated Senior High School are studying an interdisciplinary unit (IDU) on the theme of prejudice and stereotypes. The social studies, drama, journalism, and English language arts teachers have collaborated on the unit that has, as one of its key goals, the heightened awareness of racism and the need for tolerance in society. The teachers involved in this curricular project have planned learning situations that are designed to challenge prevalent beliefs and attitudes and to examine societal stereotypes. Some of the activities ask students to move out of their comfort zones. Students will be required to complete a wide variety of assignments including performances, personal journals, reviews of media, and role plays. The culminating activity for this unit will be a public presentation featuring student performances by the students in the gymnasium. The teachers have been careful to use the various content area curriculum learning outcomes established by the provincial Department of Education to direct their planning; the lessons and assessment activities are aligned with the mandated outcomes.

Ms Kyrisck-Clarke, a young English teacher in the senior high, has become known for her creative lessons that require students to examine their beliefs in a critical way. Her students have been enthusiastic about English this year and she has won the respect of both students and parents for her hard work and dedication to the school and community. Ms Kyrisck-Clarke has given hours of her time outside the classroom to coach drama, advise the yearbook staff, and plan fund raising activities.

Throughout the year, Ms Kyrisck-Clarke has become concerned that her students' views are narrow and that they have a hard time appreciating differences in race, religion, and political beliefs. The views they have expressed in discussions about world events, such as the ongoing violence in the Middle East, and injustices in the treatment of Canadian Aboriginal Peoples, have convinced her that the students would benefit from sensitivity exercises. As a result, she is one of the forces behind the development of the IDU.

One of the key learning activities in the unit is the completion of personal journals. These journals are not assessed for grammar and spelling and students are encouraged to be truthful, spontaneous, and personal in their journal entries. One of the prompts given for a journal entry is for students to examine the various ways in which their families demonstrate intolerance and how that has influenced their beliefs. Ms Kyrisck-Clarke responds to the journal entries and, through these exchanges with her students, she often challenges their opinions. She frequently asks students to rethink their positions on various topics.

After reading Shakespeare's *Merchant of Venice*, one of the literature selections in the IDU, Ms Kyrisck-Clarke asks students to put themselves in the role of Shylock and to write about how he might feel about being persecuted by the citizens of Venice. Further, she assigns a class debate in which students are asked to justify Shylock's plan to extract a pound of flesh from Antonio if the loan cannot be repaid.

Midway through the IDU, the Grade 11 teachers involved in the project meet and enthusiastically reflect on their progress with the unit and share suggestions and offer ideas to one another. The feeling is that this collaborative effort has been a positive one and there are plans to continue with this type of curriculum development. The plans are underway for the end-of-unit public presentation for the public.

Shortly after the meeting, the teachers are called to an emergency meeting in the main office. The principal, Ms Haines, looks distressed as she asks the teachers to gather with her in the school conference room. She passes around copies of a letter written on behalf of concerned community members. The teachers register shock as they read the contents of the letter; it is a serious attack on the IDU content and assignments. Ms Haines has prepared a piece of chart paper outlining the concerns. Many of them seem to point at the work being done in Ms Kyrisck-Clarke's classes.

The complaints are outlined as follows:

- Concern from the local clergy about students being asked to play a role assuming a religion other than Christianity
- Outrage from parents about students being encouraged to "reveal" family beliefs and share examples of prejudice in their homes
- Disapproval from the community about students partaking in a debate that supports violence against others in the form of "extracting a pound of flesh"
- Objections to the process of challenging student beliefs

The letter ends with a demand that the focus of the IDU change to a more "factual" one and that teachers refrain from expressing their own beliefs and trying to influence their students' belief systems. One of the quotes from the letter reads, "It is up to parents and the church to teach the morals and values that we see fit to teach our children. It is the job of the school to teach the basic skills required to succeed in the world of work."

The teachers look as if they have been physically attacked as they prepare to listen to how Ms Haines expects them to respond to these serious concerns.

Questions

1. What were the purposes/goals of the IDU? Are there other ways in which the IDU goals could be met?

2. What is your opinion of the assignments given by Ms Kyrisck-Clarke?

3. Since the teachers were careful to align the contents of the IDU with the provincially mandated curriculum learning outcomes, do the complaints have any merit?

4. Examine the specific complaints made to the school regarding the IDU. How should the school respond to these?

5. How would you feel if you were a member of the IDU team and realized that most of the complaints were actually directed at Ms Kyrisck-Clarke? Would you get involved in another collaborative curriculum development effort?

6. Interview a teacher about his/her experiences with curriculum development. Has this teacher ever experienced a situation similar to the one portrayed in this case study?

7. Would this approach be as likely to provoke such a reaction from the public in a culturally diverse urban setting?

8. What does this show beginning teachers about the relationship between the cultural and social milieu and curriculum development?

Like curriculum planners, textbook authors and publishers are influenced by trends in education and by social issues. In response to criticism, for example, publishers now tend to avoid bias in terms of gender, religion, class, race, and culture. However, because the goal of business is profit, publishers are most responsive to market trends and customer preferences. They are often reluctant to risk losing sales by including subjects that are controversial or that may be offensive to their bigger customers. They may also modify textbooks to appeal to decision makers in populous provinces, such as Ontario and British Columbia, where province-wide adoptions are possible.

Educators have criticized textbooks for inoffensiveness to the point of blandness, for artificially lowered reading levels (called "dumbing down"), and for using pedagogically questionable gimmicks to hold students' attention. "The quality problem [with textbooks also] encompasses [f]actors such as poor writing, poor content 'coverage,' and failure to engage students in the skills needed to create the knowledge contained in a particular area of study" (Sowell 1996, 158). Although the publishing industry continually responds to such criticisms, you would be wise to follow systematic guidelines in evaluating and selecting textbooks and other curriculum materials.

What Reform Efforts Have Affected the Curriculum?

The content of the curricula in Canada's schools has undergone significant changes since the colonial period. These modifications came about as the goals of the schools were debated, additional needs of society became evident, and the characteristics of student populations shifted.

The following list is a sampling of goals the schools have set for themselves at different times in our history.

- Prepare students to carry out religious and family responsibilities
- Provide employers with a source of literate workers
- Promote the notion of multiculturalism and bilingualism
- Reduce crime, poverty, and injustice
- Help our country compete in the world economy
- Educate students for intelligent participation in a democratic society

Vocational goals for the curriculum were most prominent from 1860 to 1920. The turn of the century brought with it many changes that profoundly influenced the curriculum. The dawning of the machine age altered the nature of industry, transportation, and communication. The growth of cities and the influx of immigrants resulted in new functions for all social institutions, and home life was forever changed.

It is interesting to examine the emphasis of early twentieth century Canadian curriculum. The *Register of the Attendance, Studies, and General Standing of the Pupils, and Statistics of the School* prescribed by the Council of Public Instruction, Nova Scotia, outlined the program of studies for the public schools of Nova Scotia for the year 1911 as the following subjects:

- Physical Education and Military Drill
- Vocal Music
- Hygiene and Temperance
- Moral and Patriotic Duties
- Good Manners
- Nature Study
- Spelling and Dictation
- Reading and Elocution
- English
- Writing
- Drawing
- Arithmetic
- Geography and History
- Manual Training

Since 1920, schools have been expected to provide educational opportunities for all Canadians. During this period, curricula have been developed to meet the needs and differences of many diverse student groups, such as students who are disabled, bilingual, gifted, or delinquent, or who have special needs.

The Progressive Curriculum

The concern for educating all our youth has drawn much of its initial energy from the **progressive education movement.** During the 1920s, the Progressive Education Association reacted against the earlier emphasis on the mental disciplines and called for elementary schools to develop curricula based on the needs and interests of all students. Throughout the 1930s, progressive ideas were promoted on the secondary level as well.

Though there was no single set of beliefs that united all Progressives, there was general agreement that students should be involved in activities that parallel those found in society. Furthermore, those activities should engage students' natural interests and contribute to their self-fulfillment. With these guidelines in mind, the progressive education movement expanded the curriculum to include such topics as home economics, health, family living, citizenship, and wood shop.

The Inquiry-Based Curriculum

The publication of Jerome Bruner's short book, *The Process of Education,* in 1960 marked another important influence on curriculum development. Bruner's book synthesized current ideas about intelligence and how to motivate students to learn. Bruner believed that students should learn the "methods of inquiry" common to the academic disciplines. For example, in an **inquiry-based curriculum,** instead of learning isolated facts about chemistry, students would learn the principles of inquiry common to the discipline of chemistry. In short, students would learn to think like chemists; they would be able to use principles from chemistry to solve problems independently.

Bruner's ideas were used as a rationale for making the curriculum more rigorous at all levels. As he pointed out in an often-quoted statement in *The Process of Education,* "Any subject can be taught effectively in some intellectually honest form to any child at any stage of development" (1960, 33). Bruner advocated a spiral curriculum wherein children would encounter the disciplines at ever-increasing levels of complexity as they progressed through school. Thus elementary students could be taught physics in a manner that would pave the way for their learning more complex principles of physics in high school.

The Relevancy-Based Curriculum

The push for a rigorous academic core curriculum was offset in the mid-1960s by a call for a **relevancy-based curriculum.** Many educators, student groups, and political activists charged that school curricula were unresponsive to social issues and significant changes in our culture. At some schools, largely high schools, students actually demonstrated against educational programs they felt were not relevant to their needs and concerns. In response to this pressure, educators began to add more courses to the curriculum, increase the number of elective and remedial courses offered, and experiment with new ways of teaching. This concern with relevancy continued until the back-to-basics movement began in the mid-1970s.

The Core Curriculum

The school reform movement of the 1980s led to provinces reviewing their curriculum and the result was that many Departments of Education increased the number of required courses for graduation, or **core curriculum**. For example, in Saskatchewan, credit requirements were increased from 21 to 24 in 1987. The current Saskatchewan Core Curriculum principles include reinforcing of teaching basic skills and an expanded range of new knowledge and skills to the curriculum.

The two major components of Core Curriculum are the *Required Areas of Study and the Common Essential Learnings.* Seven Required Areas of Study form the framework for the curriculum. Six categories of Common Essential Learnings are to be incorporated in an appropriate manner into all courses of study offered in Saskatchewan schools. To meet community and student needs at the local level, provision is made within the Core Curriculum to offer Locally Determined Options. In recognition of the diverse needs of students, provision is made through the Adaptive Dimension for teachers to adapt instruction.

Required Areas of Study Within the Core Curriculum

- Language arts
- Mathematics
- Science
- Social studies

- Health education
- Arts education
- Physical education

Each required area has unique knowledge, skills, and values that are essential for all students at the elementary, Middle, and Secondary Levels. The Required Areas of Study, therefore, are included throughout the school program from the Elementary to Secondary Levels (Saskatchewan Government Policy Document of Core Curriculum: www.sasked.gov.sk.ca/docs/policy/corecurr_pta/intro.html).

Performance-Based Education

A recent approach to reforming the curriculum to ensure that all students learn and perform at higher levels is known as **performance-based** or **outcome-based education.** The performance-based approach focuses on assessing students' mastery of a set of rigorous learning goals or outcomes. Opponents to performance-based education have expressed concern about the content of the outcomes, who determines them, and how they will be assessed.

The Canadian Curriculum Scene: Web Resources

Most Canadian provinces and territories have similar approaches to their curricular program of studies. The following regional, provincial, and territorial curriculum websites provide information about core curriculum for individual provinces and territories.

Atlantic Provinces Education Foundation (APEF) Documents http://apef-fepa.org

Western Canadian Protocol for Collaboration in Basic Education, Kindergarten to Grade 12 www.wcp.ca

Alberta Learning ednet.edc.gov.ab.ca/k_12/curriculum/

B.C. Ministry of Education, Program Standards and Education Resources Branch www.bced.gov.bc/irp/curric/

Manitoba Curriculum Development, Implementation, and Assessment www.edu.gov.mb.ca/metks4/curricul/index.html

New Brunswick www.gnb.ca/0000/anglophone-e.asp#1

Newfoundland and Labrador Division of Program Development www.stemnet.nf.ca/DepEd/Program/index.html

Northwest Territories Curriculum http://siksik.learnnet.nt.ca

Nova Scotia http://doc-depot.ednet.ns.ca

Ontario Curriculum and Policy Documents www.edu.gov.on.ca/eng/document/curricul/curricul.html

Prince Edward Island www.edu.pe.ca/

Quebec Ministere de l'Education Curriculum Publications www.meq.gouv.qc/GR-PUB/menu-curricu-a.htm

Saskatchewan Department of Education Curriculum and Instruction Branch www.sasked.gov.sk.ca/curr_inst/

Yukon Educational Student Network www.yesnet.yk.ca

Is standardized testing an effective way to measure curricular outcomes?

The topic of standardized assessment raises controversy and sharp differences of opinion; the effects of standardized testing on educational curriculum and standards in today's schools are debatable. W. Todd Rogers, of the University of Alberta, states, "We are witnessing in Canada today, as in other countries, a marked increase in the use of tests and assessment" (Rogers 1999, 329).

Standardized tests are given and scored in the same way, no matter where or when they are given, so that scores of all students can be compared. The common format for these tests is multiple choice. Examples of standardized tests include achievement tests and commercial tests such as the Canadian Test of Basic Skills (CTBS) and the Canadian Achievement Tests (CAT).

All Canadian provinces engage in some form of large-scale assessment. Some provinces test at Grades 3, 6, 9, and 12, while others test at Grades 4, 7, 10, and 12. Some provincial testing is done yearly, while other provinces test every two or three years. The Council of Ministers of Education (CMEC) operates Canada's existing national assessment program, the School Achievement Indicators (SAIP). The SAIP tests are given to 13- and 16-year-old students across the country in the core subject areas of reading, writing, math, and science. The tests are given randomly, and are used to determine if students know more or less than what is expected, and to assist provincial departments of education in making curricular decisions. A number of provinces also participate in international assessment programs, such as the Third International Math and Science Study (TIMSS) (MacDonald n.d.).

What do you think? Is the use of standardized testing an effective way to measure curricula outcomes?

Yes, the use of standardized testing is an effective way to measure curricula outcomes.

"Whatever exists, exists in some amount; to measure it is simply to know its varying amounts."

—*Edward Thorndike*

Standardized testing can serve as a basis for comparing academic results across schools, school boards, provinces, and nations. The data can help schools to make the necessary improvements to curriculum to help students develop the skills they need to compete globally. Standardized tests can reveal information about the average performance of the education system and provide a basis for decisions about educational policies based on evidence.

Mark Holmes (2001) of the Canadian Test Centre, maintains that "A national test is the only efficient way of putting individual, classroom, and school learning of basic skills into a national context. It does not show what was taught, but it does show what has and has not been learned."

He counters the criticism that such assessment tools encourage teachers to "teach to the test." Holmes claims that "Teaching to the test is generally a good thing; young people should be prepared in the basic skills of reading comprehension, language usage, and mathematical computation and problem solving, the kinds of things national tests measure."

In response to the argument that publication of test results can lead to misuse of results for comparison purposes, Holmes argues, "certainly it is inappropriate to judge the competence of teachers or schools simply on the basis of test results of any kind, whether standardized or teacher created." He argues that the knowledge that can be generated from such tests "can be useful in helping to select the most useful teaching methodologies for the students in question."

The Society for the Advancement of Excellence in Education document, *Student Assessment in Canada*, calls for a broad level of testing in all provinces. Helen Raham of the Society for the Advancement of Excellence in Education (SAEE) contends that:

Those provinces [with strong testing programs] seem to be giving their students an advantage through strong assessment programs … At the moment, Alberta, B.C. and Quebec seem to have the strongest systems and it is interesting that they have the strongest results in national and international tests. (Smyth 2001, A1)

Raham further believes that accountability systems can help schools use performance data to improve schools and student learning.

No, the use of standardized testing is not an effective way to measure curricula outcomes.

Not everything that counts can be counted, and not everything that can be counted counts.

—*Albert Einstein*

Student assessment and evaluation practices need to be fair and based on curriculum objectives and implementation. The Alberta Teachers' Association (ATA) (2002) describes teacher evaluation as an effective way of assessing what students know and are able to do. It claims that externally designed evaluation tools are seldom appropriate, and are not adapted to the individual classroom context.

A popular argument against the use of standardized testing is that it does not capture the nature or essence of teaching, and that it measures a narrow range of skills. Most critics of this form of assessment are concerned with the following:

Schools, teachers, and students may be harmed.
Results may be misinterpreted by the public.

Some of the perceived harm includes the fear that the pressure of standardized testing may lead to "teaching to the test" at the exclusion of higher order skills. Standardized tests are generally multiple choice, constructed by outside people or organizations, and administered as single assessments in a "pencil and paper" format. They tend to measure lower-order recall thinking at the expense of higher-order thinking, such as analyzing and synthesizing. They do not offer opportunities for students to demonstrate many of the skills inherent in the current curricula, such as open-ended problem-solving, application of technology, creative presentation, and effective communication. The tests simply fail to address the full range of curricular learning outcomes.

Wide-scale standardized tests are administered to large numbers of students, and as such are very general in nature. This leads to mismatches between test questions and the enacted curriculum. For example, in 1996, the TIMSS reported test-curriculum matches ranging from 53 percent in one province to 98 percent in another (Stewart 2002).

Another criticism of the standardized test assessment approach centres around the expense of administering such tests, especially in a time of financial restraint in education budgets. The money spent on such evaluation is not spent on staffing, curriculum materials, and professional development. For example, in June of 2001, the Ontario Ministry of Education estimated that a new expanded testing program would cost $16 million annually, in addition to the $30 million currently being spent on testing (Stewart 2002).

Misinterpretation of results is another main argument against large-scale assessment. The media coverage of such data has resulted in school rankings in many provinces. Test results are issued with little explanation, preventing objective analysis.

Where do you stand on this issue?

1. What are the key points in each argument?

2. With which argument do you agree the most? What other points could you make to defend your position?

3. Propose a means other than standardized testing to hold schools accountable and provide parents with information about their children's proficiency in basic skills.

4. Search the internet for articles on the topic of assessment and evaluation of educational outcomes.

Recommended Sources

British Columbia Teachers' Federation. (1997). "Opportunities to Learn: Accountability in Education in British Columbia." Retrieved November 6, 2003 from www.bctf.ca/publications/briefs/ocg/

Raham, H. (1999, Spring). Assessment practices Education Analyst (2), 1. Retrieved October 20, 2003 from www.saee.bc.ca/art2_6.html.

Raham, H. (1998, July-August). Policy Options. Building school success through accountability. www.irpp.org/po/archive/po0798.htm

Simner, M. L. (2000). Joint position statement by the Canadian Psychological Association and the Canadian Association of School Psychologists on the Canadian press coverage of the province-wide achievement test results. Retrieved October 20, 2003 from www.cpa.ca/documents/joint_position.html.

Alberta Teachers Association. (2001, February). Teachers and parents need to fight standardized testing.

Gaskell, J. & Vogel, D. (2000, March). Fraser Institute ranking fails as a measure of school quality." Retrieved October 20, 2003 from www.policyalternatives.ca/bc/opinion38.html

Elementary Teachers' Federation of Ontario. (2001, May). Assessment and accountability: Why standardized testing is the wrong answer.

Canadian Teachers' Federation. (2000). Assessment and Evaluation. Retrieved October 20, 2003 from www.ctf-fce.ca/en/default.htm

Future Direction of Canadian Education: A National Influence

In September 1993, the Council of Ministers of Education, Canada endorsed the Victoria Declaration which outlined a plan for future directions in Canadian education. The Declaration outlined the following beliefs held in common by all Ministers.

> We believe that education is a lifelong learning process. We also believe that the future of our society depends on informed and educated citizens who, while fulfilling their own goals of personal and professional development, contribute to the social, economic, and cultural development of their community and country as a whole. Beyond our borders, Canadian education should reflect the priorities of Canadians while contributing to strengthening Canada's place internationally.

> In February 1995, the Council of Ministers of Education, Canada adopted the Pan-Canadian Protocol for Collaboration on School curriculum. The protocol acknowledges that education is a provincial and territorial responsibility, while recognizing that interjurisdictional cooperation can contribute to improving the quality of education in the country. In keeping with the protocol, participating jurisdictions believe that sharing human and financial resources can increase the quality and efficiency of the curriculum development processes in Canada (Council of Ministers of Education, Canada).

What Are Some Current Subject-Area Trends?

The final section of this chapter examines briefly some of the current trends and issues regarding what is taught in elementary, middle, junior high, and high schools. See Appendix 8.1 for selected subject-area references for curriculum planning.

Reading and Writing

The importance of attaining a minimum level of literacy in our society cannot be underestimated; the language arts are the tools through which students learn in nearly all other areas of the curriculum. Most students who are deficient in reading and writing skills are at a significant disadvantage when it comes to seeking employment or additional education.

The teaching of reading at all levels should focus on acquiring basic comprehension skills and learning to appreciate literature in its various forms: novels, essays, poetry, short stories, and so on. Reading teachers, however, are currently far from united as to how these aims should be realized. Does instruction in phonics enhance reading comprehension? Is a whole-language approach to the teaching of reading superior to teaching isolated decoding and comprehension skills? Should children be taught the alphabet before learning to read? Although media coverage frequently dichotomizes the teaching of reading between the phonics approach and the whole-language approach, Cheeks, Flippo, and Lindsey (1997, 130) contend that "this polarization is more political than representative of the real issues. Those who advocate for whole language do not believe that phonics is not important. Instead they argue about how it should be presented to students."

The following comments by a Grade 1 teacher reflect the position that many teachers have taken regarding the "reading wars": "I don't think there is one best method of teaching reading or one best program. What I have done over my twenty-seven years is pick what I think works and incorporate it" (Smolkin 1999, 1A). The eclectic approach to teaching reading is also advocated by the International Reading Association, which stated that "there is no single method or single combination of methods that can successfully teach all children to read. Therefore, teachers must be familiar with a wide range

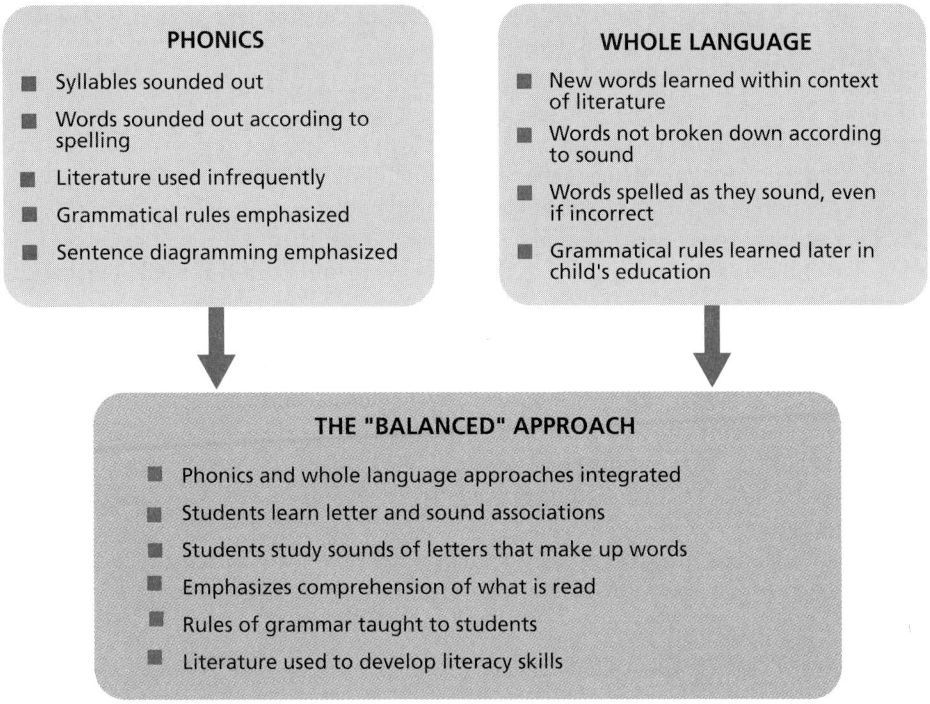

Figure 8.3

A "balanced" approach
to teaching reading and
writing

PHONICS

- Syllables sounded out
- Words sounded out according to spelling
- Literature used infrequently
- Grammatical rules emphasized
- Sentence diagramming emphasized

WHOLE LANGUAGE

- New words learned within context of literature
- Words not broken down according to sound
- Words spelled as they sound, even if incorrect
- Grammatical rules learned later in child's education

THE "BALANCED" APPROACH

- Phonics and whole language approaches integrated
- Students learn letter and sound associations
- Students study sounds of letters that make up words
- Emphasizes comprehension of what is read
- Rules of grammar taught to students
- Literature used to develop literacy skills

of methods for teaching reading and a strong knowledge of the children in their care so they can create the appropriate balance of methods needed for each child" (International Reading Association 1999). As part of a trend to "deescalate" the reading wars, then, many schools that emphasized a whole-language approach during the 1990s, began to shift to a "balanced" approach at the start of the new decade (see Figure 8.3).

Advocates of the **whole-language approach** believe that reading is part of general language development, not an isolated skill students learn apart from listening, speaking, and writing. Teachers in whole-language classrooms seldom use textbooks; instead, young students write stories and learn to read from their writing, and older students read literature that is closely related to their everyday experiences.

During the last two decades, several new approaches have been incorporated into the language arts curriculum. Many English teachers have reduced the amount of time spent on grammar, electing instead to teach grammar as needed within the context of a writing program. English teachers also have generally broadened their view of literature to include more contemporary forms of writing and the literary contributions of minority or ethnic writers. Teaching in the English classroom now frequently includes such techniques as creative writing, drama, journal writing, guided fantasy exercises, and group discussions. In addition, many teachers are using computers to explore new ways to teach students reading and writing.

After three years of collaborative development, the International Reading Association and the National Council of Teachers of English in the United States released voluntary national standards for English-language arts in 1996. Debate over these standards continues to stimulate discussion and debate about the goals of language arts instruction.

Based on their review of literacy research, Cheeks, Flippo, and Lindsey (1997, 83–84) recommend that teachers do the following to develop children's language abilities:

1. Allow many opportunities for social imaginative play and other verbal peer interaction, which enhance language and cognitive development.

2. Develop learning activities that integrate listening, speaking, reading, and writing (oral and written language).
3. Use art, music, and drama activities to further develop language opportunities.
4. Read many books and stories to children every day.
5. Choose books and stories that you believe will be of high interest to children and will further stimulate their interest in reading books.
6. Give children opportunities to respond to the books and stories you read.
7. Reread favourite stories as often as children request them.
8. Give children opportunities to retell and/or act out stories in their own words after listening to you read them.
9. Give children many opportunities to make their own books. Children can dictate stories as the teacher writes the stories down in the children's own words. Children also can write their own books using scribble writing, pictures, and invented spellings to tell their stories in their own words.
10. Give children many opportunities to share with others the stories they write.
11. Accept "less than perfect" readings, retellings, writing, and other literacy attempts for all children.
12. Provide classroom activities and an environment that enhances the idea that literacy is part of communication and that meaning is essential for communication to take place.

The Canadian Council of Teachers of English Language Arts (CCTLA) and its provincial affiliates have not published national standards, but they are associated with the National Council of Teachers of English (NCTE) and the International Reading Association (IRA) and follow many of the standards established by these organizations. There appears to be consistency in English Language Arts Curriculum documents throughout the country. The Western Canadian Protocol for Collaboration in Basic Education (British Columbia, Alberta, Saskatchewan, Manitoba, Nunavut, and Yukon) accepted a Common Curriculum Framework for English Language Arts in 1998. The Atlantic Provinces Education Foundation (Nova Scotia, New Brunswick, Prince Edward Island, and Newfoundland and Labrador), and the ministries of Quebec and Ontario all recognize the importance of language and communications skills in society skills, and they embrace the concept that literacy has moved beyond print, encompassing media literacy and other ways of representing language.

Mathematics

Although there is no pan-Canadian framework in mathematics curriculum, most provinces are following similar approaches to this content area. The current teaching approaches in mathematics curriculum embrace a constructivist, learner-centred focus with the learning goal of mathematical literacy. The new math curriculums across Canada emphasize problem solving and inquiry approaches. For example, the Common Curriculum Framework for K–12 Mathematics (Western Canadian Protocol for collaboration in Basic Education, 1998a) incorporates the following seven interrelated mathematical processes:

- Communication
- Connections
- Estimation and mental mathematics
- Problem solving
- Reasoning
- Technology
- Visualization

The curriculum development process in Canada has tended to draw on such sources as the National Council of Teachers of Mathematics (NCTM) Curriculum and Evaluation Standards for Mathematics. This American organization has widespread membership in Canada. Since it began working on the *Standards 2000* project, a set of pre K–12 standards to be released in spring 2000, the National Council of Teachers of Mathematics (NCTM) has made it clear that basic mathematical skills for the new century should consist of more than computation skills. *Standards 2000* emphasizes five mathematical content standards (number and operation; patterns, functions, and algebra; geometry and spatial sense; measurement; and data analysis, statistics, and probability) that students should study with increasing breadth and depth as they move through the grades. In addition, *Standards 2000* emphasizes five mathematical processes through which students should acquire and use their mathematical knowledge: problem solving, reasoning and proof, communication, connections, and representation (National Council of Teachers of Mathematics 1998).

What is needed is **problem-centred learning,** in which students work in small groups on problems that have many or open-ended solutions. Rather than memorizing facts, working on sets of problems in textbooks, and competing against their classmates, students discover concepts, solve problems similar to those they will encounter in life, and learn to cooperate in small groups. For example, one mathematics-reform group developed a curriculum unit on testing blood for diseases that asks students to use quadratic and cubic equations to decide when to pool samples of blood rather than test each sample individually (Viadero 1996, 33). The use of manipulative materials such as Cuisinnaire rods, balance beams, counting sticks, and measuring scales also has positive effects on students' achievement in mathematics. For instance, Washington State University researcher David Slavit (1998, 280) found that "combining hands-on, visually-based activities with mathematical discussions [can increase] students' structural understanding of the geometric concepts of similarity and congruence. Observing students perform these activities confirmed ... the educational importance of 'doing' mathematics."

Science and Technology

Current science curriculum approaches underline the need for students to learn more science and to acquire scientific knowledge, skills, and processes through an inquiry, discovery, or problem-centred method. The teacher's primary role is to guide students in their search for knowledge rather than to act solely as a source of information and/or right answers.

The first joint development project initiated by the Council of Canadian Ministers of Education's 1995 common frameworks for curriculums was in the content area of science learning outcomes. This common set of guidelines lays out a framework comprised of a vision for scientific literacy in Canada and outlines learning outcomes. These outcomes include attitudes, knowledge, and skills for students to become inquirers and problem solvers. The website of the Council of Ministers of Education, Canada, at www.cmec.ca/science/framework/, says that science education aims to do the following:

- Encourage students at all grade levels to develop a critical sense of wonder and curiosity about scientific and technological endeavours.
- Enable students to use science and technology to acquire new knowledge and solve problems so that they may improve the quality of their lives and the lives of others.

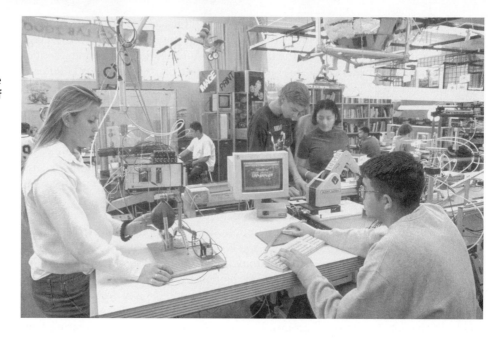

- Prepare students to critically address science-related societal, economic, ethical, and environmental issues.
- Provide students with a foundation in science that creates opportunities for them to pursue progressively higher levels of study, that prepares them for science-related occupations, and that engages them in science-related hobbies appropriate to their interests and abilities.
- Develop, in students of varying aptitudes and interests, knowledge of the wide variety of careers related to science, technology, and the environment.

Four foundation statements of science learning guide the development of science curriculums across Canada:

- Foundation 1: Science, technology, society, and the environment
- Foundation 2: Skills
- Foundation 3: Knowledge
- Foundation 4: Attitudes

This framework emphasizes a constructivist approach to science learning and encourages learner-centred approaches. The framework is intended to be used as a guide rather than a prescription for science curriculum development and the selection of learning resources.

Social Studies

Goals for the social studies lack the precision that we find in other subject areas. Consider, for example, Charles Beard's comment in 1938 that the social studies aim at the "creation of rich and many-sided personalities, equipped with practical knowledge and inspired by ideals so that they can make their way and fulfill their mission in a changing society which is part of a world complex" (1938, 179). Consider also the following ten "strands" from the National Council for the Social Studies' (1994) *Expectations of Excellence: Curriculum Standards for Social Studies:*

1. Culture and cultural diversity
2. Human beings' views of themselves over time
3. People, places, and environments
4. Individual development and identity
5. Interactions among individuals, groups, and institutions
6. How structures of power, authority, and governance are changed
7. The production, distribution, and consumption of goods and services
8. Relationships among science, technology, and society
9. Global interdependence
10. Citizenship in a democratic society

The Western Canadian Protocol for Collaboration in Basic Education (2000, 6) has adopted the following formal definition for social studies:

> Social studies is the study of people in relation to each other and their world. It is an interdisciplinary subject that draws upon history, geography, economics, law, political science, and other disciplines. Social studies focuses on people's relationships with their social, physical, spiritual, cultural, economic, political, and technological environments. Social studies helps students become active and responsible citizens within their communities, locally, nationally, and globally, in a complex and changing world.

Canada does not have national guidelines or standards in the social studies curriculum area but common themes can be identified in the various provinces and territories. The Atlantic Provinces Education Foundation (APEF) (199, 12) identifies the following six strands to categorize social studies content, along with general outcomes for each strand.

1. *Citizenship, power, and governance.* Students need to understand the rights and responsibilities of citizenship and the origins, functions, and sources of power, authority, and governance.
2. *Individuals, societies, and economic decisions.* Students need to make responsible economic decisions, both as individuals and as members of society.
3. *People, place, and environment.* Students need to understand how people, places, and the environment interact.
4. *Culture and diversity.* Students need to understand culture, diversity, and worldview, and to recognize similarities and differences among personal, cultural, racial, and ethnic perspectives.
5. *Interdependence.* Students need to understand that relationships among individuals, societies, and the environment—locally, nationally, and globally—are interdependent, and the relationships have implications for a sustainable future.
6. *Time, continuity, and change.* Students need to understand the past and how it affects the present and the future.

The social studies curriculum has been expanded in recent years to keep pace with societal trends; specifically, courses or units in African Canadian and Aboriginal studies and women's history have been developed to give voice to minorities whose stories had previously been ignored. Efforts will continue to be made in this content area to address such issues as racial, ethnic, cultural, gender, and socio-economic biases and promote multiculturalism, diversity, and anti-discrimination in society.

The social studies curriculum has also experienced a rapid expansion of information related to the proliferation of the internet. This development underlines the need for opportunities within the curriculum to develop media literate students who can critically interpret and analyze information.

How can educational software change the roles of teachers and students?

Educational software enables students to experience events or study phenomena that they could not witness firsthand. By integrating educational software into various learning tasks and across subject areas, teachers can provide students with learning experiences that would have been impossible a few years ago. Most important, careful and purposeful use of educational software changes the roles of teachers and students and enhances students' higher order and problem-solving skills.

As you read the following two classroom vignettes, consider how the use of educational software changes the roles of teachers and students. Then, individually or with the rest of your class, reflect on the questions that follow the vignettes.

Vignette #1

When five of her students consistently had trouble understanding early geometry concepts, and all began to have poor attitudes about their own abilities, Ms Johnson turned to problem-solving software as another tool to provide a useful context for their learning. Over the course of two weeks, she introduced the group to the problem-solving activities in *Snootz Math Trek.*

[Her] students concentrated on only one of the five thinking activities in *Snootz,* the one that dealt with the shape puzzles in Al's Garage. The *Snootz*

characters engaged students, and the exposure to the quality problem-solving activities made light bulbs turn on in their heads.

Speaking with them individually over the next several weeks, Ms Johnson realized that not only were the students demonstrating proficiency with problem-solving strategies, but that they were feeling confident about what they knew. One student even offered to show one of the top math students how to use the software (Bitter and Pierson 1999, 94).

Vignette #2

One of the most difficult areas of the Grade 8 language arts curriculum to teach effectively, according to Mrs. Hancock, is poetry. Students just are not interested. [She] was, therefore, most interested when she found the program *In My Own Voice: Multicultural Poets on Identity.*

Mrs. Hancock feels that all good writers have a writing environment that is comfortable to them and inspires them to write, and she was amazed that this software simulates such a rich environment. In the *Writer Space,* students can access all of the program resources. They can visit a gallery of artistic images and hear the poems that were inspired by the art. Students can study one poet's

Second-Language Instruction

The majority of Canadian students take their school courses in English or French, Canada's two official languages. The federal government funds French and English instruction as second languages. Publicly-funded schooling in either language is guaranteed "where numbers warrant" and is decided on a case-by-case basis. In Quebec, only a child whose parent was educated in English can attend an English-language public school (UN Reporting Category: Education, Leisure, and Cultural Activities). Canada has also been in the forefront of the French Immersion field, with a variety of programs.

French is one of the official languages of Canada and is spoken by over 6.7 million Canadians and more than 300 million people worldwide. Many jobs in Canada require French language skills. An Ipso-Reid survey shows that most young Canadians believe that knowing English and French improves job opportunities (Turnbull 2000).

style by reading a collection of his or her poems and hear in the poet's own words how each poem was created. They can examine the actual text of each poem to see examples of the unique capitalization, punctuation, and physical layout that is acceptable in poetry. Budding poets can even choose from a selection of background music to further frame the writing mood.

Over the next several weeks, students worked individually or in pairs to write and rewrite their own original poems using the writing tool *In My Own Voice*. When they all had poems they were proud of, Mrs. Hancock planned one more extension to the project.

The students used another tool program called *Blocks in Motion* to design an electronic illustration to accompany their poems. They used the various backgrounds and motions to create a scene they envisioned when they thought about their poem. Once each student had

finished experimenting and each had designed a finished visual representation of their poem, a recording was made of each student poet reading his or her poem. The audio recordings would play in an electronic slide show of the student creations.

The class held a gallery day when Ms Johnson invited other classes to visit the poets. Not only had students learned about poetry, but they had personally experienced what it feels like to be a poet (Bitter and Pierson 1999, 100).

1. In addition to the content and processes students learn through the use of educational software, what "lessons" might they learn through the "hidden curriculum" created by educational software?

2. In regard to the subject area and grade level for which you are preparing to teach, what are the advantages and disadvantages of teaching concepts with and without educational software?

3. Based on your experiences, is educational software educationally sound? Does some software rely too heavily on "bells and whistles" to entertain students?

4. To what extent is quality educational software currently available for the subject area and grade level for which you are preparing to teach?

Canadian Parents for French (CPF) was formed in 1977 to help increase student success rates in French as a second language. The CPF Report on The State of French Second Language Education in Canada (2002) notes that of the seven provincial or territorial jurisdictions west of Ontario, only in the Yukon is French compulsory for any part of a student's career, and even there it is only required from Grades 3 to 8. In February 2000, Canadian Heritage and the Council of Ministers of Education, Canada, signed a memorandum of understanding to provide quality second-language instruction in primary and secondary schools. The bilateral agreements that the Canadian Heritage Department signed with the provinces and territories contain action plans and contributed $42.7 million to the provinces and territories (Canadian Heritage 2002).

In **core French**, the second language is taught in periods that vary in length from school to school. Provinces may recommend a basic core French structure and the school boards may also influence the program. The aims of core French are as follows:

- Basic communication skills
- Language knowledge
- An appreciation of French culture in Canada and beyond

(*Source*: Turnbull 2000)

Core French concentrates on speaking, reading, listening, and writing in French. As of the year 2000, two million elementary students, and approximately one million secondary students, were taking core French. The trend in core French instruction is teaching through themes designed to interest students by considering learners' life experiences, intellectual development, and interests. Core French now aims to expose students to more spoken French and to use their skills to communicate in real-life situations. In the beginning, curriculum emphasizes listening and speaking. Later, the emphasis on reading and writing increases. Core curriculum also features learning about Francophone culture, with an emphasis on French-speaking Canada.

About 317 000 Canadian students are in **French Immersion** programs. In immersion, instruction is mostly in French. Subjects like math, science, and music are taught in French. The language is the medium and not the object of instruction. The goal of immersion is for learners to achieve a level of fluency to function well in a French-speaking community, work in a French-speaking community, or pursue postsecondary education in French. The Canadian Association of Immersion Teachers (CAIT) works to promote and improve immersion programs in Canada.

The Canadian Association of Second Language Teachers (CASLT) is a national organization that promotes the advancement of second language opportunities. There are no national standards for second language teaching in Canada, but CASLT (2003) has issued the following statement of beliefs on www.caslt.org to act as a guide:

- We believe that being able to communicate in a second language contributes to the full development of the human potential.
- We believe that every individual is capable of learning a second language according to his or her needs, interests, and abilities.
- We believe that the opportunity to learn a second language is a fundamental human right.
- We believe that second language learning is an essential component of a formal education.

The Arts

More than any other area of the curriculum, the arts have held an insecure position. When schools have faced budgetary cutbacks or pressure to raise scores on basic skills tests, a cost-conscious public has often considered the elimination of music and art. The arts as a means of expression are especially important in the context of current educational reform. "Hard" evidence on the importance of the arts has appeared in the media, academic journals, and various national reports. *Arts Education: Basic to Learning*, a report by the Northwest Regional Educational Laboratory, points out the following:

- In 1995 College Board testing, students who studied the arts for at least four years score 59 points higher on the verbal portion of the SAT, and 44 points higher on math, than students with no experience or coursework in the arts.
- According to a 1997 report from the Department of Education, "Children naturally sing, dance, draw, and role-play in an effort to understand the world around them

and communicate their thoughts about it. A growing body of evidence demonstrates that when their caretakers engage them in these activities early in life on a regular basis, they are helping to wire the children's brains for successful learning."

- In studies at [the] University of California at Irvine, IQ scores go up among college students who listen to classical recordings immediately before testing—a phenomenon nicknamed the "Mozart Effect."
- Arts education programs are related to safer and more orderly school environments.
- Schools with strong arts programs report better attendance, increased graduation rates, improved multicultural understanding, greater community support, invigorated faculty, and the development of higher-order thinking skills, creativity, and problem-solving ability among students.
- The arts serve students with special needs, including those who are in danger of falling through the cracks of the educational system, and allow success "for people who have been defined as failures" (Northwest Regional Educational Laboratory, 1999, 5).

Typically, elementary art and music are limited to one period a week, and this instruction is given either by regular teachers or by special teachers who travel from school to school. In addition, most elementary students have occasional opportunities to use crayons, watercolours, clay, and other art materials as they learn in other subject areas. And, from time to time, many children even have the opportunity to experience dance, puppetry, role-play, pantomime, and crafts.

At the middle and junior high level, instruction in art and music becomes more structured, as well as more voluntary. Students may choose from band, chorus, arts, and crafts. At the high school level, art and music are usually offered as electives.

Physical Education

The ultimate aim of physical education is to promote physical activities that develop a desire in the individual to maintain physical fitness throughout life. More specifically, the National Association for Sport and Physical Education (U.S.) has stated that a physically educated student does the following:

1. Demonstrates competency in many movement forms and proficiency in a few movement forms.
2. Applies movement concepts and principles to the learning and development of motor skills.
3. Exhibits a physically active lifestyle.
4. Achieves and maintains a health-enhancing level of physical fitness.
5. Demonstrates responsible personal and social behaviour in physical activity settings.
6. Demonstrates understanding and respect for differences among people in physical activity settings.
7. Understands that physical activity provides opportunities for enjoyment, challenge, self-expression, and social interaction (National Association for Sport and Physical Education 1999).

In addition to their participation in activities, students in physical education programs may receive instruction in health and nutrition, sex education, and driver education.

At one time, physical education programs consisted largely of highly competitive team sports. Many children, less aggressive and competitive than their peers, did not do well in such programs and experienced a lowered sense of self-esteem. Gradually, instructors began to offer activities designed to meet the needs and abilities of all students, not just the athletically talented. In addition to traditional team sports such as football, baseball, and basketball, and individual sports such as swimming and wrestling, many students in Grades K–12 may now participate in a broad array of physical activities, including aerobics, archery, badminton, dodgeball, folk and square dancing, gymnastics, handball, hockey, table tennis, golf, racquetball, shuffleboard, skating, volleyball, soccer, and yoga.

The Canadian Association for Health, Physical Education, Recreation and Dance is an advocacy group that lobbies for health and fitness programs in schools and communities. Although there are no pan-Canadian standards in the area of physical education curricula, most provinces endorse the Quality Daily Education program standards of daily activity of 30 to 60 min that emphasize enjoyment, health, personal fulfillment, and success (CAHPERD 1998).

School-to-Work Transitions

In the mid 1990s, many high schools formed partnerships with the private sector and began to develop school-to-work programs to address current and future needs in industry. In many provinces, **school-to-work programs** and **Cooperative Education programs** offer students the opportunity to develop employability skills and explore career options. For example, the objectives of Cooperative Education programs in New Brunswick are as follows:

- Provide students with an opportunity to gain knowledge and work experience in a career area of their choice.
- Assist students in developing and expanding employability skills.
- Foster positive student expectations and attitudes toward self, others, school, and work.
- Develop awareness of better accessibility to students in various occupations.
- Encourage cooperation between the business community and educational system.
- Provide employers with a talent pool of trained and prepared potential employees.

The program allows students to participate in a regular school program while at the same time developing employability skills through participation in 40–55 h of in-school instruction and 125–195 h of non-paid experience.

In Nova Scotia, the School-to-Work Transition program involves a school program offered in Grades 11 and 12 that features an in-school component and a work experience component. The objective of the program is to facilitate transitions from school to work by providing skills that might increase high school students' likelihood of becoming employed in desirable jobs. It is also designed to help students make better educational and occupational choices and to gain realistic expectations about future occupations.

Implemented in the fall of 2002, the new Ontario high school program reflects a belief in the importance of out of class career-related experiences for students. It requires all school boards to offer co-operative education, work experience, and school-to-work transition programs. In addition, students are also required to participate in 40 h of community involvement that will give them additional experience outside the classroom.

Curriculum will likely continue to focus on opportunities that take students outside the traditional walls of the classroom to develop knowledge, confidence, and skills to help them in the workplace.

SUMMARY

What Is Taught in Schools?

- There are many different definitions for the term *curriculum*. A general definition is that *curriculum* refers to the experiences, both planned and unplanned, that either enhance or impede the education and growth of students.

- There are four curricula that all students experience. In addition to learning what teachers intend to teach (the explicit curriculum), students learn from the hidden curriculum, the null curriculum, and extracurricular/cocurricular programs.

- From school policies to national politics, many factors influence what is taught (and not taught) in the schools.

How Is the School Curriculum Developed?

- Curricula are based on the needs and interests of students and also reflect a variety of professional, commercial, local, provincial, national, and international pressures.

- Teachers must be prepared to assume important roles in the curriculum development process, especially in developing student-centred and integrated curricula.

What Reform Efforts Have Affected the Curriculum?

- Historical forces affecting the aims of education have influenced curriculum reform. In any historical period, curriculum content reflects society's beliefs and values about education.

- Recent systematic efforts to establish curriculum reforms have focused on curriculum standards, core curricula, and education for equity and excellence.

What Are Some Current Subject-Area Trends?

- Alternative curricula for literacy, multicultural curricula, character education, art as curriculum, problem-centred learning, thinking skills, computer literacy, and career education are examples of curriculum trends today.

- Curriculum trends also involve, for example, redefining foreign language study and sex/health education, developing school-to-work programs, providing for active and authentic learning, determining what students will need to know and be able to do in the twenty-first century, and establishing standards in the content areas.

KEY TERMS AND CONCEPTS

Cooperative Education programs, 320
core curriculum, 306
core French, 317
curriculum, 294
explicit curriculum, 295

extracurricular/cocurricular programs, 297
French Immersion, 318
hidden curriculum, 295
inquiry-based curriculum, 306

integrated curriculum, 299
null curriculum, 296
outcome-based education, 307
performance-based education, 307

APPLICATIONS AND ACTIVITIES

Teacher's Journal

1. List in order of importance the five factors that you believe have the greatest impact on the curriculum. Then list the five factors that you believe *ideally* should have the greatest influence. What differences do you notice between your actual and ideal lists? What might be done to reduce the differences between the two lists?

2. Reflect on the 12 000 or so hours that you have spent as a student in K–12 class-rooms. What did the nonexplicit curricula in the classes teach you about yourself?

3. What religious and political emphases affected your learning as a student in elementary school or high school? Which experiences do you view as having been positive for you? Which do you view as having been negative for you?

4. In your opinion, how should teachers and schools respond to censorship issues in the curricula and complaints about the content of instructional materials?

5. What is your opinion of the current emphasis on preparing students for the world of work as the chief aim of education? What influences have created this emphasis? What curriculum goals might be sacrificed through a focus on turning out good employees?

Teacher's Database

1. Visit the online ERIC Clearinghouse for a curricular area you plan to teach, and record information for your portfolio on the resources available to you as a teacher in that content area.

2. Survey the internet to begin locating and bookmarking websites, schools, networks, and teacher discussion groups that you could use to help develop a subject-area curriculum for your students.

3. Find the professional curriculum standards for your subject area(s) online and compare them to the curriculum standards for that subject area in a province where you plan to teach. For example, you might download the National Council for Teachers of Mathematics (NCTM) standards and then compare them with the mathematics curriculum in the province where you plan to teach.

Observations and Interviews

1. Spend a half-day at school at the level you plan to teach and record your impressions regarding the types of curricula. If possible, chat briefly with administrators, teachers, and students about your impressions. Include observations of students outside the classroom during the school day.

2. As a collaborative project, conduct an informal survey on what people think are the four most important subjects to be taught at the elementary, middle, junior, and senior high levels. Compare your data with the information in this chapter.

3. With classmates, as an experiment, practice the process of curriculum development described in this chapter. Assign some members of the group to observe and report on their observations in relation to concepts presented in this chapter.

Professional Portfolio

Compare and contrast two or more textbooks or curriculum guides that are currently used by teachers to teach a unit in a subject area and at a grade level you are preparing to teach. Assess the strengths and weaknesses of the unit in each textbook or curriculum guide. Would you use the materials in your classroom? How would you improve them? What other curriculum materials would you incorporate? How would you integrate educational technology? How would you adapt the curriculum for the unit for individual students according to their needs and characteristics?

Appendix 8.1

The following are among the many recently published resources available for curriculum planning in the various subject areas. Many of these materials are available in online and CD-ROM versions as well as print.

Reading and Writing

Publications

Becoming a Reader: A Developmental Approach to Reading Instruction, 2nd ed. Michael P. O'Donnell and Margo Wood. Boston: Allyn and Bacon, 1999.

Best Books for Beginning Readers. Thomas G. Gunning. Boston: Allyn and Bacon, 1998.

Children's Inquiry: Using Language to Make Sense of the World. Judith Wells Lindfors. *Teaching for a Tolerant World, Grades K-6*. Judith P. Robertson (Ed.). New York: Teachers College Press, 1999.

Children's Writing: Perspectives from Research. Karin L. Dahl and Nancy Farnan. Newark, DE: International Reading Association, 1998.

Essentials of Children's Literature, 3rd ed. Carol Lynch-Brown and Carl M. Tomlinson. Boston: Allyn and Bacon, 1999.

Essentials of Elementary Language Arts, 2nd ed. Margo Wood. Boston: Allyn and Bacon, 1999.

Ideas Plus: Book Fifteen. Champaign, IL: National Council of Teachers of English, 1997.

Learning in Living Color: Using Literature to Incorporate Multicultural Education into the Primary Curriculum. Alora Valdez. Boston: Allyn and Bacon, 1999.

Literacy Instruction in Half- and Whole-Day Kindergartens: Research to Practice. Lesley Mandel Morrow, Dorothy S. Strickland, and Deborah Gee Woo. Newark, DE: International Reading Association, 1998.

NAEP 1998 Reading Report Card for the Nation and States. Washington, DC: National Assessment of Educational Progress, 1999.

Practical Applications of the Language Experience: Looking Back, Looking Forward. Olga G. Nelson and Wayne M. Linek. Boston: Allyn and Bacon, 1999.

Popular Culture in the Classroom: Teaching and Researching Critical Media Literacy. Donna E. Alvermann, Jennifer S. Moon, and Margaret C. Hagood. Newark, DE: International Reading Association, 1999.

Resilient Children: Stories of Poverty, Drug Exposure, and Literacy Development. Diane Barone. Newark, DE: International Reading Association, 1999.

Scaffolding Emergent Literacy: A Child-centered Approach for Preschool through Grade 5. Anne K. Soderman, Kara M. Gregory, and Louise T. O'Neill. Boston: Allyn and Bacon, 1999.

Teaching Children to Read and Write: Becoming an Influential Teacher, 2nd ed. Boston: Allyn and Bacon, 1999.

Teaching Language Arts: A Student- and Response-Centered Classroom, 3rd ed. Connie Cox. Boston: Allyn and Bacon, 1999.

Teaching Reading in the 21st Century, web ed. Michael F. Graves, Connie Juel, and Bonnie B. Graves. Boston: Allyn and Bacon, 1999.

Teaching Writing in Middle and Secondary Schools: Theory, Research and Practice. Margot Iris Soven. Boston: Allyn and Bacon, 1999.

Writing Framework and Specifications for the 1998 National Assessment of Educational Progress. Washington, DC: National Assessment of Educational Progress, 1999.

Journals
English Education
English Journal
Language Arts
The Reading Teacher

Web Site
The Canadian Council for Teachers of English Language Arts
www.cctela.ca

Mathematics

Publications

Activities for Junior High School and Middle School Mathematics, Vol. 2. Kenneth E. Easterday, F. Morgan Simpson, and Tommy Smith. Reston, VA: National Council of Teachers of Mathematics, 1998.

Essentials of Elementary Mathematics, 2nd ed. C. Alan Riedesel and James E. Schwartz. Boston: Allyn and Bacon, 1999.

Future Basics: Developing Numerical Power. Randall Charles and Joanne Lobato. Reston, VA: National Council of Supervisors of Mathematics, 1998.

Mathematics in the Middle. Larry Leutzinger (ed.). Reston, VA: National Council of Teachers of Mathematics, and Columbus, OH: National Middle School Association, 1998.

Middle Grades Mathematics Textbooks: A Benchmark-based Evaluation (book and CD-ROM). American Association for the Advancement of Science. New York: Oxford University Press, 1999.

School Policies and Practices Affecting Instruction in Mathematics. Evelyn F. Hawkins, Frances B. Stancavage, and John A. Dossey. Washington, DC: National Assessment of Educational Progress (NAEP), 1998.

Spreadsheet Activities in Middle School Mathematics, 2nd ed., *revised for Macintosh and ClarisWorks.* John C. Russell. Reston, VA: National Council of Teachers of Mathematics, 1998.

Teacher-made Aids for Elementary School Mathematics: Readings from The Arithmetic Teacher *and* Teaching Children Mathematics, Vol. 3. Carole J. Reesink (ed.). Reston, VA: National Council of Teachers of Mathematics, 1998.

Teaching Mathematics: A Sourcebook of Aids, Activities, and Strategies, 3rd ed. Max A. Sobel and Evan M. Maletsky. Boston: Allyn and Bacon, 1999.

The Wonderful World of Mathematics: A Critically Annotated List of Children's Books in Mathematics, 2nd ed. Diane Thiessen, Margaret Matthais, and Jacquelin Smith. Reston, VA: National Council of Teachers of Mathematics, 1998.

Journals
Arithmetic Teacher
The Journal of Computers in Mathematics and Science Teaching
Mathematics Teacher
School Science and Mathematics

Web Site
Math Central mathcentral.uregina.ca/ SchoolNet Resource Pages
www.schoolnet.ca/home/e/resources/

Science and Technology

Publications
Atlas of Science Literacy: Mapping K–12 Learning Goals. American Association for the Advancement of Science. New York: Oxford University Press, 2000.

Benchmarks for Science Literacy: A Tool for Curriculum Reform. American Association for the Advancement of Science. New York: Oxford University Press, 1993.

Blueprints for Reform: Science, Mathematics, and Technology Education. American Association for the Advancement of Science. New York: Oxford University Press, 1998.

Designs for Science Literacy. American Association for the Advancement of Science. New York: Oxford University Press, 1999.

Discovering Elementary Science: Method, Content, and Problem-solving Activities, 2nd ed. Boston: Allyn and Bacon, 1999.

Essentials of Elementary Science. Daniel C. Dobey, Robert J. Beichner, Sharon L. Raimondi. Boston: Allyn and Bacon, 1999.

Resources for Science Literacy: Professional Development, Helping Teachers Understand and Use Science Literacy Goals. (CD-ROM and companion paperback). American Association for the Advancement of Science. New York: Oxford University Press, 1997.

Science for All Children: Lessons for Constructing Understanding. Ralph Martin, Colleen Sexton, and Jack Gerlovich. Boston: Allyn and Bacon, 1999.

Journals
American Biology Teacher
Physics Teacher
School Science and Mathematics
Science and Children
Science Education
Science Teacher
Studies in Science Education

Web Sites
The Common Framework for Science Learning
www.cmec.ca/science/framework

Yes I Can! Science
http://yesican.yorku.ca

Canadian Curriculum Resources
www.aldershot.ednet.ns.ca/curriculum/ CanadianREsources/canadiansubjects/ science.html

Manipulatives and Resources: The Ontario Science Curriculum
www.exclusiveeducational.ca/science.html

The Canadian Science and Engineering Hall of Fame
www.science-tech.nmstc.ca/english/about/ hallfame/u_main_e.cfm

Canada Science and Technology Museum
www.science-tech.nmstc.ca

Saskatchewan Science Centre
www.sasksciencecentre.com

Social Studies and Geography

Publications
Because We Can Change the World: A Practical Guide to Building Cooperative, Inclusive, Classroom Communities. Mara Sapon-Shevin. Boston: Allyn and Bacon, 1999.

Essentials of Elementary Social Studies. Thomas N. Turner. Boston: Allyn and Bacon, 1999.

Appendix 8.1 *(continued)*

Classroom-Ready Activities for Teaching History and Geography in Grades 7–12. Thomas P. Ruff and Jennifer T. Nelson. Boston: Allyn and Bacon, 1998.

Global Perspectives for Educators. Carlos F. Diaz, Byron G. Massialas, and John A. Xanthopoulos. Boston: Allyn and Bacon, 1999.

Middle Grades Social Studies: Teaching and Learning for Active and Responsible Citizenship, 2nd ed. Michael G. Allen and Robert L. Stevens. Boston: Allyn and Bacon, 1998.

Teaching for a Tolerant World, Grades K–6. Judith P. Robertson (ed.). Champaign, IL: National Council of Teachers of English, 1999.

Teaching for a Tolerant World, Grades 9–12. Carol Danks and Leatrice B. Rabinsky (eds.). Champaign, IL: National Council of Teachers of English, 1999.

Journals
History Teacher
Social Education
The Social Studies
Social Studies and the Young Learner
Social Studies Journal

Web Sites
Canadian Heritage
www.canadianheritage.gc.ca/index_e.cfm

Statistics Canada
www.statcan.ca

Canada's Parliament
www.parl.gc.ca

Canadian War Museum
www.civilizations.ca/cwme/asp

Canadian Online History
canadahistory.about.com/cs/history/

Federal and Provincial Human Rights Commission
www.chrc-ccdp.ca

Gander Academy's Theme-Related Resources on the World Wide Web
www.stemnet.nf.ca/CITE/themes.html

Human Rights Internet
www.hri.ca/welcome.asp

Humanities Canada
www.fedcan.ca/

Communication Canada
www.communication.gc.ca/

Online Resources for Canadian Heritage
www.civilization.ca/orch/www00_e.html

National Council for Social Studies
www.ncss.org

Foreign Languages

Second Language Education

Publications
Content-Based Instruction in Foreign Language Education: Models and Methods. Stephen B. Stryker and Betty Lou Leaver. Washington, DC: Georgetown University Press, 1997.

Language and Cognitive Development in Second Language Learning: Educational Implications for Children and Adults. Virginia Gonzalez. Boston: Allyn and Bacon, 1999.

Technology-Enhanced Language Learning. Michael D. Bush and Robert M. Terry (eds.). Lincolnwood, IL: National Textbook Co., 1997.

Understanding Learning Styles in the Second Language Classroom. Joy M. Reide (ed.). Upper Saddle River, NJ: Prentice Hall Regents, 1998.

Journals
Modern Language Journal
Modern Language Quarterly
Modern Languages

Web Sites
The Canadian Association of Second Language Teachers
www.calt.org

Language Training Canada
ww.edu.psc-cfp.gc.ca

The Arts

Publications
The Arts in Children's Lives: Aesthetic Education in Early Childhood. Mary Renck Lalongo and Laurie Nicholson Stamp. Boston: Allyn and Bacon, 1997.

Learning in and Through Arts: A Guide to Discipline-based Art Education. Stephen Mark Dobbs. Los Angeles: Getty Education Institute for the Arts, 1998.

The Quiet Evolution: Changing the Face of Arts Education. Brent Wilson. Los Angeles: Getty Education Institute for the Arts, 1996.

Journals
Art Education
Music Educator's Journal
School Arts

Physical Education

Publications

Concepts of Physical Education: What Every Student Needs to Know. Reston, VA: National Association for Sport and Physical Education, 1998.

Dynamic Physical Education for Elementary School Children, 12th ed. Robert P. Pangrazi. Boston: Allyn and Bacon, 1998.

Eastern District Association's Guidelines for Physical Education Programs: Standards, Objectives, and Assessments for Grades K-12. Steveda F. Chepko and Ree K. Arnold. Boston: Allyn and Bacon, 1999.

Moving into the Future: National Physical Education Standards: A Guide to Content and Assessment. Reston, VA: National Association for Sport and Physical Education, 1995.

Physical Activity for Children: A Statement of Guidelines. Reston, VA: National Association for Sport and Physical Education, 1998.

Physical Education Methods for Classroom Teachers. Human Kinetics with Bonnie Pettifor. Champaign, IL: Human Kinetics, 1999.

Journals

Journal for Physical Education, Recreation and Dance Journal of Health Education Research Quarterly for Exercise and Sport Strategies

Web Sites

Canadian Fitness and Lifestyle Research Institute
www.cflri.ca

Health Canada
www.hc-sc.gc.ca

PACE Canada
www.pace-canada.org/links3.htm

The Canadian Association of Health Physical Education Recreation and Dance
www.cahperd.ca

The Canadian Health Network
www.canadian-health-network.ca

Vocational Education

Publications

Career and Technical Educator's Survival Guide. Alexandria, VA: Association for Career and Technical Education, 1999.

Curriculum Development in Vocational and Technical Education: Planning, Content, and Implementation, 5th ed. Curtis R. Finch and John R. Crunkilton. Boston: Allyn and Bacon, 1999.

High Skill, High-Wage Jobs. Kristen J. Amundson. Alexandria, VA: Association for Career and Technical Education, 1998.

Making the Case—for School-to-Careers and Vocational Education. Alexandria, VA: Association for Career and Technical Education, 1997.

Taking the Worry out of Work-based Learning: The Law, Labor & School-to-Careers. Alice Potosky. Alexandria, VA: Association for Career and Technical Education, 1998.

Teaching Your Occupation to Others: A Guide to Surviving the First Year. Paul A. Bott. Boston: Allyn and Bacon, 1998.

The Dog Did It! And Other Classroom Stories from Vocational Educators. Alexandria, VA: Association for Career and Technical Education, 1998.

Journals

The Career Development Quarterly
Career Education
Techniques: Connecting Education and Careers

Teaching
with Technology

*Media and technologies [may]
greatly expand the range of teaching,
learning, and communication
modalities available to teachers and
students, but at bottom their only
value is in helping us to do other
things well—engage students deeply
in a topic, help them take more
responsibility for their learning, help
them learn to communicate clearly
about their work and their ideas.*

—Cornelia Brunner and William Tally
The New Media Literacy Handbook, 1999

focus questions

1. How are educational tools and technologies influencing schools?
2. What technologies are available for teaching?
3. What is the state of computer technology in the Canadian classroom?
4. What are the effects of computer technology on learning?
5. Should technology be at the forefront of efforts to improve schools?

At the South Shore Alternative High School in the Southwest District School Board, James Turner's Grade 11 Canadian History class is preparing for their Heritage Canada/YM+YWCA exchange to a community on Baffin Island. James wants to give his students a sense of where they are going and the people they will be meeting there. This includes how the Nunavut came to govern themselves and how they support themselves in the face of an economic reality very different from that of Atlantic Canada. The Grade 11 History curriculum has the following main themes: governance, sovereignty, justice, and development. The creation of a computer activity requires students to work with their own computer disc containing documents that have them complete tasks concerning each of the course themes in relation to the Nunavut region and its people. Each task features a link to a specific website, information, and links to other related sites. There is a series of questions that may be answered directly on the student disc; this enables the student to edit and revise their work as they complete their tasks. In addition, the students may contact Baffin Island school children and residents who will act as key pals to provide more information for their assignment.

In the Queen Charlotte School in District 50, the Technological Supported Program for the Visually Impaired provides such assistive technology aids as a Braille printer to produce transcribed texts and class materials. A special large screen monitor and CPU with large font and high contrast settings has been developed for the network. A Braille light enables students to take class notes. The students have Jaws software to use while researching, emailing, and chatting on the internet.

This same school district offers a Remote Adult Education Program to provide courses for adults living on another island that does not provide an adult learning centre. Students are provided with spare computers that become available when school computer labs are updated. The adult learners can connect to the school server through an 800 number phone line that is provided for them.

Sources: James Turner, teacher at South Shore Alternative High School in the Southwest Regional School Board in Nova Scotia; Canada's SchoolNet Network of Innovative Schools www.schoolnet.ca/nis-rei/e/members/view_school.asp?sid=40

In the previous contrasting settings, students and teachers are using computer technology in very different ways. The Grade 11 History teacher uses computers to present information to students and to encourage them to expand their understanding of cultural diversity. Further, technology encourages the development of research, writing, and communication skills. In the Queen Charlotte School District, visually impaired students are provided with tools to assist them in the learning process. For the adult learners living in remote island locations, technology is the tool that enables them to avail themselves of formal learning opportunities from their own communities. Although these examples are strikingly different, they are similar in that teachers are using the computer as a "tool" to achieve their educational goals and to create particular kinds of learning environments.

How Are Educational Tools and Technologies Influencing Schools?

Elijah Knockwood's elementary classroom looks like those of talented teachers everywhere—lively, filled with displays of students' work, photos of field trips, and information-filled posters. A closer look, however, reveals how computers have transformed teaching and learning in his classroom. Several computers in the room allow students to communicate via the internet with other students in Germany, Holland, Russia, and Australia. Knockwood's students also use child-oriented "search engines" like *Yahooligans*! and KidsLink to search for information about whales, the Brazilian rain forest, or the planet Mars on the web. They go to "chat rooms" or "newsgroups" for children, where they can "talk" to other children around the world or participate in various global networking projects for children.

Knockwood's classroom and the classrooms featured in this chapter's opening scenario are representative of how recently developed technologies have transformed the learning environments in thousands of schools around the country. Moreover, the pace of change shows no signs of letting up—as one technology expert said, "We may well assume that we haven't seen anything yet. [If] present trends continue, it seems not unreasonable to expect that digital technologies will have an impact on our classrooms proportionate to that of writing and the printing press" (Withrow 1997, 4). Similarly, foremost futurist, Marvin Cetron, has predicted that "Computers will free educators to adopt much more sophisticated, effective, and rewarding styles of teaching. Future teachers will be facilitators, monitors, and catalysts, rather than lecturers and taskmasters" (Cetron 1997, 19–20).

Technology and the Challenge to Schools

The internet, web, and related telecommunications technologies have the potential to transform teaching and learning. However, one of the education issues for the twenty-first century is how committed are teachers, administrators, policymakers, parents, and the general public to enabling students to realize the full impact that technology can have on their learning?

Additionally, educators must develop new assessment techniques to evaluate students' learning that occurs through the use of advanced telecommunications like the internet and the web. The number of correct responses on homework, quizzes, and examinations will no longer suffice to measure students' learning. "If teachers want students to be able to use ditto masters, then they shouldn't spend thousands of dollars on systems that support computer-assisted instruction. If teachers want to reinforce their didactic role and their role as information providers, then they should also leave computers alone" (Morton 1996, 419).

In its *School Technology and Readiness Report*, the CEO Forum on Education and Technology (1999) called on teachers to incorporate technologies to create "new learning environments" that enable students to develop higher-order thinking skills to research, analyze, and creatively solve problems in the future. The following chart contrasts the "traditional" and "new" learning environments envisioned by the Forum.

Traditional Learning Environment	New Learning Environment
Teacher-centred instruction ⟶	Student-centred learning
Single-sense stimulation ⟶	Multisensory stimulation
Single-path progression ⟶	Multipath progression
Single medium ⟶	Multimedia
Isolated work ⟶	Collaborative work
Information delivery ⟶	Information exchange
Passive learning ⟶	Active/exploratory/inquiry-based learning
Factual, knowledge-based ⟶	Critical thinking and informed decision making
Reactive response ⟶	Proactive/planner action
Isolated, artificial context ⟶	Authentic, real-world context

When you think about your future as a teacher who will be expected to use technology to create a "new learning environment," you may find that future at once exciting and intimidating, enticing, and threatening. You may ask, will I be ready to meet the challenge of integrating technologies into my teaching? In a very real sense, it is in the hands of people like you to develop new ways to use new technologies in the classrooms of tomorrow. The following "Professional Reflection" is designed to help you begin the process of planning for that future.

Following is a list of educational technologies and instructional strategies that are currently changing teaching and learning. For each, indicate with an X whether you are "proficient," "somewhat proficient," or "not proficient" with that technology or strategy. Then indicate whether you are "highly committed," "somewhat committed," "opposed," or "neutral" toward using that technology or strategy in your teaching. Space is provided for you to add technologies and strategies not on the list.

After responding to the items, reflect on those to which you are "highly committed" to integrating into your teaching. What steps will you take from this point on to ensure that those technologies and strategies will, in fact, be part of your teaching in the future?

Technology or Instructional Strategy	Proficiency Level			Commitment to Using			
	Proficient	Somewhat proficient	Not proficient	Highly committed	Somewhat committed	Opposed	Neutral
1. Student networking via computer							
2. Video teleconferencing							
3. Interactive multimedia/ hypermedia							
4. Web page authoring							
5. CD-ROMs/ DVD							
6. Computer assisted instruction (CAI)							
7. Word processing							
8. Desktop publishing							
9. Presentation graphics							
10. Spreadsheets/graphing							
11. Databases							
12. email							
13. Attaching files to email							
14. Newsgroups							
15. Electronic gradebook							
16. Information retrieval on the web							
17. Networking with a file server							
18. Scanners							
19. Faxes							
20. Digital cameras							
21. Video cameras							
22. Other _____							
23. Other _____							

What Technologies Are Available for Teaching?

To enhance their classroom instruction, today's teachers can draw from a dazzling array of technological devices. Little more than a decade ago, the technology available to teachers who wished to use more than the chalkboard was limited to an overhead projector, a 16-mm movie projector, a tape recorder, and, in a few forward-looking school districts, television sets. Today, teachers and students use ever-more-powerful desktop and laptop computers with built-in modems, faxes, and CD-ROM players; videodisc players; camcorders; optical scanners; speech and music synthesizers; laser printers, digital cameras, and LCD projection panels. In addition, they use sophisticated software for web browsing, email, word processing, desktop publishing, presentation graphics, spreadsheets, databases, and multimedia applications.

Although the array of currently available technology for the classroom is dazzling, Marvin Cetron predicts that future technologies will be even more impressive. He contends that by 2010 an "Information Appliance" (IA) "should be on the desks of most American students." The same might be expected in Canadian schools.

> The IA will be a computer, a fax machine, and a copier. Its 20 by 30 inch flat colour screen will be half multimedia display and half picture-phone. Two buttons will set it to translate automatically among any of nine common languages, enabling users who don't speak the same language to communicate.

> This new one-box-does-all data center will handle all our information and communication needs. Radio, 500 television channels (many designed for the classroom), email, web access, and all forms of personal computing will come through the IA. Aimed at consumers, its controls will be simple enough for small children to use. And because it will contain more raw computing power than today's top-of-the-line PCs, it will run educational software as sophisticated as any now available for multi-user classroom systems (Cetron 1997, 21).

While the term *educational technology* is usually taken to mean computers in the classroom, many different forms of technology have influenced education. If we broadly define **educational technology** as inventions that enable teachers to reach their goals more effectively, it is clear that for some time teachers have been integrating into their classrooms many forms of educational technology, from the humble chalkboard to the overhead projector. One technology that has had a long and perhaps controversial history in education is television.

The Television Revolution

The television revolution began with great optimism. David Sarnoff, who founded NBC and introduced the first colour television at the New York World's Fair in 1939, confidently predicted that television was "destined to provide greater knowledge to larger numbers of people, truer perception of the meaning of current events, more accurate appraisal of men in public life, and a broader understanding of the needs and aspirations of our fellow human beings" (Sarnoff 1940). Since that time, television has become an omnipresent feature of life. According to Statistics Canada (1999), 99 percent of Canadian households own a radio and a television set. Fifty-nine percent have two television sets, and more than a third have at least three. Eighty-one percent of all homes have cable television. The number of hours of television watched by Canadians per week increases with age. For example, in the 2–11 and 12–17 age groups, children spend an average of 15.5 h per week watching television. The average for the 18–24 age group is 15.7 h of television viewing per week.

Critics of television point out that it encourages passivity in the young, may be linked to increases in violence and crime, often reinforces sexual and ethnic stereotypes, retards growth and development, and may be linked to learning disorders. Psychologist Jerome Singers contends that "most [heavy-viewing] kids show lower information, lower reading recognition or readiness to reading, [and] lower reading levels; [and they] tend to show lower imaginativeness and less complex language usage" (quoted in Shenk 1998, 61). Some say that television robs children of the time they need to do homework, to read and reflect, and to build bonds with family members and others through interaction.

However, television can enhance students' learning. Excellent educational programs are aired by the Canadian Broadcasting Company (CBC), the Public Broadcasting Service (PBS), and by some cable and other commercial networks. Television has also had a positive impact on how students are taught in schools. With the increased availability of video equipment, many schools have begun to have students produce their own television documentaries, news programs, oral histories, and dramas. Many schools have closed-circuit television systems that teachers use to prepare instructional materials for students in the district, and many districts have **distance learning networks** that use two-way, interactive telecommunications to provide enrichment instruction to students in remote areas or staff development to teachers.

The Computer Revolution

In a two-part report aired on 25 and 26 March, 2002, CBC's "The National" visited Canadian schools that have fully incorporated computer technology in their classrooms. One of these, Elmwood, a private girls' school in Ottawa, demonstrates what is possible if costs are not an issue. Grade 10 and 11 Elmwood students each have their own laptops and carry them with them constantly, plugging them in before class begins. This gives them the opportunity to look over the day's lesson, make notes of anything they want to record, and capture snapshots of anything written on the board. Blackboards have been replaced by large computer screens connected to student laptops. With this widespread availability, the possibilities for enhancing the teaching/learning experience through computer technology are endless.

Although personal computers may not have transformed all schools so that all students have learning experiences like those at Elmwood, computers have had a significant impact on education. Like the dawn of the television era 60 years earlier, the widespread availability of personal computers has been heralded as a technological innovation that will change the teaching–learning process. As Bill Gates, founder of Microsoft, predicted in *The Road Ahead* (Gates, Myhrvold, and Rinearson 1996), "I expect education of all kinds to improve significantly within the next decade ... information technology will empower people of all ages, both inside and outside the classroom, to learn more easily, enjoyably, and successfully than ever before."

Computers and Instruction

Since the early 1980s, the use of computers to enhance instruction has grown steadily. Two of the more common approaches are computer-assisted instruction (CAI) (sometimes called computer-*aided* instruction) and computer-managed instruction (CMI). **Computer-assisted instruction (CAI)** relies on computer programs that provide students with highly structured drill-and-practice exercises or tutorials. Research has shown CAI to be effective with at-risk students and students with disabilities because it accommodates their special needs and instruction is appropriately paced (Bialo 1989; Jones 1994;

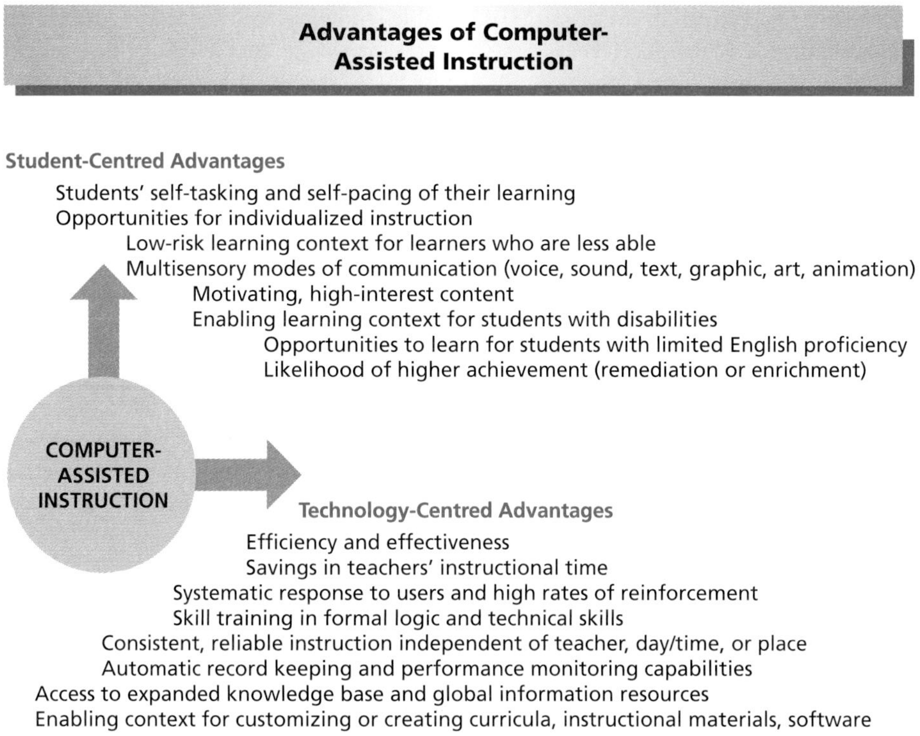

Figure 9.1

Advantages of
computer-assisted
instruction (CAI)

Advantages of Computer-Assisted Instruction

Student-Centred Advantages

Students' self-tasking and self-pacing of their learning
Opportunities for individualized instruction
Low-risk learning context for learners who are less able
Multisensory modes of communication (voice, sound, text, graphic, art, animation)
Motivating, high-interest content
Enabling learning context for students with disabilities
Opportunities to learn for students with limited English proficiency
Likelihood of higher achievement (remediation or enrichment)

COMPUTER-ASSISTED INSTRUCTION

Technology-Centred Advantages

Efficiency and effectiveness
Savings in teachers' instructional time
Systematic response to users and high rates of reinforcement
Skill training in formal logic and technical skills
Consistent, reliable instruction independent of teacher, day/time, or place
Automatic record keeping and performance monitoring capabilities
Access to expanded knowledge base and global information resources
Enabling context for customizing or creating curricula, instructional materials, software

Kozma et al. 1992; Norris 1994; Signer 1991). Moreover, CAI can provide students with a more positive, supportive environment for learning; students can avoid embarrassment since their inevitable mistakes while learning are not exposed to peers. Figure 9.1 presents several additional student-centred and technology-centred advantages of CAI.

Computer-managed instruction (CMI) relies on programs that evaluate and diagnose students' needs and then, based on that assessment, guide them through the next steps in their learning. CMI also records students' progress for teachers to monitor. CAI and CMI can result in reduced teacher–student interactions, if the teacher interprets his or her role as primarily that of record keeper or manager. On the other hand, CAI and CMI can enhance teacher–student interactions: "Freed from the necessity of conducting routine drills and performing many management duties, the teacher has more time to be the vital human link between student and knowledge. The computer does not supplant teachers; it supports them" (Bitter and Pierson 1999, 249).

An increasingly popular approach to computer-based instruction is computer-enhanced instruction (CEI). Unlike CAI and CMI, **computer-enhanced instruction (CEI)** is less structured and more inquiry-oriented. Unlike CAI or CMI, teachers in CEI play a critical role in facilitating interactions between computer and student—teachers "are [essential] to the learning process, because simply seating students in front of their computers to surf the Net will not result in the same learning curve as when teachers assign well-designed projects in which students use the Net to gather information" (Kirkpatrick and Cuban 1998).

Some schools are using another inquiry-oriented approach to enhancing instruction with computers—the microcomputer-based laboratory (MBL), sometimes called CBL (computer-based laboratory). Through probes and sensors attached to computers,

microcomputer-based laboratories (MBL) enable students to measure and graph data such as light, sound temperature, voltage, skin resistance, magnetic field, and heat flow. Students can gather data in the school laboratory or use a battery-operated interface to gather data in the field. For example, Concord Consortium, a nonprofit research and development organization dedicated to developing new ways to use technology in teaching, has developed MBL curriculum materials that enable students to learn about rain forests by using a sensor to gather local data for such variables as humidity, light, dissolved oxygen in rivers and streams, and acid rain. Students then compare local data with those obtained in an actual rain forest.

The Magic of Media

Personal computers have so revolutionized the instructional media available to teachers that today it is no exaggeration to refer to the "magic" of media. Some of the most exciting forms of media magic involve CD-ROMs, DVDs, and interactive multimedia. Recent advances in computer technology have made it possible for students to become much more active in shaping their learning experiences. On a **CD-ROM**, students can access the equivalent of about 270 000 pages of text, about nine hundred 300-page books; or on a Digital Videodisk (**DVD**) they can access the equivalent of about 54 000 photographic slides. Computer-supported **interactive multimedia** allow students to integrate information from huge text, audio, and video libraries.

Hypermedia

Systems consisting of computer, CD-ROM drive, DVD player, video monitor, and speakers now allow students to control and present sound, video images, text, and graphics with an almost limitless array of possibilities. Students who use such hypermedia systems, the most familiar of which is the web, can follow their curiosity, browse through enormous amounts of information, and develop creative solutions for multidimensional, real-life problem situations. Online databases in many fields are changing the way students conduct library research, as more computerized reference works—such as directories, dictionaries, and encyclopedias—become available.

The term **hypermedia** refers to documents composed of text, audio, and visual information stored in a computer and accessed by the user in a nonlinear fashion. "Rather than reading an information space sequentially in a pre-determined order, a user of [hypermedia] explores the information space in his or her own order, usually based on his or her interests" (Schwartz and Beichner 1999, 56), with the computer used to "link" related segments of information into larger "webs" or networks. A hypermedia system is an effective learning tool because it allows students to actively construct their own learning experiences based on their interests, preferences, and learning styles.

Computer Simulations

For students, computer simulations can be engaging and very motivational. Simulations model complex, multidimensional events in the real world and can range from the lemonade stand that elementary school students plan and run vicariously, practicing basic arithmetic and problem-solving skills, to a mock trial, which law students can participate in via videodisc and computer. As learners work their way through a simulation, they make decisions at critical points, enter their decisions into the computer, and then receive feedback on the consequences of those decisions.

Currently available **computer-based simulations** provide students with contextually rich learning experiences, from visiting the great museums of the world, to exploring the bottom of the Pacific Ocean, to experiencing what it was like to be a pioneer setting out in a wagon train travelling west. Figure 9.2, for example, shows a household water use simulator from *Exploring the Nardoo,* a CD-ROM program that focuses on a range of water management investigations related to the Nardoo, an imaginary river in Australia. The *Nardoo* program, developed by the Interactive Multimedia Learning Laboratory at the University of Wollongong in Australia, requires students to solve problems, measure, synthesize data, and communicate findings as they "conduct" research at the Water Research Centre. After students enter the number of baths, showers, toilet flushes, dish washings, car washes, and so on a hypothetical family uses per day, the simulator calculates the family's water usage and compares it with national averages. Students then implement various water-saving strategies throughout the household and rerun the simulation to determine the amount of water saved.

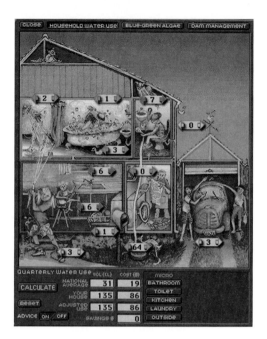

Figure 9.2

Household water use simulator from *Exploring the Nardoo*

Source: Interactive Multimedia Learning Laboratory, Faculty of Education, University of Wollongong, Wollongong, New South Wales, Australia. Used with permission.

Home–School Communication Systems

Computer-based home–school communication systems such as the Phone Master Notification System are helping busy teachers and parents exchange information. Interfacing a computer program with its computer-based student records can enable teachers to use a "Talking Gradebook" to communicate students' progress to parents. Or, by using a touchtone phone and entering a teacher's room number, students and parents can access homework assignments, test scores, and current grades. Increasingly, schools are using sophisticated **home–school communication systems** to strengthen their educational programs. Some communication systems even include a "tip line" that uses voice disguising to provide students with an anonymous, safe way to provide tips to help reduce school violence. Schools are also using home–school communication systems to disseminate the following kinds of information:

- absence and tardy parent notification
- PTA/PTO/SAC information
- invitations to school events
- school cancellations, early dismissals
- teacher reminders for assignments/activities
- lunch menus
- reminders of School Board meetings
- bus schedules
- congratulatory calls
- club information

The Internet

Observers estimate that the amount of information in the world doubles every 900 days (Bitter and Pierson 1999); the **internet,** consisting of thousands of interconnected computers around the globe, and the **web** (the most popular "entrance" to the internet) make available to teachers and students much of this information. As Table 9.1 shows, the size of the web has increased exponentially since 1995. In addition, newsgroups and chat rooms on the internet enable teachers and students to communicate with people around the world.

Teaching for
Excellence

Prime Minister's Award for Teaching Excellence Recipients: Stephen Gallagher and Jay Willman

Stephen Gallagher,
W.P Wagner School of Science and Technology,
Edmonton, Alberta

Jay Willman,
R. B. Russell Vocational High School,
Winnipeg, Manitoba

Stephen Gallagher, a physics, math, and calculus teacher, views technology as neither friend nor foe; he sees it as a tool. To Gallagher, technology is any machine or tool that expands and extends the users' natural abilities. New technologies are ideal for streamlining learning tasks. Computers, browser programs, and multimedia presentations illustrate complex processes such as the working of a carburetor or a chemical reaction more clearly and accurately than does a printed page. In these cases, technology clears the way for real learning.

Students in Gallagher's physics class, for example, dissect cattle eyeballs and intently compare the structures in the eyeball with the mechanisms of a dismantled video camera. Gallagher uses whatever technology that works to get his point across. "I want to match the technology to the learning task, and do it well," says Gallagher. And it doesn't matter if the technology is sophisticated or simple.

Gallagher's math students string plastic bags (a simple and cheap technology) weighted with volleyballs from the cafeteria ceiling to experiment and explore the mathematics of trigonometric curves. They monitor the swinging pendulums with a Calculator Based Ranger (CBR) connected to a graphing calculator (both considerably more sophisticated technologies) to display results. With technology's help, students grasp the difference between various equations quickly and easily, allowing for more time for hands-on experimentation. "They get really excited and the room buzzes," Gallagher reports. "They try different ways of swinging the pendulum, different places to measure the results and can see the mathematical results right away."

Jay Willman sees technology as a system or "any combination of human, machine, and idea that completes a task." The possibility of change inspires Willman as he works to create new structures for learning that benefit at-risk students such as those he teaches. At-risk students typically have poor reading and writing skills and struggle with social problems such as extreme poverty. "Many people in the community would never think of going to the library, even if they could get to it," says Willman. "Our school, right at the centre of the neighbourhood, is the obvious place to make computers and other technologies easily and freely available for research and learning." Providing a wide variety of learning programs and multimedia experiences allows transient, at-risk students, those without computers at home and the wider community to gain much needed exposure and experience with a computer.

Technology helps Jay Willman have the greatest effect he can have on a maximum number of students every day. He uses video technology to enhance a drama course called Community Action. Students create and present plays dealing with critical issues for inner-city youth. For a presentation on glue sniffing, Willman and his students videotaped a number of First Nations elders talking about why young people shouldn't sniff. For the presentation, Willman wrapped a screen onto a teepee shape and had the elementary audiences sit inside. "When our character was faced with the opportunity to sniff, the elders' faces and voices surrounded him, all talking about why he shouldn't. Then the narrator morphed into an eagle and flew away. You could see the impact on the kids. It was powerful."

Source: Reproduced with the permission of the Minister of Public Works and Government Services, 2003. Prime Minister's awards for teaching excellence: Exemplary practices. *Forging Alliances*. Retrieved 26 February, 2003, from http://pma-ppm.ic.gc/exemplary/1999/technology.htm

Table 9.1

Growth of the internet and the web

	1995	1999	2003
		Numbers (worldwide)	
People online*	26 million	179 million	605.6 million
Websites	230 million	4.4 million	9.04 million
Hosts (computers connected to internet)	6.64 million	43.23 million	171.6 million
pages	18 million	829 million	5 billion

*Figures include both adults and children
Note: Numbers are estimates.

Sources: Data compiled from Nua Ltd, Internet Surveys, 2003; Internet Software Consortium (ISC), 1999; *Adobe Magazine, 10*(2), 100, Spring 1999; Viz Marketing Ltd, 2003; Online Computer Library Centre, 2003; and Robert H. Zakon, Hobbes' Internet Timeline, 1999.

Newsgroups

Through **newsgroups,** students can create electronic bulletin boards of their own and discuss topics of mutual interest with students at other schools, in the same community, or around the world. Messages are "posted" on the bulletin board for others to read at their convenience. When students "visit" a newsgroup, they will find messages arranged by subject and author, with responses listed beneath the original message.

Chat Rooms

Students can also participate in "live" discussions held in a chat room. **Chat rooms** use internet Relay Chat (IRC) technology and allow users to participate in live, online, typed discussions. In some chat rooms, students can talk to online experts in a wide array of fields and receive immediate responses to their questions.

KIDLINK, a well-known chat room for children ages 10 to 15, is carefully monitored and open only to registered users. The goal of KIDLINK is to promote global dialogue among young people, and students must answer four questions when they register: (1) "Who am I?" (2) "What do I want to be when I grow up?" (3) "How do I want the world to be better when I grow up?" and (4) "What can I do now to make this happen?" Teacher-leaders of KIDLINK organize and monitor numerous projects; for example, the ongoing Family History Project has the following goals:

- To bring history alive for students by assisting them in learning how their family participated in "real" history
- To learn how previous generations actually lived, values they had, customs they practiced, and so on
- To promote creative writing skills
- To develop research and note-taking skills by "digging" around in the family tree
- To learn about other cultures by sharing with each other on the Kidproj list (an email list of participants)
- To increase computer skills by using word processing programs, perhaps drawing or graphics programs, email, listservs, and the web
- To learn more about community resources in individual geographical areas (Schwartz and Beichner 1999, 119–120).

highlights

Can the internet enhance school–home communication and parental involvement?

As the following table from the Fifth Phi Delta Kappa Poll of Teachers' Attitudes toward the Public Schools shows, both teachers and members of the public believe that traditional forms of communication such as newsletters and open houses are much more effective than internet chat rooms. Why do you think the internet is not seen as a more effective vehicle for school–home communication? Do parents who have the ability to communicate with schools and teachers via the internet have an unfair advantage over parents who do not have access to the internet? What suggestions do you have for how schools might use the internet more effectively to foster communication with their constituencies?

Here are some ways in which public schools try to open lines of communication with citizens. In your opinion, how effective do you think each of the following would be?

	Very and somewhat effective		Very effective	Somewhat effective	Not very effective	Not at all effective
	Teachers %	Public %	Teachers %	Teachers %	Teachers %	Teachers %
Public school newsletters	84	87 (2)	33	51	14	2
Public school open houses	81	89 (1)	35	46	15	3
Public school news hotlines	71	77 (5)	21	50	25	3
Neighbourhood discussion groups	66	81 (4)	19	47	28	6
Open hearings	62	85 (3)	16	46	32	6
Televised school board meetings	60	74 (6)	16	45	33	7
Internet "chat rooms" set up by your local school	55	63 (7)	13	42	34	11

(Numbers in parentheses indicate where the item ranks with the public. Not all rows add to 100 percent because of rounding.)

Source: Carol A. Langdon, "The Fifth Phi Delta Kappa Poll of Teachers' Attitudes Toward the Public Schools," *Phi Delta Kappan,* April 1999, p. 618.

Videoconferencing

Video conferences can be held over the internet if users have video cameras connected to their computers and CUWorld, Yahoo Messenger, or similar software installed. As with any educational technology, care must be taken that **videoconferencing** is more than a "high tech" way for teachers to lecture to passive students at other locations. "Videoconferencing best supports meaningful learning by helping diverse learners to collaborate and converse with each other in order to solve problems and construct meaning" (Jonassen, Peck, and Wilson 1999, 82)

What Is the State of Computer Technology in the Canadian Classroom?

As the chapter illustrates, an array of technologies is available for teacher use in the classroom. However, the availability and use of these tools for teaching and learning are two factors that have an influence on the power of technology to impact education. To what extent and how are teachers actually using new technologies? How accessible is technology to students?

How "Wired" Are the Schools?

Statistics Canada information reveals that the majority of Canadian schools are connected to the internet for educational purposes. However, despite the fact that 90 percent of Canadian Schools are online, education systems face significant challenges as they move towards effectively integrating this technology in the teaching/learning process.

According to a 1999 Statistics Canada survey of more than 4000 Canadian schools, more than 9 out of every 10 students at the elementary, middle, and secondary levels in Canada attended schools that had access to the internet. The national ratios of students per internet connected computer were 7:1 at the secondary level, 8:1 at the middle school, and 9:1 at the elementary level. The range of ratios varies from a low of 5:1 for secondary students in Manitoba to a high of 15:1 for elementary students in Nova Scotia. In some provinces—Prince Edward Island and New Brunswick, for example—all schools were connected to the internet at the time of the survey. (Statistics Canada 1999)

Regarding the location of internet connected computers in Canadian schools, the survey revealed that 59 percent of computers are located in computer labs, 32 percent in classrooms, and 9 percent in other areas of the schools.

Principals and school personnel reported a number of obstacles to fuller use of computer technology in the classroom; the most prominent were a lack of sufficient computers and insufficient professional development opportunities for teachers. In the Statistics Canada survey, principals cited a need for more computers in the classroom and more time for teachers to prepare courses that require the use of computers and to explore ways to integrate computer technology effectively into their curriculum. In addition, the principals observed that teachers needed more opportunities to upgrade their computer knowledge and skills and that the schools required technical support to maintain the computers and solve minor problems. (Statistics Canada 1999).

Progress

Progress is being made: the 1999 Statistics Canada survey concluded that there were, on average, seven students per computer in secondary schools. Seventy-three percent of students attended a middle or high school that had its own site on the web. In general, computers were more available to students in higher grades. Mathematics was the subject most likely to be taught in all three levels of schools using instructional software.

Most elementary students had access to software for word processing, encyclopedias on CD-ROM, spreadsheet packages, databases, and internet browsers. Additionally, middle and secondary students had widespread access to software for graphics, presentation, and programming.

The following chart presents the findings according to school level and content area:

Percentage of students attending a school using software according to school level and content area

	Math	Geography	Primary Language Instruction	Informatics
Elementary School	87	64	56	—
Middle School	76	57	—	53
Secondary School	79	64	—	75

Source: Based on information from Statistics Canada. Computer technology in schools. The Daily, October 12, 1999. Retrieved November 1, 2003 from www.statcan.ca/Daily/English/991012/d991012a.htm

Training and professional development opportunities and types of training taken vary considerably among teachers. Only about 30 percent of students at all three levels attended a school where it was mandatory for all teachers to take at least a basic computer-training course. Similarly, only 22 percent of students attended a school where it was mandatory for all teachers to take courses on a regular basis to keep up to date with new technological knowledge and skills. However, about 79 percent of the students were in a school where a large number of teachers had taken at least some basic computer courses. The course most frequently provided for teachers was an introductory application course.

"One Bite At A Time!"

The Canadian principal of a new high tech elementary school, Cheryl Scotland-Moxon, describes how her school staff has embraced technology:

During the past year I have had the opportunity, in my capacity as principal, to experience first hand all the trials, tribulations, and triumphs information technology creates in a new school. When we opened our doors to our new high tech elementary school in October of 2001, it seemed that we went from famine to feast. The amount of new technology we now had compared to what we used in the old building was overwhelming. Also overwhelming were the numerous challenges of what to do with all the new information technology. A saying frequently used at our school is, "You must eat the elephant one bite at a time." In other words, we had to realize that professional development opportunities were scarce, and no amount of complaining about being ill trained to use the technology was going to make it easier on us.

We realized that everyone had a different comfort zone with using and integrating technology in their teaching. Trying to use technology in a way to support curriculum was a greater task for those teachers who did not have any computer background. A balance needed to be struck with first learning how to use the technology tools, understanding the potential of the tools, and then using the tools to create quality, high level learning activities. These are all areas in which we continue to learn and grow. The teachers all have their own individual continuum of learning to integrate technology into their teaching. Given the demands of the curriculum, it was not very long before everyone clearly understood that technology is not curriculum. Rather, technology is a wonderful tool with endless possibilities to support the curriculum.

The challenge for teachers is learning from others, having opportunities to share and observe firsthand examples of quality technology integration in the curriculum and time to become "tech savvy." For educators to accomplish this feat, many things are needed. This takes time, personal motivation on behalf of the teacher to learn, support from the school administrator, support from the School Board, and from colleagues. It also means that we keep in balance our work in technology integration with all the other demands of the classroom. Remember, one bite at a time!

Source: Reprinted with permission from Cheryl Scotland-Moxon.

What Are the Effects of Computer Technology on Learning?

The use of computers and other technologies in schools has grown enormously since the early 1980s, and, as a director of the North Central Regional Education Laboratory noted, "For policymakers, the honeymoon for technology is over. They are starting to say, 'Show us the results'" (Williams 1999). In addition to information about the effects of technology on learning, there is a realization that "no one knows for certain [h]ow it is used" or "how much it is used" (Mehlinger 1996, 403). Since educational technology is a tool to help teachers teach more effectively, how it is used is critical. For example, one science teacher might use computers primarily for student drills on science terminology, while another science teacher might have students use computer simulations to determine the impact of urbanization on animal populations. The lack of information about how technology is being used in the schools aside, research results are just now beginning to appear on the long-term effects of technology on learning.

Apple Classrooms of Tomorrow (ACOT)

One of the most informative research studies is based on the Apple Classrooms of Tomorrow (ACOT) project launched in seven K–12 classrooms in 1986. Participating students and teachers each received two computers—one for school and one for home. Eight years later, study results indicated that all ACOT students performed as well as they were expected without computers, and some performed better. More important, perhaps, "the ACOT students routinely and without prompting employed inquiry, collaboration, and technological and problem-solving skills" (Mehlinger 1996, 405). Also, 90 percent of ACOT students went on to college after graduating from high school, while only 15 percent of non-ACOT students did. Furthermore, the behaviour of ACOT teachers also changed—they worked "more as mentors and less as presenters of information" (Mehlinger 1996, 404).

An additional positive finding of the ACOT study was how teachers gradually began to use the computers in new ways in the classroom. "When [ACOT] teachers were able to move past that pervasive teacher-centred view of education, students and teachers, as communities of learners, were able to benefit from the range of individual areas of expertise represented by the entire group" (Bitter and Pierson 1999, 43). Teachers rearranged their classrooms to enable students to work collaboratively on projects, and they frequently made arrangements for students who wished to stay after school to work on multimedia projects. Frequently, "Students and teachers collaborated together, with the students often in the role of expert or resource person" (Schwartz and Beichner 1999, 33–34).

Integrating Technology

Teacher participants in the ACOT study were volunteers, many of whom had little experience with educational technology. As with teachers learning any new instructional strategy, the ACOT teachers frequently struggled to adjust to their new computer-filled rooms. Researchers found that the teachers progressed through five distinct stages as they integrated the technology into their teaching (Sandholtz, Ringstaff, and Dwyer 1997).

1. *Entry stage*—For many teachers, this was a period of painful growth and discomfort; learning to use computers presented challenges similar to those faced by beginning teachers.
2. *Adoption stage*—Becoming more proactive toward the challenge of integrating computers, teachers began to teach students how to use the computers and software.
3. *Adaptation stage*—Teachers turned from teaching the technology to using the technology as a tool to teach content.
4. *Appropriation stage*—Teachers moved from merely accommodating computers in their daily routines to personally exploring new teaching possibilities afforded by the technology.
5. *Invention stage*—Eager to move beyond teacher-centred instruction, teachers began to collaborate with peers in developing authentic, inquiry-oriented learning activities.

As informative as the ACOT study has been, it is important to remember that the project was funded by a computer manufacturer; thus, the outcomes might have been influenced by commercial bias and/or the expectation that computers *could not* have had anything other than a significant positive influence on teaching and learning. In fact, Schwartz and Beichner (1999, 34) suggest that the ACOT project "epitomizes what might be termed the 'Emperor's New Clothes' perspective on technology in education. [To] take the ACOT reports at face value would be to accept the notion that technology is the panacea that education has been searching for ages."

Findings from Other Research Studies

A powerful way to determine whether certain educational practices actually influence students' learning is to conduct *meta-analyses*, that is, to "take the findings from single studies and calculate a way to compare them with each other. The goal is to synthesize the findings statistically and determine what the studies reveal when examined all together" (Kirkpatrick and Cuban 1998). One such meta-analysis reviewed the results of 133 research studies on educational technology from 1990 through 1994. The results of that study follow:

- Educational technology has a significant positive impact on achievement in all subject areas, across all levels of school, and in regular classrooms as well as those for special-needs students.
- Educational technology has positive effects on student attitudes.
- The degree of effectiveness is influenced by the student population, the instructional design, the teacher's role, how students are grouped, and the levels of student access to technology.
- Technology makes instruction more student-centred, encourages cooperative learning, and stimulates increased teacher–student interaction.
- Positive changes in the learning environment evolve over time and do not occur quickly (Mehlinger 1996, 405).

Another meta-analysis conducted by Heather Kirkpatrick and Larry Cuban (1998) at Stanford University also addressed the complications and difficulties involved in determining the effects of computers on learning, particularly when much of the research in that area is methodologically flawed. Research studies, they pointed out, "are of little use unless they elaborate the children's ages, the subject, the software used, the kinds of outcomes that were sought, and how the study was done." With these limitations in mind, the following is a brief summary of Kirkpatrick and Cuban's findings:

1. Seven of the single studies of elementary and secondary students yielded positive findings related to achievement and attitude change, while seven studies yielded negative or mixed findings.
2. Ten of the single studies on the effectiveness of computers to teach in core areas such as mathematics, reading, science, and social studies yielded results ranging from very positive to "cautiously negative."
3. Ten meta-analyses found higher levels of student achievement in computer-using classrooms.
4. Five meta-analyses found that student attitudes improved and students learned more in less time in computer-using classrooms.

On the basis of their meta-analysis of the research, much of it was considered methodologically flawed due to a lack of scientific controls, and Kirkpatrick and Cuban conclude that "we are unable to ascertain whether computers in classrooms have in fact been or will be the boon they have promised to be."

The ambiguities of research on computer-based instruction aside, it is clear that educational technology *can* have positive effects on learning and teaching, and indications are that technology will influence all aspects of education even more in the 21st century. Thus the question to be asked about the effectiveness of educational technology is not, "Is it effective?" Instead, the question should be ... "How and under what circumstances does educational technology enhance students' learning?" As more funds are made available to purchase hardware and software, train teachers, and provide technical support, the benefits of classroom media magic will become even more widespread.

Should Technology Be at the Forefront of Efforts to Improve Schools?

Daily, the mass media feature stories on schools and classrooms that have been transformed through the use of computer-based modes of teaching and learning. Additional reports appear regularly describing the development of new technologies that hold further promise for the improvement of education. The advantages outlined in these reports include:

- Systematic, well-structured, and consistent lessons
- The ability of students to pace their learning
- The ability of teachers to accommodate their students' varied learning styles and preferred paces of learning
- Opportunities for students in rural and remote areas to interact with students and teachers in diversely populated urban and suburban areas
- Increased record-keeping efficiency, which allows teachers to spend more time with students
- Immediate feedback and reinforcement for students

These students receive immediate feedback and reinforcement, are more engaged and motivated, and are acquiring important twenty-first century workplace skills by using computers at school. Should computers and other technology be at the forefront of efforts to improve schools?

- Improved student engagement and motivation that result from learning materials with colour, music, video, and animated graphics
- More effective assessment of students' learning
- Cost effectiveness
- The acquisition of computer literacy skills needed for the twenty-first century workplace

For several years, some people have been questioning the role of technology in improving schools. An *Atlantic Monthly* cover story titled "The Computer Delusion" even suggested that spending money on computers in the classroom was a form of "malpractice" (Oppenheimer 1997). Some critics, like Stanford professor Larry Cuban, believe it is misguided to assume that teaching will benefit from the use of computers, as have other forms of work:

> The essence of teaching is a knowledgeable, caring adult building a relationship with one or more students to help them learn what the teacher, community, and parents believe to be important. It is an intertwining of emotional and intellectual bonds that gives a tone and texture to teaching and learning unlike what occurs in other work environments. The lure of higher productivity in teaching and learning via computer technologies, however, has seduced reformers to treat teaching like other forms of labor that gained productivity after automation (Cuban 1999a).

Elsewhere, Cuban (1999b) suggests several seldom-considered factors that might account for why the increase in available educational technologies is not reflected in more effective use of technology in the classroom:

- *Contradictory advice from experts*—During the last two decades, Cuban points out, teachers have been presented with an "ever-shifting menu of advice" about what computer skills to teach students, ranging from how to program computers in the 1980s to how to do hypertext programming or HTML in the 1990s.
- *Intractable working conditions*—While technology has transformed most workplaces, conditions of teaching have changed little. As "people for whom rollerblades would be in order to meet the day's obligations," Cuban says, teachers are hard pressed to find time and energy to integrate new technologies into their teaching.

- *The inherent unreliability of the technology*—Software malfunctions, servers that crash, and the continual need for computers with more memory and speed are among the problems Cuban notes.
- *Policymakers' disrespect for teachers' opinions*—Teachers are seldom consulted about which machines and software are most appropriate and reliable for their teaching.

Other critics, like *Chicago Tribune* columnist Bob Greene, are clear about the place of computers in the classroom: He has an answer for how the next generation of children can be helped to be academically successful. "It all comes down to computers in the classroom. Get rid of them" (Greene 1999). Critics like Greene believe that computers can have a dampening effect on the intellectual development of children, not unlike television, and should not be used extensively in the classroom until the high school level. As Greene puts it: "We are not doing [children] any favours by plopping them in front of yet another set of screens and programming them to tap and stare away."

Will computer technology help schools develop the kind of students and citizens the nation needs? Is there a "fit" between the undeniable power of computers and the educational goals we seek? Are there more cost-effective ways to achieve these educational goals? These are among the difficult questions that are being addressed as the role of technology in educational reform is being debated.

The Opposition: Computers *Will Not* Improve Education

Among the first to question the role of technology in the classroom was Clifford Stoll, one of the pioneers of the internet. In *Silicon Snake Oil: Second Thoughts on the Information Highway* (1996, 127), Stoll points out that "Our schools face serious problems, including overcrowded classrooms, teacher incompetence, and lack of security. Local education budgets hardly cover salaries, books, and paper. Computers address none of these problems. They're expensive, quickly become obsolete, and drain scarce capital budgets. Yet school administrators want them desperately."

Similarly, others critics have cautioned the public against pushing schools into the computer revolution. A sampling of their comments follow:

> Penetration of the education market with computer-based technology has depended more on effective conditioning of the market through a barrage of advertising and ideology than on the effectiveness of the technologies themselves (Noble 1996, 20).

> I do not go as far back as the radio and Victrola, but I am old enough to remember when 16-millimeter film was to be the sure-cure. Then closed-circuit television. Then 8-millimeter film. Then teacher-proof textbooks. Now computers. I know a false god when I see one (Postman, 1995).

The Advocates: Computers *Will* Improve Education

Despite media stories and articles critical of the call for more computers in schools, enthusiasm for technology in schools remains strong. For example, in an MCI nationwide poll in 1998, almost 60 percent of the public answered "a great amount" when asked, "How much do you think computers have helped improve student learning?" (Trotter 1998, 6). Following are two comments that rebut arguments against computers in the schools.

Is the use of technology in schools overemphasized?

According to futurists, students will continue to use more and more technology in the coming years. Is this good news or bad? Many say that it is great news! They claim that failing to use such technological advances will shortchange children and prevent them from fully participating in the global village of the future. Others disagree and direct educators to ask *why, to what end,* and *what* regarding the uses of technology, not just *how* and *how soon.* They believe that educators are unthinkingly accepting technology without evaluating its impact on the curriculum, student learning, and the social settings for education.

Where do you stand on this issue? Do you think that the use of technology in schools is being overemphasized?

The use of technology in schools is not overemphasized.

Technology is not overemphasized in education today, and schools would be foolish to turn their backs on the world of information available to them through the internet, CD-ROMs, and computer programs. In addition to making grading and record-keeping easier for teachers, educational technology can expand their instructional capabilities beyond what was imagined just a few years ago.

For instance, in *Curriculum Update* Larry Mann (1998) describes the benefits of using the website *GlobaLearn.* He reports the experiences of fans of the site such as Christy Harmon, a resource teacher in Grades K–5, who uses *GlobaLearn* in her special education and English as a Second Language programs. Through the multimedia site her students are able to interact with live remote expedition teams around the world in activities that develop the skills, awareness, and determination they will need to become responsible stewards of the Earth. Harmon's students research their subjects online and then prepare and present their reports in PowerPoint productions. They also prefer to use internet encyclopedias rather than those in their school libraries because they have more pictures and include videos. Her students are stretching their knowledge and perspectives, and Harmon observes, "I look forward to seeing what these kids can do with their lives....

They are so good at this at such a young age."

Interacting on the internet is also equalizing. Upper- and lower-income students, those with and without special needs, classroom stars, and shy students, even young and old, have equal voices and equal respect on the internet. And for students at risk of dropping out of school, educational technology in alternative schools can be the life raft that keeps them afloat. Working with computers, they can learn at their own pace and make mistakes out of the sight of critical peers.

Educational technology is not an end in itself but a tool to use. To avoid using it, whatever the reason, is to limit learning possibilities. Motion pictures, videos, and television, once viewed as threats to education, have become generally accepted in classrooms. The advances in today's educational technology will do the same. Knowing how and when to use them will make the difference.

The use of technology in schools is overemphasized.

The use of technology in schools is overemphasized, distracting educators from what should be their focus—students, their learning, and their lives. Technology depersonalizes education, distancing students from each other and their teachers. Computers are not sensitive to students' needs. They don't notice when a student's work habits, communication, demeanour, grooming, or dress change abruptly, signalling trouble. They don't know when a student is discouraged, sad, lonely, fearful, or "stuck" in his or her learning. Computers are poor substitutes for true companions. They do not laugh, commiserate, or share warmly with their users. Clearly, they cannot provide the human dimension that is needed so greatly in today's society.

The utilitarian goals of technology are inadequate for students' education for life. We are told that students need technology to keep up in a competitive global economy. But is the purpose of education solely to prepare workers for the economy? In an article entitled "Visions of Sugarplums: The Future of Technology, Education, and the Schools," Stephen Kerr suggests four improved goals for education, all of them clustering around essential human concerns:

[F]irst, a focus on the acquisition of knowledge as a tool for self-discovery and liberation ... second, self-esteem and a feeling of self-worth; third, respect for others with differing values and characteristics; and fourth ... a "democratic world view," a willingness to participate in the affairs of democratic society (Kerr 1999).

Educational technology is not essential to achieve any of these goals.

Failure to consider the ways that technology can shape or change the curriculum and the school culture can have serious consequences. When technology is approached this way, the tail begins to wag the dog. The available technology begins to determine what will be taught and what values will be stressed, rather than the reverse.

Even more serious are the dangers of students' exposure to knowledge we don't want them to have, like the listings on one webpage index reported by Daniel Okrent of *Time* a month after the Littleton, Colorado, incident: "'Counterfeit Money,' 'Hot-Wiring Cars,' 'Breaking into Houses,' 'Thermite Bombs,' and 'Tennis Ball Bombs.'" Okrent observes that communication with another on the internet is actually interaction with the facsimile of a human being and explains:

I remember passing through the study in our house when my 13-year-old daughter was engaged in a chat with someone who said she was a 15-year-old Californian named Cheryl. It occurred to me—and I suggested to my daughter—that her chatmate, with whom she was sharing the sort of intimacies a 13-year-old will indulge in, could just as likely be a 53-year-old backwoods hermit named Earl. It was a nauseating thought to both of us (Okrent 1999).

Finally, instruction by teachers cannot be replaced by technology. Brain research and the constructivist approach to learning confirm that live adults need to be present and ready to scaffold students' efforts when needed. Children and youths should have committed, dynamic adults to

believe in them, to encourage them when they fail, and to celebrate with them when they succeed. Technology, no matter how advanced, cannot replace the direction and care of a good teacher.

Where do you stand on this issue?

1. Which side do you take, and which arguments do you prefer? Why?

2. What can you add to defend your position?

3. What are your experiences with educational technology?

4. What guidelines would you propose for a balanced, healthy, and beneficial use of educational technology and of the internet in particular?

Recommended Sources

Cetron, M. (1997). Reform and tomorrow's schools. *TECHNOS Quarterly*, 6(1), 19–22.

Kerr, S. T. (1999). Visions of sugarplums: The future of technology, education, and the schools. In M. J. Early and K. J. Rehage (Eds.). *Issues in curriculum: A selection of chapters from past NSSE yearbooks, Part II.* Chicago, IL: The National Society for the Study of Education.

Mann. L. (1998, Summer). Getting global with technology. *Curriculum Update.*

Okrent, D. (1999, May 10). Raising kids online: What can parents do? *Time.*

Postman, N. (1995, October 9). Virtual students, digital classrooms. *The Nation.*

Withrow, F. B. (1997, June). Technology in education and the next twenty-five years. *T. H. E. Journal (Technological Horizons in Education),* 1–4.

It has become fashionable to say that computers in education are a bust. [However,] the new media can positively change the role of the teacher and student, shifting education from broadcast to interactive learning. When done effectively, [the] results are dramatic (Tapscott July 6, 1999).

Using technology to aid learning-disabled students improve literacy skills has been a real stepping stone to learning for my students and myself. The motivation and enthusiasm displayed each class is proof that learning with technology is extremely advantageous. The students are being creative, experimental, and collaborative (Ann Robichaud, Resource Teacher June 2003).

Canadian Curriculum Websites

Canadian curriculum is the responsibility of the individual provinces and territories. For a thorough analysis of the role of educational technology in various curriculums across Canada, refer to the following regional, provincial, and territorial curriculum sites:

Regional Curriculum Websites

Atlantic Provinces Education Foundation (APEF) Documents
http://apef-fepa.org

Western Canadian Protocol for Collaboration in Basic Education, Kindergarten to Grade 12:
www.wcp.ca

Alberta Learning
http://ednet.edc.gov.ab.ca/k_12/curriculum/

BC Ministry of Education, Program Standards and Education Resources Branch
www.bced.gov.bc.ca/irp/curric/

Manitoba Curriculum Development, Implementation, and Assessment
www.edu.gov.mb.ca/metks4/cuuricul/index.html

New Brunswick
www.gnb.ca/0000/anglophone-e.asp#1

Newfoundland and Labrador Division of Program Development
www.stemnet.nf.ca/DeptEd/Program/index.html

Northwest Territories Curriculum
http://siksik.learnernet.nt.ca

Nova Scotia
http://doc-depot.ednet.ns.ca

Ontario Curriculum and Policy Documents
www.edu.gov.on.ca/eng/document/curricul/curricul.html

Prince Edward Island
www.edu.pe.ca

Quebec Ministère de l'Education: Curriculum Publications
www.meq.gouv.qc.ca/GR-PUB/menu-curricu-a.htm

Saskatchewan Department of Education: Curriculum and Instruction Branch
www.sasked.gov.sk.ca/curr_inst/

Yukon Educational Student Network
www.yesnet.yk.ca/

Fortunately, teachers, along with others who have an interest in education, are becoming more sophisticated in understanding the strengths and limitations of technology as a tool to promote learning. They know full well that "If [they] bring in these technologies and don't think ahead to how they'll be used to promote learning and the acquisition of skills, then the only thing that will change in school is the electric bill" (educational technology expert quoted in Goldberg 1998). They also know that, like another educational tool—the book—the computer *can* be a powerful, almost unlimited medium for instruction and learning, if they carefully reflect on *how* it will further the attainment of the goals and aspirations they have for their students.

SUMMARY

How Are Educational Tools and Technologies Influencing Schools?

- Technology is a tool teachers can use to achieve educational goals and to create particular kinds of learning environments.

- Technology can provide students with a structured, efficient instructional delivery system, or it can spark their interest in open-ended, inquiry-oriented learning.

- In many schools and classrooms, technology has already transformed teaching and learning; however, teachers, administrators, policymakers, and parents must realize that advanced telecommunications will require new approaches to teaching and assessing students' learning.

What Technologies Are Available for Teaching?

- Through technologies such as two-way interactive telecommunications, CD-ROM players, interactive multimedia, computer simulations, and hypermedia, teachers are creating learning environments that allow students to become more active in shaping their learning experiences.

- If *educational technology* is broadly defined as inventions that enable teachers to reach their goals more effectively, then it is clear that for some time all teachers have been using various forms of educational "technology."

- Three common uses of computers in instruction are computer-assisted instruction (CAI), computer-managed instruction (CMI), and computer-enhanced instruction (CEI).

- Some schools have microcomputer-based laboratories (MBL) that students use to gather and analyze various kinds of data.

- Newsgroups, chat rooms, and videoconferencing on the internet enable teachers and students to communicate with people around the world.

What Is the State of Computer Technology in the Canadian Classroom?

- Teachers most frequently use the internet to gather information and resources for teaching.

- Teachers who have classroom access to the internet are more likely than those without access to communicate via email and to post information and student work on the web.

- After word processing and using CD-ROM references, performing "research" on the web is the most common teacher-directed use of computers by students.

What Are the Effects of Computer Technology on Learning?

- Although how and to what extent computers and other technologies are being used in schools is not known, research indicates that technology has a positive impact on students' achievement and attitudes.

- The Apple Classrooms of Tomorrow (ACOT) project showed that teachers progress through five stages as they integrate technology into teaching: entry, adoption, adaptation, appropriation, and invention.

- Single research studies and meta-analyses of large numbers of single studies indicate that the effects of computers on students' learning are varied—some report learning gains, some don't, and others report "mixed" outcomes.

- In spite of the ambiguities of research on computer-based instruction, it is clear that technology *can* have positive effects on learning.

Should Technology Be at the Forefront of Efforts to Improve Schools?

- Some critics feel strongly that computers do not aid education, and are a drain on scarce capital funds, while several polls have indicated a great deal of support among the general public for computers in the classroom.

KEY TERMS AND CONCEPTS

CD-ROM, 336
chat rooms, 339
computer-assisted
    instruction
    (CAI), 334
computer-based
    simulations, 337
computer-enhanced
    instruction
    (CEI), 335

computer-managed
    instruction (CMI), 335
distance learning
    networks, 334
DVD, 336
educational
    technology, 333
home–school
    communication
    systems, 337

hypermedia, 336
interactive
    multimedia, 336
internet, 337
microcomputer-based
    laboratories
    (MBL), 336
newsgroups, 339
videoconferencing, 340
web, 337

APPLICATIONS AND ACTIVITIES

Teacher's Journal

1. In your opinion, what are the most important benefits of technology for education, and what are its most important drawbacks?

2. What impact has television had on your life? What steps might teachers take to increase the educational benefits of television in society?

3. A concern voiced by some is that the use of computers in education will lead to a depersonalization of the teacher–learner relationship. How valid is this concern?

4. Write a scenario forecasting how technology will change the teaching profession during the next two decades; during the next four decades.

Teacher's Database

1. With classmates, join or start an online discussion on one or more of the following topics or on another topic in Chapter 9.

   - computer simulations
   - educational software
   - computer-assisted instruction (CAI)
   - educational technology
   - computer-managed instruction (CMI)
   - hypermedia
   - computer-enhanced instruction (CEI)
   - interactive multimedia

2. Find out more about educational newsgroups and distance learning networks. How might you use newsgroups or distance learning networks in your preparation as a teacher? As a teacher, how might you and your students use these two forms of educational technology? What knowledge and skills do you need to start or participate in an educational newsgroup or distance learning network? Using the internet, develop a list of resources for both.

Observations and Interviews

1. Survey a local school district to determine the educational technologies used by teachers. How and how often are these technologies used for instruction? What is the availability of computers and software for student use?

2. Find an online chat room frequented by teachers and enter (or initiate) a discussion on educational technology. What are the teachers' views of integrating technology into the classroom? What technologies, software, and instructional activities have they found most effective?

Professional Portfolio

Prepare a catalogue of interactive multimedia resources and materials that you will use as a teacher. For each entry, include an annotation that briefly describes the resource materials, how you will use them, and where they may be obtained. As with the selection of any curriculum materials, try to find evidence of effectiveness, such as results of field tests, published reviews of educational software, awards, or testimonials from educators. View and report on at least one program you have included in your personal catalogue. Explain in your report how you will integrate this multimedia resource into your curriculum.

Appendix 9.1

Criteria for Evaluating Software Programs

	Poor	Fair	Excellent
User friendliness			
How easy is it to start the program?	❏	❏	❏
Is there an overview or site map for the program?	❏	❏	❏
Can students easily control the pace of the program?	❏	❏	❏
Can students exit the program easily?	❏	❏	❏
Can students create their own paths through the program and develop their own links among elements?	❏	❏	❏
After first-time use, can students bypass introductory or orientation material?	❏	❏	❏
Does the program include useful hotlinks to internet sites?	❏	❏	❏
Inclusiveness			
Can students with hearing or visual impairments make full use of the program?	❏	❏	❏
Can students navigate the program by making simple keystrokes with one hand?	❏	❏	❏
Does the material avoid stereotypes and reflect sensitivity to racial, cultural, and gender differences?	❏	❏	❏
Textual Material			
How accurate and thorough is the content?	❏	❏	❏
Is the content well organized and clearly presented?	❏	❏	❏
Is the textual content searchable?	❏	❏	❏
Can the content be integrated into the curriculum?	❏	❏	❏
Images			
Is the image resolution high quality?	❏	❏	❏
Is the layout attractive, "user friendly," and uncluttered?	❏	❏	❏
Do the graphics and colours enhance instruction?	❏	❏	❏
How true are the colours of the images?	❏	❏	❏
Are the images large enough?	❏	❏	❏
Does the program have a zoom feature that indicates the power of magnification?	❏	❏	❏
Does the program make effective use of video and animation?	❏	❏	❏
Audio			
Are the audio clips high quality?	❏	❏	❏
Does the audio enhance instruction?	❏	❏	❏
Technical			
Is installation of the program easy and trouble-free?	❏	❏	❏
Are instructions clear and easy to follow?	❏	❏	❏
Is user-friendly online help available?	❏	❏	❏
Are technical support people easy to reach, helpful, and courteous?	❏	❏	❏
Motivational			
Does the program capture and hold students' interest?	❏	❏	❏
Are students eager to use the program again?	❏	❏	❏
Does the program give appropriate, motivational feedback?	❏	❏	❏
Does the program provide prompts or cues to promote students' learning?	❏	❏	❏

Appendix 9.2

Criteria for Evaluating Websites

	Poor	Fair	Excellent

Authoritativeness

The author(s) are respected authorities in the field. ☐ ☐ ☐
The author(s) are knowledgeable. ☐ ☐ ☐
The author(s) provide a list of credentials and/or educational background. ☐ ☐ ☐
The author(s) represent respected, credible institutions or organizations. ☐ ☐ ☐
Complete information on references (or sources) is provided. ☐ ☐ ☐
Information for contacting the author(s) and webmaster is provided. ☐ ☐ ☐

Comprehensiveness

All facets of the subject are covered. ☐ ☐ ☐
Sufficient detail is provided at the site. ☐ ☐ ☐
Information provided is accurate. ☐ ☐ ☐
Political, ideological, and other biases are not evident. ☐ ☐ ☐

Presentation

Graphics serve an educational, rather than decorative, purpose. ☐ ☐ ☐
Links are provided to related sites. ☐ ☐ ☐
What icons stand for is clear and unambiguous. ☐ ☐ ☐
The website loads quickly. ☐ ☐ ☐
The website is stable and seldom, if ever, nonfunctional. ☐ ☐ ☐

Timeliness

The original website was produced recently. ☐ ☐ ☐
The website is updated and/or revised regularly. ☐ ☐ ☐
Links given at the website are up-to-date and reliable. ☐ ☐ ☐

part four

Your Teaching Future

dear mentor

On Being Involved in Your Educational Community

Dear Mentor,

I am in the process of completing my degree and earning my teaching certificate. I have always been active in the social issues of my community. How can I, as a teacher, be active in my school's decisions about education reform? What opportunities should I look for?

Sincerely,
Sara Waltmire

ear Sara,

I, too, have been involved consistently in the social issues of my community. When I started teaching, I wanted to bring those issues into my school. I have come up with some pretty unusual math lessons on community, diversity, and other social issues. I also saw opportunities for students to be involved in serving others. We started a community service club and planned activities with a local food bank and a children's hospital. A few months after the club began, I learned a valuable lesson: One of the students who had taken the lead in organizing and supporting the club's activities was in much need of help herself. Her family was in financial and personal turmoil. Sometimes she had to look after herself. But still, she managed to be a good student.

Because my life had been sheltered from many of the realities of the world, I did not realize that the people who needed help weren't just "out there" somewhere but were also right inside my classroom. Problems at home are not left outside school on the steps; they travel with the student and impact everything that happens in that child's life and education. All children, whatever challenges life has put in their path, deserve a safe place to learn and construct their understanding of the world. I began to realize that changing what went on in my classroom alone was not enough. If I wanted to create real change, I had to become involved in reforming education on a wider plane.

First, I began participating on a district Pre-Algebra committee whose goal was to get input about what was working and what was not from as many teachers as possible. I was concerned that I did not have much to offer. However, on that committee I found other teachers who confront many of the same problems I did, and who wanted to make a change. We wrote a new curriculum to address the varied learning styles of our students. Participating in this project led to more projects and more people who are working to improve education.

Join in a committee, a project, or a seminar. Speak out at every chance you get. Be an advocate for kids. Sooner than you think, you will have more opportunities to serve and people asking you to help than you will have time for. One thing of which I am certain—that has been proven to me time and again—is that teachers are the most creative, devoted, and caring people you will meet. In my travels, I have met teachers from all over Canada, and I have been amazed by the different challenges we face. At the same time, if I talk with them at length, I discover that underneath it all, we are faced with many of the same challenges. We are a great community of educators working together on the critical assignment of educating children and youth.

Sincerely,

Diane Crim, Math Teacher

Teachers As Educational Leaders

Leadership is first and foremost about making effective decisions. If the leader makes good decisions, everything else will fall into place. The leader must ensure that the organization objectively evaluates what is known and makes his or her decision on the basis of research, facts and rationality.

—A classroom teacher
Educational Leadership: Cunningham and Cordeiro, Pearson Education Inc., 2003, p.2

1. To what extent is teaching a full profession?

2. What is professionalism in teaching?

3. To what professional organizations do teachers belong?

4. What new leadership roles for teachers are emerging?

5. How do teachers contribute to educational research?

6. How are teachers providing leadership for school development and curriculum improvement?

It is November of your fifth year of teaching, and you are attending a "task force" meeting of the steering committee for a province-wide teacher network launched that September. The Department of Education has divided the province into twelve regions, and you have been elected by your peers to be the network leader for your region. The network is based on the premise that teachers should have opportunities to participate in, and lead, professional development activities of their own choosing, such as curriculum workshops, leadership institutes, internships, and conferences.

This two-day meeting at the Department of Education will begin the process of designing a series of two-week summer institutes for teachers. The institutes will be invitational, and institute "fellows" will be selected by the steering committee after an extensive application and interview process. One institute will be held in each region throughout the province, and teachers will receive a $600 stipend plus expenses for attending. To disseminate the knowledge and skills they acquire and to further develop their leadership abilities, the institute fellows will design and deliver staff development programs at their home schools.

The committee chair, a teacher from a school in the province's largest city, has just laid out the group's task for the next two days. "By the end of the day tomorrow, we need to have identified which institutes will be offered in each region. Also, we need to have a game plan for how each of you will facilitate the development of the summer institute in your region."

"Well, the way I see it," says the teacher next to you, "the institutes should accomplish at least two major purposes. First, they should provide teachers with ways to increase their effectiveness in the classroom by acquiring new strategies and materials. Second, and just as important, the institutes should give teachers opportunities to play key leadership roles in school improvement efforts around the province."

"That's right," says another teacher. "Teachers should recognize that the institutes give them a voice and meaningful opportunities to function as professionals."

"What I like about the institutes," says the teacher across the table from you, "is that they give teachers a chance to break out of the role of passively *receiving* inservice training. It's no different for teachers than it is for students—we learn best by actively shaping our learning environment and constructing meaning."

As several members of the group, including you, nod in agreement, you reflect on what you've just heard. What does it really mean to be a professional? What are the characteristics of a profession, and to what extent does teaching reflect those characteristics? What new leadership roles for teachers are emerging? What leadership roles will you play in educational improvement?

Educational improvement, as the preceding scenario illustrates, is continuing to change dramatically what it means to be a teacher. Provincially-sponsored teacher networks, the professionalization of teaching, shared decision making, peer review, and mentor teacher programs are just a few of the changes that are providing unprecedented opportunities for teachers to assume new leadership roles beyond the classroom. In addition, as Joseph Murphy points out in "Reconnecting Teaching and School Administration: A Call for a Unified Profession," approaches to educational leadership are becoming more collaborative and participatory:

> The hierarchical, bureaucratic organizational structures that have defined schools over the past 80 years are giving way to more decentralized and more professionally controlled systems that create new designs for school management. In these new postindustrial educational organizations, there are important shifts in roles, relationships, and responsibilities: traditional patterns of relationships are altered, authority flows are less hierarchical, role definitions are both more general and flexible, leadership is connected to competence for needed tasks rather than to formal position, and independence and isolation are replaced by cooperative work (Murphy 1999).

We have referred to teaching as a **profession** throughout this book; however, if we compare teaching with other professions—law and medicine, for example—we find

Yes	Uncertain	No	
○	○	○	1. Professionals are allowed to institutionalize a monopoly of essential knowledge and services. For example, only lawyers may practice law; only physicians may practice medicine.
○	○	○	2. Professionals are able to practice their occupation with a high degree of autonomy. They are not closely supervised, and they have frequent opportunities to make their own decisions about important aspects of their work. Professional autonomy also implies an obligation to perform responsibly, to self-supervise, and to be dedicated to providing a service rather than meeting minimum requirements of the job.
○	○	○	3. Professionals must typically undergo a lengthy period of education and/or training before they may enter professional practice. Furthermore, professionals usually must undergo a lengthy induction period following their formal education or training.
○	○	○	4. Professionals perform an essential service for their clients and are devoted to continuous development of their ability to deliver this service. This service emphasizes intellectual rather than physical techniques.
○	○	○	5. Professionals have control over their governance, their socialization into the occupation, and research connected with their occupation.
○	○	○	6. Members of a profession form their own vocational associations, which have control over admissions to the profession, educational standards, examinations and licensing, career development, ethical and performance standards, and professional discipline.
○	○	○	7. The knowledge and skills held by professionals are not usually available to nonprofessionals.
○	○	○	8. Professionals enjoy a high level of public trust and are able to deliver services that are clearly superior to those available elsewhere.
○	○	○	9. Professionals are granted a high level of prestige and higher-than-average financial rewards.

some significant differences. As a result of these differences, current opinion is divided as to whether teaching actually is a full profession. Some have labelled teaching a *semi*-profession (Etzioni 1969), an *emerging* profession (Howsam et al. 1976), an *uncertain* profession (Powell 1980), an *imperilled* profession (Duke 1984; Sykes 1983; Freedman, Jackson, and Botes 1983; Boyer 1990), an *endangered* profession (Goodlad 1983b), and a *not-quite* profession (Goodlad 1990)!

Figure 10.1

Does teaching meet the criteria for a profession?

To What Extent Is Teaching a Full Profession?

We use the terms *professional* and *profession* quite frequently, usually without thinking about their meanings. Professionals "possess a high degree of specialized *theoretical knowledge*, along with methods and techniques for applying this knowledge in their day-to-day work.... [and they] are united by a high degree of in-group solidarity, stemming from their common training and common adherence to certain doctrines and methods" (Abrahamsson 1971, 11–12).

From several sociologists and educators who have studied teaching come additional characteristics of occupations that are highly professionalized, summarized in Figure 10.1: Does teaching meet the criteria for a profession. Before reading further, reflect on each characteristic and decide whether it applies to teaching. Then, continue reading about the extent to which teaching satisfies each of these commonly agreed-upon characteristics of full professions. Do our perceptions agree with yours?

Institutional Monopoly of Services

On one hand, teachers do have a monopoly of services. As a rule, only those who are certified members of the profession may teach in public schools. On the other hand, the varied requirements we find for certification and for teaching in private schools weaken this monopoly. In addition, any claim teachers might have as exclusive providers of a service is further eroded by the practice of provincial educational systems approving temporary, or emergency, certification measures to deal with temporary teacher shortages—a move that establishes teaching as the only profession that allows non-certified individuals to practice the profession. This practice is likely to become more widespread in the next five to eight years as some provinces will lose 40–50 percent of their teaching force to retirement. Dealing with the resultant teacher shortage presently poses, and will continue to pose, serious problems for almost all educational jurisdictions within the country.

Perhaps the most significant argument against teachers claiming to be the exclusive providers of a service, however, is the fact that a great deal of teaching occurs in informal, non-school settings and is done by people who are not teachers. Every day, thousands of people teach various kinds of how-to-do-it skills: how to water-ski, how to make dogs more obedient, how to make pasta from scratch, how to tune a car's engine, and how to meditate.

Teacher Autonomy

In one sense teachers have considerable autonomy. They usually work behind a closed classroom door, and only seldom is their work observed by another adult. In fact, one of the norms among teachers is that the classroom is a castle of sorts, and teacher privacy a closely guarded right. Although the performance of new teachers may be observed and evaluated on a regular basis by supervisors, veteran teachers are observed much less frequently, and they usually enjoy a high degree of autonomy.

Teachers also have extensive freedom regarding how they structure the classroom environment. They may emphasize discussions as opposed to lectures. They may set certain requirements for some students and not for others. They may delegate responsibilities to one class and not another. And, within the guidelines set by local and provincial/territorial authorities, teachers may determine much of the content they teach.

There are, however, constraints placed on teachers and their work. Teachers, unlike doctors and lawyers, must accept all the "clients" who are sent to them. Only with the permission of a school's administrator can a teacher "reject" a student assigned to him or her.

Teachers must also agree to teach what department of education and local officials say they must. Moreover, the work of teachers is subject to a higher level of public scrutiny than that found in other professions. Because the public provides "clients" (students) and pays for schools, it has a significant say regarding the work of teachers. Nevertheless, it has been suggested that some "levelling" of professions will occur in Canada during the early 21st century: "More of the work of the traditional high-status professions, particularly medicine, will occur in bureaucratic or large organizational settings under the watchful eye of managers. [While] doctors are accepting more and more regulation, the school teachers ... will slowly break out of long-established bureaucratic hierarchies and share more of the autonomy previously enjoyed by members of the high-status professions" (Grant and Murray 1999, 231–32).

Years of Education and Training

As sociologist Amitai Etzioni (1969) points out in his classic discussion of the "semi-professions," the training of teachers is less lengthy than that required for other professionals—lawyers and physicians, for example. The initial professional component of teacher education programs is the shortest of all the professions. However, as we learned in Chapter 2, Canadian colleges and universities offer a variety of teacher-education models with Alberta's being one of the shortest and Nova Scotia's one of the longest. Additionally, many institutions now offer education degrees at the Master and doctoral levels. If the number of longer Bachelor of Education graduate-level teacher education programs continues to grow, the professional status of teaching will definitely be enhanced.

In most professions, new members must undergo a prescribed induction period. Physicians, for example, must serve an internship or residency before beginning practice, and most lawyers begin as clerks in law firms. In contrast, teachers usually do not go through a formal induction period before assuming full responsibility for their work. Practice teaching comes closest to serving as an induction period, but it is often relatively short, informal, and lacking in uniformity.

Provision of Essential Service

Although it is generally acknowledged that teachers provide a service that is vital to the well-being of individuals and groups, the public does need to be reminded of this fact from time to time. This importance was driven home on a large scale during the early1980s and 1990s when several reports called for school improvement because:

> Every moment in the lives of teachers and pupils brings critical decisions of motivation, reinforcement, reward, ego enhancement and goal direction. Proper professional decisions enhance learning and life; improper decisions send the learner towards incremental death in openness to experience and in ability to learn and contribute. Doctors and lawyers probably have neither more nor less to do with life, death, and freedom than do teachers (Howsam et al. 1976, 15).

Degree of Self-Governance

The limited freedom of teachers to govern themselves has detracted from the overall status of the profession. In many provinces and territories, licensing guidelines are set by government officials who may or may not be educators; and at the local level, decision-making power usually resides with local boards of education, largely made up of people who have never taught. As a result, teachers have had little or no say over what they teach, when they teach, whom they teach, and, in extreme instances, *how* they teach.

However, recent efforts to professionalize teaching are creating new roles for teachers and expanded opportunities to govern important aspects of their work. Within some educational jurisdictions, teachers have a louder voice in decisions related to curriculum development, staffing, budget, and the day-to-day operation of schools. In other areas, such as Ontario, Atlantic Canada, and parts of western Canada, however, teachers are expected to teach to Essential Learning Outcomes. In some of these areas there are also externally designed examinations, set by departments of education, which must be administered to students by teachers. The result is a possible net decline in the degree of teacher autonomy.

Although teachers and principals differ significantly in the amount of influence or control they believe teachers have, teachers may experience greater degrees of self-governance as principals respond to increasing pressure to become more effective at facilitating collaborative, emergent approaches to leadership (Parkay, Shindler, and Oaks 1997). Writing in *So You Want to Be a Teacher* (1996, 79) Rod Dolmage states that what teachers "talk about are challenges, autonomy, recognition, personal growth and a sense of collegiality and belonging." With the teacher shortage making it easier for teachers to move from one jurisdiction to another, school districts which refuse to accommodate these important teacher needs will almost certainly experience significant difficulties in retaining the services of their teaching forces.

Professional Associations

Teachers, like other professionals, have formed a number of vocational associations that are vitally concerned with issues such as admission to the profession, educational standards, examinations and licensing, career development, ethical and performance standards, and professional discipline. It is clear, though, that provincial and territorial teacher organizations have not progressed as far as other professions have in gaining control of these areas.

Professional Knowledge and Skills

Professionals are granted a certain status because they possess knowledge and skills not normally held by the general public. Within the profession of teaching, however, the requirements for membership are less precise. In spite of the ongoing efforts of educational researchers, there is less than unanimous agreement on the knowledge and skills considered necessary to teach. This lack of agreement is reflected in the varied programs at colleges and universities that offer teachers' education programs.

Level of Public Trust

The level of trust the public extends to teachers as professionals varies greatly. On the one hand, the public appears to have great confidence in the work that teachers do. Because of its faith in the teaching profession, the public invests teachers with considerable power over its children. For the most part, parents willingly allow their children to be molded and influenced by teachers, and this willingness must be based on a high degree of trust. In addition, most parents expect their children to obey and respect teachers. However, the burgeoning number of parents who are electing to send their children to Canada's independent (private) schools is a certain indication that many parents are not satisfied with the level of education offered by public schools.

Though all professions have some members who might be described as unprofessional, teaching is especially vulnerable to such charges. The sheer size of the teaching force makes it difficult to maintain consistently high professional standards. Moreover, teaching is subject to a level of public scrutiny and control that other, more established, professions traditionally have not tolerated. However, the era of widespread public trust may be running out for these other professions as well. Mushrooming malpractice suits against doctors, for example, may be a sign that here, too, public confidence has significantly eroded.

Prestige, Benefits, and Pay

As mentioned in Chapter 1, teachers are viewed as having higher social status than most of the population; however, this higher status is based on level of education attained rather than wealth. Thus, teachers have not received salaries in keeping with other professions requiring approximately the same amount of schooling. However, because of the grid system on which teachers are paid, they can reach their maximum salary levels at a fairly early stage in their careers. This differs from other professions where maximum income levels are reached at a much later point in individual careers.

What Is Professionalism in Teaching?

The current goal among teachers, teacher educators, policymakers, and the general public is to make teaching a full profession. Toward this end, teachers are willing to take risks and learn new roles as they press for greater self-governance, better working conditions, and increased financial rewards. In addition, teachers are acquiring the analytical skills needed to understand and provide leadership for the complex processes of educational reform. The following sections look at the three key dimensions of professionalism in teaching presented in Figure 10.2: professional behaviour, lifelong learning, and involvement in the profession.

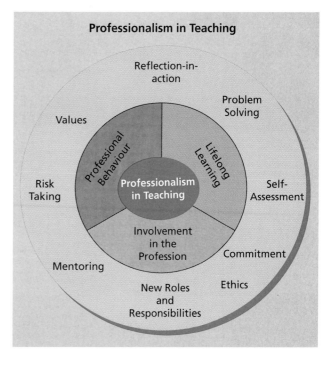

Figure 10.2

Professionalism in teaching

Professional Behaviour

Professional teachers are guided by a specific set of values. They have made a deep and lasting commitment to professional practice. They have also adopted a high standard of professional ethics and model behaviours that are in accord with that code of ethics. The professional teacher also engages in serious, reflective thought about how to teach more effectively and does this by continually examining experiences to improve practice.

Reflection-in-Action

Donald Schön (1983, 1987, and 1991) has described this professional behaviour as **reflection-in-action,** and he describes how a teacher might use it to solve a problem in the classroom:

> An artful teacher sees a child's difficulty in learning to read not as a defect in the child but as a defect "of his [or her] own instruction." And because the child's difficulties may be unique, the teacher cannot assume that his [or her] repertoire of explanations will suffice, even though they are "at the tongue's end." The teacher must be ready to invent new methods and must "endeavor to develop in himself [or herself] the ability of discovering them" (1983, 66).

The professional teacher Schön describes makes careful, sensitive observations of classroom events, reflects on the meaning of those observations, and then decides to act in a certain way. Steven Lacy, an exemplary elementary teacher, describes the reflective decision-making process this way:

Our effectiveness as teachers is not reflected in the materials and structures of our pedagogy as much as it is in the countless decisions we make every day, decisions that are made in an instant. [D]o I help him with that problem or let him struggle? Do I pursue her question or stick with the lesson? Does this behaviour need to be punished or ignored? Does this composition need to be criticized or praised? (Levey 1996, 2–3)

Becoming a Mentor

Because of their positions and their encounters with young people, teachers may find opportunities to become mentors to some of their students. Accepting this responsibility is another example of professional behaviour. The role of **mentor** is unique in several ways. First, mentorship develops naturally and is not an automatic part of teaching, nor can it be assigned to anyone. True mentorships grow from teaching relationships and cannot be artificially promoted. Second, the role of mentor is a *comprehensive* one: Mentors express broad interest in those whom they mentor. Third, the role of mentor is *mutually* recognized by student and teacher; both realize that their relationship has a special "depth." Fourth, the role of mentor is significant and has the potential to change the quality and direction of students' lives. And fifth, the opportunity to work with a mentor is free, what Gehrke (1988) terms the mentor's "gift of care."

The longer you teach, the more you will encounter opportunities for mentorships to develop, discovering that you can mentor less experienced teachers and student teachers as well as students. The rewards that come from the unique role of mentor are among the most satisfying.

What characteristics distinguish teaching as a profession? What characteristics might distinguish this teacher as a professional?

Lifelong Learning

The professional teacher is dedicated to continuous learning—both about the teaching-learning process and about the subject taught. No longer is it sufficient for career teachers to obtain only a bachelor's degree and a teaching certificate. Rather, teachers are lifelong members of learning communities.

Several provinces have mandated continuing education for teachers as a condition for maintaining their teaching certificates. For example, in Nova Scotia the requirement is one hundred hours of professional development within a five-year *period (Nova Scotia Teacher Certification Handbook*, August, 2001). The content of the curriculum as well as methods and materials for teaching that content are changing so rapidly that teachers must be involved in continuous learning to maintain their professional effectiveness. In addition, we feel that teachers must practice what they preach. A teacher who is not continuously learning raises serious questions for students: If it's not important for our teachers to learn, why should we? The attitude toward learning that teachers model for students may be as important as the content they teach.

Many opportunities are available for teachers to learn new knowledge and skills. Nearly every school district makes provisions for in-service training or staff development. Topics can range from classroom-focused issues such as authentic assessment, using the internet, classroom management, integrated curricula, or learning styles to school-wide management issues such as restructuring, shared governance, or school–community partnerships. Beyond these in-service opportunities, professional teachers actively seek additional avenues for growth, as this teacher observes during her fourth year of teaching: "After realizing what it could mean to work with colleagues and support colleagues in their work, I began arranging my own 'in-service' opportunities in my building and in the professional community. Even though I am a young teacher, I learned that I too am responsible for continuing my own learning in my profession" (Visconti 1996, 154).

Learning to Become a Leader

For professional teachers, an important goal of lifelong learning is to acquire leadership skills. Successful educational reform in the twenty-first century will require teacher participation in leadership. In fact, it is quite possible that "schools of the [21st] century will be run by teams of teachers who [have] the tools, incentives, and leadership they need to accomplish their jobs" (Gerstner et al. 1994, 169).

Involvement in the Profession

Today's teachers realize that they have the most important role in the educational enterprise and that, previously, they have not had the power they needed to improve the profession. Therefore, they are taking an increasingly broader view of the decisions that, as professionals, they have the right to make, as this elementary teacher points out:

> One of the problems is legislative people deciding what the education reforms should be and how they should be handled. I think it entails a lack of trust in the teachers by these authorities, and I think it's passed on to the public by the authorities.... For example, there's all the talk about competency testing and we're going to get rid of all the bad teachers. Teachers have the feeling that they're talking about all of us. We sometimes are used as public relations by authorities. And then often they take credit for what we do (Godar 1990, 264).

Across the country, professional teachers are deeply involved with their colleagues, professional organizations, teacher educators, legislators, policy makers, and others in a push to make teaching more fully a profession. Through their behaviours and accomplishments, they are demonstrating that they are professionals, that the professional identity of teachers is becoming stronger. During the last decade, for example, teachers have become more involved in teacher education programs, teacher certification, and professional governance. And, through the efforts of scores of teacher organizations, teachers have also made gains in working conditions, salaries, and benefits.

To What Professional Organizations Do Teachers Belong?

The expanding leadership role of teachers has been supported through the activities of both national and provincial/territorial teacher organizations (Canadian Teachers' Federation). These organizations, and the scores of hardworking teachers who run them, support a variety of activities to improve teaching and schools. Through their lobbying

Martha's Leadership

The following case is based on several interviews in a research study by the second author of this book. "Martha Townsend" is a pseudonym for a woman who had taught music in urban elementary schools for 25 years. She was selected for the study because of her enthusiasm for teaching and her perseverance in the profession.

Martha Townsend smiled and nodded slightly to Teresa, the small child who stood quietly in the doorway of her music classroom, waiting to be invited in. When the girl did not move, Martha bent further in a second nod, smiled more broadly, and added in an expressive whisper, "Come in, come in. Please!" Teresa beamed and entered quickly, finding her seat among the chairs and tables grouped into a semicircle around Martha. Close behind Teresa were 20 other children, all around her age. They smiled shyly at Martha and whispered to each other as they hurried single-file to their places.

"Probably Grade 3s," the visitor guessed. "I wonder why they're so excited." The children remained enthusiastic throughout the music class. Always intent on Martha, they answered each of her questions eagerly. They smiled often, sat tall, sang with enthusiasm, and seemed to love music, Ms Townsend, or both. The visitor, a researcher studying exceptional veteran teachers, was glad she could see Martha in action.

After the children left, Martha and the researcher began the interview with open-ended questions about why Martha had persevered in teaching so long and with such enthusiasm. In her lengthy, thoughtful answers, some patterns began to emerge. The clearest was that this soft-spoken woman was a determined leader who had battled against odds to develop the school's music program. Recalling coming to the school eleven years earlier, Martha explained that there was a lack of parental support for the music program. " I went into the school and nobody showed up for the instrumental tryouts."

Persistent in her desire to develop a music program for the children, Martha arranged a music assembly for the school and community. The visiting 118-piece orchestra had won awards six years in a row. Their superb performance was well received. After the applause, Martha explained to the audience that the orchestra was not a special group of gifted musicians but instead one that she had developed in her previous school. She invited the parents to let her do the same for their children. A steady focus on her goal and her creative leadership over the years has resulted today in an impressive music program that includes a large orchestra and the participation of every class in school.

Several times a year, under Martha's leadership, over a hundred children performed to capacity crowds of appreciative parents, friends, and relatives. Several weeks after the interview, Martha single-handedly directed a musical with an extensive cast and repertoire of songs and skits—some that made the crowd burst out in laughter. The audience packed the gymnasium, filling all the seats, spilling into the side aisles, and crowding the space across the back of the gym. Parents stretched to catch sight of their children when they performed and applauded with enthusiasm for each set in the program. Martha could rightly regard her program as a success.

Martha also demonstrated leadership in her guidance of student teachers, her lobbying of school district officials, her trust-earning relationships with her principals, the workshops she presented in professional conferences, the writing she did for the province's department of education, and the college teaching she did as an adjunct professor. But of all her leadership opportunities, Martha believed that guiding her students and getting to know their families were most important. "If we really want to effect change in our society, we have to get our best minds working where it counts, and that's with the kids who don't have opportunities otherwise."

In her advice for new teachers Martha emphasized the importance of being active in the community and a resource for parents:

> It's very important that teachers not be a people who just come to the neighbourhood during school hours. I think they have to make a connection with the people who live there. And I strongly recommend that they do some volunteer work in the community. Attending things that are meaningful in the community says a lot. For instance, I just went to a Fall Festival Parade.... Our school is in a port town, so a lot of people who are just coming into the community might not have met me yet, but there I was. When the children started yelling out my name and waving, their families realized that I was there. On Monday three of the mothers came in to tell me about problems they were having. That happened because I was at the parade. They felt differently about me because they saw me in the community.

From Martha's perspective, to be a teacher is to be a leader, and the position is permanent. She tells her elementary school children and her college students, "I'm your teacher, I am always your teacher, forever, no matter how old and gray you get. I am still your teacher. If you want to come to me later and ask me something, come." And they do.

Questions

1. How did Martha handle the parents who didn't think she should teach in their children's school? What other approaches could she have tried?

2. Describe Martha's leadership style and compare it to your own.

3. How else could Martha be a leader in her school? What areas did she overlook?

4. How do you envision using your leadership skills?

activities, teacher associations acquaint legislators, policymakers, and politicians with critical issues and problems in the teaching profession. Many associations have staffs of teachers, researchers, and consultants, who produce professional publications, hold conferences, prepare grant proposals, engage in school improvement activities, and promote a positive image of teaching to the public.

The Canadian Teachers' Federation

The following is a slightly amended description of the **Canadian Teachers' Federation** mandate.

> As the national bilingual umbrella organization for teachers in this country, the Canadian Teachers' Federation has 14 provincial and territorial Member organizations representing 240 000 teachers across Canada. It is a powerful voice for the profession and provides much needed support to its Member organizations and teachers at a time when many governments have moved ahead with very regressive education agendas. The CTF's major areas of concern include: defending public education; promoting the teaching profession; providing support to Member organizations and teachers across Canada; addressing societal issues that affect the health and well-being of children and youth in Canada and abroad; and providing assistance and support to teacher colleagues in developing countries. For over 80 years it has advanced the cause of children, defended the rights of teachers, and promoted a strong public education system.
>
> The CTF intervenes whenever the interests of teachers and students are at stake. It lobbies federal departments whose work affects education, children and youth, conducts campaigns to keep commercial interests out of schools and fights to keep education out of international trade agreements. It also helps teachers in the collective bargaining process. When Member organizations head into negotiations, it provides information from across the country on teacher salaries, pensions, and the full spectrum of benefits. The CTF conducts research on education issues like workload, demographics, testing and funding, helps its Member organizations provide stronger representation for teachers, and supports teachers and Member organizations by holding seminars and conferences on educational issues. It provides research on an array of topics through its Economic Service Notes and Economic Service Bulletins, which are sent to Member organizations throughout the year. The CTF has assisted and will continue to assist all teacher organizations across Canada in difficult times. The strength and unity of 240 000 Canadian teachers provide a formidable force for any government to reckon with. The CTF's website is at www.ctf-fce.ca/.

Teacher Unions and Other Professional Organizations

Teacher unions exist in all provinces and territories, although in some jurisdictions the name used is federation rather than union. While most provinces have a single union/federation which represents all teachers, there are some exceptions. New Brunswick has two affiliated teacher unions with membership determined by whether one speaks English or French, and Quebec has a similar structure with membership determined by religion. Ontario's structure is the most complex as there are five separate affiliated unions with membership variously determined by such things as language, gender, religion, and grade-level of instruction. British Columbia's union structure is different from others as it has a College of Teachers with compulsory membership and a teachers' federation with voluntary membership. However, regardless of the actual structure of a provincial or territorial teachers' union, membership is compulsory. Dues, often in the $500/year range, are automatically deducted at source and the unions negotiate salaries and benefits on behalf of their members. In most jurisdictions the negotiations are conducted with the provincial or territorial government.

Teacher unions/federations also have an interesting dilemma. While they prefer to see themselves as equivalent to professional organizations, such as the provincial bar associations for lawyers or the colleges of physicians for medical practitioners, teacher federations often act more as trade unions than as purely professional associations. They can, and do, organize strikes, and they can, and do, discipline any of their members who fail to cooperate. The reality is that most are both unions and professional associations. By participating in the "Simulation Activity—Union Negotiations" located in Appendix 10.1 you can gain some insight into the process in which teacher unions and governments engage when settling contracts.

In addition to provincial teacher unions and the nationally based Canadian Teachers' Federation, teachers' professional interests are represented by numerous other international, national, and provincial organizations. Several of these are concerned with improving the quality of education at all levels and in all subject areas. **Phi Delta Kappa (PDK)**, for example, is an international professional and honorary fraternity of educators concerned with enhancing quality education through research and leadership activities. Founded in 1906, Phi Delta Kappa now has a membership of 166 000 and branches in most Canadian provinces. Members, who are graduate students, teachers, and administrators, belong to one of more than 668 chapters. To be initiated into Phi Delta Kappa, one must have demonstrated high academic achievement, have completed at least fifteen semester hours of graduate work in education, and have made a commitment to a career of educational service. Phi Delta Kappa members receive *Phi Delta Kappan,* a journal of education published ten times a year.

As you will see in Appendix 10.2 and Appendix 10.3, many professional associations exist for teachers of specific subject-areas, such as mathematics, English, social studies, music, physical education, as well as for teachers of specific student populations, such as exceptional learners, young children, and students with limited English proficiency.

What New Leadership Roles for Teachers Are Emerging?

Teachers' roles are changing in fundamental and positive ways at the beginning of the twenty-first century. Greater autonomy and an expanded role in educational policy-making has led to "unprecedented opportunities for today's teachers to extend their leadership roles beyond the classroom" (Gmelch and Parkay 1995, 48). To prepare for this future, today's teachers will need to develop leadership skills to a degree not needed in the past.

Teacher Involvement in Teacher Education, Certification, and Staff Development

Teacher input into key decisions about teacher preparation, certification, and staff development are important to the teaching profession. Through their involvement with professional certification standards boards (see Chapter 2), and scores of local, provincial, and national education committees, teachers are changing the character of pre- and in-service education. They serve on curriculum committees, offer workshops and

Do teachers' unions have a positive effect on education?

The public seems to be divided over whether teachers' unions have a positive effect on education. According to a Phi Delta Kappa/Gallup Poll, "27 percent believed that unions have improved the quality of the public schools, 26 percent believe that unions have hurt the public schools, and 37 percent believe that unions have made no difference" (Rose and Gallup 1998).

Opponents object that unions are too focused on increasing teachers' salaries, improving their working conditions, and protecting their jobs. Such concerns make teachers resist educational reform efforts such as the voucher system and a longer school year. Those in favour of unions believe that the unions' interests are not self-centred and that improving the quality of education for children and youth is their ultimate goal. By uniting teachers, the unions can advocate for the rights and needs of children and influence legislation on their behalf.

What do you think? Do teachers' unions have a positive effect on education?

Yes, teachers' unions have a positive effect on education.

Yes, teachers' unions do have a positive effect on education. They "protect against efforts to dismantle public education and lobby for increased funding to strengthen schools" (Noll 1999, p. 355). They bring about specific changes that increase students' opportunities to learn. They do, for example, lobby for smaller class sizes, assistance for students with special needs, and increased professional development for teachers. They have also developed codes of professional conduct for their members, award grants to teachers who have provided proposals for interesting curricular initiatives, and provided both legal and other professional assistance as a member's circumstances may require.

Most teachers' union would agree that they:

- Advance the Cause of Education for All Individuals
- Promote the Health and Welfare of Children and/or Students
- Promote Professional Excellence Among Educators

Additionally, the wide range of books, videos, and services provided by all teachers' unions are directed toward assisting teachers in their work and improving education.

No, teachers' unions do not have a positive effect on education.

Those who oppose teachers' unions believe that the unions' successes in increasing salaries have come at the cost of improvements to education. They argue that unions have increased the costs of public education while doing little to improve the final outcomes for students.

One way that opponents say unions have hurt schools is through their insistence that all teachers be paid according to the same scale. In teaching-shortage areas such as math and science, where pay in fields outside the classroom is higher, the only way to meet the demand for teachers is to pay more. Union resistance to doing so shows more caring about teachers than about the education of children and youth. Unions also resist merit pay for teachers, layoffs on any other basis than seniority, and teacher dismissal other than for the most serious of offences.

Opponents also object to teacher strikes. They believe that teachers are professionals working with human services and that they should not strike under any circumstance. "Professionals owe their primary responsibility to the needs of clients; this ethical commitment should override secondary imperatives, such as personal gain, political exigencies, or simple expedience," Linda Darling-Hammond explained in a discussion of professionalism in teaching (1993).

Where do you stand on this issue?

1. What are the strongest points in each position?
2. What do you believe? Do teachers' unions have a positive effect on education?
3. What illustrations can you add to defend your position?

Recommended Sources

Chase, B. (1999). Unions lead the fight for innovation and investment in public education. In J. W. Noll (Ed.). *Clashing views on controversial educational issues,* 10th ed. Guilford, CT: Dushkin/McGraw-Hill.

Chase, B. (1997, October 15). Restoring the impulse to dream: the right to a quality public education. *Vital speeches of the day.* City News Publishing Company.

Noll, J. W. (1999). *Taking sides: Clashing views on controversial issues,* 10th ed. Guilford, CT: Dushkin/McGraw-Hill.

Rose, L. C. and Gallup, A. M. (1998, September). The 30th annual Phi Delta Kappa/Gallup poll of the public's attitudes toward the public schools. *Phi Delta Kappan,* 41–56.

in-service sessions, and act as mentors for teachers new to the profession. Many also teach courses within schools of education on a seconded or part-time basis for there is a growing belief that such individuals can bring the true flavour of public school teaching to the university classroom. Teachers are becoming leaders within their profession. As the titles of the following books published during the 1990s suggest, the term **teacher-leader** has become part of the vocabulary of educational improvement.

- *Awakening the Sleeping Giant: Leadership Development for Teachers* (Katzenmeyer and Moller 1996).
- *Collaborative Leadership and Shared Decision Making: Teachers, Principals, and University Professors* (Clift et al. 1995).
- *Educating Teachers for Leadership and Change* (O'Hair and Odell 1995).
- *A Handbook for Teacher Leaders* (Pellicer and Anderson 1995).
- *Teachers as Leaders: Evolving Roles* (Livingston 1992).
- *Teachers as Leaders: Perspectives on the Professional Development of Teachers* (Walling 1994).
- *Who Will Save Our Schools?: Teachers as Constructivist Leaders* (Lambert et al 1996).

"In their new leadership roles, teachers are being called upon to form new partnerships with business and industry; institutions of higher education; social service agencies; professional associations; and local, and provincial governmental agencies. In this new role, teachers will be the key to promoting widespread improvement of our educational system" (Gmelch and Parkay 1995, 50–51). A brief look at the professional activities of Sandra MacQuinn, a teacher-leader who worked with the first author and a colleague on a major restructuring effort at a large urban high school, illustrates the wide-ranging roles of a teacher-leader. In addition to teaching, here are just a few of MacQuinn's leadership activities while serving as liaison and on-site coordinator of a school-university partnership.

- Writing grant proposals for teacher-developed projects
- Helping other teachers write grant proposals
- Facilitating the development of an integrated school-to-work curriculum
- Preparing newsletters to keep faculty up-to-date on restructuring
- Organizing and facilitating staff development training
- Developing connections with area businesses and arranging "job shadowing" sites for students

- Working with a community college to create an alternative school for Rogers High students at the college
- Scheduling substitute teachers to provide Rogers teachers with release-time to work on restructuring
- Making presentations on the school's restructuring at provincial and regional conferences.
- Meeting with the principal, assistant principals, professors, and others to develop short- and long-range plans for implementing site-based management; chairing meetings of the site-based council, the restructuring steering committee, and other restructuring-related committees.

At a large middle school which has several schools within a school, teachers have the following roles: coordinator of special education services and lead teacher, coordinator of the media centre responsible for schoolwide implementation of technology, and director of the school's whole-language program (Gerstner et al. 1994). At an elementary school with a shared decision making form of governance, teachers work on committees that make hiring, budget, and school policy decisions. In the words of one teacher at that school: "I'm not just a teacher in a classroom, I am a member of an organization, a company that helps to run the school. I'm not just alone in my room" (Ross and Webb 1995, 76).

Dimensions of Teacher Leadership Beyond the Classroom

Figure 10.3 illustrates ten dimensions of teacher leadership beyond the classroom. The many teachers whom we have assisted on school restructuring projects during the last few years have used these skills to reach an array of educational goals. Clearly, these teachers have modeled what Rallis (1990, 193) terms "an elevated conception of teaching."

Figure 10.3

Ten dimensions of teacher leadership beyond the classroom

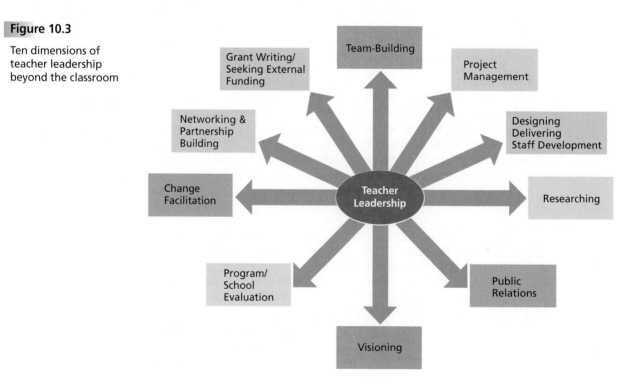

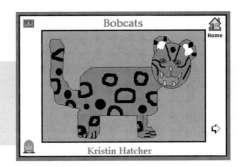

Bobcats

Home

Kristin Hatcher

How are teachers playing a leadership role in the development and dissemination of multimedia software?

As pointed out in Chapter 9, a key to the effective use of technology to enhance students' learning is the availability of high-quality educational software. Since computer-enhanced instruction (CEI) first began to be used widely in the schools during the early 1990s, there has been a consistent call for higher-quality educational software and a realization that teachers, with their deep understanding of students' learning needs, would need to play a central role in the development of that software. Educational software publishers now realize that teachers need to be involved in separating the wheat from the chaff."

In response to that call, scores of teachers have become directly involved in developing and disseminating innovative, cutting-edge educational software. Perhaps the best known teacher-developed software is Roger Wagner's *HyperStudio®*, which now has millions of worldwide users. As a science and mathematics teacher in California, Wagner launched *HyperStudio®* in 1978. According to Wagner, "We wanted to make multimedia authoring a reality for students on the humble Apple IIGS. [The] world at large sets the stage for what is happening in classrooms now. As students increasingly use electronic sources of information for their research, and see the pervasion of multimedia around them, they expect to create their own projects in the same manner"

(Davitt 1997). Currently, dozens of teachers provide Wagner with input as he continues to develop newer versions of *HyperStudio®.*

Many other teachers around the country are working with instructional technology laboratories to develop and field test multimedia software. For example, scores of teachers have collaborated with researchers to develop *Astronomy Village* and *Investigating the Solar System,* two of the most innovative computer simulations currently available.

Still other teachers are providing leadership for the integration of technology into teaching and learning environments. For example, thousands of teachers have attended Teacher-Leader Institutes, where they acquire strategies for integrating technology into education. Clearly, teachers will play three vital leadership roles in the development of multimedia software for classrooms of the twenty-first century:

- Developing and disseminating increasingly powerful versions of multimedia software
- Developing strategies for the most effective ways to use that software in the classroom
- Training other teachers to use that software

At schools around the country, teachers and principals are using a "collaborative, emergent" approach to leadership; that is, the person who provides leadership for a particular school-wide project or activity may or may not be the principal or a member of the administrative team (Parkay, Schindler and Oaks, 1997). Such schools are characterized by a "higher level of professional community" (Newmann and Wehlage 1995). They are similar to the schools Wohlstetter (1995, 24) identified as having successfully implemented site-based management (SBM): "[They] had principals who played a key role in dispersing power. [T]he principals were often described as facilitators and managers of change." In addition, teachers who accept the challenge of becoming

Figure 10.4

Five principles that
guide the actions of
teacher-leaders

Source: Adapted from
Michael Fullan and Andy
Hargreaves, *What's Worth
Fighting for in Your School?*
New York: Teachers College
Press, 1996.

Five Principles That Guide the Actions of Teacher-Leaders

PRINCIPLE 1

Teacher-leaders accept their responsibility to increase the degree and quality of daily interactions with other teachers, administrators, and staff members. They know that "even if done on a small scale regularly, this can make a very significant difference for other individual teachers and for oneself."

PRINCIPLE 2

Teacher-leaders recognize that they have a responsibility to understand and to improve the culture of the school. "Every teacher must be concerned about the health of the school as an organization. This does not mean getting obsessively involved in every aspect of school life, but it does mean taking some responsibility for the welfare of one's colleagues and the wider life of the school."

PRINCIPLE 3

Teacher-leaders recognize that every teacher is a leader, and that a teacher's leadership role will vary according to the stage of the teacher's life and career. However, "all teachers have a leadership contribution to make beyond their own classrooms and should take action accordingly."

PRINCIPLE 4

Teacher-leaders recognize that they have a responsibility to become informed about the development of educational policies as well as professional and research issues. "This does not mean having a second career as an academic. But it does mean connecting with the knowledge base for improving teaching and schools. The more knowledgeable a teacher is about global educational and professional issues, the more resourceful he or she will be for students as well as for other teachers."

PRINCIPLE 5

Teacher-leaders recognize that all teachers have a responsibility for helping to shape the quality of the next generation of teachers. Teachers can make a contribution by working with student teachers, mentoring new teachers, and supporting and praising other teachers who assume those roles.

teacher-leaders and redefining their roles to include responsibilities beyond the classroom recognize the importance of five principles Michael Fullan and Andy Hargreaves present in their book, *What's Worth Fighting for in Your School?* (1996); they use these principles to guide their professional actions (see Figure 10.4).

How Do Teachers Contribute to Educational Research?

Today's teachers play an increasingly important role in educational research. By applying research to solve practical, classroom-based problems, teachers validate the accuracy and usefulness of educational research and help researchers identify additional areas to investigate. As consumers of educational research, teachers improve their teaching, contribute to educational advancements, and enhance the professional status of teaching.

The new calls to leadership for teachers suggest that teachers' essential knowledge and skills may not differ much from those traditionally required for educational administrators. Performance requirements (domains) have been established by all provinces and territories for those who are *principal* teachers (ie., those who are the principal of a school). Which of the following domains also apply to teacher-leaders? To what extent are the knowledge and skills required of teacher-leaders and of principals becoming similar?

I. **Functional Domains**
   1. Leadership
   2. Information Collection
   3. Problem Analysis
   4. Judgment
   5. Organizational Oversight
   6. Implementation
   7. Delegation

II. **Programmatic Domains**
   8. Instructional Program
   9. Curriculum Design
   10. Student Guidance and Development
   11. Staff Development
   12. Measurement and Evaluation
   13. Resource Allocation

III. **Interpersonal Domains**
   14. Motivating Others
   15. Sensitivity
   16. Oral Expression
   17. Written Expression

IV. **Contextual Domains**
   18. Philosophical and Cultural Values
   19. Legal and Regulatory Applications
   20. Policy and Political Influences
   21. Public and Media Relationships

In addition, increasing numbers of teachers are becoming competent researchers in their own right and making important contributions to our understanding of teaching and learning. Prior to the mid 1980s, teachers were the missing "voice" in educational research. However, as teachers and staff developers Holly and McLoughlin (1989, 309) noted more than a decade ago, "We've moved from research on teachers to research with teachers and lately to research by teachers." Since their observation, we have seen the emergence of the **teacher-researcher,** the professional teacher who conducts classroom research to improve his or her teaching.

Part of being a professional is the ability to decide *how* and *when* to use research to guide one's actions. For example, Emmerich Koller, a teacher of German at a suburban high school, describes in an article he wrote for the book *Teachers Doing Research: Practical Possibilities* (Burnaford, Fischer, and Hobson 1996) how he experimented with new teaching methods based on the latest findings from brain research and "accelerated learning," a strategy for optimizing learning by integrating conscious and unconscious mental processes. After determining how and when to put that research into practice, he commented, "At age 50, after 27 years of teaching, I have found something that has made teaching very exciting again" (Koller 1996, 180).

Sources of Educational Research

Research findings are reported in scores of educational research journals (see Appendix 10.2). In addition, there are several excellent reviews of research with which you should become familiar during your professional preparation, such as the third edition of the *Handbook of Research on Teaching* (published by Macmillan, 1986), a project sponsored by the American Educational Research Association. Its more than 1000 pages synthesize research in several areas, including research on teaching at various grade levels and in various subject areas. Other comprehensive, authoritative reviews of research you might wish to consult include the following:

This teacher is conducting classroom research on the ways students come to understand a problem and to apply appropriate problem-solving skills. What are several ways the teacher might use this research as a professional?

- *Encyclopedia of Educational Research,* 6th ed., four volumes (Macmillan, 1992)
- *Handbook of Research on the Education of Young Children* (Macmillan, 1993)
- *Handbook of Research on Mathematics Teaching and Learning* (Macmillan, 1992), sponsored by the National Council of Teachers of Mathematics
- *Handbook of Research on Multicultural Education* (Macmillian, 1995)
- *Handbook of Research on Teaching the English Language Arts* (Macmillan, 1991), sponsored by the International Reading Association and the National Council of Teachers of English
- Handbook of Research on Teaching Literacy through the Communicative and Visual Arts (Macmillan, 1997)

The United States Federal Government did Canadian educational researchers a great service when it created the **Educational Resources Information Center (ERIC).** ERIC is an American information system made up of sixteen **ERIC Clearinghouses** and several adjunct clearinghouses—all coordinated by the central ERIC agency in Washington, D.C. The ERIC system, now available in most Canadian college and university libraries, contains descriptions of exemplary programs, the results of research and development efforts, and related information that can be used by teachers, administrators, and the public to improve education. Each Clearinghouse specializes in one area of education and searches out relevant documents or journal articles that are screened according to ERIC selection criteria, abstracted, and indexed.

Organizations such as the Canadian Teachers' Federation, Canadian Council for the Advancement of Education, the Canadian Council for the Advancement of Education, the Canadian Education Association, and many others (see Appendix 10.1), are devoted to high-quality, fundamental research at every level of education, with most of the research done by scholars at the host university. Among the areas these centres focus on are the processes of teaching and learning, school organization and improvement, the content of education, and factors that contribute to (or detract from) excellence in education.

Conducting Classroom Action Research

More than three decades ago, Robert Schaefer (1967, 5) posed the following questions in *The School as the Center of Inquiry*:

> Why should our schools not be staffed, gradually if you will, by scholar-teachers in command of the conceptual tools and methods of inquiry requisite to investigating the learning process as it operates in their own classroom? Why should our schools not nurture the continuing wisdom and power of such scholar-teachers?

Schaefer's vision for teaching has become a reality. Today, thousands of teachers are involved in action research to improve their teaching. Using their classrooms as "laboratories," these teacher-researchers are systematically studying the outcomes of their teaching through the application of various research methods. In addition, they are disseminating the results of their research at professional conferences and through various publications.

Simply put, **action research** is the classroom-based study by teachers, individually or collaboratively, of how to improve instruction. As in the *reflection-in-action* approach described earlier in this chapter, action research begins with a teacher-identified question, issue, or problem. How can I more effectively motivate a group of students? How do students experience the climate in my classroom? What factors limit parental participation in our school? How can our department (or teacher team) become more collegial? How does computer use in the foreign language classroom affect students' oral communication? Identification of the question to be investigated via action research is a critical step, as the staff development coordinator at an urban elementary school points out:

> As a member of the school leadership team responsible for staff development, I helped guide the process of designing and carrying out the [action research] projects. One of the major challenges in conducting action research projects for this particular group of teachers was the first step: defining the question or problem to be studied. The delicate part of the facilitator's role for this part of action research is to guide teachers toward questions that accurately represent their real concerns and to help them articulate questions in ways that clarify the important elements. If action research is to be useful and engaging, then questions must focus on significant issues related to the success of students within the classroom (Mills 2000, 130).

Action research is also "a natural part of teaching. [T]o be a teacher means to observe students and study classroom interactions, to explore a variety of effective ways of teaching and learning, and to build conceptual frameworks that can guide one's work. This is a personal as well as a professional quest, a journey toward making sense out of and finding satisfaction in one's teaching. It is the work of teacher-researchers" (Fischer 1996, 33).

Action research can be used to study almost any dimension of teaching and learning. At the beginning of the action research cycle, Mills (2000, 41) suggests developing an "action plan" consisting of these steps:

- Write an area-of-focus statement.
- Define the variables.
- Develop research questions.
- Describe the intervention or innovation.
- Describe the membership of the action research group.
- Describe negotiations that need to be undertaken.
- Develop a timeline.
- Develop a statement of resources.
- Develop data collection ideas.

Figure 10.5

Action research data
collection techniques
(The Three Es)

Source: Geoffrey E. Mills,
*Action Research: A Guide
for the Teacher Researcher.*
Upper Saddle River, NJ:
Merrill, 2000, p. 66. © 2000.
Reprinted by permission of
Prentice Hall, Inc., Upper
Saddle River, NJ.

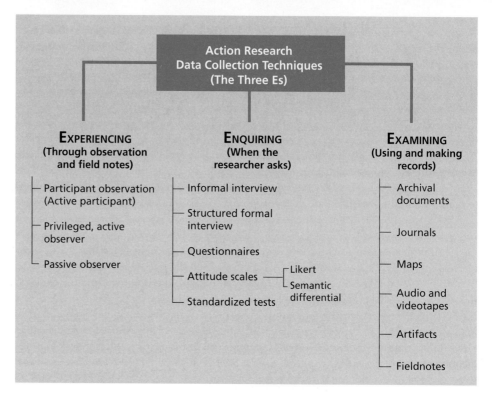

Figure 10.5 presents a "taxonomy" of data collection techniques for action research.
Not surprisingly, becoming a teacher-researcher is hard work, given the daily
demands of teaching itself. However, more schools are redefining the teacher's role to
include doing action research. These schools realize that action research can provide
data on the effectiveness of educational programs, enhance student learning, and
energize teachers for professional growth. Four teachers, all members of an action
research team, comment on the benefits of action research:

> By far the most rewarding part of working on an action research team was the
> opportunity to learn and grow with a small group of teacher colleagues. This expe-
> rience of mutual commitment provided a wonderful staff development experi-
> ence; by working with these colleagues consistently throughout the year, we were
> able to explore new ideas and take risks in the classroom with a type of "safety net"
> in place. For that reason alone, as well as our desire to explore the new questions
> and challenges raised by our research, we will continue to conduct action research
> into the effectiveness of our teaching and grading practices (Mills 2000, 97).

How Are Teachers Providing Leadership for School Development and Curriculum Improvement?

Today's teachers welcome opportunities to provide leadership for school development
and curriculum improvement. Although teachers may have played a limited role in
school governance in the past, there are currently many opportunities for teachers to
become educational leaders beyond the classroom. Figure 10.6 presents five clusters
of educational improvement, each of which will offer teachers opportunities to shape
policies during the twenty-first century.

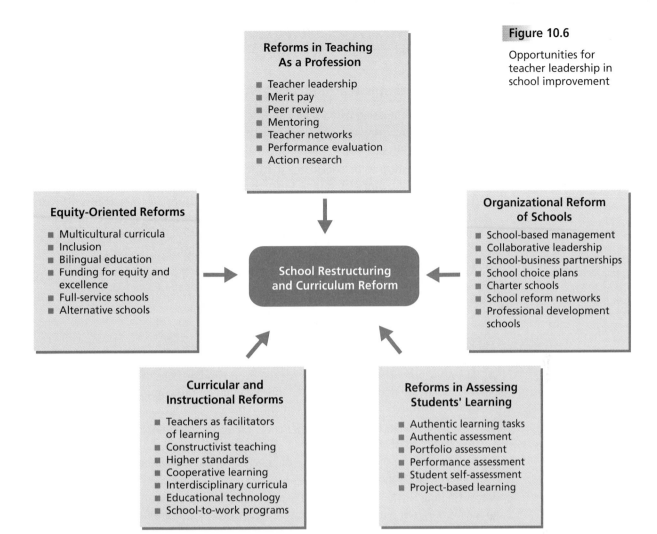

Figure 10.6

Opportunities for teacher leadership in school improvement

Reforms in Teaching As a Profession

- Teacher leadership
- Merit pay
- Peer review
- Mentoring
- Teacher networks
- Performance evaluation
- Action research

Equity-Oriented Reforms

- Multicultural curricula
- Inclusion
- Bilingual education
- Funding for equity and excellence
- Full-service schools
- Alternative schools

School Restructuring and Curriculum Reform

Organizational Reform of Schools

- School-based management
- Collaborative leadership
- School-business partnerships
- School choice plans
- Charter schools
- School reform networks
- Professional development schools

Curricular and Instructional Reforms

- Teachers as facilitators of learning
- Constructivist teaching
- Higher standards
- Cooperative learning
- Interdisciplinary curricula
- Educational technology
- School-to-work programs

Reforms in Assessing Students' Learning

- Authentic learning tasks
- Authentic assessment
- Portfolio assessment
- Performance assessment
- Student self-assessment
- Project-based learning

The key to successful school development and curriculum improvement is teacher leadership and collaboration. The following possibilities are among the many ways in which teachers can deliver the leadership required.

- Participate in professional teacher organizations
- Take part in school decisions
- Define what students need to know and be able to do
- Share ideas with colleagues
- Be a mentor to new teachers
- Improve facilities and technology
- Work with parents
- Create partnerships with the community
- Create partnerships with businesses and organizations
- Create partnerships with colleges and universities to prepare future teachers
- Become a leader in the community
- Lead efforts to make teachers more visible; communicate positive information

To What Extent Is Teaching a Full Profession?

- Teachers are assuming new leadership roles beyond the classroom as educational systems become more decentralized and approaches to school leadership become more collaborative and participatory.

- For an occupation to be considered a profession, it must satisfy several criteria. Of the following nine criteria for a profession, teaching meets some more fully than others: (1) institutional monopoly of services, (2) teacher autonomy, (3) years of education and training, (4) provision of essential service, (5) degree of self-governance, (6) professional associations, (7) professional knowledge and skills, (8) level of public trust, and (9) prestige, benefits, and pay.

- Although teaching does not currently satisfy all criteria for a profession, the collaborative efforts of individuals and groups such as the Canadian Teachers' Federation are very active in this area.

What Is Professionalism in Teaching?

- The most potent force for enhancing the professional status of teaching is for teachers to see that their actions are professional and to commit themselves to lifelong learning and active involvement in the profession.

- Professional behaviour as a teacher is characterized by reflection-in-action (the ability to observe sensitively in classrooms, reflect on those observations, and then act accordingly) and a willingness to serve as a mentor to those entering the profession.

- As lifelong learners, professional teachers actively seek opportunities for growth—from participating in training provided by a school district to arranging one's own "in-service" activities, to acquiring new leadership skills.

To What Professional Organizations Do Teachers Belong?

- Teachers help shape education as a profession through their leadership roles in local, provincial, and national teacher organizations.

- Teachers are members of professional associations for specific subject areas and student populations.

What New Leadership Roles for Teachers Are Emerging?

- Through their involvement with local, provincial, national, and international teacher organizations, teachers participate in making key decisions about teacher preparation, certification, and staff development.

- In their new role as teacher-leaders, many teachers are playing a key role beyond the classroom as they form partnerships that focus on the improvement of Canadian schools.

- Teachers who work collaboratively with principals on school improvement use ten dimensions of teacher leadership beyond the classroom: team-building, project management, designing and delivering staff development, researching, public relations, visioning, program/school evaluation, change facilitation, networking and partnership building, and grant writing/seeking external funding.

How Do Teachers Contribute to Educational Research?

- Teachers validate the accuracy and usefulness of educational research and identify additional areas to research when they put "research into practice."

- In the role of teacher-researcher, many teachers conduct action research and systematically study the outcomes of their teaching. Teachers use a five-step action research cycle to study their classrooms and improve their teaching: problem identification, planning, organization, evaluation, and action.

How Are Teachers Providing Leadership for School Development and Curriculum Improvement?

- Five "clusters" of educational improvement areas provide teachers with many opportunities to provide leadership for school improvement: reforms in teaching as a profession, equity-oriented reforms, organizational improvement of schools, improvements in assessing students' learning, and curricular and instructional improvements.

KEY TERMS AND CONCEPTS

action research, 379
Canadian Teachers' Federation (CTF), 370

Educational Resources Information Center (ERIC), 378
ERIC Clearinghouses, 378
mentor, 366

Phi Delta Kappa (PDK), 371
profession, 360
reflection-in-action, 365
teacher-leader, 373
teacher-researcher, 377

APPLICATIONS AND ACTIVITIES

Teacher's Journal

1. In your opinion, what accounts for public trust and lack of trust in the teaching profession? What might be the best way to increase that trust?

2. Visit the Canadian Teachers' Federation and review several of the most recently published articles. What topics appear to be receiving the most attention?

3. Do you plan to join a teacher's association after you graduate? What are your reasons? What advantages and disadvantages are most important to you?

Teacher's Database

1. With classmates, join or start an online discussion on one or more of the following topics or another topic in Chapter 10 of this text.

   action research   teacher leadership
   educational reform   teacher strikes
   grant writing   teacher unions
   mentoring   teacher–principal collaboration
   school improvement

2. Using your favourite search engine, gather online information and resources about school networking and teacher networking. How might online networking contribute to your preparation as a teacher? As a teacher, how might you and your students use networking in connection with your curriculum? What knowledge and skills do you need to start to participate in a school-based networking project?

Observations and Interviews

1. Survey adults who are not involved in education to get their views on teaching as a profession. What images of teachers and teaching emerge? How do you account for these views?

2. Interview teachers about their involvement in professional associations and the teachers' union. What benefits do teachers obtain from their professional involvement?

3. Find out if teacher strikes are legal in your province or territory. What risks do striking teachers face? How are disputes between teachers and school districts settled?

4. Collaborate with classmates to study a school that is involved in restructuring and participants' roles in the change process. Compare teachers' activities with the new leadership roles for teachers discussed in this chapter. Are any of the teachers involved in action research in the classroom? How does teacher research contribute to restructuring efforts?

5. Visit a school that has developed a partnership with one or more community agencies, schools of higher education, businesses, parent groups, or neighbourhood associations. Arrange to observe a planning meeting between the school and the community representatives. Write a narrative account of the meeting followed by an evaluation of the effectiveness of this partnership.

Professional Portfolio

Focusing on the grade level and subject area for which you are preparing to teach, consult several of the sources of educational research listed in this chapter and prepare a set of research findings to guide your teaching. For each entry, include a bibliographic citation and an annotation that briefly describes the research and the results of that research.

Appendix 10.1

Directions

- Each negotiation team will appoint a reporter to complete/return this sheet.
- There are 35 min available for reaching mutual agreement as to which items shall be included in the next contract.
- Failure to reach agreement will result in a strike being declared. All who go on strike will receive zero bonus points.
- Each team of union negotiators competes against every other team of union negotiators; the same situation applies to government negotiators.
- Depending on negotiating success, non-striking teams can earn up to 3 bonus points.

Union Team Members   *Government Team Members*

Team Name _____   Team Name _____
_____   _____
_____   _____
_____   _____
_____   _____

Items To Be Negotiated

1. Salaries (Every one percent increase in teacher salaries will cost the government $5 million per year)

    ____ 1% raise   ____ 4% raise ____   ____ 7% raise
    ____ 2% raise   ____ 5% raise ____   ____ 8% raise
    ____ 3% raise   ____ 6% raise ____   ____ 9 % raise

2. Insurance packages

    a. Life Insurance to be paid by the employer. (A $20 000 policy for each teacher will cost the government $1 million per year.)

    __ $10 000   __ $20 000   __ $40 000
    __ $60 000   __ $80 000   __ $100 000

    b. Salary continuation: Salary continuation costs for all teachers would be $5 million per year. The union would probably be content to have the government pay a percentage of the costs of this program.

    ____ 0% of costs ____ 20% ____ 40%
    ____ 60% ____ 80% ____ 100%

    c. Dental Care Program: Full Dental Care would cost about $5 million per year. As with salary continuation, the union would be happy to see a portion of the costs covered by the government.

    ____ 0% of costs ____ 20% ____ 40%
    ____ 60% ____ 80% ____ 100%

    d. Pharmacare Medical Program to cover drugs, eye glasses, private hospital room, and other related medical needs: This program is very expensive and would cost the government, if it paid the full costs, about $10 million per year. As with other items, the union would settle for a percentage of the costs.

    ____ 0% of costs ____ 20% ____ 40%
    ____ 60% ____ 80% ____ 100%

3. Miscellaneous items

    a. Terms of employment: The government wants greater authority to rid the schools of incompetent teachers. It sees the "seniority" clause in the present agreement as a hindrance to its aims. The union, on the other hand, feels an obligation to protect its members. The possibilities are:

    ___ Merit employment only; no seniority of any type
    ___ Renewable seniority which is good for a five-year period. Decision to be made by an independent panel of experts.
    ___ Merit employment for the first five years of teaching with seniority protection at the end of this period.
    ___ Maintain present seniority system

    b. Terms of Employment: The government is concerned that too many teachers are not keeping current with modern pedagogical practices. The possibilities are:

    ____ Require that all teachers take part in 100 h of in-service and/or university course work (in a <u>three</u> year period) to maintain their current license levels. Failure to meet this requirement would result in a teacher's license being reduced by one level (eg., a TC5 license would become a TC4).

_____ Require that all teachers take part in 100 h of in-service and/or university course work (in a <u>five</u> year period) to maintain their current license levels. Failure to meet this requirement would result in a teacher's license being reduced by one level (eg., TC5 license would become a TC4).

_____ Maintain present system with no professional development requirement.

Other Information

As negotiations start, your province/territory has just ended a four-year period of fiscal restraint. In addition, there is a new government as the result of a recent election. With four years to go before it has to renew its mandate from the people, the government feels it can be relatively tough in its negotiations with teachers. In addition, money is still tight and funds given to teachers would have to be taken from some other area of the budget.

Appendix 10.2

Canadian Education Associations

ABC Canada (a national nonprofit literacy organization) www.abc-canada.org

The ABC Canada website provides information about national literacy awareness campaigns, promotional support for local literacy groups, and research to further the development of a fully literate Canadian population.

ACELF—Association canadienne d'education de langue française a pour objectif la promotion et la defense de la langue et de la culture francaise au Canada www.acelf.ca

The organization's official website.

Association of Canadian Community Colleges www.accc.ca

The Association of Canadian Community Colleges website provides information for teachers to meet the educational and training needs of students.

Association for Canadian Home-Based Education www.flora.org/homeschool-ca/achbe/index.html

The Association for Canadian Home-Based Education website provides information about home schooling.

AMTEC—Association for Media and Technology in Education in Canada www.amtec.ca/

The official website of the Association for Media and Technology in Education in Canada.

Association for Teacher-Librarianship in Canada www.atlc.ca/

The Association for Teacher-Librarianship in Canada website provides educators with information about advocacy, cooperative planning, cooperative teaching, and resource-based instruction.

Association of Universities and Colleges of Canada www.aucc.ca

The Association of Universities and Colleges of Canada website provides information on Canadian higher education.

Bacchus Canada: The Alcohol Education Group www.bacchus.ca

The Student Life Education Company website provides resources, training, and educational materials to help Canadian students make healthy decisions about alcohol use.

Canada Student Loans Program www.hrdc-drhc.gc.ca/student_loans

The Canada Student Loans Program website provides information about qualifying, making payments, interest rates, and legislation for Canadian student loans.

Canada World Youth www.cwy-jcm.org/

The Canada World Youth website provides information to Canadian students about opportunities to travel, live, and work in different communities.

Canadian Association for Distance Education www.cade-aced.ca

The Canadian Association for Distance Education Website provides information about distance education in Canada.

Canadian Association for Health, Physical Education, Recreation, and Dance www.cahperd.ca/

The Canadian Association for Health, Physical Education, Recreation, and Dance website provides information for teachers, administrators, researchers, coaches, students, and others who have an interest in the fields of physical education, physical activity, health, fitness, sport, recreation, and dance.

Canadian Association for Media Education Organizations http://interact.uoregon.edu/MediaLit/CAMEO/index.html

The Canadian Association for Media Education Organizations provides information about promoting and developing media literacy in Canada.

Canadian Association for Pastoral Practice and Education www.cappe.org

The Canadian Association for Pastoral Practice and Education website provides information about professional education, certification, and support to people involved in pastoral care and pastoral counselling.

Canadian Association for University Continuing Education http://cauce-aepuc.ca/

The Canadian Association for University Continuing Education website provides information for deans, directors, senior administrative personnel, and practitioners, whose professional careers are in university continuing education in Canada.

Appendix 10.2 (continued)

Canadian Association of Career Educators and Employers www.cacee.com

The Canadian Association of Career Educators and Employers website provides information, advice, and services to employers, students, and career centre personnel, in the areas of career planning and student recruitment.

Canadian Association of College & University Student Services www2.cacuss.ca/cacuss

The Canadian Association of College and University Student Services website provides information for people working in post-secondary education in the student affairs or service fields.

Canadian Association of Learned Journals http://calj.icaap.org/

The Canadian Association of Learned Journals website provides information about learned journals in Canada as disseminators of scholarly work.

Canadian Association of Student Activity Advisors http://sentex.net/~casaa

The Canadian Association of Student Activity Advisors website provides information to promote and develop student leadership and activities within Canadian schools.

Canadian Association of University Teachers http://www.caut.ca

The official website of the Canadian Association of University Teachers.

Canadian Bureau for International Education www.cbie.ca

The Canadian Bureau for International Education website provides information about activities, research and services, training programs, scholarship management, and professional development for international educators.

Canadian Career Development Foundation www.ccdf.ca/

The Canadian Career Development Foundation website provides information about careers in education, government, professional associations, community, and the private sector.

Canadian Congress for Learning Opportunities for Women www.nald.ca/cclow.htm

The Canadian Congress for Learning Opportunities for Women website provides information about literacy, equity in education, and job training for women.

Canadian Council for the Advancement of Education www.stmarys.ca/partners/ccae/ccae.htm

The Canadian Council for the Advancement of Education website provides information about issues that face post-secondary institutions.

Canadian Education Association www.acea.ca

The official website of the Canadian Education Association.

Canadian Federation of Students www.cfs-fcee.ca

The Canadian Federation of Students website provides information about the group, which works with students and administrators to build a high-quality system of post-secondary education, which is accessible to all students.

Canadian Higher Education Loan Program www.iefc.com/

The Canadian Higher Education Loan Program (International Education Finance Corporation) website provides information about student loan programs for students who wish to study in foreign countries.

Canadian Institutional Researchers and Planners Association www.usask.ca/cirpal

The Canadian Institutional Researchers and Planners Association website provides information about research, policymaking, management, and planning involved in post-secondary education systems.

Canadian Organization of Campus Activities www.coca.org

The Canadian Organization of Campus Activities website provides information about campus programming that involves educational and business opportunities, resources, and services for professional staff.

Canadian Parents for French www.cpf.ca

The Canadian Parents for French website provides information about the values of French and promotes the creation of French second-language learning opportunities for young Canadians.

Canadian School Library Association www.cla.ca/divisions/csla/

The organization's official website.

Canadian University Press www.cup.ca/

The Canadian University Press website provides student news from Canada's university and college campuses.

Canadian Vocational Association www.cva.ca

The Canadian Vocational Association website provides links to various vocational resources.

Canadian Home and School Federation
cap.ic.gc.ca/chsptf/

The Canadian Home and School Federation website provides information for parents who participate in education at local and provincial levels.

Canadian Teachers' Federation www.ctf-fce.ca/

The Canadian Teachers' Federation website provides information about defending public education, promoting the teaching profession, and societal issues that affect the health and well-being of children and youth in Canada.

Centre for Entrepreneurship Education and Development www.ceed.ednet.ns.ca

The Centre for Entrepreneurship Education and Development website provides information about entrepreneurship education, research and program design, professional development, and community entrepreneurship.

Child and Family Canada www.cfc-efc.ca

The Child and Family Canada website provides information about children and families in Canada.

Council of Ministers of Education Canada
www.cmec.ca

The Council of Ministers of Education Canada website provides information about elementary, secondary, and postsecondary education.

Institute for Leadership Development
www.ildglobal.org/newsite/main.htm

The Institute for Leadership Development website provides information about critical issues concerning young professionals and young entrepreneurs around the world.

Interuniversity Services Inc www.interuniversity.ns.ca

The official website of Interuniversity Services Inc.

Junior Achievement of Canada www.jacan.org

The Junior Achievement of Canada website provides information to help students discover leadership, entrepreneurial, and workforce skills so they can achieve their highest potential.

Learning Disabilities Association of Canada
http://edu-ss10.educ.queensu.ca/~lda

The Learning Disabilities Association of Canada website provides information about the advancement of education, employment, social development, legal rights, and general well-being of people with learning disabilities.

Media Awareness Network
www.media-awareness.ca/

The Media Awareness Network website provides information about media literacy and education resources for parents and teachers.

National Literacy and Health Program
www.nlhp.cpha.ca/

The official website of the National Literacy and Health Program.

National Literacy Secretariat www.nald.ca/nls.htm

The National Literacy Secretariat provides information about literacy as an essential component for a learning society.

Ontario Native Literacy Coalition
www.nald.ca/onlc.htm

The Ontario Native Literacy Coalition website provides culturally relevant learning materials that promote a greater awareness about native literacy.

Prime Minister's Awards for Teaching Excellence
www.schoolnet.ca/pma/

The Prime Minister's Awards for Teaching Excellence website provides information about the awards that recognize the efforts of outstanding teachers in all disciplines who provide students with the tools to become good citizens, develop and grow as individuals, and contribute to Canada's growth.

Public Service Commission of Canada Training Programs Branch www.edu.psc-cfp.gc.ca

The Public Service Commission of Canada Training Programs website provides information about work-related training and career development.

SchoolNet www.schoolnet.ca

The SchoolNet website provides information about educational resources and services for teachers and students.

Science Teachers' Association of Ontario
www.stao.org/

The official website of the Science Teachers' Association of Ontario.

Service regional d'admission au collegial de Quebec
www.sraq.qc.ca/

The organization's official website.

Social Sciences and Humanities Research Council of Canada www.sshrc.ca

The Social Sciences and Humanities Research Council of Canada website provides information about university-based research and graduate training in the social sciences and humanities.

Society for the Advancement of Excellence in Education www.saee.bc.ca

The Society for the Advancement of Excellence in Education website provides information about education research to policymakers, education partners, and the public.

Writers in Electronic Residence Program www.wier.ca

The Writers In Electronic Residence website is an online program that allows classes to interact with Canadian writers as well as with peers in other classes across Canada in a collaborative writing environment.

World University Service of Canada www.wusc.ca

The World University Service of Canada website provides information about global understanding through education and training.

Source: "Canadian Education Associations," www.worldbook.com. Jan. 2004. World Book Inc., 23 Jan. 2004 <http://www2.worldbook.com/educators/pro_links_can_04.asp> Adaptation of list by permission of World Book, Inc.

Appendix 10.3

Canada-Wide Organizations

Alliance canadienne des responsables des enseignants et enseignantes en français langue maternelle
www.franco.ca/acref/

Association of Canadian College and University Teachers of English
www.mun.ca/accute/

Canadian Adventist Teachers Network
http://catnet.sdacc.org/

Canadian Association of Immersion Teachers
www.educ.sfu.ca/acpi/index-e.htm

Canadian Association of Literacy Educators
www.nald.ca/Cale.htm

Canadian Association of Second Language Teachers
www.caslt.org/

Canadian College of Teachers
www.cct-cce.com/

Canadian Council of Teachers of English Language Arts www.cctela.ca/

Canadian Music Educators Association
www.musiceducationonline.org/cmea/index.html

Contact Point (Career Counsellors)
www.contactpoint.ca/

TESL Canada www.tesl.ca/

Alberta

Alberta Social Studies Council
www.socialstudies.ab.ca/

The Alberta Teachers' Association
www.teachers.ab.ca/

College of Alberta School Superintendents
www.cass.ab.ca/

Confederation of Alberta Faculty Associations
www.ualberta.ca/~cafa/

British Columbia

British Columbia College of Teachers
http://bcct.ca/

British Columbia Teachers' Federation
www.bctf.bc.ca/home.shtml

College-Institute Educators' Associations of British Columbia
www.ciea.bc.ca/

Computer Using Educators of British Columbia
www.cuebchorizons.ca/

Confederation of University Faculty Associations of British Columbia
http://cufabc.harbour.sfu.ca/

Early Childhood Educators of British Columbia
www.cfc-efc.ca/ecebc/

GALE: Gay and Lesbian Educators of B.C.
www.galebc.org/

Vancouver Catholic Schools Teachers' Association
www.vcsta.com/

Manitoba

Computer Education Coordinators of Manitoba
www.cecm.winnipeg.mb.ca/

Manitoba Association of Computer Educators
www.manace.ca/

Manitoba Association of Teachers of English
www.mts.net/~mate1/

Manitoba Teachers of German
http://io.uwinnipeg.ca/~german/mtg.html

The Manitoba Teachers' Society
www.mbteach.org/

Science Teachers' Association of Manitoba
www.stam.mb.ca/

Technology Educators' Association of Manitoba
www.technologyeducators.mb.ca/

New Brunswick

New Brunswick Teachers' Association
www.nbta.ca/

Newfoundland

Association of Early Childhood Educators, Newfoundland and Labrador
www.cfc-efc.ca/aecenfld/

Newfoundland and Labrador Teachers' Association
www.nlta.nf.ca/

Northwest Territories

The Northwest Territories Teachers' Association
www.nwtta.nt.ca/

Appendix 10.3 *(continued)*

Nova Scotia

Association of Science Teachers
http://ast.ednet.ns.ca/main.html

Certification Council of Early Childhood Educators
of Nova Scotia
www.cfc-efc.ca/ccecens/

Nova Scotia Music Educators Association
www.nsmea.com/

Nova Scotia Teachers Union
http://www.nstu.ca/

Ontario

Association des directions et directions adjointes
des écoles franco-ontariennes
www.adfo.org/index2.shtml

Association des enseignantes et des enseignants
franco-ontariens
http://w3.franco.ca/aefo/index.html

Association for Computer Studies Educators
www.acse.net/

Association of Early Childhood Educators, Ontario
www.cfc-efc.ca/aeceo/

Catholic Principals' Council of Ontario
www.cpco.on.ca/

Design and Technology Teachers of Ontario
www.wincom.net/dtto/

Elementary Teachers' Federation of Ontario
www.etfo.on.ca/index2.htm?ETFO_token=6FT06

English Language Arts Network (Ontario)
www.elan.on.ca/

Ontario Association of Business Education
Co-ordinators
www.oabec.org/

Ontario Association of Child and Youth Counsellors
www.oacyc.org/

Ontario Association of Geographic & Environmental
Educators http://oagee.org/

Ontario Association of Police Educators
www.oape.org/

Ontario Association of Physics Teachers
www.physics.uoguelph.ca/OAPT/

Ontario Association of Teachers of German
www.oatg.org/

Ontario Business Educators' Association
www.obea.on.ca/

Ontario College of Teachers
www.oct.ca/flash.html

Ontario Confederation of University Faculty
Associations www.ocufa.on.ca/

Ontario English Catholic Teachers' Association
www.oecta.on.ca/

Ontario Family Studies Home Economics Educators'
Association www.ofsheea.ca/

Ontario Federation of Teaching Parents
www.ontariohomeschool.org/

Ontario History and Social Sciences Teachers'
Association www.ohassta.org/

Ontario Principals' Council
www.principals.on.ca/index3.htm?token=public
www.ormta.org/

Ontario School Counsellors' Association
www.osca.ca/

Ontario Secondary School Teachers' Federation
www.osstf.on.ca/

Ontario Teachers Federation
www.otffeo.on.ca/

Retired Teachers of Ontario
www.rto-ero.org/

Science Teachers' Association of Ontario
www.stao.org/

Teachers for Excellence in Education
www.geocities.com/Athens/7192/moretfe.html

Teachers Life Insurance Society (Fraternal)
www.teacherslife.com/

TESL Ontario - Teachers of English as a Second
Language of Ontario
www.teslontario.org/

Quebec

Association des enseignants en imprimerie de québec
http://home.ca.inter.net/~aeiq/

Association francophone internationale des directeurs
d'établissements scolaires (AFIDES)
http://afides.org/

Association pour les applications pédagogiques de
l'ordinateur au postsecondaire (APOP)
www.apop.qc.ca/

Association québécoise de pédagogie collégiale
www.aqpc.qc.ca/

Association québécoise du personnel de direction des
écoles www.grics.qc.ca/aqpde/index.htm

La Conférence des recteurs et des principaux
   des universités du Québec (CREPUQ)
   www.crepuq.qc.ca/

Fédération québécoise des professeures
   et professeurs d'université
   www.fqppu.qc.ca/

Fédération nationale des enseignantes
   et enseignants du Québec
   www.fneeq.qc.ca/

Saskatchewan

LEADS: League of Educational Administrators,
   Directors and Superintendents of Saskatchewan
   www.sasbo.com/LEADS-forums.html

Saskatchewan Home Economics
   Teachers' Association
   www.stf.sk.ca/prof_growth/ssc/sheta/sheta.html

Saskatchewan Teachers' Federation
   www.stf.sk.ca/

Yukon

Yukon Teachers' Association
   www.yta.yk.ca/

Source: Reprinted with permission. Retrieved November 1, 2003 from www.oise.utoronto.ca/%7Empress/eduweb/teachers.html

11

Your First Teaching Position

What I've found very helpful is to get in touch with all my kids' parents right after the first day. I tell them a bit about how I run my class, what we're going to do that year, and how pleased I am to have their child in my room. I keep it upbeat, very positive. We're going to have a great year!
—A Grade 1 teacher

focus questions

1. How will you become certified or licensed to teach?

2. Where will you teach?

3. How will you find your first teaching job?

4. What can you expect as a beginning teacher?

5. How can you become a part of your learning community?

6. How can you participate in teacher collaboration?

7. How will your performance be evaluated?

Your spring student-teaching seminar ended minutes ago; now you and three other students are seated in the faculty–student lounge enjoying coffee and talking about finding a job.

"What was the interview like?" you ask one of your classmates, upon learning that he interviewed yesterday for a position at an urban school.

"Yeah, tell us," another student adds. "I'm really anxious about interviewing. I don't know what to expect. There're so many things they could ask."

"Well, I was interviewed by the principal and two people from the district office—I think they were in personnel. At first, they asked questions like the ones we used in our seminar role plays: 'Why do you want to teach? What are your weaknesses? Use five adjectives to describe yourself.'"

"What else?" you ask, anxious to complete a mental image of the interview process so you'll be ready for your first interview next week.

"They asked me to describe a student teaching lesson that went well," he continues. "After I did that, one of them asked 'How could the lesson have been better—either for the entire class or for a certain student?' That one took some thinking."

As he goes on to reconstruct his response, you imagine how you would answer the same question.

Moments later, he says, "Then, one that really surprised me came when I was asked 'What would you do if your principal told you to discontinue a classroom activity because it was too noisy and left a mess for the custodians to clean up? But, the activity really involved the kids and they learned a lot.'"

He pauses for a sip of coffee and then continues, "Another one was, 'Give us an example of a principle that guides your teaching.'"

Impressed with the district's ability to pose challenging questions, you again imagine how you would respond.

A few minutes later, another student asks, "What about portfolios? Did they spend much time looking at yours?"

"Did they ever!" your classmate exclaims. "With my application materials I included a portfolio on CD-ROM; plus I gave them the web address for my portfolio. They were pretty impressed. It was obvious that they had looked at just about everything in the portfolio. They asked all kinds of questions. Half the questions were about how to make a digital portfolio. But they also really wanted to see things that were related to how much my students learned while I was student teaching."

With the mention of portfolios, you're reminded of tomorrow's computer lab workshop on how to create an electronic portfolio. Hopefully, you'll have a portfolio on CD-ROM that you can take to your first job interview next week. In addition, you wonder what else you should do to prepare for the interview and what steps you can follow to increase your chances of finding the best possible teaching position.

On completion of your teacher education program, you will still have several important steps to take before securing your first teaching position. Preparing well for these steps will go a long way toward helping you begin teaching with confidence.

It is natural that you feel both excited and a bit fearful when thinking about your first job. While taking the courses required in your teacher education program, you probably feel secure in your role as a student; you know what is expected of you. As a teacher, however, you will assume an entirely new role—a role that requires some time before it becomes comfortable. The aim of this chapter, then, is to help make the transition from student to professional teacher a positive, pleasant one. We first look at the steps you can take to become certified or licensed to teach and to identify current trends related to teacher supply and demand.

How Will You Become Certified or Licensed to Teach?

A **teaching certificate** is actually a license to teach. The majority of Canadian provinces and territories require completion of a professional teacher education program consisting of a minimum of 30 semester credit-hours of course work and practicum for teacher certification.

In terms of professional teacher education course work, in general, provinces and territories do not prescribe content; however, coursework in teaching methodology and educational psychology is common to all teacher education programs. With the exception of Ontario, approved teacher education programs within Canada contain a minimum 12-week practicum experience (Council of Ministers of Education 1999).

Provincial Certification Requirements

Although all jurisdictions, through the power of legislation, have the ultimate authority to change certification requirements in order to comply with the spirit of the Agreement on Internal Trade/Teaching Profession (AIT), some have contractual/protocol arrangements that require consultation with, or approval by, the profession and/or teachers' union.

Most jurisdictions have requirements that all teachers have postsecondary course work background in the subject areas of the K–12 school curriculum within their jurisdiction. This is emphasized more clearly in the preparation of secondary teachers who are expected to have some depth in the subject areas in which they teach. This is normally completed within a first degree.

In most jurisdictions, elementary teachers are also expected to have coursework in the subject areas of the curriculum. This varies from New Brunswick's requirement of coursework in general subject areas, to Ontario's acceptance of any bachelor's degree. In the case of British Columbia, the coursework requirement is 60 credits, including six credits of English, six credits of Canadian Studies, three credits of Mathematics, and three credits of Lab Science.

Some jurisdictions recognize subject areas not found in the K–12 curriculum of other jurisdictions. For example, religious studies, heritage, or international and First Nations languages are specific to a jurisdiction.

Teachers wishing to move between provinces and territories must have access to information on the requirements for qualification in each jurisdiction. Recognizing the importance of this matter, all jurisdictions publish their certification requirements on an annual basis. Jurisdictions publish their requirements on their websites and also make them available to the Council of Ministers of Education, Canada, on its website. You may contact the teacher certification contact in the province where you plan to teach. See Appendix 11.1 for a listing of information on each provincial body responsible for Teacher Certification and Teacher Classification in Canada.

Teacher Certification and Classification for Each Province:

Mobility provisions under the AIT entitle a teacher to receive a teaching credential from the receiving province or territory under the following conditions:

All applicants must:

- hold a valid teaching credential from a Canadian province or territory
- have completed a professional teacher education program consisting of a minimum of 30 semester credit-hours of coursework and practicum for teacher certification
- provide all documents required by the receiving province or territory
- satisfy any requirements of the receiving province or territory with respect to "fit and proper person," currency of practice, and language proficiency

Applicants fall into one of three (3) categories.

Category #1

Applicants who have completed a minimum of four years of postsecondary education and hold a degree(s) completed at a university that is a member of the Association of Universities and Colleges of Canada or any other university degree(s) deemed equivalent by the receiving province or territory, will be issued a teaching credential in the receiving province or territory based on the following.

An applicant who satisfies the basic requirements of the receiving province or territory will be granted a teaching credential by the receiving province or territory.

OR

An applicant who does not satisfy all requirements of the receiving province or territory will be granted a teaching credential valid for a period of time (to be determined by the receiving province or territory)—said time period to be reasonable, in the circumstances—during which time the teacher will be required to complete successfully any outstanding academic/professional preparation requirements of the receiving province or territory.

Category #2

Applicants who hold a degree/diploma in vocational, technical, or technological studies equivalent to the requirements of the receiving province or territory will be issued a teaching credential by the receiving province or territory based on the following specifications.

Applicants who satisfy the equivalent standards, including any work experience requirements, of the receiving province or territory will be granted an appropriate teaching credential by the receiving province or territory. In some instances, the teacher may be required to complete successfully any outstanding academic/professional preparation requirements of the receiving province or territory during the validity period of the teaching credential.

Category #3

Applicants who hold a teaching credential based on academic/professional preparation that does not fall into either of the above two categories will be assessed on a case-by-case basis by the receiving province or territory, and may be granted a teaching credential in the receiving province or territory if they meet the necessary equivalent academic/professional preparation. In some instances, the teacher may be required to complete successfully any outstanding academic/professional preparation requirements of the receiving province or territory during the validity period of the teaching credential (Council of Ministers of Education, 2000).

Where Will You Teach?

When you think ahead to a career in teaching, two questions you are likely to ask yourself are, How hard will it be to find a job? and, Where will I teach? From time to time, **teacher supply and demand** figures have painted a rather bleak picture for those entering the teaching profession. At other times, finding a position in a preferred location has been relatively easy.

The number of educators (elementary and secondary schools) in Canada declined to 271 000 in 1999–2000 from 284 000 in 1991–92 and the number of students in Canadian schools increased to 4.86 million from 4.64 million (Canadian Teachers' Federation, 2000).

Approximately 45 percent of the current Canadian teaching force will be eligible to retire by 2008. According to Statistics Canada, one in five elementary-secondary school teachers in Canada in 1997 was looking for another job when surveyed two years after graduating in 1995. Many Canadian regions report significant difficulties in hiring supply teachers. Further, Canadian teachers are being offered significant financial incentives to teach in the United States and in other countries (Canadian Teachers' Federation, 2000).

A recent empirical study of possible teacher shortages was conducted by the Canadian Teachers Federation in October of 2000. This was a survey of senior administrators responding from 272 of 490 public school boards across Canada and the sample was stratified by size of district, based on enrolments. Survey highlights include:

- Recruiting has been getting more difficult over the past four years.
- Teacher shortages are the most prevalent in science subjects in the past four years (science, chemistry, biology, physics).
- Shortages in some areas vary by language of instruction and/or rural versus non-rural (Canadian Teachers' Federation 2002).

A Favourable Job Market

The description of the trends in demand and supply of teachers due to retirement and attrition does not lead to the firm conclusion that there will be shortages of teachers overall. There are differing views on this important issue, but there does seem to be little disagreement that there are increasing shortages in certain subjects, such as math, science, and technology.

With very low unemployment rates in the occupations of elementary and secondary teaching, the supply of new, additional workers very much depends on the output of graduates from teacher training programs. While there may be different prospects for actual employment gains based on changes in funding, policy, and limited growth in the youth population, the majority of these openings are expected to occur from the workers who are retiring. The results, showing an increased requirement over the 1998 to 2008 period compared to the 1988 to 1998 decade, suggest that the supply of new graduates should be at least the same or somewhat larger (The Steering Group for the Situational Analysis of Canada's Education Sector Human Resources, January 2002, iv).

The ease with which you will find your first teaching position is also related to your area of specialization and to the part of the country where you wish to locate. In mid-February of each year, the various school boards around the country accept applications from both experienced teachers, and also teacher candidates still completing their courses.

Finding a Teaching Position in Canada

Finding a teaching position in Canada requires a plan. For current employment opportunities, the following job-search resources may be helpful:

- *The Education Canada Network* has developed a website to assist job seekers: www.educationcanada.com/
  This site has teaching positions posted from the individual school districts/divisions across Canada. A feature of the website is the Education Canada Resume Registry where visitors can post, edit, renew, or delete their own resume for free. Employers are provided with user ID's and passwords to search the resume database.
- *Apply to Teach Network (ATTN)* is a recruitment database for teachers, school boards, and hiring principals: www.attn.org/
- A registration fee is required.
- *Jobs in Education* also assists job seekers: www.jobsineducation.com/
- Some assistance in locating employment is provided free of charge by the Canada Employment Centres, which are located in all main population centres. In Quebec, inquiries should be directed to the nearest Centre Travail. However, not all teaching vacancies are listed with these centres.

- Lists of school boards may be obtained from the provincial authorities and inquiries regarding possible vacancies made directly to the boards: www.cdnsba.org/
- It is, however, considered a breach of professional ethics to apply for a position in an area where the board's relationship with the teachers has been declared unsatisfactory by the teachers' association.
- Those seeking positions in private schools should get in touch with the clearing-house for applicants to Canadian Independent Schools: www.cais.ca/

Most teaching positions are advertised in local newspapers between February and June, with duties commencing September of the following school year. Vacancies may occur during the school year. Applicants must generally be present in Canada and available for interviews. School principals frequently conduct interviews for positions in their schools.

When considering supply and demand estimates, remember that jobs are to be had in oversupplied areas. Job hunting will be more competitive, though, and you may have to relocate to another region of the country.

Other Career Opportunities for Teachers

There are also a great many non-teaching jobs in education and education-related fields, such as principal, assistant principal, librarian, and counsellor. In addition, there are many jobs that, although removed from the world of the classroom, would nevertheless enable you to use your teaching skills.

The following outline lists several places other than schools where individuals with teaching backgrounds are often employed. The number of education-related careers is likely to increase in the coming decades.

Industry
- Publishers
- Educational materials and equipment suppliers
- Specialized educational service firms
- Communications industries
- Research and development firms
- Management consulting firms
- Education and training consultants

Government
- Jobs in provincial departments of education

Education-Related Associations
- Research centres and foundations
- Professional associations such as Teachers' Associations or Teachers' Unions

Community Organizations
- Community action programs—neighbourhood health centres, legal services
- Social service agencies—Boy Scouts, Girl Scouts, YMCAs and YWCAs, boys' and girls' clubs, women's shelters, etc.
- Adult education centres
- Museums
- Hospitals

How Will You Find Your First Teaching Job?

During the last year of your teacher education program, you will probably become increasingly concerned about finding a teaching position. The "Job Search Timetable Checklist" presented in Appendix 11.2 may help you plan your job search. Also, Figure 11.1 presents an overview of the data and impressions that more than 200 school hiring officials consider most important when they are considering first-time teachers for employment. In the remainder of this section we discuss five critical steps in that sequence: finding out about teaching vacancies, preparing a résumé, writing letters of inquiry and letters of application, being interviewed, and selecting a position.

Finding Out about Teaching Vacancies

Your college or university probably has a **placement service** designed to help graduates find jobs. On a regular basis, placement offices usually publish lists of vacancies, which are posted and, in many cases, mailed to students who have registered with the office and set up a credentials file. In addition, you can use the internet to connect with other universities that have accessible online placement services.

A **credentials file** (known as placement papers at some institutions) usually includes the following: background information on the applicant, the type of position sought, a list of courses taken, performance evaluations by the applicant's cooperative teacher, and three or more letters of recommendation. With each job application, the candidate requests that his or her credentials be sent to the appropriate person at the school district, or the school district itself may request the applicant's papers. Placement offices usually charge a small fee for each time a candidate's papers are sent out.

A job announcement describes the position and its requirements and provides the name and address of the individual to contact at the school district. For each position you are interested in, send a letter of application to the appropriate person along with your résumé. In addition, you may have your placement office send your credentials file. Placement offices also frequently set up on-campus interviews between candidates and representatives of school district personnel departments.

Personal networking will play an important role in landing the right job. Let people know you are looking for a job—friends, teachers at schools you've attended, faculty at the school where you student teach, and people you meet at workshops and conferences. Also, with access to the internet, you can conduct a global job search and even make your résumé available to millions of people.

Job Fairs

Some provinces have used the concept of **job fairs** to advertise and fill teaching positions. Job fairs are designed to bring potential teachers to one location for interviews and information sessions. The procedures used for job fairs vary from province to province. There are usually a number of school boards present and some have specific job openings while others will give candidates a general idea of possible upcoming positions. A common practice is for job fair organizers to offer and require an online registration for the job fair.

Job fairs for beginning teachers usually operate like a market place where each school or school board has its own table or area and candidates visit with the administrators or senior board personnel to talk about positions. Often candidates are given

Figure 11.1

Moving from "candidate" to "teacher"

Note: Items arranged in order of importance.

Source: Adapted from Judy McEnany and Patricia Reuss, "Fascinating Facts for First-Time Teachers," *1999 Job Search Handbook for Educators,* American Association for Employment in Education, p. 31. Used with permission.

CANDIDATE

Employers evaluate first-time teachers' job applications for:

(a) Letters of recommendation from public school personnel
(b) A mentoring teacher's evaluation
(c) Examples of teaching skills and classroom management skills
(d) Experience with specific programs used in the school district
(e) Number of certifications which the candidate holds
   (eg., elementary *and* special education).

Employers evaluate first-time teachers' academic preparation for:

(a) Knowledge of subject matter
(b) Success in student teaching
(c) Computer knowledge and skill

Important factors about candidates' work experience in paid employment not related to teaching include:

(a) A positive work ethic
(b) Punctuality
(c) Good quality work
(d) Low absenteeism

The following factors influence the decision to invite an applicant for an interview:

(a) Correct spelling, punctuation, and English usage of the candidate's application
(b) Letters of recommendation from those who have seen the candidate work with students
(c) Neatness of the applicant's materials
(d) Evaluation from the mentoring teacher

Employers use interview questions to assess the ways in which first-time teachers respond to:

(a) "Real life" and "what if" situations
(b) Classroom management issues
(c) Enthusiasm about teaching
(d) Demonstrating their knowledge of subject matter
(e) Describing and evaluating their own strengths
(f) Structured questions that range from impersonal to personal

In evaluating interviews, employers look for the following:

(a) The candidate's commitment to teaching
(b) Knowledge of the teaching field
(c) Interpersonal skills
(d) The candidate's understanding of the role of a teacher
(e) Professional judgment

TEACHER

a specific time to arrive at the fair location. These fairs give beginning teachers the opportunity to network, participate in interview situations, and gain an understanding of the hiring process of various school districts.

Candidates attending job fairs should take along a carefully prepared resume, a letter of inquiry, and be prepared for being interviewed. Potential employers may have specific vacancies and candidates may be prepared to offer a contract on that day, especially in the specialty areas that are hard to fill such as technology, music, French, and science.

Preparing Your Résumé

A **résumé** presents a concise summary of an individual's professional experiences, education, and skills. Résumés must be typed and preferably no longer than one page, two pages at most. Though there is no right way to prepare a résumé, it should present—in a neat, systematic way—key information that will help an employer determine your suitability for a particular position. Because your résumé will most likely be your first contact with an employer, it must make a good impression.

Ordinarily, a résumé contains the following information:

- Personal data
- Education
- Certificates held
- Experience
- Activities and interests
- Honours and offices held
- Professional memberships
- References

Figure 11.2 on page 404 is a résumé prepared by Linda M. Abbott that you can use as a model. This is only one form of résumé; a variety of résumé samples may be found at the following URL from Concordia University: http://caps.concordia.ca/students/artsscience/resumesamples.shtml

To prepare an effective résumé, read "Résumé Advice for Educators" in Appendix 11.3.

Writing Letters of Inquiry and Application

As a job seeker, you will most likely have occasion to write two kinds of letters: letters of inquiry and letters of application. A **letter of inquiry** is used to determine if a school district has, or anticipates, any teaching vacancies. This type of letter states your general qualifications and requests procedures to be followed in making a formal application (see Figure 11.3 on page 405). A letter of inquiry should also include your résumé as well as a self-addressed, stamped envelope for the school district's convenience. Be prepared not to receive a reply for each letter of inquiry you send out. Many school districts are unable to respond to all inquiries.

A **letter of application** (often called a cover letter) indicates your interest in a particular position and outlines your qualifications for that job. As most districts have several vacancies at any given time, it is important that the first sentence of your letter refer to the specific position for which you are applying. The body of the letter should then highlight why you would be an excellent choice to fill that position. Also, inform the reader that your credentials file will be sent on request or is being sent by your placement office. Close the letter by expressing your availability for an interview (see Figure 11.4 on page 406).

Linda M. Abbott

Personal Data

Address and Phone: 641 Montbeck Crescent

Mississauga, Ontario L5G 1P4

905-891-1248

Education

Bachelor of Arts (English), Queen's University, Kingston, Ontario, May 2001

Bachelor of Education, Faculty of Education, Queen's University, Ontario, May 2003

Certificates Held

Major Area: Elementary/Middle School Education, K-8

Minor Area: Bilingual Education

Experience

Student Teaching, Greenbank Middle School, 168 Greenbank Road, Nepean, Ontario K2H 5V2, Spring 2001 and 2002. Cooperating teacher: Mrs. Becky Jones. Observed, assisted, and taught regular and accelerated Grade 3 classes in a multilingual setting. Organized after-school tutoring program and developed a unit on using the web in the classroom. Attended site-based council meetings with Mrs. Jones and assisted in the development of community-based partnerships.

Camp counsellor and Recreation Director, YWCA Summer Camp, Nepean, Ontario. Directed summer recreation programs consisting of 10 counsellors and 140 elementary aged girls.

Volunteer Telephone Counsellor, Nepean Crisis Hotline, June 1999–June 2001

Activities and Interests

Nepean Historical Society, Secretary, 2001

Member, Queen's University Community Service Learning Centre

Hobbies: Jogging, Aerobics, Piano, Water Skiing

Honours

Bachelor of Arts with Honours, Queen's University, June 2001

Queen's University Faculty of Education Scholarship

Professional Memberships

Ontario Council of Elementary Educators

Second Language Teachers of Ontario

Instructional Technology Skills

Word processing, internet and web, optical scanner, interactive whiteboard, LCD projection panel, NovaNet (computer-based learning system, multimedia skills)

Career Objective

Seeking K-8 position in multicultural/multilingual setting

References

References and credentials file available upon request.

Figure 11.2

Résumé

Linda M. Abbott
641 Montbeck Crescent
Mississauga, Ontario L5G 1P4

April 5, 2003

Dr. Lawrence Walker
Human Resources Department
Ottawa-Carleton District School Board
133 Greenbank Road
Nepean, Ontario K2H 6L3

Dear Mr. Walker:

This letter is to express my interest in a teaching position with the Ottawa-Carleton School Board. Specifically, I would like to know if you anticipate any vacancies at the elementary level for the fall of 2003. This May I will receive my Bachelor of Education degree from Queen's University in Kingston, Ontario. My specialization area is teaching English as a second language.

As a student teacher during the past two years, I taught regular and accelerated Grade 3 classes at Greenbank Elementary/Middle School in Nepean, Ontario. One class had 25 students, three of whom were diagnosed with learning disabilities. At Greenbank School, I introduced students to science resources on the web, and each student learned to send email messages to students in other countries.

My education at Queen's University, I believe, has prepared me well to teach in today's classrooms. I have had a course that focuses on meeting the needs of at-risk learners, and my area of specialization in bilingual education has prepared me to meet the challenges of working with students from diverse linguistic backgrounds. If possible, I would like a position that would allow me to develop programs for students with non-English backgrounds.

Enclosed you will find my résumé, which provides additional information about my experience and activities. If there are any positions for which you think I might be suited, please send application materials in the enclosed, self-addressed envelope. I appreciate your consideration, and I look forward to hearing from you.

Sincerely,

Linda M. Abbott

Linda M Abbott

Figure 11.3

Letter of Inquiry

Participating in a Job Interview

The interview is one of the most important steps in your search for an appropriate position. As the dialogue in the scenario at the beginning of this chapter suggests, school district representatives may ask a wide range of questions, both structured and open-ended.

In some districts, you might be interviewed by the principal only; in others, the superintendent, the principal, and the department chairperson might interview you; and in still others, classroom teachers might interview you. Regardless of format, the interview enables the district to obtain more specific information regarding your probable success as an employee, and it gives you an opportunity to ask questions about what it is like to teach in the district. By asking questions yourself, you demonstrate your interest in working in the district. Appendix 11.4 presents "Critical Information to

Linda M. Abbott
641 Montbeck Crescent
Mississauga, Ontario L5G 1P4

May 5, 2003

Dr. Lawrence Walker
Human Resources Department
Ottawa-Carleton District School Board
133 Greenbank Road
Nepean, Ontario K2H 6L3

Dear Mr. Walker:

This letter is in support of my application for the position of Grade 4 teacher at Elgin Street Public School. This May I will receive my Bachelor of Education degree from Queen's University in Kingston, Ontario. My specialization area is teaching English as a second language.

As my enclosed resume indicates, I just completed my student teaching at Greenbank Elementary/Middle School in Nepean, Ontario. During that 20 week period, I taught regular and accelerated Grade 3 classes. One class had 25 students, 3 of whom were diagnosed with learning disabilities. I also organized an after-school tutoring program and assisted my cooperating teacher in developing community-based partnerships.

A major interest of mine is using technology in the classroom. I am familiar with various hypermedia programs and NovaNET, a computer-based learning system. At Greenbank Elementary School, I introduced students to science resources on the web, and each student learned to send email messages to students in other countries.

As a result of my rewarding experiences at Greenbank Elementary School and in light of my preparation in bilingual education, I believe I could make a significant contribution to the educational program at Elgin Street Public School.

I have arranged for my credentials to be forwarded from Queen's University's placement office. If you require additional information of any sort, please feel free to contact me. At your convenience, I am available for an interview in Nepean. I thank you in advance for your consideration.

Sincerely,

Linda M. Abbott

Linda M Abbott

Figure 11.4

Letter of Application

Know about School Districts," which can be used to formulate questions. In addition, at some point in the interview process you may wish to present brief highlights from your professional portfolio. Or, if you have created internet and/or CD-ROM versions of your portfolio, you could give the hiring official(s) the URL for the portfolio or a copy of the CD-ROM itself.

Accepting an Offer

One day you are notified that a school district would like to hire you. Your job search efforts have paid off! In the competition for positions, you have been successful. However, accepting your first teaching position is a major personal and professional step. Before signing a contract with a district, you should carefully consider job-related questions such as the following:

What questions might you be asked in an interview for a teaching position? What questions should you have about the teaching position? about the school?

- In regard to my abilities and education, am I suited to this position?
- Would I like to work with this school's students, administrative staff, and teachers?
- Is the salary I am being offered sufficient?
- Will this position likely be permanent?
- Would I like to live in or near this community?
- Would the cost of living in this community enable me to live comfortably?
- Are opportunities for continuing education readily available?

If you accept the offer, you will need to return a signed contract to the district along with a short letter confirming your acceptance. As a professional courtesy, you should notify other districts to which you have applied that you have accepted a position elsewhere. The following Professional Reflection can help you identify the type of school that would be most satisfying for your first teaching position.

Professional Reflection   What elements are essential for your job satisfaction?

Job satisfaction as a teacher depends on many factors: the size and location of a school; the backgrounds of students; the surrounding community; and the climate, or culture, of the school itself, to name a few. The following sentence completion items can help you determine what conditions are essential for your job satisfaction. Write your responses on a separate sheet or in your teacher's journal. For each item, write at least a few additional sentences to elaborate on how you completed the sentence.

1. Ideally, my first position would be teaching students who had the following backgrounds and characteristics:
2. For me, an ideal work setting would be a school that
3. My fellow teachers would help me during my first year of teaching by
4. When not in school, my colleagues and I would enjoy
5. My principal and/or supervisor would appreciate the way I
6. In his or her feedback on my teaching, my principal and/or supervisor would be most impressed with
7. During my first year at the school I would volunteer to
8. Five years after I began teaching at this school, I would like to be

How can you create an electronic professional portfolio?

As this chapter's opening scenario suggested, job candidates can use technology to create internet-accessible and CD-ROM versions of a professional portfolio. The possibilities for creating a digital portfolio that uses a computer to record information are endless. Although it is beyond the scope of this Technology Highlights feature to present in detail all the steps involved in preparing an electronic portfolio, what follows is a broad outline of how to prepare internet-accessible and CD-ROM versions of your portfolio. A helpful article on how to prepare an electronic portfolio is Helen Barrett's "Create Your Own Electronic Portfolio (Using Off-the-Shelf Software)" in the April 2000 *Learning & Leading with Technology*. In addition, your university's computer lab probably provides training in hypermedia techniques necessary to create an electronic portfolio.

The first step in compiling an electronic portfolio is the same as that for a traditional portfolio—identify and organize the materials to include in the portfolio. In the case of an electronic portfolio, however, the contents will be in the form of text, sound, graphics, and video data that a computer can access and manipulate.

To create an internet-accessible version of an electronic portfolio, you must use an HTML (hypertext markup language) web editor such as Macromedia Dreamweaver, Adobe GoLive, or Microsoft FrontPage. If you want to include video and/or audio clips, you also need a video input device, or webcam. Today's HTML editors function much like word processing programs, and, unlike early editors, they don't require knowledge of complex HTML programming. HTML editors are based on WYSIWYG—"what you see is what you get"—which means you don't see a myriad of formatting "tags"; the program inserts the tags automatically. To create internet-accessible material with an editor, the user formats desired material and saves it as an HTML file. To add

What Can You Expect As a Beginning Teacher?

Once you accept the professional challenge of teaching, it is important to prepare well in advance of the first day of school. In addition to reviewing the material you will teach, you should use this time to find out all you can about the school's students, the surrounding community, and the way the school operates. Also reflect on your expectations.

The First Day

The first day of school can be both exciting and frightening, as the following veteran teacher acknowledges; however, if the teacher is well prepared, he or she can use anxiety to set a positive tone for the rest of the school year:

> The anxiety level for both teachers and students about [the] first day is high. Taking advantage of these feelings can make for a good beginning.

> Students like to have guidelines on how the class will be run as well as what is expected of them academically. I always begin by welcoming the students into my class and immediately giving them something to do. I hand them their textbook and an index card. On the card, they write their name, address, telephone number, and book number.

hyperlinks, the user highlights the desired material, clicks on a "link" button, and then types in the URL (uniform resource locator, or internet address).

Another approach to making an internet-accessible portfolio is to "print" your data to PDF (portable document format) files using Adobe Acrobat. Once the files are placed on the internet, they are accessible by using the Acrobat Reader plug-in available for free on the internet. Remember that you will need access to a server on which to publish your internet-accessible electronic portfolio. Check with your college or university, or with your internet service provider, to see whether they make any server space available to you for personal websites such as this.

You can use any of several different software tools to create an electronic portfolio in CD-ROM format. Each CD-ROM can store up to 650 megabytes of data and costs about $2.00 if purchased by the hundred. The most common approach to making a CD-ROM is to use a hypermedia "card" program, or "authoring" tool, such as HyperStudio. A hypermedia program allows you to integrate different forms of media into a single file and then, using a CD-ROM burner, place the data on a CD-ROM. HTML files (Web documents) can also be "burned" onto a CD-ROM and then be accessed using a web browser.

By creating digital versions of items that appear in a traditional portfolio and skillfully using video and audio clips, you can enhance the presentation of your professional portfolio. For example, you can include voiceover explanations of your performance while teaching, or you can include scanned images of certificates, awards, photographs, or completed projects. Clearly, "digital portfolios are more than just electronic file cabinets. The technological enhancements add markedly to the value of a portfolio" (Weidmer 1998, 586).

While the students are filling out their cards and looking at the textbook, I set up my seating chart and verify attendance. Within ten minutes of meeting the students, I begin my first lesson. By keeping clerical chores to a minimum, I try to have more time on task. After a closure activity, somewhere in the middle of the class period I take a few minutes to explain how their grade will be determined, the rules of the class, and when extra help sessions are available.

Next, we deal with some curriculum content, and then I make a homework assignment. I tell the students that any homework assignment will be written on the chalkboard every day in the same location.

Setting high standards on the first day makes the following days easier. We will always need to monitor and adjust, but this will be within the framework set on the first day (Burden and Byrd 1999, 177).

Creating a pleasant, learning-oriented climate on the first day, as this teacher has done, will contribute greatly to your success during the first year. On the first day, students are eager to learn and are hopeful that the year will be a productive one. In addition, nearly all students will be naturally receptive to what you have to say. To them, you are a new, unknown quantity, and one of their initial concerns is to find out what kind of a teacher you will be. It is therefore critical that you be well organized and ready to take charge.

Advice from Experienced Teachers

In our work with schools and teachers, we have gathered recommendations on preparing for the first day from experienced K–12 teachers in urban, suburban, and rural schools. Teachers' recommendations focus on planning, establishing effective management practices, and following through on decisions.

> There are little things you can do, such as having a personal note attached to a pencil welcoming each child. You may want to do a few little tricks in science class or read them your favourite children's story. But, don't put all your energy into the first day and have that day be the highlight of the year. Be well prepared and have plenty of things to do. Don't worry if you don't get everything done. Remember, you have all year.
>
> —Middle school science teacher

> It really helps on the first day to have plenty of material to cover and things to do. I'd recommend taking the material you plan to cover that day and doubling it. It's better to have too much than to run out. What you don't use the first day, you use the next. It takes a while to get a feeling for how fast the kids are going to go.
>
> —Grade 3 teacher

> The first day is a good time to go over rules and procedures for the year. But don't overdo it. Be very clear and specific about your expectations for classroom behaviour.
>
> —Grade 6 teacher

> From the beginning, it's important to do what you're there to do—that's teach. Teach the class something, maybe review material they learned last year. That lets them know that you're in charge, you expect them to learn. They'll look to you for direction—as long as you give it to them, you're fine.
>
> —Junior high language arts teacher

How Can You Become a Part of Your Learning Community?

Your success in your first year of teaching will be determined by the relationships you develop with the pupils, their families, your colleagues, school administrators, and other members of the school community. All of these groups contribute to your effectiveness as a teacher, but the relationships you establish with students will be the most important (and complex) you will have as a teacher.

Relationships with Students

The quality of your relationships with students will depend in large measure on your knowledge of students and commitment to improving your interactions with them. As one teacher put it:

> Students respond to praise, compliments, and encouragement. I must know the subject matter, but also have a lot of patience, mental energy, and selflessness. I have found that you have to be encouraging even to the most negative students, or they can make your life miserable. Even though you might know the subject matter, you will not be a successful teacher if you can't motivate your students by talking with them, not at them (Burden and Byrd 1999, 290).

Your relationships with students will have many dimensions. Principally, you must see that each student learns as much as possible; this is your primary responsibility as a professional teacher. You will need to establish relationships with a great diversity of students based on mutual respect, caring, and concern. Without attention to this personal realm, your effectiveness as a teacher will be limited. In addition, teachers are significant models for students' attitudes and behaviours.

Relationships with Colleagues and Staff

Each working day, you will be in close contact with other teachers and staff members. As the experience of the following teacher suggests, it will definitely be to your advantage to establish friendly, professional relationships with them:

> I was on a staff with a group of teachers who really supported me. They made it a part of their day to come into my room and see how I was doing and to share things. They made it easy to ask questions and work with them. They started me on the track of cooperating with other teachers and sharing my successes and failures with them.

> They did such a good job of taking care of each other that my needs were always met. I had plenty of supplies, counselling help, administrative help. The school was a community. Anything I needed to be successful was provided.

During your first few months at the school, it would be wise to communicate to colleagues that you are willing to learn all you can about your new job and to be a team player. In most schools it is common practice to give junior faculty members less desirable assignments, reserving the more desirable ones for senior faculty. By demonstrating your willingness to take on these responsibilities with good humour and to give them your best effort, you will do much to establish yourself as a valuable faculty member. Appendix 11.5, "Negotiating a School's Culture: A Political Roadmap for the First-Year Teacher," provides additional suggestions for developing collaborative relationships with colleagues and staff.

Your colleagues may also appreciate learning from you about new approaches and materials—if you share in a manner that doesn't make others feel inferior. The following comments by a high school department chair, for example, illustrate a first-year French teacher's positive influence on others:

> She won the respect of all her colleagues in the school who have dealt with her almost immediately, not because she's so competent in French and not because she's so competent as a teacher, but because she handles everything with such sensitivity and sensibleness.

> Because of the way she operates—which is quietly but effectively—she has raised the whole tenor of expectations in the department. We have some very fine faculty in French, but I would speculate they don't see their group self-image as intellectuals but rather as "people people." Because of what Elizabeth has brought to the school: the knowledge about how to use computers, her knowledge of foreign language oral proficiency, her knowledge of French film and French authors, she has kind of lifted everybody up and helped her colleagues see themselves in a little bit different light and to improve professionally (Dollase 1992, 49).

It is important that you get along with your colleagues and contribute to a spirit of professional cooperation or **collegiality** in the school. Some you will enjoy being around; others you may wish to avoid. Some will express obvious enthusiasm for teaching; others may be bitter and pessimistic about their work. Be pleasant and friendly with both types. Accept their advice with a smile, and then act on what you believe is worthwhile.

Relationships with Administrators

Pay particular attention to the relationships you develop with administrators, department heads, and supervisors. Though your contacts with them will not be as frequent as with other teachers, they can do much to ensure your initial success. They are well aware of the difficulties you might encounter as a first-year teacher, and they are there to help you succeed.

The principal of your new school will, most likely, be the one to introduce you to other teachers, members of the administrative team, and staff. He or she should inform you if there are assistant principals or department heads who can help you enforce school rules, keep accurate records, and obtain supplies, for example. The principal may also assign an experienced teacher to serve as a mentor during your first year. In addition, your principal will indicate his or her availability to discuss issues of concern, and you should not hesitate to do so if the need arises.

Relationships with Parents

Developing positive connections with your students' parents can contribute significantly to students' success and to your success as a teacher. In reality, teachers and parents are partners—both concerned with the learning and growth of the children in their care. As U.S. Secretary of Education Richard Riley pointed out, "Parents, teachers and school officials working closely together are proven ingredients for success in our nation's schools" (Riley 1999). Unfortunately, research indicates that mothers typically spend less than Riley's recommended 30 min per day talking with or reading to their children, and fathers spend less than 15 min. The time parents spend interacting with their children differs as much as five times from family to family (Sadker and Sadker 1994).

It is important that you become acquainted with parents at school functions, at meetings of the Parent–Teacher Association or Organization (PTA or PTO), at various community events, and in other social situations. To develop good communication with parents, you will need to be sensitive to their needs, such as their work schedules and the language spoken at home.

By maintaining contact with parents and encouraging them to become involved in their children's education, you can significantly enhance the achievement of your students. Figure 11.5, based on interviews with the parents and guardians of almost 17 000 K–12 students, shows that parental involvement is associated with higher levels of student achievement, more positive attitudes toward school, greater participation in extracurricular activities, fewer suspensions and expulsions, and fewer grade repetitions. In light of such significant findings, it is important that you be willing to take the extra time and energy to pursue strategies such as the following for involving parents:

- Ask parents to read aloud to the child, to listen to the child read, and to sign homework papers.
- Encourage parents to drill students on math and spelling and to help with homework lessons.
- Encourage parents to discuss school activities with their children and suggest ways parents can help teach their children at home. For example, a simple home activity might be alphabetizing books; a more complex one would be using kitchen supplies in an elementary science experiment.
- Send home suggestions for games or group activities related to the child's schoolwork that parent and child can play together.

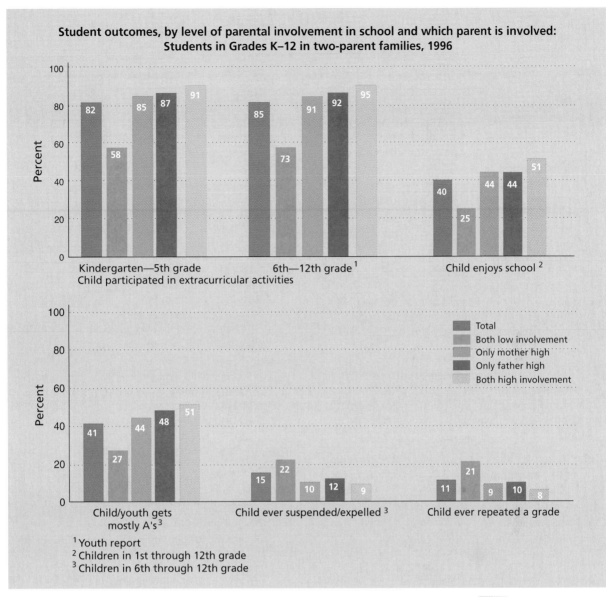

Student outcomes, by level of parental involvement in school and which parent is involved: Students in Grades K–12 in two-parent families, 1996

Child participated in extracurricular activities

Kindergarten—5th grade: 82, 58, 85, 87, 91
6th—12th grade [1]: 85, 73, 91, 92, 95
Child enjoys school [2]: 40, 25, 44, 44, 51

Legend:
- Total
- Both low involvement
- Only mother high
- Only father high
- Both high involvement

Child/youth gets mostly A's [3]: 41, 27, 44, 48, 51
Child ever suspended/expelled [3]: 15, 22, 10, 12, 9
Child ever repeated a grade: 11, 21, 9, 10, 8

[1] Youth report
[2] Children in 1st through 12th grade
[3] Children in 6th through 12th grade

Figure 11.5

Student outcomes, by level of parental involvement and which parent is involved: Students in grades K–12 in two-parent families, 1996.

Source: U.S. Department of Education, National Center for Education Statistics. *Fathers' Involvement in Their Children's School,* NCES 98–091, by Christine Winquist Nord, DeeAnn Brimhall, and Jerry West, Washington, DC, 1997, p. 55.]

- Encourage parents to participate in school activities such as a sports booster club, career day, and music and drama events.
- Involve parents in their children's learning by having them co-sign learning contracts and serve as guest speakers.

Family involvement resources are also available on the internet through the National Parent Information Network (NPIN), a project sponsored by the ERIC system. (For information, call (800) 583-4135.) NPIN resources include information for parents on child development, testing, working with teachers, and home learning activities. Ask ERIC Question & Answer Service provides forums for parents and teachers to address mutual concerns, listings of useful and inexpensive learning materials, and descriptions of model parent involvement programs. Other online resources for parental involvement in schools can be obtained from the Consortium for School Networking.

Should teachers be required to make home visits?

ome visits by teachers were a common practice in the past, but more recently, teachers have limited their communication with parents to their own classrooms. From earlier days of schooling, when families had their children's teachers over for Sunday dinner, to the 1970s, when teachers in many districts were required to have conferences with every parent, even if that meant catching them at home or on a tractor plowing the fields, teachers connected with families outside of their classrooms. By the 1990s, the situation had changed significantly. Parent conferences were still required, but teachers' home visits were a rarity.

Why would this happen? What caused the change? Has anything been lost because teachers no longer visit their students and parents in their homes?

Many articles in education journals emphasize the importance of parent involvement in children's education and teacher–parent partnerships. However, they rarely mention that teachers should make home visits to strengthen connections with parents. Instead, the suggested settings for launching parent programs are the classroom, school, or a "neutral" location.

In an article on "Expanding Parental Involvement in Canadian Schools," Mary McKenna and J. Douglas Willms write that "studies of parental involvement in Alberta and British Columbia found that parents who were of lower socioeconomic status, or who spoke English as their second language, were less likely to be directly involved as volunteers or to participate in school governance." The writers identify the nature of the schools themselves as a barrier to involvement. "Schools are middle-class institutions, which value middle-class language patterns, authority relations, and organizational structures" (McKenna and Willms, 1998, 3–4).

According to Anne Lewis, author of "Helping Young Urban Parents Educate Themselves and Their Children," an *ERIC/CUE Digest,* the literature on parent involvement describes parent–school communications as formal, one-way transactions, from the school to the parent. She notes that "parents complain that their most personal communication with schools usually only occurs because of a problem or crisis" (Lewis 1992).

Perhaps home visits are returning, however. In addition to traditional strategies for involving parents, such as "open houses, fund-raising fairs, parent conferences, volunteers, intergenerational literacy programs, and advisory and policy councils," Lewis adds new ideas, including "parent centers, family support programs, such as home visits and parenting workshops, and school and community organization partnerships with universities, businesses, civic groups and such" (Lewis 1992).

What do you think? Is it time to revive the practice of requiring teachers to make home visits?

Yes, teachers should be required to make home visits.

Home visits can be informative, helpful, and a good way to connect with parents. A 30-year veteran Grade 3 teacher explained that his twice-a-year home visits are invaluable. For years, in August before the school year begins and in December, at the middle of the school year, he has made it a practice to visit each of his students' homes. In the summer he tells the parents how pleased he is that their child will be in his class and explains his goals for the coming school year. In December he returns to update them and learn about their interests and concerns. "It's time consuming," he admits, "but it is well worth the effort."

Home visits can help teachers better understand their students. One teacher, concerned about a child's inattentiveness, made a home visit that, she says, turned out to be an "eye opener. They didn't have a door. Somehow the door had been removed and they just had a blanket up." The teacher then understood the cause of the student's problem. "I realized he probably couldn't sleep because there was this traffic going by. And he didn't have a bed, he was on a pallet. Those kinds of things are important to know." She returned from the visit feeling a connection with the family and closer to the child.

Making such connections is the most important reason for home visits. However, teachers must conduct them in the right spirit. They should not appear to be inspecting the home, checking up on family members' activities, or judging the parents. Instead they should genuinely respect parents and family members and seek to learn from them if the visits are to be beneficial.

In an often-cited article entitled "School/Family/Community Partnerships: Caring for the Children We Share," Joyce Epstein (1995) recommends that home visits be conducted "at transition points to preschool, elementary, middle, and high school." She also recommends holding "neighborhood meetings to help families understand schools and to help schools understand families."

No, teachers should not be required to make home visits.

Requiring teachers to make home visits would be a mistake for several reasons. First, if teachers are less sensitive and respectful, such visits would be counterproductive. Also, teachers who prefer not to visit in their students' homes but do so because they are required to may show their discomfort or conduct their visits in a perfunctory manner, thus defeating the purpose of such visits.

Secondly, depending on the neighbourhood, the teacher's familiarity with it, and the teacher's professional experience, home visits could actually be dangerous for the teacher. An inexperienced teacher visiting in an unfamiliar, violence-prone neighbourhood at the wrong time would be taking a risk making home visits.

Third, depending on the teacher's experience and sensitivity, home visits could embarrass or even anger parents. If parents felt they were being judged as inadequate or believed that the teacher was investigating them, the home visit would be a failure.

Finally, teachers do not need to make home visits in order to connect with parents. They can make parents feel welcome and valued through phone calls, personal notes, after school visits, and meetings in their classrooms. There is no need to impose on parents at home.

It is one thing for teachers to make home visits at the invitation of parents and quite another to be *required* to. Because of all these potential problems, administrators should not require teachers to make home visits.

Where do you stand on this Issue?

1. Are you in favour of teachers making home visits? Why or why not?

2. What have your home visit experiences been as a student or parent? How would you feel as a novice teacher about making home visits?

3. How could an inexperienced teacher learn about making home visits?

4. How could teachers protect their safety in making home visits into dangerous neighbourhoods?

5. What other means can you recommend for better understanding a student's home situation? For connecting with parents?

Recommended Sources

Arlin, P. K. (1990). Teaching as conversation. *Educational Leadership*, 48, 82–85.

Arlin, P. K. (1999). The wise teacher. *Theory into Practice*, 38, 12–17.

Epstein, J. (1995, May). School/family/community partnerships: Caring for the children we share. *Phi Delta Kappan, 76* (9), 701–712.

Lewis, A. (1992). Helping young urban parents educate themselves and their children. *ERIC/CUE Digest,* No. 85.

McKenna, M. & Wilms, J.D. (1998, September). Expanding parental involvement in Canadian schools. *Policy Brief,* Atlantic Centre for Policy Research, University of New Brunswick, 3–4.

Community Relations

Communities provide significant support for the education of their young people and determine the character of their schools. In addition, communities often help their schools by recruiting volunteers, providing financial support for special projects, and operating homework hotline programs. For example, school–community partnerships have been formed through business and community connections in parts of Canada.

- Canadian businesses have recognized the need to have their employees knowledgeable about their children's schools and programs. Businesses such as State Farm Insurance have given their employees notification that if they wish to volunteer at their children's school, that they will be given a day's pay to do so. It is their belief that these good corporate citizen policies make for stronger and happier parents and a more productive workforce.

- Service clubs and business associations develop strong partnerships with the education community. Examples in New Brunswick include the Lions Quest program for self esteem building sponsored by the Lions Club and the Fredericton Chamber of Commerce that published for schools a directory of businesses who want to help out by making presentations or offering job placements for students.
- Safety of school children is another concern of businesses. The New Brunswick Telephone Company has a safe blue telephone truck operating in the Perth Andover area. Whenever children feel they have a problem or need help from an adult, they simply walk up to a telephone employee. Employees have offered to help children in whatever manner is necessary (Love 1994).

How Can You Participate in Teacher Collaboration?

The relationships that build a learning community involve **collaboration**—working together, sharing decision making, and solving problems. As a member of a dynamic, changing profession, your efforts to collaborate will result in an increased understanding of the teaching–learning process and improved learning for all students. By working with others on school governance, curriculum development, school–community partnerships, and educational reform, you will play an important role in enhancing the professional status of teachers.

The heart of collaboration is meaningful, authentic relationships among professionals. Such relationships, of course, do not occur naturally; they require commitment and hard work. Friend and Bursuck (1999, 72–74) have identified seven characteristics of collaboration which are summarized in the following:

- Collaboration is voluntary; teachers make a personal choice to collaborate.
- Collaboration is based on parity; all individuals' contributions are valued equally.
- Collaboration requires a shared goal.
- Collaboration includes shared responsibility for key decisions.
- Collaboration includes shared accountability for outcomes.
- Collaboration is based on shared resources; each teacher contributes something— time, expertise, space, equipment, or other resource.
- Collaboration is emergent; as teachers work together, the degree of shared decision making, trust, and respect increases.

Schools that support the essential elements of collaboration are collegial schools "characterized by purposeful adult interactions about improving schoolwide teaching and learning" (Glickman, Gordon, and Ross-Gordon 1998, 5–6). In the following, we examine four expressions of teacher collaboration: peer coaching, staff development, team teaching, and co-teaching.

Peer Coaching

Experienced teachers traditionally help novice teachers, but more formal peer coaching programs extend the benefits of collaboration to more teachers. **Peer coaching** is an arrangement whereby teachers grow professionally by observing one another's teaching and providing constructive feedback. The practice encourages teachers to learn together in an emotionally safe environment. According to Bruce Joyce and Marsha

Weil (2000, 440), peer coaching is an effective way to create communities of professional educators, and all teachers should be members of coaching teams.

If we had our way, *all* school faculties would be divided into coaching teams—that is, teams who regularly observe one another's teaching and learn from watching one another and the students. In short, we recommend the development of a "coaching environment" in which all personnel see themselves as coaches.

Through teacher-to-teacher support and collaboration, peer coaching programs improve teacher morale and teaching effectiveness.

Staff Development

Increasingly, teachers are contributing to the design of staff development programs that encourage collaboration, risk-taking, and experimentation. Some programs, for example, give teachers the opportunity to meet with other teachers at similar grade levels or in similar content areas for the purpose of sharing ideas, strategies, and solutions to problems. A day or part of a day may be devoted to this kind of workshop or idea exchange. Teachers are frequently given released time from regular duties to visit other schools and observe exemplary programs in action.

What are some forms of professional collaboration in which you will participate as a teacher? In what types of co-teaching arrangements might these teachers cooperate?

Team Teaching

In **team teaching** arrangements, teachers share the responsibility for two or more classes, dividing up the subject areas between them, with one preparing lessons in mathematics, science, and health, for instance, while the other plans instruction in reading and language arts. The division of responsibility may also be made in terms of the performance levels of the children, so that, for example, one teacher may teach the lowest- and highest-ability reading groups and the middle math group, while the other teaches the middle-ability reading groups and the lowest and highest mathematics group. In many schools, team teaching arrangements are so extensive that children move from classroom to classroom for 40- to 50-min periods just as students do at the high school level.

The practice of team teaching is often limited by student enrolments and budget constraints. As integrated curricula and the need for special knowledge and skills increase, however, the use of collegial support teams (CSTs) will become more common. A **collegial support team (CST)** provides teachers with a "safe zone" for professional growth, as one teacher commented:

[The CST] allows me much discretion as to the areas I'd like to strengthen. Therefore, I am truly growing with no fear of being labelled or singled out as the "teacher who is having problems." I am aware of problem spheres and I work to correct these with the aid of my colleagues (Johnson and Brown 1998, 89).

The members of a team make wide-ranging decisions about the instruction of students assigned to the team, such as when to use large-group instruction or small-group instruction, how teaching tasks will be divided, and how time, materials, and other resources will be allocated.

Co-Teaching

In **co-teaching** arrangements, two or more teachers, such as a classroom teacher and a special education teacher or other specialist, teach together in the same classroom.

Co-teaching builds on the strengths of two teachers and provides increased learning opportunities for all students (Friend and Bursuck 1999). Typically, co-teaching arrangements occur during a set period of time each day or on certain days of the week. Among the several possible co-teaching variations, Friend and Bursuck (1999) have identified the following:

- *One teach, one support*—one teacher leads the lesson; the other assists.
- *Station teaching*—the lesson is divided into two parts; one teacher teaches one part to half of the students while the other teaches the other part to the rest. The groups then switch and the teachers repeat their part of the lesson. If students can work independently, a third group may be formed, or a volunteer may teach at a third station.
- *Parallel teaching*—a class is divided in half, and each teacher instructs half the class individually.
- *Alternative teaching*—a class is divided into one large group and one small group. For example, one teacher may provide remediation or enrichment to the small group, while the other teacher instructs the large group.

How Will Your Performance Be Evaluated?

Most teachers are evaluated on a regular basis to determine whether their performance measures up to acceptable standards, if they are able to create and sustain effective learning environments for students. Performance criteria used to evaluate teachers vary and are usually determined by the school principal, district office, the school board, or a provincial education agency. In most schools, the principal or a member of the leadership team evaluates teachers.

Teacher evaluations serve many purposes: to determine whether teachers should be retained, receive tenure, or be given merit pay. Evaluations also help teachers assess their effectiveness and develop strategies for self-improvement. National studies indicate that "teachers want to be observed more, they want more feedback, and they want to talk more with other professionals about improving learning for their students" (Glickman, Gordon, and Ross-Gordon 1998, 313).

Quantitative and Qualitative Evaluation

Typically, supervisors use quantitative or qualitative approaches (or a combination) to evaluate teachers' classroom performance. **Quantitative evaluation** includes pencil-and-paper rating forms the supervisor uses to record classroom events and behaviours objectively in terms of their number or frequency. For example, a supervisor might focus on the teacher's verbal behaviours—questioning, answering, praising, giving directions, and critiquing.

Prime Minister's Award for Teaching Excellence Recipient: Paul Barrett

Parents and teachers have a common interest: helping children grow up to be good citizens, part of a community, and with a job to take care of themselves and family. The teacher profiled in this Teaching for Excellence feature demonstrates how alliances between parents and teachers can be built for the benefit of children and programs.

Paul Barrett,
Cobequid Educational Centre, Truro, Nova Scotia

As a music teacher at Cobequid Educational Centre, Paul Barrett leads an ambitious extracurricular band program that includes award-winning junior, senior, jazz, and stage bands and a jazz choir. Barrett credits the program's success to the parents, the small army of volunteers who stepped in to rescue the band when its funding was cut and now help run every aspect of the band program, from fundraising to organizing trips.

Involving parents in school programs allows students to see their parents and teachers interact in a different context. "And what they get to see is everybody working together as a community," says Barrett. "The magic that comes when parents and teachers collaborate, or when a well-tuned band plays in perfect harmony," says Paul Barrett, "has to be built on a firm foundation."

Organized parental involvement starts with a meeting, Barrett advises, to elect a core group of officials—a president, vice-president, and treasurer. Barrett suggests this approach even if only a handful of people volunteer to start with. "It is much harder to start something in a school where there is no existing culture of parent groups. The thing I suggest to someone in that position is to start with a core group and see what they can build up."

It does mean that the teacher has to learn to trust in other people's abilities. "When I first began I had a tendency to do everything myself because that way I could be sure it would get done. It took a long time to train myself out of that."

Reproduced with the permission of the Minister of Public Works and Government Services, 2003. Government of Canada (1999). Prime Minister's awards for teaching excellence: Exemplary practices. *Forging Alliances*. Retrieved 19 February, from http://pma-ppm.ic.gc.ca/exemplary/1999/forging.htm

Qualitative evaluation, in contrast, includes written, open-ended narrative descriptions of classroom events in terms of their qualities. These more subjective measures are equally valuable in identifying teachers' weaknesses and strengths. In addition, qualitative evaluation can capture the complexities and subtleties of classroom life that might not be reflected in a quantitative approach to evaluation.

Clinical Supervision

Many supervisors follow the four-step **clinical supervision** model in which the supervisor first holds a preconference with the teacher, then observes in the classroom, analyzes and interprets observation data, and finally holds a postconference with the teacher (Anderson and Snyder 1993; Goldhammer, Anderson, and Krajewski 1993; Pajak 1993; Smyth 1995; Acheson and Gall 1997). During the preconference, the teacher and supervisor schedule a classroom observation and determine its purpose and focus and the method of observation to be used. At the postconference, the teacher and supervisor discuss the analysis of observation data and jointly develop a plan for instructional improvement.

Fulfilling the clinical supervision model is difficult and time-consuming, and time-pressed administrators must often modify the approach. For example, Kim Marshall, principal at a Boston elementary school with 39 teachers, makes four random, unannounced five-minute visits to classrooms each day. This schedule allows him to observe every teacher during a two-week period, and each teacher about 19 times during a year. To make the most of his five-minute classroom visits, he follows these guidelines:

■ Be a perceptive observer in order to capture something interesting and helpful to say during the feedback session.
■ Give teachers a mixture of praise, affirmation, suggestions, and criticism.
■ When sharing critical observations with teachers, be tactful and nonthreatening but totally honest.
■ Use good judgment about when to deliver criticism and when to hold off (Marshall 1996, 344).

Regardless of the approach a school district will use to evaluate your performance as a beginning teacher, remember that evaluation will assist your professional growth and development. Experienced teachers report that periodic feedback and assistance from knowledgeable, sensitive supervisors is very beneficial; such evaluation results in "improved teacher reflection and higher-order thought, more collegiality, openness, and communication, greater teacher retention, less anxiety and burnout, greater teacher autonomy and efficacy, improved attitudes, improved teaching behaviours, and better student achievement and attitudes" (Glickman, Gordon, and Ross-Gordon, 1998, 317).

SUMMARY

How Will You Become Certified Or Licensed To Teach?

■ Mobility provisions under the Agreement on Internal Trade/Teaching Profession entitle a teacher to receive a teaching credential from the receiving province or territory under the following conditions. All applicants must:
■ Hold a valid teaching credential from a Canadian province or territory.
■ Have completed a professional teacher education program consisting of a minimum of 30 semester credit-hours of course work and practicum for teacher certification.
■ Provide all documents required by the receiving province or territory.
■ Satisfy any requirements of the receiving province or territory with respect to "fit and proper person," currency of practice, and language proficiency.

Where Will You Teach?

Teacher supply and demand in content areas and geographic regions influences finding a teaching position.

A recent empirical study of possible teaching shortages revealed the following:

■ Recruiting has been getting more difficult over the past four years.
■ Teacher shortages are the most prevalent in science subjects in the past four years (science, chemistry, biology, physics).

- Shortages in some areas vary by language of instruction and/or rural versus non-rural.
- Education-related career opportunities for teachers include principal, assistant principal, librarian, counsellor, and teaching roles in government and the private sector.

How Will You Find Your First Teaching Job?

- Information about teaching vacancies may be obtained through placement services, provincial departments of education, and personal networking on the internet.
- A résumé is a concise summary of an individual's experiences, education, and skills. A letter of inquiry is used to find out if a school district has any teaching vacancies, and a letter of application (or cover letter) indicates an individual's interest in and qualifications for a teaching position.

What Can You Expect As a Beginning Teacher?

- Beginning teachers should prepare instructional strategies and materials and learn about their students and the community well in advance of the first day of school.
- Experienced teachers' recommendations for beginning teachers focus on planning, organizing, and following through.

How Can You Become a Part of Your Learning Community?

- The learning community includes students, their families, colleagues, and members of the community.
- Research indicates that parental involvement is a key factor in children's academic achievement.
- Training programs, hotlines, referral networks, and partnership programs are among the resources teachers can use to involve parents and members of the community.

How Can You Participate in Teacher Collaboration?

- Teachers collaborate through participation in school governance, curriculum development, school-community partnerships, and educational reform.
- Four approaches to teacher collaboration are peer coaching, staff development, team teaching, and co-teaching.

How Will Your Performance Be Evaluated?

- Performance criteria for evaluating teachers are developed by school principals, districts, school boards, or provinces.
- Quantitative approaches to teacher evaluation focus on the incidence, frequency, or amount of teacher or student behaviour in various categories.
- Qualitative approaches to teacher evaluation are usually written narratives focusing on the qualities of classrooms and events, such as classroom climate and teaching style.

clinical supervision, 419
collaboration, 416
collegial support team
    (CST), 417
collegiality, 411
co-teaching, 418
credentials file, 401

job fairs, 401
letter of application, 403
letter of inquiry, 403
peer coaching, 416
placement service, 401
qualitative
    evaluation, 419

quantitative
    evaluation, 418
résumé, 403
teacher supply and
    demand, 398
teaching certificate, 396
team teaching, 417

APPLICATIONS AND ACTIVITIES

Teacher's Journal

1. Record in your journal your plan for becoming certified or licensed to teach.

2. Develop answers to possible interview questions and brainstorm questions to ask.

3. Envision your first day as a teacher and describe what you see.

4. When you become a teacher, in what collaborations and partnerships will you participate? How might these activities contribute to your effectiveness as a teacher? How might your involvement enhance students' learning and your relationships with them?

Observations and Interviews

1. If you can arrange it, observe the first day of classes at a local school. What strategies did the teachers use to begin the year on a positive, task-oriented note? What evidence did you see that the teachers followed the advice given by the experienced teachers in this chapter?

2. Survey teachers at a local school to get information about how they prepare for the first day of school.

3. Prepare a questionnaire and then survey a group of experienced teachers for their recollections about the triumphs and defeats they experienced as beginning teachers. What lessons are evident in their responses to your questionnaire? Are there common themes that characterize the triumphs they recall? The defeats?

4. Interview teachers and administrators about their experiences with professional collaboration and parental involvement. What examples do they provide, and how do these reflect the seven characteristics of collaboration presented in this chapter? How do students benefit from collaboration and parental involvement? What suggestions do the teachers and administrators have for improving collaboration and parental involvement?

Professional Portfolio

1. Draft a preliminary professional résumé. Review the section in this chapter titled "Preparing Your Résumé" and "Résumé Advice for Educators" in Appendix 11.3. In addition, examine the résumé prepared by Linda M. Abbott (Figure 11.2).

In your résumé, under "Personal Data," provide a current address and a permanent address. Also, under "Education," specify an anticipated graduation date. Under "Experience," include work experience that indicates your ability to work with people. Begin with your most recent experiences and present information in reverse chronological order.

When you have finished your preliminary résumé, critique it against "Résumé Advice for Educators."

2. Draft an essay describing what you will bring to your first year of teaching. It may help to review the essay you wrote for the Chapter 1 portfolio entry on what has drawn you to teaching.

Appendix 11.1

Listed below is information on each provincial body responsible for Teacher Certification and Teacher Classification in Canada.

Teacher Certification and Classification for each Province

Province	Certification	Qualification
British Columbia	British Columbia College of Teachers 405–1385 West 8th Avenue Vancouver, British Columbia V6H 3V9 Tel: (604) 731-8170 Fax: (604) 731-9142	Teacher Qualification Service #106–1525 West 8th Avenue Vancouver, British Columbia V6J 1T5 (jointly sponsored by teacher and trustee associations) Tel: (604) 736-5484 Fax: (604) 736-6591
Alberta	Director Teacher Certification and Development Department of Education Devonian Building, West Tower 11160 Jasper Avenue NW Edmonton, Alberta T5K 0L2	Teacher Qualifications Service The Alberta Teachers' Association Barnett House 11010–142 Street NW Edmonton, Alberta T5N 2R1
Saskatchewan	Registrar Provincial Examinations, Student and Teacher Services Saskatchewan Education 1500–4th Avenue Regina, Saskatchewan S4P 3V7	
Manitoba	Director Professional Certification Unit Department of Education and Training Legislative Building 450 Broadway Winnipeg, Manitoba R3C 0V8	
Ontario	Ontario College of Teachers 121 Bloor Street East, 6th Floor Toronto, Ontario M4W 3M5	Qualifications Evaluation Council of Ontario 1260 Bay Street Toronto, Ontario M5R 2B9 Certification Department Ontario Secondary School Teachers' Federation 60 Mobile Drive Toronto, Ontario M4A 2P3

Appendix 11.1 *(continued)*

Province	Certification	Qualification
Quebec	Direction des ressources humaines Permis et brevets d'enseignement Ministère de l'Éducation Édifice Marie-Guyart 1035, rue de La Chevrotière Québec G1R 5A5	Direction générale des ressources humaines Direction de la classification Ministère de l'Éducation Édifice Marie-Guyart 1035, rue de La Chevrotière Québec G1R 5A5
New Brunswick	Director Human Resources Department of Education P.O. Box 6000 Fredericton, New Brunswick E3B 5H1	
Nova Scotia	Registrar's Office Teacher Certification Department of Education P.O. Box 578 Halifax, Nova Scotia B3J 2S9	
Prince Edward Island	Registrar, Department of Education and Human Resources P.O. Box 2000 Charlottetown, P.E.I. C1A 7N8	
Newfoundland	Registrar, Teacher Certification and Records Section Division of School Services Department of Education Confederation Building, West Block, P.O. Box 8700 St. John's, NF A1B 4J6 Tel: (709) 729-3020	
Northwest Territories	Registrar Department of Education, Culture and Employment P.O. Box 1320 Yellowknife, N.W.T. X1A 2L9 Tel: (867) 873-7392	
Yukon	Mr. Bill Ferguson Senior Consultant Department of Education Territorial Government of the Yukon P.O. Box 2703 Whitehorse, Yukon Y1A 2C6	Reproduced with permission from the Canadian Teachers' Federation website: www.ctf-fce.ca/e/tic/appenc.htm

Appendix 11.2

Job Search Timetable Checklist

This checklist is designed to help graduating students who are seeking teaching positions make the best use of their time as they conduct job searches. We encourage you to use this checklist in conjunction with the services and resources available from your college or university career planning and placement office.

August/September (12 months prior to employment)	_____ Attend any applicable orientations/workshops offered by your college placement office.
	_____ Register with your college placement office and inquire about career services.
October (11 months prior to employment)	_____ Begin to define career goals by determining the types, sizes, and geographic locations of school systems in which you have an interest.
	_____ Begin to identify references and ask them to prepare letters of recommendation for your credential or placement files.
	_____ See a counsellor at your college placement office to discuss your job-search plan.
November (10 months prior to employment)	_____ Check to see that you are properly registered at your college placement office.
	_____ Begin developing a résumé and a basic cover letter.
	_____ Begin networking by contacting friends, faculty members, etc., to inform them of your career plans. If possible, give them a copy of your résumé.
December/January (8–9 months prior to employment)	_____ Finalize your résumé and make arrangements for it to be reproduced. You may want to get some tips on résumé reproduction from your college placement office.
	_____ Attend any career planning and placement workshops designed for education majors.
	_____ Use the directories available at your college placement office to develop a list of school systems in which you have an interest.
	_____ Contact school systems to request application materials.
	_____ If applying to out-of-province school systems, contact the appropriate Provincial Departments of Education to determine testing requirements.
February (7 months prior to employment)	_____ Check the status of your credential or placement file at your college placement office.
	_____ Send completed applications to school systems, with a résumé and cover letter.
	_____ Inquire about school systems which will be recruiting at your college placement office, and about the procedures for interviewing with them.
March/April (5–6 months prior to employment)	_____ Research school systems with which you will be interviewing.
	_____ Interview on campus and follow up with thank you letters.
	_____ Continue to follow up by phone with school systems of interest.
	_____ Begin monitoring the job vacancy listings available at your college placement office.
May/August (1–4 months prior to employment)	_____ Just before graduation, check to be sure you are completely registered with your college placement office, and that your credential or placement file is in good order.
	_____ Maintain communication with your network of contacts.

Appendix 11.2 *(continued)*

May/August *(continued)* (1–4 months prior to employment)	_____ Subscribe to your college placement office's job vacancy bulletin. _____ Revise your résumé and cover letter if necessary. _____ Interview off campus and follow up with thank you letters. _____ If relocating away from campus, contact a college placement office in the area to which you are moving and inquire about available services. _____ Continue to monitor job vacancy listings and apply when qualified and interested. _____ Begin considering job offers. Ask for more time to consider offers, if necessary. _____ Accept the best job offer. Inform those associated with your search of your acceptance.

Adapted from material originally prepared at Miami University of Ohio.

Source: American Association for Employment in Education (AAEE), *1999 Job Search Handbook for Educators*. Evanston, IL: American Association for Employment in Education, p. 10. The *Handbook* is available for US $8.00 from AAEE.

Appendix 11.3

A modern-day résumé is a written advertisement focused on a prospective employer. In a résumé, however, the "product" being advertised is you, the candidate.

Many job applicants become confused about what to include on a résumé. This article covers the most common informational categories, but you should strive to include any information that you feel will enhance your chances of being selected for an interview.

Seeking the "Perfect" Résumé

Just as every individual is different, each résumé presents a distinct combination of skills, abilities, and qualifications about its author. This is why it is impossible to find a perfect sample résumé and simply copy it. Your background is unique, and cannot be found in a book. However, reviewing other résumés will certainly be helpful because they will provide a rich supply of ideas and perspectives for your document.

While the perfect résumé may be an elusive concept, excellent résumés have many characteristics in common. An excellent résumé is one to two pages in length. It is free of typographical errors, produced on high-quality bond paper, accentuates your most salient qualities and qualifications, is organized and easy to read, and conveys a sense of who you are to the reader. This is easier said than done!

You need to remember that in today's job market, school principals are inundated with résumés. One or two pages is about the maximum they are willing to read about each candidate. As a prospective teacher, a résumé with any typographical error is a signal that you are poorly prepared to instruct others, so be sure to have your final document read by others, until all errors are eliminated.

Résumés for teaching and résumés for business have both similarities and differences. Organization, style, appearance, neatness, and punctuation issues apply to both. (If you need help with these issues, you will find useful books on the topic in your institution's career planning and placement office or at local bookstores.) However, educators' résumés typically include additional categories: student teaching, clinical experience, and certification information.

As you work to write the "perfect" résumé you will undoubtedly receive a variety of well-intentioned advice, and some of it will be conflicting. Everyone will have an opinion to offer. One of your most difficult tasks will be to evaluate what you hear. Pursue different opinions, and then decide what makes sense for you.

Statement of Teaching Objective

It is appropriate to include a "Career Objective" or "Teaching Objective" statement on your résumé. While optional, this statement is highly recommended because it helps identify the specific areas in which you wish to teach. Consider the advantages and disadvantages of the following three sample objectives, then develop your own to fit your requirements.

1. Elementary Teaching Position, K–6.
2. Seeking a classroom position in the upper elementary grades that provides an opportunity to facilitate academic, social, and personal growth of students.
3. Secondary or middle school position in science/math, in a suburban location. Qualified and interested in coaching track, volleyball, or swimming.

Objective "A" is descriptive and to the point. However, additional elements are incorporated into examples "B" and "C." Objective "C" is well thought out and developed, although unless you intend to decline all offers other than those in suburban locations, you should avoid using a phrase which defines location too tightly. The reader will assume that you mean what you say.

Student Teaching Information

It is important that beginning teachers provide information about their student teaching experiences. Do not assume that all student teaching experiences are alike, and therefore need not be described. Some principals remain interested in your student teaching experience even after you have several years of professional experience.

Review the two examples below, and then develop a section that accurately portrays your own experience.

1. Robert Bateman Secondary School
   Abbotsford, British Columbia
   Student Teacher
   Taught Grade 11 chemistry and math courses in an open classroom format. Coordinated field study trips, and a "Careers in Science" day.

2. St. Elizabeth Elementary School
   Ottawa, Ontario
   Student Teacher
   September–December, 1997

Observed, assisted, and taught regular and accelerated classes. Developed daily lesson and unit plans. Assisted in after-school tutoring program. Coordinated a revised parent conference format that increased teacher–parent interaction. Refined an existing computer database for classroom record keeping.

Note how the examples include pertinent details of student teaching experiences beyond the routine aspects. It is this information that demonstrates ways in which you made yourself valuable. In your narrative, try to focus on how your presence made something better to make your experience stand out from those who merely developed lesson plans and assisted teachers.

Past Employment Information

Normally, an employer wants to know about your last ten years of professional experience. As a prospective teacher, you should include any experiences in which you worked with K–12-age individuals. Examples of pertinent positions would include camp counsellor, teacher's aide, tutor, Scout troop leader, and so forth.

Many candidates dismiss nonteaching experiences as unrelated, and fail to include them on their résumés. However, principals and school administrators can draw valuable inferences regarding your work habits from this information. Dependability, responsibility, and leadership potential are just a few of the desirable traits you can document with information about jobs you have held.

Related Activities and Interests

Information about activities and interests helps you present the image of a well-rounded and versatile teacher. The following categories represent just a few of the areas you may want to include.

- Volunteer activities
- Professional memberships
- Special interests
- Honours and awards
- Committee work
- Training
- Study abroad
- Community involvement
- Fluency in languages other than English
- Computer skills
- Leadership activities
- Professional development activities
- Class projects
- Scholarships

Remember, the more areas of knowledge and expertise that you demonstrate, the more likely you are to become a desirable candidate in the eyes of school administrators. School districts actively seek candidates who are flexible and willing to take on a variety of tasks in the school.

A Few Final Do's and Don't's

Make sure that your résumé is not a jigsaw puzzle of unrelated odds and ends, expecting that the principal will be able to piece them together. If those who receive your résumé have to work hard to figure it out, it is likely that they will just move on to the next résumé!

When your résumé is complete, print your final copy on a laser-jet printer, and have copies made at a printing service on high-quality, bond paper. Conservative paper—white, off-white, or ivory—is always suitable. Your printing service can help you select a paper which has matching envelopes to enhance your presentation. Be sure to purchase blank paper that matches your résumé so your cover letters will also match your presentation package.

Writing your résumé should be an introspective, exhilarating, positive, pat-yourself-on-the-back experience. If you approach it with this spirit, your résumé will be one of which you are justifiably proud.

Source: Lorn B. Coleman, *1999 Job Search Handbook for Educators.* Evanston, IL: American Association for Employment Education, pp. 16–17. Used with permission.

Appendix 11.4

In your interviews with K–12 school district administrators, it is very important that you know as much as possible about the school, district, and community in which you might be employed. You might want to visit the district while classes are in session and to visit the department and building in which you might be working. If at all possible, try to meet the department head and/or building principal by whom you would be supervised. Also, you should be prepared to ask about concerns and issues related to your employment that are of interest to you.

The following are topics about which job applicants typically have questions:

District

- Type of district (elementary, high school, or unit)
- History and development of the district
- Characteristics of the student population and community
- Size of the district (number of elementary, junior high/middle, and high schools)
- Central office administrators and their roles
- Grades included at each level of education

Curriculum

- Courses in the curriculum in your discipline and their content, sequence, prerequisites, and status as electives or required courses
- Typical schedule of courses in the curriculum (first and/or second semester courses)
- Textbook and supplementary materials, the recency of their adoption, and district adoption procedures
- Availability of AV materials and equipment for classroom use
- New and/or innovative curriculum developments in your discipline in recent years
- Curriculum developments currently being planned

Students

- Type and size of student body in which a position is available
- Typical class size
- Procedures for student placement
- Characteristics of entering and exiting students (ie., number or percentage who are enrolled in vocational and college preparatory curricula and the number or percentage who enroll in college on graduation).

Instructional Assignment

- Reasons why the position is available (enrolment increase, retirement, resignation, etc.)
- Number and type of teaching preparations (ie., self-contained classes or team-taught classes)
- Other instructional assignments
- Methods and frequency of teacher evaluation
- Availability of summer employment
- Assignments on department, school, or district committees
- Duties in the supervision/sponsorship of student activities
- Starting and ending dates of employment
- Contract length

Faculty

- Number of administrators in the building and their responsibilities
- Size of the faculty within departments and the building
- Number of new teachers hired each year
- Special interests and/or expertise of faculty

Student Services

- Student clubs, organizations, and sports
- Counselling and guidance personnel and services
- Social worker, school nurse, librarian, and other support staff and their roles

Community

- Community support for education
- Involvement of parents and other community members in the school program
- Recreational and other facilities in the community
- Demographic information about community residents
- Cost of living and housing in the community

Salary and Fringe Benefits

- District salary schedule
- Pay for extracurricular responsibilities
- Reimbursement policies for graduate study
- District requirements for continuing professional education
- Vacation and sick leave, personal leave, and other leave policies

Appendix 11.4 *(continued)*

- Substitute teacher procedures
- Payroll schedule
- Medical insurance

Selection Procedures

- Number and type of interviews that job candidates can expect

- Individuals involved in the preliminary screening of candidates, interviews, and the final selection
- District requirements for residency of staff
- Final Suggestions
- Be certain to read your employment contract carefully before signing it.

Source: Jan E. Kilby, *The ASCUS Annual 1988: A Job Search Handbook for Educators.* Addison, IL: Association for School, College and University Staffing, p. 16. Used with permission.

Appendix 11.5

Congratulations! You've completed your teacher education training program, become certified, and been offered a teaching position! As you begin your assignment, it is essential to keep in mind that successful teachers possess skills in many areas: teaching ability, content knowledge, interpersonal relations and communications, and those nebulous areas—"etiquette, politics, and culture."

Etiquette, Politics, and Culture

What do those words—*etiquette, politics, and culture*—mean, and what impact do they have on first-year teachers? Some refer to these as the "informal structure" of schools, the "rites of passage" that new teachers must experience.

■ Every school has formal and informal cultures and political structures. Learn about these structures as soon as possible. Become acquainted with the informal leaders. The sooner you understand the established culture at the school—whether it is participating in football pools, sitting at a particular table at lunch, or joining in after school activities—the sooner you will be considered effective and involved.

■ Watch, listen, learn to ask questions! Know who to ask! Frequently, colleagues are available for assistance during those first days of school, but once classes begin, you may be left on your own. Ask for help, watch what others do, and be an intuitive observer.

■ Seek a mentor. New teachers all need someone to turn to for guidance and support. Identify another teacher you respect and like, and ask that teacher to provide information, counselling, and encouragement.

■ Volunteer! Join the PTA, work at the school carnival, chaperone a school dance. Become involved with curriculum committees. You'll get to meet many people this way, and your fellow teachers will respect your involvement.

■ Volunteer, but don't be "pushy," and don't intrude. Be available as others invite you into the group.

■ Distinguish between the "good guys" and the "bad guys." Identify the positive staff members and join their team. Avoid the complaining, negative teachers. When you walk into the teacher's lounge and hear a teaching colleague criticizing the principal or ridiculing a student, walk the other way!

■ Be a role model for students. Yes, students may need friends, but you're more than that—you're their teacher. Have well-prepared lessons, be fair and consistent, and provide a positive learning environment.

■ Be professional—look the part and act the part. Work on your wardrobe. Weed out the casual, informal clothes that make you look like a college—or high school—student. Exude an aura of dependability and professionalism.

■ Accept the fact that you're the expert! Remember, you are the teacher. Parents and students look to you as the one with all the answers. Don't let them down!

■ Be open, yet sensitive, in dealing with parents. Whenever you talk to a mom or a dad about one of their children, you are talking about an extension of their very beings. Understand that they may be very sensitive and may react emotionally about little Farhad or Susie. Be clear and concise, but tactful and kind.

■ Watch what you say and where you say it. Be honest and open, but sensitive to the informal culture of the school. Don't criticize the school secretary to an aide who may be her best friend. Don't complain about a student in the faculty lounge. Don't talk about school problems in the grocery store.

Meet the Challenge

New teachers face the challenges of discipline and classroom management, motivation of students, assessment of students' needs and abilities, heavy teaching loads, insufficient preparation time, and building appropriate relationships with fellow teachers, administrators, and parents. However, beginning teachers often have the most difficulty adjusting to the emotional rigours—the politics and etiquette—of the job. Remember:

■ Focus on the positive; avoid the negative.
■ Teaching can be lonely; find a friend.
■ Be patient—wisdom takes time to acquire.
■ Learn to love teaching!
■ Be the best you can be!

The job of teaching is an incredibly challenging one. You will need to give a total commitment to your role as a teacher. But don't confuse something that's difficult with something that's negative. The excitement of teaching is embodied in hard work, meeting challenges, and accomplishing goals.

As time passes (and with help from others), you will learn to work more efficiently and figure out easier and better ways to do those things that at first seemed so difficult. You will have mastered the school's formal and informal structures!

Accept the challenge—be your best—and you'll find that you will be appreciated, respected, and perhaps even loved! You are a teacher—there is no better or more rewarding career!

Source: Mary Lee Howe in American Association for Employment in Education, *1995 Job Search Handbook for Educators,* Evanston, IL: Association for School, College and University Staffing, Inc., p. 31. Used with permission.

12

Education Issues for the Twenty-First Century

At the turn of the century, more and more educators are working in a world of intensifying and rapid change.... New technologies, greater cultural diversity, the skills called for in a changing economy, restructured approaches to administration and management, and a more sophisticated knowledge-base about teaching and learning, are all pulling students and their teachers in new directions.

—Mission Statement excerpt
International Centre for Educational Change
Ontario Institute for Studies in Education
University of Toronto

focus questions

1. What knowledge and skills will prepare students for a global information age?

2. How can schools and teachers provide an outstanding education for all learners?

3. How can community-based partnerships address social problems that hinder students' learning?

4. How will the fledgling charter school movement affect equity and excellence in education?

5. What can teachers and schools learn from international education?

6. What is our vision for the future of education?

H ow will education change during the twenty-first century? What new school–community linkages will help schools meet the needs of all learners? In what ways will teachers' professional lives become more collaborative and oriented toward system-wide reform? How likely is it that, as a teacher, you will have experiences similar to the following?

After a short drive through early-morning traffic less heavy than usual, you arrive at school in time for a 7:30 AM meeting of your school's Teacher Leadership Team (TLT), a group that makes curricular and instructional decisions for the school. The TLT also works directly with the school's Site-Based Council (SBC), which makes budget, personnel, and other policy decisions. SBC members include three teachers, the principal, five community members, and two professors from a nearby university.

Like most schools around the country, the changing demographics of the nation are reflected in an increasingly diverse student population at your school. About 15 percent of students are from families who live below the poverty line, and one in eight students is learning with English as a second language. According to a district survey, students represent 18 different language groups with Arabic being second to English as the most prevalent tongue. Overall, students at your school score in the top percentiles on provincial examinations; 50 percent of students go on to college, and 15 percent enrol in other forms of postsecondary programs.

With a few minutes before the meeting begins, you enter the classroom of another TLT member. Both of you were selected to be part of a nationwide network of teachers who will field test an interactive computer simulation developed by an instructional technology laboratory at a major university. Last week you both received the beta-test (trial) software, field-test guidelines, and registration materials for a four-day preparatory workshop to be held at the university. The university is paying for travel plus expenses, as well as providing a stipend.

"Well, did you have a chance to try out the software?" you ask upon entering the room. "I did last night, and it looks pretty impressive. I'm anxious to see what the kids think."

"I haven't had a chance yet; I've been preparing for this morning's TLT meeting," your friend says, pausing momentarily as she staples handouts arranged in neat stacks on top of her desk. Last spring she was elected to be one of the school's two curriculum coordinators. At today's TLT meeting, she and the other coordinator are presenting a model for school-wide curriculum integration. "What do we have to do as field testers?" she asks, continuing with her stapling task. "I just glanced at the field-test guidelines."

"Well, actually quite a lot, but I think it'll be interesting," you say. "The lab wants us to use the software every day for three weeks. Also, collect student performance data on a regular basis and samples of students' work. Plus, students will complete a survey at the beginning and at the end of the field test. That's about it ... oh, I forgot, they want us to do some student interviews ... there's a set of constructivist-oriented questions we're supposed to use. Basically, the lab wants us to develop a picture of students' problem-solving strategies as they work through the simulation."

"That does sound interesting," your friend says.

"Right. Well, I better get out of here and let you finish getting ready for the TLT meeting," you say.

Walking down the hallway to the conference room, you think about how satisfying it is to teach at your school. Teachers are hard-working and share a strong commitment to good teaching and to building a collegial professional community. Ample leadership opportunities, common planning periods, stimulating colleagues who are professionally involved, and solid support from the district and community are just a few of the factors that make working conditions at your school very positive.

Though no one has an educational crystal ball that can give a totally accurate glimpse of how the profession of teaching will evolve during the twenty-first century and how students will be taught, powerful forces are shaping schools and teaching in the directions just outlined. Moreover, thousands of teachers are collaborating and playing key leadership roles in shaping that future; and, today, hundreds of schools have professional communities identical to that described in the preceding scenario. We believe that the conditions under which teachers will work in this century will provide a dramatic contrast to those that many teachers experienced throughout much of the previous century. Isolation, lack of autonomy and self-governance, and few chances for professional growth are being replaced by collaboration, empowerment, stronger professionalism, and opportunities to provide leadership for educational change.

What Knowledge and Skills Will Prepare Students for a Global Information Age?

What knowledge and skills will students need to succeed in a global information age? Teachers in every generation have asked that question. At the beginning of the twenty-first century, the answer is confounded by conflicting theories, expectations, and values. One thing everyone agrees on, however, is that increasing cultural diversity in Canada and other countries and increasing global economic interdependence will call for communication and cooperation skills. People will need to be able to live together well and use environmental resources wisely. To equip students to do this, teachers will need to dedicate themselves to ensuring that all students develop knowledge, skills, attitudes, and values in nine key areas (see Figure 12.1). Though these nine areas of learning will not be all that students will need, learning in these areas will best enable them to meet the challenges of the future.

Literacy in Language, Mathematics, and Science

To solve the problems of the future, students will need to be able to write and speak clearly and succinctly. To access critical information from enormous data banks, they will need to be able to read complex material with a high degree of comprehension. Moreover, the continued development of "user-friendly" technologies such as voice-activated computers and reading machines will not reduce the need for high-level language arts literacy. In addition to strong skills in reading and writing, students will also need to be able to apply mathematical and scientific concepts to solve new problems. For example, they will need to be able to analyze unfamiliar situations, pose appropriate questions, use trial-and-error methods to gather and evaluate relevant data, and summarize results.

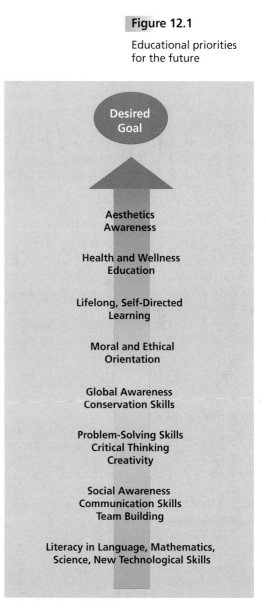

Figure 12.1

Educational priorities for the future

Desired Goal

Aesthetics Awareness

Health and Wellness Education

Lifelong, Self-Directed Learning

Moral and Ethical Orientation

Global Awareness Conservation Skills

Problem-Solving Skills Critical Thinking Creativity

Social Awareness Communication Skills Team Building

Literacy in Language, Mathematics, Science, New Technological Skills

New Technology Skills

Students of the future will also need to attain high levels of skill in computer-based technologies. To teach students skills in accessing the vast stores of information that computers routinely handle today, our nation's schools will become more technologically rich and teachers more technologically sophisticated. No longer able to resist the "irresistible force" of Information Age technology (Mehlinger 1996), schools will join the larger society where "the computer is a symbol of the future and all that is good about it" (Morton 1996, 417). In such an environment, students will not only learn to use computers as "tools" to access information—they will use computers to communicate worldwide and to generate creative solutions to real-world problems.

Problem Solving, Critical Thinking, and Creativity

Students of the future will need to be able to think rather than to remember. Although the information that students learn in schools may become outdated or useless, the thinking processes they acquire will not. These processes focus on the ability to find, obtain, and use information resources for solving problems or taking advantage of opportunities. Students will need to learn how to cope with change, how to anticipate alternative future developments, how to think critically, and how to analyze and synthesize large amounts of complex data.

Forecasts about the future share one thing in common—they place a priority on creative thinking to solve future problems. The acquisition of structured bodies of knowledge, while important, is not sufficient preparation for the future. Students must learn to think creatively to solve unforeseen problems. Students who are stretched to develop their creativity today will become the adults who invent ways to solve tomorrow's problems.

Can creative thinking be taught? William J. J. Gordon (1968, 1971a, 1971b, 1975), who has devoted his career to the study of creativity, believes it can. Gordon developed synectics, a teaching method based on the thinking process that is designed to

What knowledge and skills for the twenty-first century does this learning activity support? What else will students need to know and be able to do in the future?

"teach" creativity through the use of metaphor and analogy. **Synectics** is based on the assumptions that (1) creativity is important; (2) creativity is not mysterious; (3) in all fields, creative invention draws from the same underlying intellectual processes; and (4) the creativity of individuals and groups is similar (Joyce, Weil, and Calhoun 2000).

Social Awareness, Communication Skills, and Team Building

Tomorrow's students must be able to communicate with people from diverse cultures. The ability to create a better world in the future, then, will surely depend on our willingness to celebrate our rich diversity through the kind of communication that leads to understanding, friendly social relations, and the building of cohesive teams. "[T]he classroom should be a laboratory for collaborative decision making and team building" (Uchida, Cetron, and McKenzie 1996, 8).

An important lesson for students will be to learn that poverty, discrimination, violence, crime, and unequal opportunities, wherever they occur, affect us all. To solve these and other social problems, students will need to become socially aware, politically active, and skilled in conflict resolution strategies.

Global Awareness and Conservation Skills

Tomorrow's students will need to recognize the interconnectedness they share with all countries and with all people. Our survival may depend on being able to participate intelligently in a global economy and respond intelligently to global threats to security, health, environmental quality, and other factors affecting the quality of human life. The curriculum of the future must emphasize cultural diversity, interdependence, respect for the views and values held by others, an orientation toward international cooperation for resolving global issues, and practical knowledge and skills on, for example, the conservation of natural energy resources.

Health and Wellness Education

With ever-increasing health care costs, the spread of diseases such as AIDS, increased risks of cancer, and longer life spans, it is imperative that students of the future acquire appropriate knowledge, skills, and attitudes in the area of health education. To live healthy lives, then, students of tomorrow will need consumer education to select from among an increasingly complex array of health care services. In addition, they will need to be able to make informed choices among alternatives for the prevention or treatment of problems relating to substance abuse, nutrition, fitness, and mental health. Sex education, still a matter for debate in some communities, seems more critical today than at any time in the past.

Moral and Ethical Orientation

The school culture and the curriculum reflect both national and community values. The traditional practice of using values-clarification activities in the classroom, however, has been criticized by some for promoting relativism at the expense of family values or religious doctrines. Yet, as we witness the effects of violence in schools, racial intolerance, sexual exploitation of children, drunk driving, white-collar crime, false advertising, unethical business practices, excessive litigation, and so on, many citizens are calling for schools to pay more attention to issues of public morality and ethical behaviour. "[T]o survive and prosper in the twenty-first century, students will need self-discipline, which entails an ethical code and the ability to set and assess progress toward their own goals" (Uchida, Cetron, and McKenzie 1996, 17). In response to harassment and intimidation that can lead to violence in the hallways, for example, many Canadian schools have implemented anger management programs similar to the Second Step program created by the Seattle-Based Committee for Children. According to a teacher at a school that begins the year with Second Step lessons for all students, "We have created a culture in our school that says we all recognize that some things just aren't accepted" (Gutloff 1999).

Aesthetic Awareness

Another challenge for teachers and schools is to encourage creativity and greater appreciation for the arts. Many observers of Canadian education point out that emotional, spiritual, aesthetic, and reflective, or meditative, dimensions of life receive less emphasis than analytical thinking and practical life skills. Although literature and drama are standard fare in curricula, for example, most students know little about music, painting, and sculpture. Public school students are rarely taught art history or principles of design or other criteria for evaluating creative works. As a result, students may lack the concepts and experiences that lead to an appreciation of beauty and the development of aesthetic judgment.

Lifelong Self-Directed Learning

The key educational priority that should guide teachers of the future is to create within each student the ability, and the desire, to continue self-directed learning throughout his or her life.

It has often been said that one of the primary purposes of schooling is for students to learn how to learn. In a world characterized by rapid social, technological, economic, and political changes, all persons must take responsibility for their own learning. Career changes will be the norm, and continuing education over a lifetime will be necessary.

How Can Schools and Teachers Provide an Outstanding Education for All Learners?

Although we don't know exactly how teaching will change during the twenty-first century, we do know that teachers will continue to have a professional and moral obligation to reach all learners, many of whom will be from environments that provide little support for education. Imagine, for example, that one of your students is Dolores, described in the following scenario.

> Fifteen-year-old Dolores and her twin brother, Frank, live with their mother in a housing project in a poor section of the city. Their mother divorced her third husband two years ago, after she learned that he had been sexually abusing Dolores. Since then, Dolores' mother has been struggling to make ends meet with her job as a custodian at a hospital. Two evenings a week, she goes to a neighbourhood centre to learn English. She hopes to become proficient enough in English to get a job as a secretary.

Dolores wishes her mother and Frank didn't fight so much. The fights usually revolve around Frank missing school and his drinking. Just last night, for example, Frank came home drunk and he and his mother got into another big fight. When she accused him of being involved in a street gang, Frank stormed out and went to spend the night at his cousin's apartment two blocks away.

At 6:30 that morning, Dolores awoke just as her mother left for work. The hinges on the apartment door, painted over by a careless maintenance worker, creaked loudly as she closed the door behind her. Dolores felt reassured by the sound of her mother locking the dead bolt—the apartment beneath them had been burglarized last week. Like Frank, she wasn't getting along well with her mother lately, so it would be nice to have the apartment to herself while she got ready for school.

Dolores got up slowly, stretched, and looked around the cluttered living room of the one-bedroom apartment. Her mother slept in the bedroom, and Frank, when he wasn't out all night or at his cousin's, slept on the other couch in the living room.

She had had trouble sleeping last night. Now that it was winter, the radiator next to the beige couch on which she slept clanked and hissed most of the night. Also, she was worried—two weeks ago a doctor at the neighbourhood clinic confirmed that she was pregnant. Yesterday, she finally got up enough courage to tell her boyfriend. He got angry with her and said he "wasn't gonna be no father."

Dolores knew she ought to be seeing a doctor, but she dreaded going to the clinic alone. Her mother took a day off from work—without pay—when she went two weeks ago. Right after that, her mother complained about missing work and said, "Don't expect me to take off from work every time you go to the clinic. You should have thought about that before you got in trouble."

Later that morning, Dolores is in your class, sitting in her usual spot in the middle of the back row. While your students work on an in-class writing assignment, you glance at Dolores and wonder why she hasn't been paying attention during the last few weeks like she usually does. At that moment, Dolores, wearing the same clothes she wore yesterday, stifles a yawn.

As you continue to move about the room, checking on students' progress and answering an occasional question, you wonder if you should talk with Dolores after class. You don't want to pry into her life outside of school, but you're worried about what might be causing her to act differently.

Although the family will continue to remain a prominent part of our culture, evidence indicates that many children, like Dolores and Frank, live in families that are under acute stress. Soaring numbers of runaway children and cases of child abuse suggest that the family is in trouble. In addition, teachers will continue to find that more and more of their students are from families that are smaller, have working mothers, have a single parent present, or have unrelated adults living in the home.

Equity for All Students

A dominant political force in the twenty-first century will be continued demands for equity in all sectors of Canadian life, particularly education. For example, the legalities of school funding laws will be challenged where inequities are perceived, and tax reform measures will be adopted to promote equitable school funding. Classroom teachers will continue to be held accountable for treating all students equitably.

An Exemplary School

The following case describes a prototypical exemplary urban elementary school, "Paul Robeson Elementary School," as compiled by Gloria Ladson-Billings, an award-winning researcher and author. Not a futuristic school, the school is an example for today—incorporating the best practices and perspectives that Ladson-Billings observed in eight classrooms that she studied over a two-year period. Consider Ladson-Billings' Robeson School as presented and then project it 20 years into the future. How might it be different and even better?

Paul Robeson Elementary School is located in a low-income predominantly ethnic community. More than merely a school, Robeson is a neighbourhood centre and gathering place that is open from 6:00 AM to 10:00 PM It includes a daycare centre, a preschool, a health clinic, and a job training centre. Local civic and church groups use the school as a meeting place. If one needs information about the community, the school is the likely place to locate it.

The banner across the main hallway of the school reads, "It takes a whole village to educate a child." Robeson's teaching staff is multicultural. The teaching staff has representatives from a variety of racial and ethnic backgrounds. However, every credentialed adult at Robeson, not just the teachers, teaches a class—the principal, the counsellor, the special teachers. This means that classes are relatively small—12 to 15 students. There are no "pull out" programs, such as those that require students to be taken out of their regular classrooms to receive remedial instruction while simultaneously depriving them of the instruction that is occurring in the regular class. There is no separate class for students evaluated as learning-disabled. Instead, students with learning disabilities are integrated into the regular classrooms and receive additional attention with the help of teachers' aides, the classroom teacher, and more advanced peers.

Robeson has one requirement—that its students be successful. The curriculum is rigorous and exciting. The student learning is organized around problems and issues. For example, one fourth-grade class is studying how cities develop. The students have studied cities in Europe, Africa, and Asia. They are studying their own city. They have taken trips to City Hall and have seen the city council in action. The mayor visited their classroom. In current events they read about the city news. Groups of students are working on solutions to problems specific to their city. The problems include the city's budget deficit, homelessness, the poor conditions of roads, and crime—particularly drug-related crime.

The students have read Carl Sandburg's poetry and they have studied architecture—buildings and bridges. They have studied geography and urban planning. They have written letters to the editor of a city newspaper about conditions in the city and in their neighbourhood. Each student is an "expert" in some aspect of cities. Together they are planning an exhibition that will be shown in the evening so that their parents and other community members can attend.

All students at Robeson Elementary participate in a community service program. The students in the primary grades usually participate as a class group. Community service activities include visiting a local nursing home, where students participate in the Adopt-a-Grandparent program. They also participate in neighbourhood cleanup days and recycling drives. The older students develop their own community service projects, which are approved by their teachers. They usually work in small groups or in pairs. Occasionally, an intermediate class will take on a project such as becoming readers at the local library, volunteering in the pediatric ward of the hospital, and planting and maintaining a community garden.

Parents play an important role at Robeson. Each household is assessed 20 h of volunteer service to the school. Some volunteer one hour a week in the classroom. Others participate in the school's Artists and Scholars in Residence program. Parents who participate in the local church choir offer their musical skills. Others share their cooking, sewing, knitting, woodworking, or athletic talents.

School governance at Robeson involves the principal, the teachers, the parents, and the students. The school council meets once a month to discuss the curriculum, instruction, personnel, and finances. The council members determine school policy and hiring and firing issues, and they constitute the school's disciplinary board.

One of Robeson's unique qualities is its residence program. By working with local social-service agencies Robeson obtained use of a renovated small apartment building nearby to house students whose family lives are in turmoil. Under the best circumstances students spend only a short time at the residence; in some unfortunate cases they spend the entire year there. By living in a centre in their own community, they do not have to leave Robeson or the neighbourhood they know. The residence is not for students with disciplinary problems. It is designed simply to alleviate family stresses.

As a testament to the success of Robeson Elementary School, its students score above the national norm on standardized tests, but Robeson does not make a fuss over its test score performance. The school community knows that in a caring, supportive environment where all of the children are made to feel special, test scores are but one of the marks of accomplishment that can be expected.

Questions

1. What features of this school are exemplary?

2. What societal problems are addressed by the school? How?

3. Do you agree with the school's perspective on test scores? Why or why not?

4. How would you add to this exemplary school to make it an ideal school for the year 2020?

5. Design your own ideal school, making it a rural, urban, suburban, or virtual school in the year 2020.

Source: Reprinted with permission from Gloria Ladson-Billings, The Dreamkeepers: Successful Teachers of African American Children. San Francisco, Jossey-Bass, 1994. Selection from pp. 140–42.

In Chapter 5, you learned about the importance of preparing multicultural instructional materials and strategies to meet the learning needs of students from diverse cultural, ethnic, and linguistic backgrounds. In Chapter 6, you learned how to create an inclusive classroom to meet the needs of all students, regardless of their developmental levels, intelligences, abilities, or disabilities. In addition, you should create a learning environment in which high-achieving and low-achieving students are treated the same. Thomas Good and Jere Brophy (2000) reviewed the research in this area and found that several teacher behaviours indicated unequal treatment of students. The behaviours identified include waiting less time for them to answer questions, interacting with them less frequently, giving less feedback, calling on them less often, seating them farther way, failing to accept and use their ideas, smiling at them less often, making less eye contact, praising them less, demanding less, grading their tests differently, and rewarding inappropriate behaviours.

Effective teachers establish respectful relationships with *all* students; they listen to them; they give frequent feedback and opportunities to ask questions; and they demand higher-level performance. In their assessment of student's learning, they give special attention to the questions they ask of students. Research indicates that most questions teachers ask are **lower-order questions,** those that assess students' abilities to recall specific information. Effective teachers, however, also ask **higher-order questions** that demand more critical thinking and answers to questions such as, Why? What if ... ? In addition, to reach all learners and prepare them for the future, effective teachers provide students with active, authentic learning experiences.

Active, Authentic Learning

Since the 1970s, educational researchers have increased our understanding of the learning process. Though learning theorists and researchers disagree about a definition for *learning,* most agree that **learning** "occurs when experience causes a relatively permanent change in an individual's knowledge or behavior" (Woolfolk 1998, 204). Research into multiple intelligences and multicultural learning modes has broadened our understanding of this definition of learning. In addition, research in the fields of neurophysiology, neuropsychology, and cognitive science will continue to expand our understanding of how people think and learn.

Our growing understanding of learning indicates that all students learn best when they are actively involved in authentic activities that connect with the "real world." Small-group activities, cooperative learning arrangements, field trips, experiments, and integrated curricula are among the instructional methods you should incorporate into your professional repertoire.

How Can Community-Based Partnerships Address Social Problems That Hinder Students' Learning?

Earlier in this book, we examined social problems that affect schools and place students at risk of dropping out: poverty, family stress, substance abuse, violence and crime, teen pregnancy, HIV/AIDS, and suicide (see Chapter 5). We also looked at intervention programs schools have developed to ensure the optimum behavioural, social, and academic adjustment of at-risk children and adolescents to their school experiences: peer counselling, full-service schools, school-based inter-professional case management, compensatory education, and alternative schools and curricula. Here, we describe innovative, community-based partnerships that some schools have developed recently to prevent social problems from hindering students' learning.

The range of school-community partnerships found in today's schools is extensive. For example, as the "Interactive Organizational Model" in Figure 12.2 illustrates, Exeter High School in suburban Toronto has developed partnerships with 13 community organizations and more than 100 employers. Through Exeter's Partners in Learning program, business, industry, service clubs, and social service agencies make significant contributions to students' learning.

The Community As a Resource for Schools

To assist schools in addressing the social problems that impact students, many communities are acting in the spirit of a recommendation made by Ernest Boyer: "Perhaps the time has come to organize, in every community, not just a *school* board, but a *children's* board. The goal would be to integrate children's services and build, in every community, a friendly, supportive environment for children" (Boyer 1995, 169). In partnerships between communities and schools, individuals, civic organizations, or businesses select a school or are selected by a school to work together for the good of students. The ultimate goals of such projects are to provide students with better school experiences and to assist students at risk.

Civic Organizations

To develop additional sources of funding, many local school districts have established partnerships with community groups interested in improving educational opportunities in the schools. Some groups, such as the Lions Club, have actively supported a variety of school projects. Others adopt or sponsor schools and enrich their educational programs by providing funding, resources, or services.

Volunteer Mentor Programs

Mentorship is a trend in community-based partnerships today, especially with students at risk. Parents, business leaders, professionals, and peers volunteer to work with students in neighbourhood schools. Goals might include dropout prevention, high achievement, improved self-esteem, and healthy decision making. Troubleshooting on lifestyle issues often plays a role, especially in communities plagued by drug dealing, gang rivalry, casual violence, and crime. Mentors from organizations such as " Big Brothers and Big Sisters of Canada" also model success for participating children and adolescents.

Corporate-Education Partnerships

Business involvement in schools has taken many forms, including, for example, contributions of funds or materials needed by a school, release time for employees to visit classrooms, adopt-a-school programs, cash grants for pilot projects and teacher development, educational use of corporate facilities and expertise, employee participation, and student scholarship programs. Extending beyond advocacy, private sector efforts include job initiatives for disadvantaged youths, in-service programs for teachers, management training for school administrators, minority education and faculty development, and even construction of school buildings.

Student Activities and Clubs
- Ambassadors
- Art
- Band/Choir/Chamber Band/Stage Band
- Bowling
- Chess
- Culinary
- Design
- Drama
- Fish-On
- Interact (Junior Rotarians)
- Math Clinic
- OSAID
- Outers
- Sign Language
- Ski
- Squash
- Technology
- Weight Training
- Welding
- Woodworking
- Youth Alive

Support Staff
- Secretarial
- LAN Administrator
- Custodial

Departments
- Art
- Business
- English
- Family Studies
- Geography
- History
- Library Media
- Mathematics
- Moderns
- Music
- Physical & Health Education
- Science
- Technology
- Special Education
- Student Services
- Work Education

Community Groups
- Exeter Citizenship
- Exeter Intergenerational
- Tech Advisory
- Music Advisory
- OISE/U of T
- Ontario Hydro
- Durham Regional Police
- C.A.M.C.
- McDonalds
- Durham Health and the Youth Council
- Rogers Cablesystem
- School Town Library
- Bell Canada Pioneers
- Over 100 employers for Work Education Program

MISSION STATEMENT

Exeter High School is committed to excellence through innovative academic and technological programming within a culture of mutual respect, community involvement, and partnerships.

School Growth Team

Administration Team

Department Heads

Student Council

School Community Council

Student Athletic Associations
- Alpine Skiing
- Archery
- Badminton
- Baseball
- Cross Country Running
- GoH
- Field Hockey
- Hockey
- Soccer
- Softball
- Swimming
- Tennis
- Track & Field
- Volleyball
- Wrestling

Task Forces
- Integrated Curriculum
- Curriculum Focus Day
- Exam Scheduling
- Staff Supervision

Committees
- Ethnocultural
- P.D.
- Beautification
- Safe Schools
- Wellness
- Evaluation
- Specialization Years
- Public Relations
- Site Management Team
- Schoolwide Action Research
- Health & Safety
- New Teachers
- Computers

Activity Groups
- Breakfast Club
- Food and Toy Drive
- Graduation/Junior Awards
- Open House
- Picture Day
- Sunshine Club
- Transition Years
- United Way
- School Profile
- Citizenship
- Intergenerational
- Yearbook

Liason Groups
- Group 1
- Group 2
- Group 3
- Group 4
- Group 5
- Group 6
- Group 7
- Group 8

Figure 12.2

Exeter High School interactive organizational model

Source: Gordon Cawelti, *Portraits of Six Benchmark Schools: Diverse Approaches to Improving Student Achievement.* Arlington, VA: Educational Research Service, 1999, p. 32. Used with permission.

This involvement of the business community with education is not without its critics. Maude Barlow, in her article *The Assault on Canadian Schools* (1995, 1-8), points out, in the strongest of language, that the efforts of transnational corporations to infiltrate Canadian schools is a serious problem which must be addressed. She writes about the United States, where Burger King operates fully accredited high schools, as does its main competitor, McDonalds Corporation, and also of New Zealand, where "students are writing exams brought to them by Reebok and Coca Cola … [with] the corporate logos on each exam." (Barlow 1995, 7) In addition to contributing more resources to education, chief executive officers of 99 Canadian corporations surveyed by the *Financial Post* "said they should be, and very soon would be, in the schools (Barlow 1995, 7).

Schools As Resources for Communities

The view that schools should serve as multipurpose resources *for* the community is a shift from the more traditional perspective of schools needing community support to meet the needs of students affected by social problems. By focusing not only on the development of children and youth, but on their families as well, schools ultimately enhance the ability of students to learn. As Ernest Boyer (1995, 168) puts it, "No arbitrary line can be drawn between the school and life outside. Every [school] should take the lead in organizing a *referral service*—a community safety net for children that links students and their families to support agencies in the region—to clinics, family support and counseling centers, and religious institutions."

Beyond the School Day

Many schools and school districts are serving their communities by providing educational and recreational programs before and after the traditional school day and during the summers. Increasingly, educational policymakers recognize that the traditional school year of approximately 190 days is not the best arrangement to meet students' learning needs. As the RCM Research Corporation, a nonprofit group that studies issues in educational change, points out: "Historically, time has been the glue that has bonded the traditions of our public school system—i.e., equal class periods, no school during summer months, 12 years of schooling, etc.,—and, as a result, the use of time has become sacrosanct, 'We have always done it this way!' How time is used by schools often has more to do with administrative convenience than it does with what is best educationally for the student" (RCM Research Corporation 1998). In 2003, for example, British Columbia considered having the regular school day extended in length while reducing the actual number of school days per week to four from the more customary five. In the late 1990s some Nova Scotia school districts also considered, but eventually rejected, a similar possibility.

Proposals for year-round schools and educationally oriented weekend and after-school programs address the educational and developmental needs of students impacted by social problems. While Canadian provinces and territories have yet to make substantive changes to the regular school year, examples of what might eventually take place can be found in the United States. There, according to the San Diego–based National Association for Year-Round Education, more than 2800 public schools now extend their calendars into the summer, and more than two million students go to school year-round. In Austin, Texas, for example, schools can participate in an Optional Extended Year (OEY) program that allows them to provide additional instruction in reading and mathematics to students at risk of being retained a grade. Schools participating in

OEY can choose from among four school day options: (1) extended day, (2) extended week, (3) intersession of year-round schools, and (4) summer school (Idol 1998; Washington 1998). Futurist Marvin Cetron predicts that, soon, "schools will educate and train both children and adults around the clock: the academic day will stretch to seven hours for children; adults will work a 32-hour week and prepare for their next job in the remaining time" (Uchida, Cetron, and McKenzie 1996, 35).

Programs that extend beyond the traditional school day also address the needs of parents and the requirements of the work world. Every day, thousands of elementary-age, "latchkey" children arrive home to an empty house. As one elementary teacher said, "Many of my students just hang around at the end of every day. They ask what they can do to help me. Often there's no one at home, and they're afraid to go home or spend time on the streets" (Boyer 1995, 165).

After-school educational and recreational programs are designed to (1) provide children with supervision at times when they might become involved in antisocial activities, (2) provide enrichment experiences to widen children's perspectives and increase their socialization, and (3) improve the academic achievement of children not achieving at their potential during regular school hours (Fashola 1999). Ernest Boyer argues that schools should adapt their schedules to those of the workplace so that parents can become more involved in their children's education, and that businesses, too, should give parents more flexible work schedules. Drawing on the model of Japan, Boyer suggests that the beginning of the school year could be a holiday to free parents to attend opening day ceremonies and celebrate the launching and continuation of education in the same way that we celebrate its ending.

Although some research indicates that extended school days and school calendars have a positive influence on achievement (Gandara and Fish 1994; Center for Research on Effective Schooling for Disadvantaged Students 1992), the Center for Research on the Education of Students Placed at Risk (CRESPAR) at Johns Hopkins University concluded that "there is no straightforward answer to the question of what works best in after-school programs" (Fashola 1999). According to CRESPAR, few studies of the effects of after-school programs on measures such as achievement or reduction of antisocial behaviour meet minimal standards for research design. Nevertheless, CRESPAR found that after-school programs with stronger evidence of effectiveness had four elements: training for staff, program structure, evaluation of program effectiveness, and planning that includes families and children (Fashola 1999).

Social Services

In response to the increasing number of at-risk and violence-prone children and youth, many schools are also providing an array of social services to students, their families, and their communities. The following comments by three female students highlight the acute need for support services for at-risk youth who can turn to aggression and violence in a futile attempt to bolster their fragile self-esteem and to cope with the pain in their lives. All three girls have been involved in violent altercations in and around their schools, and all three frequently use alcohol and illegal drugs.

Fifteen-year-old "Mary" has been physically abused by both her father and mother, and she was raped when she was 14. "Linda," also 15 years old, was sexually molested during a four-year period by a family acquaintance, and she endures constant physical and psychological abuse from her father. Fourteen-year-old "Jenny" is obsessed with death and suicide, and she aspires to join a gang.

> When you're smoking dope, you just break out laughing, you don't feel like punching people because it's just too hard. It takes too much.... You're mellow.... You just want to sit there and trip out on everybody.... It's even good for school work. When

I used to get stoned all the time last year, I remember, I used to sit in class and do my work because I didn't want the teacher to catch me, and this year I'm getting failing marks 'cause I'm not doing my work 'cause I'm never stoned (Mary).

I just know I got a lot of hatred.... And there's this one person [Jenny], and it just kinda happened after she mouthed me off, I was just like totally freaked with her and now I just want to slam her head into something. I wanna shoot her with a gun or something. I wanna kill her.... If I could get away with it I'd kill her. I wouldn't necessarily kill her, but I'd get her good. I just want to teach her a lesson. I'd beat the crap out of her. She's pissed me off so badly. I just want to give her two black eyes. Then I'd be fine. I'd have gotten the last word in (Linda).

I like fighting. It's exciting. I like the power of being able to beat up people. Like, if I fight them, and I'm winning, I feel good about myself, and I think of myself as tough.... I'm not scared of anybody, so that feels good. My friends are scared of a lot of people, and I go "Oh yeah, but I'm not scared of them.... All these people in grade eight at that junior high are scared of me, they don't even know me, and they're scared of me. It makes me feel powerful (Jenny) (Artz 1999, 127, 136, 157).

In Chapter 5, we looked at how some schools provide educational, medical, social and/or human services, and how the school-based inter-professional case management model uses case managers to deliver services to at-risk students and their families. Although many believe that schools should not provide such services, an increase in the number of at-risk students like Mary, Linda, and Jenny suggest that the trend is likely to continue, with more schools requiring a service agency "which brings together all of the community agencies concerned with children, coordinates the services, increases support, and prepares a report card on progress" (Boyer 1995, 169). More social initiatives such as parent support groups, infant nurseries, and programs for students with special needs, are likely to form a more prominent part of future Canadian schooling.

How Will the Fledgling Charter School Movement Affect Equity and Excellence in Education?

One of the most interesting experiments in Canadian education during the last decade has been the development of charter schools. While there are only ten such schools in Canada, all in Alberta, these schools present a new direction in educational reform. Charter schools offer a modern and flexible approach to the complex teaching environment of today. While held fully accountable to a publicly elected government body, they control their own budget, staffing, programs, and services, to better meet the needs of their students.

Charter schools are independent, innovative, outcome-based, public schools. "The charter school concept allows a group of teachers, parents, or others who share similar interests and views about education to organize and operate a school. Charters can be granted by a local school district or by the province. In effect, charter schools offer a model for restructuring that gives greater autonomy to individual schools and promotes school choice by increasing the range of options available to parents and students within the public schools system" (Wohlstetter and Anderson 1994, 486).

To open a charter school, an original charter (or agreement) is signed by the school's founders and a sponsor (usually the local school board). The charter specifies the learning outcomes that students will master before they continue their studies. Charter schools, which usually operate in the manner of autonomous school districts (a feature that distinguishes them from the alternative schools that many school districts operate), are public schools and must teach all students. If admission requests for a charter school exceed the number of available openings, students are selected by a draw.

Because charter schools are designed to promote the development of new teaching strategies that can be used at other public schools, they can prove to be an effective tool for promoting educational reform and the professionalization of teaching in the future. Moreover, charter schools give teachers unprecedented leadership opportunities and the ability to respond quickly to students' needs:

> [We had] the chance to create a school that takes into account the approaches we know will work. We listen to what the students want and need, because we ask them. And each day we ask ourselves if we are doing things the best way we can. We also have the flexibility to respond. We can change the curriculum to meet these needs as soon as we see them. Anywhere else it would take a year to change. It is much better than anything we have known in the traditional setting (North Central Regional Education Laboratory 1993, 3).

Murnane and Levy (1996) suggest that charter schools are "too new to have a track record," and they should not be seen as a "magic bullet" that will dramatically, and with little effort, improve students' achievement. In addition, they suggest four questions that observers should pose to determine whether individual charter schools promote both equity and excellence.

- Does the charter school commit itself to a goal, such as mastery of critical skills for all its students, or will it emphasize other goals?
- Does the charter school commit itself to serve a fair share of the most difficult-to-educate children, and does it have a strategy for attracting such children—or will it discourage applications from such children?
- Does the charter school's contract with the school district provide enough time and enough financial support for the school to persevere and learn from the mistakes that are inevitable in any ambitious new venture?
- Does the charter school commit itself to providing information about student achievement that will allow parents to make sound judgments about the quality of the education their children are receiving (Murnane and Levy 1996, 113)?

The United States and For-Profit Schools

Other than a short-lived experiment in Nova Scotia with Public-Private Partnership (P–3) schools, there are no for-profit schools in Canada. However, in the United States—which often provides us with a hint of future educational directions—one of the most controversial educational issues for the twenty-first century is the practice of turning the operation of public schools over to private, for-profit companies. Advocates of **privatization** believe privately operated schools are more efficient; they reduce costs and maximize "production"—that is, student achievement. Opponents, however, are concerned that profit, rather than increasing student achievement, is the real driving force behind **for-profit schools**. Critics of for-profit schools are also concerned that school districts may not be vigilant enough in monitoring the performance of private education companies.

Like Maude Barlow, Canadian essayist and novelist John Ralston Saul is very concerned about the possible privatization of our schools. In his article "In Defense of Public Education" (Saul 2002, 12) he states that "Our country has been built, from the very beginnings of its democratic system 150 years ago, upon a happy linkage between democracy and public education." He makes the additional comment that "if society and its leaders are not willing to fund the [educational] system, then we

How does Canada compare to other countries regarding the importance of information technology in the curriculum?

Students leaving school today, both in Canada and around the world, will compete for jobs in a global economy that is powerfully influenced by information technology. In many respects, the "coin of the realm" for the global economy of the twenty-first century will be neither raw materials nor labour but information. As a result, the place of information technology in the school curriculum is critical.

Figure 12.3 shows the percentage of the public in eleven OECD (Organization for Economic Co-operation and Development) countries who gave information technology and technical studies a rating of either "essential" or "very important" in the school curriculum. (Unfortunately, Canada was not included in this study, with the result that where Canadians stand on this issue stands is

only an estimate.) Information technology (eg., computing and database management) was viewed as relatively more important than technical studies (eg., metal shop and drafting) in all countries except Spain, where they were viewed as nearly the same. It is noteworthy that the United States public, more than the public in the other countries, views information technology as especially important. To what extent do you believe the *actual* emphasis on information technology in school curricula reflects the importance the Canadian public attaches to instruction in information technology? As a teacher, what role can you play in ensuring that your students acquire the information technology skills they will need for their future in a global economy?

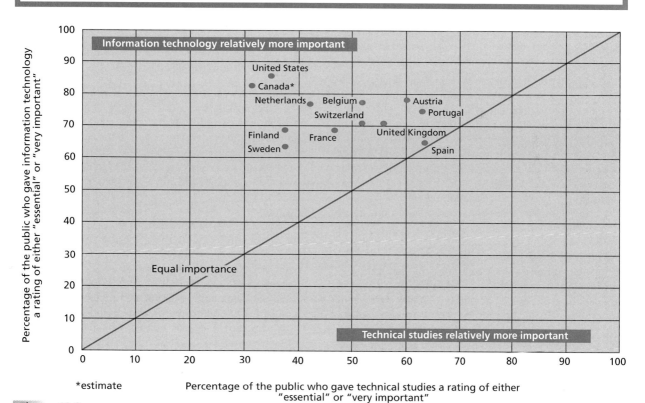

Figure 12.3

The importance of information technology and technical studies: An international perspective.

Source: Public Attitudes Toward Secondary Education: The United States in an International Context. Washington, DC: U.S. Department of Education, 1997.

Should Canada emulate the United States' for-profit school model?

Would businesses do a better job running public schools in Canada than the provincial, government-based system? Should businesses make a profit from schools? Should taxpayers contribute funds to schools that in turn give businesses profits? With the rise of privatization of education in the late 1990s, people were beginning to ask such questions.

With some now starting to refer to the education system as an "education industry," *The Economist,* a London publication, reported on privatization of US education (1999b), noting that

... the government says that the country spends a total of $625 billion a year on education—more than it devotes to pensions or defence [sic]—and predicts that spending per pupil will rise by 40% over the next decade. Private companies currently have only 13% of the market.... But International Data Corporation, a consultancy, reckons that this share will expand to 25% over the next two decades.

US businesses privatize schools in three ways: establishing for-profit charter schools, placing public schools under corporate management (for example, the Edison Schools), and providing supplementary services such as testing and coaching (for example, the Sylvan Learning Systems). The "education industry" covers schooling from preschool through college, with the former in particular regarded as a "boom area."

Teachers' unions and education scholars and writers expressed alarm over the expansion of privatization. Henry Giroux criticized its advocates:

They view education primarily as a commercial venture in which the only form of citizenship offered to young people is consumerism. Yet reducing public education to the ideological imperatives of corporate culture works against the critical social demands of educating citizens who can sustain and develop inclusive democratic identities, relations, and public spheres. (Giroux 1999)

Education researchers questioned the merit and ethics of commercializing education. In a study of eleven for-profit schools in western Michigan, Christy Lancaster Dykgraaf, and Shirley Kane Lewis concluded that the emergence of such schools was "cause for concern," adding, "Issues related to cost-cutting strategies, communication, and public ownership of the public schools deserve serious attention if these charter schools are to

match the expectations and meet the needs of the constituencies they are intended to serve" (1998).

In April 1999, Henry Levin, Stanford education professor and leader of the Accelerated Schools Project, moved to Columbia University to head the new National Center for the Study of Privatization in Education. According to an *Education Week* issue paper (1999, July 29), Levin "hopes to conduct neutral research, without any political pull from conservatives or liberals, on the impact of privatization to advance the debate about vouchers, charter schools, and private companies in education."

While the experts are evaluating the matter, what do you think about the move toward privatization? Is this an effective way to improve education?

Yes, privatization is an effective way to improve education.

The country's poor record in student achievement compared to that in other countries makes it imperative to do something different. U.S. businesses and colleges complain about the inadequate skills and limited knowledge of high school graduates. What the country has been doing has not been working. Now the problem is too great to ignore. As the world news journal, *The Economist* (1999b), observes:

America spends more of its GDP on education than most countries, yet it gets mediocre results. Children in Asia and Europe often trounce their American counterparts in standardised [sic] scholastic tests. More than 40 percent of American ten-year-olds cannot pass a basic reading test; as many as 42 million adults are functionally illiterate. Part of the reason for this dismal performance is that close to half of the $6500 spent on each child is eaten up by "non-instructional services"—mostly administration.

The best solution is to combine business expertise with government regulation to spend education money more effectively. "Government's oversight function and its responsiveness to the needs of citizens can be retained while taking advantage of private enterprise's ability to be more efficient, reduce costs, and maximize production—in this case, student achievement," *Education Week* observed (1999, July 29).

Many believe that the competition that free enterprise provides will motivate schools to improve. Others believe privatization will bring fresh ideas to a weary education system. Michael R. Sandler, the chief executive officer for EduVentures, is quoted in a May 1999 *Education Week* article as saying, "The true agents of change for education reform in the twenty-first century are going to be the innovative for-profit enterprises built by education entrepreneurs" (Walsh 1999). And *The Economist* (1999, Jan. 16) reported that "Such schemes free education from the stifling grip of teaching unions and bureaucrats." With the freedom to innovate and the unique perspectives and know-how of business, for-profit charter schools and corporate management of public schools may breathe new life into education in the U.S.

No, privatization is not an effective way to improve education.

Most of the arguments against privatization fall into two broad areas—reductionism of education and alteration of the purpose of schools.

Privatization reduces education by narrowing the curriculum, standardizing the way it is taught, and devaluing the gifts of teachers. Because for-profit schools and management corporations need to demonstrate that they are effective, they must specify exactly what will be learned and then be able to prove that students have learned it. Accountability is the prime focus; and the narrower and more standardized the curriculum, the easier it is to assess. Curricula also become limited to that which can be tested. Lessons regarding attitudes, values, correct behaviour, creative expression, leadership, art, music, sports, speech, and drama all are difficult to assess. As a consequence they tend to be set aside or given limited focus so that teachers and students can prepare for tests on core curricula. Similarly, the instruction teachers provide is strictly prescribed to maximize the likelihood that test scores rise. Teachers' abilities to enrich school experiences and make learning meaningful are squelched by the standardization process and assessment focus.

More serious is privatization's impact on the direction and purpose of schools. Its focus on profit, integration of commercialism in curricula, and preparation of students as consumers is a far cry from the original purposes of schools—to prepare students to lead morally good lives and be good and informed citizens able to participate in a democratic government. Henry Giroux, a passionate voice against the corporatizing of U.S. education, writes that advocates of privatization are attempting to "transform public education from a public good, benefiting all students, to a private

good designed to expand the profits of investors, educate students as consumers, and train young people for the low-paying jobs of the new global marketplace" (Giroux 1999). He observes that these advocates critique U.S. education by viewing it separate from the social conditions in society:

Stripped of a language of social responsibility advocates of privatization reject the assumption that school failure might be better understood within the political, economic, and social dynamics of poverty, joblessness, sexism, race and class discrimination, unequal funding, or a diminished tax base.

Privatization of education serves the profit interests of businesses, not the good of students and the country. Citizens need to be wary.

Where do you stand on this issue?

1. Which are the best arguments on each side of this issue?

2. Where do you stand on this issue? Why do you hold this position?

3. What are the potential costs if either side has complete control of education?

4. Update yourself on this issue by following it on the web through Ebscohost or First Search. In First Search choose "all data bases" and then explore Wilson Select and PerAbs for full text articles.

Recommended Sources

AFT on the Issues (1999, July). Vouchers and the accountability dilemma.

Kane, S. and Dykgraaf, C. L. (1998, October). For-profit charter schools: What the public needs to know. *Educational Leadership, V. 56*(2), 51–53.

The Economist (1999a, January 16). A contract on schools: Why handing education over to companies can make sense.

The Economist (1999, January 16). Reading, writing and enrichment: Private money is pouring into American education—and transforming it.

Education Week on the Web (1999, July 29). Issue Paper: Privatization of public education.

Giroux, H. A. (1999, Winter). Schools for sale: public education, corporate culture, and the citizen-consumer. *The Educational Forum, 63*(2), 140–49.

Nathan, J. (1998, March). Heat and light in the charter school movement. *Phi Delta Kappan 79*(7), 499–505.

Pipho, C. (1999, February). The profit side of education. *Phi Delta Kappan, 80*(6), 421–22.

Walsh, M. (1999, May). Two reports offer bright outlook for education industry. *Education Week, 18*(36), 5.

collectively, and they specifically, must all take responsibility for the decline of our own children and the children of our fellow citizens" (Saul 2002, 12). Whether Canadian schools will succumb to the private sector's desire to become more deeply involved in education as a business initiative is an unsettled issue. For an examination of the arguments for and against for-profit schools, see the "where do you stand?" feature on pages 452–453.

What Can Teachers and Schools Learn from International Education?

The world has truly become smaller and more interconnected as telecommunications, cyberspace, and travel by jet bring diverse people and countries together. As we continue to move closer together, it is clear that education is crucial to the well-being of every country and to the world as a whole. "For teachers, on whom the quality of education ultimately depends, the challenges and opportunities the twenty-first century will bring are remarkably similar worldwide, and there is much the [we] can learn from other countries about the conditions that promote the ability of teachers and students to deal with that future" (Parkay and Oaks 1998). For example, an observation in a *Bangkok Post* editorial on the need to prepare Thai youth for a changing world echoes calls for educational improvement in Canada. "The country's policy planners [s]hould seriously review and revamp the national education system to effectively prepare our youths [for] the next century" (Sricharatchanya 1996, 15). Similarly, a community leader's comments about educating young substance abusers in Bangkok's Ban Don Muslim community could apply to youth in scores of Canadian communities: "We are in an age of cultural instability. Children are exposed to both good and bad things. [I]t's hard to resist the influences and attitudes from the outside world that are pulling at the children's feelings" (Rithdee 1996, 11). Lastly, the curriculum goals at Shiose Junior High School in Nishinomiya, Japan, are based on Japan's fifteenth Council for Education and would "fit" Canadian junior high schools as well; according to principal Akio Inoue (1996, 1), "Students will acquire the ability to survive in a changing society, that is, students will study, think and make judgments on their own initiative. It is also important that we provide a proper balance of knowledge, morality, and physical health, and that we nurture humanity and physical strength for that purpose." As a result of the universal challenges that confront educators, we are entering an era of increasing cross-national exchanges that focus on sharing resources, ideas, and expertise for the improvement of education worldwide.

Comparative Education

As the nations of the world continue to become more interdependent, educational policies and practices will be influenced increasingly by **comparative education,** the study of educational practices in other countries. Comparative education studies show how school systems in other countries work and how Canadian students compare with students in other countries on certain measures of schooling and achievement. In addition, research in comparative education enables professionals to share information about successful innovations internationally. Teachers can collaborate on global education projects and test change models that other countries have used to help match educational and societal needs and goals.

Table 12.1 and Table 12.2 contain the results of an international study by the Organization for Economic Cooperation and Development (OECD) on the reading, mathematical, and scientific literacy skills of students near the ends of their high school careers. This study, conducted in 2000, indicates wide disparities between developed and developing countries. While Canada as a whole ranks significantly above the OECD average in all three areas, within the area of literacy skills there are several provinces which are not rated as highly.

However, one must be careful when interpreting the results of cross-national studies of education achievement. David Berliner and Bruce Biddle (1995, 63) offer these cautions when interpreting such data.

- Few studies have yet focused on the unique values and strengths of each country's educational system.
- Many studies can be affected by sampling biases and inconsistent methods for gathering data.
- Many or most results of such studies are subject to differences in curricula—in opportunities to learn—in the countries studied.
- Aggregate results can be misleading because of the huge range of school quality in most countries—ranging from marvellous to terrible.

In a comparative study of Japanese education, Harry Wray (1999, 137) concludes that Japan's system of national examinations "reinforce[s] excessive conformity, passivity, standardization, anxiety, group consciousness, and controlled education." Wray goes on to say that "Excessive emphasis on passing entrance examinations plays a contributing role in killing most students' interest in studying and scholarship after entering a university, especially for those outside the science, engineering, and medical areas. Students exhausted by the dehumanizing methodology lose motivation and curiosity" (Wray 1999, 138). Additionally, provincial examinations have been criticized because they encourage students to take a narrow view of learning, and tend to emphasize lower-order thinking skills that can be assessed easily by pencil-and-paper measures. As one Japanese university student confided to Wray: "In elementary school we had many occasions to give our opinions; however, after we entered junior high school, we did not get such opportunities because all the studies are for high school entrance examinations, and all the studies in high school are for university entrance examinations. One who is considered 'intelligent' is one who can get good grades, not those who have their own opinions" (Wray 1999, 137).

Lessons from Other Countries

The previous comments about Japanese education aside, Canadian educators can learn a great deal from their colleagues around the world regarding what works and what doesn't work in other countries. When considering the possibility of adopting practices from other countries, however, it is important to remember that educational practices reflect the surrounding culture. When one country tries to adopt a method used elsewhere, a lack of support from the larger society may doom the new practice to failure. In addition, it is important to realize that the successes of another country's educational system may require sacrifices that are unacceptable to our way of life. Nevertheless, there are many practices in other countries that Canadian educators and policymakers might consider.

Table 12.1

Reading, mathematical, and scientific literacy

Mathematical Literacy

Countries	Main performance on the mathematical literacy scale		Range of possible rank order positions	
	Mean	S.E	Upper	Lower
Countries statistically significantly above the OECD average				
Japan	557	(5.5)	1	3
Korea	547	(2.8)	2	3
New Zealand	537	(3.1)	4	8
Finland	536	(2.1)	4	7
Australia	533	(3.5)	4	9
Canada	533	(1.4)	5	8
Switzerland	529	(4.4)	4	10
United Kingdom	529	(2.5)	6	10
Belgium	520	(3.9)	9	15
France	517	(2.7)	10	15
Austria	515	(2.5)	10	16
Denmark	514	(2.4)	10	16
Iceland	514	(2.3)	11	16
Liechtenstein[2]	514	(7.0)	9	18
Sweden	510	(2.5)	13	17
Countries not statistically different from the OECD average				
Ireland	503	(2.7)	16	19
Norway	499	(2.8)	17	20
Czech Republic	498	(2.8)	17	20
United States	493	(7.6)	16	23
Countries statistically significantly below the OECD average				
Germany	490	(2.5)	20	22
Hungary	488	(4.0)	20	23
Russian Fed.[2]	478	(5.5)	21	25
Spain	476	(3.1)	23	25
Poland	470	(5.5)	23	26
Latvia[2]	463	(4.5)	25	28
Italy	457	(2.9)	26	28
Portugal	454	(4.1)	26	29
Greece	447	(5.6)	27	30
Luxembourg	446	(2.0)	29	30
Mexico	387	(3.4)	31	31
Brazil[2]	334	(3.7)	32	32
Netherlands[1]	—	—	1	4

Scientific Literacy

Countries	Main performance on the scientific literacy scale		Range of possible rank order positions	
	Mean	S.E	Upper	Lower
Countries statistically significantly above the OECD average				
Korea	552	(2.7)	1	2
Japan	550	(5.5)	1	2
Finland	538	(2.5)	3	4
United Kingdom	532	(2.7)	3	7
Canada	529	(1.6)	4	8
New Zealand	528	(2.4)	4	8
Australia	528	(3.5)	4	8
Austria	519	(2.5)	8	10
Ireland	513	(3.2)	8	12
Sweden	512	(2.5)	9	13
Czech Republic	511	(2.4)	10	13
Countries not statistically different from the OECD average				
France	500	(3.2)	13	18
Norway	500	(2.7)	13	18
United States	499	(7.3)	11	21
Hungary	496	(4.2)	13	21
Iceland	496	(2.2)	14	20
Belgium	496	(4.3)	13	21
Switzerland	496	(4.4)	13	21
Countries statistically significantly below the OECD average				
Spain	491	(3.0)	16	22
Germany	487	(2.4)	19	23
Poland	483	(5.1)	19	25
Denmark	481	(2.8)	21	25
Italy	478	(3.1)	22	25
Liechtenstein[2]	476	(7.1)	20	26
Greece	461	(4.9)	25	29
Russian Fed.[2]	460	(4.7)	26	29
Latvia[2]	460	(5.6)	25	29
Portugal	459	(4.0)	26	29
Luxembourg	443	(2.3)	30	30
Mexico	422	(3.2)	31	31
Brazil[2]	375	(3.3)	32	32
Netherlands[1]	—	—	3	14

Reading Literacy

Countries	Main performance on the combined reading literacy scale		Range of possible rank order positions	
	Mean	S.E	Upper	Lower
Countries statistically significantly above the OECD average				
Finland	546	(2.6)	1	1
Canada	534	(1.6)	2	4
New Zealand	529	(2.8)	2	8
Australia	528	(3.5)	2	9
Ireland	527	(3.2)	3	9
Korea	525	(2.4)	4	9
United Kingdom	523	(2.6)	5	9
Japan	522	(5.2)	3	10
Sweden	516	(2.2)	9	11
Austria	507	(2.4)	11	16
Belgium	507	(3.6)	11	16
Iceland	507	(1.5)	11	15
Countries not statistically different from the OECD average				
Norway	505	(2.8)	11	16
France	505	(2.7)	11	16
United States	504	(7.0)	10	20
Denmark	497	(2.4)	16	19
Switzerland	494	(4.2)	16	21
Countries statistically significantly below the OECD average				
Spain	493	(2.7)	17	21
Czech Republic	492	(2.4)	17	21
Italy	487	(2.9)	19	24
Germany	484	(2.5)	21	25
Liechtenstein[2]	483	(4.1)	20	26
Hungary	480	(4.0)	21	26
Poland	479	(4.5)	21	27
Greece	474	(5.0)	23	28
Portugal	470	(4.5)	24	28
Russian Fed.[2]	462	(4.2)	27	29
Latvia[2]	458	(5.3)	27	29
Luxembourg	441	(1.6)	30	30
Mexico	422	(3.3)	31	31
Brazil[2]	396	(3.1)	32	32
Netherlands[1]	—	—	2	14

[1] Response rate is too low to ensure comparability (see Annex A3).
[2] Non-OECD country

Source: Reproduced with permission from the Organization for Economic Co-operation and Development.

Table 12.2

Reading literacy scores by province

Alberta	550
British Columbia	538
Ontario	533
Quebec	536
Manitoba	529
Saskatchewan	528
Nova Scotia	521
Prince Edward Island	517
Newfoundland	517
New Brunswick	501

Source: Organization for Economic Cooperation and Development (OECD), 2001.

Support for Teachers and Teaching

In many other countries, teachers and the profession of teaching receive a level of societal support that surpasses that experienced by teachers in Canada. For example, teachers in many countries are accorded greater respect than their Canadian counterparts; and, as Figure 12.4 shows, the salary range (as a ratio of per-capita Gross Domestic Product) for teachers in Japan, the UK, Italy, Germany, and the United States. While Canada was not included in this study, it is likely that the results for our country would roughly approximate those of the United States (Science and Engineering, March, 2003).

In addition, most Canadian teachers have about one hour or less per day for planning, and Canadian high school teachers teach about 30 classes a week, compared with 20 by teachers in Germany and fewer than 20 by Japanese teachers. While teachers from these latter two countries have over 15 h per week to work collaboratively on school-based endeavours, little such time is available to Canadian teachers. Among Western countries the number of contracted hours is quite variable. In Switzerland, the total number of in-class hours worked by elementary teachers during the school year is 1085; in Canada and United States, the contact hours are in the 950 range; while in Norway and Sweden, the average is approximately 650 h (OECD 1994, 60).

Other countries also invest their resources in hiring more teachers, who make up a statistically higher proportion of total staff than is the case in Canada. While exact

Figure 12.4

Ratio of teacher salaries (starting and maximum) per-capita GDP, by education level and career point

Source: Organization for Economic Co-operation and Development, Center for Educational Research and Innovation, International Indicators, 2001.

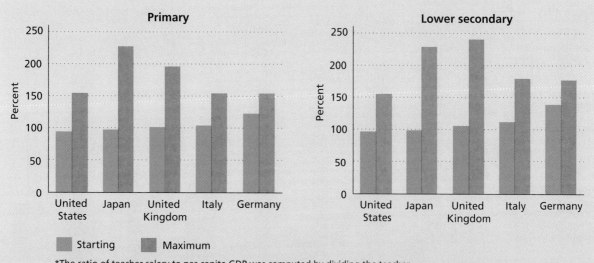

*The ratio of teacher salary to per-capita GDP was computed by dividing the teacher salary figure by the GDP per capita and multiplying by 100. A value of 100 indicates that teachers are paid the same as the GDP per capita.

data for the Canadian context are not available, in the United States (see Figure 12.5), where teaching loads are comparable, a 1996 study noted that "too many people and resources are allocated to activities outside of classrooms, sitting on the sidelines rather than the front lines of teaching and learning." Many countries also invest more resources in beginning-teacher support programs. They provide novice teachers with experiences that are, as the following practices indicate, more positive than those of their Canadian counterparts.

1. New teachers are viewed as professionals on a continuum, with increasing levels of experience and responsibility; novice teachers are not expected to do the same job as experienced teachers without significant support.
2. New teachers are nurtured and not left to flounder on their own; interaction with other teachers is maximized.
3. Teacher induction is a purposive and valued activity.
4. Schools possess a culture of shared responsibility and support, in which all or most of the school's staff contributes to the development and nurturing of the new teacher.
5. Assessment of new teachers is downplayed.

Parental Involvement

The powerful influence of parental involvement on students' achievement is well documented (Booth and Dunn 1996; Buzzell 1996; ERIC Clearinghouse 1993; Epstein 1992). Japan probably leads the world when it comes to parental involvement in education. Japanese mothers frequently go to great lengths to ensure that their children get the most out of the school's curriculum. The *kyoiku mama* (literally, education mother) will tutor her child, wait for hours in lines to register her child for periodic national exams, prepare healthy snacks for the child to eat while studying, forego television so her child can study in quiet, and ensure that her child arrives on time for calligraphy, piano, swimming, or martial arts lessons. Though few Canadian parents might wish to assume the role of the *kyoiku parent*, it seems clear that Canadian students would benefit from greater parental involvement.

Figure 12.5

Comparisons of educational staff by function

Source: Organization for Economic Cooperation and Development (OECD), *Education at a Glance: OECD Indicators.* Paris, OECD, 1995, table, p. 31, pp. 176–77. Taken from National Commission on Teaching and America's Future, *What Matters Most: Teaching for America's Future.* New York, National Commission on Teaching and America's Future, p. 15.

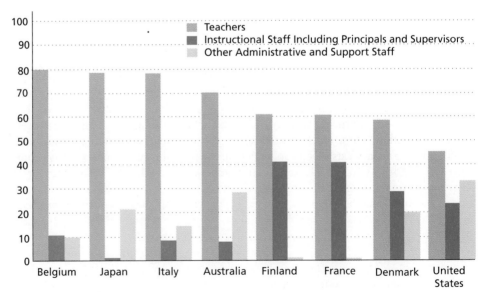

Pressure to Excel

There have been many calls to make Canadian schooling more rigourous—a longer school calendar, longer school days, more homework, and harder examinations, for example, have all been proposed. These changes, it is assumed, would increase student achievement and find favour with the majority of the public that wants greater academic rigour in the schools. More often than not, Japan, Korea, and other Asian countries are held up as models for the direction Canadian education might emulate.

But should Canadian schools be patterned after schools in these countries? Several of those who have studied and experienced Asian schools are beginning to think not. For example, Paul George (1995), who studied the Japanese public school his son attended for two years, reports in *The Japanese Secondary School: A Closer Look* that large numbers of students, deprived of sleep from having attended *jukus* (cram schools) to do well on college entrance exams, waste time in school, having been told by their *juku* instructors not to pay attention to their teachers. Additionally, a teacher of English in rural Japan reports that 70 percent of students at her school attend *jukus* and frequently are awake past midnight (Bracy 1996). According to Gerald Bracey (1996, 128), if parents want their children to achieve at the level of Asian students, which is often only a few percentage points higher on standardized examinations, they must understand the sacrifices made by Asian students and their parents and be prepared to adhere to these guidelines:

1. [W]hen their children come home from public school, they should feed them and then ship them off to a private school or tutor until 10 PM; most youngsters, both elementary and secondary, will need to go to school all day on Sunday, too.
2. [They should] spend 20 to 30 percent of their income on [a]fter-school schools.
3. [W]hen their children turn four, they should take them on their knees and tell them, "You are big boys and girls now, so you need to start practicing for college entrance examinations" (Bracey 1996, 128).

In addition, Canadian students would need to realize that "if they sleep four hours a night, they will get into college, but if they sleep five hours a night, they won't; they must study instead" (Bracey 1996, 128).

What Is Our Vision for the Future of Education?

Imagine that it is the year 2020, and we are visiting Westside Elementary school, a school in a medium-sized city. All of the teachers at Westside are fully certified and have salaries which are on a par with those of other professionals with comparable education and training. About half of the 55 teachers at Westside have also earned advanced professional certification. These teachers are known as lead teachers and may earn as much as $85 000 per year. Westside has no principal; the school is run by an executive committee of five lead teachers elected by all teachers at the school. One of these lead teachers is elected to serve as committee chair for a two-year period. In addition, the school has several student interns and educational assistants who are assigned to lead teachers as part of their graduate-level teacher-preparation program. Finally, teachers are assisted by a diagnostician; hypermedia specialist; computer specialist; video specialist; social worker; school psychologist; four counsellors; special remediation teachers in reading, writing, mathematics, and oral communication; bilingual and ESL teachers; and special-needs teachers.

What vision of the school of the future does this photograph suggest? What might you add to the image to achieve a broader perspective on tomorrow's teachers and learners?

Westside Elementary operates many programs that illustrate the close ties the school has developed with parents, community agencies, and businesses. The school houses a daycare centre that provides after-school employment for several students from the nearby high school. On weekends and on Monday, Wednesday, and Friday evenings, the school is used for adult education and for various community group activities. Executives from three local businesses spend one day a month at the school visiting with classes and telling students about their work. Students from a nearby college participate in a tutoring program at Westside, and the college has several on-campus summer enrichment programs for Westside students.

Westside has a school-based health clinic that offers health care services and a counselling centre that provides individual and family counselling. In addition, from time to time Westside teachers and students participate in service-learning activities in the community. At the present time, for example, the Grade 5 classes are helping the city develop a new recycling program.

All the facilities at Westside—classrooms, library, multimedia learning centre, gymnasium, the cafeteria, and private offices for teachers—have been designed to create a teaching/learning environment free of all health and safety hazards. The cafeteria, for example, serves meals based on findings from nutrition research about the best foods and methods of cooking. The school is carpeted, and classrooms are soundproofed and well lit. Throughout, the walls are painted in soft pastels tastefully accented with potted plants, paintings, wall hangings, and large murals depicting life in different cultures.

The dress, language, and behaviours of teacher, students, and support personnel at Westside reflect a rich array of cultural backgrounds. In the cafeteria, for example, it is impossible not to hear several languages being spoken and to see at least a few students and teachers wearing non-Western clothing. From the displays of students' work on bulletin boards in hallways and in classrooms, to the international menu offered in the cafeteria, there is ample evidence that Westside is truly a multicultural school and that gender, race, and class biases have been eliminated.

Each teacher at Westside is a member of a teaching team and spends at least part of his or her teaching time working with other members of the team. Furthermore, teachers determine their schedules, and every effort is made to assign teachers according to their particular teaching expertise. Students attend Westside by choice for its excellent teachers; its curricular emphasis on problem solving, human relations, creative thinking, and critical thinking; and its programs for helping at-risk students achieve academic success.

Instruction at Westside is supplemented by the latest technologies. The school subscribes to several computer databases and cable television services, which teachers and students use regularly. The hypermedia learning centre has an extensive collection of CD-ROMs and computer software, much of it written by Westside teachers. The centre also has virtual-reality interactive videodisc systems, workstations equipped with the latest robotics, and an extensive lab with voice-activated computers. The computer-supported interactive multimedia in the centre use the CD-ROM format and the more advanced Integrated Services Digital Network (ISDN) delivery system based on the optical fiber.

Every classroom has a video camera, fax machine, hypermedia system, and telephone that, in addition to everyday use, are used frequently during satellite video teleconferences with business executives, artists, scientists, scholars, and students at schools in other states and countries. Westside Elementary's technological capabilities permit students to move their education beyond the classroom walls, as they determine much of how, when, where, and what they learn.

Tomorrow's Teacher

Teaching and the conditions under which teachers work may change in some fundamental and positive ways during the next two decades. Teaching will become increasingly professionalized, for example, through such changes as more lengthy and rigorous preservice training programs, salary increases that put teaching on a par with other professions requiring similar education, and greater teacher autonomy and an expanded role for teachers in educational policy making. There will be more male teachers who are African-Canadians, Arabic and Asian, or members of other ethnic and racial groups. There will be greater recognition for high-performing teachers and schools through such mechanisms as merit pay plans, master teacher programs, and career ladders. Tomorrow's teachers will achieve new and higher levels of specialization. The traditional teaching job will be divided into parts. Some of the new jobs may be the following:

- Learning diagnostician
- Researcher for software programs
- Courseware writer
- Curriculum designer
- Mental health diagnostician
- Evaluator of learning performances
- Evaluator of social skills
- Small-group learning facilitator
- Large-group learning facilitator
- Media-instruction producer
- Home-based instruction designer
- Home-based instruction monitor

Though we cannot claim to have handed you an educational crystal ball so that you can ready yourself for the future, we hope you have gained both knowledge and inspiration from our observations in this chapter. Certainly, visions of the future, such as the one of Westside Elementary, will not become a reality without a lot of dedication and hard work. The creation of schools like Westside will require commitment and vision on the part of professional teachers like you.

Professional Reflection — What does the future hold for your province or territory?

Predict the future of education in your province or territory in terms of the following list of innovations and trends. Rate each development according to whether it already exists in your state or when you think it will become common practice in the schools—within the next five or the next 15 years. If you don't know the status of a particular development in your province, find out. Add at least one new item representing a trend in your province that does not appear on the list. When you have finished rating the items, share your results with your classmates. What reasons or evidence will you give for your predictions?

Innovation//Trend	Now	Within 5 years	Within 15 years	Not likely
1. Alternative/authentic assessment of students' learning	____	____	____	____
2. Cross-age tutoring/mentoring	____	____	____	____
3. Peer counselling/peer coaching	____	____	____	____
4. Faculty teams/team teaching	____	____	____	____
5. Business–school partnerships	____	____	____	____
6. Community–school teaming	____	____	____	____
7. School-based clinics/counselling centres	____	____	____	____
8. Organized after-school programs	____	____	____	____
9. Year-round schools	____	____	____	____
10. School development	____	____	____	____
11. Equity in school funding	____	____	____	____
12. Open enrollment/school choice	____	____	____	____
13. Telephones in the classroom	____	____	____	____
14. Student computer networking	____	____	____	____
15. Video teleconferencing	____	____	____	____
16. Interactive multimedia/hypermedia	____	____	____	____
17. Multimedia distance learning	____	____	____	____
18. Sex education	____	____	____	____
19. AIDS education	____	____	____	____
20. Character education curricula	____	____	____	____
21. Globalism/multiculturalism	____	____	____	____

(continued) Innovation//Trend	Now	Within 5 years	Within 15 years	Not likely
22. Aesthetics orientation	____	____	____	____
23. Alcohol and drug intervention	____	____	____	____
24. Reduction of gender bias	____	____	____	____
25. Reduction of racial/ethnic prejudice	____	____	____	____
26. Inclusion of students who have special needs	____	____	____	____
27. Teacher empowerment	____	____	____	____
28. Constructivist teaching approaches	____	____	____	____
29. Charter schools	____	____	____	____
30. Corporate-education partnerships	____	____	____	____
31. For-profit schools	____	____	____	____
32. _____	____	____	____	____
33. _____	____	____	____	____

SUMMARY

What Knowledge and Skills Will Prepare Students for a Global Information Age?

- Conflicting theories, expectations, and values make it difficult to answer what students need to know and be able to do in the future; however, increasing cultural diversity and global economic interdependence call for communication and cooperation skills and wise use of environmental resources.

- To meet the challenges of the future, students will need knowledge, skills, attitudes, and values in nine key areas: literacy in language, mathematics, and science; new technological skills; problem solving, critical thinking, and creativity; social awareness, communication skills, and team building; global awareness and conservation skills; health and wellness education; moral and ethical orientation; aesthetics awareness; and lifelong, self-directed learning.

How Can Schools and Teachers Provide an Outstanding Education for All Learners?

- To reach all learners, teachers must understand how some families are under acute stress, how crime and violence impact students' lives, and how to develop multicultural curricula and instructional repertoires that develop the potentialities of students from varied backgrounds.

- In addition to preparing multicultural instructional materials and strategies for students from diverse cultural, ethnic, and linguistic backgrounds, teachers treat students equitably when they treat high- and low-achieving students the same. Research has identified several teacher behaviours that reflect inequitable treatment of low-achieving students: waiting less time for them to answer questions, interacting with them less frequently, giving them less feedback, calling on them less often, seating them farther away, failing to accept and use their ideas, smiling at them less often, making less eye contact, praising them less, demanding less, grading their tests differently, and rewarding inappropriate behaviours.

- Effective teachers establish positive relationships with all students by listening to them, giving frequent feedback and opportunities to ask questions, and demanding higher-level performance by asking higher-order questions that require more critical thinking.

- To reach all learners, teachers should provide them with active, authentic learning experiences.

How Can Community-Based Partnerships Address Social Problems That Hinder Students' Learning?

- Communities help schools address social problems that hinder students' learning by providing various kinds of support.

- Civic organizations raise money for schools, sponsor teams, recognize student achievement, award scholarships, sponsor volunteer mentor programs, and provide other resources and services to enrich students' learning.

- Corporate–education partnerships provide schools with resources, release time for employees to visit schools, scholarships, job initiatives for disadvantaged youth, in-service programs for teachers, and management training for school administrators.

- Schools serve as resources for their communities by providing educational and recreational programs before and after the school day, and by providing health and social services.

How Will the Fledgling Charter School Movement Affect Equity and Excellence in Education?

- Charter schools and U.S. for-profit schools, both part of the privatization movement, were developed in response to perceived inadequacies of the public schools.

- Charter schools are independent, innovative, outcome-based public schools started by a group of teachers, parents, or others who obtain a charter from a local school district, a province, or the federal government.

What Can Teachers and Schools Learn from International Education?

- The challenges and opportunities for teachers in the twenty-first century are remarkably similar worldwide, and teachers in different countries can learn much from one another. Comparative education, the study of educational practices in other countries, enables educators to collaborate internationally.

- A study conducted by the Organization for Economic Cooperation and Development (OECD) indicates that Canadian schools are among the best in the world.

- Education in many other countries is centralized and teachers follow a national curriculum. In Canada each province and territory is responsible for the education of its children.

- Many other countries tend to provide greater support for teachers and teaching and have greater parental involvement, two practices that would benefit Canadian education. However, pressure for students in other countries to excel is often extreme.

- Many other countries provide greater support for teachers and the teaching profession, have greater parental involvement, and take more steps to nurture beginning teachers.

What Is Our Vision for the Future of Education?

- It is not unrealistic to imagine that teachers in schools during the year 2020 will be well-paid, self-governing professionals who have developed specialized areas of expertise. This vision becomes more possible with each teacher who makes a commitment to its realization.

KEY TERMS AND CONCEPTS

charter schools, 449
comparative education, 454
for-profit schools, 450

higher-order questions, 444
learning, 444
lower-order questions, 444

privatization
movement, 450
synectics, 439

APPLICATIONS AND ACTIVITIES

Teacher's Journal

1. Write a scenario forecasting how the teaching profession will change during the next two decades.

2. Select one of the following areas and develop several forecasts for changes that will occur during the next two decades: energy, environment, food, the economy, governance, family structure, demographics, global relations, media, and technology. On what current data are your forecasts based? How might these changes affect teaching and learning?

3. Think about two children you know and project them into the future, twenty years from now. What skills are they likely to need? Which talents should help them? How can schools better promote the development of these skills and talents?

1. Begin at the web home pages for the Organization for Economic Cooperation and Development (OECD) and the Canadian Teachers' Federation (CTF) and gather information on educational systems in other countries. In what areas of the curriculum and at what levels is the achievement of Canadian students at or above the international average? What conclusions about the strengths and weaknesses of Canadian schools can you draw from your analysis of these data?

2. Explore the field of international education or comparative education and talk to teaching professionals in other countries online. For example, you might ask them what they see as the greatest challenge facing educators in their respective countries. Or, you might ask them about working conditions for teachers—that is, number of students taught, time for planning, professional responsibilities beyond the classroom, and so on.

Observations and Interviews

1. Interview the principal at a local or nearby school and ask him or her to describe what the school will be like in ten years. Now interview several teachers at the school. Compare the forecasts of the principal with those of the teachers. What might account for any differences you find?

2. Search for examples of school–community partnership arrangements in the local school district. Find out if these partnerships are progressing and propose a specific new one based on your knowledge of the community.

Professional Portfolio

1. Prepare a portfolio entry of instructional resources—curriculum guides, teaching tips, assessment strategies, relevant professional associations, books and articles, software, and online resources—related to one of the nine areas of learning students will need to meet the challenges of the future (i.e., literacy in language, mathematics, and science; new technological skills; problem solving, critical thinking, and creativity; social awareness, communication skills, and team building; global awareness and conservation skills; health and wellness education; moral and ethical orientation; aesthetics awareness; and lifelong, self-directed learning). For each entry include a brief annotation describing the materials, how you will use them, and where they may be obtained. After you have prepared this portfolio entry, meet with your classmates and exchange information.

References

Abrahamsson, B. (1971). *Military professionalization and political power.* Stockholm: Allmanna Forlagret.

Acheson, A. A., and Gall, M. D. (1997). *Techniques in the clinical supervision of teachers: Preservice and inservice applications,* 4th ed. New York: Longman.

Adler, M. (1982). *The paideia proposal: An educational manifesto.* New York: Macmillan.

Adler, M. (1984). *The paideia program: An educational syllabus.* New York: Macmillan.

Alan Guttmacher Institute. (1999). *Teenage pregnancy: Overall trends and state-by-state information.* New York: Alan Guttmacher Institute.

*Alberta Teachers Association. (2001, April 3). Teachers and parents need to fight standardized testing. *The Learning Team, Volume 3.* Retrieved November 1, 2003 from www.teachers.ab.ca/resources/ata.learningteam/index.cfm?p_ID=1809&Volume=4&Issue=3

*Alberta Teachers' Assocation. (2002). Safe and caring schools. Retrieved November 1, 2003 from www.teachers.ab.ca/safe/Recognition.htm

Alexander, C. J. (1998). Studying the experiences of gay and lesbian youth. *Journal of Gay and Lesbian Social Services, 8.*

*Allan, R. (2001). In my world: A citizenship initiative and a progressive account of teacher change. *Research Connections Canada (VII).* 105-115. Canadian Childcare Federation.

American Association for the Advancement of Science. (1999). *Middle grades mathematics textbooks: a benchmark-based evaluation.* New York: Oxford University Press, 1999.

American Association for the Advancement of Science. (2000). *Atlas of science literacy goals: mapping K–12 learning goals.* New York: Oxford University Press.

American Association of University Women (AAUW). (1992). *How schools shortchange girls: The AAUW report.* Researched by The Wellesley College Center for Research on Women. Washington, DC: AAUW Educational Foundation.

American Association of University Women (AAUW). (1993). *Hostile hallways: The AAUW survey on sexual harassment in America's schools.* New York: Louis Harris and Associates.

American Federation of Teachers. (1998b). *Teacher salaries in the 100 largest cities, 1996–97.* Washington, DC: American Federation of Teachers.

American Federation of Teachers. (1999a). [Online]. AFT on the issues: Vouchers and the accountability dilemma. Retrieved July 1999 from www. aft.org

Anderson, J. D. (1997). Supporting the invisible minority. *Educational Leadership, 54,* 65–68.

Anderson, R. E., and Ronnkvist, A. (1999). The presence of computers in American schools. The University of California, Irvine, and the University of Minnesota, Center for Research on Information Technology and Organizations.

Anderson, R. H., and Snyder, K. J. (Eds.), (1993). *Clinical supervision: Coaching for higher performance.* Lancaster, PA: Technomic.

Application of Bay v. State Board of Education, 233 Ore. 609, 378 P.2d 558 (1963).

Aristotle. (1941). *Politics* (Book VIII). In Richard McKoen (Ed.), *The basic works of Aristotle.* New York: Random House.

Artz, S. (1999). *Sex, power, and the violent school girl.* New York: Teachers College Press.

Ashton-Warner, S. (1963). *Teacher.* New York: Simon and Schuster.

Ballantine, J. H. (1997). *The sociology of education: A systematic analysis,* 4th ed. Upper Saddle River, NJ: Prentice Hall.

Banks, J. A. (1997). *Teaching strategies for ethnic studies,* 6th ed. Boston: Allyn and Bacon.

Banks, J. A., and Banks, C. A. (Eds.), (1997). *Multicultural education: Issues and perspectives,* 3rd ed. Boston: Allyn and Bacon.

*Barlow, M. (1995). The assault on Canadian schools. *The Canadian Administrator, 35,* 1.

Barman, J., McCaskill, D., and Hebert, Y. (1986). *Indian education in Canada volume 1: The legacy.* Vancouver: University of British Columbia Press.

Barrett, H. (2000, April). Create your own electronic portfolio (using off-the-shelf software). *Learning and Leading with Technology.*

Battles v. Anne Arundel County Board of Education, 904 F. Supp. 471 (Md. 1995), aff'd, 95 F.3d 41 (4th Cir. 1996).

Bennett, C. I. (1999). *Comprehensive multicultural education: Theory and practice,* 4th ed. Boston: Allyn and Bacon.

Besner, H. F., and Spungin, C. I. (1995). *Gay and lesbian students: Understanding their needs.* Washington, DC: Taylor and Francis.

*Best, C. *The Best guide to Canadian legal research.* Retrieved November 1, 2003 from www.legalresearch.org/

*Bezeau, L. M. (2002). *Educational administration for Canadian teachers.* Retrieved June 9, 2003 from www.unb.ca/education/bezeau/eact/eactcvp.html

Bialo, E. (1989). Computers and at-risk youth: A partial solution to a complex problem. *Classroom Computer Learning, 9*(4), 48–55.

Bitter, G. G., and Pierson, M. E. (1999). *Using technology in the classroom.* Boston: Allyn and Bacon.

Bloom, B. S. (1981). *All our children learning: A primer for parents, teachers, and other educators.* New York: McGraw-Hill.

Board of Education of Oklahoma City Public Schools v. Dowell, 498 U.S. 237, 249–50 (1991).

Boleman, L. G., and Deal, T. E. (1994). *Becoming a teacher leader: From isolation to collaboration.* Thousand Oaks, CA: Corwin Press.

Booth, A., and Dunn, J. F. (Eds.), (1996). *Family–school links: How do they affect educational outcomes?* Mahwah, NJ: Lawrence Erlbaum Associates, Publishers.

Borich, G. D. (1996). *Effective teaching methods,* 3rd ed. Englewood Cliffs, NJ: Merrill.

*Bowman, J. (2002, August 29). In depth: Education. *CBC News Online.* Retrieved October 24, 2003 from www.cbc.ca/news/features/school_boards.html

Boyer, E. (1990). Teaching in America. In M. Kysilka (Ed.), *Honor in Teaching: Reflections.* West Lafayette, ID: Kappa Delta Pi.

Boyer, E. (1995). *The basic school: A community for learning.* Princeton, NJ: The Carnegie Foundation for the Advancement of Teaching.

Boyer, E. L. (1983). *High school: A report on secondary education in America.* New York: Harper.

Bracey, G. W. (1993). "Now then, Mr. Kohlberg, about moral development in women..." In G. Hass, and F. W. Parkay (Eds.), *Curriculum planning: A new approach,* 6th ed. Boston: Allyn and Bacon, 165–66.

Bracey, G. W. (1996, October). The sixth Bracey report on the condition of public education. *Phi Delta Kappan,* 127–38.

Bracey, G. W. (1999, March). Getting along without national standards. *Phi Delta Kappan, 80*(7), 548–50.

Bradley, A. (1997, April 30). Staying in the game. *Education Week on the Web.*

Brameld, T. (1959). Imperatives for a reconstructed philosophy of education. *School and Society, 87.*

*Brien, K. (2002, January). School discipline and the law: Perspective of high school vice-principals. Paper presented for the University of Calgary Online Conference *Linking Educational Research and Practice.* Retrieved October 24, 2003 from www.ucalgary.ca/~lrussell/brien.html

*British Columbia Teachers' Federation. (2003). Code of ethics. In *Members' guide to the BCTF 2003-2004.* Retrieved October 3, 2003 from www.bctf.ca/about/MembersGuide/

*British Columbia Teachers' Federation. (1997, June). Opportunities to learn: Accountability in education in British Columbia. A brief to the Minister of Education, Skills, and Training. Retrieved November 10, 2003 from www.bctf.ca/publications/briefs/ocg/

(items with an asterisk are new to this edition)

Brown, F. B., Kohrs, D., and Lanzarro, C. (1991). The academic costs and consequences of extracurricular participation in high school. Paper presented at the Annual Meeting of Educational Research Association.

Brown v. Hot, Sexy and Safer Productions, Inc., 68 F. 3d 525 (1st Cir. 1995), cert. denied, 116 S. Ct. 1044 (1996).

Bruner, C., and Bennett, D. (1997). Technology and gender: Differences in masculine and feminine views. *NASSP Bulletin, 81,* 46–51.

Bruner, J. S. (1960). *The process of education.* New York: Random House.

Bryk, A. S., Sebring, P. B., Kerbow, D., Rollow, S., and Easton, J. Q. (1998). *Charting Chicago school reform: Democratic localism as a lever for change.* Boulder, CO: Westview Press.

Bucky, P. A. (1992). *The private Albert Einstein.* Kansas City: Andrews and McMeel.

Burnaford, G., Fischer, J., and Hobson, D. (1996). *Teachers doing research: Practical possibilities.* Mahwah, NJ: Lawrence Erlbaum Associates.

*Burstall, K. (1993, Spring). The quality teacher. *Aviso.* Nova Scotia Teachers Union.

Buzzell, J. B. (1996). *School and family partnerships: Case studies for regular and special educators.* Albany, NY: Delmar Publishers.

*Calgary Board of Education. (2001). *Character education.* Calgary, Alberta.

Calkins, L. (1991). *Listening between the lines.* Portsmouth, NH: Heinemann.

*Canada Safety Council. (2001, July). Risk management for schools. *News: (XLV),* 3. Retrieved July 21, 2003 from www.safety-council.org/news/sc/2001/sch-riskmgt.html

*Canada Safety Council. (2002). How safe are school field trips? Retrieved July 18, 2003 from www.safety-council.org/info/child/Anchor-Managin-19189#Anchor-Managin-19189

*Canadian Association for Health, Physical Education, Recreation and Dance. (1998). Quality daily physical education. Retrieved October 20, 2003 from www.cahperd.ca/e/qdpe/index.htm

*Canadian Association of Second Language Teachers. (2003). Beliefs. Retrieved November 3, 2003 from www.caslt.org/Info/mission.htm#beliefs

*Canadian Educational Policy and Administration Network. (1999). Education governance in Canada: trends and implications. Retrieved October 3, 2003 from www.cepan.ca/rrnew/sg/xcanchart.htm

*Canadian Education Research Information System (CERIS). (n.d.) Introduction to Canadian education. Retrieved June 10, 2003 from http://ceris.schoolnet.ca/e/EdCanIntro.html

*Canadian Heritage. (2000). Launch of the 1999–2000 official languages programs for students. Retrieved on November 3, 2003 from:www.cmec.ca/releases/olplaunche.stm

*Canadian Teachers' Federation. (n.d.). Salaries and fringe benefits. Retrieved January 18, 2003 from www.ctf-fce.ca/E/TIC/salaries.htm

*Canadian Teachers' Federation (n.d.) Becoming a teacher. Retrieved Novermber 3, 2003 from www.ctf-fce.ca/en/teaching/teaching.htm#d

*Canadian Teachers' Federation. (n.d.). Standardized testing: Undermining equity in education. Retrieved November 15, 2003 from www.ctf-fce.ca/en/issues/assessment/testing-policy.html

*Canadian Teachers' Federation. (2000). Assessment and evaluation. Retrieved November 15, 2003 from www.ctf-fce.ca/en/issues/assessment/testing-policy.html

*Canadian Teachers' Federation. (2001). Workplace Survey. Retrieved November, 2003 from www.ctf-fce.ca/en/press/2001/workplc.htm.

*Canadian Teachers' Federation. (2003). What is CTF? Retrieved November 1, 2003 from www.ctf-fce.ca/en/default.htm.

Cantor, L. (1989). Assertive Discipline—more than names on the board and marbles in a jar. *Phi Delta Kappan,* 71(1), 57–61.

Carmichael, L. B. (1981). *McDonogh 15: The making of a school.* New York: Avon Books.

Cawelti, G. (1999). *Portraits of six benchmark schools: Diverse approaches to improving student achievement.* Arlington, VA: Educational Research Service.

*CBC's *The National.* (2002, March 25). Program title unknown. Producer and director unknown. Toronto: Canadian Broadcasting Corporation.

Center for Research on Effective Schooling for Disadvantaged Students. (1992). Helping students who fall behind, Report No. 22. Baltimore, MD: The Johns Hopkins University.

Center for the Study and Prevention of Violence, University of Colorado at Boulder. (1998). Response to the Columbine school incident. Retrieved April 21, 1999 from www.colorado.edu/cspv

Centers for Disease Control and Prevention. (1998a). Characteristics of health education among secondary schools—school health education profiles, 1996. Atlanta, GA: Centers for Disease Control and Prevention.

Centers for Disease Control and Prevention. (1998b). *Youth risk behavior surveillance—United States, 1997.* Atlanta, GA: Centers for Disease Control and Prevention.

CEO Forum on Education and Technology. (1999). *School Technology and Readiness Report.* Washington, DC: CEO Forum on Education and Technology.

Cetron, M. (1997). Reform and tomorrow's schools. *TECHNOS,* 61, 19–22.

*Chase, B. (1997, October 15). Restoring the impulse to dream: The right to a quality public education. *Vital Speeches of the Day,* 20–23.

*Chase, B. (1999). Teachers lead the fight for innovation and investment in public education. In J. W. Noll (Ed.), *Taking sides: Clashing views on controversial issues* 10th ed. Guilford, CT: McGraw–Hill.

Chaskin, R. J., and Rauner, D. M. (1995, May). Youth and caring: An introduction. *Phi Delta Kappan.*

Cheeks, E. H., Flippo, R. F., and Lindsey, J. D. (1997). *Reading for success in elementary schools.* Madison, WI: Brown and Benchmark.

Clift, R. T., et al. (1995). *Collaborative leadership and shared decision making: Teachers, principals, and university professors.* New York: Teachers College Press.

Codell, E. R. (1999). *Educating Esmé.* Chapel Hill, NC: Algonquin Books.

Cohn, M. M., and Kottkamp, R. B. (1993). *Teachers: The missing voice in education.* Albany, NY: State University of New York Press.

Coladarci, T., and Cobb, C. D. (1996). Extracurricular participation, school size, and achievement and self-esteem among high school students: A national look. *Journal of Research in Rural Education,* 12(2), 92–103.

Comber, C., et al. (1997). The effects of age, gender and computer experience upon computer attitudes. *Educational Research,* 39, 123–33.

Combs, A. (1979). *Myths in education: Beliefs that hinder progress and their alternatives.* Boston: Allyn and Bacon.

Comer, J. P. (1997). *Waiting for a miracle: Why schools can't solve our problems—and how we can.* New York: Dutton.

Committee for Economic Development. (1994). *Putting learning first: Governing and managing schools for high achievement.* New York: Research and Policy Committee, Committee for Economic Development.

Cornbleth, C. (1990). *Curriculum in context.* London: the Falmer Press.

Cornfield v. Connsolidated High School District No 230, F.2d 1316 (7th Cir. 1993).

Costa, A. L. (1984). A reaction to Hunter's knowing, teaching, and supervising. In P. L. Hosford (Ed.), *Using what we know about teaching.* Alexandria, VA: Association for Supervision and Curriculum Development.

*Council of Ministers on Education. (1995, February). Pan-Canadian protocol for collaboration on school curriculum. Retreived November 3, 2003 from www.cmec.ca/protocol-eng.htm

Counts, G. (1932). *Dare the school build a new social order?* New York: The John Day Company.

*Covell, K., & Howe, R. B. (2000). Moral education through the 3r's: rights, respect, and responsibility. *Journal of Moral Education, 30 (1),* 31-43.

*Cunningham, W. G., and Cordeiro, P. A. (2001). *Educational leadership: A problem-based approach.* Toronto: Allyn and Bacon, 2.

Curtis v. School Committee of Falmouth, 652 N.E. 2d 580 (Mass. 1995), *cert. denied*, 116 S. Ct. 753 (1996).

Curwin, R. and Mendler, A. (1988, October) Packaged discipline programs: Let the buyer beware. *Educational Leadership*, 46(6), 68–71.

Curwin, R., and Mendler, A. (1989, March). We repeat, let the buyer beware: A response to Canter. *Educational Leadership*, 46(6), 83.

Daniels, C. B. (1984). Quality of educational materials: A marketing perspective. In F. W. Parkay, S. Obrien, and M. Hennesey, (Eds.), *Quest for quality: Improving basic skills instruction in the 1980s*. Lanham, MD: University Press of America.

Darling-Hammond, L. (1999). Educating teachers for the next century: Rethinking practice and policy. In G. A. Griffin (Ed.), *The education of teachers: Ninety–eighth yearbook of the National Society for the Study of Education*. Chicago: University of Chicago Press.

Darling-Hammond, L., Wise, A. E., and Klein, S. P. (1995). *A license to teach: Building a profession for 21st–century schools*. Boulder, CO: Westview Press.

Davis, G. A., and Rimm, S. B. (1998). *Education of the gifted and talented*, 4th ed. Boston: Allyn and Bacon.

Davis v. Meek, 344 F. Supp. 298 N.D. Ohio (1972).

Davis v. Monroe County Board of Education, Supp. 97–843. Georgia (1999).

Davitt, J. (1997, January 3). The ultimate good shepherd. *Times Educational Supplement*.

Deal, T. E., and Peterson, K. D. (1999). *Shaping school culture: The heart of leadership*. San Francisco: Jossey–Bass Publishers.

Dean v. Board of Education, 523 A. 2d 1059 (Md. App. 1987).

Department of Health and Human Services. (1999). *Profile of homelessness in America*. Washington, DC: Department of Health and Human Services.

*Department of Justice Canada. (1982). *Canadian charter of rights and freedoms*. Retrieved October 3, 2003 from http://laws.justice.gc.ca/en/Charter/. Enacted as Schedule B to the Canada Act 1982 (U.K.) c. 11, which came into force on April 17, 1982.

Dewey, J. (1900). *The school and society*. Chicago: University of Chicago Press.

Dewey, J. (1902). *The child and the curriculum*. Chicago: University of Chicago Press.

Dewey, J. (1916). *Democracy and education: An introduction to the philosophy of education*. New York: Macmillan.

Dobbs, S. M. (1998). *Learning in and through arts: A guide to discipline-based art education*. Los Angeles: Getty Education Institute for the Arts.

Dollase, R. H. (1992). *Voices of beginning teachers: Visions and realities*. New York: Teachers College Press.

Dolmage, R. (1996). *So you want to be a teacher*. Toronto: Harcourt Brace and Company, Canada, 79.

Doyle, W. (1986). Classroom organization and management. In M. Wittrock (Ed.), *Handbook of research on teaching*, 3rd ed. New York: Macmillan.

Duffy, G., and Roehler, L. (1989). The tension between information-giving and mediation: Perspectives on instructional explanation and teacher change. In J. Brophy (Ed.), *Advances in research on teaching*, Vol. 1. Greenwich, CT: JAI Press.

Duke, D. L. (1984). *Teaching—the imperiled profession*. Albany, NY: State University of New York Press.

Durlak, J. A. (1995). *School-based prevention programs for children and adolescents*. Thousand Oaks, CA: Sage Publications.

Dykgraaf, C. L., and Kane, S. (1998, October). For-profit charter schools: What the public needs to know. *Educational Leadership*, 56(2), 51–53.

*Earl, L. M. (1999). Assessment and accountability in education: improvement or surveillance? *Education Canada* 39(3), 4-6.

Economist. (1999a, January 16). A contract on schools: Why handing education over to companies can make sense.

Economist. (1999b, January 16). Reading, writing, and enrichment: Private money is pouring into American education—and transforming it.

*education@canada. (n.d.) International gateway to education in Canada. Retrieved June 10, 2003 from www.educationcanada.cmec.ca/EN/EdSys/over.php

Education law reporter: Elementary and secondary schools. (1994). Untitled article in *Volume (6)*, 49.

Education Week. (1996b, April 24). Virginia governor victorious in rejecting Goals 2000.

Education Week. (1997). Staying in the game.

Education Week. (1998, September 9). New teachers are hot commodity.

Education Week. (1999a, March 31). N.M. governor digs in his heels on vouchers.

Education Week. (1999b, April 14). States increasingly flexing their policy muscle.

Education Week. (1999d, May 26). Clinton ESEA plan targets accountability.

Education Week. (1999e, June 2). Substituting the privilege of choice for the right to equality.

Education Week on the Web. (1999, July 29). Issue paper: Privatization of public education.

Edwards, A. T. (1997). Let's stop ignoring our gay and lesbian youth. *Educational Leadership*, 54.

Edwards, P., and Young, L. (1992). Beyond parents: family, community, and school involvement. *Phi Delta Kappan*, 74(1), 72, 74, 76, 78, 80.

Edwards v. Aguillard, 482 U.S. 578(1987).

Eisner, E. (1994). *The educational imagination: On the design and evaluation of school programs*, 3rd ed. New York: Macmillan.

Eisner, E. W. (1998). *The kind of schools we need: Personal essays*. Portsmouth, NH: Heinemann.

Elam, S. M., Rose, L. C., and Gallup, A. (1994, September). The 26th annual Phi Delta Kappan/Gallup Poll of the public's attitudes toward the public schools. *Phi Delta Kappan*, 41–56.

Emerson, R., Fretz, R., and Shaw, L. (1995). Writing ethnographic field notes. Chicago: University of Chicago Press.

Epstein, J. (1995, May). School/family/community partnerships: Caring for the children we share. *Phi Delta Kappan*, 76(9), 701–12.

Epstein, J. L. (1992). School and family partnerships. In M. C. Alkin (Ed.), *Encyclopedia of educational research*, 6th ed. New York: Macmillan.

ERIC Clearinghouse. (1993). *Value search: Parent involvement in the educational process*. Eugene, OR: ERIC Clearinghouse on Educational Management.

Erikson, E. H. (1963). *Childhood and society*. New York: W. W. Norton.

Erikson, E. H. (1997). *The life cycle completed: Extended version with new chapters on the ninth stage of development by Joan M. Erikson*. New York: W.W. Norton and Company.

*Erskine-Cullen, E., and Sinclair, A. M. (March 1996). Preparing teachers for urban schools: A view from the field. *Canadian Journal of Educational Administration and Policy, Issue Six*. Retrieved November 1, 2003 from www.umanitoba.ca/publications/cjeap/issue1/issue6.htm

Essex, N. L. (1999). *School law and the public schools: A practical guide for educational leaders*. Boston: Allyn and Bacon.

Etzioni, A. (1969). *The semi-professions and their organization: Teachers, nurses, social workers*. New York: Free Press.

Etzioni, A. (1999, June 9). The truths we must face to curb youth violence. *Education Week on the Web*.

Evertson, C. M., Emmer, E. T., Clements, R. S., and Worsham, M. E. (1997). *Classroom management for elementary teachers*, 4th ed. Boston: Allyn and Bacon.

Fashola, O. (1999). *Review of extended-day and after-school programs and their effectiveness*. Johns Hopkins University: Center for Research on the Education of Students Placed at Risk.

Feldhusen, J. F. (1997). Educating teachers for work with talented youth. In N. Colangelo and G. A. Davis (Eds.), *Handbook of gifted education*. Boston: Allyn and Bacon.

Felsenthal, H. (1982, March). Factors influencing school effectiveness: An ecological analysis of an "effective" school. Paper presented at the Annual Meeting of the American Educational Research Association, New York.

*Fleming, T. (1997, November). Provincial initiatives to restructure Canadian school governance in the 1990s. *Canadian Journal of Education Administration and*

Policy (11). Retrieved May 26, 2003 from www.umanitoba.ca/publications/cjeap/articles/thomasfleming.html

Franz, K. R. (1996, Autumn). Toward a critical social consciousness in children: multicultural peace education in a first grade classroom. *Theory into Practice, 35*(4), 264–70.

Freedman, S., Jackson, J., and Botes, K. (1983). Teaching: An imperiled profession. In L. Shulman, and G. Sykes, (Eds.), (1983). *Handbook of teaching and policy.* New York: Longman.

Freeman, M. (1993). Whither children: Protection, participation and autonomy? *Manitoba Law Journal (22)*, 307.

Friend, M., and Bursuck, W. D. (1999). Including students with special needs: A practical guide for classroom teachers, 2nd ed. Boston: Allyn and Bacon.

*Froese-Germain, B. (1991). Standardized testing: Undermining equity in education. Ottawa: Canadian Teachers' Federation. Retrieved October 24, 2003 from www.nlta.nf.ca/HTML_Files/html_pages/publications/bulletins/feb2000/fb00resouc.html

Fuligni, A. J., and Stevenson, H. W. (1995). Home environment and school learning. In Lorin W. Anderson (Ed.), *International encyclopedia of teaching and teacher education,* 2nd ed. Oxford: Pergamon, 378–82.

Fullan, M., and Hargreaves, A. (1996). *What's worth fighting for in your school?* New York: Teachers College Press.

Fuller, B., Burr, E., Huerta, L., Puryear, S., and Wexler, E. (1999). *School choice: Abundant hopes, scarce evidence on results.* University of California–Berkeley and Stanford University: Policy Analysis for California Education.

Gagné, R. M. (1974). *Essentials of learning for instruction.* Hinsdale, IL: Dryden.

Gagné, R. M. (1977). *The conditions of learning,* 3rd ed. New York: Holt, Rinehart and Winston.

Gallup, G. H. (1975, September). The 7th annual Gallup poll of the public's attitudes toward the public schools. *Phi Delta Kappan,* 227–41.

Gandara, P., and Fish, J. (Spring 1994). Year-round schooling as an avenue to major structural reform. *Educational Evaluation and Policy Analysis, 16.*

Garbarino, J. (1999). *Lost boys: Why our sons turn violent and how we can save them.* New York: Free Press.

Gardner, H. (1983). *Frames of mind.* New York: Basic Books.

Gardner, H. (1995, November). Reflections on multiple intelligences: Myths and messages. *Phi Delta Kappan,* 200–03, 206–09.

Gardner, H. (1999). *The disciplined mind: What all students should understand.* New York: Simon and Schuster.

Gaskell, J. (1995). *Secondary schools in Canada: The national report of the exemplary schools project.* Toronto: Canadian Education Association.

Gates, B., Myhrvold, N., and Rinearson, P. M. (1996). *The road ahead.* New York: Penguin.

George, P. (1995). *The Japanese secondary school: A closer look.* Columbus, OH: National Middle School Association; and Reston, VA: National Association of Secondary School Principals.

Gerber, S. B. (1996). Extracurricular activities and academic achievement. *Journal of Research and Development in Education, 30*(1), 42–50.

Gerstner, L. V., Semerad, R. D., Doyle, D. P., and Johnston, W. B. (1994). *Reinventing education: Entrepreneurship in America's public schools.* New York: Dutton.

Giroux, H. A. (1999, Winter). Schools for sale: Public education, corporate culture, and the citizen-consumer. *The Educational Forum, 63*(2), 140–49.

Glasser, W. R. (1997, April). A new look at school failure and school success. *Phi Delta Kappan,* 596–602.

Glasser, W. R. (1998a). *Quality school,* 3rd ed. New York: Harper Perennial.

Glasser, W. R. (1998b). *The quality school teacher: Specific suggestions for teachers who are trying to implement the lead-management ideas of the quality school.* New York: Harper Perennial.

Glasser, W. R. (1998c). *Choice theory: A new psychology of personal freedom.* New York: HarperCollins.

Glasser, W. R., and Dotson, K. L. (1998). *Choice theory in the classroom.* New York: Harper Perennial.

Glickman, C. D. (1993). *Renewing America's schools: A guide for school-based action.* San Francisco: Jossey-Bass.

Glickman, C. D. (1998). *Revolutionizing America's schools.* San Francisco: Jossey-Bass.

Glickman, C., Gordon, S. P., and Ross-Gordon, J. M. (1998). *Supervision of instruction: A developmental approach,* 4th ed. Boston: Allyn and Bacon.

Gmelch, W. H., and Parkay, F. W. (1995). Changing roles and occupational stress in the teaching profession. In M. J. O'Hair, and S. J. Odell (Eds.), *Educating teachers for leadership and change: Teacher education yearbook III.* Thousand Oaks, CA: Corwin Press, 46–65.

Godar, J. (1990). *Teachers talk.* Macomb, IL: Glenbridge Publishing.

Goldberg, D. (1998). Does technology make the grade? *Family Circle PC World.*

Goldhammer, R., Anderson, R. H., and Krajewski, R. J. (1993). *Clinical supervision: Special methods for the supervision of teachers,* 3rd ed. Fort Worth, TX: Harcourt Brace Jovanovich.

Goleman, D. (1997). *Emotional intelligence.* New York: Bantam Books.

Goleman, D. (1998). *Working with emotional intelligence.* New York: Bantam Books.

Good, T. E., and Brophy, J. E. (1997). *Looking in classrooms,* 7th ed. New York: Longman.

Good, T. E., and Brophy, J. E. (2000). *Looking in classrooms,* 8th ed. Boston: Pearson Publishing.

Good, T. E., and Grouws, D. (1979). The Missouri mathematics effectiveness project: An experimental study in fourth-grade classrooms. *Journal of Educational Psychology, 71,* 355–62.

Goodlad, J. I. (1983a, April). What some schools and classrooms teach. *Educational Leadership,* 8–19.

Goodlad, J. (1983b, Spring). Teaching: An endangered profession. *Teachers College Record,* 575–78.

Goodlad, J. (1990). *Teachers for our nation's schools.* San Francisco: Jossey-Bass.

Gordon, W. J. J. (1968). *Making it strange,* Books 1 and 2. Evanston, IL: Harper and Row.

Gordon, W. J. J. (1971a). *Invent-o-rama.* Cambridge, MA: Porpoise Books.

Gordon, W. J. J. (1971b). *What color is sleep?* Cambridge, MA: Porpoise Books.

Gordon, W. J. J. (1975). *Strange and familiar,* Book 1. Cambridge, MA: Porpoise Books.

Goss v. Lopez, 419 U.S. 565 (1975).

*Government of Canada. (2001). Prime Minister's awards for teaching excellence: Exemplary practices. http://pma-ppm.ic.gc.ca/bio01-e.asp?prov=al

Grant, C. A. (1978). Education that is multicultural: Isn't that what we mean? *Journal of Teacher Education, 29*(5), 45–58.

Grant, C. A. (1994, Winter). Challenging the myths about multicultural education. *Multicultural Education,* 4–9.

Grant, P. G., Richard, K. J., and Parkay, F. W. (1996, April). *Using video cases to promote reflection among preservice teachers: A qualitative inquiry.* Paper presented at the Annual Meeting of the American Educational Research Association, New York.

Greene, B. (1999, July 7). A 21st century idea for schools: Log off and learn. *Chicago Tribune,* Sec. 2, p. 1.

Greene, M. (1995). What counts as philosophy of education? In Wendy Kohli (Ed.), *Critical conversations in philosophy of education.* New York: Routledge.

Griego-Jones, T. (1996). Reconstructing bilingual education from a multicultural perspective. In C. A. Grant, and M. L. Gomez (Eds.), *Making schooling multicultural: Campus and classroom.* Englewood Cliffs, NJ: Merrill.

Griffin, G. A. (1999). Changes in teacher education: Looking to the future. In G. A. Griffin (Ed.), *The education of teachers: Ninety–eighth yearbook of the National Society for the Study of Education* (pp. 1–28). Chicago: University of Chicago Press.

Grossman, D., and Siddle, P. (1999). Combat. In L. Kurtz (Ed.), *The encyclopedia of violence, peace, and conflict.* San Diego: Academic Press.

Gutloff, K. (1999, October). Anger in the halls. *NEA Today,* 8–9.

Haberman, M. (1996). Selecting and preparing urban teachers. In J. Sikula (Ed.), *The second handbook of research on teacher education* (pp. 747–60). New York: Macmillan.

Hadderman, M. (1998). Charter schools. *ERIC Digest, 118.*

Hallahan, D. P., and Kauffman, J. M. (2000). *Exceptional children: Introduction to special education,* 8th ed. Boston: Allyn and Bacon.

Hammett, R. F. (1997). Computers in schools: White boys only? *English Quarterly 28,* 1.

Hankins, K. H. (1998). Cacophony to Symphony: Memoirs in Teacher Research. *Harvard Educational Review, 68*(1), 80–95.

Hansen, D. T. (1995). *The call to teach.* New York: Teachers College Press.

*Hanvey, R. (November 2001). *Children and youth with special needs.* Ottawa: Canadian Council on Social Development. Retrieved November, 2003 from www.ccsd.ca

Hardman, M. L., Drew, C. J., and Egan, M. W. (1999). *Human exceptionality: Society, School, and family,* 6th ed. Boston: Allyn and Bacon.

Health. (June 1999). New York: Family Media, Inc.

Hedges, L. V. (1996). Quoted in Hedges finds boys and girls both disadvantaged in school. *Education News.* The Department of Education, University of Chicago.

Henriques, M. E. (1997, May). Increasing literacy among kindergartners through cross-age training. *Young Children,* 42–47.

Henry, E., Huntley, J., McKamey, C., and Harper, L. (1995). *To be a teacher: Voices from the classroom.* Thousand Oaks, CA: Corwin Press.

Henry, M. (1993). *School cultures: Universes of meaning in private schools.* Norwood, NJ: Ablex.

Henry, M. E. (1996). *Parent–school collaboration: Feminist organizational structures and school leadership.* Albany, NY: State University of New York Press.

Herbert, B. (1993, June 27). Listen to the children. *New York Times,* OP–ED.

Hoff, D. (1999, January 13). With 2000 looming, chances of meeting national goals iffy. *Education Week on the web.*

Hole, S. (1998). Teacher as rain dancer. *Harvard Educational Review, 68*(3), 413 –21.

Holland, A., and Andre, T. (1987, Winter). Participation in extracurricular activities in secondary schools. *Review of Educational Research,* 437–466.

Holly, M. L., and McLoughlin, C. (Eds.), (1989). *Perspectives on teacher professional development.* New York: Falmer Press.

Holt v. Shelton, 341 F. Supp. 821 (M.D. Tenn. 1972).

Holt–Reynolds, D. (1999). Good readers, good teachers? Subject matter expertise as a challenge in learning to teach. *Harvard Educational Review, 69*(1), 29–50.

Hopkins, B. J., and Wendel, F. C. (1997). *Creating school-community-business partnerships.* Bloomington, IN: Phi Delta Kappa Educational Foundation.

Howsam, R. B., Corrigan, D. C., Denemark, G. W., and Nash, R. J. (1976). *Educating a profession.* Washington, DC: American Association of Colleges for Teacher Education.

Hutchins, R. M. (1963). *A conversation on education.* Santa Barbara, CA: Fund for the Republic.

Idol, L. (1998). Optional extended year program, Feedback, Publ. No. 97.20. Austin Independent School District, TX, Office of Program Evaluation.

Igoa, C. (1995). *The inner world of the immigrant child.* New York: Lawrence Erlbaum Associates, Publishers.

Imber, M., and van Geel, T. (1993). *Education law.* New York: McGraw-Hill, Inc.

Inoue, A. (1996, October 10). *Creating schools with special characteristics.* Paper presented at the eighth Washington State University College of Education/Nishinomiya Education Board Education Seminar. Washington State University, Pullman.

International Reading Association. (1999, April). *Using multiple methods of beginning reading instruction.* Newark, DE: International Reading Association.

*Irwin, Annette. (1999). Acadia's use of technology. Retrieved October 10, 2003 from http://plato.acadiau.ca/courses/comm/e2/Website/annette.htm

Jackson, P. (1990). *Life in classrooms.* New York: Teachers College Press.

* Jeary, J. (2001). *Character education.* Calgary Board of Education.

Jersild, A. (1955). *When teachers face themselves.* New York: Teachers College Press.

Johnson, D. W., and Johnson, R. T. (1999). *Learning together and alone: Cooperative, competitive, and individualistic learning,* 5th ed. Boston: Allyn and Bacon.

Johnson, J., and Immerwahr, J. (1994). *First things first: What Americans expect from the public schools, a report from Public Agenda.* New York: Public Agenda.

Johnson, M. (1926). The educational principles of the School of Organic Education, Fairhope, Alabama. In G. M. Whipple, (Ed.), *The twenty–sixth yearbook of the National Society for the Study of Education.* Bloomington, IL: Public School Publishing Company.

Johnson, M. J., and Brown, L. (1998). Collegial support teams. In D. J. McIntyre, and D. M. Byrd (Eds.), *Strategies for career-long teacher education: Teacher education yearbook VI.* Thousand Oaks, CA: Corwin Press.

Jonassen, D. H., Peck, K. L., and Wilson, B. G. (1999). *Learning with technology: A constructivist perspective.* Upper Saddle River, NJ: Merrill.

Jones, J. (1994). Integrated learning systems for diverse learners. *Media and Methods 31*(3).

Jones, J. M. (1981). The concept of racism and its changing reality. In B. D. Bowser and R. G. Hunt (Eds.), *Impacts of racism on white Americans.* Beverly Hills, CA: Sage.

Jordan, K. M., Vaughan, J.S., and Woodworth, K. J. (1997). I will survive: Lesbian, gay, and bisexual youths' experience of high school. *Journal of Gay and Lesbian Social Services, 7,* 17–33.

Jordan, W. J., and Nettles, S. M. (1999). *How students invest their time out of school: Effects on school engagement, perceptions of life chances, and achievement.* Baltimore, MD: Center for Research on the Education of Students Placed at Risk.

Joyce, B., Weil, M., and Calhoun, E. (2000). *Models of teaching,* 6th ed. Boston: Allyn and Bacon.

Katzenmeyer, G. M., and Moller, G. (1996). *Awakening the sleeping giant: Leadership development for teachers.* Thousand Oaks, CA: Corwin Press.

Kerr, S. T. (1999). Visions of sugarplums: The future of technology, education, and the schools. In *Issues in curriculum: A selection of chapters from past NSSE yearbooks: Ninety–eighth yearbook of the National Society for the Study of Education, Part II.* Chicago: University of Chicago Press.

King, S. H. (1993, Summer). The limited presence of African-American teachers. *Review of Educational Research.*

Kirkpatrick, H., and Cuban, L. (1998). Computers make kids smarter—right? *TECHNOS Quarterly 7*(2), 26–31.

Kleinfeld, J. (1998). *The myth that schools shortchange girls: Social science in the service of deception.* Washington, DC: Women's Freedom Network.

Knupfer, N. N. (1998). Gender divisions across technology advertisements and the WWW: Implications for educational equity. *Theory into Practice 37*(1), 54–63.

Kohl, H. R. (1967). *36 children.* New York: Signet.

Kohlberg, L. (2000). The cognitive-developmental approach to moral education. In F. W. Parkay, and G. Hass, (Eds.), *Curriculum planning: A contemporary approach,* 7th ed. Boston: Allyn and Bacon, 136–48.

Kohn, A. (1997, February). How not to teach values: A critical look at character education. *Phi Delta Kappan,* 428–39.

Koller, E. (1996). Overcoming paradigm paralysis: A high school teacher revists foreign language education. In G. Burnaford, J. Fischer, and D. Hobson, (Eds.), *Teachers doing research: Practical possibilities.* Mahwah, NJ: Lawrence Erlbaum Associates.

Kounin, J. (1970). *Discipline and group management in classrooms.* New York: Holt, Rinehart and Winston.

Kozma, R., et al. (1992). Technology and the fate of at-risk students. *Education and Urban Society 24*(4), 440–53..

Krogh, S. L. (2000). Weaving the web. In F. W. Parkay, and G. Hass, (Eds.), *Curriculum planning: A contemporary approach,* 7th ed. Boston: Allyn and Bacon, 338–41.

*Kuehn, L. (1993). BC teachers: Lower job satisfaction. Retrieved January 21, 2003 from www.bctf.ca/ResearchReports/93wlc02/

Ladson-Billings, G. (1994). *The dreamkeepers: Successful teachers of African American children.* San Francisco: Jossey-Bass.

Lambert, L., et al. (1996). *Who will save our schools?: Teachers as constructivist leaders.* Thousand Oaks, CA: Corwin Press.

*Learning Disabilities Association of Canada. (2002, January). *Official definition of learning disabilities.* Retrieved October 3, 2003 from www.ldac-taac.ca/english/defined/definew.htm

Lee, V. E., Chen, X., and Smerdon, B. A. (1996). *The influence of school climate on gender differences in the achievement and engagement of young adolescents.* American Association of University Women.

Levey, S. (1996). *Starting from scratch: One classroom builds its own curriculum.* Portsmouth, NH: Heinemann.

Levy, F. (1996, October). What General Motors can teach U.S. schools about the proper role of markets in education reform. *Phi Delta Kappan,* 108–14.

Lewis, A. (1992). Helping young urban parents educate themselves and their children. *ERIC/CUE Digest, 85.*

Lewis, J. F. (1995, September). Saying no to vouchers: What is the price of democracy? *NASSP Bulletin,* 45–51.

Lewis, R. B., and Doorlag, D. H. (1999). *Teaching special students in general education classrooms,* 5th ed. Upper Saddle River, NJ: Merrill.

Lickona, T. (1998, February). A more complex analysis is needed. *Phi Delta Kappan,* 449–54.

Lieberman, A. (1990). Foreword. In S. Mei–ling Yee, (Eds.), *Careers in the classroom: When teaching is more than a job.* New York: Teachers College Press.

Lightfoot, S. L. (1982). *The good high school: Portraits of character and culture.* New York: Basic Books.

Lindsay, D. (1996, March 13). N.Y. bills give teachers power to oust pupils. *Education Week.*

Livingston, C. (Ed.), (1992). *Teachers as leaders: Evolving roles.* Washington, DC: National Education Association.

Louis Harris and Associates. (1990). *The Metropolitan Life survey of the American teacher 1990: New teachers: Expectations and ideals.* New York: Louis Harris and Associates.

Louis Harris and Associates. (1995). *The Metropolitan Life survey of the American teacher, 1984–1995: Old problems, new challenges.* New York: Louis Harris and Associates.

*Love, K. M. (1994). We've only just begun … in New Brunswick. Journal of the

Canadian Association of Community Education (5). Retrieved November 16, 2003 from:www.nald.ca/cace/journal/net3.htm

*MacDonald, T. (2001).To test or not to test: A question of accountability in Canadian schools. Retrieved on November 3, 2003 from www.policy.ca/archive/20010622.php3

*MacKay, A. W., and Sutherland, L. I. (1992). *Teachers and the law: A practical guide for educators.* Toronto: Edmond Montgomery Publications.

MacNaughton, R. H., and Johns, F. A. (1991, September). Developing a successful schoolwide discipline program. *NASSP Bulletin,* 47–57.

Madaus, G. F. (1999). The influence of testing on the curriculum. In M. J. Early and K. J. Rehage (Eds.), *Issues in curriculum: A selection of chapters from past NSSE yearbooks: Ninety-eighth yearbook of the National Society for the Study of Education, Part II* (pp. 73–111). Chicago: University of Chicago Press.

Mahoney, J., and Cairns, R. B. (1997). Do extracurricular activities protect against early school dropout? *Developmental Psychology, 33*(2), 241–53.

Mann, H. (1868). Annual reports on education. In Mary Mann (Ed.), *The life and works of Horace Mann,* Vol. 3. Boston: Horace B. Fuller.

Mann, L. (1998, Summer). Getting global with technology. *Curriculum Update.*

Manning, M. L., and Baruth, L. G. (1996). *Multicultural education of children and adolescents.* Boston: Allyn and Bacon.

Manzo, K. K. (1999, June 2). States setting strategies to reduce mistakes in textbooks. *Education Week on the Web.*

Marcus v. Rowley 695 F.2d 1171 (9th Cir. 1983).

Marks, H. M., Newmann, F. M., and Gamoran, A. (1996). Does authentic pedagogy increase student achievement? In F. M. Newmann, et al. (Eds.), *Authentic achievement: Restructuring schools for intellectual quality.* San Francisco: Jossey-Bass Publishers, 49–76.

Marshall, K. (1996, January). How I confronted HSPS (hyperactive superficial principal syndrome) and began to deal with the heart of the matter. *Phi Delta Kappan,* 336–45.

Maslow, A. (1954). *Motivation and personality.* New York: Basic Books.

Maslow, A. (1962). *Toward a psychology of being.* New York: Basic Books.

*McBeath, A. (2002, April). Untitled. *Educational Leadership,* 15.

McCarthy, M. M., Cambron-McCabe, N. H., and Thomas, S. B. (1998). *Public school law: Teachers' and students' rights,* 4th ed. Boston: Allyn and Bacon.

*McCoubrey, S., and Sitch, G. (2001). Instructor's guide: Teaching students' rights to pre-service and beginning teachers. *Education and Law Journal (11).*

McGhan, B. (1997, Winter). Compulsory school attendance: An idea past its prime? *The Educational Forum,* 134–39.

Mehlinger, H. D. (1996, February). School reform in the Information Age. *Phi Delta Kappan,* 400–07

Miami Herald. (1999, April 26). It's clear sailing for school vouchers: Legislators agree on tuition plan.

Mills, G. E. (2000). *Action research: A guide for the teacher researcher.* Upper Saddle River, NJ: Merrill.

Modi, M., Konstantopoulos, S., and Hedges, L. V. (1998). Predictors of academic giftedness among U.S. high school students: Evidence from a nationally representative multivariate analysis. Paper presented at the Annual Meeting of the American Educational Research Association, San Diego. Eric Document No. ED422-356.

Molino, F. (1999). My students, my children. In M. K. Rand, and S. Shelton-Colangelo, (Eds.), *Voices of student teachers: Cases from the field.* (pp. 55–56). Upper Saddle River: Merrill.

Moore, D. R. (1992). Voice and choice in Chicago. In W. H. Clune, and J. F. Witte (Eds.), *Choice and control in American education: Volume II. The practice of choice, decentralization and school restructuring.* Philadelphia: Falmer Press.

Moran v. School District No. 7, 350 F. Supp. 1180 (DC Mont. 1972).

Morris, J. E., and Curtis, K. E. (1983, March/April). Legal issues relating to field-based experiences in teacher education. *Journal of Teacher Education,* 2–6.

Morris, V. C., and Pai, Y. (1994). *Philosophy and the American school: An introduction to the philosophy of education.* Lanham, MD: University Press of America.

Morrison v. State Board of Education, 82 Cal. Rptr. 175, 461 P.2d 375 (Cal. 1969).

Morton, C. (1996, February). The modern land of Laputa: Where computers are used in education. *Phi Delta Kappan,* 416–19.

Moyers, B. D. (1989). *A world of ideas: Conversations with thoughtful men and women.* New York: Doubleday.

Murphy, J. (1999, April). Reconnecting teaching and school administration: A call for a unified profession. Paper presented at the Annual Meeting of the American Educational Research Association, Montreal.

Murray v. Pittsburgh Board of Public Education, 919 F. Supp. 838 (Pa. 1996).

Nash, R. J. (1997). *Answering the "virtuecrats": A moral conversation on character education.* New York: Teachers College Press.

Nathan, J. (1998, March). Heat and light in the charter school movement. *Phi Delta Kappan, 79*(7), 499–505.

National Assessment of Educational Progress (NAEP). (1996). *Measuring essential learning in science.* Washington, DC: National Assessment Governing Board, U.S. Department of Education.

National Assessment of Educational Progress (NAEP). (1999). *The nation's report card.* Washington, DC: Office of Educational Research and Improvement.

National Association for Sport and Physical Education. (1999). *National standards for physical education.* Reston, VA: National Association for Sport and Physical Education.

National Association for Year–Round Education. (1999). History of year–round education. San Diego, CA: National Association for Year–Round Education. Retrieved from www.nayre.org

National Commission on Civic Renewal. (1998). *A Nation of Spectators.* College Park, MD: National Commission on Civic Renewal.

National Council for Accreditation of Teacher Education (NCATE). (1997a). *Standards for accreditation of teacher education.* Washington, DC: National Council for Accreditation of Teacher Education (NCATE).

National Council for Accreditation of Teacher Education (NCATE). (1997b). *Standards, procedures, and policies for the accreditation of professional education units.* Washington, DC: National Council for Accreditation of Teacher Education (NCATE).

National Council for Accreditation of Teacher Education (NCATE). (1999). *NCATE: Did you know?* Washington, DC: National Council for Accreditation of Teacher Education (NCATE).

National Council for the Social Studies. (1994). *Expect excellence: Curriculum standards for the social studies.* Washington, DC: National Council for the Social Studies.

National Council of Teachers of Mathematics. (1998). *Principles and standards for school mathematics: Discussion draft.* Reston, VA: National Council of Teachers of Mathematics.

National Education Goals Panel. (1998). *The national education goals report: Building a nation of learners, 1998.* Washington, DC: U.S. Government Printing Office.

National Education Goals Panel. (1999). National Education Goals Panel recommends that goals be renamed "America's Education Goals" and continue beyond the year 2000. Press Release, National Education Goals Panel.

National Institute for Mental Health. (1999). *Suicide fact sheet.* Washington, DC: National Institute for Mental Health.

National Joint Committee on Learning Disabilities. (1997). *Operationalizing the NJCLD definition of learning disabilities for ongoing assessment in schools.* Rockville, MD: National Joint Committee on Learning Disabilities.

National Trade and Professional Associations of the United States, 34th ed. (1999). B. Downs, S. E. White, and A. G. Wood, (Eds.), New York: Columbia Books, Inc.

Neill, A. S. (1960). *Summerhill: A radical approach to child rearing.* New York: Hart.

Nelson, J. L., Carlson, K., and Palonsky, S. B. (2000). *Critical issues in education: A dialectic approach,* 4th ed. New York: McGraw–Hill.

Newmann, F. M., et al. (Eds.), (1996). *Authentic achievement: Restructuring schools for intellectual quality.* San Francisco: Jossey-Bass.

Newmann, F. M., and Wehlage, G. G. (1995). *Successful school restructuring: A report to the public and educators by the Center on Organization and Restructuring of Schools.* Madison, WI: University of Wisconsin, Center on Organization and Restructuring of Schools.

Noble, D. (1996, November). Mad rushes into the future: The overselling of educational technology. *Educational Leadership,* 18–23.

Noddings, N. (1995, May). Teaching themes of care. *Phi Delta Kappan,* 76(9), 675–79.

Noll, J. W. (Ed.), (1999). *Taking sides: Clashing views on controversial educational issues,* 10th ed. Guilford, CT: McGraw–Hill.

Norris, C. (1994). Computing and the classroom: Teaching the at–risk student. *Computing Teacher* 21(5), 12, 14.

North Central Regional Educational Laboratory. (1993). *Policy briefs, report 1, 1993.* Elmhurst, IL: NCREL

Northwest Regional Educational Laboratory. (1999). *Arts education: Basic to learning.* Portland: Northwest Regional Educational Laboratory.

*Nova Scotia Department of Education. (1996). *Special education policy manual.*

*Nova Scotia Department of Education. (2001). *Nova Scotia teacher certification handbook.*

*Nova Scotia Education and Culture. (1999). Foundation for the Atlantic Canada social studies curriculum. Halifax, NS: Atlantic Provinces Education Foundation, 16–27.

Okrent, D. (1999, May 10). Raising kids online: What can parents do? *Time,* 38–43.

*Ontario Human Rights Commission. (December, 2001). Report of the Ontario Human Rights Commission

Oppenheimer, T. (1997, July). The computer delusion. *The Atlantic Monthly,* 45–62.

*Osborne, K. (1999). *Education: A guide to the Canadian school debate—or, who wants what and why?* Montreal: Penguin/McGill Institute.

*Ottawa-Carlton District School Board (Board Procedure PR.585.CUR, June, 2000.

Ozmon, H. W., and Craver, S. M. (1999). *Philosophical foundations of education,* 6th ed. Upper Saddle River, NJ: Merrill.

Pajak, E. (1993). *Approaches to clinical supervision: Alternatives for improving instruction.* Norwood, MA: Christopher-Gordon.

Paliokas, K. L., and Rist, R. C. (1996, April 3). School Uniforms: Do they reduce violence—or just make us feel better? *Education Week,* 61(7), 46–49.

Pang, V. O. (1994, December). Why do we need this class: Multicultural education for teachers. *Phi Delta Kappan.*

*Pansegrau, M. (1997). Public education governance undergoes facelift as change sweeps nation's school boards. *Spectrum (Fall).* Retrieved October 3, 2003 from www.cdnsba.org/energyinnovators/articles.html.

Parkay, F. W. (Summer 1988). Reflections of a protégé. *Theory into Practice,* 195–200.

Parkay, F. W., and Hass, G. (2000). *Curriculum planning: A contemporary approach,* 7th ed. Boston: Allyn and Bacon.

Parkay, F. W., and Oaks, M. M. (1998, April 15). *Promoting the professional development of teachers: What the U.S. can learn from other countries.* Paper presented at the Annual Meeting of the American Educational Research Association, San Diego.

Parkay, F. W., Shindler, J., and Oaks, M. M. (1997, January). Creating a climate for collaborative, emergent leadership at an urban high school: Exploring the stressors, role changes, and paradoxes of restructuring. *International Journal of Educational Reform,* 64–74.

Pellicer, L.O., and Anderson, L. W. (1995). *A handbook for teacher leaders.* Thousand Oaks, CA: Corwin Press.

Piirto, J. (1999). *Talented children and adults: Their development and education.* Upper Saddle River, NJ: Merrill.

Pipho, C. (1999, February). The profit side of education. *Phi Delta Kappan,* 80(6), 421–22.

Pitton, D. E. (1998). *Stories of student teaching: A case approach to the student teaching experience.* Upper Saddle River, NJ: Merrill.

*Popham, W. J. (1999, May 12). Commentary: Assessment apathy. *Education Week on the Web.*

*Portelli, J., and Solomon, R. P. (2001). *A wolf in sheep's clothing: The erosion of democracy in education.* Calgary, Alberta: Detselig Enterprises Ltd, 136.

Posner, G. J. (1993). *Field experience: A guide to reflective teaching,* 3rd ed. New York: Longman.

Postman, N. (1995, October 9). Virtual students, digital classroom. *The Nation.*

Powell, A. G. (1980). *The uncertain profession: Harvard and the search for educational authority.* Cambridge, MA: Harvard University Press.

Power, E. J. (1982). *Philosophy of education: Studies in philosophies, schooling, and educational policies.* Englewood Cliffs, NJ: Prentice Hall.

*Proudfoot, A., and Hutchings, L. (1998). *Teacher beware: A legal primer for the classroom teacher.* Calgary: Detselig Enterprises Ltd.

*Queen's Printer of Ontario. (2002). *Ontario teacher qualifying test information booklet*. Toronto: Ontario Ministry of Education, 4.

*Queen's Printer of Ontario. (2002). Teacher performance appraisal manual and approved forms and guidelines. Toronto: Ontario Ministry of Education, 75.

*Raham, H. (1999, Spring). Assessment practices. *Education Analyst (2)*, 1. Retrieved October 20, 2003 from www.saee.bc.ca/art2_6.html.

Rallis, S. F. (1990). Professional teachers and restructured schools: Leadership challenges. In B. Mitchell, and L. L. Cunningham, (Eds.), *Educational leadership and changing contexts of families, communities, and schools* (89th NSSE yearbook). Chicago: University of Chicago Press.

Ravitz, J. L., Wong, Y. T., and Becker, H. J. (1999). Report to participants. The University of California, Irvine, and The University of Minnesota: Center for Research on Information Technology and Organizations.

RCM Research Corporation. (1998). *Time: Critical issues in educational change*. Portsmouth, NH: RCM Research Corporation.

Renzulli, J. S. (1998). The three–ring conception of giftedness. In S. M. Baum, S. M. Reis, and L. R. Maxfield, (Eds.), *Nurturing the gifts and talents of primary grade students*. Mansfield Center, CT: Creative Learning Press.

Rice, R., and Walsh, C. E. (1996). Equity at risk: The problem with state and federal education reform efforts. In C. Walsh (Ed.), *Education reform and social change: Multicultural voices, struggles, and visions*. Mahwah, NJ: Lawrence Erlbaum Associates, Publishers.

Riley, R. W. (1998, August 19). Research shows teachers, schools work hard on parental involvement; parents want even more partnerships. Press release. Washington, DC.

Ripple, R. E., and Rockcastle, V. E. (Eds.), (1964). *Piaget rediscovered: A report of the conference on cognitive studies and curriculum development*. Ithaca, NY: Cornell University, School of Education.

Rithdee, K. (1996, November 3–9). Fighting drugs with faith. *The Bangkok Post Sunday Magazine*.

*Roehr Institute. (2000). *Count us in: A demographic overview of childhood and disability in Canada*.

Rogers, C. (1961). *On becoming a person*. Boston: Houghton Mifflin.

Rogers, C. (1974). *Freedom to learn*. Columbus, OH: Merrill.

Rogers, C. (1982). *Freedom to learn in the eighties*. Columbus, OH: Merrill.

Rogers, K. (1991). *The relationship of grouping practices to the education of the gifted and talented learner*. Storrs, CT: University of Connecticut, National Research Center on the Gifted and Talented.

*Rogers, W. T. (1999, Winter). Introduction to measurement and evaluation: Current and future research directions for the new millennium. *Alberta Journal of Educational Research, Volume XLV (4)*.

Romans v. Crenshaw, 354 F. Supp. 868 (S.D. Tex. 1972).

Romer, R. (2000). Today standards—tomorrow success. In F. W. Parkay, and G. Hass, (Eds.), *Curriculum planning: A contemporary approach*, 7th ed. Boston: Allyn and Bacon, 314–17.

Rosenshine, B. (1988). Explicit teaching. In D. Berliner and B. Rosenshine (Eds.), *Talks to teachers*. New York: Random House.

Rosenshine, B. (1995). Advances in research on instruction. *The Journal of Educational Research, 88(5)*, 262–268.

Rosenshine, B., and Stevens, R. (1986). Teaching functions. In Merlin C. Wittrock (Ed.), *Handbook of research on teaching*, 3rd ed. New York: Macmillan.

Rosenshine, B., Meister, C., and Chapman, S. (1996). Teaching students to generate questions: A review of the intervention studies. *Review of Educational Research, 66(2)*, 181–221.

Ross, D. D., and Webb, R. B. (1995). Implementing shared decision making at Brooksville Elementary School. In A. Lieberman (Ed.), *The work of restructuring schools: Building from the ground up*. New York: Teachers College Press.

Sadker, M., and Sadker, D. (1994). *Failing at fairness: How our schools cheat girls*. New York: Touchstone.

Sallie Mae Corporation. (1995). *A report from the 1994 Sallie Mae symposium on quality education*. Washington, DC: Sallie Mae Corporation.

Salovey, P., and Sluyter, D. J. (Eds.), (1997). *Emotional development and emotional intelligence: Educational implications*. New York: Basic Books.

Sandholtz, J. J., Ringstaff, C., and Dwyer, D. C. (1997). *Teaching with technology: Creating student-centered classrooms*. New York: Teachers College Press.

Sarnoff, D. (1940). Foreword to L. R. Lohr. *Television broadcasting*. New York. McGraw-Hill.

Sartre, Jean-Paul. (1972). Existentialism. In John Martin Rich (Ed.), *Readings in the philosophy of education*. Belmont, CA: Wadsworth.

*Saskatchewan School Trustees Association. (1997). Canadian educational governance update. Retrieved June 12, 2003 from www.ssta.sk.ca/research/governance/csbacan.htm

*Saskatchewan Teachers' Federation. (2003, September). Teacher salary classification in Saskatchewan. Retrieved October 3, 2003 from www.stf.sk.ca/prof_growth/pdf/teacher_classification.pdf

*Saul, J. R. (2002). In defense of public education. *Horizons*. Ottawa: Canadian Teachers' Federation, 12.

Schaefer, R. (1967). *The school as the center of inquiry*. New York: Harper and Row.

Schifter, D. (Ed.), (1996). *What's happening in math class? Envisioning new practices through teacher narratives, Vol. 1*. New York: Teachers College Press.

Schmuck, R. A., and Schmuck, P. A. (1997). *Group processes in the classroom*, 7th ed. Madison, WI: Brown and Benchmark.

Schnaiberg, L. (1995, November 1). Record increase in special-education students reported. *Education Week on the Web*.

Schnaiberg, L. (1996, June 12). Staying home from school. *Education Week on the Web*.

Schneider, R. B., and Barone, D. (1997, Spring). Cross-age tutoring. *Childhood Education*, 136–143.

Schön, D. (1983). *The reflective practitioner: How professionals think in action*. New York: Basic Books.

Schön, D. (1987). *Educating the reflective practitioner: Toward a new design for teaching and learning in the professions*. San Francisco: Jossey-Bass.

Schön, D. (1991). *The reflective turn: Case studies in an on educational practice*. New York: Teachers College Press.

Schwartz, J. E., and Beichner, R. J. (1999). *Essentials of educational technology*. Boston: Allyn and Bacon.

Schwartz, W. (1995, December). Opportunity to learn standards: Their impact on urban education. *ERIC/CUE Digest*, 110.

Schwebel, A. J., et al. (1996). *The student teacher's handbook*, 3rd ed. Mahwah, NJ: Lawrence Erlbaum Associates.

Scopes, J. (1966). *Center of the storm*. New York: Holt, Rinehart, and Winston.

Scoville v. Board of Education of Joliet Township High School District 204, cert. denied, 400 U.S. 826, 91 S. Ct. 51 (1970); 425 F.2d 10 (7th Cir. 1971).

Sears, J. T. (1991). Educators, homosexuality and homosexual students: Are personal feelings related to professional beliefs? *Journal of Homosexuality, 22*.

Sharan, Y., and Sharan, S. (1989/1990, December/January). Group investigation expands cooperative learning. *Educational Leadership*, 17–21.

Shenk, D. (1998). *Data smog: Surviving the information age*. New York: HarperEdge.

Sigalit, U., and Van Lehn, K. (1995). STEPS: A simulated, tutorable physics student. *Journal of Artificial Intelligence in Education, 6(4)*, 405–37.

Signer, B. (1991). CAI and at–risk minority urban high school students. *Journal of Research on Computing in Education, 24(2)*.

Singer, A. (1994, December). Reflections on multiculturalism. *Phi Delta Kappan*, 284–88.

Sizer, T. (1997a). *Horace's compromise: The dilemma of the American high school*, 3rd ed. Boston: Houghton Mifflin.

Sizer, T. (1997b). *Horace's school: Re-designing the American high school*. Boston: Houghton Mifflin.

Sizer, T. (1997c). *Horace's hope: What works for the American high school.* Boston: Houghton Mifflin.

Sizer, T. and Sizer, N. (1999). *The students are watching: Schools and the moral contract.* Boston: Beacon Press.

Skinner, B. F. (1972). Utopia through the control of human behavior. In J. M. Rich (Ed.), *Readings in the philosophy of education.* Belmont, CA: Wadsworth.

Slavin, R. E. (2000). *Educational psychology: Theory and practice,* 6th ed. Boston: Allyn and Bacon.

Slavit, D. (1998). Above and beyond AAA: The similarity and congruence of polygons. *Mathematics Teaching in the Middle School, 3*(4), 276–280.

Smith, D. D. (1998). *Introduction to special education: Teaching in an age of challenge,* 2nd ed. Boston: Allyn and Bacon.

Smith, K. B., and Meier, K. K. (1995). *The case against school choice: Politics, markets, and fools.* Armonk, NY: M.E. Sharpe.

Smith v. Archbishop of St. Louis, 632, S.W. 2d 516 (Mo. app. 1982).

Smith v. Board of School Commissioners of Mobile County, 655 F. Supp. 939 (S. D. Ala.), *rev'd,* 827 F.2d 684 (11th Cir. 1987).

Smolkin, R. (1999, February 27–28). The reading debate rages. *Moscow-Pullman Daily News,* 1A, 10A.

Smyth, J. W. (1995). *Clinical supervision: Collaborative learning about teaching.* New York: State Mutual Book and Periodical Service.

*Smythe, J. (2001, June 12). Provinces urged to test students vigorously.http://www.policy.ca/archive/20010622.php3-_ednref5#_ednref5 *National Post,* A1. Retrieved November 3, 2002 from www.policy.ca/archive/20010622.php3

Sommers, C. H. (1994). *Who stole feminism?: How women have betrayed women.* New York: Simon and Schuster.

Sommers, C. H. (1996, June 12). Where the boys are. *Education Week on the Web.*

Sowell, E. J. (1996). *Curriculum: An integrative introduction.* Boston: Allyn and Bacon.

Spring, J. (1998). *Conflict of interests: The politics of American education,* 3rd ed. Boston: McGraw Hill.

Spring, J. (1999). *American education,* 8th ed. New York: McGraw–Hill.

Sricharatchanya, P. (1996, November 5). Education reforms are also crucial. *Bangkok Post.*

*Statistics Canada. (1999, October 12). Computer technology in schools. *The Daily,* catalogue number 11-001-XIE. Retrieved November 1, 2003 from www.statcan.ca/Daily/English/991012/d991012a.htm

*Statistics Canada. (2001a). *A profile of disability in Canada.* Catalogue No. 89-577-XIE. Ottawa: Housing, Family and Social Statistics Division. Retrieved October 2003 from www.hrdc-drhc.gc.ca/sp-ps/arb-dgra/publications/research/2001docs/PALS/89-577-XIE01001.pdf.

*Statistics Canada. (2001b). Canada's ethnocultural portrait: The changing mosaic. Retrieved October 11 from www12.statcan.ca/english/census01/Products/Analytic/companion/etoimm/canada.cfm

*Statistics Canada. (2002, July 17). Crime Statistics. *The Daily.* Retrieved October 1, 2003 from URL http://www.statcan.ca/Daily/English/020717/d020717b.htm

*Statistics Canada. (2002, November 25). Reading performance of students in rural and urban schools. *The Daily.* Retrieved November 3, 2003 from www.statcan.ca/Daily/English/021125/d021125b.htm

*St. Boniface School Division No. 4. Appendix I: Indicators of good practice. *Teacher supervision.* Retrieved October 3, 2003 from www.stboniface.winnipeg.mb.ca/tsdev-ai.htm.

St. Michel, T. (1995). *Effective substitute teachers: Myth, mayhem, or magic?* Thousand Oaks, CA: Corwin Press.

Stanford, B. H. (1992). Gender equity in the classroom. In D. A. Byrnes and G. Kiger (Eds.), *Common bonds: Anti–bias teaching in a diverse society.* Wheaton, MD: Association for Childhood Education International.

Steinberg, A. (1999, March/April). The human cost of over-reliance on tests. *Harvard Education Letter.*

Steinberg, L., Dornbusch, S., and Brown, B. (1996). *Beyond the classroom: Why school reform has failed and what parents need to do.* New York: Simon and Schuster.

Sternberg, R. J. (1996, March). Myths, countermyths, and truths about intelligence. *Educational Researcher,* 11–16.

*Stewart, M. (2002, February 20). The perils of testing: A submission to the commission on the future of health care in Canada. Prince Edward Island Teachers' Federation. Retrieved November 3, 2003 from: www.peitf.com/FromThePresident.htm

Stoll, C. (1996). *Silicon snake oil: Second thoughts on the information highway.* New York: Anchor.

Stover, D. (1992, March). The at-risk kids schools ignore. *The Executive Educator,* 28–31.

*Sussel, T. (1995). *Canada's legal revolution: Public education, the Charter and human rights.* Toronto: Edmond Montgomery Ltd.

Sykes, G. (1983, October). Contradictions, ironies, and promises unfulfilled: A contemporary account of the status of teaching. *Phi Delta Kappan,* 87–93.

Tapscott, D. (1999, July 6,). Kids, technology and the schools. *Computerworld.*

*Taylor, A. R., and Tubianosac, T. R. (2001, May). Student assessment in Canada: improving the learning environment through effective evaluation. SAEE Research Series #9. Available from www.saee.bc.ca/research_rpt.html#Assessment

Tellijohann, S. K., and Price, J. H. (1993). A qualitative examination of adolescent homosexuals' life experiences: Ramifications for secondary school personnel. *Journal of Homosexuality, 26.*

Terman, L. M., and Oden, M. H. (1947). The gifted child grows up. In L. M. Terman (Ed.), *Genetic studies of genius,* Vol. 4. Stanford, CA: Stanford University Press.

Terman, L. M., and Oden, M. H. (1959). The gifted group in mid–life. In L. M. Terman (Ed.), *Genetic studies of genius,* Vol. 5. Stanford, CA: Stanford University Press.

Terman, L. M., Baldwin, B. T., and Bronson, E. (1925). Mental and physical traits of a thousand gifted children. In L. M. Terman (Ed.), *Genetic studies of genius,* vol. 1. Stanford, CA: Stanford University Press.

Terry, W. (1993, February). Make things better for somebody. *Parade Magazine.*

Thelen, H. A. (1960). *Education and the human quest.* New York: Harper and Row.

Thelen, H. A. (1981). *The classroom society: The construction of educational experience.* London: Croom Helm.

Tombari, M. L., and Borich, G. D. (1999). *Authentic assessment in the classroom: Applications and practice.* Upper Saddle River, NJ: Merrill.

Tozer, S. E., Violas, P. C., and Senese, G. (1993). *School and society: Educational practice as social expression.* New York: McGraw-Hill.

Trotter, A. (1998, October 1). A question of effectiveness. *Education Week on the Web.*

*Turnbull, M. (2000). Introduction: What is core French? *Core French FAQ.* Retrieved October 11, 2003 from www.cpfnb.com/core_FAQ/CoreFAQ.html

Tyler, R. (1949). *Basic principles of curriculum and instruction.* Chicago: University of Chicago.

Uchida, D., Cetron, M., and McKenzie, F. (1996). *Preparing students for the 21st century.* Arlington, VA: American Association of School Administrators.

U.S. Department of Education. (1996b). *Manual on school uniforms.* Washington, DC: U. S. Department of Education.

U.S. Department of Education. (1997). *From students of teaching to teachers of students.* Washington, DC: U.S. Department of Education.

U.S. Department of Education. (1999a). [Online]. Safe schools, healthy schools: Remarks as prepared for delivery by U.S. Secretary of Education Richard W. Riley. http://www.ed.gov/Speeches/04–1999/990430.html [1999, April 30].

U.S. Department of Education. (1999b). *Schools with IDEAs that work.* Washington, DC: U.S. Department of Education.

U.S. Department of Education and International Institute on Education. (1996). *A splintered vision: An investigation of U.S. science and mathematics education.* Washington, DC.

U.S. Department of Health and Human Services. (1998, October 27). *Improving Head Start: A success story.* Washington, DC: U.S. Department of Health and Human Services.

U.S. Department of Justice. (1996). *1995 national youth gang survey*. Washington, DC: U.S. Department of Justice.

Unified School Dist. No 241 v. Swanson, 717 P.2d 526 (Kan.App.1986).

The University of Memphis. (1994/95, Winter). Technology provides field experiences. *Perspectives*. Memphis: University of Memphis, College of Education.

Utay, C., and Utay, J. (1997). Peer–assisted learning: The effects of cooperative learning and cross–age peer tutoring with word processing on writing skills of students with learning disabilities. *Journal of Computing in Childhood Education*, 8.

Valenza, J. K. (1997). Girls + technology = turnoff? *Technology Connections*, 3.

van Manen, M. (1991) *The tact of teaching: The meaning of pedagogical thoughtfulness*. Albany, NY: State University of New York Press.

Vaughn, S., Bos, C. S., and Schumm, J. S. (1997). *Teaching mainstreamed, diverse, and at-risk students in the general education classroom*. Boston: Allyn and Bacon.

Viadero, D. (1996, May 8). Math texts are multiplying. *Education Week*.

Viadero, D. (1999, January). [Untitled article]. *Education Week, 10*(4), 23.

Visconti, K. (1996). Stay in or get out? A "twenty–something" teacher looks at the profession. In G. Burnaford, J. Fischer, and D. Hobson, (Eds.), *Teachers doing research: Practical possibilities*. Mahwah, NJ: Lawrence Erlbaum Associates.

Vygotsky, L. S. (1978). *Mind in society: The development of higher mental process*. Cambridge, MA: Harvard University Press.

Vygotsky, L. S. (1986). *Thought and language*. Cambridge, MA: MIT Press.

*Wagner, K. (1998). Choice in public education. *Policy Watch*. Vancouver: Society for the Advancement of Excellence in Public Education. Retrieved October 24, 2002 from www.saee.bc.ca/policywa. html#Choice

Walberg, H. J., and Greenberg, R. C. (1997, May). Using the learning environment inventory. *Educational Leadership*, 45–47.

Walberg, H. J., and Niemiec, R. P. (1994, May). Is Chicago school reform working? *Phi Delta Kappan*, 713–715.

Walberg, H. J., and Niemiec, R. P. (1996, May 22). Can the Chicago reforms work? *Education Week on the Web*.

Waller, W. (1932). *The sociology of teaching*. New York: Wiley.

Walling, D. R. (Ed.), (1994). *Teachers as leaders: Perspectives on the professional development of teachers*. Bloomington, IN: Phi Delta Kappa Educational Foundation.

Walsh, M. (1999a, April 2). Conservatives join effort to pull the plug on Channel One. *Education Week on the Web*.

Walsh, M. (1999b, April 14). Most Edison schools report rise in test scores. *Education Week on the Web*.

Walsh, M. (1999c, May). Two reports offer bright outlook for education industry. *Education Week, 18*(36), 5.

Walsh, M. (1999d, May 5). Shootings raise host of legal questions. *Education Week on the Web*.

Walsh, M. (1999e, May 26). Nader, Schlafly lambaste Channel One at Senate hearing. *Education Week on the Web*.

Walsh, M. (1999f, September 8). Edison Project, now Edison Schools Inc., plans to go public. *Education Week on the Web*.

Walters, L. S. (1999, January/February). What makes a good school violence prevention program? *Harvard Education Letter*.

Walthers, K. (1995, September). Saying yes to vouchers: Perception, choice, and the educational response. *NAASP Bulletin*, 52–61.

Washington State Department of Health, Non–Infectious Disease and Conditions Epidemiology Section. (1994). *Youth violence and associated risk factors: An epidemiological view of the literature*. Olympia, WA: Washington State Department of Health, Non–Infectious Disease and Conditions Epidemiology Section.

Washington, W. (1998). Optional extended year program feedback. Austin Independent School District, TX, Department of Accountability, Student Services, and Research.

Wasserman, S. (1994, April). Using cases to study teaching. *Phi Delta Kappan*, 602–11.

*Watkinson, A. (1999). *Education, students' rights and the Charter*. Saskatoon: Purich Publishing Ltd.

Webb, L. D., Metha, A., and Jordan, K. F. (1999). *Foundations of American education*, 3rd ed. Englewood Cliffs, NJ: Prentice Hall.

Wechsler, D. (1958). *The Measurement and appraisal of adult intelligence*, 4th ed. Baltimore: Williams and Wilkins.

Weidmer, T. L. (1998). Digital portfolios: Capturing and demonstrating skills and levels of performance. *Phi Delta Kappan, 79*(8), 586–589.

*Weinberg, P. (2000, September 3). Public schools, private dollars: How cash strapped schools wheel and deal with corporate donors. *Eye Weekly*. Retrieved October 24, 2003 from www.eye.net/eye/issue/issue_03.09.00/news/schools.html

West, A. M. (1980). *The National Education Association: The power base for education*. New York: Free Press.

West v. Board of Education of City of New York, 187 N. Y. S.2d 88 8 A.D. 2d 291 (N.Y. App. 1959).

*Western Canadian Protocol for Collaboraton in Basic Education. (2000). Retrieved October 20, 2003 from www.wcp.ca/

White, K. A. (1997). A matter of policy. *Education Week on the Web*. www. edweek. org/sreports/tc/policy/po–n.htm

Whitely, B. E. (1997). Gender differences in computer–related attitudes and behavior: A meta–analysis. *Computers in Human Behavior, 13*.

Williams, J. (1999, April 18). Urban schools' obstacles hindering technology. *Milwaukee Journal Sentinel*.

Willingham, W. W., and Cole, N. S. (1997). *Gender and fair assessment*. Mahwah, NJ: Lawrence Erlbaum Associates.

*Wilson, J. D., Stamp, R. M., and Audet, L. P. (1970). *Canadian education : A history*. Scarborough: Prentice Hall of Canada Ltd.

Withrow, F. B. (1997). Technology in education and the next twenty-five years. *T.H.E. Journal, 2411*, 59–61.

Wohlstetter, P. (1995, September). Getting school-based management right: What works and what doesn't. *Phi Delta Kappan*, 22–24, 26.

Wohlstetter, P., and Anderson, L. (1994, February). What can U.S. charter schools learn from England's grant-maintained schools? *Phi Delta Kappan*, 486–491.

Wolfgang, C. H. (1999). *Solving discipline problems: Methods and models for today's teachers*, 4th ed. Boston: Allyn and Bacon.

Woolfolk, A. E. (1998). *Educational psychology*, 7th ed. Boston: Allyn and Bacon.

Woolfolk, A. E. (1995). *Educational psychology*, 6th ed. Boston: Allyn and Bacon.

Worldbook. Canadian education associations. In *Educator resource centre*. Retrieved November 1, 2003 from *Worldbook* www2.worldbook.com/educators/pro_links_can_04.asp

Yahoo Internet Life. (1999). America's 100 most wired colleges.

Yamamoto, K., Davis, O. L. Jr., Dylak, S., Whittaker, J., Marsh, C., and van der Westhuizen, P C. (1996, Spring). Across six nations: Stressful events in the lives of children. *Child Psychiatry and Human Development*, 139–150.

Young, C. (1999). *Ceasefire! Why women and men must join forces to achieve true equality*. New York: Free Press.

Zehm, S. J., and Kottler, J. A. (1993). *On being a teacher: The human dimension*. Newbury Park, CA: Corwin Press.

Glossary

A

Academic learning time (p. 266): the amount of time students spend working on academic tasks with a high level of success (80 percent or higher).

Action research (p. 379): classroom-based study, by teachers, of how to improve their instruction.

Aesthetics (p. 83): the branch of axiology concerned with values related to beauty and art.

Aims of education (p. 162): what a society believes the broad, general purposes of education should be—for example, socialization, achievement, personal growth, and social improvement.

Allocated time (p. 266): the amount of time teachers allocate for instruction in various areas of the curriculum.

Alternative school (p. 194): a small, highly individualized school separate from a regular school; designed to meet the needs of students at risk.

American tradition (p. 92): an approach to education which the frontier experience of the United States modified to make it more practical than the British model upon which it was originally based.

Assertive discipline (p. 271): an approach to classroom discipline requiring that teachers establish firm, clear guidelines for student behaviour and follow through with consequences for misbehaviour.

Assessment (p. 279): the process of gathering information related to how much students have learned.

Assistive technology (p. 234): technological advances (usually computer-based) that help exceptional students learn and communicate.

Attention deficit disorder (ADD) (p. 228): a learning disability characterized by difficulty in concentrating on learning.

Attention deficit hyperactivity disorder (ADHD) (p. 228): a learning disability characterized by difficulty in remaining still so that one can concentrate on learning.

Authentic assessments (p. 282): an approach to assessing students' learning that requires them to solve problems or work on tasks that approximate as much as possible those they will encounter beyond the classroom.

Authentic learning tasks (p. 265): learning activities that enable students to see the connections between classroom learning and the world beyond the classroom.

Axiology (p. 83): the study of values, including the identification of criteria for determining what is valuable.

B

Behaviourism (p. 89): a philosophical orientation based on behaviouristic psychology that maintains that environmental factors shape people's behavior.

Between-class ability grouping (p. 263): the practice of grouping students at the middle and high school levels for instruction on the basis of ability or achievement, often called *tracking*.

Block scheduling (p. 267): a high school scheduling arrangement that provides longer blocks of time each class period, with fewer periods each day.

British North America Act (BNA Act) (pp. 101, 125): 1867 act that established Canada as a nation and laid the framework for public institutions such as schools.

Burnout (p. 20): an acute level of stress resulting in job dissatisfaction, emotional and physical exhaustion, and an inability to cope effectively.

C

Canadian Charter of Rights and Freedoms (p. 232): 1982 document which enshrined the rights and freedoms in the form of a document, the Charter, to serve as the guiding law of the land and applies to all levels of government.

Canadian Parents for French (p. 131): nation-wide volunteer organization to promote teaching of French in schools, especially French Immersion programs.

Canadian School Board Association (p. 128): national voice of school boards in Canada, comprised of ten provincial school board associations.

Canadian Teachers' Federation (CTF) (p. 370): national bilingual Canadian organization with 240 000 members from all provinces and territories.

Caring classroom (p. 260): a classroom in which the teacher communicates clearly an attitude of caring about students' learning and their overall well-being.

CD-ROM (p. 336): a small plastic disk (usually 4.72 or 5.25 inches in diameter) that holds 600 or more megabytes of information that can be read by a computer.

CEGEP (p. 107): (collège d'enseignement général et professional) a Quebec junior college that students can attend for one or two years of study.

Character education (p. 214): an approach to education that emphasizes the teaching of values, moral reasoning, and the development of "good" character.

Charter schools (p. 449): independent schools, often founded by teachers, that are given a charter to operate by a school district, province, or national government, with the provision that students must demonstrate mastery of predetermined outcomes.

Chat rooms (p. 339): internet sites where students can participate in on-line discussions by typing in their comments and questions.

Child abuse (p. 149): any kind of harm that causes injury to a child, including physical, sexual, emotional, and neglect.

Choice theory (p. 267): an approach to classroom management, developed by psychiatrist William Glasser, based on a belief that students will usually make good choices (i.e., behave in an acceptable manner) if they experience success in the classroom and know that teachers care about them.

Classroom climate (p. 257): the atmosphere or quality of life in a classroom, determined by how individuals interact with one another.

Classroom culture (p. 169): the "way of life" characteristic of a classroom group; determined by the social dimensions of the group and the physical characteristics of the setting.

Classroom management (p. 267): day-to-day teacher control of student behaviour and learning, including discipline.

Classroom organization (p. 263): how teachers and students in a school are grouped for instruction and how time is allocated in classrooms.

Clinical supervision (p. 419): a four-step model supervisors follow in making teacher performance evaluations.

Code of ethics (p. 137): a set of guidelines that defines appropriate behaviour for professionals.

Cognitive development (p. 210): the process of acquiring the intellectual ability to learn from interaction with one's environment.

Cognitive science (p. 90): the study of the learning process that focuses on how individuals manipulate symbols and process information.

Collaboration (p. 416): the practice of working together, sharing decision making, and solving problems among professionals.

Collaborative consultation (p. 238): an approach in which a classroom teacher meets with one or more other professionals (such as a special educator, school psychologist, or resource teacher) to focus on the learning needs of one or more students.

Collective bargaining (p. 141): a process followed by employers and employees in negotiating salaries, hours, and working conditions; in most states, school boards must negotiate contracts with teacher organizations.

Collegial support team (CST) (p. 417): a team of teachers—created according to subject area, grade level, or teacher interests and expertise—who support one another's professional growth.

Collegiality (p. 411): a spirit of cooperation and mutual helpfulness among professionals.

Comparative education (p. 454): the comparative study of educational practices in different countries.

Computer-assisted instruction (CAI) (p. 334): the use of computers to provide individualized drill-and-practice exercises or tutorials to students.

Computer-based simulations (p. 337): computer programs that present the user with multifaceted problem situations similar to those they will encounter in real life.

Computer-enhanced instruction (CEI) (p. 335): the use of computers to provide students with inquiry-oriented learning experiences such as simulations and problem-solving activities.

Computer-managed instruction (CMI) (p. 335): the use of computers to evaluate and diagnose students' learning needs and record students' progress for teachers to monitor.

Concrete operations stage (p. 211): the stage of cognitive development (seven to eleven years of age) proposed by Jean Piaget in which the individual develops the ability to use logical thought to solve concrete problems.

Constitution Act of 1982 (p. 125): act granting Canada its own constitution, the most notable section being the Charter of Rights and Freedoms entrenched as Part 1 of the Constitution of Canada.

Constructivism (p. 89): a psychological orientation that views learning as an active process in which learners *construct* understanding of the material they learn—in contrast to the view that teachers transmit academic content to students in small segments.

Constructivist teaching (p. 275): a method of teaching based on students' prior knowledge of the topic and the processes they use to *construct* meaning.

Cooperative Education programs (p. 320): programs designed to develop employability skills and help students explore career options by offering both an in-school and a work experience component.

Cooperative learning (p. 263): an approach to teaching in which students work in small groups, or teams, sharing the work and helping one another complete assignments.

Copyright laws (p. 141): laws limiting the use of photocopies, videotapes, and computer software programs.

Core curriculum (p. 306): a set of fundamental courses or learning experiences that are part of the curriculum for all students at a school.

Core French (p. 317): second language instruction that emphasizes basic communication skills, language knowledge, and appreciation of French culture.

Corporal punishment (p. 147): physical punishment applied to a student by a school employee as a disciplinary measure.

Co-teaching (p. 418): an arrangement whereby two or more teachers teach together in the same classroom.

Council of Ministers of Education, Canada (p. 126): established in 1967, acts as a forum for provincial and territorial ministers of education to meet and discuss matters of mutual interest.

Credentials file (p. 401): a file set up for students registered in a teacher placement office at a college or university, which includes background information on the applicant, the type of position desired, transcripts, performance evaluations, and letters of recommendation.

Cross-age tutoring (p. 277): a tutoring arrangement in which older students tutor younger students; evidence indicates that cross-age tutoring has positive effects on the attitudes and achievement of tutee and tutor.

Cultural identity (p. 172): an overall sense of oneself, derived from the extent of one's participation in various subcultures within the national macroculture.

Culture (p. 170): the way of life common to a group of people; includes knowledge deemed important, shared meanings, norms, values, attitudes, ideals, and view of the world.

Curriculum (p. 294): the school experiences, both planned and unplanned, that enhance (and sometimes impede) the education and growth of students.

D

Dame -schools (p. 92): colonial schools, usually held in the homes of widows or housewives, for teaching children basic reading, writing, and mathematical skills.

Democratic classrooms (p. 267): a classroom in which the teacher's leadership style encourages students to take more power and responsibility for their learning.

Departmentalization (p. 169): an organizational arrangement for schools in which students move from classroom to classroom for instruction in different subject areas.

Department of education (p. 127): the provincial government ministry responsible for all aspects of education.

Deputy Minister of Education (p. 127): appointed civil servant whose position is directly below the Minister of Education, responsible for the day-to-day management of the Department of Education.

Direct instruction (p. 274): a systematic instructional method focusing on the transmission of knowledge and skills from the teacher to the students.

Discovery learning (p. 276): an approach to teaching that gives students opportunities to inquire into subjects so that they "discover" knowledge for themselves.

Distance learning networks (p. 334): two-way, interactive telecommunications systems used to deliver instruction to students at various locations.

Diversity (p. 170): differences among people in regard to gender, race, ethnicity, culture, and socioeconomic status.

Due process (p. 139): a set of specific guidelines that must be followed to protect individuals from arbitrary, capricious treatment by those in authority.

Duty of care (p. 145): special obligation of teachers to prevent reasonably foreseeable harm to those under their supervision. Duties often clarified through regulations, school board bylaws, policy statements, and job descriptions.

DVD (p. 336): Similar to a CD-ROM, a DVD holds much more information, and is generally regarded to be a technological advancement over the CD-ROM.

E

Education Act (p. 127): provincial statutes that create an education system and provides for its management and funding.

Educational philosophy (p. 79): a set of ideas and beliefs about education that guide the professional behaviour of educators.

Educational Resources Information Center (ERIC) (p. 378): a national information system made up of sixteen clearinghouses that disseminate descriptions of exemplary programs, results of research and development efforts, and related information.

Educational technology (p. 333): computers, software, multimedia systems, and advanced telecommunications systems used to enhance the teaching-learning process.

Emotional intelligence (p. 163): a level of awareness and understanding of one's emotions that allows the person to achieve personal growth and self-actualization.

English tradition (p. 92): a model of education based upon church control, class, and separate schools for boys and girls.

Epistemology (p. 82): a branch of philosophy concerned with the nature of knowledge and what it means to know something.

ERIC Clearinghouses (p. 378): sixteen Educational Resources Information Center Clearinghouses that disseminate descriptions of exemplary educational programs, the results of research and development efforts, and related information.

Essentialism (p. 85): formulated in part as a response to progressivism, this philosophical orientation holds that a core of common knowledge about the real world should be transmitted to students in a systematic, disciplined way.

Ethical dilemmas (p. 139): problem situations in which an ethical response is difficult to determine; that is, no single response can be called "right" or "wrong."

Ethics (p. 83): a branch of philosophy concerned with principles of conduct and determining what is good and evil, right and wrong, in human behaviour.

Ethnic group (p. 172): individuals within a larger culture who share a racial or cultural identity and a set of beliefs, values, and attitudes and who consider themselves members of a distinct group or subculture.

Ethnicity (p. 195): a shared feeling of common identity that derives, in part, from a common ancestry, common values, and common experiences.

Evaluation (p. 282): making judgments about, or assigning a value to, measurements of students' learning.

Exceptional learners (p. 225): students whose growth and development deviate from the norm to the extent that their educational needs can be met more effectively through a modification of regular school programs.

Existentialism (p. 85): a philosophical orientation that emphasizes the individual's experiences and maintains that each individual must determine his or her own meaning of existence.

Explicit curriculum (p. 295): the behaviour, attitudes, and knowledge that a school intends to teach students.

Extracurricular/cocurricular programs (p. 297): school-sponsored activities students may pursue outside of, or in addition to, academic study.

F

Field experiences (p. 53): opportunities for teachers-in-training to experience firsthand the world of the teacher, by observing, tutoring, and instructing small groups.

Formal operations stage (p. 211): the stage of cognitive development (eleven to fifteen years of age) proposed by Jean Piaget in which cognitive abilities reach their highest level of development.

Formative evaluation (p. 282): an assessment, or diagnosis, of students' learning for the purpose of planning instruction.

For-profit schools (p. 450): schools that are operated, for profit, by private educational corporations.

French Immersion (p. 318): program whereby all, or nearly all, curriculum instruction is in French.

French tradition (p. 92): based upon church-controlled schools with classes often taught by members of the clergy.

Fringe benefits (p. 14): benefits (i.e., medical insurance, retirement, and tax-deferred investment opportunities) that are given to teachers in addition to base salary.

Full inclusion (p. 234): the policy and process of including exceptional learners in general education classrooms.

G

Gender bias (p. 182): subtle bias or discrimination on the basis of gender;

reduces the likelihood that the target of the bias will develop to the full extent of his or her capabilities.

Gender-fair classroom (p. 182): education that is free of bias or discrimination on the basis of gender.

Gifted and talented (p. 229): exceptional learners who demonstrate high intelligence, high creativity, high achievement, or special talent(s).

Grievance (p. 141): a formal complaint filed by an employee against his or her employer or supervisor.

Group investigation (p. 277): an approach to teaching in which the teacher facilitates learning by creating an environment that allows students to determine what they will study and how.

H

Hidden curriculum (p. 295): the behaviours, attitudes, and knowledge the school culture unintentionally teaches students.

Hierarchy of needs (p. 219): a set of seven needs, from the basic needs for survival and safety to the need for self-actualization, that motivate human behaviour.

Higher-order questions (p. 444): questions that require the ability to engage in complex modes of thought (synthesis, analysis, and evaluation, for example).

Home-school communication systems (p. 337): computer-based systems that allow schools to disseminate information to parents and, in turn, enable parents to communicate directly with school personnel.

Home -schooling (p. 114): the practice of parents taking on the role of teacher and educating their children at home.

Humanism (p. 88): a philosophy based on the belief that individuals control their own destinies through the application of their intelligence and learning.

Humanistic psychology (p. 88): an orientation to human behaviour that emphasizes personal freedom, choice, awareness, and personal responsibility.

Hutterite schools (p. 114): operated by the Hutterites, a religious group found mainly in Western Canada.

Hypermedia (p. 336): an interactive instructional system consisting of a computer, CD-ROM drive, videodisc player, video monitor, and speakers. Hypermedia systems allow students to control and present sound, video images, text, and graphics in an almost limitless array of possibilities.

I

Inclusion (p. 234: the practice of integrating all students with disabilities into general education classes.

Independent schools (p. 113): also known as private schools which charge a tuition fee.

Individual racism (p. 174): the prejudicial belief that one's ethnic or racial group is superior to others.

Individualized education plan (IEP) (p. 232): a plan for meeting an exceptional learner's educational needs, specifying goals, objectives, services, and procedures for evaluating progress.

Information processing (p. 276): a branch of cognitive science concerned with how individuals use long- and short-term memory to acquire information and solve problems.

Inquiry-based curriculum (p. 306): a curriculum that teaches not only the content but also the thought processes of a discipline.

Inquiry learning (p. 276): an approach to teaching that gives students opportunities to explore, or *inquire* into, subjects so that they develop their own answers to problem situations.

In-service workshops (p. 64): on-site professional development programs in which teachers meet to learn new techniques, develop curricular materials, share ideas, or solve problems.

Institution (p. 165): any organization a society establishes to maintain, and improve, its way of life.

Institutional racism (p. 174): institutional policies and practices, intentional or not, that result in racial inequities.

Instructional goals (p. 278): general statements of purpose that guide schools and teachers as they develop instructional programs.

Integrated curriculum (p. 299): a school curriculum that draws from two or more subject areas and focuses on a theme or concept rather than on a single subject.

Intelligence (p. 222): the ability to learn; the cognitive capacity for thinking.

Interactive multimedia (p. 336): computer-supported media that allow the user to interact with a vast, non-linear, multimedia database to combine textual, audio, and video information.

Interactive teaching (p. 27): teaching characterized by face-to-face interactions between teachers and students in contrast to preactive teaching.

The internet (pp. 65, 337): many interconnected computer networks created for the rapid dissemination of vast amounts of information around the world.

J

Job analysis (p. 47): a procedure for determining the knowledge and skills needed for a job.

Job fairs (p. 401): information sessions that bring teacher candidates and potential employees together to provide information about job openings.

K

Knowledge base (p. 46): the body of knowledge that represents what teachers need to know and be able to do.

L

Latchkey children (p. 187): children who, because of family circumstances, must spend part of each day unsupervised by a parent or guardian.

Learning (p. 444): changes in behaviour the individual makes in response to environmental stimuli; the acquisition and organization of knowledge and skills.

Learning disability (LD) (p. 227): a limitation in one's ability to take in, organize, remember, and express information.

Learning objectives (p. 279): specific, measurable outcomes of learning that students are to demonstrate.

Learning styles (p. 223): cognitive, affective, and physiological behaviours through which an individual learns most effectively; determined by a combination of hereditary and environmental influences.

Least restrictive environment (p. 233): an educational program that meets a disabled student's special needs in a manner that is identical, insofar as possible, to that provided to students in general education classrooms.

Letter of application (p. 403): a letter written in application for a specific teaching vacancy in a school district.

Letter of inquiry (p. 403): a letter written to a school district inquiring about teaching vacancies.

Liability (p. 147): responsibility for damages or harm.

Logic (p. 84): a branch of philosophy concerned with the processes of reasoning and the identification of rules that will enable thinkers to reach valid conclusions.

Lower-order questions (p. 444): questions that require students to recall specific information.

M

Mainstreaming (p. 234): providing students with the least restrictive academic environment in which they may comfortably learn the curriculum.

Mastery learning (p. 274): an approach to instruction based on the assumptions that (1) virtually all students can learn material if given enough time and taught appropriately and (2) learning is enhanced if students can progress in small, sequenced steps.

Measurement (p. 282): the gathering of data that indicate how much students have learned.

Mentor (pp. 63, 366): a wise, knowledgeable individual who provides guidance and encouragement to someone.

Mentoring (p. 62): an intensive form of teaching in which a wise and experienced teacher (the mentor) inducts a student (the protégé) into a professional way of life.

Metaphysics (p. 82): a branch of philosophy concerned with the nature of reality.

Microcomputer-based laboratories (MBL) (p. 336): the use of computers to gather and then analyze data that students have collected in a school laboratory or in the field.

Microteaching (p. 55): a brief, single-concept lesson taught by a teacher education student to a small group of students; usually designed to give the education student an opportunity to practice a specific teaching skill.

Minister of Education (p. 127): elected cabinet minister with the formal responsibility for the provincial Department of Education and its staff.

Minorities (p. 195): groups of people who share certain characteristics and are smaller in number than the majority of a population.

Modelling (p. 275): the process of "thinking out loud," which teachers use to make students aware of the reasoning involved in learning new material.

Modes of teaching (p. 30): different aspects of the teaching function—for example, teaching as a way of being, as a creative endeavour, as a live performance, and so on.

Montessorri Method (p. 113): a method of teaching, developed by Maria Montessori, based on a prescribed set of materials and physical exercises to develop children's knowledge and skills.

Moral reasoning (p. 210): the reasoning process people follow to decide what is right or wrong.

Multicultural curriculum (p. 178): a school curriculum that addresses the needs and backgrounds of all students regardless of their cultural identity and includes the cultural perspectives, or "voices," of people who have previously been silent or marginalized.

Multicultural education (p. 175): education that provides equal educational opportunities to all students—regardless of socioeconomic status; gender; or ethnic, racial, or cultural backgrounds—and is dedicated to reducing prejudice and celebrating the rich diversity of multicultural life.

Multiculturalism (p. 174): a set of beliefs based on the importance of seeing the world from different cultural frames of reference and valuing the diversity of cultures in the global community.

Multiple intelligences (p. 223): a perspective on intellectual ability, proposed by Howard Gardner, suggesting that there are at least seven types of human intelligence.

N

Negligence (p. 145): failure to exercise reasonable, prudent care in providing for the safety of others.

Newsgroups (p. 339): internet sites where students can post and exchange information on electronic bulletin boards.

Normal schools (p. 92): schools that focus on the preparation of teachers.

Null curriculum (p. 296): the intellectual processes and subject content that schools do not teach.

O

Observations (p. 53): field experiences wherein a teacher education student observes a specific aspect of classroom life such as the students, the teacher, the interactions between the two, the structure of the lesson, or the setting.

Open-space schools (p. 169): schools that have large instructional areas with movable walls and furniture that can be rearranged easily.

Opportunity to learn (OTL) (p. 266): the time during which a teacher provides students with challenging content and appropriate instructional strategies to learn that content.

Outcome-based education (p. 307): an educational reform that focuses on developing students' ability to demonstrate mastery of certain desired outcomes or performances.

Outcome-based teacher education (p. 47): an approach to teacher education emphasizing outcomes (what teachers should be able to do, think, and feel) rather than the courses they should take.

P

Parochial schools (p. 92): schools founded on religious beliefs.

Pedagogical content knowledge (p. 43): the knowledge accomplished teachers possess regarding how to present subject matter to students though the use of analogies, metaphors, experiments, demonstrations, illustrations, and other instructional strategies.

Peer coaching (p. 416): an arrangement whereby teachers grow professionally by observing one another's teaching and providing constructive feedback.

Peer counselling (p. 193): an arrangement whereby students, monitored by a school counsellor or teacher, counsel one another in such areas as low achievement, interpersonal problems, substance abuse, and career planning.

Peer-mediated instruction (p. 277): approaches to teaching, such as cooperative learning and group investigation, that utilize the social relationships among students to promote their learning.

Peer-tutoring (p. 277): an arrangement whereby students tutor other students in the same classroom or at the same grade level.

Perennialism (p. 84): a philosophical orientation that emphasizes the ideas contained in the Great Books and maintains that the true purpose of education is the discovery of the universal, or perennial, truths of life.

Performance assessment (p. 282): the process of determining what students can *do* as well as what they know.

Performance-based education (p. 307): an educational reform that focuses on developing students' ability to demonstrate mastery of certain desired performances or outcomes.

Performance-based teacher education (p. 47): an approach to teacher education emphasizing performances (what teachers should be able to do, think, and feel) rather than the courses they should take.

Personal-development view (p. 46): the belief that teachers become more effective by increasing their self-knowledge and developing themselves as persons.

Petites écoles (p. 92): early schools within the French tradition that provided a rudimentary education.

Phi Delta Kappa (PDK) (p. 371): a professional and honorary fraternity of educators with 650 chapters and 130 000 members.

Placement service (p. 401): a school, government, or commercial service that matches job applicants with job openings and arranges contacts between employers and prospective employees.

Portfolio assessment (p. 282): the process of determining how much students have learned by examining collections of work that document their learning over time.

Practicum (p. 57): a short field-based experience during which teacher education students spend time observing and assisting in classrooms.

Preactive teaching (p. 27): the stage of teaching when a teacher prepares to teach or reflects on previous teaching experiences in contrast with interactive teaching.

Preoperational stage (p. 211): the stage of cognitive development (two to seven years of age), proposed by Jean Piaget, in which the individual begins to use language and symbols to think of objects and people outside of the immediate environment.

Privatization (p. 450): moving an organization or institution from public (government) ownership to private ownership.

Problem-centred learning (p. 313): an approach to instruction in which students work in small groups on problems that have many or open-ended solutions.

Profession (p. 360): an occupation that requires a high level of expertise, including advanced study in a specialized field, adherence to a code of ethics, and the ability to work without close supervision.

Professional empowerment (p. 20): a trend for teachers to have expanded opportunities to make decisions that affect their professional lives.

Professional portfolio (pp. 37, 60): a collection of various kinds of evidence (e.g., projects, written work, and video demonstrations of skills) documenting the achievement and performance of individuals in an area of professional practice..

Progressive education movement (p. 305): a movement during the 1920s and 1930s to create schools that emphasized democracy, children's interests and needs, and closer connections between school and community.

Progressivism (p. 86): a philosophical orientation based on the belief that life is evolving in a positive direction, that people may be trusted to act in their own best interests, and that education should focus on the needs and interests of students.

Prosocial values (p. 163): values such as honesty, patriotism, fairness, and civility that promote the well-being of a society.

Psychosocial crisis (p. 211): a life crisis at one of eight different stages of growth and development. According to psychologist Erik Erikson, individuals must resolve each crisis to reach the next stage.

Psychosocial development (p. 210): the progression of an individual through various stages of psychological and social development.

Public private partnerships (p. 133): partnerships, sometimes referred to as P3s, between local school districts with the private sector, includes funds or materials for a variety of school needs.

Q

Qualitative evaluation (p. 419): the appraisal of teacher performance through the use of written, open-ended descriptions of classroom events in terms of their qualities.

Quantitative evaluation (p. 418): the appraisal of teacher performance by recording classroom events in terms of their number or frequency; for example, teacher verbal behaviours such as questioning, praising, or critiquing.

R

Race (p. 172): a concept of human variation used to distinguish people on the basis of biological traits and characteristics.

Realities of teaching (p. 21): actual conditions teachers face in the classroom; the demands as well as the rewards..

Reflection (p. 63: the process of thinking carefully and deliberately about the outcomes of one's teaching.

Reflection-in-action (p. 365): the process of engaging in serious, reflective thought about improving one's professional practice while one is engaged in that practice.

Reflective teaching log (p. 59): a journal of classroom observations in which the teacher education student systematically analyzes specific episodes of teaching.

Relevancy-based curriculum (p. 306): a curriculum that is relevant to students' needs, interests, and concerns about social issues.

Research-based competencies (p. 47): specific behaviours that educational research has identified as characteristic of effective teachers.

Résumé (p. 403): a concise summary of an individual's professional experiences and education.

S

Scaffolding (p. 275): an approach to teaching based on the student's current level of understanding and ability; the teacher varies the amount of help given (e.g., clues, encouragement, or suggestions) to students based on their moment-to-moment understanding of the material being learned.

School Advisory Councils (p. 128): councils mandated at school levels to allow and encourage parents and community members to become involved in school level decision making

School-based interprofessional case management (p. 194): an approach to education in which professionally trained case managers work directly with teachers, the community, and families to coordinate and deliver appropriate services to at-risk students and their families.

School-based management (p. 132): various approaches to school improvement in which teachers, principals, students, parents, and community members manage individual schools and share in the decision-making processes.

School boards (p. 128): the primary governing body of a local school district.

School choice (p. 132): various proposals that would allow parents to choose the schools their children attend.

School culture (p. 168): the collective "way of life" characteristic of a school; a set of beliefs, values, traditions, and ways of thinking and behaving that distinguish it from other schools.

School-to-work programs (p. 320): educational programs, often developed collaboratively by schools and industry, that emphasize the transfer of knowledge and skills learned at school to the job setting.

School traditions (p. 169): those elements of a school's culture that are handed down from year to year.

School-within-a-school (p. 194): an alternative school (within a regular school) designed to meet the needs of students at risk.

School year (p. 107: the required number of days required for students to attend school.

Scottish tradition (p. 93): offered both elementary and secondary education to boys and girls in combined classes regardless of their social class.

Self-assessment (p. 63): the process of measuring one's growth in regard to the knowledge, skills, and attitudes possessed by professional teachers.

Self-contained classroom (p. 168): an organizational structure for schools in which one teacher instructs a group of students (typically, twenty to thirty) in a single classroom.

Separate schools (p. 98): publicly funded schools based upon religious or language.

Sex-role socialization (p. 180): socially expected behaviour patterns conveyed to individuals on the basis of gender.

Sex-role stereotyping (p. 180): beliefs that subtly encourage males and females to conform to certain behavioural norms regardless of abilities and interests.

Social reconstructionism (p. 87): a philosophical orientation based on the belief that social problems can be solved by changing, or *reconstructing*, society.

Socratic questioning (p. 84): a method of questioning designed to lead students to see errors and inconsistencies in their thinking, based on questioning strategies used by Socrates.

Special education (p. 231): a teaching specialty for meeting the special educational needs of exceptional learners.

Stages of development (p. 210): predictable stages through which individuals pass as they progress through life.

Standard of care (p. 145): level of care expected of school personnel, level of care to be that of careful or prudent parents in the care of their own children.

State agents (p. 148): teacher in the role and carrying out the duties as defined in education statutes, Charter of Rights and Freedoms, provincial human rights codes.

Stereotyping (p. 174): the process of attributing behavioral characteristics to all members of a group; formulated on the basis of limited experiences with and information about the group, coupled with an unwillingness to examine prejudices.

Student-centred curriculum (p. 299): curricula that are organized around students' needs and interests.

Student diversity (p. 8): differences among students in regard to gender, race, ethnicity, culture, and socioeconomic status.

Student-mobility rates (p. 16): the proportion of students within a school or district who move during an academic year.

Student variability (p. 8): differences among students in regard to their developmental needs, interests, abilities, and disabilities.

Students at risk (p. 185): students whose living conditions and backgrounds place them at risk for dropping out of school.

Students with disabilities (p. 226): students who need special education services because they possess one or more of the following disabilities: learning disabilities, speech or language impairments, mental retardation, serious emotional disturbance, hearing impairments, orthopedic impairments, visual impairments, or other health impairments.

Substitute teaching (p. 60): Temporary teachers who replace regular teachers absent due to illness, family responsibilities, personal reasons, or professional workshops and conferences.

Successful school (p. 183): schools characterized by a high degree of student learning, results that surpass those expected from comparable schools, and steady improvement rather than decline.

Summative evaluation (p. 282): an assessment of student learning made for the purpose of assigning grades at the end of a unit, semester, or year and deciding whether students are ready to proceed to the next phase of their education.

Superintendent (p. 131): the chief administrator of a school district.

Supply teaching (p. 60): Temporary teachers who replace regular teachers absent due to illness, family responsibilities, personal reasons, or professional workshops and conferences.

Synectics (p. 439): a method for "teaching" creativity through the use of metaphors and analogies.

T

Teacher accountability (p. 30): society's expectations that teachers will adhere to high professional and moral standards and create effective learning environments for all students.

Teacher centres (p. 65): centres where teachers provide other teachers with instructional materials and new methods and where teachers can exchange ideas.

Teacher-leader (p. 373): a teacher who assumes a key leadership role in the improvement and/or day-to-day operation of a school.

Teacher-researcher (p. 377): a teacher who regularly conducts classroom research to improve his or her teaching.

Teacher-student ratios (p. 16): a ratio that expresses the number of students taught by a teacher.

Teacher supply and demand (p. 398): the number of school-age students compared to the number of available teachers; may also be projected based on estimated numbers of students and teachers.

Teachers' thought processes (p. 28): the thoughts that guide teachers' actions in classrooms. These thoughts typically consist of thoughts related to planning, theories and beliefs, and interactive thoughts and decisions.

Teaching certificate (p. 396): a license to teach issued by a province or, in a few cases, a large city.

Teaching simulations (p. 56): an activity in which teacher education students participate in role-plays designed to create situations comparable to those actually encountered by teachers.

Team teaching (p. 417): an arrangement whereby a team of teachers teaches a group of students equal in number to what the teachers would have in their self-contained classrooms.

Time on task (p. 266): the amount of time students are actively and directly engaged in learning tasks.

Tort liability (p. 145): conditions that would permit the filing of legal charges against a professional for breach of duty and/or behaving in a negligent manner.

Tyler rationale (p. 298): a four-step model for curriculum development in which teachers identify purposes, select learning experiences, organize experiences, and evaluate.

V

Vicarious liability (p. 147): responsibility of an employer for damage caused by an employee, even though the employer may not have done anything wrong.

Videoconferencing (p. 340): the use of computer-mounted video cameras to conduct two-way interactive conferences over the internet.

Virtual schools (p. 114): offer public schools programs over the internet.

W

Web (p. 337): the most popular connection to the internet; composed of home pages, which users access through browser programs such as Netscape Communicator, Microsoft Internet Explorer, or America Online.

Whole-language approach (p. 311): the practice of teaching language skills (listening, reading, and writing) as part of students' everyday experiences rather than as isolated experiences.

Within-class ability grouping (p. 263): the practice of creating small, homogeneous groups of students within a single classroom for the purpose of instruction, usually in reading or mathematics, at the elementary level.

Y

Youth Criminal Justice Act (p. 143): act replacing the Young Offenders' Act to ensure criminal justice for youth; emphasizes rehabilitation and reintegration of youth.

Name Index

Montessori, M., 113–114
Moyers, B., 20–21
Murnane, R.J., 450

N
Nash, R., 217–218
Noddings, N., 261
Noll, J.W., 142
Nowell, A., 181

O
Okrent, D., 349

P
Pang, V.O., 178
Parkay, F., 62
Paul, D.N., 105
Pavlov, I., 89
Percy, W., 44
Peterson, K., 165, 168
Piaget, J., 210–212, 215
Popham, W.J., 281

R
Raham, H., 308
Rallis, S.F., 374
Renzulli, J.S., 230
Riley, R., 191, 192, 412
Rogers, C., 89
Rogers, W.T., 308
Rosenshine, B., 43, 45
Ross, V.L., 189–190

S
Salovey, P., 223
Sandler, M.R., 453
Sarnoff, D., 333
Sartre, J.-P., 87
Saul, J.R., 450
Schaefer, R., 379
Schmuck, P., 259
Schmuck, R., 259
Schön, D., 365
Schubert, W.H., 292
Scotland-Moxon, C., 342
Senese, G., 180
Seward, B., 97
Simon, T., 222
Singers, J., 342
Skinner, B.F., 89
Slavin, R., 223
Slavit, D., 313
Sluyter, D., 223
Smerdon, B.A., 181
Socrates, 84
Sommers, C.H., 181
Spring, J., 139, 165
Steinberg, A., 281
Stoll, C., 347
Sutherland, L.I., 145

T
Tagore, R., 27
Tally, W., 328
Terman, L., 222, 226

Thelen, H.A., 265
Thorndike, E.L., 107
Tozer, S.E., 180
Turner, J., 283
Tyler, R., 298

V
Vanderhoeden-Bracken, S., 4
van Manen, M., 27
Violas, P.C., 180
Vygotsky, L.S., 276

W
Wagner, 133
Wagner, R., 375
Walberg, H., 261
Ward, W.A., 358
Watson, J.B., 89
Wechsler, D., 222
Weil, M., 273, 416
Willingham, W., 181
Willman, J., 338
Willms, J.D., 414
Wilson, Y., 179
Wohlstetter, P., 375
Wolfgang, C., 272
Woolfolk, A.E., 27, 230, 259, 275
Wray, H., 455

Y
Yamamoto, K., 220
Yoong, D., 174
Young, C., 181

Subject Index